Africa, Asia, Europe and the F

Caucasus

Australia, New Zealand and the Pacific

India: States

ID	Name
1	Arunachal Pradesh
2	Assam
3	Chandigarh
4	Delhi
5	Haryana
6	Jharkhand
7	Manipur
8	Meghalaya
9	Mizoram
10	Nagaland
11	Sikkim
12	Tripura

Russia: Administrative divisions

ID	Name	ID	Name	ID	Name	ID	Name	ID	Name	ID	Name
1	Adygea	10	Ingushetia	19	Kostroma	28	Nizhny Novgorod	37	Ryazan	46	Tula
2	Astrakhan	11	Ivanovo	20	Krasnodar	29	North Ossetia	38	St Petersburg City	47	Tver
3	Bashkortostan	12	Kabardino-Balkaria	21	Kursk	30	Novgorod	39	Samara	48	Udmurtia
4	Belgorod	13	Kaliningrad	22	Leningrad	31	Orel	40	Saratov	49	Ul'yanovsk
5	Bryansk	14	Kalmykia	23	Lipetsk	32	Orenburg	41	Smolensk	50	Vladimir
6	Chechnya	15	Kaluga	24	Mari El	33	Penza	42	Stavropol'	51	Volgograd
7	Chelyabinsk	16	Karachay-Cherkessia	25	Mordovia	34	Perm	43	Sverdlovsk	52	Vologda
8	Chuvashia	17	Karelia	26	Moskva	35	Pskov	44	Tambov	53	Voronezh
9	Dagestan	18	Kirov	27	Murmansk	36	Rostov	45	Tatarstan	54	Yaroslavl'

HISTORY, TRENDS AND POSSIBILITIES

The Future of the Global Church

Patrick Johnstone

Authentic

This edition first published in the UK and Commonwealth 2011 by Authentic Media Limited

52 Presley Way, Crownhill, Milton Keynes, MK8 0ES, UK

www.authenticmedia.co.uk

British Library Cataloguing in Publication Data

A catalogue record for this book is available from the British Library.

ISBN: 978-1-85078-966-6

Scripture quotations, unless otherwise stated, are from the New Revised Standard Version Bible: Anglicized Edition, copyright 1989, 1995 by the Division of Christian Education of the National Council of the Churches of Christ in the United States of America. Used by permission. All rights reserved.

Enquiries about translation rights should be sent to The Piquant Agency

PO Box 83, Carlisle, CA3 9GR, United Kingdom

info@piquant.net

Cover design by Projectluz.com

Book design by 2at.com

This book published in the US by Biblica (ISBN 978-1-60657-132-3).

Printed in the United States of America

CONTENTS

Note: *Notes* appear on the concluding page of each chapter.

PREFACE

This book is the fulfilment of a 30-year dream. For four decades, I found out all I could about the nations of the world for the production of six editions of *Operation World* and it gave me a unique and exciting overview of the progress of the Gospel around the world. Indeed, I have seen so much of what God has done, it has made me an optimist! Anecdotal evidence of God's amazing acts around the world in recent years is borne out by the meticulously assembled data we have gathered—all confirming what God promised us in the Bible.

The original challenge to me to compile this data came from Hans von Staden, the founder and leader of the Dorothea Mission, with which I served for 16 years in southern Africa. The aim was to provide information for believers so that they could pray—a primary focus being a series of "weeks of prayer for the world" held in many parts of Africa and Europe. My research was intended to summon Christians to prayer and action for world evangelization.

In the course of preparing successive editions of *Operation World*, we built up a remarkable network of loyal informants, a unique body of knowledge and a range of resources that needed to be made more widely available. *Operation World* became a widely used source of facts about the world and fuel for prayer. Sales of the books, in English and some 16 other languages, can only be estimated, but the cumulative total may soon approach 3 million copies. In 2002, I handed over the work of compiling a new edition to Jason Mandryk, who was responsible for the excellent seventh edition published in 2010. This gave me new freedom and opportunity to realize my dream.

Over time, I graduated from pencil-and-paper calculations and portable typewriters in urban slums in southern Africa to sophisticated databases, networked computers and extensive use of the internet as I engaged in a global ministry as a member of WEC International as well as being involved with many different networks and movements.

For the past six years, I have sought to interpret what all the data I have gathered might tell us about the progress of world evangelization, and even to examine the hints that present trends might give us about the prospects for the cause of God's Kingdom in the coming generation. There will certainly be many surprises, and yet many of the macro-developments in the political, economic and (especially) religious realms have built a momentum over the last 60 years that is likely to be maintained—unless some global catastrophe occurs, or a dramatic outpouring of the Spirit of God in answer to prayer.

My concern in designing this book is that passion and vision be paramount. My longing is that this book will be used by my Heavenly Father to inspire many others and hasten the day when "the earth will be full of the knowledge of the LORD as the waters cover the sea"!

Patrick Johnstone
WEC International
Wisbech, England

ABOUT THE AUTHOR

Patrick Johnstone was brought up in England as the eldest of six siblings, children of an Irish father and a Dutch mother. He was converted to Christ in 1959 during his first year as a student at Bristol University, while reading Chemistry in preparation to become a research scientist. At a Christian Union meeting, he heard Glyndwr Davies speak about the evangelistic work of the Dorothea Mission in urban townships in southern Africa, and he rose to the challenge and committed his life to serve as a missionary evangelist. He went to South Africa in 1962, completing his theological training at the Dorothea Mission Bible College in Pretoria.

It was during this time that he met Jill Amsden, a fellow worker from the UK serving in the Dorothea Mission. Patrick and Jill eventually were able to marry in 1968 on their first home leave. Thereafter, they served together in Zimbabwe, where their three children, Peter, Timothy and Ruth, were all born.

During his first six-year term on the field, Patrick served in Kenya, South Africa and Zimbabwe (then Rhodesia). In the last of these, he led the first Dorothea Mission team in evangelistic outreach in towns and cities across the country. He learnt a number of African languages, including siNdebele, chiShona and Afrikaans, and also became involved in translating part of the New Testament into chiNambya, a language spoken in northwest Zimbabwe.

It was during this time that he also began the work of gathering data about the world both to inform prayer and for the first editions of *Operation World*. The first printed booklet with that title, which came out in 1965, was just 30 pages long. The second edition appeared in 1973 and covered nearly every country of the world. It was reprinted several years later by Ralph Winter of the USCWM, and also prompted George Verwer to set in motion an OM-backed rewrite of the book for global distribution. This was completed in 1978 and led to many openings for wider ministry. The impact of *Operation World* is incalculable. Over 2.5 million copies have been distributed around the world in seven editions and some 16 languages, and the book has played a key role in developing the global vision of African, Latin American and Asian missions.

The 1978 edition also led to some big changes in Patrick's ministry. The first was to join the OM ship, the MV *Logos*, for a year in Asia and the Pacific in 1979. The second followed an invitation to become part of the leadership team of WEC International, a large pioneer church-planting mission. Patrick's main responsibilities in 1980 were strategy and research and he worked in that role for the next 22 years, playing a part in the considerable growth of the mission as it addressed new unreached peoples and countries. For six years, he was also WEC's deputy international director.

Patrick was long involved with the Lausanne Movement. During the 1980s, he was a member of the Strategy Working Group that helped to formulate many of the definitions for its ethno-linguistic people-group databases. In the '90s, he was co-leader with John Robb of World Vision of the "unreached peoples track" of the AD2000 and Beyond Movement. He has worked closely with David Barrett and Todd Johnson of the *WCE* and other researchers in sharing information and developing databases, and also played a part in the formation of Global Mapping International (GMI) and the Joshua Project and its listing of people groups.

Jill became ill with cancer in 1990 but she continued to write her children's version of *Operation World* and had almost completed it by the time of her death in 1992. The book was published as *You Can Change the World,* and later (by Daphne Spraggett) as *Window on the World*.

In 1995, Patrick married Robyn Erwin from the US, who had been a co-worker with Jill before her death. Patrick and Robyn now live in Cambridgeshire, England, where they currently serve as regional directors for WEC's European bases.

ACKNOWLEDGEMENTS

It is almost impossible to name all who have contributed in some way to this book. Here are some to whom I would like to express my thanks:

The thousands of informants and respondents around the world who provided the millions of pieces of data on which *Operation World* and this book were based.

The Piquant team. Pieter Kwant, our literary agent (and much more), who believed in me and was confident that I could deliver the goods—even when I doubted it myself; Elria Kwant, who with perseverance succeeded in bringing together all the text, graphics and editorial contributions into the final product in your hands; and Dave, their son, who did all the typesetting in New Zealand. It was courageous to take on this project with no clear assurance that it could even be a viable product. The failure of the original publishers, the global economic crisis and the very different reading habits of this new generation all made this unusual book a risky undertaking.

Editors. Huw Spanner, who tenaciously edited the original manuscript and transformed my quaint neologisms, frustrating inconsistencies and confusing word order into meaningful prose; and Margaret Bardsley, who meticulously proofread the final manuscript and suggested a great number of last-minute improvements.

Photographers. Several photographers kindly gave us permission to use their images: Adam Beattie, Elizabeth Daymond, Paul Hattaway, Elizabeth Hempel, David Jones, Pieter Kwant, Timothy Kwant, Carol Pantridge, David Phillips and Betty Spackman. We also used images courtesy of Langham Partnership International, the Lausanne Movement (Cape Town 2010), OM International and Samaritan's Purse (Bolivia).

Jason Mandryk and the Operation World 2010 team, who have relieved me from the time-consuming writing for *Operation World* and readily furnished me with the results of their more recent research as they were writing the 2010 edition. The book was completed too late for me to do more than draw on some of its conclusions, but the overall trends I have predicted have not been challenged by their new data.

The Global Mapping International team, without whom neither the mapping for the book nor the publishing of all the electronic components of the project would have been possible—and particularly Mike O'Rear and Bill Dickson, who oversaw the process and kept my computers running; Bryan Nicholson, who prepared the original maps that I then adapted; and Loren Muelius, whose years of work made possible the language-polygon maps which became an integral part of this book.

The World Christian Encyclopedia team. I owe thanks first to David Barrett, for his encyclopedic knowledge and innovative ideas, which have contributed to many of the concepts I have used in this book, and for enabling me to draw upon information in the unique WCD database. There has been considerable mutual sharing of data between the two extant global Christian databases (for the WCE and for *Operation World*), leading to very different applications. Second, to Todd Johnson, for his continuing support as we both worked on our graphical productions—in his case, *The Atlas of Global Christianity* published in 2010 (too late for me to make much reference to it).

The publishers. Biblica in the US and Koorong (Authentic Media) in Australia and the UK, who at fairly short notice took on the challenge of publishing this book after all our early plans foundered when the original publishers shut down in 2009.

Then, there were the encouragers along the way who also believed in the project: notably, Darrell Dorr of USCWM, Justin Long of Pioneers, Jim Haney, the Southern Baptist International Mission Board's director of research, and my dear colleagues in WEC International, who released me from many other duties to undertake this work—especially Trevor and Jen Kallmier, our international directors and accountability partners.

Finally, I thank God for my dear wife, Robyn, who constantly challenged me to come out of the dream world of false optimism where I all too often took refuge, to be realistic about what was possible in this complex project.

The Future of the Global Church is dedicated to the growing global army of proclaimers of the Good News who are passionate to see Jesus return in glory with the task of world evangelization complete. May this book give them tools to increase still further the involvement of believers in praying, giving and going!

Patrick Johnstone

INTRODUCTION

Many elements were brought together in *The Future of the Global Church*. These are some of them:

1. Graphics. In 1979, Jill, my first wife, and I left Africa and the Dorothea Mission (where the first three editions of *Operation World* were written) to join the international leadership team of WEC International in the UK as directors for research. Our journey took us round the world as we ministered for a year on the OM ship MV *Logos*.

At that time, I began to develop visual images that I could use to represent to Christian conferences in various countries all that God was doing in the world and what still remained to be done. I drew maps by hand to show on an overhead projector, then a fairly new technology. During our travels, the ship docked in Melbourne, Australia. Once more I used my growing collection of acetates, but someone came to the ship's director and complained about their poor quality. This dismayed me, and I resolved that when I reached the UK I would master the techniques required to make more professional transparencies. This I did, using acetate shading and one of the first laser photocopiers to reproduce good type for the lettering, which was all painstakingly assembled by hand on acetate sheets.

This developed into a large operation employing a photographic photocopier to provide acetates for use by others around the world. The advent of personal computers with graphics capability again changed everything, and over time we were able to switch to database-linked mapping and high-quality graphics software, which became the basis for all the graphics designed for both this book and its electronic supplements. The sophistication of current software pushed me into a difficult, five-year learning curve to master the elements I needed. Without the help of the Global Mapping International team, it would not have been possible. There were many times in the seven years I spent producing this book when I almost gave up, but the work is now complete.

2. History. I love maps, and especially historical ones. However, as I pored over many atlases I realized that no one had pulled information together, century by century, to show the rise and fall of empires and the advances and retreats of the Church around the world. This book reviews 2,000 years of that history over 42 pages.

3. Demographics. Our world faces challenges and potential crises in the 21st Century. I have selected nine factors that I consider the most important and have sought to give an indication of where present trends may lead and how they may affect Christian ministry. Some of my conclusions may surprise readers. They may also prove to be either perspicacious or incorrect—time will tell!

4. Evangelicals. For many people, the focus on statistics on Evangelicals has been one of the unique and valuable contributions of *Operation World*. This book covers all branches of Christianity but majors on renewal and evangelical movements, for which we have extensive statistics. This helps to clarify future challenges for ministry if we are to give all of humankind the opportunity to find a personal relationship with God through the Lord Jesus Christ. A major part of the book therefore examines the unfinished task of world evangelization.

5. Peoples. With others, I have worked for many years compiling lists of the world's languages and people groups, which has given me an extensive knowledge of this complex field. In this book, I have sought to bring some order and clarity to it, to aid understanding and facilitate ministry by elaborating for the first time the classification of the world's peoples into 15 "affinity blocs" and around 250 "people clusters".

6. Electronic media. The rapid technological advances since 1980 are transforming the way people obtain and use information. Many commentators postulate the death of printed books as everything is transferred to electronic media. Here I have sought to combine the two, with most of our information being made available as soon as practicable on DVD or in electronic form accessible via the internet and even downloadable to a Kindle, iPad or other reading devices. The limited length of this book inevitably means that a lot of information has, painfully, been left out, as well as any fuller analysis of the information that is included. However, the electronic extensions of this book have allowed us to publish more. We have posted most of the appendices and bibliographies on our website, and have also made available most of our databases with the sourced statistics on which the graphics in this book are based. There is also a range of downloadable PowerPoint slides, both individual and in sets, with extensive speaker notes, which elaborate on the contents of this book. To find out how to access this material, see pages 241–42.

7. **The internet.** A book of this nature would not have been possible without extensive use of the internet, and so there are many internet addresses and hot links provided in the electronic versions of this book. We trust they will all still be valid when we go to press!

How to use this book

This book is designed to be used in many different ways by many kinds of readers:

Christians passionate about the extension of God's Kingdom. This is a passionate book. It cites statistics in such a way as to stir hearts. Nearly every page has a spiritual application to challenge or provoke thought–presented in a special text box entitled "Food for Thought" or "Burning Question for Today". Such readers may find that this book can be used on its own, without reference to its electronic supplements. It is also a useful companion to *Operation World*.

The facts are marshalled so that Christians may pray and become actively involved in God's mission to win for His Son a perfected Bride. Accuracy and academic rigour are vital, and I trust they have been achieved–I cite accessible sources for all the information given here. Nonetheless, the true purpose of the book is to give glory to God for the wonders He is now performing all over our world and to communicate a vision for the completion of the task of world evangelization.

Christian congregations. This is also a book to empower Christian congregations. A few copies stocked in the church library or in the hands of the missions committee can be a valuable source of information to provide a wider perspective on our present world and the one that is emerging and to give meaning and strategic direction to ministry both locally and further afield.

The basic sets of PowerPoint slides on the DVD of the book can be a good resource for pastors, leaders and prayer coordinators, who will be able to put any of the diagrams and maps up on a screen. A wider and richer selection of PowerPoint slides with animations and even voice-over recordings are also available on the internet–see page 241. Ownership of this book gives access to these resources, some free of charge and some at a modest price.

Disciplers and teachers. Each chapter has its own particular focus and can be integrated in an existing course or expanded into an additional module. There are many aspects of this book that are unique for

teaching–demographics from a Christian perspective, comparative religion or the history of the Church, the growth and spread of Christianity, renewal and revival or Evangelicalism–examining the unevangelized world or presenting a new analysis of people groups and their evangelization. The book advances an overview, and the extensive range of PowerPoint slides communicates the facts.

Mobilizers. Mobilizers need tools appropriate for our digital world to gain the attention of a new generation and get it involved in working for world evangelization. This book is a unique resource presenting many aspects of Christian ministry, not least the challenges it faces in the decades ahead, but all within the context of a positive account of what God is already doing. All the PowerPoint slides come with extensive speaker notes similar to (and often considerably expanded from) the text of the book itself. These slides can also be incorporated in personal slide sets used to inspire people to pray and get involved.

Missionaries. Many missionaries making presentations while on home leave need broader back-up materials to intersperse with those relating to their own ministries and countries, and to set what they are doing in the context of the wider patterns of developments around the world. The electronic supplements mentioned above can provide just such materials.

For these users, some of the electronic formats, including PDF files of individual pages, may prove to be a useful way to take both this book and *Operation World* with them when they are travelling.

Researchers and academics. Behind all the information presented in this book is a range of extensive databases on Excel spreadsheets that contain all the raw data we have used (and their sources). In addition there are step-by-step explanations of how we derived the figures cited in the diagrams and maps in this book. For access to this valuable information, see page 241.

Finally, there is much in this book and its expanded electronic supplements that has never been published before. As this is all essentially the work of one person, it is likely to contain biases and quirks–and there will be topics left entirely untreated. For these, I must take responsibility. Nonetheless, I trust that readers will find in these pages an inspiring worldview that offers a perspective very different from that presented by the pessimistic secular media. May it provide both encouragement and challenge so that we will more fully engage in ministry to our needy world, now and in future!

Patrick Johnstone

COLOUR CODES

This book is meant to be visual. A lot of information is compressed into a small space and presented in a varied and innovative way. In the maps, tables and diagrams, I have used colours and abbreviations as consistently as possible. These two pages cover the main colour schemes and labels used for the recurring themes. Mostly I have used three-hue colour ramps with gradations in tint appropriate to the context.

General

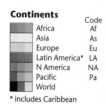

Continents

		Code
	Africa	Af
	Asia	As
	Europe	Eu
	Latin America*	LA
	N America	NA
	Pacific	Pa
	World	

* includes Caribbean

The six continents referred to throughout are as defined by the UN, except that I have used the term "the Pacific" rather than "Oceania". The colour range used for each is shown here. The two-letter abbreviations are important—they are used separately and in combination (AfAsLA or EuNAPa) throughout the book.

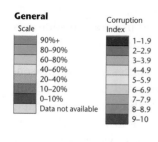

General

Scale
- 90%+
- 80–90%
- 60–80%
- 40–60%
- 20–40%
- 10–20%
- 0–10%
- Data not available

Corruption Index
- 1–1.9
- 2–2.9
- 3–3.9
- 4–4.9
- 5–5.9
- 6–6.9
- 7–7.9
- 8–8.9
- 9–10

I have used colour gradations in diagrams and maps to indicate percentage ranges. Here are two examples with eight or nine data intervals or indices showing high/low, good/bad or positive/negative. Green is usually the higher or better, red or blue the lower or worse.

Maps. This book contains many maps. They are all based on countries and territories and the borders they had in 2000–04. Outside Chapter 2, all maps—including future projections—refer to the international borders in 2000 so as to enable direct comparisons over time (though I recognize that many borders changed substantially over the course of the 20th Century). I have made no allowance for recently established states such as Montenegro, Kosovo and S Sudan.

Statistics. Many readers find statistics a challenge. In this book I have simplified and summarized very large amounts of data. See pages 241–42 to find out how more detailed data can be accessed via the website supporting this book.

I have rounded many figures up or down for the sake of clarity, which means that often percentages do not add up to 100.

Errors are inevitable. Please notify the publishers should you come across any so that, in time, they may be listed on the website.

Labelling. To avoid unnecessary clutter, I have labelled the maps sparingly and only where relevant to the accompanying text. Please refer to the more detailed maps on the inside covers to identify countries (in the front) and affinity blocs, people clusters and people group (in the back). Abbreviations are listed on page xiv.

The font sizes used strike a balance, I hope, between legibility and the economical use of space.

History

Dominant Religion
- Ethnic religions
- Secular/mixed
- Hindu/Buddhist
- Muslim
- Catholic
- Orthodox
- Protestant/other

Chapter 2 reviews on its left-hand pages the major empires in each century. The religious affiliation of their rulers is indicated by the colours shown here—each empire has its own unique shade. Note that ethnic religions are in this case denoted by shades of brown.

State of Christianity
- Politicized Christendom
- Christian majority/state
- Conversion by coercion
- Reformation & State involvement
- Active Christian witness/renewal
- Stagnating Christianity
- Christian decline
- Severe Christian decline
- Persecution of Christians
- Severe persecution
- Early Christian renewal movements
- Muslim control or majority

The right-hand pages in Chapter 2 look at the advances and retreats of Christianity in each century and its interactions with political systems and rulers. Christian renewal and persecution are indicated with colour and cross-hatching.

The pie charts draw largely on the data on martyrs in the *World Christian Encyclopedia*. The definition of martyrdom is broad and includes all who were killed because of the faith they professed. It enabled us to estimate the number of martyrs in each century in each of the six Christian "megablocs", shown in the right-hand pie. The left-hand pie represents the persecutors who were responsible—the size of each segment indicates the proportion of the century's martyrs that they killed.

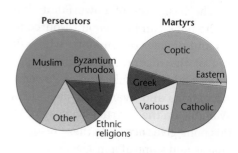

Persecutors | Martyrs

Religions

Religions

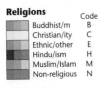

	Code
Buddhist/m	B
Christian/ity	C
Ethnic/other	E
Hindu/ism	H
Muslim/Islam	M
Non-religious	N

I have grouped the world's religions in six major categories. Adherents are counted on the basis of how they identify themselves. Each religion has its own colour range as shown here, and is referred to by the one-letter abbreviation listed here.

In Chapter 3, religious affiliation by people/language is presented in a way that distinguishes between indigenous and immigrant peoples. There are two layers of colour on each map. The percentage religious affiliation for each indigenous people/language with a specific language area is shown in the upper-layer colouring. Everywhere else, the underlying colour shows, representing the religious affiliation of indigenous people who speak the national or majority language or one spoken nationwide. This layer is only visible when there is no upper-layer local language area. Immigrant peoples/languages are represented by a circle in or close to each country. The size of the circle is proportionate to the size of the immigrant population; the colour shading in the circle represents the percentage affiliation for the religion in question.

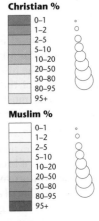

Religious Scales

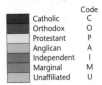

B	E	H	M	N	%
					0–1
					1–2
					2–5
					5–10
					10–20
					20–50
					50–80
					80–95
					95+

I have developed colour ramps for each of the six main religious categories, which broadly match the colours shown above. Darker colours generally represent higher percentages.

Christianity

I have generally used the colour yellow, symbolizing light, to represent—depending on context—Christians, Protestants and Evangelicals in particular.

The Orthodox include several different ancient churches which may have little or no relationship with each other (see p107). The Independents include all the denominations and networks established more recently, also those that are entirely indigenous in origin (see p112).

Christian Megablocs

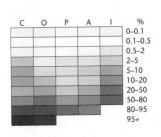

	Code
Catholic	C
Orthodox	O
Protestant	P
Anglican	A
Independent	I
Marginal	M
Unaffiliated	U

All denominations are categorized in six megablocs ("traditions", "confessions" or "streams"). I have used the one-letter abbreviations widely, sometimes coupled together, eg "PIA" in Chapter 4.

C	O	P	A	I	%
					0–0.1
					0.1–0.5
					0.5–2
					2–5
					5–10
					10–20
					20–50
					50–80
					80–95
					95+

I have assigned three-hued colour ramps to five of the megablocs—the Marginals are too few in number to be mapped in this book—based on the colour scheme shown above. These colours are used extensively in the maps in Chapter 4. Catholics (p104) and Anglicans (p110) are single-denomination megablocs.

Christian Renewal Movements

	Evangelical
	Pentecostal
	Other charismatic

These colours distinguish between Evangelicals, Pentecostals and other Charismatics in Chapter 5. Note that the categories overlap—all Pentecostals are, by definition, both Charismatics and Evangelicals. See pages 121 and 141.

Pentecostals are included in the statistics for both Evangelicals and Charismatics. I have used red to draw attention to areas with a small percentage of Evangelicals.

Pentecostal/ charismatic %

%
0–0.1
0.1–0.5
0.5–1
1–2
2–5
5–10
10–20
20–30
30–50

Evangelical %

%
0–0.2
0.2–0.5
0.5–1
1–2
2–5
5–10
10–20
20–50
50+

Evangelization

I have used two different approaches in Chapter 7 to indicate the impact of Christian ministry on the unevangelized. This colour scheme refers to the "percent evangelized" figures derived by the WCE (with further statistical input from the figures for Evangelicals in *Operation World*). The "nominal" figures are only estimates.

My second approach uses two simple criteria to define unreached/unevangelized peoples as being less than 5% Christian and less than 2% evangelical. The colour scheme expands into four categories: the least, the less, the more and the largely evangelized.

Evangelized % (WCD perspective)

Unevangelized [WCD]
Evangelized non-Christian [WCD]
Non-evangelical Christian [OW]
Evangelical [OW]
Nominal evangelical
Nominal/unevangelized "Christian"
Marginally evangelized non-Christian

**Evangelized %
(Operation World/FGC)**

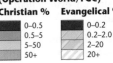

Christian %	Evangelical %
0–0.5	0–0.2
0.5–5	0.2–2.0
5–50	2–20
50+	20+

DEFINITIONS

10/40 Window the region of the Eastern hemisphere between latitudes 10° and 40° north of the equator, covering North Africa, the Middle East and most of Asia. This window contains most of the world's areas of greatest physical and spiritual needs, most of the world's least evangelized peoples and most of the governments that actively oppose Christianity. See page 162.

adherents followers of a particular religion, church or philosophy. This is a broad category based on self-identification rather than on proven practice or devotion. It includes professing and *affiliated* adults and their children (practising and non-practising) in a given area or country. It refers to those who, if not under coercion, would claim to have a religion even if their adherence is only *nominal*. For *Christian adherents*, see page 93.

adult members people (aged at least 12 or 18, depending on the *denomination*) who are communicants or full church members. Statistics for adult members are recorded in the "members" column in the denominations table in *Operation World*. In this book we use inclusive figures (*adherents*) for Christian totals.

affiliated Christians all who are considered as belonging to organized churches. It includes full members, their children and regular participants in church activities, those who represent the whole Christian community. [Statistics for affiliated Christians are recorded under "Affiliates" in the *denominations* table, as well as under "pop %" and "affiliates" columns (as an absolute number) in the megabloc table in *Operation World* and were used to derive denominational figures in Chapter 4 here.]

AfAsLA An acronym I coined for this book for Africa, Asia and Latin America. This is a neutral term I use in preference to more inaccurate or possibly condescending terms such as "third world", "*developing world*", "global south", which I use sparingly. See pages 3, 13 (HDI), 101.

affinity bloc See page 169.

Anglicans one of the six Christian *megablocs* described in this book. See pages 100, 111.

anti-semitism See note 34 on page 92.

awakening a movement of the Holy Spirit that includes a significant turning to God among the unconverted. See page 132.

born-again believers those who by grace and through faith in the atoning work of Christ have been regenerated by the Holy Spirit. The phrase is often used to denote those who claim an *evangelical* conversion experience. See also page 140.

Catholics one of the six Christian *megablocs* described in this book. See page 105.

Charismatics/charismatic pertains to those who testify to having had a renewing experience of the Holy Spirit and who exercise the gifts of the Spirit, such as speaking in tongues, healing, prophecy and miracles. The charismatic renewal, or "Second Wave" Pentecostalism, has generally remained within the established *denominations*. The later "Third Wave" renewal movement has been less closely associated with formal Pentecostalism or the charismatic move-

ment. Second and Third Wave charismatics are considered as a single grouping in this book. Operation World's global survey of *denominations* assessed the percentage of *affiliated Christians* in each of the world's 37,500 *denominations*, from 1990 to 2010, that identified themselves as *Charismatics*. See page 121.

Christians people who professes to be Christians (Matthew 10:32 and Romans 10:9). The term embraces all traditions and confessions of Christianity and does not indicate the degree of commitment or theological orthodoxy. See page 93.

Church the universal, invisible Church and also its manifestations in *denominations*, national and international bodies

church a local fellowship of believers. "Church planting" means the starting of a church or a network of churches.

cross-cultural missionaries full-time *Christian* workers sent out/commissioned by a *church* or mission agency to work among people of a different culture, within their own country or abroad. See also page 226.

denomination an association or network of local congregations, linked together formally or informally, within any given country. Note that in this book international denominations are counted multiple times according to the number of countries in which they are present. See also page 115.

developed world the industrialized nations of the world. See EuNAPa

developing world See AfAsLA.

ethnic religions a generic term for a variety of informal religions, such as ancestor worship, animism, fetishism, shamanism and spiritism. In this book I have broadened the term to also include all more formal religious groups that are ethnically based, such as Baha'i, Druze, Jainism, Judaism, Sikhism, Shinto, Taoism, Yezidis etc. See page 87.

ethno-linguistic group see page 168. In this book, transnational ethno-linguistic groups are counted multiple times according to the number of countries where they have an identifiable community.

EuNAPa used in preference to "the *West*" or "*developed world*" for Europe, North America and the countries of the Pacific. See also *AfAsLA*.

Evangelicals/evangelical See pages 121, 140. Evangelicals are largely *Protestant, Independent* or *Anglican* though some are *Catholic* or *Orthodox*. They constitute one of the transconfessional/transbloc movements examined in this book. How Evangelicals are defined, and the statistics relating to them are fundamental to the contents of this book and form the basis for assessing the number of evangelical *Christians* and their spectacular numerical growth over the past few decades. *Operation World* classes as "Evangelicals": a) all *affiliated* Christians in *denominations* that are definitively evangelical in theology; b) those affiliated Christians in denominations that are not wholly evangelical who themselves have evangelical beliefs. This is a definition based on theology; it does not mean all evangelicals as defined above are *born-again*. In many nations, only 10–40% of Evangelicals may have had a conversion experience and regularly attend *church* services. However, using the term in this way does show how many people associate themselves with churches where the Gospel is being proclaimed. See Chapter 6.

evangelism   activity by *Christians* to spread the Gospel

evangelization   the process of proclaiming the Gospel globally or regionally. See pages 161–63.

evangelized   the state of having had the Gospel communicated and offered in such a way that the hearer becomes aware of the claims of Christ and the need to obey and follow Him. Possibly 1.7–1.9 billion people fall within this category in 2010. See pages 161–63, 168, 172.

evangelized non-Christian world   non-Christians who have been, or are likely to have been, exposed to the Gospel. The equivalent of *World B*. See pages 161–62.

First, Second and Third Worlds   the political division of the world during the Cold War (1946–99). See page 101. See also *AfAsLA, EuNAPa*.

First Wave charismatics   members of classical *Pentecostal denominations*

Great Commission   See page 21.

gross domestic product (GDP)   the total market value of all goods and services produced by a country each year, usually quoted as a per capita figure. See page 12.

home missionaries (or domestic missionaries)   full-time Christian workers who spread the Gospel (often cross-culturally) in their own country. See *cross-cultural missionaries*.

Independents   one of the six Christian *megablocs* described in this book. It includes recent breakaways from *denominations* in other megablocs, as well as indigenous denominations not started by foreign missionaries and post-denominational networks. See page 112.

Islamism   a set of ideologies holding that Islam is not only a religion but also a political system, emphasizing the following: enforcement of *shari'a* law (on Muslims); pan-Islamic political unity; and the elimination of non-Islamic, particularly Western, influences in the Muslim world. In its most extreme form, its activist zealots embrace suicidal terrorism to become a "martyr" for the cause. See page 76.

Marginals   a stream of Christianity treated as a *megabloc* in this book, comprising marginal or fringe Christian groups. See page 114.

megabloc/Christian megabloc   See page 100 and page 138, note 8.

migrants   a generic term that covers all who move from their area of origin. I have used it mainly for labourers who have every intention of returning home once their contracted work is completed. An immigrant is an incoming migrant, usually arriving with the intent to settle in a new land. An emigrant is a migrant who leaves their home area with the intent to settle elsewhere. See page 4.

missionary   See page 226. See the FGC website for a fuller definition. In this book I have sought to reconcile differing definitions by dividing all missionaries into three categories: foreign, *cross-cultural* and *home*/domestic. Foreign missionaries are cross-cultural unless they work in expatriate communities of their own culture.

Nevius principles   the principles of self-government, self-support and self-propagation that underlie the mission strategy for planting viable *churches* formulated originally by pioneering 19th-Century American missionary John Nevius

nominal believers   those who profess to belong to a religion but are not really committed to its tenets or practices. See page 93.

Orthodox   one of the six Christian *megablocs* described in this book. See page 107 and page 120, note 19.

Pentecostals/pentecostal   pertains to charismatic Christians *affiliated* to *denominations* committed to a pentecostal theology, usually including a post-conversion experience of baptism in the Spirit and exercising the gifts of the Spirit. See page 121, 126.

people cluster   See page 169.

people movement   See page 132.

peoples/languages   a term used in Chapter 7 of this book to reconcile the Joshua Project listing of *ethno-linguistic* people groups with the mapped language polygons derived from the *The Ethnologue*. In more than 85% of the records, the ethno-linguistic people group and its spoken language are congruent, but I use this "mongrel" term to include the exceptions. See page 172.

Protestant   one of the six Christian *megablocs* described in this book. See page 108.

reached   See *unreached*.

renewal movement   See page 124.

revival   the restoration to living faith of believers/*churches* that had experienced the regenerating power of the Holy Spirit but subsequently became cold, worldly and ineffective. It is often wrongly applied to evangelistic campaigns. See page132.

Second Wave charismatics   Christians who have experienced renewal within mainstream, non-pentecostal *denominations*

syncretism   the attempt to synthesize elements of different religious systems into a single body of belief and practice. Baha'ism, for instance, is a synthesis of Islamic, Christian and other religious beliefs. Some African Independent *Churches* have sought to synthesize elements of Christianity with pre-Christian traditional beliefs. See page 121.

Third Wave charismatics   Christians in newer *charismatic denominations* or post-denominational networks

transconfessional movement   a term applied in this book to *Evangelicals, Charismatics* and *Pentecostals*, as each of these can be found in more than one of the six Christian *megablocs*. See page 121.

unreached   an *ethno-linguistic* people group among whom there is no viable indigenous community of believing *Christians* with adequate numbers and resources to *evangelize* their own people without outside (*cross-cultural*) assistance.

West/Western   see *EuNAPa*.

Worlds A/B/C   terms used in the WCD to describe respectively the "*unevangelized*", "*evangelized*" and "*Christian*" worlds. They are defined more fully on the map on page 162.

ABBREVIATIONS

A   Anglican

ABs   affinity blocs, see Definitions

Af   Africa

AfAsLA   Africa, Asia and Latin America, see Definitions

AGR/Ann Gr   annual growth rate

AICs   African Independent Churches

AIDS   acquired immune deficiency syndrome

AIM   AIM International: Africa Inland Mission International

As   Asia

B   Buddhist(s)

BBBs   believers from a Buddhist background

BMBs   believers from a Muslim background

C   Catholic(s)

CMS   Church Missionary Society

Congo, DR   Democratic Republic of the Congo (Congo-DR)

CPA   Christian Patriotic Association, the officially recognized association of churches in China (see also TSPM)

E   East

Eu   Europe

EU   European Union

EUMC   European Monitoring Centre on Racism and Xenophobia

EuNAPa   Europe, North America and Pacific, see Definitions

Ev, Evang   Evangelical(s)

FGC   *The Future of the Global Church*

GDP   gross domestic product

GMI   Global Mapping International

GNP   gross national product

H   Hindu(s)

HDI   human development index

HIV   human immunodeficiency virus

HK   Hong Kong

HRE   Holy Roman Empire

I/Indep   Independent(s), see Definitions

IMB   International Mission Board (of the Southern Baptist Churches)

IPCC   Intergovernmental Panel on Climate Change, see note 14, page 32

J   Jews

JAARS   Jungle Aviation and Radio Service (a sister organization to WBT)

JP/L   Joshua Project/List

LA   Latin America (including Central America and the Caribbean)

LCWE   Lausanne Committee for World Evangelization. now LM

LM   Lausanne Movement

MANI   Movement for African National Initiatives

M   Muslim(s); also used for Marginal Christians (depending on context)

ME, M East   Middle East

MENA   Middle East and North Africa

N   North, non-religious (non-rel)

NA   North America

N/non-rel   non-religious

OECD   Organisation for Economic Co-operation and Development, see Fig 1.37, page 14

OM   Operation Mobilisation

OW   *Operation World,* when not italic it refers to the database

Pa   Pacific

PCs   people clusters

PGs   people groups

PIA   Protestant/Independent/Anglican

PJRN   Persekutuan Jaringan Riset Nasional=Indonesian National Research Network

PNG   Papua New Guinea

P/pop   population

R/rel   religion/religious

S   South

SIL-WBT   Summer Institute of Linguistics—Wycliffe Bible Translators

SIM   Serving in Mission, an interdenominational agency that has had a variety of names with the same acronym

SNNP   Southern Nations Nationalities and Peoples (Region)

TB   tuberculosis

TCM/s   trans-confessional Movement(s): in *Operation World* this is termed "Trans-Bloc groups"

TSPM   Three-Self Patriotic Movement, the official government body that oversees registered churches of the CPA

UAE   United Arab Emirates

UK   The United Kingdom of Great Britain and Northern Ireland, used in preference to "Britain"/"Great Britain"

UN   United Nations

US, USA   United States of America

USCWM   US Center for World Mission

USDs   United States Dollar(s) ($)

USSR   Union of Soviet Socialist Republics—preferred use the Soviet Union

W   West

WCD   World Christian Database, the online database of the *World Christian Encyclopedia* (WCE)

WCE   *World Christian Encyclopedia*

WCH   *World Christian Handbook* (1947–1968)

WEA   World Evangelical Alliance, formerly World Evangelical Fellowship

WEC   WEC International: Worldwide Evangelization for Christ

WEF   World Evangelical Fellowship, see WEA

WMC   World Missionary Council

WVS   world values survey

YWAM   Youth With A Mission

Demography: Nine Global Challenges

Without doubt, the future holds many surprises. For example, who could have foreseen:

▲ **natural disasters** such as the Asian tsunamis in December 2004 and March 2011, or earlier cataclysms such as the eruptions of super-volcanoes that have decisively changed the course of human history?

▲ **catastrophic pandemics** such as AIDS, emerging in 1980, or the bubonic plague that wiped out much of the world's population on at least three occasions in the last two millennia? What other new (or even mutated old) diseases may suddenly become global killers?

▲ **the collapse of Communism in Europe**—without a conflict—from its apogee in 1974–76 to the tearing down of the Berlin Wall in 1989?

▲ the rise of China, from the nadir of Mao's "cultural revolution" to its ascendancy as an industrial giant 30 years later, still Communist but transformed by capitalism?

▲ **the growing influence of religion** (despite Western secularist predictions of its imminent demise)? The unexpected resurgence of a militant form of Islam has created a new, "asymmetric" superpower, while attempts to eradicate religion in Communist China have actually so indigenized Christianity that China could soon become a major force in global Evangelicalism.

Predicting the future is dangerous![1] Past and present trends hint at what might be. How should these mould Christian ministry in obedience to the Great Commission? In this first chapter I focus on nine factors that will impact our world (not a comprehensive account as other important topics have been omitted). The content of this chapter informs the conclusions in subsequent chapters.

Population

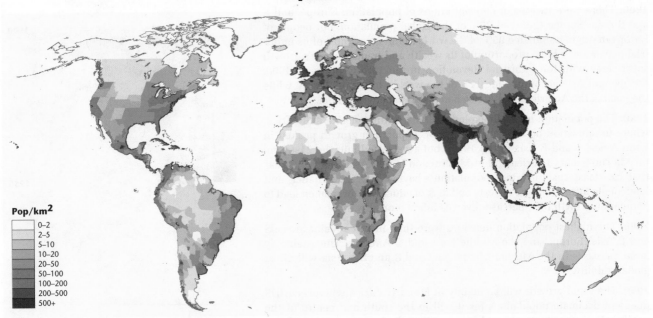

Pop/km²
0–2
2–5
5–10
10–20
20–50
50–100
100–200
200–500
500+

Fig 1.1 *The population density in 2010 by the 3000+ provinces of the 243 countries of the world*

The population disparities are huge. Note where the concentrations are on this map. Subsequent maps will show changes in density by country from 1900 to 2050. Two-thirds of the world's population live within 500 km of a coast. This has benefits for wealth generation and trade, but there are dangers in more low-lying areas if climate change causes a significant rise in sea levels.

Often, the threat to the world's more populous, fertile and civilized regions has come from its apparent wildernesses. Great empires have been overthrown by invaders such as the Medes, Goths, Huns, Mongols, Arabs and Turks. Is it from the "wastes" of N Africa and C Asia that destruction might come in the 21st Century?

Future projections of population are based on many assumptions. The UN population database is the primary source used throughout this book. I have used the 2004 database median projections, but adjusted a few national statistics where there were significant changes in 2006 and 2008. I have also drawn upon other UN databases for longer-range projections for country and city populations. The UN also gives high and low projections, which are displayed in Fig 1.2. The peaking of the world's population at around 9 billion in 2050 will place huge demands on global resources and ecosystems. The dire predictions of unrestricted population growth are therefore unlikely to be fully realized.

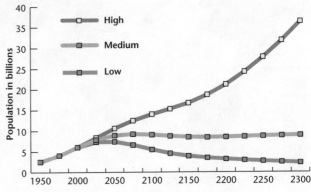

Fig 1.2 *Global population projections, 2000–2300*

POPULATION

In Fig 1.3 the growth of the world's population is shown for each of the six inhabited continents, the smallest being the Pacific, which includes Australia and nearly all the Pacific island territories. Note the colouring used for each continent, which I have employed fairly consistently throughout this book.

The area of each circle is proportionate to the population. Most of the diagrams and statistics I have used cover the 20th Century, with projections to the middle of the 21st.

The minimal growth in Europe is a contrast to every other continent. The populations of the Americas and the Pacific are growing as a result of both birth rate and considerable immigration. Africa and Asia's growth is almost entirely down to birth rate.

The world maps in Fig 1.5 show the population changes by country over the 20th Century with projections to 2050. Note

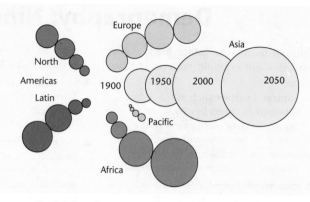

Fig 1.3 *Population growth by continent, 1900–2050*

that here, and throughout the book, country borders that were valid in 2000 are used for the whole period 1900–2050, so that comparisons can be made. This period has seen the most dramatic growth in population in the history of the world. In this, the 20th Century is likely to prove unique in terms of both population growth and mass migrations across continents. By 2050 we shall probably be nearing an equilibrium, but massive population movements will continue. Compare the situation at the 50-year markers in Fig 1.5.

1900: There were two major concentrations of population: Europe, and E and S Asia. Europe then had 25% of the global population, but people of European origin dominated 95% of the world's land mass, most of its industrial power and a huge proportion of its wealth and trade. Europe's growth spurt came with the Industrial Revolution in the 19th Century. In 1900, Europe and Asia accounted for 84% of the world's total population, while the Pacific, the Americas and Africa had just 16% between them.

1950: The population began to explode in Asia, Latin America and Africa, where urbanization became a major factor. Population growth peaked in Latin America and E Asia in the 1990s, but accelerated into the 21st Century in sub-Saharan Africa and in Muslim and Hindu Asia—the very areas that can least sustain larger populations—having poor governance and inadequate infrastructure. Poverty and lack of education for women lead to population growth rate increases even as infant mortality increases.

2000: The highest population densities were then in three major areas: S and E Asia, Europe and the Middle East, and C America. Unsustainably large increases in the Muslim Middle East and S and SW Asia will affect global stability.

2050: The rapid growth will be mainly in E and W Africa wherever AIDS does not decimate populations (as it will in the south and centre of the continent). Generally speaking, Africa has seen the lowest economic development despite being resource-rich. Corruption, tribalism, the distorting effects of aid dependence and lack of investment in education and infrastructure are to blame. The future is bleak without political, social and economic improvements. In 2050, Europe's population will have dropped to a mere 7% (and the West's to 12.6%) of the world's population—for a definition of 'the West' see page xiii.

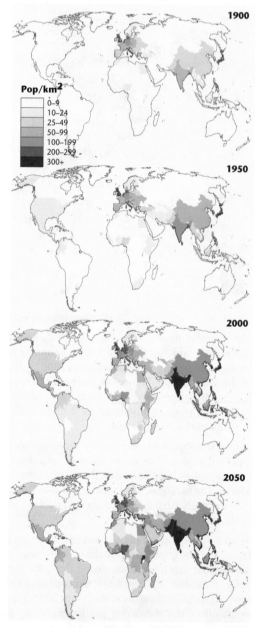

Fig 1.5 *Changing population densities, 1900–2050*

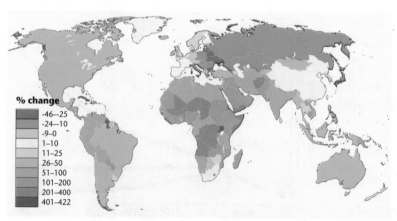

Fig 1.4 *Population change projection, 2000–50*

The population of the more developed world peaked with the post-Second-World-War baby boom around 1960. Fig 1.6 compares the more and less developed worlds by plotting the population estimates for those aged under five and adults aged 25–29[2] for each five-year period respectively. Globally, there is likely to be a peak in births around 2015, and an adult population peak around 2040–60.

Likely trends in the 21st Century: the world's most populous countries

In 1950, it was mainly industrialized, developed countries that topped the list. This changed in the second half of the 20th Century as birth rates plummeted in developed countries while those of the developing world peaked in the 1990s.

By 2000, the two most populous countries, India and China, were nearly equal in population and countries in the developing world began to dominate the list. Only five developed countries remained on the list. Generally the fastest biological growth (i.e. birth rate minus death rate) was Muslim.

In 2050, growth will be mainly in populations that are Muslim or African or both. Of the original developed countries, only two will remain on the list; but Mexico and Brazil will by then be joining the more developed countries.

By 2100, population growth will be highest in Muslim countries in Africa and Asia. It is likely that many of them will suffer severe shortages of food, water and resources and their impoverished millions will be forced to migrate to a Europe whose own population is shrinking.

The next 60 years will be ones of huge disparities between those parts of the world where population is already declining and those where it continues to grow. Only after this period is the global population likely to plateau. These disparities will create tensions within countries, as much of the growth will occur in places afflicted by corruption, inequality, lack of healthy development and generally inadequate education, infrastructure or resources.[3] The deprived poor will either fight to take their share or migrate to earn it.

In *the more developed world,* birth rates have fallen dramatically as a result of greater wealth, education and birth control, and the breakdown of families. By 2000, the populations of most developed countries were in decline. Only those with high immigration from the less developed world remained steady or grew.

In *the less developed world,* the population explosion was generated by industrialization, urbanization, improvements in agriculture, water quality and health care. The constraints upon it have ranged from China's harsh one-child policy to the involuntary limitation imposed by the AIDS pandemic in southern Africa. In most Muslim countries there are few controls on population growth, yet economic development is slowest there and the prospect is greatest that poverty will increase and water supplies will prove inadequate. This could make the Muslim world a demographic time bomb for the next two or three generations, provoking militancy, wars and massive emigrations.

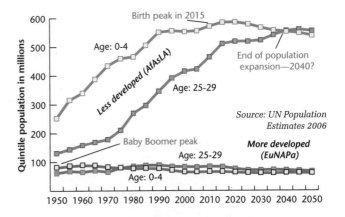

Fig 1.6 *Total population estimates for those under five and adults aged 25–29, 1950–2050*

Burning Question for Today

Growing population and poverty are linked. In poorer countries, people see having children as the best insurance for the future. Little of the financial aid that is given in less developed countries addresses the root problems or leads to sustainable, replicable changes.

▲ How should governmental, NGO and Christian aid best be administered to achieve these things?

Global stability may depend on how we help the poorer nations to secure a viable, hopeful future—failure could lead to ecological disaster, social collapse and huge migrations of people.

	1950	mil	2000	mil	2050	mil	2100	mil
1	China	555	China	1275	India	1531	India	1458
2	India	358	India	1017	China	1395	China	1182
3	USA	158	USA	285	USA	409	USA	437
4	Russia	103	Indonesia	212	Pakistan	349	Pakistan	409
5	Japan	84	Brazil	172	Indonesia	294	Nigeria	303
6	Indonesia	80	Russia	146	Nigeria	259	Indonesia	273
7	Germany	68	Pakistan	143	Bangladesh	255	Bangladesh	260
8	Brazil	54	Bangladesh	138	Brazil	233	Ethiopia	222
9	UK	50	Japan	127	Ethiopia	171	Brazil	212
10	Italy	47	Nigeria	115	Congo, DR	152	Congo, DR	203
11	France	42	Mexico	99	Mexico	140	Uganda	167
12	Bangladesh	42	Germany	82	Egypt	127	Yemen	144
13	Pakistan	40	Vietnam	78	Philippines	127	Egypt	132
14	Ukraine	37	Philippines	76	Vietnam	118	Philippines	129
15	Nigeria	30	Turkey	68	Japan	110	Mexico	128
16	Spain	28	Egypt	68	Iran	106	Vietnam	110
17	Mexico	28	Iran	66	Uganda	103	Niger	99
18	Vietnam	27	Ethiopia	66	Russia	102	Iran	98
19	Poland	25	Thailand	61	Turkey	98	Turkey	90
20	Egypt	22	France	59	Yemen	84	Afghanistan	90

☐ Muslims >80%   ☐ Muslims 30–80%   ☐ Muslims 10–30%   ☐ Refugee / migrant source

Fig 1.7 *Population: the top 20 countries, 1950–2100*

Figs 1.8 and 1.9 give statistics for the 10 countries receiving the most foreign-born migrants in 2001. One in 35 (191 million) of the world's population is a registered migrant. More than 30 million are illegal international migrants.[4] Few governments' censuses differentiate between locally-born and foreign-born members of ethnic-minority communities, so these communities are generally larger than official statistics indicate. The scale of movement of people from one continent to another is unprecedented in history, and will be a major preoccupation for governments for much of the 21st Century. It is vital that we all realize the social, cultural, economic, political and spiritual implications and prepare for this inevitable, unstoppable reality. Fig 1.8 shows that there is a massive flow of people to the West.[5] In Fig 1.9 most countries are smaller in size with high levels of migrant labour. In Western countries (Switzerland, Australia, Canada) and Israel these settlers are moving to reside in a new land. Most of the rest are migrant workers in the oil-producing Middle East or Singapore

Country	Population in millions	% of all migrants	Major migrant communities of 20th and 21st Centuries
United States	38.4	20.2	European, African, Asian, Latin Am
Russia	12.1	6.4	Russian from former Soviet states
Germany	10.1	5.3	German from E Europe, Turks
France	6.4	3.4	North African, Black African
Saudi Arabia	6.4	3.3	Various
Canada	6.1	3.2	European, Asian, Latin American
India	5.7	3.0	South Asian, Tibetan
UK	5.4	2.8	Caribbean, South Asian, E European
Spain	4.7	2.2	North African, Latin American
Australia	4.1	2.2	European, Asian
Other countries	91.2	48.0	
World total	190.6	100.0	

Fig 1.8 *Top 10 countries for foreign-born migrants (as a % of all migrants)*

Country	Population in millions	% migrants	Major migrant communities of 20th and 21st Centuries
UAE	3.2	71.4	Global variety, Arab, Asian
Kuwait	1.7	62.1	Global variety, Arab, Asian
Singapore	1.8	42.6	Global variety, Asian, Caucasian
Israel	2.6	39.6	Returning Jews
Jordan	2.2	39.0	Arab, especially Palestinian
Saudi Arabia	6.4	25.9	Global variety, Arab, Asian
Oman	0.6	24.5	Global cariety, Arab, Asian
Switzerland	1.6	22.9	Europeans, Turks, Arabs
Australia	4.1	20.3	European, Asian, Middle Eastern
Canada	6.1	18.9	European, Asian, Hispanic

Fig 1.9 *Top 10 countries for foreign-born migrants (as a % of the country's population)*

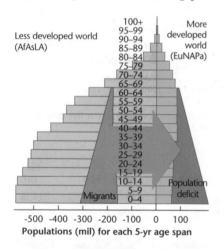

Fig 1.10 *Projected flow of immigrants to the West by 2025*

who will return to their homelands when their contracts end.

In Fig 1.10, the projected population pyramids for the less developed and more developed worlds are shown side by side for 2025. By that date, falling birth rates in the developed world will have created a population deficit, which will be made up, legally or illegally, from the poorer parts of the world until the global population begins to stabilize.

Fig 1.11 estimates a further 170 million migrants by 2050 if the current migration flow patterns do not change. Possible horrific demographic catastrophes—some are suggested in the table—most of which would affect Muslim-majority regions, could greatly increase that number and add to the large and growing Muslim communities that are least willing to assimilate into their host countries and cultures.

EuNAPa	Population 2050 (mil)	Migration gain/ loss (mil)	Catastrophe refugees (mil)	Possible catastrophe scenarios - both natural and through human causes
N America	438	+100	?	Nuclear terror incident: Yellowstone supervolcano
W and C Europe	430	+50		
Australasia	39	+18		
Rest of world			an additional:	There will be many surprises such as:
N Africa	312	–18.7	–40	Drought; failure of Nile flood; massive civil unrest
Sub-Saharan Africa	1,626	–15.5	–20	Wars, breakdown of economies
China (E Asia)	1,369	–18.5	–40	Breakdown of totalitarianism; civil war in China
The Pacific	985	–28.0	–15	Major volcanic eruption
C and S Asia	2,495	–26.8	–50	Wars in southern Asia or Muslim S and C Asia
Middle East	383	–2.8	–30	Sunni-Shia Muslim or water wars–nuclear?
E Europe	224	–19.0		
Latin America	783	–41.0	–25	Effects of climate change on rainfall patterns
World totals	9,039	Migrants: 170 mil 2000–2050?		Refugees an unknown extra number

Fig 1.11 *Possible migration patterns, 2000–50*

Demographic changes as a result of migration

It is helpful to survey the demographic implications of migration patterns over the first half of the 21st Century.[6] The global overview is followed by a look at the three 'worlds'—First (the West), Second (the Soviet bloc) and Third—as they were in the latter part of the 20th Century, and then at the West itself. The pie charts draw attention to the two components of the world population that will change the most: the shrinking Caucasian population (people of European origin) and the expanding and spreading Muslim population.

The pies in Figs 1.12 and 1.13 show the effects on the make-up of various populations of probable migration patterns during the first half of the 21st Century. The world population is divided into two broad ethnic categories: Caucasian (European-origin) and non-Caucasian. Both are then also divided into Muslim and non-Muslim, since it is the Muslim component that may prove most challenging politically, socially and spiritually during the 21st Century. The global Muslim population is likely to grow as fast as the Caucasian population shrinks (from 15.6% in 2000 to 8.4% in 2050 of the world population).

Fig 1.12 shows the proportions of these four groups in each of the three 'worlds'. There are likely to be two significant flows of migrants—Muslims to the West and Chinese to Siberia. These are represented by the red arrows, with the width of each arrow indicating approximately the size of the flow. The enlarged pink arrow represents what is likely to occur if there are major crises and wars in the Middle East, which will affect Europe proportionately more.

In Fig 1.13, the same categories are used. The two pies for the West from Fig 1.12 above reappear, but inverted and enlarged. The West is then separated into N America and Europe (using statistics for the 27 countries of the EU). Note:

▲ the increasing numbers of Muslims in the West, and especially Europe, even though the influx of non-Muslims is not much smaller than that of Muslims

▲ the increasing numbers of non-Muslims in Europe and (especially) the US—in the latter case, the larger increase is that of Hispanics and Asians

▲ The increase in the number of Caucasian Muslims is likely to be low and will largely be the result of Muslim men marrying non-Muslims.

▲ Muslims are likely to comprise 17% of Europe's population in 2050 at present rates of immigration, but the percentage could be higher if political, economic or natural disasters afflict the Middle East.

▲ By 2050, Caucasians will probably be a minority in N America.

▲ By 2050, Muslims could make up 28% of the population in France, over 20% in Bulgaria, the Netherlands and Italy and over 15% in Germany, Switzerland, Spain, Portugal, the UK and Greece. Most of this percentage growth will be due to immigration and to a higher birth rate among first-generation immigrants.

The final bar charts (Figs 1.14 and 1.15) look in more detail at the changes in composition of the population of two countries, the US and New Zealand, over the period 2000–50. In both cases, the Caucasian component will probably fall below 50% of the population.

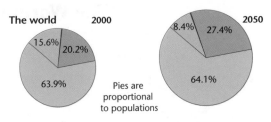

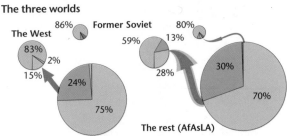

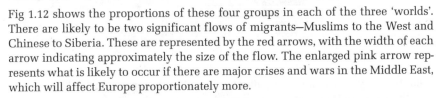

Fig 1.12 *Migration and demographic change, 2000–50*

Caucasian non-Muslim — Other Muslim
Caucasian Muslims — Other non-Muslim

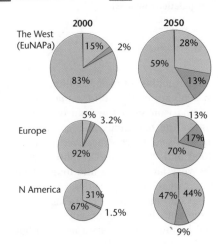

Fig 1.13 *Demographic change in the West, 2000–50*

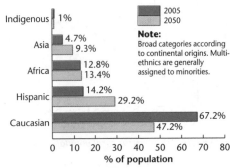

Fig 1.14 *Projected demographic change in the US, 2005–50*

Note: Broad categories according to continental origins. Multi-ethnics are generally assigned to minorities.

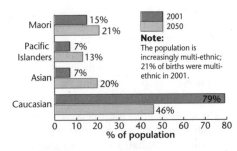

Fig 1.15 *Projected demographic change in New Zealand, 2001–50*

Note: The population is increasingly multi-ethnic; 21% of births were multi-ethnic in 2001.

Burning Question

The developed world may be more vulnerable than many realize. The Roman Empire in AD 200 looked strong but had been critically weakened. The world population had been halved by famine and pandemics. The Roman elite suffered a collapse of its birth rate as a result of immorality, family breakdown and lead poisoning. There were not the leaders or soldiers to defend the empire.

Hungry, desperate Asian peoples pushed westwards, driving Germanic peoples into the weakened empire and ultimately destroying it. A moral and spiritual fall of the Caucasian peoples is happening now before our eyes.

▲ Can Christians today rise to the challenge and forge a new community amid the collapse of the old, just as Christians did as the Roman Empire disintegrated?

The World's Megacities in 2000

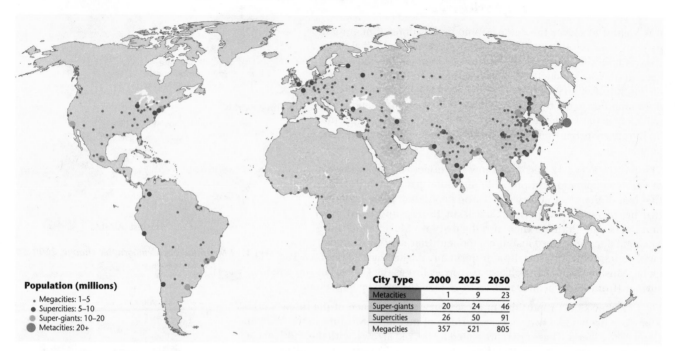

Population (millions)
- Megacities: 1–5
- Supercities: 5–10
- Super-giants: 10–20
- Metacities: 20+

City Type	2000	2025	2050
Metacities	1	9	23
Super-giants	20	24	46
Supercities	26	50	91
Megacities	357	521	805

All megacities[7] of over 1 million people in 2000 are marked on the map above. Comparison with the map on page 7 shows the enormous changes we can expect as cities grow massively between 2000 and 2050. The UN now divides the very largest cities into four categories: megacities, supercities, super-giant cities and meta-cities. These last are so large that they function across provincial boundaries and even national borders. There was only one meta-city in 2000, but they will increasingly dominate the world in the latter part of this century (see insert table on map above).

Urbanization is a global fact today that cannot be ignored. Throughout history, cities have set the trends and been sources of innovation and cultural change. Yet two thousand years ago the Roman and Chinese empires were only 5% urban. In 1800, only 3% of humankind lived in cities. It is estimated that in 2100 the figure will be nearly 90%. It was probably in 2007/08 that the world's population first became predominantly urban (see Fig 1.16).

By 2000, four continents were overwhelmingly urban. Africa and Asia were still mostly rural, but this is projected to change rapidly over the first half of the present century as many countries become industrialized.

The 21st Century will be the first urban century in history. This fact will affect every area of life, and mould the shape of Christian ministries in the future.

Most of the world's 10 most populous cities in 2000 were in the more developed world. By 2050, only Tokyo will remain in that list. There will probably be 23 metacities in 2050. All of the 10 most populous cities will be in Asia or Africa, and five of them will be in S Asia. Lagos is likely to be the largest city in the world. Of the top 10, only Shanghai and Tokyo are likely to be highly developed. Shanghai will possibly be the world's leading financial and industrial city. Most of the meta-cities will be vast, poorly governed and chaotic, with a huge proportion of their population living in slums in dire poverty.[8]

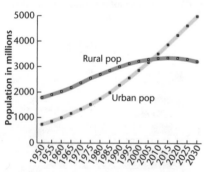

Fig 1.16 *Urban versus rural population*

Food for Thought

The urbanization of the world has important implications for quality of life in every area of human activity: cultural, social, linguistic and spiritual. Christian ministry will be affected enormously. Too many of us are hankering or preparing for a world that no longer exists.

▲ How should this realization influence our strategic planning and our emphases in training and ministry?

Top 10 Cities in 2000		Top 10 Cities in 2025		Top 10 Cities in 2050	
City, Country	**mil**	**City, Country**	**mil**	**City, Country**	**mil**
Tokyo, Japan	28	Mumbai, India	30	Lagos, Nigeria	64
Mexico City	18	Lagos, Nigeria	30	Mumbai, India	50
Mumbai, India	18	Tokyo, Japan	29	Karachi, Pakistan	50
São Paulo, Brazil	17	Karachi, Pakistan	25	Dhaka, Bangladesh	49
New York, USA	17	Dhaka, Bangladesh	24	Kolkata, India	34
Shanghai, China	14	Kolkata, India	21	Kinshasa, Congo-DR	34
Lagos, Nigeria	13	Mexico City	21	Delhi, India	33
Los Angeles, USA	13	São Paulo, Brazil	21	Shanghai, China	30
Kolkata, India	13	Shanghai, China	21	Addis Ababa, Eth	30
Buenos Aires, Arg	12	Delhi, India	20	Tokyo, Japan	30

Fig 1.17 *The world's 10 most populous cities*

The World's Megacities by 2050

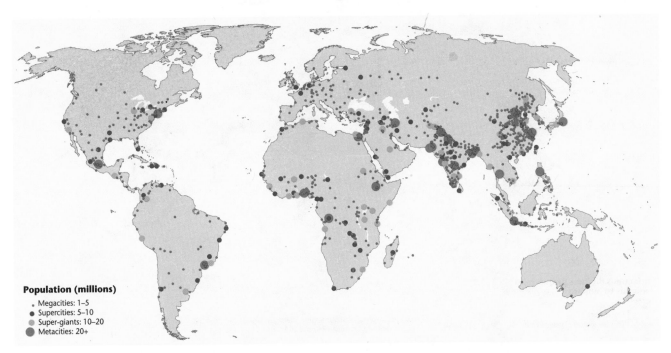

Population (millions)
- Megacities: 1–5
- Supercities: 5–10
- Super-giants: 10–20
- Metacities: 20+

Compare the map above with the one on page 6, opposite. The massive growth of cities in AfAsLA (see pxii) in contrast to the more static situation in EuNAPa is evident. By 2050, there may be only one city in Europe with well over 10 million inhabitants—and that will be Istanbul.

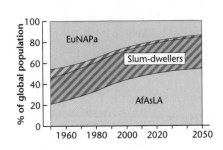

Fig 1.18 *The global distribution of city- and slum-dwellers, 1945–2045*

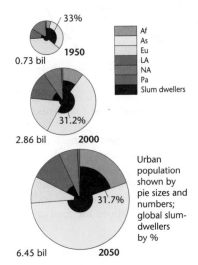

33%
1950
0.73 bil

31.2%
2.86 bil **2000**

31.7%
6.45 bil **2050**

Af
As
Eu
LA
NA
Pa
Slum dwellers

Urban population shown by pie sizes and numbers; global slum-dwellers by %

Fig 1.19 *City- and slum-dwellers by continent, 1950–2050*

The challenge of poverty

The rate of urbanization by continent is shown in Fig 1.18. By 2050, 71% of humankind will live in cities, and of these 85% will be in AfAsLA. The total of urbanites in 2050 will equal the total world population in 2008. The shaded strip on the graph shows the changes in the proportion of city-dwellers living in slums in EuNAPa and AfAsLA. By 2050, slum-dwellers will constitute 23% of the world's population, or nearly 2 billion people.

Note the minimal change in the global percentages for slum-dwellers (the black sectors) in Fig 1.19. Despite all the efforts of governments and NGOs to alleviate poverty in AfAsLA, the proportion of humankind living in slums is unlikely to be reduced by much over the next 40 years. Indeed, while the percentage of slum-dwellers in Asia and Latin America may fall, there will be a marked increase in Africa unless there is a radical change towards efficient governance. The situation in that continent will probably be horrific, with over 40% (840 million) of all Africans living in slums. Who will win the hearts and minds of these destitute, desperate people? In many countries, it has been Islamist movements that have had the greatest success in providing help—with strings—and thereby recruiting many for their violent agendas. Christians have so much to offer: a new identity in Christ, a caring community and hope for the future.

Township dwellings near Cape Town (photo by A Beattie), above, and The Waterfront by night (photo courtesy Lausanne Movement), below.

Burning Question for Today

Indigenous, grass-roots Christian movements have made an impact on the urban poor—especially in China, Latin America and parts of Africa.

▲ How much have foreign mission agencies contributed to the spiritual and physical needs of the large proportion of humankind that lives in urban slums?

Disease Hotspots, Past and Future

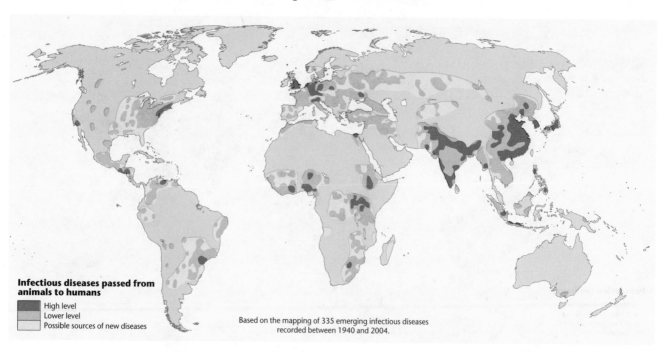

Infectious diseases passed from animals to humans
- High level
- Lower level
- Possible sources of new diseases

Based on the mapping of 335 emerging infectious diseases recorded between 1940 and 2004.

Medical science has cut child mortality, increased life expectancy and enhanced our ability to cure sicknesses. However, many viruses, bacteria and parasites are becoming immune to vaccines, antibiotics and pesticides. New diseases such as AIDS and SARS, Nipah fever, Ebola, bird flu, MRSA and "mad cow disease" have jumped species, some to create fearsome pandemics. The proximity of dense populations to domestic animals or wildlife increases the incidence of such diseases.

Zoonosis: an infectious disease that naturally occurs among animals or birds but can be transmitted to humans. Most diseases and plagues are zoonotic in origin, including perhaps smallpox, measles, diphtheria and the common cold. Some zoonotic diseases, such as anthrax, rabies and psittacosis, pass only from animal to human, not human to human unless they mutate. Others, such as flu, bubonic plague, TB and SARS, are highly infectious between humans and can become pandemics, leading to enormous loss of life.

The map above shows where 335 such zoonotic diseases have originated since 1940, and where new diseases could appear. Serious pandemics that wiped out a large part of the world's population have been a major factor in human history. The first known pandemics were bubonic plague in c950 BC (1 Samuel 5–6) and AD 541–750, smallpox (AD 165–80) and the Black Death (1343–50). Other major endemic diseases include leprosy, measles, polio, cholera and Spanish flu. Only one major disease has been eradicated from the earth—smallpox—though polio, too, could soon follow.

Food for Thought

Christians have always been at the forefront in the caring professions. In post-colonial times, medical missions have not had the same importance, for health care has been seen as a responsibility of government. Are we likely to need a new generation of Christian agencies to cope with future challenges that may be too large for governments to handle?

Mexico—a case study

The arrival of the Spanish in Mexico was catastrophic for the indigenous population (see Fig 1.20). First, the local population was decimated by the smallpox brought by the conquistadors, and then the indigenous, rodent-borne haemorrhaging fever known locally as *cocoliztli,* flared up as a result of a 40-year drought and jumped species to the human population, who, no longer having the strength to resist the invaders, were crushed and enslaved.[9] Estimates for population figures vary widely, but it is likely that the pre-conquest population was reduced by 90–95%.

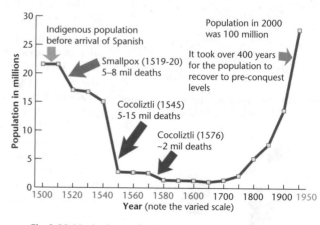

Fig 1.20 *Mexico's population collapse in the 16th Century*

Such catastrophic declines could happen again. Population pressure, climate change, global trade and travel all increase the risk of the spread of old and new diseases that could be disastrous for humans, livestock, wildlife, crops and plant life. The modification of DNA in plants and animals by scientists also has possibly global implications for good or evil.

The human immunodeficiency virus (HIV) is a terrifying enemy that most likely jumped species in W Africa from chimpanzees to humans some time in the 20th Century. It strikes at the heart of modern culture because it is transmitted mainly through sexual promiscuity and substance abuse. It devastates family life by killing parents and breadwinners. There appears to be little prospect of finding a complete cure, even though research has led to the development of drugs that inhibit the development and spread of the disease. But will these expensive drugs be made available for sufferers in poorer countries?

Fig 1.21 shows the areas of the world most affected—Africa most tragically, but increasingly Russia and S and SE Asia, too. The challenge of HIV is daunting for sufferers and those who are, or should be, caring for them and their families. In 2004–06, UN estimates of the number of sufferers were somewhat reduced, though it is hard to tell whether that is due to better analysis and reporting or an undercount. By 2005, 25 million people had died as a result of HIV, and this figure is increasing by 2–3 million every year. In 2006, there were 2 million children living with HIV. There were 15 million under 17 who had lost one or both parents to AIDS, of whom 12 million lived in Africa.[10] The table below lists the 10 countries known to be most afflicted with the disease.

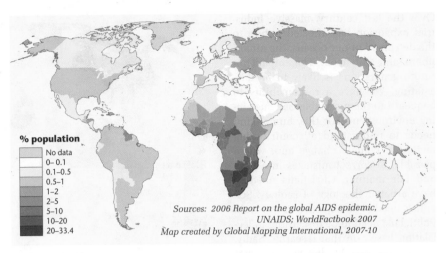

Fig 1.21 *The AIDS pandemic: HIV prevalence among adults aged 15–49*

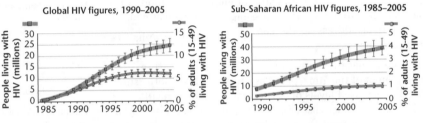

Fig 1.23 *People living with HIV: worldwide and in sub-Saharan Africa*

Country	Number
India	5,700,000
S Africa	5,500,000
Nigeria	2,900,000
Mozambique	1,800,000
Zimbabwe	1,700,000
Tanzania	1,400,000
Kenya	1,300,000
USA	1,200,000
Zambia	1,100,000
Congo, DR	1,000,000

Fig 1.22 *The 10 countries with the most adults and children living with HIV*

In Fig 1.23, the 2006 figures for HIV worldwide and in sub-Saharan Africa are compared. The upper lines show the absolute number of living sufferers and the lower lines the percentage of the population that has the virus.

Those in wealthier countries are living longer as a result of better drugs, which have reduced the death rate (though not necessarily the infection rate). The difficulty of measuring the incidence of HIV/AIDS means that the margin

for error is considerable, as the vertical max/min lines indicate. This is also shown in Fig 1.24, where margins for error are high in war-torn or failing states such as Swaziland and Zimbabwe, whose health services were barely functioning in 2006.

AIDS in Africa

Of the 10 countries most afflicted by HIV/AIDS, all but two are in Africa (Fig 1.22), with the centre and south of the continent most affected. In Fig 1.24, a portion of the flag of each country is used. The height of the oval shield indicates the possible maximum and minimum, and the width the more probable actual percentage. Uganda is the only country in the world that has faced up to the tragedy and reduced the percentage of its population with HIV, with the adult infection rate down from about 15% in the early 1990s to an estimated 6.7% in 2005. Once the worst-affected country in the world,

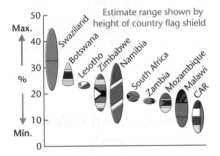

Fig 1.24 *The 10 African countries with the most adults (15–49) living with HIV*

Uganda is no longer even in the top 10. The main factor in this success was the widespread application of Christian moral standards.

Although some governments, NGOs and churches have made notable efforts to reduce infection rates and set up infrastructures to cope with the needs of victims, carers and the bereaved, too little has been done. Sadly, the active involvement of most African churches has been poor.

Burning Question for Today

The Church is the only network with the human resources, moral imperative and spiritual motivation to deal with the root causes of the spread of HIV (sexual promiscuity and substance abuse) and help its victims by providing local, self-sustaining mechanisms for survival, a loving community for the present and real hope for the future.

▲ How can the Church worldwide, and in Africa especially, be mobilized to help people living with HIV?

Over the last century, massive industrial expansion has affected nature to the detriment of our oceans, the atmosphere and life itself. The impact on future generations is likely to be devastating. We have a responsibility to bequeath to them a viable, self-sustaining environment. For this, humankind needs to understand all contributing factors to climate change and, where possible, to correct mistakes in a wise and fair manner. Christians need to have a better theology of ecology. Scientists need to be objective in research. Politicians need to be discerning in legislation based on that research. Sadly, there are many hidden agendas and much emotion in the current debate. Note how opposing views are often tackled by attacking the messenger rather than addressing the content of the message.

Despite its negative press, CO_2 is a key component of the atmosphere essential to life. Increased levels of CO_2 promote plant life and increase crop yields but also retain more of the sun's heat—the "greenhouse effect". Fig 1.25 shows the variation in CO_2 emissions per person between countries and regions. The huge disparity between the richer and poorer nations is both an indictment and a challenge that hinders all efforts to find agreement on how to reduce CO_2 emissions.

Science and global warming

The scientific evidence that global warming is solely or largely due to human production of CO_2 is not adequately established. No one knows the relative contributions to global cooling and warming over aeons of time of natural cycles (sunspot activity, changes in the planet's orbit, geo-magnetic reversal etc), catastrophic events (volcanoes, comets) and human activities. Nor is the science of atmospheric CO_2 well enough understood for it to make sense to seek to limit it by spending trillions of dollars heavily subsidizing "green" energy and investing in other ways to reduce emissions. Focusing on the contribution of human-generated CO_2 alone is not only unscientific but also dangerous, and possibly economically suicidal, for those countries that espouse such policies.[11] In times to come, it may be seen that the trillions of dollars should have been spent on dealing with air, water-table and ocean pollution, water management and the side-effects of man-made chemicals (plastics, drugs,

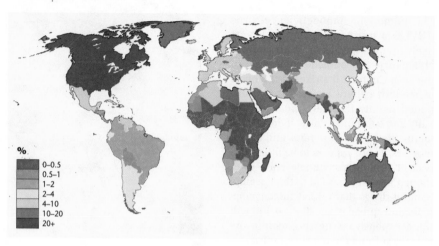

Fig 1.25 *CO_2 emissions per country*

dyes, food preservatives etc).

The graphs in Fig 1.26 are an illustration of this. Both show the results of research sponsored by the UN.[12] The two reports became the basis for international conferences[13] and much debate on climate change. The 1996 graph shows the estimated average temperatures for Europe since AD 800 based on many different "data sets" of scientific observation. The Medieval Warm Period (when Greenland supported farming and there was limited Arctic pack ice) is clearly visible. This was followed by the Little Ice Age, when Europe's climate became much colder. These changes were not caused by human activity. The 2001 graph, produced by Mann, Bradley and Hughes with corrections in 2004, was based on a more limited data set. It dispensed with the peaks and troughs of the earlier 1996 graph and supported alarming predictions of impending temperature rises—it is the bend in the graph line that gained it its nickname "the hockey stick". There is evidence that a global cooling cycle may have begun around 2000.[14]

Climate change happens and indeed is inevitable. Human history and the Earth itself provide abundant evidence of both multiple cycles of change and cataclysms. To these we add the impact of human activity over the past few centuries. The complex interplay between them all is only now beginning to be recognized. There are other possible sce-

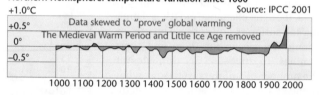

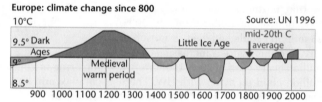

Fig 1.26 *The doubtful science of global warming*

narios that could be far more traumatic than CO_2-induced climate change.

An added box in Fig 1.27 on page 11 shows research estimates for levels of CO_2 in the atmosphere and also of global temperatures between 1950 and 2007. This shows that CO_2 levels are now higher than at any time over the four most recent ice ages.

Food for Thought

As Christians, we should be passionate about God's creation as His appointed stewards. We should be in the forefront in protecting and improving our environment and managing the finite resources of our earth-home. Yet the debate on climate change is charged with emotion, partisan politics and economic protectionism. We must be more objective in weighing the evidence and actively supporting viable solutions, living for God's glory and by His standards even if it means bearing a Celtic Cross. The Celtic Cross has a circle at its heart that symbolizes God's creation.

Cyclic changes

The larger graph in Fig 1.27 shows cyclic changes observed in history. There are also other cycles such as levels of sunspot activity and solar energy, changes in the Earth's orbit and reversals of its magnetic poles. No one knows how much these affect climate. This graph illustrates several cycles. These results were gained from analysis of temperature and CO_2 levels from air bubbles trapped in Antarctic ice over the past 420,000 years. This provides evidence of four ice ages and briefer warm periods such as we are now experiencing. No one yet knows what causes the alternating cold and warm periods, but it appears we should perhaps fear another ice age more than a warming! It is also interesting that this graph shows that when you compare changing levels of temperature and CO_2, the latter lags behind. Does rising temperature cause higher CO_2 levels rather than the other way round or does each reinforce the other? In a few decades we may be worrying about how we can heat the Earth up to ensure continued food production!

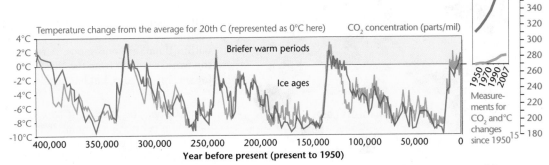

Fig 1.27 Temperature and CO_2 concentration in the atmosphere over the past 420,000 years [16]

Cataclysmic changes

Only in the last few decades has the evidence of massive and sudden climate changes accumulated. There has been speculation about interference from another planet (a possible cause of the biblical flood?) and collisions with comets and their impact on life on earth. More common would appear to be volcanic eruptions—the largest of these coming from what we now call "super-volcanoes".[17] All of these are beyond our ability to predict or control. Fig 1.28 lists some of the larger eruptions in prehistoric (green) and historic (red) times, with a measure of the volume of material they ejected into the atmosphere and a brief description of their global impact.

Some components of the atmosphere enhance the greenhouse effect, notably increased levels of water vapour, CO_2, methane, nitrous oxide etc. There are other substances that cause global dimming or cooling—greater cloud cover, aircraft vapour trails, extended ice or snow cover and volcanic eruptions that spew out sulphur dioxide (SO_2), all of which reflect the sun's heat into space. Could atmospheric engineering with stratospheric SO_2 counteract the effects of CO_2?

Food for Thought

There are numerous events described or foretold in the Bible, not least by Jesus Himself, that are specifically catastrophic. We should not be surprised when such things occur.

▲ Are we preparing Christians not to be overwhelmed by such events but to be ready to minister to the millions who could be affected?

We are warned that the end of time will be cataclysmic (2 Peter 3) and will come only after the Gospel has been preached throughout the whole world (Matthew 24:14).

▲ Are we ready for Jesus' appearing, having fully obeyed His commission?

Volcano	Vol km³	Age/ year	Impact on earth and humankind
Yellowstone, USA	2,500	2.2 mil	Unknown, but probably similar to Lake Toba below; possibly 80-90% mortality of most animal species
Yellowstone, USA	1,000	640,000	Unknown; much of vegetation and life likely to have died in the decades of famine and darkness that followed
Lake Toba, Indonesia	2,800	75,000	80-90% mortality of most animal species and followed by a 1,000-year deepening of the last Ice Age
Lake Taupo, New Zealand	1,170	26,500	Effects on climate would have been global with darkness, major famines and droughts
Santorini, Greece	100	?1620 BC	End of Minoan civilization; radically affected the whole Middle East and beyond with famines and droughts.
Lake Taupo, New Zealand	100	AD 181	Half the world's population perished in the droughts, famines and plagues that followed. Roman Empire fatally weakened
Krakatoa, Indonesia	100+	535	Over 100 million died in famines, wars and plagues. Existing civilizations weakened or collapsed. Aided rise of Vikings and Islam
Laki, Iceland	14	1783	Disastrous for Northern Hemisphere. Famines in Europe and Middle East. One of stimuli for unrest in France and the French Revolution.
Tambora, Indonesia	160	1815	1815 was the year without a summer worldwide. Weather patterns affected. The entire population of Sumbawa Island died.
Krakatoa, Indonesia	25	1883	The explosion heard 5000 km away; tsunami noticed in London UK. Over 36,000 people lost their lives.
St Helens, USA	4	1980	Local devastation; loss of 57 lives. Some global cooling
Pinatubo, Philippines	10	1991	Huge quantities of sulphur dioxide enlarged the Antarctic ozone hole. Globe cooled by 0.4°C. Main effects were localized.

Fig 1.28 Volcanoes and climate change

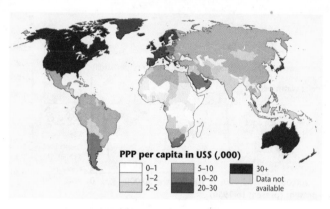

Fig 1.29 *National wealth in 2004*

PPP per capita in US$ (,000)

0–1	5–10	30+
1–2	10–20	Data not
2–5	20–30	available

The world distribution of wealth

Before the Industrial Revolution there was little difference in living standards between nations across the world. The disparities today between rich and poor nations, and individuals within them, are enormous. A remarkable redistribution of the world's wealth from the West to the rest has been evident for several decades, but has accelerated since 2008.

Gross Domestic Product (GDP): GDP is a measure of the size of a country's economy.[18] It represents the total market value of all goods and services produced by that country over a single year. Dividing GDP by population allows a reasonable comparison of per-capita incomes between countries. The GDP-PPP adjusts for the relative difference in purchasing power between countries, and therefore makes possible a fairer comparison.

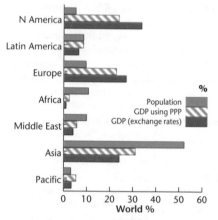

Fig 1.30 *Comparison of GDP, GDP-PPP and population by continent in 2000*

Fig 1.29 shows the startling disparities between countries, with the poorest being in C and W Africa. In the 18th Century most trade was in agricultural produce. Colonial rule and industrialization transferred much of the world's wealth to the West and Japan. The centuries-long technological advantage enjoyed by China, India and the Muslim Middle East was then lost to the West. The technology of the East (from making paper to making steel) was used to develop mass-production industries that created new wealth.

Capitalism was the primary mechanism—though its inherent greed was challenged and constrained by the moral and ethical standards of Christianity, whose underpinning helped to disseminate its gains in the West. The current loss of this lies at the heart of the global financial disasters since 2007.

Fig 1.30 shows the major regions of the world and differences in population and GDP. The hatched middle bar shows the adjustment produced by the PPP calculation (a US dollar goes further in a poorer country). Globalization is rapidly reversing the flow of wealth, from the old industrial countries to the new ones in Asia. Sadly, Africa has been abused and neglected, but its economic uplift may come from China and India as they scour the world for resources for their own massive indus-

trialization. Most of the Middle East would resemble Africa were it not for its vast, but unevenly distributed, oil reserves—and one day still may do without major political and social change.

A survey in 2006[19] analyzed the total assets of each country, rather than its annual income (see Figs 1.29 and 1.31). N America, Europe and the richer Asian countries possess 87% of the world's wealth and just 13% is shared by the rest. The wealth of Brazil, China and India is set to increase rapidly—hastened by the calamitous banking crisis in the West from 2008 on. The amoral greed of financiers and bankers and their speculations also damaged the credibility of both capitalism and democracy, which were inspired by biblical ethics. Much of the poorer world's oil revenues, as well as money amassed by its corrupt politicians, has been invested in the richer countries and provided some of the capital for these speculative adventures. In 2000, household wealth worldwide averaged $20,500 per family. The individuals who constitute the world's richest 10% own 85% of its assets—and the richest 2% own 50%. The poorest 50% of humankind own only 1% of the world's assets.

The pie chart in Fig 1.32 shows the distribution of wealth between the regions of the world even more starkly.

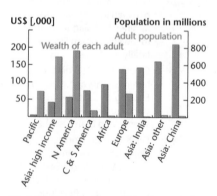

Fig 1.31 *Household wealth and population by continent in 2000*

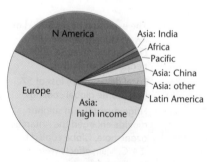

Fig 1.32 *Global distribution of household wealth in 2000*

Food for Thought

The growing disparities between rich and poor bode ill for future global stability. Raising the standard of living of the poor to that of the rich is not sustainable. The initiative lies with the wealthy but is unlikely to be taken willingly by them.

▲ In what ways can we, as individual Christians and in our churches, encourage each other to be responsible consumers—and encourage our politicians to move our society in the same direction—as part of our biblical calling as God's representatives on earth?

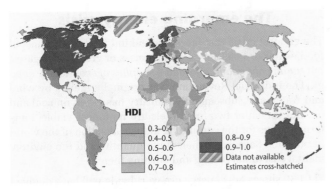

Fig 1.33 *World Human Development Index (HDI), 2004*

Fig 1.33 uses the UN definition of "developed" countries (HDI>0.8), "middle level" countries (0.5–0.8) and "less developed" countries (<0.5). There has been relatively little improvement over the last 50 years, especially in Africa. Many factors contribute to this: borders drawn by imperial powers in the 19th Century divided peoples and produced unviable states, corrupt governments stole their countries' wealth and failed to bring development, and old resurgent diseases (malaria, sleeping sickness, bilharzia, TB), as well as new diseases such as AIDS, have caused devastation.

The Human Development Index (HDI):

HDI is a composite scale[20] that assesses the quality of life in every country in the world using statistics on life expectancy, literacy, education, standard of living and GDP per capita. It is a global standard for measuring development and the success of government policies and helps to set the direction of the policies of UN agencies. I have used the data from 2004 and 2006 on these pages.

Corruption

Corruption is defined as "the misuse of entrusted power for private gain" (Transparency International [TI]). Fig 1.34 is based on the TI Corruption Index. This does not measure less severely punished "white collar" crime by businesses and individuals, which is estimated to have cost nearly $600 billion in the US in 2005. Nor does it measure the higher cost of the 2008 financial crash, and its aftermath, caused by speculative gambling by rich-world bankers and financiers.

The cost of corruption:

To the global economy: About 10–20% of global GDP is spent on bribery—about $US1 trillion in 2005.[21]

To political parties and governments: Worldwide, an estimated US$400 billion a year is lost to corruption in awarding government contracts, and 20–50% of aid to developing countries is stolen before it can reach its intended recipients.

To police forces and legal systems: Loss of respect and trust—they are usually the worst offenders for demanding bribes or kickbacks.

To individuals: Every year, over 10% of humankind pay a bribe.

To freedom: Corruption increases the gap between rich and poor, cripples meaningful development and limits democratic, legal and economic reform.

The Great Recession and "Banksters". Low interest rates and easy credit made possible excessive borrowing by individuals and banks. Greed trumped wisdom. Housing "bubbles", together with rising oil and food prices, provoked an inevitable crash and a banking crisis in 2008. These have become known as the Great Recession. Massive amounts of public money were poured into the ailing banking system to forestall a deep depression. The only ones who seem to have benefited have been the bankers themselves. It is with some justification that bankers and financiers have been labelled "banksters". The cost to countries and individuals has been enormous. Recovery will take years. This cost is illustrated in figures shown in Fig 1.35 for the UK and US. The national debt and the cost of the bailout for the banks and finance industry are shown in relation to the GDP.[22]

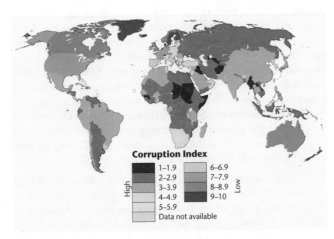

Fig 1.34 *Perceived levels of corruption in 2007*

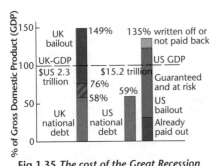

Fig 1.35 *The cost of the Great Recession*

Food for Thought

▲ Is it right to blame only the world's poorer countries for their endemic corruption?

Arguably, the richer countries are just as guilty in stimulating corruption by giving unfair local subsidies and inappropriate or unaudited aid and by supporting unsavoury regimes in countries of strategic importance. Likewise, international banks provide secret accounts for poorer-world kleptocrats in rich-world tax havens that are ostensibly free of corruption.

Burning Question for Today

Christians cannot afford to be complacent! In 2008, US$390 billion was given to Christian causes,[23] but $25 billion of that was probably embezzled, and further billions wasted on inappropriate "aid".

▲ How can Christians apply biblical ethics to economics and also be wisely and prayerfully generous in their giving for the sake of the Kingdom?

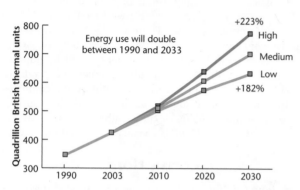

Fig 1.36 *Total primary-energy consumption worldwide*

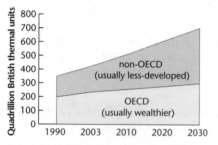

Fig 1.37 *Comparison of primary-energy consumption in OECD and non-OECD countries*

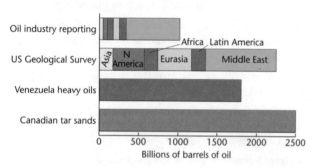

Fig 1.38 *Global oil reserves as estimated in 2000*

Suburban street in Kawasaki, Japan (photo by PJK)

Food for Thought

Committed Christians of the 18th and 19th Centuries spoke out against the sinful structures of the society of their time and effected dramatic changes in promoting prison reform and education, opposing slavery and colonial exploitation and many other areas.

▲ Where are the Christian leaders of the 21st Century who will challenge structures and vested interests that protect and manipulate the lucrative oil trade?

The emerging energy crisis

The greatest crisis that faces humankind is not a shortage of food, water or health care or an excess of greenhouse gases, but *finding abundant, affordable supplies of eco-friendly energy*. The Industrial Revolution was originally fuelled by wind and water, and subsequently industry has relied on coal and oil. But the latter two fossil fuels are no longer viable, long-term options for the continuing industrialization of the world in our time because of their finite quantity and the environmental cost of harvesting and burning them.

Fig 1.36 shows how energy use worldwide will have doubled between 1990 and 2030. Pollution and eco-degradation will therefore increase proportionately. That energy use could be higher if no action is taken to reduce it (the "high alternative"), or it could be lower with more vigorous action by most countries (the "low alternative"). International agreements such as the Kyoto Protocol are likely to have only a marginal impact because they are limited to just one component of the problem: CO_2. The enormous cost and the need for all countries actively to participate make any significant global agreement unlikely.[24] Any major alternative to fossil fuels will have to be economically viable or it will not be accepted as a solution.

As much of the world's industry moves from the wealthier democracies of the OECD to poorer countries (see Fig 1.37), their energy needs will grow exponentially.[25] Most of this growth is now being supplied by burning coal or oil. The consequent ecological damage could be severe. China and India's polluted cities are evidence of this, as are dying sea-shelf ecosystems around the world. The richer countries want to limit global emissions of CO_2, but other countries blame them for creating the problem in the first place and insist they must pay for it, while they themselves must be allowed to emit more CO_2 so that they can catch up economically.

Today, oil reserves are running down. Fig 1.38 shows recent estimates of those reserves. "Peak oil" is the term used to refer to the point when the rate of production reaches its maximum, after which it will decline. The increase in the price of crude oil in 2006–08 and again in 2010–11 suggests that we may soon reach that point.

The world's limited oil reserves. Oil companies reckon that global oil reserves are half what the US Geological Survey estimates (see Fig 1.38). Both alike exclude the vast reserves of heavy oils and tar sands in Canada and Venezuela and the global shale gas resources (not shown on this graph): these would greatly extend the availability of oil far into the future, but their exploitation would be eco-hostile, if potentially profitable. High oil prices also expose underinvestment in exploration and in developing alternative sources of energy while oil prices were low. The only long-term solution is to find ways to generate energy cheaply and locally without harming food production or the environment in the process. This could be achieved in this century if there were the will and the commitment. What could be the future sources of such energy? On page 15 some possible options are suggested.

Oil has often proved a curse to countries that possess it. Few major oil-producing countries have used their revenues wisely. Many have been corrupted by them, with elites becoming super-wealthy while ordinary people rarely benefit. This has distorted international politics, encouraged crime and corruption, provoked wars and helped to finance the arms trade—both legal and illegal. It also contributed to the global financial crisis that started in 2008.

The world's present energy sources

Fig 1.39 presents an assessment of total energy production worldwide in 2006. The larger column labels the five main source categories, three of which are fossil fuels. The smaller column subdivides sources of renewable energy (all scaled to the right-hand 10% scale). The fossil fuels are coal, oil and gas. Burning these fuels returns to the atmosphere the CO_2 that aeons ago was sequestered in the Earth's crust. The 89% of our energy now sourced in this way may be reduced to 75% by 2050, but it will take deep levels of commitment internationally to achieve this!

Nuclear energy can be produced by splitting radioactive elements such as uranium, thorium and plutonium. Known sources of uranium ore may last only 70 years, but fast-breeder reactors can create further fuel as a by-product,

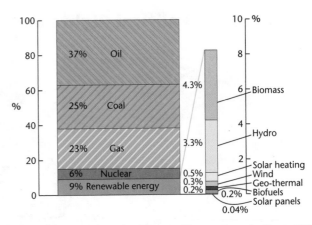

Fig 1.39 *Renewable and non-renewable energy production in 2006*

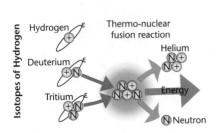

Fig 1.40 *Thermonuclear energy: three isotopes of hydrogen*

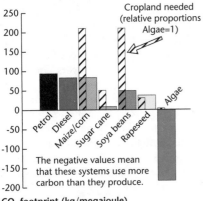

CO₂ footprint (kg/megajoule)

Fig 1.41 *Generating energy from biofuels*

which could serve for hundreds more years. The downside is the cost of constructing and eventually dismantling nuclear power stations and the difficulties of disposing of the radioactive waste safely. There is also the risk of accidents such as the explosion at the Soviet Chernobyl reactor in 1986, and Japan's tsunami and Fukushima nuclear disaster of 2011. The overall costs and the need for government subsidies make this an unlikely and unpalatable energy source in the long term.

Renewable energy can be harvested from sources such as sunlight, wind, ground heat, tides and biofuels. Energy from such sources could increase from 9% of all energy produced in 2006 to around 15–18% in 2030. With existing technology, renewable energy cannot replace fossil fuels; it will help to reduce the proportion of our energy derived from them, though not the amount, and it may not even reduce our carbon footprint. Most current sources are subject to daily and seasonal changes in weather patterns. Some will never be commercially viable, ecologically desirable or even an appropriate use of resources. Any energy source that has to rely on subsidies to be commercially viable cannot be a good solution.

The world's possible future energy sources

Thermonuclear fusion is the fundamental energy that powers the universe. Hitherto, we have succeeded only in replicating this in weapons of mass destruction. Efforts to harness it over half a century have so far failed. Fig 1.40 shows the most attainable of these thermonuclear reactions, using "heavy water" or the slightly heavier isotope of hydrogen (deuterium) that represents 0.015% of all hydrogen atoms in naturally occurring water. The even heavier tritium is mildly radioactive and can be

made in a nuclear reactor. These two form the basis of a low-radiation reaction that could produce the energy we need. One cubic kilometre of seawater contains enough deuterium to power the world for many years.

The exploitation of *biofuels* is a major area of research. How effective are they? Fig 1.41 presents a recent assessment of the comparative energy yields and carbon footprints of different crops.[26] Maize and soya beans require a lot of land and have a large footprint. Rapeseed or palm oil and sugar are better, but still need much land and water. Given the world food and water crises that are now developing, setting aside agricultural land for fuel production will raise food prices further, thereby provoking widespread social unrest as it lowers the standard of living for many. A better prospect is the farming of *oil-producing algae* and bacteria, which require a feedstock of sewage, nitrogen and CO_2 and are best cultivated on otherwise unproductive land. The fact that sewage could become a marketable commodity for producing energy in deserts is a win-win situation![27]

What of the future for energy? The present crisis may prove to be a transition from 250 years of a fossil-fuel economy to one of almost unlimited green energy based on nuclear fusion and the heat of the desert, turned into electricity by solar panels[28] and algae farms. Present efforts to exploit the tides, the wind and the sun and to plants crops to harvest bio-oils are too costly in terms of resources and too dependent on weather, the seasons and the Earth's rotation for these to become major sources of energy. How many wind farms will there be in 50 years' time? Their electricity production is far lower, more costly and less reliable than their advocates dare admit!

Food for Thought

▲ Have we allowed our addiction to oil and other fossil fuels to make us look for the wrong answers to the damage they cause and their possible demise as major sources of energy?

Trillions of dollars are currently committed by our governments to an interim patch-up.

▲ Would it be wiser to spend the money on the basic research into better alternatives not yet being tapped, and then in due course switch to them.

Political Rights and Civil Liberties in 2007

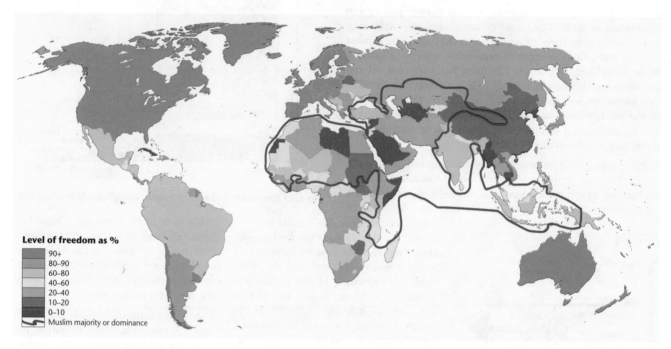

Level of freedom as %

- 90+
- 80–90
- 60–80
- 40–60
- 20–40
- 10–20
- 0–10
- Muslim majority or dominance

The Universal Declaration of Human Rights

Everyone is entitled to all the rights and freedoms set forth in this Declaration, without distinction of any kind, such as race, colour, sex, language, religion, political or other opinion, national or social origin, property, birth or other status. Furthermore, no distinction shall be made on the basis of the political, jurisdictional or international status of the country or territory to which a person belongs, whether it be independent, trust, non-self-governing or under any other limitation of sovereignty.

United Nations, 1948, and the International Bill of Human Rights, 1989

Nearly every member state of the UN was in favour of this Declaration and the subsequent Bill, but by 2007 less than half of them were applying the terms to which they had agreed. These form much of the basis for international law.[29] Freedom House in the US has devised a composite index that measures political rights and civil liberties.[30] Both the map above and Fig 1.42 are based on this. With only a few exceptions, it is the influence of Christianity on cultures and nations that has promoted these freedoms. Religious freedom and democracy

often then create stability and wealth. Conversely, note the area of Muslim majority or dominance where truly democratic government is rare and civil liberties are few. In few Marxist-, nationalist- or Muslim-ruled states is there religious freedom.

Fig 1.42 gives an overview of the tumultuous 20th Century. Note how levels of freedom have increased. In 1900, few democracies had universal suffrage for both men and women. True freedom was at its lowest ebb after the Axis powers conquered wide swathes of Europe and Asia in 1942, at a time when colonial and Communist powers controlled much of the rest of the world. There has been steady, if slow, improvement since the subsequent demise of Fascism, colonialism and Communism. This is likely to continue, though at an even slower pace. The greatest threats to human freedom are presented by nationalistic dictatorships (such as Eritrea, Myanmar, N Korea and Uzbekistan), collapsed states (such as the two Congos, Somalia and Zimbabwe) or Muslim states that implement aspects of *shari'a* law.

We can rejoice over the great increase in political, civil and religious liberty since 1945—yet the challenge remains that there are many countries where people do not enjoy such freedoms. It is often those very countries where the Gospel of the Lord Jesus Christ is least known and proclaimed and where Christians are persecuted for their faith.

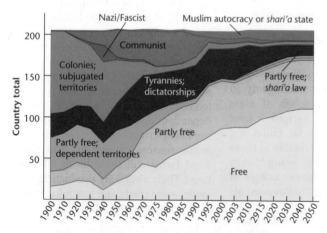

Fig 1.42 *Global political freedom, 1900–2050*

Food for Thought

For the many countries where freedom is seriously restricted, the first priority is individual and corporate prayer—for the rulers, and for avenues by which the Gospel can be proclaimed. There are many global prayer movements, but it is in the Church in the West that intercessory prayer is least treasured and practised.

▲ Why have so many professing Christian politicians failed to live up to biblical standards of morality?

▲ Where are the 21st-Century Christians who will challenge evil customs, structures of sin, tyranny and institutionalized greed?

Conflicts of the First Decade of the 21st Century

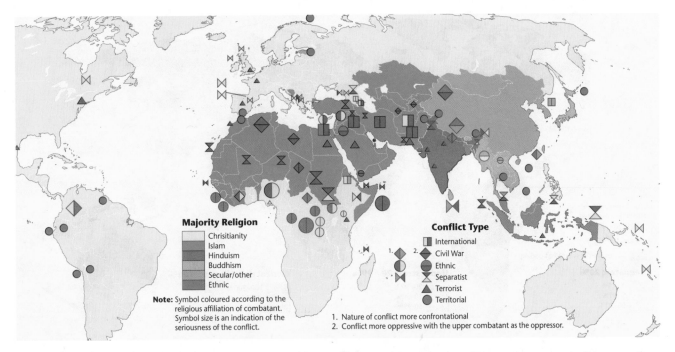

Majority Religion
- Chrisitianity
- Islam
- Hinduism
- Buddhism
- Secular/other
- Ethnic

Note: Symbol coloured according to the religious affiliation of combatant. Symbol size is an indication of the seriousness of the conflict.

Conflict Type
- International
- Civil War
- Ethnic
- Separatist
- Terrorist
- Territorial

1. Nature of conflict more confrontational
2. Conflict more oppressive with the upper combatant as the oppressor.

Current and emerging conflicts will deeply affect the life and witness of the Church in the 21st Century. Much of the 20th Century was dominated by global conflicts based on distorted, anti-religious Western ideologies—Fascism, Nazism and Communism—that emerged from the Enlightenment. After the Second World War, we lived under the threat of nuclear war between the Western and Communist blocs, but the Third World War never broke out.[31] The euphoria at the collapse of Communism in Europe raised the hope that there would at last be real peace and progress without the threat of war hanging over us. It was a forlorn hope. The map above shows this. Note how many involve Muslims.

The 21st Century opened with the "9/11" terrorist attacks on the US, following the Islamist al-Qa'ida's declaration of war on the "Crusaders" and the corrupt Muslim states that deal with them. Religion has returned as a significant component of present and likely future wars, though many of these may not be specifically religious in nature. This map uses symbols to denote the religious background of combatants and the oppressive or confrontational nature of the conflicts in 2000–11. A Third World War between superpowers looks unlikely for the foreseeable future, but we are involved in a global "asymmetric war" instigated by Islamist networks with a vision for Islam's global dominance.

Fig 1.43 is based on an analysis of the 74 significant wars and conflicts over territory that were waged between 2000 and 2008—some of which had their beginnings in the 20th Century. The death rates for both sides in these wars are indicated by the black bars and bottom scale. Note that the total number of dead in these wars was around 12 million, but many of these are represented in the bar chart in more than one column. Sadly, the high death toll in conflicts involving Christians is largely due to genocide—purportedly Christians killing Christians in Congo-DR, Rwanda and Burundi, or Muslims seeking to eliminate any Christian presence in Indonesia, Nigeria and Sudan. The likely future scenario will be for regional, civil and ethnic wars, and wars instigated by radical Islamist terrorism.

Although "Christian" nations are involved in many of these conflicts, very few of those shown on the map are instigated by Christians because of their faith. In present times, Christians are involved more because they are victims, or citizens of countries engaged in military involvements that have a professing Christian majority.

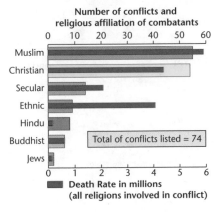

Number of conflicts and religious affiliation of combatants

Total of conflicts listed = 74

Death Rate in millions
(all religions involved in conflict)

Fig 1.43 *Conflicts of the first decade of the 21st Century*

Burning Question for Today

The Lord Jesus warned us that there would be wars and turmoil in the world until His return in glory. He also pronounced peacemakers blessed. Many today condemn religion, including Christianity, as a cause of conflict, and sadly this accusation has some truth in it—though most forget that the worst mass murderers of the last century were actively anti-Christian (eg Stalin, Hitler, Mao, Pol Pot).

▲ How can we, as followers of the Prince of Peace, stand up for the democratic freedoms and civil liberties bequeathed to us by our Christian heritage and be effective peacemakers in a world full of hatred, violence and war?

Global Water Use Projected by 2050

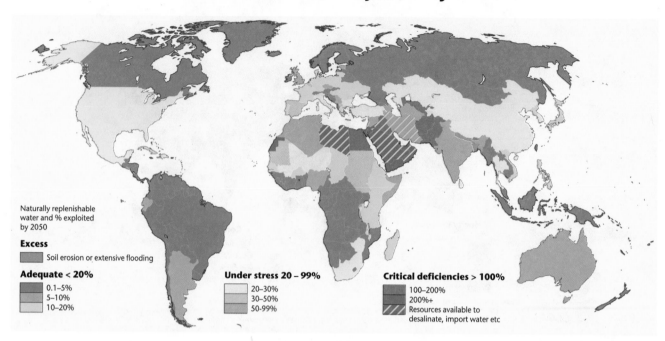

Naturally replenishable water and % exploited by 2050

Excess
- ▨ Soil erosion or extensive flooding

Adequate < 20%
- 0.1–5%
- 5–10%
- 10–20%

Under stress 20 – 99%
- 20–30%
- 30–50%
- 50–99%

Critical deficiencies > 100%
- 100–200%
- 200+
- ▨ Resources available to desalinate, import water etc

Population growth, rising living standards and the industrialization of many parts of the developing world all put pressure on water resources. The map above, based on UN statistics,[32] shows the varying levels of stress. The challenges range from too much water in Nepal and Bangladesh to far too little in some parts of the Middle East and N Africa. The UN estimated that in 2003 over 40% of the world's population did not have access to clean water or lived in areas with serious water pollution. If major climate change occurs, this figure could rise dramatically.

The problems are greatest in Muslim (and especially Arab) countries, where population growth is highest and water supplies limited. Those in desperate need will either fight or flee to areas where water is available. There are solutions to this growing crisis, but they require good governance and much investment: the conservation and recycling of water must be improved; new, affordable methods of desalination must be found; and unsustainable water subsidies for agriculture should be ended. Failure to do this will impoverish billions, provoking large-scale migrations and even war.

Israel and Palestine: an example

Fig 1.44 shows the inequality since Israel's occupation of the West Bank and the Golan Heights in 1967's Six Day War. Israel controls almost the entire water supply of the Jordan Basin west of the river and allocates only 11% to the Palestinians who comprise nearly half the population.

The conflict between Israel and the Arabs over Palestine is one of the longest-standing and most intractable conflicts in the world today. Both Palestinians

and Jews claim the land, based on their religious beliefs and histories. This is a conflict over land and water that negatively impacts the region and indeed the wider world. Any valid settlement of this dispute will require an equitable sharing of water. The two maps that follow show the political complexities (Fig 1.45) and the hydrological situation (Fig 1.46 on p19) in Israel/Palestine.[33]

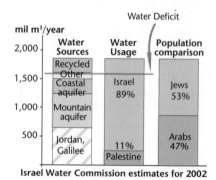

Fig 1.44 *Supply and use of water in Israel/Palestine in 2002*

Fig 1.45 *Political map of Israel/Palestine in 2008*

Burning Question for Today

The conflict between the Israelis and the Palestinians has polarized Christian opinion between those who support Israel blindly because of their eschatology[34] and those who sympathize with the manifestly unjust treatment of the Palestinians. This damages the ability of the Church to help Arabs and Jews to find peace through the Cross of Christ.

▲ How can Christians help to find a solution rather than aggravate the problem?

Major River Systems of the World in the 21st Century

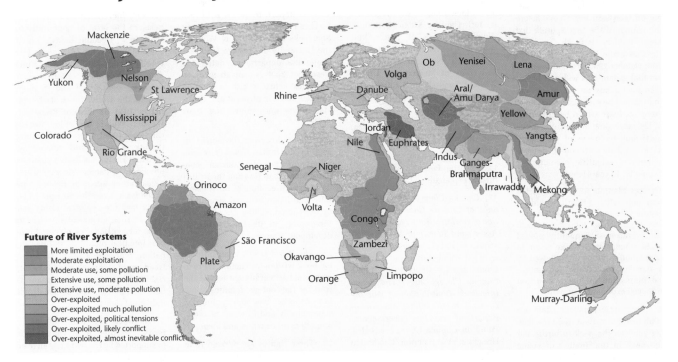

Future of River Systems

- More limited exploitation
- Moderate exploitation
- Moderate use, some pollution
- Extensive use, some pollution
- Extensive use, moderate pollution
- Over-exploited
- Over-exploited much pollution
- Over-exploited, political tensions
- Over-exploited, likely conflict
- Over-exploited, almost inevitable conflict

Industrialization and population growth strain global resources. Water is the most basic resource for life, but also one of the most threatened. Without it, manufacturing, energy generation and food production would all be impossible. The pollution of river systems and seas and the shrinking per-capita availability of water will seriously affect the quality of life of most of the world's population in coming decades. The map above shows the levels of threat that will face 37 of the world's most important river systems. Even the less stressed systems are in danger.[35] Over-exploitation is a problem in nearly every part of the world. Many countries depend on stressed international river systems such as the Nile, the Indus, the Amur and the Mekong, where there is likely to be serious friction. In extreme situations, as with the Jordan, Aral&Amu-Darya and Tigris-Euphrates systems, this could lead, or has already led, to international wars. The next 50 years are critical. Failure to find solutions could decisively tip the balance towards ecological catastrophes that would affect agriculture, health, biodiversity, climate and the productivity of the seas.[36]

Israel and Palestine: an example (continued)

The Palestinian *intifadas* or uprisings since 1988 led to immense suffering and poverty. Most cross-border employment came to a halt. The tit-for-tat killings between the two sides continue endlessly. It is easy to see how this has generated anger, hatred and vengefulness on both sides. Suicide bombings prompted Israel to build a massive wall inside Palestinian territory, which has only a few gates. This is still under construction and no one is sure of its final route, but one possibility is shown on this map. The wall is having a devastating impact on the West Bank, obstructing family life, employment, the movement of people and normal flows of water. Tragically, the descendants of the people the Nazis imprisoned in ghettos have themselves created ghettos for the Palestinians. The conflict has fuelled extremism on both sides. This has impacted both the once-large number of Palestinian Christians (many of whom have now emigrated) and the small but growing number of Messianic Jews. The honour/shame cultures that influence both Judaism and Islam complicate any efforts to find a solution.

Future of River Systems

- Israel–pre-1967 bordets
- Palestinian Authority (PA)
- Israeli Wall under construction
- Coastal and Mountain aquifers
- Jordan River basin

Fig 1.46 *Israel, Palestine and water in 2008*

Food for Thought

Water is vital for all life and every human activity. Every item we use has a "water embedment" figure. A pair of jeans takes nearly 11,000 litres (73 bathfuls) of water, a kilogram of beef nearly 4,000, a single cup of coffee 140 litres.[37]

Many countries need to export food and industrial products in order to survive economically but they may in effect be exporting their limited supplies of water. Water availability may prove to be one of the most critical factors in the global economy and politics in the 21st Century.

1.   I remember well as a boy in 1956 hearing Harold Spencer Jones, then Britain's Astronomer Royal, saying on television two weeks before the launch of the first Sputnik that Man would never reach the moon. He also wrote in *New Scientist* on 10th October 1958: "I am of the opinion that generations will pass before man ever lands on the moon and that, should he eventually succeed in doing so, there would be little hope of his succeeding in returning to the Earth and telling us of his experiences." A demonstration of the inexactness of scientific prediction—it happened 10 years later!

Thomas Malthus in 1798 predicted that population growth would be exponential and would outstrip the linear growth of food production. His premises subsequently proved to be incorrect. An explosion in population growth was followed by a deceleration, while technological innovation in food production achieved exponential growth.

2.   Source: UN population database 2050 medium variant. Note the time lag between the peak in births and the peak in the number of young adults. Fuller details of sources are given on the DVD and the website.

3.   Examples of failed or failing states include: Somalia, which has turned to piracy; Haiti, a nation of refugees; Pakistan and Yemen, both havens for violent Islamism; and N Korea, a nuclear-armed gulag.

4.   "People trafficking is now a bigger business than drug trafficking ...Between 400,000 and 500,000 migrants are smuggled into the European Union each year" (*The Economist*); "The United States estimated in 2002 that 300,000 to 400,000 unauthorized foreigners crossed its borders every year" (UNHCR—the original PDF article can be found at: citeseerx.ist.psu.edu/viewdoc/download?doi=10.1.1.61.4528.pdf)

5.   Russia and India's immigrants are mostly returning ethnic Russians or Indians born abroad.

6.   Source: International Organization for Migration (http://www.iom.int/jahia/Jahia/lang/en/pid/1 et al). The latest report of the IOM: http://publications.iom.int/bookstore/free/WMR_2010_ENGLISH.pdf contains later statistics than those used in this book.

7.   Megacities are defined as all conurbations of over 1 million people. These can include cities and suburbs outside recognized municipal boundaries. I have followed the UN definitions for megacities of over 5 million: supercities (5–10m), supergiants (10–20m) and meta-cities (20m+).

8.   These figures were derived and extrapolated from the UN statistics and World Christian Database. One wonders whether such vast cities could ever develop or function—if they do, their level of stress and deprivation will be a huge challenge.

9.   "Megadrought and Megadeath in 16th Century Mexico", Rodolfo Acuna-Soto, David W Stahle, Malcolm K Cleaveland and Matthew D Therrell (National Autonomous University of Mexico and University of Arkansas), April 2002 (http://origin.cdc.gov/ncidod/EID/vol-8no4/01-0175.htm)

10.   See http://data.unaids.org/pub/GlobalReport/ 2006/2006_GR_CH02_en.pdf.

11.   See the PowerPoint notes for further explanation.

12.   *Climate Change 1995: The Science of Climate Change—Contribution of Working Group I to the Second Assessment Report of the Intergovernmental Panel on Climate Change*, eds. J T Houghton et al (London: Cambridge University Press, 1996); *Climate Change 2001: The Scientific Basis—Contribution of Working Group I to the Third Assessment Report of the Intergovernmental Panel on Climate Change*, eds. J T Houghton et al (London: Cambridge University Press, 2001)

13.   The Kyoto Protocol of 1997, which was supplemented in 2007

14.   There is much on the internet that supports both the concept of global warming and global cooling. There is considerable debate about whether there has been continued fast global warming since 1998 or whether there has been a plateauing or even decline in global temperatures. See this website: http://notrickszone.com/2011/01/22/signs-of-strengthening-global-cooling/. This contains an interesting graph with the IPCC projections of rapid warming and other projections concerning a cyclic warming and cooling cycle related to sun spot activity. The two successive N Hemisphere cold winters of 2009/10 and 2010/11 would seem to support the alternative. The next two decades will provide evidence as to which is more correct.

15.   As measured on the top of the volcano Mauna Loa in Hawaii. See http://www.eoearth.org/article/Mauna_Loa_curve.

16.   "Climate and Atmospheric History of the Past 420,000 Years from the Vostok Ice Core in Antarctica", J R Petit, J Jouzel et al, *Nature* 399 (3 June 1999), pp429–36

17.   The eruption of Krakatoa in AD 535–36 was devastating and caused 11 years of famine and plague. It led to the collapse of empires and ushered in the Dark Ages (most aptly named!). See http://ezinearticles.com/?Days-of-Darkness-(AD-535-AD-546)&id=202540.

18.   In *Operation World* 2001, we used Gross National Product figures for each country. GNP differs from Gross Domestic Product in that it also includes total foreign inward investment.

19.   The report, by James B Davies, Susanna Sandstrom, Anthony Shorrocks and Edward N Wolff of the University of Western Ontario's economics department, dated 5th December 2006, sought to measure countries' actual wealth in 2000 by calculating their physical and financial assets and subtracting their debts.

20.   The index was developed in 1990 by the Indian Nobel-Prize-winner Amartya Sen, the Pakistani economist Mahbub ul Haq and the British development economist Sir Richard Jolly, and has been used since then by the United Nations Development Programme in its annual human development report.

21.   *The World is Flat* is an influential book written by Thomas L Friedman. His basic argument is that the world is flat—not geographically but in every other way now: politically, economically and in terms of trade, migration, information and ideas.

22.   These figures are derived from the International Monetary Fund 2010 Report, CIA World Factbook 2010 and the UK Office for National Statistics. The CIA and UK-ONS use different ways of measuring national debt—the CIA's higher figure is indicated by the cross-hatching.

23.   Figures derived from David Barrett's Christian statistical review for 2008 in the *International Bulletin for Missions Research* of January 2008.

24.   The Kyoto Protocol, 1997 (supplemented in 2007)

25.   The Organisation for Economic Co-operation and Development, consisting of 25 industrialized democracies

26.   "Biofuels and Biodiversity: Principles for Creating Better Policies for Biofuel Production", Martha J Groom, Elizabeth M Gray, Patricia A Townsend, *Conservation Biology*, vol 22 no 3, pp602–09

27.   Oil-generating algae that consume three of the principal unwanted by-products of human activity—sewage, nitrogen compounds and CO_2—to produce a fuel that can be burnt in existing engines may seem too good to be true, but viable strains of algae that do this are being developed. It is calculated that 5,000 km^2 could one day meet the current fuel needs of the whole of the US.

28.   Since writing this a new enterprise to exploit solar energy in the world's deserts has been launched: http://www.desertec.org/?gclid=CM6pvYbsuagCFQUKfAod_2ASCg

29.   The full document can be found at http://www.un.org/Overview/rights.html. Over time, this was followed by other covenants and protocols that were subsumed in the International Bill of Human Rights in 1989.

30.   Freedom House has sought to measure the level of conformity to these in a "freedom index", which can be found on the DVD under File FreedomIndex-07April08.xls. Freedom House defines itself as "a clear voice for democracy and freedom around the world. Since its founding in 1941 by Eleanor Roosevelt, Wendell Willkie and other Americans concerned with the mounting threats to peace and democracy, Freedom House has been a vigorous proponent of democratic values and a steadfast opponent of dictatorships of the far left and the far right." The index measures political rights and civil liberties, giving equal weight to these seven categories: electoral process, political pluralism and participation, functioning of government, freedom of expression and belief, rights of association and organization, rule of law, and personal and individual rights.

31.   Between 1947 and 1990, many proxy wars, often local, were fought or supported by the two sides all over the world, resulting in as many as 20 million deaths.

32.   I have extrapolated future projections from 2030 to 2050. See http://www.fao.org/nr/water/aquastat/water_res/index.stm.

33.   A good analysis of this conflict over water, by Chuck Spinney and dated June 2003, can be found at http://www.prorev.com/mideastwater.pdf I have also drawn on other materials in compiling the maps. The actual route of the West Bank wall has not officially been published, and there are likely to be changes. See http://www.btselem.org/download/separation_barrier_map_eng.pdf.

34.   The strongly premillennial and dispensational views of the "end times" among some Christians influence Western policies and give credence to the Muslim perception that these policies are Christian and anti-Muslim.

35.   The destruction of rainforests in Brazil, SE Asia and Indonesia, the use of mercury in illegal gold extraction in the Amazon area and the pollution of Arctic systems with mining all pose a serious threat.

36.   The PowerPoint notes cover these river systems and the prognosis more thoroughly.

37.   http://news.bbc.co.uk/1/hi/sci/tech/8628832.stm

History: 20 Centuries AD

The aim of this book is that we as Christians should be better prepared for ministry in the 21st Century. Some knowledge of history is essential if we are to understand our world and communicate the Gospel in a relevant way.

I look back in this section at the world's history in the light of the Great Commission, which I believe is the key to history. This is a philosophy of history that could well be seen as looking at the world through rose-tinted glasses—Mark Twain's quote (right) is relevant here! Yet I believe passionately that history is "His story" of redemptive acts in human affairs. God *is* in control. Jesus reigns *now*.

History seems to be merely a catalogue of suffering, greed, lust for power, cruelty and bloodshed in which humankind stumbles from one tragedy to another. Yet there is another level of history centred on God's Kingdom. It addresses rather the heroic faith and exploits of the often hated, despised and persecuted body of people who have met with God through faith in Jesus Christ and obeyed His Last Command. They have decisively influenced our world for good in every realm of human life.

This section is designed to show these two sides. For both, I have given a few key dates with some observations relevant to our ministry in the 21st Century. On the left-hand page is a summary of each century in terms of its politics, wars and movements of peoples and the religious affiliations of its rulers. I have also included developments in political Christianity. Often, such factors as these are catalysts for the advance of the Gospel, or barriers to its progress. On the right-hand page, I have attempted to show something of the spiritual world and the growth or decline in vitality of visible Christendom (also see pp121ff); also which Christians suffered martyrdom, and by whom they were being persecuted.

The Great Commission

The Great Commission is at the heart of what Jesus wanted to communicate to His disciples after He had risen from the dead. There are five recorded instances in Scripture of this command. In each, there is a different set of circumstances and a different focus for the disciples' intended ministry. Fig 2.1 lists them.

The final words of Jesus before His ascension, which give His strategy for His Church, are illustrated in Fig 2.2. This strategy was of relevance to the disciples, but it took some years before they grasped its significance and obeyed (see p23).

These words are just as relevant to all Christians in all times and all places. We are all involved. This command has a geographical aspect, applying the Gospel locally and moving out further afield to distant locations, as well as a cultural aspect, applying the Gospel to closely related cultural communities and moving out to more foreign cultures, as Fig 2.3 indicates.

John of Montecorvino, 13th-C Catholic missionary to China

The 16th-Century Reformers did not rediscover the Great Commission (see p53). It took another 300 years for Protestants to wake up to the need for mission, while the Catholic Church continued to send missionaries all over the world. Many excuses can be made,[2] but the legacy worldwide in theology, leadership training, congregational structures and practice that resulted from this tragic failure are still with us.

> "Those who cannot learn from history are doomed to repeat it."
> George Santayana

> "History is more or less bunk."
> Henry Ford

> "When Americans say something is history, they mean it is no longer relevant. When Europeans say the same thing, they usually mean the opposite." Javier Solana[1]

> "A historian who would convey the truth must lie. Often he must enlarge the truth by diameters, otherwise his reader would not be able to see it."
> Mark Twain

Bible Text	Ministry Focus
Mark 16:15	Evangelizing
Matthew 28:18-20	Church planting
Luke 24:46-49	Teaching
John 20:21	Sending
Acts 1:8	Global Strategy

Fig 2.1 *Christ's resurrection commands*

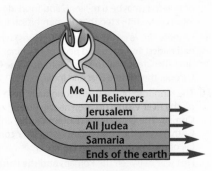

Me
All Believers
Jerusalem
All Judea
Samaria
Ends of the earth

Fig 2.2 *Acts 1:8*

Burning Questions for Today

Obedience is called for in the 21st Century if we are to complete the Great Commission. For most churches today, missions still remains an optional extra, a fad, an inconvenient relic of the colonial era, not a central reason for the existence of the Church. Others define "mission" as any ministry activity aimed at the (mostly local) unchurched, while they ignore activity aimed at the global discipling of peoples required by the Great Commission in Acts 1:8.

▲ Why has the Great Commission become the Great Omission for much of the Church?

▲ Can any congregation that does not make Jesus' Last Command fundamental to a global ministry claim to be truly biblical and evangelical?

▲ How biblical is your congregation, training institution or agency with regard to the Last Command of Jesus?

To Disciples	In time	For Ministry
Themselves	All ages and centuries	Everyone involved
Jerusalem	To own area	To cities
All Judea	To own country	To countries
Samaria	To ethnic minorities	To people groups
End of the earth	To whole world	To all society

Fig 2.3 *The Meaning of the Great Commission*

The Empires of AD 100

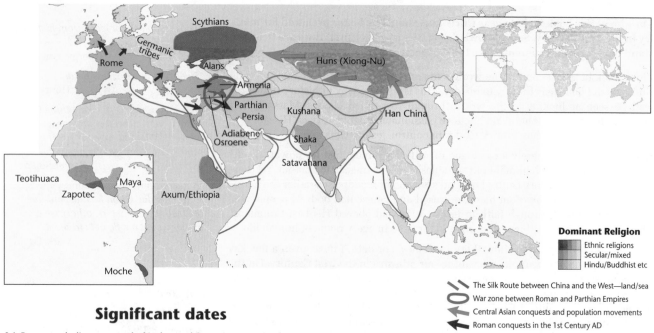

Dominant Religion
- Ethnic religions
- Secular/mixed
- Hindu/Buddhist etc

〜〜 The Silk Route between China and the West—land/sea
◯ War zone between Roman and Parthian Empires
← Central Asian conquests and population movements
◀ Roman conquests in the 1st Century AD

Significant dates

06 Rome took direct control of Judea and Samaria—a major factor facilitating the later spread of Christianity.

25 The foundation of the Later Han dynasty in China. China was the most advanced civilization and foremost industrial power until Europe began to exploit her inventions in the 16th Century. The Silk Routes were now functioning effectively for the first time.

43 Romans began the conquest of Britain. Britain was fairly densely populated (maybe 6 million), and more developed and intensively cultivated than Roman historians acknowledged.

48 Chinese drove out the Xiong-Nu (Huns) who for three centuries had raided and occupied parts of N China. The Chinese then built the Great Wall to keep them out. The Huns later invaded Europe, the Middle East and India.

50 The Kingdom of the Goths (originally from Scandinavia) founded on the river Vistula (in present-day Poland) and then in the Crimea. The Ostrogoths (Eastern Goths) and Visigoths (Western Goths) were the "barbarians" who later contributed most to the fall of the Western Roman Empire.

53 First war between the Romans and the Parthian Persians, ending in AD 58 in compromise over Armenia. It was followed over six centuries by more than 21 wars between the two empires. This struggle contributed to the separate development of Western and Eastern Christianity.

58 Nero became Emperor of Rome. He was the first Emperor specifically to persecute Christians. There followed 10 periods of state-sanctioned persecution up to 310, with over a million martyred.

Buddhism reached China. It was to become the chief rival to Eastern Christianity for the hearts of the Chinese.

66 The Jewish Revolt started. It was crushed by Vespasian and his son Titus. Jerusalem and the Temple were destroyed in AD 70, and an estimated 600,000 people died and 90,000 were enslaved.[3] The large Jewish diaspora was the launch pad for evangelism within and beyond the Roman Empire, but from now on the Christian Church became truly multicultural and predominantly Gentile in composition.

69 Vespasian became Emperor of Rome. Titus succeeded him in AD 79 and Rome entered its golden era of peace and prosperity.

The hand of God in history

A world prepared—Greek learning and language, widely disseminated and known, Rome's sprawling empire and *pax Romana*, cultural diversity, good communications, a generally stable economy and multiple religions made possible the rapid spread of the Gospel.

The world's first globalization—in trade, the mingling of cultures, transfer of ideas, huge movements of population in the Jewish diaspora and migrations of whole peoples

Religious freedoms and a ferment of new ideas—the Romans permitted all religious views that did not threaten the Empire. The Jews expected the imminent appearance of the Messiah. The Zoroastrians in Persia were seeking enlightenment—as shown by the coming of the wise men at the birth of Jesus. The Greeks were constantly searching out new ideas. Buddhism was spreading through India and into China, causing much religious debate.

Christians were politically powerless, social misfits but spiritually dynamic, making astonishing progress in the first few centuries.

Globalization	Period	Cause of ending
Silk Route	100 BC–AD 200	Decline of Rome and China
Islamic	800–1000	The Crusades
Post-Napoleonic	1815–1884	European nationalism
Post Cold War	1990–	Migrations? Islamism?

Fig 2.4 *History's four globalizations*

Food for Thought

The coming of Jesus was in a unique time when many strands converged (Galatians 4:4). One of these was the first globalization. There are many parallels to our situation today in the early stages of the fourth and most comprehensive globalization. Every previous globalization has provided open trade routes, relative peace and a transfer of ideas that has given fresh impetus to world evangelization.

▲ Should we not expect this time, too, to give us a new day for the Gospel in the 21st Century?

The Itineraries of the Apostles

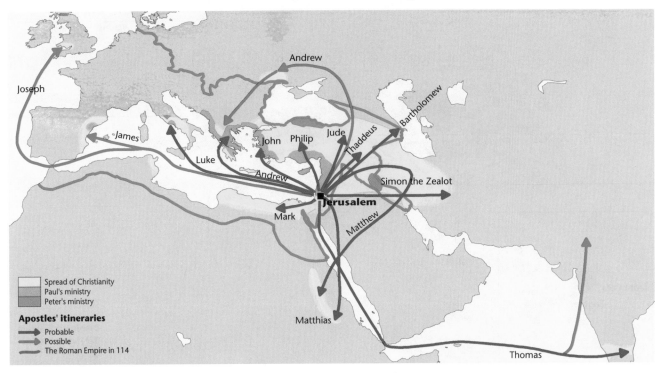

- Spread of Christianity
- Paul's ministry
- Peter's ministry

Apostles' itineraries
- → Probable
- → Possible
- — The Roman Empire in 114

Significant dates

4 BC Jesus born in Bethlehem

AD 26 Baptism of Jesus and the start of His three and a half years of ministry to Jews and also Gentiles.

30 Crucifixion and resurrection of Jesus, followed by the Great Commission and Day of Pentecost—the birth of the Church.

31 Conversion of Paul, "the Apostle to the Gentiles". His ministry began the internationalization of the Church.

36 Philip won Samaritans to Christ. The first non-Jewish congregations started; first Christians in Nubian Meroe (Ethiopia)—the homeland of the Ethiopian eunuch.

38 Peter preached to Romans. Cornelius was converted, the first of a multitude of Roman citizens who embraced Christianity over the next four centuries.

39 The Church in Antioch founded, a multicultural congregation that became the base for the first wave of missionary advance to the Gentiles.

42 First Christians in Britain. The King of the Silures, in present-day S Wales, converted—possibly the first ruler in the world to become a Christian.[4]

44 Peter and many other apostles left Jerusalem—half a generation after Pentecost, a delay that weakened its initial impetus.

45 Paul's missionary journeys began, and Christianity soon became more Gentile than Jewish.

48 The Gospel reached Persia—the birth of the Assyrian Church, which developed autonomously as one of the most significant and missions-minded branches of the Church.

49 First Council in Jerusalem, in which Gentile converts were released from having to keep Jewish law

50 Paul's second missionary journey, and the evangelization of Phrygia and Galatia (in present-day Turkey) and Greece

52 Thomas travelled to India. He was martyred there in AD 72.

53 Paul's third missionary journey and the evangelization of Macedonia, and maybe Illyricum (present-day Croatia and Montenegro)

58 Paul arrested in Jerusalem. Evangelization of Malta

60 The Kingdom of Osrhoene, an Aramaic-speaking buffer state between the Roman and Persian Empires, evangelized. By AD 100, it was the first independent state to become Christian.

64 First Imperial persecution of Christians, under Nero. Paul and Peter martyred in Rome

65 Gospel of Mark written, followed by Luke (AD 70), Matthew and John (both AD 75)

70 Matthew martyred in Ethiopia

91 Second Imperial persecution of Christians, under Diocletian

96 Book of Revelation written by John, the last book of the Bible to be completed

Church office and Christian maturity

Why did the five Christ-given ministries essential for the development of a mature Church (Ephesians 4:11–13) die out or become distorted so quickly? Did the early Christians lose the apostolic vision for world evangelization and replace it with church politics? The apostolic succession of 2 Timothy 2:2 to empower a new generation of leaders rapidly degenerated into a striving for position and the development of rituals to build an enduring hierarchy. These five ministries should be seen as a sequence of developing ministries as the churches grow rather than as a pyramid of power (see Fig 2.5).

Food for Thought

The Acts of the Apostles records only a few apostles' ministries. Most of the apostles' widespread ministries are known to us through Christian tradition and records written generations later. Some of the dates and stories are open to challenge and revision, but the essential historicity of their ministries, as shown in the map above, is certain.

▲ Have we a passion for world evangelization as they did?

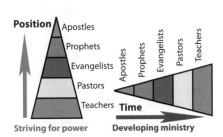

Fig 2.5 *Position or succession?*

The Empires of AD 200

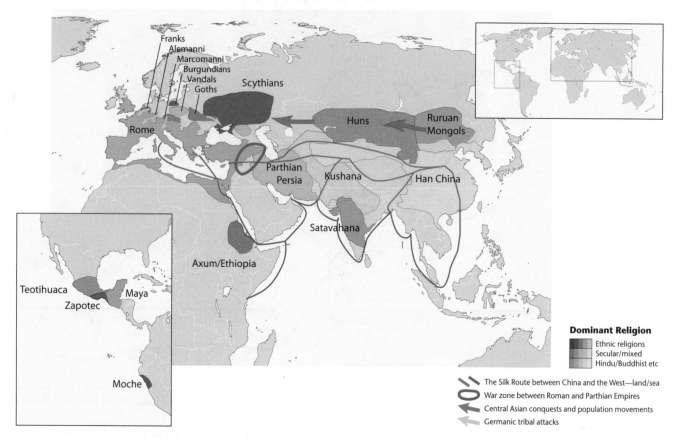

Franks
Alemanni
Marcomanni
Burgundians
Vandals
Goths
Scythians
Rome
Huns
Ruruan Mongols
Parthian Persia
Kushana
Han China
Satavahana
Axum/Ethiopia
Teotihuaca
Zapotec
Maya
Moche

Dominant Religion
Ethnic religions
Secular/mixed
Hindu/Buddhist etc

The Silk Route between China and the West—land/sea
War zone between Roman and Parthian Empires
Central Asian conquests and population movements
Germanic tribal attacks

Significant dates

100 Rome, with over a million inhabitants the world's largest city, became a magnet for wealth, immigration—and invasion.

Buddhism spread through China and SE Asia, and deeply influenced the Kushan Empire and India's various empires.

105 The Chinese developed the technology to make high-quality paper from bamboo.

110 Split in Buddhism between the Mahayana (mainly in Tibet, Mongolia, S Asia and China) and Theravada (SE Asia) sects in a convention called by the Kushan emperor Kanishka. This division persists today.

117 Hadrian became Emperor of Rome, whose territory now reached its greatest geographical extent. Thereafter, a rapid succession of bad emperors, along with civil war, famine, lead poisoning and foreign invasion, caused Rome's decline.

127 Hadrian's Wall completed, protecting the subjugated part of Great Britain from the difficult and warlike, non-Celtic Pictish/Caledonian peoples to the north. (The Celtic Scots still lived in Ireland at this time, only settling on Scotland's west coast in the 3rd Century onwards.)

132 Jewish rebellion led by the "messiah" Bar Kochbar, followed by the final dispersal of the Jews. Thereafter, no significant numbers of Jews lived in the Promised Land for nearly 1,800 years.

152 Mongol peoples displaced the Xiong-Nu (Huns) from present-day Mongolia. Over the next two centuries, the Xiong-Nu were to move west and wreak havoc across much of Asia and Europe.

167 Plague killed 25% of the population of the Roman Empire—more in the cities where unsanitary conditions increased prevalence of all diseases. Urban life and industry were more successful in cultures where drinking tea became widespread.

186 Eruption of the super-volcano Taupo in New Zealand, followed by global cooling, causing famine, civil unrest and massive migration worldwide, including the barbarian invasions of Rome, Persia and India and the collapse of the Han Chinese empire

Solemnly and slowly, with his index finger extended, Napoleon Bonaparte in the 19th Century outlined a great stretch of country on a map of the world. "There," he growled, "is a sleeping giant. Let him sleep! If he wakes, he will shake the world." That sleeping giant was China.

Invention	Date	Significance
Silk	c6000 BC	Created global trading
Tea	unknown	Urban life made safer
Compass	c300 BC	Ocean travel, mapping
Paper	AD 105	Education for all possible
Gunpowder	c.AD 200	Changed balance of power
Printing	1045	Books and Bible availability

Fig 2.6 Chinese inventions that changed the world

Food for Thought

In the 2nd Century the two superpowers of the time, Rome and China, made contact. The catalyst was trade in silk, the almost magical fabric whose secret China long concealed. The Silk Route shown on the map above was significant: the Romans were outstanding in war, administration, law and engineering, but it was the smuggling of Chinese inventions to the West that laid the foundations for the industrialization of the modern world.

▲ Should we be surprised as China reclaims her intellectual riches now that this giant has awoken?

▲ What impact will she have by 2050—with a probably vast and vibrant Church emerging from persecution at the same time?

The Christian World of AD 100–200

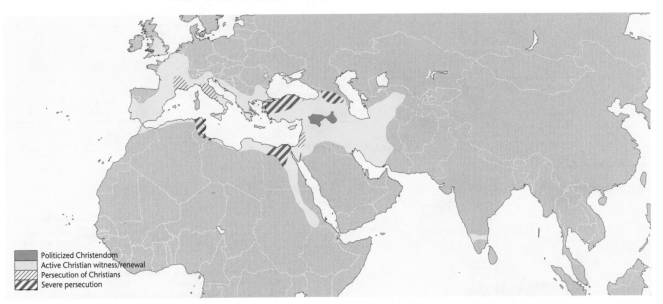

Politicized Christendom
Active Christian witness/renewal
Persecution of Christians
Severe persecution

Significant dates

110 Third Imperial persecution of Christians under Trajan. Martyrdom was becoming increasingly common and deeply affected the development of Christianity. Note the shading on the map above indicating areas where persecution was documented in the 2nd Century. Note also Fig 2.7.

140 Celtic Christian kingdom in S Wales, loosely under the umbrella of the Roman Empire

150 The Old Testament translated into Latin. The translation of the New Testament was completed in 190.

156 Montanism appeared in Phrygia, and then spread throughout the Roman Empire, especially Asia Minor and N Africa. This movement, which in some ways resembled Pentecostalism and the Charismatic movement in the 20th Century, sought to restore spiritual gifts, pursue holiness and prepare for the return of the Lord Jesus. It was, on the whole, theologically biblical—but it was a threat to secular and hierarchical trends in the Church and so was vigorously maligned, condemned and opposed.

165 Fourth Imperial persecution of Christians, albeit a minor one

170 First translation of the Scriptures into the Coptic language of Egypt

177 Abgar VIII, king of Osrhoene (straddling present-day Syria and Iraq), converted.

180 Ireneus, the first great post-apostolic theological writer, became bishop of Lyons. He contributed to the establishment of the canons of the Old and New Testaments (which were only finally decided in 393) and spoke out against the Gnostic heresy sweeping the Church in the 2nd Century.

195 Widespread conversion to Christianity in N Africa and what are now France, Spain and Britain and elsewhere. Nearly every Roman province had some Christian witness.

196 Christians present on the Caspian Sea coast and in Kurdistan, Bactria (a province straddling present-day Afghanistan, Pakistan and Tajikistan) and the Hindu Kush in the Kushan Empire

Key Statistics: 100–200	100	200
World population (millions)	180	192
Christians (millions)	1.4	4.7
Christians as % of world population	0.8%	2.5%
Christian martyrs during 101–200		81,000

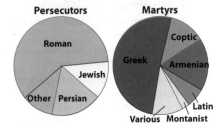

Persecutors

Roman
Jewish
Other Persian

Martyrs

Coptic
Greek
Armenian
Latin
Various Montanist

Fig 2.7 *Who persecuted whom in the 2nd Century*

The Coptic cross used by early Gnostic Christians in Egypt

Burning Questions for Today

▲ Why did the Church lose its apostolic character, servant leadership and Great Commission "DNA" so quickly?

▲ By the middle of this century, apostles, prophets and evangelists were no longer mentioned and church hierarchies were emerging with bishops and popes. About half a generation after Pentecost, nearly all the original apostles had been scattered far from Jerusalem. What happened? See Fig 2.8.

▲ Renewal movements seem to be needed every half generation to bring Christians back to their first love and commitment to Jesus' Last Command. The charismatic Montanists were rejected because they upset the emerging order and control of ecclesiastical life. Has this not been the oft repeated experience of the Church right up to the present day?

Ephesians 4:11		after 300
Ministries	**Acceptance**	**Hierarchies**
Apostles	✗	Popes
Prophets	✗	Archbishops
Evangelists	?	Bishops
Pastors	✓	Priests
Teachers	✓	Theologians

Fig 2.8 *The five "Ephesian" ministries*

The Empires of AD 300

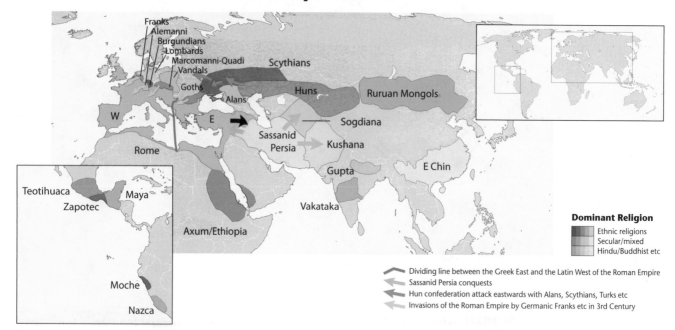

Dominant Religion
- Ethnic religions
- Secular/mixed
- Hindu/Buddhist etc

➤ Dividing line between the Greek East and the Latin West of the Roman Empire
➤ Sassanid Persia conquests
➤ Hun confederation attack eastwards with Alans, Scythians, Turks etc
➤ Invasions of the Roman Empire by Germanic Franks etc in 3rd Century

Significant dates

215 Mani born in Persia. He founded the heresy Manicheanism, which mixed Christianity with Zoroastrianism and Buddhism. Though he was executed by the Persians in 276, his teachings spread throughout Asia and proved to be formidable competition for Christian missionaries. It died out, together with Eastern Christianity, during the expansion of the Mongol Empire.

200 The Chinese invent gunpowder and begin to exploit it for military purposes.

220 Fall of Han dynasty in China, followed by four centuries of short-lived kingdoms ruled by warlords

224 Sassanids came to power in Persia and by 226 had overthrown the religiously tolerant Parthian Empire. Zoroastrianism became the state religion in 272 and Christians, seen as allies of the arch-enemy, Rome, were severely persecuted.

250 Sassanids, Persian-speaking people originating from China, began conquest of Kushana. The Persian-related Sogdians, the great traders of the Silk Route, became subject to Sassanid Persia.

Start of the classical period of Mayan civilization, with advanced urban societies and knowledge of astronomy and mathematics.

251 Emperor Decius defeated by invading Goths who had probably come from the Scandinavian island of Gotland and migrated south through present-day Poland to the Baltic. In 257, the Goths split into Ostrogoths (who later attacked the Eastern Roman Empire) and Visigoths (who later attacked the Western Roman Empire).

252 Plague killed 25% of the population of the Roman Empire, which came to rely on foreign mercenaries. Fear of disease and death made Romans open to witness by Christians who cared for the sick despite the dangers.

268 First major Goth incursion into the Roman Empire finally halted at the Battle of Naissus (now Nis, in Serbia). The Visigoths were ultimately to destroy the Western Roman Empire 150 years later.

275 Buddhism established as the state religion in Sri Lanka. It continued to spread throughout SE Asia.

285 First partition of the Roman Empire into East and West

The growth and challenge of Buddhism

The founder of Buddhism, Gautama, lived and taught in NE India around 500 BC, but the new religion did not really take root on the subcontinent until the conversion of the great Mauryan emperor Ashoka in 261 BC. Thereafter for a thousand years it had great influence in India alongside Hinduism. It was virtually eliminated in its land of origin through persecution by various Hindu rulers and invading Huns and, later, Muslims. It had spread to Sri Lanka, Kushana and Sogdiana by 200 BC, and then along the Silk Route to China by the 1st Century AD, all over SE Asia between the 1st and 5th Centuries AD, to Korea by 372 and Tibet in the 7th Century. It was the principal rival to Eastern Christianity in C and E Asia between 600 and 1400, and ultimately took lasting root. Its influence on the West since the 1950s has been marked, with many converts and many more sympathizers.

Inside a Thai Buddhist temple today (photo by PJK)

Food for Thought

Many Buddhist concepts—such as atheism, evolution, vegetarianism, meditation and reincarnation—have become part of Western culture.

▲ Has our Christian theology been adequately developed to counter them?

▲ Does their respect for the Dalai Lama blind Westerners to the spiritual needs of Buddhists?

The Spread of Christianity in AD 200–300

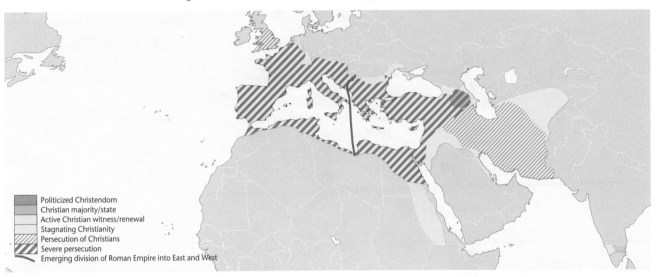

Politicized Christendom
Christian majority/state
Active Christian witness/renewal
Stagnating Christianity
Persecution of Christians
Severe persecution
Emerging division of Roman Empire into East and West

Significant dates

Progress

250 Completion of the Peshitta-Syriac Bible, which became the most important book for the expansion of both the Jacobite and the Nestorian Eastern Churches into Asia. Syriac (Aramaic) became the medium for teaching, writing and training Christian leaders.

260 Edict of toleration of Christians in the Roman Empire, a temporary respite before the worst persecution under Diocletian 43 years later

270 Rise of monasticism in Egypt, which was to spread across the Christian world and stimulate a new interest and involvement in missions—especially in the Coptic, Celtic and Eastern Churches

280 Christians significant in C Asia. By 410, about 25% of the population of present-day Uzbekistan was Christian.

287 In Armenia large numbers began to become Christian. The king was converted in 295. Christianity became the state religion in 301.

300 Advances of Christianity into NW Arabia, down the coast of the Persian Gulf, into Crimea, the southern Caspian coast, C Asia, Ireland etc. Huge growth in numbers despite unprecedented levels of persecution

Setbacks

202 Fifth Imperial persecution of Christians under Septimus Severus. It ended with his death in 211.

225 Persecution of Eastern Christians in Persia began with the revival of Zoroastrianism as the state religion. There were then about 250,000 Persian Christians.

230 The Persian Emperor severely persecuted Christians in Armenia, killing over 10,000. The Armenian Church was virtually exterminated. A further wave of persecution in 287 caused another 20,000 deaths.

235 Sixth Imperial persecution of Christians under Maximinus until his death in 238

249 Seventh Imperial persecution of Christians until 251

257 Eighth Imperial persecution of Christians under Valerian until 260

300 Indian and Ethiopian/Nubian Christians became isolated and went into decline.

Christians and martyrdom

The place of martyrdom in Christian history is important, as the map above and Figs 2.9 and 2.10 show. The upper line in Fig 2.10 shows the percentage of all Christians killed in that century, the coloured area the percentage by the major persecutor, and the lower line the percentage by all other persecutors. Note who the major persecutors were—the facts are surprising! Many Christians have laid down their lives for their faith. There are major peaks—the early centuries (Romans and Persians), the 13th and 14th Centuries (Mongols and Muslims) and the 20th Century (Marxists). Orthodox Christians comprise over 60% of the 70 million martyrs.

Ichthus (Greek acronym meaning 'fish'), an early Christian secret symbol

Key Statistics: 200–300	200	300
World population (millions)	192	192
Christians (millions)	4.7	14.3
Christians as % of world population	2.5%	7.5%
Christian martyrs during 201–300	c.399,000	

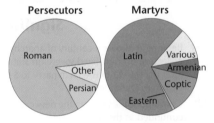

Fig 2.9 *Who persecuted whom in the 3rd Century*

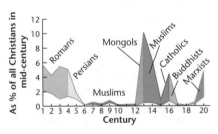

Fig 2.10 *The major persecutors of the Church*

Burning Questions for Today

Nearly 60% of all martyrs since AD 30 lost their lives in the 20th Century.

▲ How many will be martyred in the 21st Century?

▲ Ought we not to be prepared for such an eventuality? (2 Timothy 3:12)

The Empires of AD 400

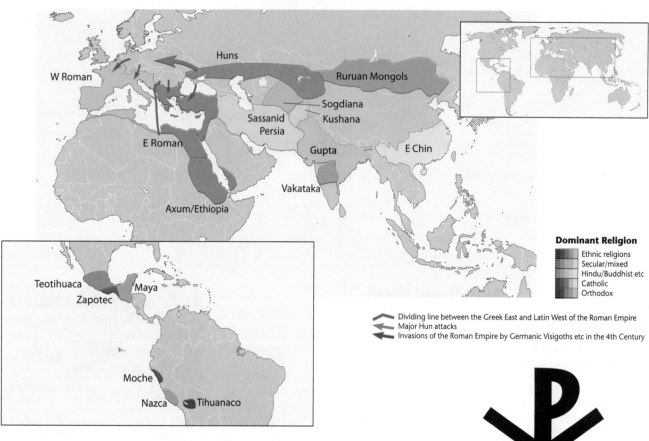

Dominant Religion

- Ethnic religions
- Secular/mixed
- Hindu/Buddhist etc
- Catholic
- Orthodox

Dividing line between the Greek East and Latin West of the Roman Empire
Major Hun attacks
Invasions of the Roman Empire by Germanic Visigoths etc in the 4th Century

Significant dates

304 Beginning of over a century of anarchy in China. The Sixteen Kingdoms were a collection of short-lived sovereign states in and around China proper from 304 to 439 after the retreat of the Jin dynasty to S China and before the establishment of the Northern Dynasties.

320 Constantinople became the new capital of a Christianized Roman Empire, and continued as the Greek-speaking capital of the Byzantine Empire until it fell to the Ottoman Turks in 1453.

324 Constantine became emperor of both eastern and western parts of the Roman Empire. After his death in 337, his sons split the Empire: Constantine II took present-day Spain, France and Britain; Constans I took Italy, N Africa and the Balkans; Constantius II took the East.

350 The Chinese repelled an invasion by the Ruruan (Juan-Juan), who in turn drove the Hsiung-nu (Huns) west towards the Ural Mountains and the Caspian Sea. The Turkic-speaking Huns moved into Europe, settling on the plains between the Urals and the Carpathian Mountains.

360 The Hun invasion of Europe triggered a chain reaction as C European (mainly Germanic) peoples moved into the Roman Empire as refugees and often conquerors, and ultimately as destroyers of the Western Roman Empire.

363 Emperor Julian the Apostate died defeated while attempting to invade the Sassanid kingdom of Persia, which then recaptured Nisibis and Armenia. The general Valentinian became Roman Emperor.

376 Visigoths allowed to settle within the Empire. In 378, they defeated the Roman army at Hadrianopolis.

385 In the west, the Roman Empire began to disintegrate as a result of massive incursions of barbarians—Franks, Burgundians, Vandals, Lombards, Goths, Huns etc.

395 Theodosius divided the Roman Empire into western and eastern empires, with Milan and Constantinople as their respective capitals.

The chi-rho monogram of Emperor Constantine

The politicization of the Church

This century saw an astonishing change as the persecuting pagan Roman Empire was won over by Christianity. Though dramatic, this "victory" proved to be a major setback that still affects the Church today. From it emerged a Church-State alliance, or (as some would call it) the "Constantinian captivity" of the Church. All five ministries of Ephesians 4:11 either became defunct or were neutralized where this happened (see Fig 8.1 on p225). The main body of the Church had already lost its apostolic ministry; now it lost its prophetic and evangelistic ministries, and its pastoral and teaching ministries became tied to the State.

Food for Thought

The "state of the Church" maps on subsequent pages give a startling illustration of the effect of the Church's new relationship with the State.

▲ How far has this "captivity" affected Christian world-view and ministries today—in attitudes to politics and power in "Christian" countries, in leadership styles and in discipling, evangelizing and world outreach?

The State of the Church in AD 300–400

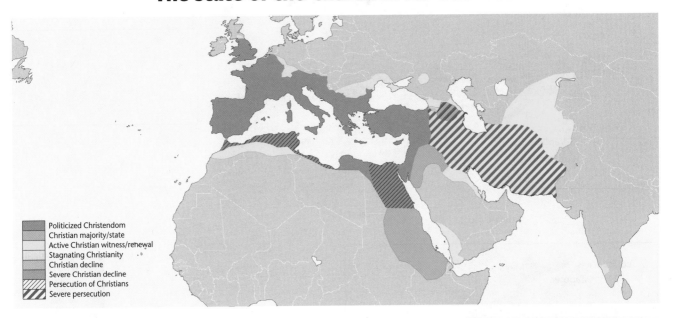

Politicized Christendom
Christian majority/state
Active Christian witness/renewal
Stagnating Christianity
Christian decline
Severe Christian decline
Persecution of Christians
Severe persecution

Significant dates

Progress

301 Armenia became a Christian state. To this day, Armenians have held on to their faith tenaciously over nearly two millennia of persecution by Romans, Persians and Muslims.

313 Edict of Milan, whereby Emperor Constantine legalized Christianity—hard on the heels of the worst persecution ever experienced by the Church

325 Council of Nicea convened by Constantine. It resulted in the Nicene Creed and condemned the christology of Arius.

328 Arrival of organized Christianity in Ethiopia and founding of the Ethiopian Orthodox Church

329 Beginning of monasticism with the establishment of the first monastery in Egypt. This movement deeply affected the whole Church for the next 13 centuries and became the principal means of spreading Christianity.

334 Merv in C Asia became a bishopric of the Eastern Church.

342 First (Eastern) church in Aden, Arabia, followed in 350 by a church on Socotra Island in the Indian Ocean (which survived until the 15th Century)

350 The three Nubian kingdoms of the Upper Nile became officially Coptic Christian, remaining so until conquered by Islam in the 16th Century.

360 The Gospel reached the Picts in Scotland through Celtic missionaries.

393 The Council of Hippo finally agreed the 27 books of the New Testament. Seven books had been disputed.

Setbacks

303 Tenth Imperial persecution of Christians ordered by Diocletian. Maybe 750,000 were killed over 10 years.

311 Church in N Africa divided by Donatist controversy. Donatists were more strict about receiving back those who had renounced their faith under persecution. Constantine initiated a four-year state persecution of Donatists in N Africa that killed over 10,000.

318 Arianism propounded—a major heresy, denying the deity of Christ, that divided the Church for 500 years. Many of the invading Germanic peoples adopted Arian Christianity.

327 Savage persecution in the Persian Empire until 402

361 Emperor Julian the Apostate sought to revive paganism in the Roman Empire to displace Christianity.

364 Vandals became Arian Christians.

380 Emperor Theodosius I pronounced Christianity the state religion of the Roman Empire. This "victory" was disastrous for the spiritual well-being and ministry of the Church.

Monasticism

The rise of monasticism was a response to the increasing carnality and politicization of the Church, and was fundamental to the development of Christianity. It took various forms: wandering monks (in the early centuries, and later the Franciscans), village communities (Patrick and the Celtic Church), ascetic hermits (Anthony of Egypt), cenobites (Egypt and the Eastern Nestorians) and highly disciplined monasteries (the Benedictines). The monastic system preserved

Key Statistics: 300–400	300	400
World population (millions)	192	186
Christians (millions)	14.3	25
Christians as % of world population	7.5%	13.4%
Christian martyrs during 301–400	962,000	

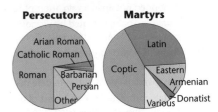

Persecutors | **Martyrs**

Fig 2.11 *Who persecuted whom in the 4th Century*

Burning Questions for Today

We may question the theological basis, the self-centred asceticism and the motivation of monks but we cannot deny their dedication and their impact on the world.

▲ How far have we shied away in modern Evangelicalism from the desire for holiness and willingness to suffer for God?

▲ Have we lost the meaning of cross-bearing, of life-time commitment for the extension of God's Kingdom?

learning, set standards of holy living and became a source of Christian charity and, for 1,500 years, virtually the only post-apostolic mechanism for spreading Christianity to non-Christians.

The Empires of AD 500

Significant dates

410 Alaric, the Visigoth king, captured Rome. Roman legions abandoned Britain in a vain attempt to defend their capital.

416 Vandals in Spain, defeated by Visigoths, migrated to take possession of N Africa, Sardinia, Corsica etc.

419 Moche people of present-day northern Peru built the Temple of the Sun.

436 Huns invaded Persia but were defeated by Sassanid Persians.

439 Vandals completed the conquest of the Maghreb in N Africa. As Arian Christians, they persecuted the Catholic and Donatist Latin and Berber populations they had conquered.

440 Huns advanced west to attack the Eastern Roman Empire and the Balkans.

450 The Mongolian Ruruan (Juan-Juan) empire gained control of territories from Manchuria to Lake Balkash in present-day Kazakhstan.

451 Attila and his Hun armies were checked in present-day France, thwarting his efforts to overcome the stricken Western Roman Empire and conquer Europe. The Huns finally quit Europe in 470. Their huge empire lasted just a few decades but it decisively changed the history of Europe, C Asia and India.

455 Vandals sacked Rome.

476 The end of the Western Roman Empire, as the Arian Christian Visigoth Odoacer deposed the Western Roman Emperor Romulus Augustulus and became king of Italy. The conquest was complete by 493.

478 First Shinto shrines built in Japan

484 Gupta Empire in India defeated by Hephthalite Hun invaders from C Asia. The Hun Empire dominated C Asia until 587.

A world and Church divided

The Western Roman Empire collapsed in chaos after being invaded by tribes from C Europe and Asia, and the same fate almost befell the Eastern Empire. Successive ecumenical Christian councils had kept the Church more or less united, with centres of power in Rome, Antioch, Constantinople, Jerusalem and Alexandria; but in this century the first irreconcilable schism occurred over efforts to define how Christ could be at the same time both God and man.[5] The positions of the Monophysite Churches of Armenia, Syria, Egypt, Nubia and Ethiopia and the Nestorian Church[6] of eastern Mesopotamia and Persia were rejected by the Council of Chalcedon. The Latin Roman and the Greek Orthodox Churches became known as the Chalcedonian Churches, but over subsequent centuries they, too, drifted apart until the Great Schism between them in 1054.

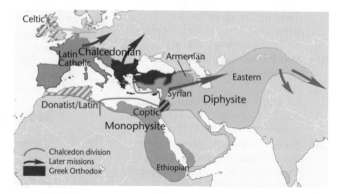

Fig 2.12 *The four main "sending" branches of Christianity in 500*

Food for Thought

Fig 2.12 shows where the four main missionary-sending branches of Christianity predominated. A difficult theological dispute deeply damaged the spiritual unity of the Church, but the real issues were relationship breakdowns, national politics and differences of language and culture. The globalization of the Church in the 21st Century will compel us to face the same type of issues.

The State of the Church in AD 400–500

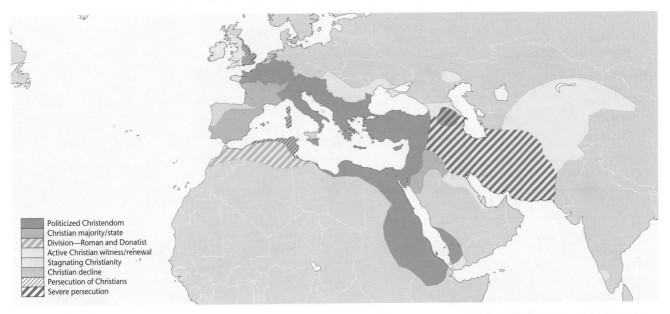

Legend:
- Politicized Christendom
- Christian majority/state
- Division—Roman and Donatist
- Active Christian witness/renewal
- Stagnating Christianity
- Christian decline
- Persecution of Christians
- Severe persecution

Significant dates

Progress

400 About 25% of C Asia and Persia was by now Christian, mainly worshipping in Syriac while using local languages for witnessing and producing some literature in indigenous Turkic and Iranic languages. By 425, the first bishops had been ordained for Herat (in present-day Afghanistan) and Samarkand (in Uzbekistan).

404 Jerome completed the Vulgate Bible in Latin.

410 Yemei converted in Persia. He later returned home to evangelize Yemen, which then had a Jewish king.

411 Augustine published his book *The City of God*, probably one of the most important and foundational theological works ever written—especially for the Western Church.

420 The first Arab tribe became Christian, though the Bible was not translated into Arabic until after the death of Mohammed.

432 Patrick, the Celtic Briton, began his successful evangelization of Ireland, founding the Celtic Church which became first a repository of learning in a world collapsing into chaos and then the source of one of the most dynamic missionary movements in history.

496 Clovis, king of the Franks, became a Christian in Rheims. The Frankish Empire was later the main bulwark against Islam for the political survival of Christendom.

497 The first deliberate attempt by the Eastern Church to send missionaries to C Asia—some reaching China

Setbacks

410 The Eastern (Persian/Nestorian) Church became independent of Rome and Constantinople. It was later declared heretical by councils in Ephesus (431) and Chalcedon (451).

420 Zoroastrian Persian persecution of Christians, followed by further persecutions in 448 and 470. Over 250,000 were killed over the century.

451 The Council of Chalcedon condemned both Monophysitism (Christ had only one nature, which combined both the divine and the human in one person) and Diphysitism (or, crudely, Nestorianism, for which Christ had two distinct and separate natures). This led to the irretrievable division of the Church into three major theological streams by 486 (cf Fig 2.12 on p30).

Cross-cultural missions in the early Church

The Holy Spirit came upon the disciples at Pentecost and they declared the mighty works of God in many languages. He showed that the Gospel must be proclaimed in other tongues. The first wave of evangelism by the Apostles used a language that was not their mother tongue. Sadly, for four centuries thereafter there is little evidence that their successors went beyond the use of Syriac (Aramaic), Greek or Latin. However, where they did, the Church flourished and withstood persecution for millennia—notably the Copts in Egypt and the Armenians in the Caucasus. The only major missionary movements that bore much fruit in the next 1,500 years were those of the Celtic

Key Statistics: 400–500	400	500
World population (millions)	186	190
Christians (millions)	25	37.8
Christians as % of world population	13.4%	19.9%
Christian martyrs during 401–500	575,000	

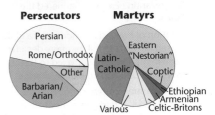

Fig 2.13 *Who persecuted whom in the 5th Century*

Burning Question for Today

The barbarian tribes were evangelized not by mainstream Christians but by Arians, who were considered heretics, and then by Irish saints who started by learning the local cultures.

▲ How far do 21st-Century mission efforts fail in this very area with their preference for English, Western cultural imperialism and lack of long-term commitment?

and Eastern Churches, which laid great emphasis on the Scriptures, prayer and adaptation to local culture. Patrick was one of the greatest cross-cultural missionaries of all time, changing a nation, the Irish, who then changed much of Europe in one of the most successful discipling processes ever developed.

The Empires of AD 600

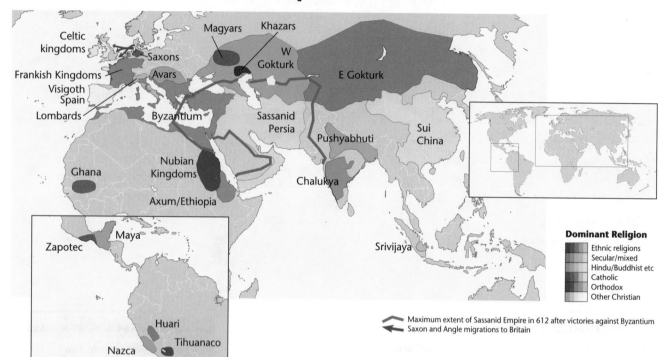

Dominant Religion
- Ethnic religions
- Secular/mixed
- Hindu/Buddhist etc
- Catholic
- Orthodox
- Other Christian

Maximum extent of Sassanid Empire in 612 after victories against Byzantium
Saxon and Angle migrations to Britain

Significant dates

510 Huns invaded India, destroying the Gupta Empire.

525 Monophysite Christian Ethiopia conquered Yemen.

533 The Byzantine Empire conquered the Vandal kingdom of N Africa.

535 Eruption of Krakatoa in Indonesia, a global catastrophe that caused harvests to fail for many decades. Famine, plague and huge migrations of people led to the collapse of empires all over the world and wholesale changes of religious affiliation.

536 The Byzantine Empire conquered the Ostrogoths in northern Italy. By 554, it had gained control of all Italy but, owing to the massive depopulation of this land, soon lost much of it to the Lombards.

541 Half the population of Europe and the Middle East was wiped out by bubonic plague over the following decade. Urban life declined drastically where the plague wreaked the worst havoc.

552 The Gok Turks (Blue Turks) under Bumin Khan defeated the Mongols and established a vast empire stretching from Manchuria to the Aral Sea. This then split into the Western and Eastern Khanates.

559 Huns devastated much of Byzantine Europe, but were checked at the gates of Constantinople.

568 Germanic Lombards, part pagan, part Arian Christian, invaded northern Italy after being defeated by the Mongol-related Avars. They gradually conquered much of central Italy as well.

570 Persians ejected the Ethiopians from Yemen, which by then had a mixed population of pagans, Jews and Christians.

A 19th-C artist's impression of the active volcano on Krakatoa

Volcano	Date	Effect
Taupo, New Zealand	186	Famine, plague, decline of Rome
Krakatoa, Indonesia	535	Global famine for seven years, plague, fall of empires
Laki, Iceland	1786	Famines in Europe and the Middle East, which helped to provoke the French Revolution

Fig 2.14 *Volcanoes and history*

Food for Thought

We live in a time when there is growing concern that human activity is causing global warming and precipitating climate change. This is a valid concern that touches on our responsibility to care for the Earth (Genesis 1:28–30). However, throughout history it has been huge "acts of God" that have had the most dramatic effect. Unpredictable, violent natural cataclysms[7] have shaped not only our planet but also human history as, apparently inexplicable and often not even known to their victims, they have radically altered human existence with global cooling, famines and resultant plagues provoking massive political, social and religious changes—as the table indicates.

▲ Are we prepared for the unexpected in our more densely populated world, with the poorer countries far less able to cope with mega-disasters which could overwhelm human efforts to control global warming?

The Christian World of AD 500–600

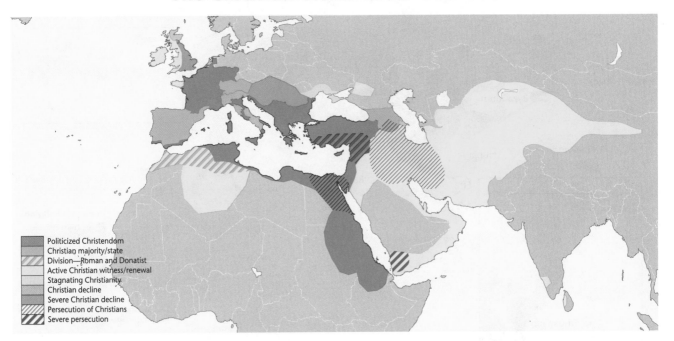

Politicized Christendom
Christian majority/state
Division—Roman and Donatist
Active Christian witness/renewal
Stagnating Christianity
Christian decline
Severe Christian decline
Persecution of Christians
Severe persecution

Significant dates

Progress

500 Syrian monks established a monastery in Ethiopia, which gradually became Monophysite in doctrine and linked to the Coptic Church in Egypt.

505 Benedict founded the first monastery in Italy, introducing monasticism to the Latin West.

510 Beginning of the Celtic missionary movement as itinerant monks went out over the next four centuries to evangelize new pagan immigrants across N and C Europe

516 Burgundians migrating into southeast France turned to Christianity.

543 The Nubian kingdom in present-day Sudan adopted Monophysite Christianity and became linked to the Coptic Church in Egypt.

563 Columba began evangelizing Scotland from the Isle of Iona. Ultimately, Iona was to be a crucial base for missionaries to the whole of Europe.

587 Visigoths in Spain started to become Catholic Christians.

590 The Irish monk Columbanus founded monasteries all over what are now France, Germany and northern Italy.

596 Augustine came to England to evangelize the Saxons. By this time, much of north and central England was already being evangelized by the Celtic Church.

Setbacks

512 West Syrian (Jacobite) Church became Monophysite, and was then severely persecuted by Byzantine Greek Orthodox Christians.

523 By 500 the Najran kingdom in Yemen contained many Monophysite Christians, but in this year its Jewish king, Masruq, murdered 30,000 Arab Christians.

533 Sixth wave of Persian persecution of Eastern Christians

Key Statistics: 500–600	500	600
World population (millions)	190	185
Christians (millions)	37.8	39.9
Christians as % of world population	19.9%	21.5%
Christian martyrs during 501–600	74,000	

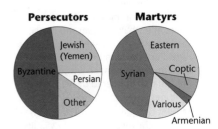

Persecutors   **Martyrs**

Fig 2.15 *Who persecuted whom in the 6th Century*

Missions in times of crisis

The huge loss of life, destruction of empires and mass migrations of the 6th Century crippled the military and political powers of the day. Organized Christianity fared just as badly. Yet it was the Christians on the fringes—the Celts, the Berbers of N Africa and the heavily persecuted Eastern Christians—who took up the missionary task. Much of the outreach of the Celtic Christians into Germanic-ruled Europe and of the Eastern Christians eastwards towards China was not organized as such but arose spontaneously out of their perceived calling as Christians. It was these believers, not the hierarchies of the Latin or Greek Churches, that undertook this work. These early missionaries learnt local languages and cultures and by adapting their approach were extraordinarily successful. Church history rarely recalls their achievements—the Catholics either ignored the work of the Celts or claimed it as their own, and later the Mongols destroyed much of the evidence for the astonishing work of the Eastern Christians.

Burning Question for Today

The 21st Century could be similar to the 6th, with huge numbers of economic migrants "invading" Europe and the West as the Middle East and C Asia once again experience great trauma and, possibly, major religious and ethnic conflicts and "water wars".

▲ Will we respond to crisis as Christians then did and see the chaos as a God-given opportunity for the Gospel?

The Empires of AD 700

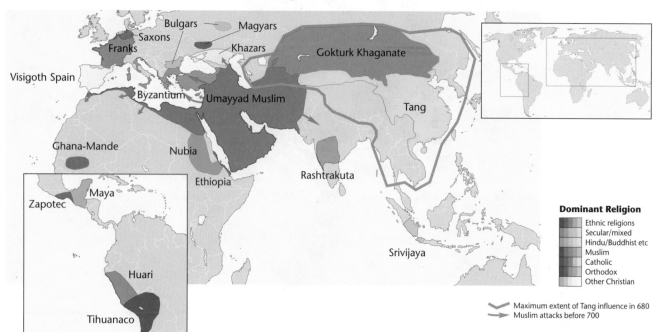

Bulgars
Magyars
Saxons
Franks
Khazars
Gokturk Khaganate
Visigoth Spain
Byzantium
Umayyad Muslim
Tang
Ghana-Mande
Nubia
Ethiopia
Rashtrakuta
Zapotec
Maya
Huari
Srivijaya
Tihuanaco

Dominant Religion
- Ethnic religions
- Secular/mixed
- Hindu/Buddhist etc
- Muslim
- Catholic
- Orthodox
- Other Christian

Maximum extent of Tang influence in 680
Muslim attacks before 700

Significant dates

601 Turks under the command of Tardu besieged China's capital, Xian.

621 Buddhism declared the state religion of Japan

622 Mohammed fled from Mecca to Medina (Hegira). In the process, Islam changed from being a tolerant religion to a militant one.

632 Death of Mohammed

636 Muslim Arab armies defeated the forces of both Byzantium and Persia, the two greatest military powers of the time. Persia succumbed and became Muslim. Byzantium recovered and was only finally conquered by Islam eight centuries later.

639 Muslim conquest of Egypt, followed by mass conversions from Christianity to Islam

650 Muslim conquest of Persia

661 Arab Muslim Umayyad dynasty established with its capital in Damascus. The Ummayads were Arab descendants of a distant relative of Mohammed.

674 Arab armies reached the river Indus in present-day Pakistan.

680 Murder of Hussein in Karbala, in present-day Iraq, and the beginning of the major division of Islam between Sunni and Shi'a over who or what was to succeed him. The Sunnis adopted a political, patriarchal caliphate, the Shi'a a theocracy.

686 Khitan Mongols from Manchuria invaded China.

691 Buddhism declared the state religion of China

697 All N Africa captured by Muslim armies

Islam's challenge to Christianity

In six centuries, the Christian message had succeeded in winning a fifth of humankind despite intense opposition and 2,500,000 martyrs, and had spread as far as the Atlantic in the west and China in the east. This growth ended as Islam swept through most of the major areas of Christian power or influence in this and the centuries that followed. Muslims collectively became the world's new superpower—note the green shading at the heart of Fig 2.16. They dominated international trade routes for the next millennium, as the graph shows, while Christianity became a fringe religion until the 16th Century, when Europeans took control of the world's sea lanes.

Two Millennia of Superpowers

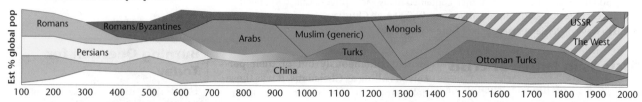

Romans
Romans/Byzantines
Persians
Arabs
Muslim (generic)
Mongols
USSR
The West
Turks
Ottoman Turks
China

Est % global pop

100 200 300 400 500 600 700 800 900 1000 1100 1200 1300 1400 1500 1600 1700 1800 1900 2000

Fig 2.16 *Two millennia of superpowers: the growth and decline of major world powers over the Christian era*

Food for Thought

Between the 7th and 16th Centuries, Christianity suffered huge losses to Islam—losses that were reversed only with the modern missionary movement of the last 200 years. Now a resurgent and angry Islam wants to recover its own losses and avenge the humiliations, real or perceived, of the past 500 years. Do Westerners comprehend how long and painful the history between us has been? Knowledge of this history is essential if we are to understand Islamism in the 21st Century. We can conquer only through love, not (as we have tried in the past) with temporal weapons of war, legislation, dialogue and compromise.

▲ How can we learn and practise such love?

▲ What does this imply for 21st-Century ministry as Muslim expansion is renewed?

The Christian World of AD 600–700

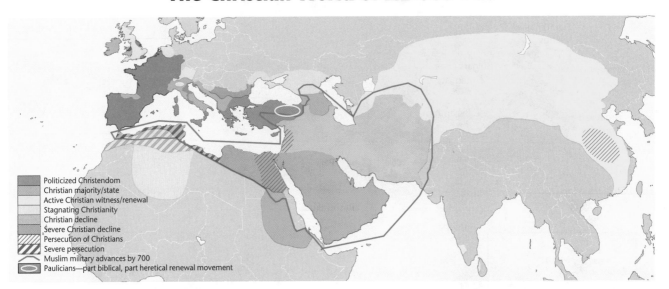

Politicized Christendom
Christian majority/state
Active Christian witness/renewal
Stagnating Christianity
Christian decline
Severe Christian decline
Persecution of Christians
Severe persecution
Muslim military advances by 700
Paulicians—part biblical, part heretical renewal movement

Significant dates

Progress

600 A large proportion of Uighurs of C Asia and W China were by this time Eastern Christians. There were then an estimated 8 million Christians among C Asian peoples.

612 Celtic missionaries evangelized the Alemanni in present-day Switzerland and the Lombards of northern Italy.

635 The Persian missionary Alopen reached China and planted the first churches there. He translated the Scriptures into Chinese for the Emperor, who permitted Christians to witness and plant churches.

640 Revivalist Paulicians emerged in Asia Minor, emphasizing the writings of Paul and seeking to rectify "errors" of Orthodoxy such as the use of icons. These precursors of the Cathars or Albigenses in France were a largely biblical renewal movement, a kind of proto-Reformation, who sought to return to the simple holiness of the Apostles (though they had some divergent doctrines, mixed with some non-Christian elements).

650 Celtic missionaries evangelized what is now the Netherlands. Willibrord from England, the great apostle to the Frisians, began his ministry there in 695.

Many Turks in C Asia were by now Christians (see Fig 2.16 on p34).

Before Muslims invaded Egypt, N Africa had some 3 million Coptic Christians and 5 million Berber Christians.

First Christians in present-day Croatia and Mongolia

Setbacks

615 Persians captured Jerusalem and massacred 90,000 Christians. They then invaded Egypt and killed 10,000 Copts.

616 The king of Northumberland chose Catholicism over the Celtic tradition and then severely persecuted the Celtic Church in Wales.

617 Vikings massacred 54 monks on the Hebridean isle of Eigg, the first of many attacks on Christian communities over the centuries to come.

628 The last Zoroastrian Persian persecution of Christians. By this time, some 30–40% of Persians were Eastern or Syrian Christians.

637 Arabs captured Jerusalem and killed 80,000 Greek Christians. The city was to remain in Muslim hands for 462 years.

663 Synod of Whitby established Catholicism in Britain at the expense of Celtic Christianity.

683 The Empress of China began persecuting Christians, though Eastern Christians remained influential for two centuries.

700 Arab destruction of the N African Church. All Christian priests were killed or enslaved. The Arabs claim they had to fight 10 wars to eradicate Christianity among the Berbers.

Key Statistics: 600–700	600	700
World population (millions)	185	205
Christians (millions)	39.9	40.6
Christians as % of world population	21.5%	19.8%
Christian martyrs during 601–700	229,000	

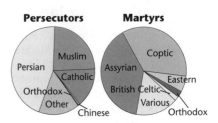

Fig 2.17 *Who persecuted whom in the 7th Century*

Burning Question for Today

Islam will be one of the formative ideologies of the 21st Century and will not just fade away. We need to understand Islam and its history and teachings and know how to share the Good News with Muslims in a relevant and appealing way.

▲ We have the answer in Christ that every true Muslim seeks, but do we really believe that?

Disaster for Christendom

It is hard for us now to comprehend the magnitude of the disaster for Christendom represented by the eruption of Islam out of the deserts of Arabia. In a mere few years, three of the five major leadership centres of Christianity—Jerusalem, Alexandria and Antioch—were overwhelmed, as well as the key centres of the Eastern Church, Adiabene and Edessa, from which much of Asia was being evangelized. Although Islam derives much from Christianity, the Qur'an openly denounces the core tenets of our faith and in many respects Islam is utterly different from Christianity: in its theology (the attributes of Allah, works rather than grace, lack of assurance of salvation etc), world-view (fatalism, lack of hope) and culture (honour/shame).

The Empires of AD 800

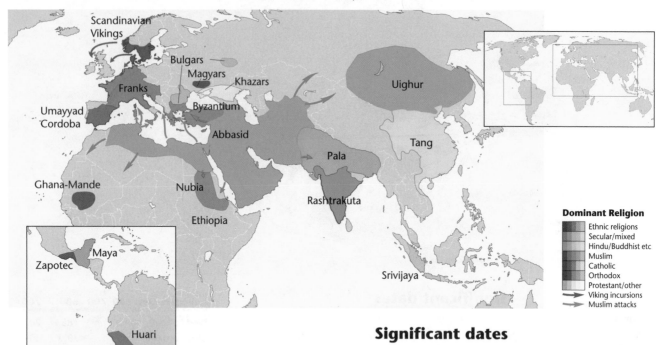

Islamic expansion

By 800, Muslims ruled the key central areas of the Old World. The Mediterranean had become virtually a Muslim lake. By that time, Muslims probably numbered just over 10 million, but they ruled a much larger number of Christians (note Fig 2.18). Over 40% (16 million) of all Christians by then lived under Muslim rule and were reduced to second-class, *dhimmi* status by Islamic laws and taxes. Huge numbers of Christians and Zoroastrians as well as pagans either were forced to embrace Islam or found it economically or politically expedient to do so. Islam's goal was total world conquest, as it remains in the 21st Century.

Significant dates

711 Arabs invaded the Iberian Peninsula and conquered all but the very north of Visigothic Spain.

Arabs captured Samarkand in C Asia, with its large Christian population, and the Sindh in India.

718 Arabs failed to take Constantinople. Byzantium remained an eastern bastion for Christianity for a further seven centuries, falling in the end largely as a result of the atrocious behaviour of the Catholic Crusaders towards the Orthodox Greeks of the declining empire.

Arabs dominant in Sardinia until 900

732 Charles Martel defeated the Arabs at Poitiers in France, ending their efforts to conquer Europe for Islam from the west. The second attempt was to come from the east seven centuries later when the Ottoman Turks invaded.

744 Turkic-speaking Uighurs (many Manicheans or Christians) conquered the Gok Turk Eastern Khanate as allies of the Chinese Tang dynasty and expanded from Lake Balkash to Lake Baikal, with their capital in Kara-Balgasun. They developed the first Turkic alphabet (still used by the Mongols today).

750 The Abbasids eliminated their Umayyad Muslim rulers, then moved the capital of the Caliphate from Damascus to Baghdad. The Abbasids were Arab descendants of another branch of Mohammed's family. They remained the supreme leaders of Islam until their defeat by the Mongols in 1258.

751 Arabs defeated a Chinese army in present-day Kyrgyzstan, ending Chinese domination of C Asia.

787 Danes and Vikings began the invasion and conquest of England.

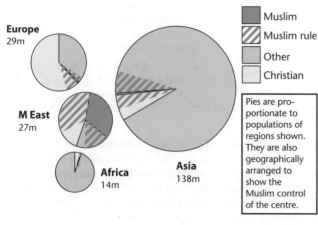

Europe
29m

M East
27m

Africa
14m

Asia
138m

Muslim
Muslim rule
Other
Christian

Pies are proportionate to populations of regions shown. They are also geographically arranged to show the Muslim control of the centre.

Fig 2.18 *Religious affiliation by region in 800*

Food for Thought

Muslims assume that Christians, as supposed inferiors, will show deference to Islam and so they expect every freedom and privilege wherever they reside but see no reason to reciprocate once they gain control. Their political dominance in the past did not depend on them being in a majority but was achieved by the manipulation of existing systems to their advantage.

▲ Why do we need to heed this history?

The patterns of the 8th Century may be repeated in the 21st. By contrast, we should also note how many Orthodox Christians suffered extraordinary humiliation, hardship and sometimes terrible persecution from this time on, but they held on, and still constitute a significant minority in the Middle East today.

The Christian World of AD 700–800

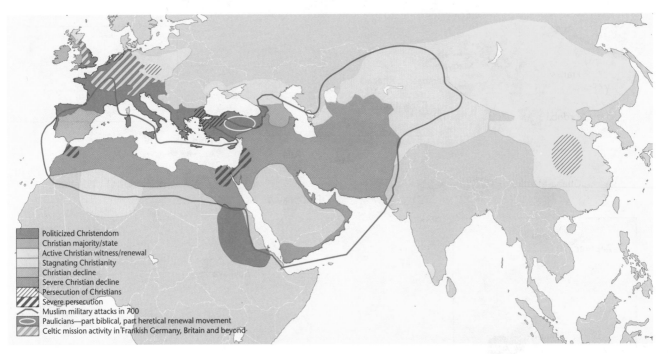

Politicized Christendom
Christian majority/state
Active Christian witness/renewal
Stagnating Christianity
Christian decline
Severe Christian decline
Persecution of Christians
Severe persecution
Muslim military attacks in 700
Paulicians—part biblical, part heretical renewal movement
Celtic mission activity in Frankish Germany, Britain and beyond

Significant dates

Progress

700 The Lombards of Italy were by this time all Catholic.

715 The Celtic missionary Boniface embarked on his evangelization of Germanic peoples. In 724, he felled an oak tree sacred to the god Thor and so discredited paganism.

750 The Arabic Bible completed. What if Mohammed had been able to read the Scriptures in his lifetime?

781 The highpoint of the first Eastern (Nestorian) missionary effort in China. Most of the Christians were expatriates, but there was a large though uncounted minority of Chinese.

790 First bishop appointed for Eastern Christians in Tibet

Setbacks

707 Great slaughter of Berber Christians in Tangiers by Arab conquerors

712 The second imperial persecution of Eastern Christians in China, in the city of Changan

725 Controversy broke out in the Byzantine Empire and the Orthodox Church over the use or non-use of icons in churches. It was to last a century.

774 Charlemagne conquered Saxony and compelled all the Saxons to be baptized. In 780, he slaughtered 4,500 who refused. By 804, all Saxons had become Catholic. Much of present-day Germany was "Christianized" by these means but was not converted to the new faith.

793 Lindisfarne burnt by Danish raiders. In 806, 80 monks were massacred. In 867, the abbey was destroyed.

Models of mission

The Celtic Church released thousands of missionary pilgrims who scattered across Scotland and then spread through W and C Europe, founding monasteries and evangelizing. Their aim was discipling Christians[8] to serve the Lord among the non-Latin-speaking peoples that had flooded across Europe. By using local languages and understanding local cultures, they achieved some astonishing successes. Their aim was to convert individuals and then educate them so that they could study their faith as true disciples. Eastern Christians[9] took a similar approach, and from this emerged a more indigenous expression of Christianity in Europe and C Asia. Note the yellow areas in the map above.

An alternative model was developed by Augustine and the Catholic Church in Britain in 597, and by Charlemagne as his empire expanded into German tribal areas, using power politics, money, the co-option of political leaders and even the threat of death to enforce conversion. Those thus persuaded or bludgeoned had a foreign religion with a foreign language (Latin) imposed on them that ignored local cultural sensitivities.

Key Statistics: 700–800	700	800
World population (millions)	205	218
Christians (millions)	40.6	40.7
Christians as % of world population	19.8%	18.7%
Christian martyrs during 701–800	133,000	

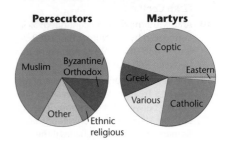

Fig 2.19 *Who persecuted whom in the 8th Century*

Burning Question for Today

The advantage of the Celtic missionaries was that they had no political power. Sadly, the unique Celtic Church was later overwhelmed by the Catholic Church, and the Eastern Church of Central and East Asia was eliminated by persecution by Muslims, Mongols and Chinese.

▲ Which model of missions will we follow in the 21st Century?

Our record of evangelizing E Europe and Mongolia through cultural imperialism after the fall of the Iron Curtain in 1989 would seem to indicate that we have not learnt the higher way!

The Empires of AD 900

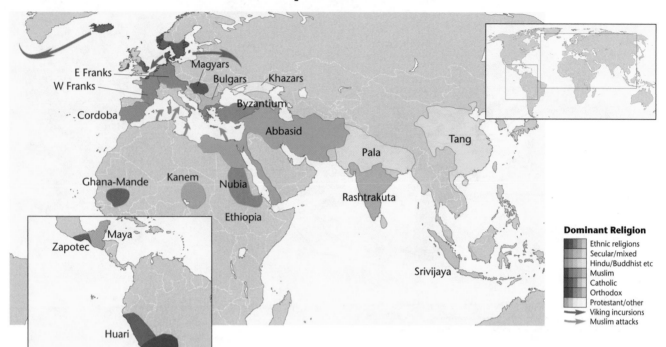

Significant dates

804 Charlemagne conquered all of Germany as far as the Elbe. This was the second of five attempts at European "union", after Rome's in the 2nd Century. Other attempts were made by the Hapsburgs (16th Century), Napoleon (19th Century) and Hitler (20th Century).

810 Arab Muslim advances continued: Sicily in 810-965 (until conquered by the Normans in 1060-90), Crete in 826, southern Italy in 838 (the Arabs sacked Rome in 844, but were ejected between 860 and 916), Malta in 869.

814 The death of Charlemagne and emergence of a new Europe. The 843 Treaty of Verdun finally partitioned Charlemagne's empire between his grandsons: Ludwig II ruled the East Franks, Lothaire I the Middle Franks (and was given the title of Holy Roman Emperor) and Charles II the West Franks. These three kingdoms ultimately developed into, respectively, Germany, Italy and France. Other new kingdoms were established in Denmark (803), Sweden (820), Scotland (848) and Norway (872).

829 Egbert, king of Wessex, won much of southern England. In 837, Danes attacked Wessex, initiating a century of conquest. In 871, Alfred the Great began his reign. He died in 899, after successfully resisting the Danes and uniting Saxon England.

830 Normans (Vikings) began their invasion of northern France ("Normandy"—which was to be the base for the later conquest of England and southern Italy) and northern Germany. In 885, Normans besieged Paris.

840 Kyrgyz destroyed the Uighur empire and pushed the Uighurs west to the Tarim Basin in what is now NW China.

845 The Chinese Emperor Wu-tsung persecuted Christians (and also Buddhists), which ultimately put an end to the first Christian mission to China. Thereafter, the Chinese adopt a mix of Taoism and Buddhism and Confucian ethics.

856 Norwegians conquered Scotland's Northern and Western Isles, the Isle of Man and eastern Ireland, where they founded the kingdom of Dublin.

860 The kingdom of Castile in northern Spain came to prominence. Eventually, in 1492, it ejected the Muslims from Spain and founded the Spanish Empire.

Viking raids along the coasts of N and W Europe devastated economies and hindered both commerce and Christian mission. The Vikings of Scandinavia traded and plundered as far afield as Murmansk, Constantinople, Greenland and Morocco. After 900, they converted to Christianity and their destructive influence waned.

874 The Norwegian Viking chieftain Ingolfur Arnarson settled in hitherto uninhabited Iceland. In 930 the first Althing was held in Iceland—the oldest parliament in Europe.

890 The Magyars were expelled from southern Russia, migrating to the Danube and settling in what is now Hungary in 896.

The geographical fragmentation of Christianity

The fragmentation of Christendom and Christian witness by 900 was extraordinary. The combined assaults of the Muslim Arabs on the states bordering the Mediterranean and the vigorously pagan Vikings on Europe's northern and western coasts and along the rivers of E Europe effectively cut off communication and trade. Links with the Christians of NW Africa and Asia were severed, leaving those communities isolated. The map opposite shows how the Muslim advance separated the two Christian areas from each other. Just two principal bastions of Christendom remained, the Frankish Empire in the west and Byzantium in the east—but both were energetically subverting or suppressing any renewal movements, even as millions of Christians in Muslim areas were going over to Islam. It was another 900 years before the Church recovered the momentum it had lost for effective mission work.

Burning Question for Today

Today, the Church is under similar assault, from a jihadist Islamist movement and the new paganism of humanistic secularism. It is in danger of giving up on the very purpose of its existence.

▲ Could blind tolerance and compromise replace a global passion for mission?

The Christian World of AD 800–900

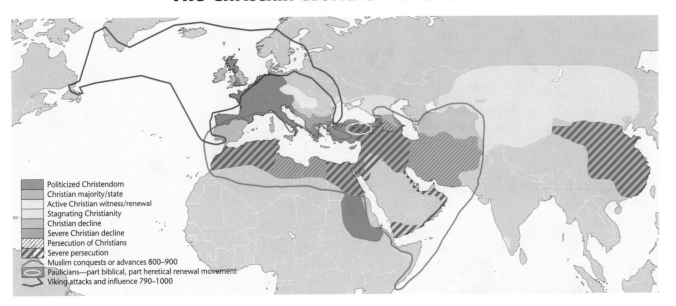

- Politicized Christendom
- Christian majority/state
- Active Christian witness/renewal
- Stagnating Christianity
- Christian decline
- Severe Christian decline
- Persecution of Christians
- Severe persecution
- Muslim conquests or advances 800–900
- Paulicians—part biblical, part heretical renewal movement
- Viking attacks and influence 790–1000

Significant dates

Progress

800 Charlemagne crowned "Holy Roman Emperor" by the Pope—an event that would establish both the papacy's claim to confer kingship and the close political link between State and Church that would shape the next thousand years of European history.

825 Migration of Syriac-speaking Persian Christians to join the Malabar Christians in India

845 Western Czech leaders embraced Christianity. In 864, Boris, Czar of the Bulgars, was baptized.

850 Christianity was now the principal religion of many peoples between the Caspian and Xinjiang—but it was under threat from Islam.

862 Cyril developed the Cyrillic alphabet in Moravia—crucial to the translation of Scripture into the Slavic languages and the evangelization of the Slavs in the next century.

Setbacks

806 Iona Monastery sacked by Vikings. Their wide-ranging, destructive raids did much to end Celtic missions.

832 Caliph Mamun massacred the Copts after an uprising. By 837, most churches in Egypt had been demolished.

835 China's third imperial persecution of Buddhists and Eastern Christians. In 845, 40,000 hermitages and temples and 4,600 monasteries (containing 265,500 monks and nuns) were destroyed or closed.

847 Savage persecution of Paulicians (see entry under 640 on p35), largely in Anatolia by the Byzantines, who crushed a major revolt in 874. There were 100,000 martyrs.

The Abbasid Caliph Mutawakkil began a major, 14-year persecution of both Christians and Muslim sects. Many churches in Mesopotamia (present-day Iraq) were destroyed.

870 Final eradication of Eastern Christianity in the Arabian Peninsula.

878 In China, the port city of Kan-fu (Canton) fell to anti-foreign peasant rebels who then slaughtered 120,000 of its inhabitants—Muslim, Jewish, Christian and Zoroastrian.

Key Statistics: 800–900	800	900
World population (millions)	218	238
Christians (millions)	40.7	40.8
Christians as % of world population	18.7%	17.1%
Christian martyrs during 801–900	329,000	

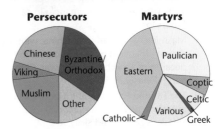

Persecutors — **Martyrs**

Fig 2.20 *Who persecuted whom in the 9th Century*

Burning Question for Today

It is tragic that so much of the growth of Islam was due to the failures of the Church—its politicization, its declining spirituality, its lack of spiritual unity, its loss of vision, its failures to translate the Bible into local languages and to witness to non-Christians etc.

▲ Will the 21st-Century Church fail for the same reasons?

Different denominations and fragmentation of the Church

In Fig 2.21, the two middle columns show the common Western perspective that the Christian world was either Catholic (Latin, western) or Orthodox (Greek, eastern). This is an over-simplification. The inaccurate term "Orthodox" covers several different theological positions as well as a variety of liturgical languages: Chalcedonian (Greek and later Slavic), Monophysite (Coptic, Nubian, Ethiopian, Armenian, Georgian and Jacobite Syrian) and Eastern/Nestorian (Syrian, Persian, C Asian and Malabar Indian).

These are the major streams of Christianity that emerged from the theological and cultural differences of the 4th–6th Centuries—and then came the advance of Islam that, geographically, separated them further. Fig 2.21 shows the position in 800, before further mass defections to Islam during the 9th Century.

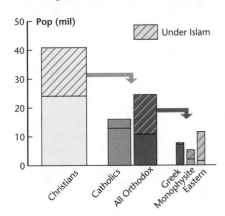

Fig 2.21 *The composition of the Church in 800*

The Empires of AD 1000

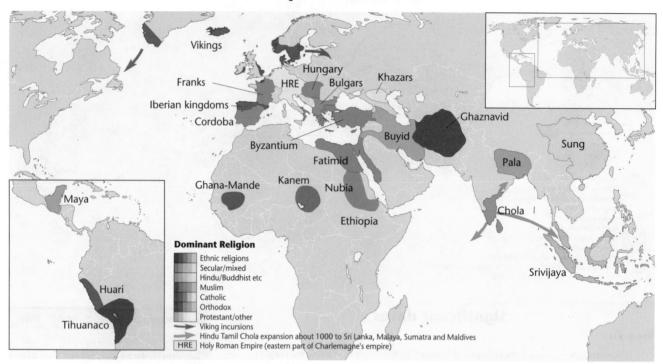

Significant dates

900 Discovery of Greenland by Vikings, who settled there in 982

The "Christian" reconquest of Spain began. In 934, a Moorish army was defeated at Simancas in central Spain. In 939, the Moors lost Madrid.

907 Massive changes afflicted China, with the fall of the Tang dynasty followed by the "Epoch of the Five Dynasties" and decades of anarchy and civil war. China was reunited under the Sung dynasty in 979.

909 The Fatimid Empire in the Maghreb, N Africa founded by al-Mahdi, who declared himself Caliph. In 948, Fatimid Saracens conquered Sicily. In 967, the Fatimids conquered Egypt and the Arab Middle East.

911 West Franks gave the dukedom of Normandy to Rollo, the leader of invading Norman Vikings. This was the start of the many Norman conquests in France, Britain, Ireland and southern Italy.

Demise of the kingdom of the East Franks, which disintegrated into many states under the umbrella of the Holy Roman Empire. In 962, Otto I was crowned emperor. The (largely Germanic) HRE became one of the bulwarks of the papacy. It was to endure until 1806, when Napoleon abolished it. Germany was not unified until 1871.

916 Mongolian Khitan Empire founded. In 925, the Khitan pushed out from their homeland in Manchuria (where they had dominated the Jurchens, or Manchus), driving the Kyrgyz west, controlling most of northern China and establishing the Liao dynasty. They were defeated by the Han Chinese in 947, though their scattered tribes were later reunited under Ghenghis Khan.

932 Buyid Empire founded in northern Persia, followed by the Ghaznavid Empire in 998 in northeast Persia. The latter then gained control of C Asia and invaded Punjab.

950 Mali Empire in W Africa founded. It became wealthy from trans-Saharan trade.

960 The Rus advanced southeast to the Khazars and expanded east as far as the Volga and also west to the Danube.

965 Byzantines forced the Arabs out of Cyprus and then in 972 conquered the Bulgarian Empire.

987 Collapse of the West Frankish kingdom, followed by the founding of the kingdom of France under the Capet dynasty

The case of Egypt

Egypt had become almost entirely Christian by 600, with a long history of heroic martyrdoms and growth under persecution and a very much longer history as a great civilization. How did a foreign power change its religion and culture so quickly, with at first minimal persecution? Egypt's Arab conquerors were originally a small minority, but they succeeded by imposing discriminatory laws and taxation. Christians were required to wear different clothes, were not allowed to ride animals, had to pay more than three times as much tax as Muslims and were restricted in what work they could do. The legal system gave them virtually no redress when they were wronged. The only way to avoid humiliation and impoverishment was to become Muslim. Later, Christians were subjected to terrible persecutions.

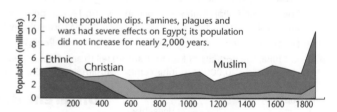

Fig 2.22 *Religious affiliation in Egypt from AD 1 to 1900*

Food for Thought

What is remarkable is the survival and continued witness of the Coptic Church, which now comprises around 10–12% of Egypt's population of 65 million. The lesson from history is that Muslims do not need to be in a majority to Islamize a country. They need only to be able to manipulate or control the legal and taxation systems.

▲ Is this something that is already well under way in 21st-Century Europe?

The Christian World of AD 900–1000

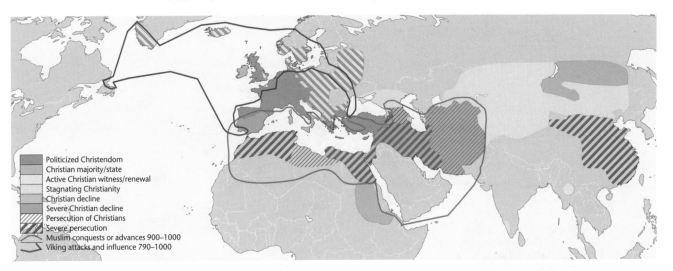

Politicized Christendom
Christian majority/state
Active Christian witness/renewal
Stagnating Christianity
Christian decline
Severe Christian decline
Persecution of Christians
Severe persecution
Muslim conquests or advances 900–1000
Viking attacks and influence 790–1000

Significant dates

Progress

916 Christianization of the Czechs, first through the Orthodox missionaries Cyril and Methodius and then through King Wenceslas, who was martyred

917 Bulgarian Orthodox Church established. By 927, Bulgaria was an Orthodox Christian country. A struggle for influence between Rome and Constantinople was one of the catalysts for the Great Schism between these two major branches of Christianity in 1056.

920 Eastern Christians reached Burma.

945 Christianity arrived in Kyiv-Rus (present-day Ukraine and Russia). In 957, King Olha became a Christian.

966 Poland became Christian, after the first Poles were won through Methodius in northern Moravia in the 860s.

980 The Scandinavian countries were Christianized—unfortunately, mainly by force or political manipulation. Harold Bluetooth united Denmark and soon after became a Christian. In 990, Christianity reached the Vikings settled in Greenland. In 993, Olav became the first Christian king of Norway (which at that time controlled Greenland, Iceland and the Shetland, Hebridean and Orkney Islands). He united it as a Christian country between 997 and 1030, and in 999 also forced the Faeroe Islanders to embrace Christianity. In 994, Olov, king of Sweden, became a Christian—though it took a further 200 years before all of Sweden was Christianized. In 1000, the Icelandic parliament decided to adopt Christianity.

988 Vladimir, ruler of Kyiv-Rus, introduced Eastern Orthodox Christianity and ordered a mass baptism of all Ukrainians and Russians.

990 The Kerait Mongolians embraced Christianity and spread its influence extensively through the Turkic and Mongolian tribes. The principal Christian tribes were the Naimans and Merkits.

997 C Europe was Christianized. Hungarians converted en masse to Catholic Christianity and the Prussians became the first of the Baltic tribes to begin to embrace it. By 999, Bohemia was fully Christianized.

Setbacks

970 Final imperial persecution of Christians in China. Christianity eradicated

996 Severe persecution of Christians in Fatimid Empire

Key Statistics: 900–1000	900	1000
World population (millions)	238	264
Christians (millions)	40.8	44.5
Christians as % of world population	17.1%	16.9%
Christian martyrs during 901–1000	80,000	

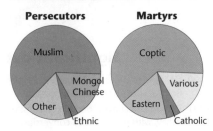

Persecutors — Muslim, Mongol Chinese, Other, Ethnic

Martyrs — Coptic, Various, Eastern, Catholic

Fig 2.23 *Who persecuted whom in the 10th Century*

Orthodox missions to the Slavs

The Greek Orthodox Church, with its ties to the Byzantine Empire, was not mission-minded. Surrounding peoples were seen as a threat—which they were!—and not as an opportunity. Two remarkable men, Cyril (or Constantine) (826–869) and Methodius (827–885), became apostles to the Slavs who had spread across E and C Europe. They were good linguists and culturally sensitive men who, despite encountering severe opposition from German Catholic priests, won the hearts of the leaders and people. Cyril developed the Glagolithic (Cyrillic) script that is used by all Orthodox Slavic peoples today, and the two men translated much of the Bible and the liturgy into Slavonic. Christianity (in their case Catholic) became indigenous to the Moravians—who in turn became a force for the Gospel in later centuries through the ministry of Jan Hus, the great 15th-Century reformer, and the launch of the first Protestant missions movement in the 18th Century.

Burning Questions for Today

It was largely through the work of Cyril and Methodius that much of C, SE and E Europe became Orthodox Christian in the 10th Century—as the map above shows. Two anointed men with a missionary calling and apostolic gifting changed the world, yet were strongly opposed by much of the established Church.

▲ Is the Church any different today?

The ministry of mission is still the only way for the nations of the world to be reconciled to God and with one another.

▲ Why has "missionary" become a negative, often embarrassing, word for Christians today?

The Empires of AD 1100

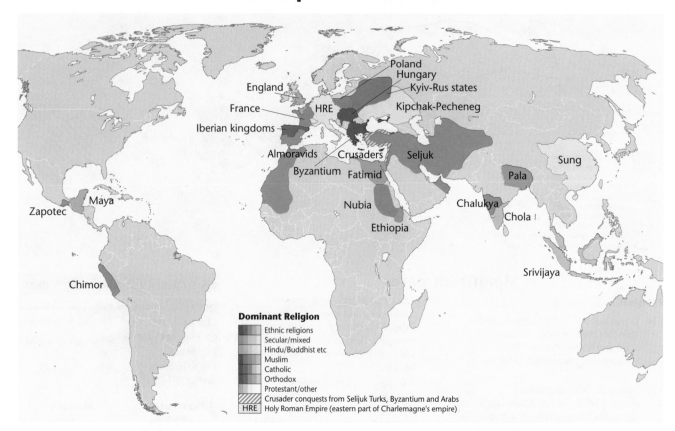

Dominant Religion
- Ethnic religions
- Secular/mixed
- Hindu/Buddhist etc
- Muslim
- Catholic
- Orthodox
- Protestant/other
- Crusader conquests from Selijuk Turks, Byzantium and Arabs
- HRE   Holy Roman Empire (eastern part of Charlemagne's empire)

Significant dates

1000 Collapse of the large Tihuanaco Empire in what is now Peru-Bolivia—possibly caused by climate change

1001 Persian Ghaznavids began conquest of Punjab and the Indus valley, with many forced conversions to Islam.

1013 Danes finally conquered all of England, only to lose it to Viking-Norman invaders from France in 1066.

1016 Normans began conquest of southern Italy, which they finally wrested from the Muslim Fatimid Empire in 1053. They then took Sicily in 1061–91 and Malta in 1091, opening the way for the Crusades.

1018 Bulgars subjugated by Byzantium

1028 Oghuz Turks from Asia migrated west and settled in the northwest corner of the Abbasid Empire. From them came both the Seljuk and the Ottoman Turk Empires. They had been largely Eastern Christian until they converted to Islam around 950. In 1040, the Seljuk Turks began their conquests in C Asia. In 1071, at the Battle of Manzikert, they decisively defeated Byzantium and seized most of Anatolia—the beginning of the end of the Byzantine Empire, and the cause of the First Crusade. From 1400 to 1900, the Ottomans were to be the Muslim world power.

1040 The Almoravids came to power in N Africa and went to war to capture both Spain and much of W Africa for a more radical expression of Islam. By this time, the great majority of Spanish in Muslim-ruled Spain had become Muslim.

1052 Pisa, a city state in what is now Italy, ejected the Arabs from Sardinia.

1061 The Kipchak (Polovets) invaded Rus. A long series of wars followed, involving huge territorial changes and loss of life, until 1235. The Kipchak were a Turkic people related to the Khazars (among whom there were Jews, Christians and some Muslims).

The Crusades and *jihad*

For Christians to resort to a "holy" war was a direct contradiction of the very spirit of the Gospel and the character of the Lord Jesus Christ. The grim legacy of the Crusades impacts Christian witness even today. Yet it must also be said that the Crusades served to check Muslim advances for 500 years, during which the Renaissance and Reformation blossomed in Western Europe.

For Muslims throughout history, *jihad* has defined the relationship between Muslims and non-Muslims. Some have interpreted it as a spiritual struggle for moral purity or as a correction of wrongs in society by word and action, but the majority have understood *jihad* as violent war to eradicate infidels and impose Islam as the global faith. It is certainly the language of the Islamists of the 21st Century. Al-Qa'ida's declaration of war against the West (or "Crusaders") in 1996 is a reality. Islamists see this conflict as a war of a thousand wounds in which the resolve of the West will be worn down to the point of surrender.

Burning Question for Today

We need to demonstrate a loving and Christian response that commends the Gospel and does not use carnal weapons (2 Corinthians 10:3–5). At the same time we should be supportive of governments pursuing realistic, wise and firm policies in response to the challenge of the Islamists. This conflict will dominate coming decades and will require long-term commitment, effort and sacrifice.

▲ What opportunities are there today for Christians to introduce Muslims to Christ?

The Church in AD 1000–1100

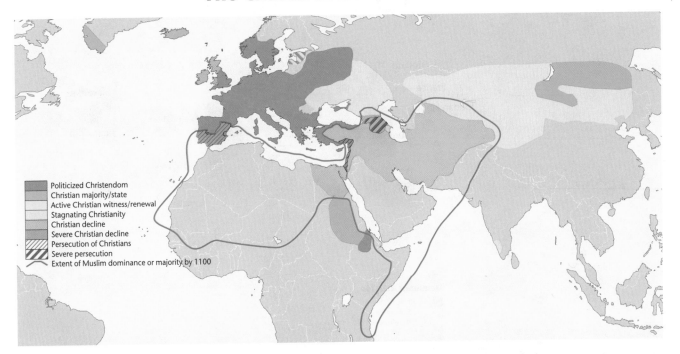

Politicized Christendom
Christian majority/state
Active Christian witness/renewal
Stagnating Christianity
Christian decline
Severe Christian decline
Persecution of Christians
Severe persecution
Extent of Muslim dominance or majority by 1100

Significant dates

Progress

1015 Russia became majority Orthodox Christian.

1020 The Eastern Church by this time had 250 dioceses and possibly 12 million Christians, all in Asia. Over 50% of the population of today's Syria, Iraq, Khorasan and other parts of C Asia was Eastern Christian. From this point on, this church went into decline but for a brief respite in the time of the Mongol Empire two centuries later.

1050 Latvia first evangelized by Russian Orthodox

Setbacks

1000 All traces of the once strong but divided church in N Africa wiped out. The indigenous Berbers became the first major non-Arab people to become wholly Muslim.

1054 Final cleavage between Western Catholic and Eastern Orthodox Christianity

1064 Armenia invaded by Seljuk Turks; 1,001 churches destroyed, 100,000 Christian Armenians massacred

1086 Battle of Zallakha in Spain, at which the Islamist Almoravid Muslims defeated the Christians.

1096 Start of the First Catholic Crusade via Constantinople (then threatened by the Seljuk Turks). This ended in 1099 with the capture of Nicea, Antioch and Jerusalem—the last of which was held by the Crusaders for over a century.

Why did the Berbers and Turks turn from Christianity to Islam?

In the 11th Century, two major peoples who were once largely Christian, the Berbers and the Turks, became strongly Muslim and also great enemies of Christendom. What went wrong? Compare them with the Ethiopians and Armenians, who suffered centuries of attacks from Islam and produced many martyrs for the faith. The latter had the Scriptures and a liturgy in their own language. Christianity had become theirs and was deeply embedded in their cultures. In contrast, the Berbers used Latin and the Turks used Syriac as their religious language. The Gospel never became part of their core culture and their language. Jesus' parable of the houses built on sand and the rock of God's word comes to mind (Matthew 7:24–27).

Since the printing of the Kabyle Berber New Testament in 1954, the Church in Algeria has grown, despite persecution, to over 50,000 Kabyle believers.

Food for Thought

Learning the local languages and cultures and then translating the Bible is essential for planting indigenous churches that will thrive for many generations. It requires years of costly work with little to show, but it is the only way.

▲ Have we lost that basic principle in today's missions thinking?

Key Statistics: 1000–1100	1000	1100
World population (millions)	264	308
Christians (millions)	44.5	51.7
Christians as % of world population	16.9%	16.8%
Christian martyrs during 1001–1100	115,000	

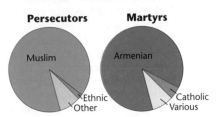

Persecutors **Martyrs**

Muslim Armenian

Ethnic Other Catholic Various

Fig 2.24 *Who persecuted whom in the 11th Century*

The Crusades left a grim legacy (Gustave Doré, 1832–83, The Battle of Antioch)

The Empires of AD 1200

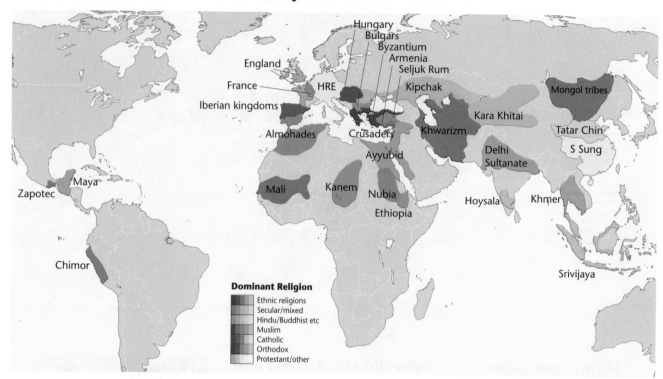

Significant dates

1100   Muslim Turkic-speaking Seljuks spread into Persia, Mesopotamia and Turkey.

1115   Jurchens (Manchus) overran the Khitans and founded the Jin dynasty in N China. The Khitans fled westwards and in 1134 founded the Kara Khitai Empire, which lasted until it was taken over by the Naiman Mongols (many of them Eastern Christians) in 1208 and they in turn were absorbed into Ghenghis Khan's Mongol Empire in 1218.

1145   The Mahdist Islamist Almohads overthrew the Almoravids in N Africa and established an empire that stretched from the Atlantic to the border of Egypt. They were intolerant of both other religions and other expressions of Islam. Many Jews and Christians were converted by force—a stimulus for Spanish violence in the reconquest of Spain and, four centuries hence, the establishment of the Inquisition to root out all but Catholicism.

1153   The population of the Maldive islands became Muslim. Many had been Eastern Christians.

1155   Pope Hadrian IV—an Englishman—issued a papal bull awarding Ireland to Henry II of England, beginning the sad involvement of England in Ireland that remains a cause of conflict even today.

1171   Saladin (Salah-ad-Din) seized power in Egypt, ending the Ismaili Shi'a Fatimid Empire and founding the Ayyubid dynasty to restore the rule of Sunni Islam. Saladin was a Kurd, born in Tikrit in what is now Iraq. He took Syria from the Crusaders In 1176, and Jerusalem in 1187. This marked the beginning of the end for the disastrous, three-century effort of European powers to defeat Islam in the Holy Land.

1173   Egypt under Saladin invaded the northern Christian Nubian kingdom, killing 130,000 and enslaving over half a million. From this point on, Christianity went into decline among the Nubians.

1175   Muslims invaded India. In the Battles of Tarain, in 1191 and 1192, they defeated Rajput forces by subterfuge, opening India to Muslim domination for the next 666 years. By 1199, all of N India was under Ghurid Muslim control.

Islam and the means for world conquest

This was the century in which Muslims resumed their march towards world conquest, defeating the European Crusaders and pushing up the Nile into Christian Nubia and eastwards into Hindu India. Most of their advances, when they were strong enough, were achieved by means of war. From a Muslim perspective, there can be no peace until Islam is globally supreme. Any peace agreement or treaty is merely an interlude while Muslims gain strength for the next advance. No binding long-term agreements with "unbelievers" are permissible in Islam, which also allows the use of deceit (*taqiyya*) to avert a threat and concealing the truth (*kitmaniyya*) to obtain advantage. The conquest of India involved both stratagems. The Rajput commander defeated the invading Muslims, but chivalrously heeded their leader's pleas for his life and freedom. The following year the Muslims returned with a bigger army. Nonetheless, they prevailed only by agreeing a truce with the Rajputs and then, when the Indian forces stood down, immediately breaking it in a night attack.

Food for Thought

Islam has not really changed and such stratagems are still used today. (Christendom is also guilty of acts of deceit in conquest—but whereas the use of deceit is part of the teaching of Islam it is contrary to Christian teaching.[10])

▲ How often are we assured by non-Muslims that Islam is a religion of peace while the Muslims who assert this continue privately to fund and support *jihad*?

▲ In the light of Islam's clear long-term goals, what worth is there in any agreements or treaties on Palestine, terror or nuclear weapons, or any undertakings to honour the laws of host countries?

▲ Do we perceive the true nature of Islam?[11]

The Church in AD 1100–1200

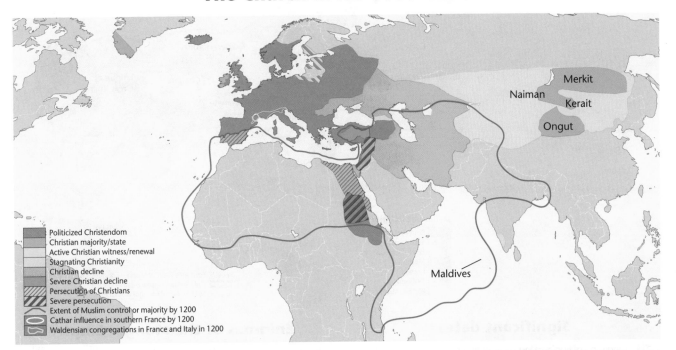

Legend:
- Politicized Christendom
- Christian majority/state
- Active Christian witness/renewal
- Stagnating Christianity
- Christian decline
- Severe Christian decline
- Persecution of Christians
- Severe persecution
- Extent of Muslim control or majority by 1200
- Cathar influence in southern France by 1200
- Waldensian congregations in France and Italy in 1200

Map labels: Merkit, Naiman, Kerait, Ongut, Maldives

Significant dates

Progress

1100 Hungary adopted Catholic Christianity as its national religion. Sweden and Poland were by now wholly Christian.

1118 The Spanish wrested Saragossa from the Muslims.

1142 Reconciliation between the West Syrian (Monophysite Jacobite) and Eastern Syrian (Nestorian) Churches, both of which used the Syriac language for their liturgies. The two communions had, respectively, 2 million and 12 million members, constituting about a quarter of all Christians at that time.

1147 The Cathars (or Albigensenses) emerged in SW France. Their syncretic reform movement spread across S France and into Italy.

1150 Ongut Turks in C Asia embraced Eastern Christianity.

1173 Waldensian reform movement began in Lyons, France. Severely persecuted for centuries, it was later strongest in N Italy.

Setbacks

1147 Start of the Second Crusade. It lasted until 1149, and was followed by a series of disastrous crusades which culminated in the fall of Jerusalem to Muslim armies in 1187.

1150 Sweden launched a first crusade against the pagan Finns. By 1250, after the third, Finland was subjugated and Catholicism widely practised. In 1180, German Teutonic knights invaded Latvia and Estonia to convert the population to Catholicism by force. This process was completed in 1212.

1171 Henry II invaded Ireland on the basis of the papal bull of 1155 and ended the independent existence of the Celtic Church there. This was followed by the English subjugation of the Celtic Church in Wales in 1292.

Key Statistics: 1100–1200	1100	1200
World population (millions)	308	357
Christians (millions)	51.7	65.7
Christians as % of world population	16.8%	18.4%
Christian martyrs during 1101–1200	169,000	

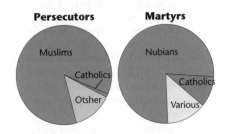

Persecutors: Muslims, Catholics, Otsher

Martyrs: Nubians, Catholics, Various

Fig 2.25 *Who persecuted whom in the 12th Century?*

Food for Thought

Reformation movements have been necessary, but very costly.

▲ Are we willing to stand up for what we believe even if it entails persecution—as it surely will as the 21st Century unfolds?

The grim logic of the Crusades

The unequal yoking of Church and State at the time of Constantine in the 4th Century had a devastating impact on the spiritual health of the Church and on its leadership structures, ministry and mission which is still affecting us in the 21st Century. Charlemagne imposed Christianity on the Saxons and others on pain of death, and the same process was still underway in the 12th Century, as the above events show.

Tragically, it was then extended to the forced conversion of Jews and Moors in the *reconquista* of Spain in the 15th Century and the Native Americans in the 16th. In the 13th Century, crusades were also launched against nascent reform movements (the Cathars and Waldensians), involving terrible slaughter. Out of these repressions of Christian "deviants" emerged the iniquitous Inquisition and the burning of heretics. The growing Reformation movement began with the Paulicians in Asia Minor, the Bogomils in the Bal-

kans and the Cathars in France (all in some respects deviating from biblical theology), but this century saw the first biblical reform movement in a Catholic-dominated area, the Waldensians. They were followed by the Lollards in England and the Hussites in Bohemia and Germany under Luther.

The Empires of AD 1300

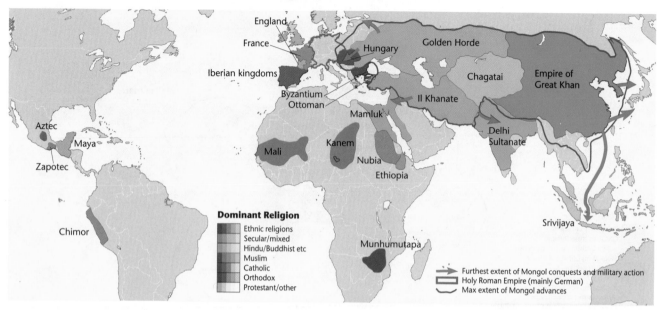

Dominant Religion
- Ethnic religions
- Secular/mixed
- Hindu/Buddhist etc
- Muslim
- Catholic
- Orthodox
- Protestant/other

→ Furthest extent of Mongol conquests and military action
▭ Holy Roman Empire (mainly German)
⌒ Max extent of Mongol advances

Significant dates

1203 King John of England lost most of his French domains. In 1215, he was forced to sign the Magna Carta, which became the eventual foundation of parliamentary democracy.

1204 Muslim armies of the Persian Ghurids conquered most of N India. In 1206, the Delhi Sultanate broke away as a separate empire. Muslim political dominance in India continued until the 18th Century.

1206 Ghenghis Khan united the Mongol and Turkic tribes to establish the Mongol Empire, which was to become the largest continuous land empire in history (see blue line on the map). The Mongols set out to conquer the world, successfully invading N China (Jin Empire) in 1211, Persia in 1218, Russia, Poland, Hungary and Bohemia in 1227–40, Korea in 1240, the Seljuk Turk Empire in 1242–43, S China in 1257–79, Mesopotamia and Syria in 1258 and India in 1526. However, their invasions of Indochina (1257), Mamluk Egypt (1260), Japan (1274), Burma (1277–83) and Java (1293) all failed.

1212 The Muslim Almohads were defeated by Christians, losing much of Spain and what is now Portugal. By 1300 they retained only Granada.

1217 Ghenghis Khan died, having divided his empire among his four sons: in the west, Hulegu founded the Ilkhanate in Persia, Batu the Golden Horde in E Europe and Chagatai his eponymous empire in C Asia—all later became Muslim; in the east, Kublai founded the Yuan dynasty of China, which was Buddhist. The Mongol Empire was effactully divided in 1259, though it reached its maximum extent in 1279 under Kublai Khan.

1267 The Aztecs settled in the Valley of Mexico. Their empire was crushed by the Spanish three centuries later.

1281 Accession of Sultan Osman in northwestern Anatolia. This was the start of the Ottoman rise to imperial power.

1282 Beginning of the Hapsburg dynasty in Austria, a regional superpower until 1918.

The Shaybanid khan Uzbek converted the Turk-Mongol Shaybanid horde to Islam. They became known as Uzbeks.

Food for Thought

Missed opportunities or selfish, short-sighted choices have had a decisive impact on the course of world history.

▲ What if we repeat the mistakes of the 13th Century in our generation?

Enigmas of the Mongol Empire

The destructiveness of the Mongol invasions (see map on p47) can overshadow the extraordinary legacy of their empire, which laid the foundations of some of the best aspects of the modern world:

▲ Good administration and communications, holding together a territory stretching for 8,000 km, with effective taxation that limited corruption and a legal system that ended intertribal warfare and vastly reduced crime

▲ Routes opened up between East and West, resulting in education and trade in goods and resources that were to stimulate both the European Renaissance and the search for a sea route to the East.

▲ A culture of tolerance that allowed all religions to make converts. In 1300, the majority religion in C Asia was Christianity; most of the Mongol leaders were shamanists, though some were Christian and many later converted to Buddhism or Islam.

▲ The unification of China and also, ultimately, Russia. The Mongols also made possible the Turkish Muslim domination of C and W Asia, SE Europe and the Mediterranean for centuries to come.

What if...

▲ the young Ghenghis Khan had become a Christian under tutelage of the Kethe Keraait king?[12]

▲ the anti-Muslim khan Hulegu had followed his conquest of Persia, Mesopotamia and Syria by conquering Egypt, the last bastion of Islam able to resist him?

▲ the West had taken up Hulegu's repeated requests for a strategic alliance to crush Islam?

▲ the Crusaders had not made a secret pact with Egypt to allow its army unhindered passage to attack the Ilkhan Mongols while they were, for a while, weak? C Asia and even Iran and Iraq might have become Christian.

▲ the Pope and Christians in the West had treated Eastern Christians as friends and not heretics?

▲ Western Christians had taken up the earlier invitation of the Mongols to teach them about Christianity?

The Church in AD 1200–1300

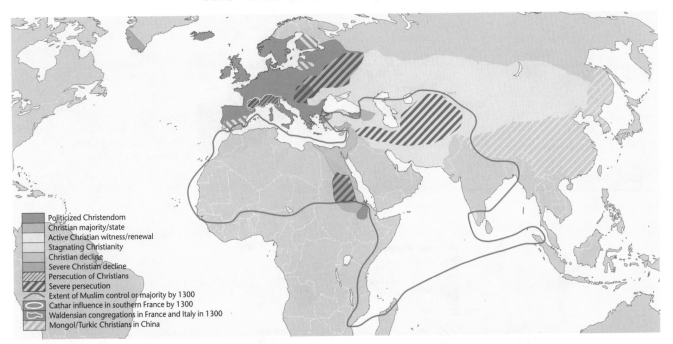

Legend:
- Politicized Christendom
- Christian majority/state
- Active Christian witness/renewal
- Stagnating Christianity
- Christian decline
- Severe Christian decline
- Persecution of Christians
- Severe persecution
- Extent of Muslim control or majority by 1300
- Cathar influence in southern France by 1300
- Waldensian congregations in France and Italy in 1300
- Mongol/Turkic Christians in China

Significant dates

Progress (some questionable)

1206 Rise of the Cathars in France. They were crushed by a papal crusade (1208–42) in which about half a million people were killed, not all of them Cathars. The Cathars were influenced by Gnosticism, Manicheanism and the Paulicians of Asia Minor.

1208 First Waldensians burnt as heretics in Strasbourg. They suffered extreme persecution but survived in northern Italy as the first biblical reform movement in the Western Church.

1214 Eastern Christianity now the dominant religion among the Turkic and Mongol tribes. The Mongol Empire created opportunity for religious change and briefly facilitated the spread of Eastern Christianity.

1227 German Crusader knights invaded Estonia from Latvia, imposed Christianity on its pagan inhabitants and ruled them for 700 years.

1271 Marco Polo travelled to China, returning to Italy in 1295. There was an abortive Catholic mission to the Mongol capital, Karakorum, in 1245.

Setbacks

1204 Crusaders captured and sacked Orthodox Constantinople and killed 30,000 Greek Orthodox in their attempt to impose Catholicism.

1214 Between now and 1258, Mongols destroyed most of the cities of C Asia, Afghanistan, Persia, Mesopotamia and Syria, many of them predominantly Christian. Perhaps 40 million people—then over 11% of the world's population—perished as a result of Mongol military actions.

1217 The disastrous series of Crusades continued. All from the Fifth to the Ninth ended in failure. By 1291, the Crusaders were conclusively defeated and expelled from Palestine.

Key Statistics: 1200–1300	1200	1300
World population (millions)	357	350
Christians (millions)	65.7	82
Christians as % of world population	18.4%	24%
Christian martyrs during 1201–1300	7,517,000	

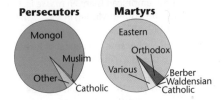

Persecutors — Mongol, Muslim, Other, Catholic

Martyrs — Eastern Orthodox, Various, Berber, Waldensian, Catholic

Fig 2.26 *Who persecuted whom in the 13th Century?*

Food For Thought

There are many parallels between the Eastern Christians in the 13th Century and the growing numbers of Evangelicals today.

▲ Could we, too, fail for similar reasons?

Why did Eastern Christians die out?

Strengths

▲ They were the most biblically oriented of the major branches of Christianity before the Reformation.

▲ They had an emphasis on learning, founding hospitals, using the Bible and training leaders and missionaries.

▲ They were trusted for their honesty, education, medical knowledge and administrative skill.

▲ They had little political influence to corrupt them.

▲ Their numbers grew despite terrible persecution, with over 12 million martyrs by 1500.

▲ They had the most fruitful and culturally sensitive missions movement before the 20th Century.

Weaknesses

▲ They were isolated from the rest of the Christian world. Little is known of their suffering and heroism.

▲ They almost always operated under non-Christian and even hostile regimes.

▲ They inadequately discipled successive generations, resulting in increasing nominalism.

▲ The educated Christians who lived in cities were slaughtered by the Mongols. The nomadic Christians who survived were often illiterate, with no leaders or teachers.

▲ Association with the Mongol conquerors led to their rejection by Muslims in the west and Chinese in the east.

The Empires of AD 1400

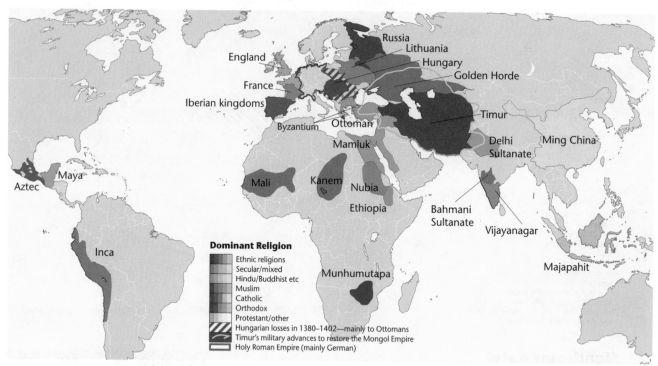

Dominant Religion
- Ethnic religions
- Secular/mixed
- Hindu/Buddhist etc
- Muslim
- Catholic
- Orthodox
- Protestant/other
- Hungarian losses in 1380–1402—mainly to Ottomans
- Timur's military advances to restore the Mongol Empire
- Holy Roman Empire (mainly German)

Significant dates

1304 Ilkhan Mongol attacks on India in 1304 and 1328 were repulsed by the Delhi Sultanate. By 1335, the Sultanate controlled almost all of India. Many lower-caste, Dalit and tribal peoples became Muslims in this period.

The Mongol khans began their conversion to Islam. The Ilkhan proclaimed himself a Shi'ite in 1304. The Golden Horde embraced Islam en masse in 1312. The Chagatai khan became a Sunni Muslim in 1322. The Ilkhanate disintegrated in 1337–53.

1328 Moscow became the capital of Russia, marking the beginning of its rise as a global power.

1330 The Black Death (probably bubonic plague) broke out in what is now Myanmar and in 1334 spread to China, where it killed nearly 70% of the population. In 1347, it reached the Middle East and Europe, where the death rate was 30–50%—higher along the Mediterranean coast and in cities. About 75 million perished worldwide.

1337 Start of the Hundred Years War between England and France. Though it ended in 1453, the antagonism between these two countries continued into the 19th Century, deeply impacting European and world history.

1354 Gallipoli captured by Ottoman Turks—their first foothold in Europe. In 1361, they established their new capital in Edirne, in what is now Bulgaria. Their advance into the Balkans continued with victory over the Slavic Serbs at the Battle of Kosovo in 1389. They conquered the Bulgars in 1396. The Muslim Ottomans dominated the Balkans and SE Europe for the next five centuries.

1365 The Turkic-speaking Mongol Timur (Tamarlane or Timur the Lame) seized the western half of the Chagatai Khanate (Transoxania) and then conquered Persia. In 1391, he defeated the Golden Horde and reached the Black Sea coast. In 1395, he sacked Baghdad. In 1398, he invaded India and crippled the Delhi Sultanate, which then went into decline. Timur's aim was to re-establish the Mongol Empire, but as a strongly Muslim entity. He died in 1405 while preparing to invade China. He was one of the greatest mass-killers of history, and Christians were a special target for his cruelty.

1368 The last Yuan Mongol emperor was overthrown and the Ming dynasty founded. China regained its independence from the Mongols.

1380 The Norwegian territories of Greenland and Iceland became Danish.

Islam spread in Sumatra and then to Malaya and the southern Philippines.

1386 Union of Poland and Lithuania established

1395 The Kazakh Horde carved out Kazakhstan from the Chagatai and Golden Hordes.

Globalization and disease

The Mongols created the first truly transcontinental ("global") empire which stimulated trade, migration and the spread of both knowledge and new religions. Initially, this favoured Christianity, but ultimately it advanced Islam and Buddhism at the expense of Christians. It also globalized disease, with the Black Death spreading along trade routes from China to Europe. This was a catastrophe for both Asia and Europe. There were lasting effects: societies across the world were changed, economies crippled and empires rendered powerless—the plague even hastened the demise of the four Mongol khanates. It ended feudalism in W Europe, and the great fear of death it inspired stimulated spiritual renewal and church reform.

Food for Thought

In the late 20th Century we had the worldwide AIDS pandemic, and in the 21st threats of other new, exotic diseases such as SARS and a mutation of bird flu which could spread like wildfire in our highly globalized and densely populated world.

▲ Are we equipped as Christians to cope with the social, economic, migrational and spiritual crises that would then be suddenly thrust upon us?

The Church in AD 1300–1400

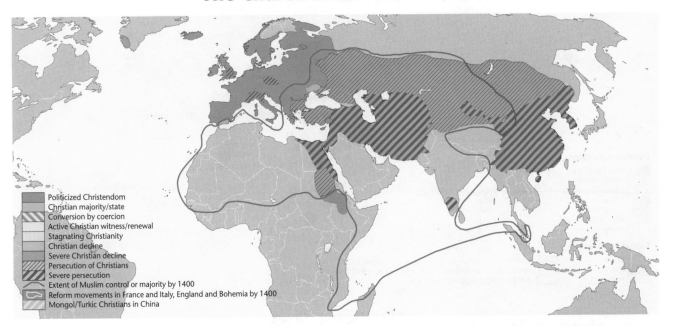

Politicized Christendom
Christian majority/state
Conversion by coercion
Active Christian witness/renewal
Stagnating Christianity
Christian decline
Severe Christian decline
Persecution of Christians
Severe persecution
Extent of Muslim control or majority by 1400
Reform movements in France and Italy, England and Bohemia by 1400
Mongol/Turkic Christians in China

Significant dates

Progress

1300 The start of the Renaissance, a cultural and philosophical revolution that moved Europe from the margins to global supremacy and opened the way for the Reformation.

1321 Dominicans began mission work in India and, in 1323, Franciscans in Indonesia.

1328 Birth of John Wycliffe, the great reformer who translated the Bible into English. He died in 1384, but despite persecution his followers, the Lollards, continued preaching as Bible evangelists. Wycliffe's writing deeply influenced Jan Hus in Bohemia-Moravia.

1369 Birth of Jan Hus in Bohemia (Czech) who initiated a pre-Reformation biblical reform movement. He was burnt at the stake as a heretic and his followers attacked by Catholic crusaders, though they won religious freedom from 1417–37.

1387 Conversion of Lithuania to Catholicism after its union with Poland in 1386

Setbacks

1301 Mamluks in Egypt systematically persecuted Christians, destroying almost all their churches. Over 335,000 Copts were martyred in the 14th Century.

1302 The Roman Pope declared himself the supreme authority in the Church and that without submission to him there is no salvation.

1305 The captive papacy based in Avignon, France and subservient to France. This was followed by the Great Schism of Western Christianity in 1378, when there were three officially elected popes.

1310 Kurds and Arabs destroyed the Christian city of Arbela in northern Mesopotamia (Iraq) and massacred 150,000 Eastern Christians.

1315 The northern Christian Nubian kingdom of Dongola embraced Islam.

1330 Muslims invaded S India and massacred nearly 200,000 Indian Syrian (Eastern) Christians.

1358 Timur destroyed much of the Eastern Church, with about 4 million killed. In 1375, he decimated the Georgian Church (150,000 dead), and in 1394 the Jacobite Church in Syria, Persia and Anatolia (200,000 dead). In 1380, the last Christian Uighurs were forced to convert to Islam in northwest China.

1399 The percentage of the global population that was Christian fell by a quarter in the 14th Century.

The paradox of Roman Catholicism

In the 14th Century, the Papacy reached its nadir with a succession of wicked men claiming to be God's representative on earth. Reformation was needed but fiercely resisted and cruelly suppressed. Yet in this same century the Catholic missions movement was launched through godly men such as Francis of Assisi and the mendicant orders they founded. Thousands of monks and priests set out to evangelize the far corners of the earth. It is their efforts that ensured the continued growth of Catholicism outside Europe. We may question their message and methodology, but we cannot question their dedication or their success—which

Key Statistics: 1300–1400	1300	1400
World population (millions)	350	315
Christians (millions)	82	56.7
Christians as % of world population	24%	18%
Christian martyrs during 1301–1400	5,570,000	

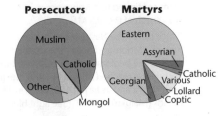

Persecutors   **Martyrs**

Fig 2.27 Who persecuted whom in the 14th Century

Mendicant order	Year founded	Strength	
		1400	**1700**
Franciscans	1209	60,000	77,000
Dominicans	1215	12,000	est 10,000
Jesuits	1534	na	22,500

Fig 2.28 Catholic missionaries in 1400 and 1700

Burning Question for Today

▲ How can 21st Century Evangelicals evangelize the world without equivalent endurance, zeal and willingness to suffer?

continued for another two centuries before the children of the Reformation themselves gained a vision for world evangelization in the 18th Century.

The Empires of AD 1500

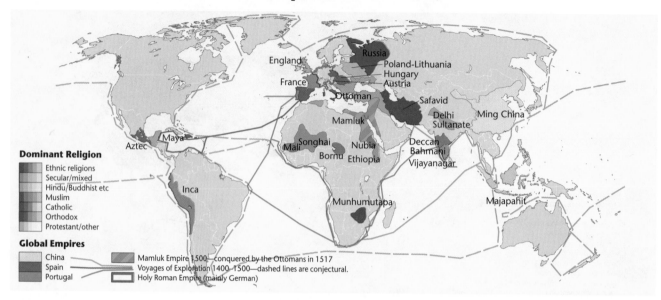

Dominant Religion
- Ethnic religions
- Secular/mixed
- Hindu/Buddhist etc
- Muslim
- Catholic
- Orthodox
- Protestant/other

Global Empires
- China
- Spain
- Portugal
- Mamluk Empire 1500—conquered by the Ottomans in 1517
- Voyages of Exploration 1400–1500—dashed lines are conjectural.
- Holy Roman Empire (mainly German)

Significant dates

1400 Timur conquered Syria and in 1402 captured the Sultan in the Ottoman Turks' first defeat in Anatolia. He died in 1405 as he prepared to invade China. His empire then disintegrated.

1401 Ottoman Turks captured Baghdad and Damascus. They then conquered Albania in 1410–78 (to hold it until 1912), Serbia in 1448–96, Constantinople in 1453, Wallachia (in what is now Romania) in 1454, Athens in 1456, Bosnia in 1463, Herzegovina in 1467, Crimea in 1475 and Croatia in 1493.

1409 Venice retook the Dalmatian coast and in 1473 captured Cyprus.

1414 Islam continued to advance among Malays, with the conversion of the first Malay ruler.

1415 Prince Henry the Navigator of Portugal seized Ceuta in N Africa from the Moors and began the exploration of Africa. This marked the beginning of the 500-year Portuguese Empire. The Portuguese reached Angola in 1488, the Indian Ocean in 1486, both Kenya and India in 1498, Brazil in 1500 and the Spice Islands (Maluku) in 1512. (See light blue lines on the map.)

1418 The Chinese produced the first integrated map of the world showing all its continents, based on the five exploratory voyages of Admiral Zheng He in 1400–23. (See orange lines on the map. That to Africa is more certain than the others.) Thereafter, the Chinese abandoned overseas exploration and trade.[13]

1434 Portugal started the European transatlantic slave trade. Over 10 million people were to be shipped from Africa to the Americas by 1850, with an estimated further 2 million dying en route.

1438 Inca rule began in Peru.

1453 End of the Franco-English Hundred Years War

1467 Final collapse of Mongol rule in Mongolia. The territories of the Mongol Empire now belonged to either the Muslim West or the Chinese East.

1469 The Timurid Empire collapsed. The Safavid Shi'a Empire was founded in Persia in 1501.

1480 Ivan, the first Tsar, liberated Russia from Mongol-Tatar domination and began pushing east into Siberia.

1492 The reconquest of Spain was completed with the capture of Granada, the last Muslim possession in the peninsula. Spain was united as a single state comprising the kingdoms of Castile and Aragon.

Columbus unwittingly "discovered" the Americas (see dark blue lines on the map.) In 1493–94, the Pope divided this "new world" between Portugal and Spain.

1494 Start of 60 years of warfare between the French and Spanish for control of Italy, which was then a medley of competing statelets and foreign-ruled territories. The war ended in 1559 with the Spanish-Austrian Hapsburgs in control and as the dominant power in Europe.

1497 Babur, a Turkic descendant of both Ghenghis Khan and Timur, became ruler of Ferghana in C Asia and founded the Persian-speaking Mughal (Mogul) dynasty that ultimately conquered India.

Spanish gold and silver from the Americas

The looted wealth of the Americas transformed both Spain and Europe. Its value in 2007 would have been about $US 3–4 trillion. It was squandered on:

▲ Territorial expansion in Italy, France and the Holy Roman Empire (modern-day Germany)—especially after the Hapsburg dynasty gained the thrones of both Spain and Austria

▲ Defending Catholic Christendom from Ottoman imperial expansion and, later, "heretical" Protestantism

▲ Humiliating France, then the most populous and best-armed state in Europe

▲ Taming the tax-rich Low Countries (especially the Netherlands), though eventually they won their independence

▲ Defending Spain's global empire against increasingly successful attacks by French, Dutch and British forces.

The negatives were a culture of exploitation rather than development in the colonies, the delay of Spanish industrialization, 150 years of overspending on costly wars to reimpose Catholicism on Europe, national impoverishment and bankruptcies. Yet ultimately this wealth financed the economic growth of N Europe, and especially the Netherlands and Britain.

Food for Thought

▲ Are there uncomfortable parallels in the way the present vast wealth of the West has been amassed and then squandered for temporal gains and not for the Kingdom of God.

The Church in AD 1400–1500

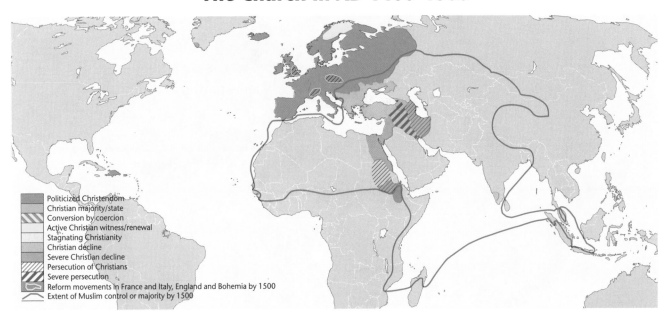

Politicized Christendom
Christian majority/state
Conversion by coercion
Active Christian witness/renewal
Stagnating Christianity
Christian decline
Severe Christian decline
Persecution of Christians
Severe persecution
Reform movements in France and Italy, England and Bohemia by 1500
Extent of Muslim control or majority by 1500

Significant dates

Progress

1419 The Hussite reformers, the Taborites, used military means to try to establish the Kingdom of God and took control of much of Bohemia and Moravia, until their defeat by Catholic forces in 1437. In 1457, the *Unitas Fratrum* (Moravian Brethren) was founded; it was to become, in 1732, the first Protestant movement to engage in missions. By 1495, the Bohemian Brethren numbered 100,000 in 400 churches.

1448 Moscow and Kiev, two metropolitans of the Orthodox Church, became independent of Constantinople, and the Russian Orthodox Church began expanding eastwards, converting local peoples to Orthodoxy.

1450 Lapps of northern Sweden evangelized by Swedes.

1454 First Christian converts in Africa through Portuguese Catholic missionaries in Senegal

1455 Gutenberg produced the first printed Bible. In 1478, Caxton printed the first book in English. The tools for an effective reformation of Christianity were now available.

1498 Birth of Girolamo Savonarola, the Italian reformer

Setbacks

1401 Sack of Baghdad by Timur. An estimated half a million Christians were killed in Mesopotamia.

1414 Council of Constance condemned heretics (Wycliffe, Hus etc) and finally settled the great Western Schism

1415 Jan Hus was burnt at the stake as a heretic. Years of persecution ensued for his followers.

1480 The Spanish Inquisition was launched, primarily to deal with superficial conversions of Jews and Muslims to Catholicism. (Possibly 12,000 were killed.) Later, it turned its attention to all heretics, including Protestants. Perhaps 3–6,000 Christians perished over the next four centuries, though some think these figures far too low.

1490 In Egypt, Nubian Christianity in the northern kingdom was eradicated by Islam. The southern kingdom became Muslim in 1499.

Christianity's dark night—the need for a new work of God

The period 1400–1500 was a desperate time for Christianity. The map above shows how a major part of the Church, spanning Asia, was brutally eliminated, while in the Middle East and N Africa Christians were in steep decline as Islam subjected them to second-class status and seasons of terrible persecution. A smaller percentage of the world population was Christian than a thousand years before. Moreover, a new Muslim power, the Ottomans, had arisen, destroying the base of Greek Orthodoxy and rapidly conquering Christian countries in SE and C Europe one after another. The only remaining bastion of Christianity was Catholic Europe, but this Catholicism was in desperate straits with a venal, corrupt and power-hungry papacy that relied more on political manipulation and the Inquisition to stifle dissent than the exercise of any spiritual gifts.

Key Statistics: 1400–1500	1400	1500
World population (millions)	315	423
Christians (millions)	56.7	75.9
Christians as % of world population	18%	17.9%
Christian martyrs during 1401–1500	599,000	

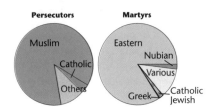

Fig 2.29 *Who persecuted whom in the 15th Century*

Yet there were signs of a new day dawning: spiritual renewal movements, prophets of reform, a hunger for something more after the devastating wars, territorial losses and plagues. That same Europe then suddenly benefited from the wealth of the Americas, and opening up of sea routes to the luxuries of Asia. It was at the darkest point that God stepped in with the advent of what we now call the Reformation, which was to lead ultimately to mission outreach and spiritual change for the world.

Burning Question for Today

▲ Do we again need a new work of the Holy Spirit in our century, in lands traditionally Christian?

The negative trends for Europe projected in this book need not happen!

The Empires of AD 1600

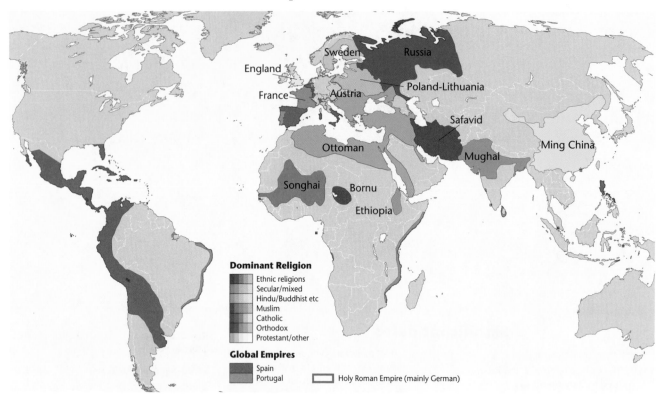

Dominant Religion
- Ethnic religions
- Secular/mixed
- Hindu/Buddhist etc
- Muslim
- Catholic
- Orthodox
- Protestant/other

Global Empires
- Spain
- Portugal
- Holy Roman Empire (mainly German)

Significant dates

1501 Safavid conquest of Persia, which became a Shi'a state

1502 Portuguese colonies established in Cochin, India, and then in Goa (1510), Malacca (1511), Ambon (Maluku) in 1513, Ceylon (1545–50), Macau (1557) and Timor (1596). In Africa, the Portuguese gained control of Zanzibar in 1503, Mozambique in 1505 and Socotra in 1506.

1504 Babur conquered Kabul in C Asia. He then advanced south, taking Kandahar in 1522 and Delhi in 1526. The Muslim Mughal Empire he founded lasted in India until 1857.

1516 Turks annexed Syria, then Egypt and Mecca in 1517, and by 1574 had advanced westwards across N Africa as far as Morocco. They also penetrated further into Europe, capturing Belgrade (Serbia) in 1521 and Moldavia in 1546. They defeated the Hungarians in the Battle of Mohacs in 1526, finishing Hungary as a major power. They captured Cyprus in 1570 with a great slaughter of Christians, and then the whole of Christian Georgia and Armenia in 1590. Two successive sieges of Vienna in 1529 failed, and the Turks were also defeated by the Venetians and Spanish in the major naval Battle of Lepanto in 1571, yet they remained a serious threat to Europe for a further century.

1519 Magellan started a circumnavigation of the globe completed by his crew in 1522.

Cortes reached the Aztec capital in Mexico, taking it in 1521. The Spanish gradually gained control of all C and S America apart from what is now Brazil, and much of N America. Spain also annexed Cuba in 1539 and the Philippines in 1564.

Charles V of Spain inherited all the Austrian Hapsburg possessions, Austria, Burgundy and the Netherlands, and used the plunder from the New World to finance a vast military expansion to gain control of Germany and Italy, limit French expansionism, confront the Ottoman Empire and crush the Reformation. Spain was to be the world's greatest power for a century or more.

1533 Ivan the Terrible became Tsar of Russia. He conquered many peoples, including the remnants of the Golden Horde: the Tatars, Chuvash and Bashkirs.

1577 Altan Khan of Mongolia converted to Tibetan Buddhism. Mongolian shamanism still continued alongside the country's official Buddhist religion.

1588 Destruction of the Spanish Armada by the English navy. This was the beginning of the eventual domination of the seas by Britain which was to open up the world for missionaries.

1590 The Emperor of Morocco annexed Timbuktu in W Africa.

1593 Beginning of Dutch colonization of the East Indies (modern-day Indonesia)

Christian imperialism?

The Mongol invasions of the 13th Century were appallingly destructive: 50% of the populations of Hungary, Russia and China perished, and possibly 90% of that of Persia. The Spanish conquest of the Americas was similarly catastrophic for the native population. By 1650, that population was perhaps 5–10 million, but we know that their numbers had fallen by 80–90% since 1492—first due to European diseases (smallpox, swine fever, measles, typhus etc) and then as a result of war, enslavement and democide.[14] This suggests a likely pre-conquest population of 50-70 million. Rich, highly developed agrarian and urban societies were, almost overnight, impoverished, humiliated, enslaved and forced to embrace the religion of their conquerors. The Aztec Empire had a population of 19–24 million, and the Inca a further 12 million.

Food for Thought

▲ Have we been objective—or has arrogance blinded us to the truth—in assessing the rich world's policies towards the poor world in the 21st Century on trade, international legislation, armaments, global warming etc?

The Church in AD 1500–1600[1]

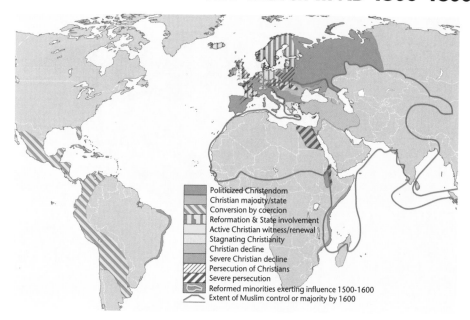

Politicized Christendom
Christian majority/state
Conversion by coercion
Reformation & State involvement
Active Christian witness/renewal
Stagnating Christianity
Christian decline
Severe Christian decline
Persecution of Christians
Severe persecution
Reformed minorities exerting influence 1500-1600
Extent of Muslim control or majority by 1600

Key Statistics: 1500–1600	1500	1600
World population (millions)	423	517
Christians (millions)	75.9	100.4
Christians as % of world population	17.9%	19.4%
Christian martyrs during 1501–1600		3,917,000

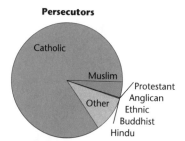

Persecutors

Catholic

Muslim

Other

Protestant
Anglican
Ethnic
Buddhist
Hindu

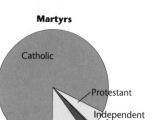

Martyrs

Catholic

Protestant

Independent

Various

Ethiopian

Fig 2.30 *Who persecuted whom in the 16th Century*

Significant dates

Progress (some of very dubious spiritual value)

1500 Portuguese Catholics met Malabar Eastern Christians in India—and sought to make these 200,000 believers into Catholics. Portuguese trade and conquest went hand-in-hand with Catholic mission. Through the Portuguese, Christianity first took root in Ghana (1503), Mozambique (1506), Burma (1544), Ceylon (1556, with 70,000 converts), Macau (by 1561 there were 5,000 Chinese Catholics), E Timor (1565) and Thailand (1567). By 1600, there were 300,000 converts in S India.

1517 Martin Luther's nailing his 95 theses to the Castle Church door in Wittenberg is seen as the start of the Reformation. In 1534, he completed the translation of the Bible into German. From 1527, Lutheranism was embraced in Scandinavia. The Reformation also made great inroads in Poland and the Baltic states until crushed in the Counter-Reformation.

1519 Ulrich Zwingli launched the Reformation in Switzerland, but died in battle seeking to impose Protestantism on Catholic cantons.

1520 The Reformation reached France, where it was strong in the south among the nobility, intelligentsia and middle class. The King tolerated the Reformers (the Huguenots) until 1534. Their number peaked in 1562 at about 2 million, or 12% of the population. Catholic persecution provoked the French Wars of Religion (1562-98). In 1572, 70,000 Huguenots were massacred on St Bartholomew's Eve. In 1589, the Protestant Henry of Navarre became King—as a Catholic. In 1592, the Edict of Nantes granted Huguenots freedom of worship and equality before the law.

1523 King Charles I of Spain ordered the mass conversion of all native Americans. Catholic spiritual conquests across the Americas were subservient to territorial expansion and the search for gold. Franciscan missionary work started in Mexico in 1529, with 6 million baptized by 1536—leaving a legacy of syncretic Catholicism today. In 1577, Franciscans reached the Philippines; by 1600, half the population of about 600,000 was Catholic.

1534 The Society of Jesus (the Jesuits) founded by Ignatius Loyola, to be endorsed by the Pope in 1540. Francis Xavier went to India in 1540 and in two years completed the conversion of the Parava caste to Catholicism; then to Malacca (60,000 Catholics by 1600) and, in 1549, Japan (300,000 Catholics by 1600, though severe persecution followed the banning of Catholicism in 1587). Jesuits started work in S America in 1549 and China in 1588. When Xavier died in 1558, the Jesuits had 1,000 missionaries and were the primary mission arm of the Catholic Church.

1533 John Calvin fled from France to Geneva. After he published his *Institutes of the Christian Religion* in 1536, he became influential as a reformer throughout Europe and from 1541 to 1564 was virtual ruler of Geneva.

1534 The Catholic king Henry VIII separated the Church of England from Rome over the issue of his divorce and remarriage. He opposed the Reformation—but also the Pope. In 1536, William Tyndale, translator of the Bible into English, was martyred in Flanders. Severe persecution under "Bloody" Queen Mary in 1553–57 aimed to restore England to Catholicism. Her short-lived predecessor, Edward VI, and her successor, Elizabeth I, were both solidly Protestant.

Setbacks

1520 Muslim suppression of the two Christian Nubian kingdoms in Sudan. The process was completed by 1606, with all Nubians forced to embrace Islam.

1527 Muslims invaded Ethiopia, to kill 20% of all Christians over the next 15 years.

1545 Start of the Council of Trent (ending in 1563). It defined Catholic dogma and formulated the Catholic response to the Reformation. These led to wars and persecution that devastated C Europe for the next 100 years.

1551 Eastern Christians split in Mesopotamia. Half became Chaldean Catholic, half kept their independence as the Ancient Apostolic Church of the East.

Food for Thought

Catholic missionaries advanced all over the world, whereas the Reformers and their successors took nearly 300 years to discover the Great Commission![15] The legacy of that failure still affects Protestant theology and practice today.

The Empires of AD 1714

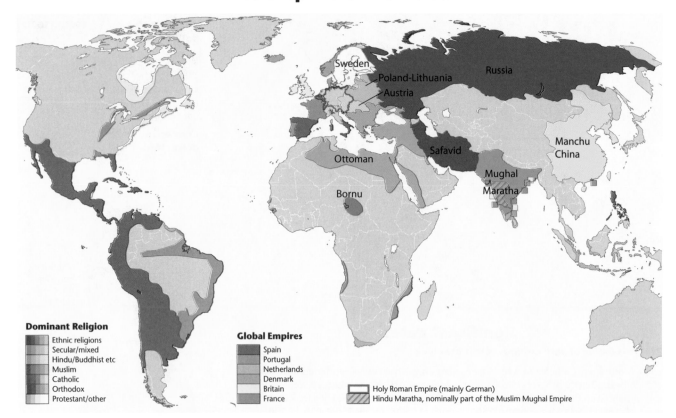

Dominant Religion
- Ethnic religions
- Secular/mixed
- Hindu/Buddhist etc
- Muslim
- Catholic
- Orthodox
- Protestant/other

Global Empires
- Spain
- Portugal
- Netherlands
- Denmark
- Britain
- France

☐ Holy Roman Empire (mainly German)
▨ Hindu Maratha, nominally part of the Muslim Mughal Empire

Significant dates

1607 First British colony in N America at Jamestown, Virginia. In 1655, the British captured Jamaica from the Spanish and expanded their Caribbean possessions.

1615 The Dutch seized the Moluccas (Maluku) from the Portuguese; many Moluccans became Protestant Christians in the following decades. They established their main base on Java in 1629, and drove the Portuguese out of W Timor in 1640, settled in S Africa in 1651 and captured Ceylon (modern-day Sri Lanka) from the Portuguese in 1656. They banned Catholicism in Ceylon, where it had 300,000 adherents.

1618 Start of the Thirty Years War. It originated in Spanish-Austrian attempts to end the Reform movement, but escalated into a war between them on the one hand and Catholic France and the Protestant states of N Europe on the other. It ended in 1648 with C Europe devastated. Germany's population had been reduced from possibly 17 million to 8 million. The power of the Hapsburgs was diminished, while that of France and Sweden was enhanced. The Netherlands' independence from Spain was recognized in the Peace of Westphalia, and the fragmentation of Germany and Switzerland into mini-states and cantons was entrenched.

1632 The Russians extended their dominion eastwards to Yakutsk, Siberia. In 1643, they explored the river Amur on China's northern border. By 1648 they had reached the Pacific Ocean, and in 1696 they arrived on the Ottoman-dominated Black Sea.

1636 Start of the English Civil War. Parliament and the (Reformed) Puritans under Oliver Cromwell had more or less destroyed the forces of King Charles I by 1645, but they then "lost the peace". In 1660, Cromwell's republican Commonwealth collapsed and the monarchy was restored, with considerable persecution of non-Anglican dissenters.

1644 End of the Ming dynasty as the Manchus conquered China

1663 French settled in Canada, founding Quebec, and then extended their possessions to the Great Lakes and down the Mississippi to found New Orleans. French settlers in N America numbered 10,000 by 1680.

1669 The Turks took Crete from Venice. In 1683, they besieged Vienna but failed to take it. In 1687, they were defeated in the second Battle of Mohacs in Hungary, and by 1699 had abandoned Hungary altogether. The slow decline of the Ottoman superpower had begun.

1688 The "Glorious Revolution" in England, as the Catholic king James II abdicated and the Protestant couple William of Orange and his wife, Mary, were invited to take the throne. This finally established the Reformation in England, and a more constitutional form of monarchy.

1701 Start of the 13-year War of the Spanish Succession. Its principal aim and outcome were to prevent a French takeover of Spain and its empire.

The Thirty Years War (1618-48) and the War of the Spanish Succession (1701-14) radically affected Europe's religious affiliations and boundaries and the shape of the growing global colonial empires.

Colonialism and missions

"Converting the heathen" was seen by Catholic and Protestant alike as the task of governments—a legacy of Constantinian Christianity. Spanish and Portuguese policy was to impose Catholicism on subject peoples. Protestants took the same view—so long as it did not interfere with commercial interests. Early Protestant missions were therefore often financed by kings and governments.[16] We now see colonialism in a negative light, but it did form a bridge for the Gospel to spread out to much of the world. It ensured 250 years of protected seed-sowing, though the full flowering of indigenous Christianity came only after colonialism ended.

Food for Thought

The 21st Century should be a time of immense harvest—but without the protection of colonialism or Christian governments, the levels of danger and the cost in lives could return to what was "normal" in apostolic times.

▲ Are we ready for this?

The Church in AD 1600–1700

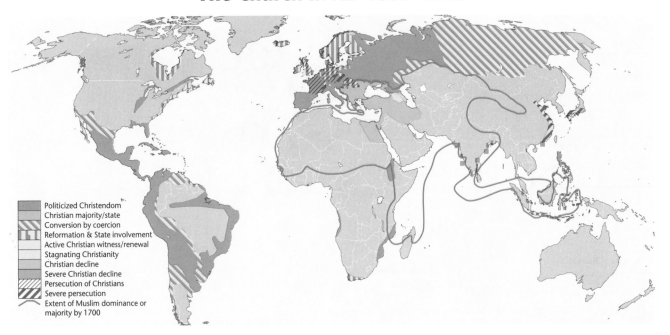

Politicized Christendom
Christian majority/state
Conversion by coercion
Reformation & State involvement
Active Christian witness/renewal
Stagnating Christianity
Christian decline
Severe Christian decline
Persecution of Christians
Severe persecution
Extent of Muslim dominance or
majority by 1700

Significant dates

Progress

1605 Robert de Nobili, a Jesuit missionary, started a ministry in S India among Brahmin Hindus—one of the first deliberate attempts by Catholics to contextualize the Christian message for non-Christians.

1607 At this point, there were just 700 Catholics in China; by 1700, there were 300,000.

1611 Publication of the "King James" or "Authorized" version of the Bible in English, which moulded the language, culture and spirituality of Britain for the next three centuries

1620 The Pilgrim Fathers left Plymouth for N America. Though not the first English settlers, they laid the foundation of the present-day United States' strong commitment to religious freedom and their evangelical heritage.

1627 In what is now Vietnam, Jesuit missionaries baptized 6,700. By 1660, there were 400,000 Christians there, but the number declined thereafter as a result of intense persecution.

1661 John Eliot from Massachusetts translated the Bible into Algonquin, the first native language in the Americas to have its own version.

1670 In India, 20,000 Bengalis converted as a result of Jesuit work.

1671 Arabic Bible published—tragically, over a thousand years after Mohammed

1698 Foundation of the Society for Promoting Christian Knowledge, the first British mission agency, which was to be the largest publisher of Christian literature in the 18th Century

Setbacks

1620 Bohemia was forced by Austria to become Catholic; 30,000 Protestants were killed and many exiled.

1637 In Japan, the extermination of Catholic Christianity began. In 1600, there were 750,000 Catholics; by 1700, 200,000 had been massacred and the Church was driven underground.

1685 In France, the Edict of Nantes, granting Huguenots freedom of worship, was revoked. Over 400,000 people fled from France, including huge numbers of its most skilled workers, who became a spiritual and economic blessing to the countries that received them.

1686 In Italy, half of the 16,000 Waldensians were massacred by Catholics.

The case for mission agencies

This century saw the last of the major wars of religion within Christendom and the beginning of mission initiatives not necessarily decided by government policy and connected with territorial expansion. At last, the Church began to recover an apostolic component in its ministry. The Catholics had their missionary orders, but Protestants had nothing comparable until societies such as the SPCK and the Danish-Halle Mission came into being (and were closely followed in the 18th Century by the extraordinary missionary effort of the Moravians from Herrnhut). This fol-

Key Statistics: 1600–1700	1600	1700
World population (millions)	517	618
Christians (millions)	100.4	129.7
Christians as % of world population	19.4%	21%
Christian martyrs during 1601–1700		360,000

Persecutors

Orthodox
Anglican
Ethnic
Various
Buddhist

Muslim

Martyrs

Japanese (RC)
Protestant
Independent
Catholic
Various

Fig 2.31 *Who persecuted whom in the 17th Century*

Food for Thought

Many people today maintain that it is local churches that should be the missionary senders and missionary agencies should be dispensed with as unbiblical. History and Scripture indicate otherwise.

▲ Are some missional churches going astray here?

lowed the pattern established in the early Church, and most notably the church of Antioch, where apostolic teams were sent out in an autonomous but accountable ministry to disciple people of all nations.

The Empires of AD 1815

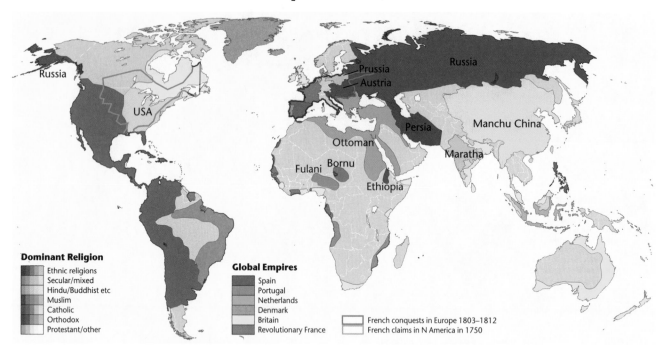

Dominant Religion
- Ethnic religions
- Secular/mixed
- Hindu/Buddhist etc
- Muslim
- Catholic
- Orthodox
- Protestant/other

Global Empires
- Spain
- Portugal
- Netherlands
- Denmark
- Britain
- Revolutionary France

French conquests in Europe 1803–1812
French claims in N America in 1750

Significant dates

1707 Union of England and Scotland, laying the foundations for the future expansion of the British Empire

Russia defeated Sweden to become a Baltic power (and eventually, by 1815, take over Finland, the Baltic states and much of Poland). In 1721, Peter the Great was declared "Emperor of All Russia" after founding his new capital, St Petersburg. In 1732, Vitus Bering mapped Russia's Arctic coast and discovered Alaska, and by 1785 Russia was a Pacific power. In 1783, it captured Crimea from the Ottomans.

1735 Persia took Georgia, Armenia and Daghestan from the Ottomans.

1744 The Saudi ruling family adopted the extreme teachings of Wahhabi Islam, which remains to this day the dominant form of Islam in that country. It was to become a key influence in the global spread of Islamism and violent *jihad* in the 21st Century.

1756 Start of the Seven Years War, the first worldwide territorial war originating in Europe. All the major European powers became involved. Prussia became the dominant power in C Europe. In 1757, the Battle of Plassey between British and French forces ensured the extension of British rule to the whole of India. In 1759, the British won Quebec from the French, making the whole of N America largely Anglophone.

1768 The English sea captain James Cook set out on the first of three voyages to the Pacific region. The fine maps he made, and the introduction of the chronometer for measuring longitude, opened up the Pacific for trade, settlement and mission work. The British colonization of Australia followed in 1788, and of New Zealand soon after.

1772 Slavery was declared illegal in Britain, but not in its colonies. Slave trading was abolished by Denmark in 1792 and by Britain in 1807, and was enforced by the British navy. The emancipation of slaves in Britain's colonies followed in 1833.

1775 The start of the Industrial Revolution, based on steam power, in Britain and the Netherlands

1776 Thirteen of Britain's N American colonies declared independence as the United States of America. After eight years of war, Britain recognized the existence of the USA in 1783 while retaining control of Canada and Newfoundland.

1786 The eruption of Mt Laki in Iceland resulted in extreme weather worldwide and extensive famine in Europe. The latter contributed to the unrest that led to the French Revolution in 1789—an event that helped to shape the history of the next two centuries.

1795 Britain took over the S African Cape from the Dutch. In the following year, the British expelled the Dutch from Ceylon.

1799 Napoleon Bonaparte gained power in France. He was declared emperor in 1804, and set about building a European empire through brilliant military conquests. He was finally defeated at Waterloo in 1815.

Who won the war for global supremacy?

The Seven Years War was a key element in the last hundred years of the struggle for dominance worldwide between France and Britain that had begun in 1689. For a century after 1815, Britain was to be the global superpower, the first major industrial giant, policing the world's oceans and ruling the largest empire ever seen. This helped to make English the world's most widely used language, to suppress the slave trade and to spread the ideals of democracy. It also opened the way for Protestant missions.

In contrast, the French lost most of their empire, their ascendancy in Europe and the pre-eminence of their language. Nonetheless, they triumphed in other ways, as the world embraced their ideas of a united Europe, a modern bureaucracy and legal structure, popular republicanism, the metric system and driving on the right. The world's prevailing ideology became that of the French Revolution, not of religion, and its terrible grandchild, Marxism, dominated the 20th Century.

That period came symbolically to an end exactly 200 years after the Revolution, with the tearing down of the Berlin Wall in 1989.

Food for Thought

Religious ideology is once more in the ascendant whether the secular-humanist West likes it or not.

▲ Have Europeans realized this?

The Church in AD 1700–1800

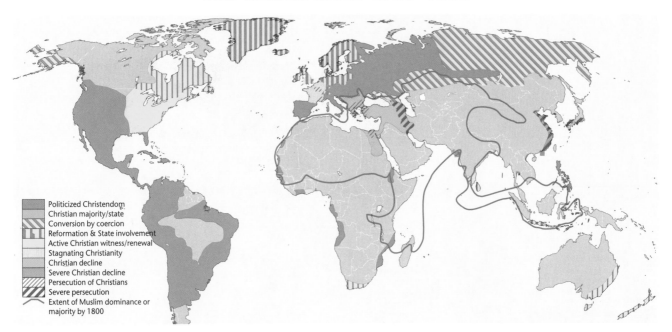

- Politicized Christendom
- Christian majority/state
- Conversion by coercion
- Reformation & State involvement
- Active Christian witness/renewal
- Stagnating Christianity
- Christian decline
- Severe Christian decline
- Persecution of Christians
- Severe persecution
- Extent of Muslim dominance or majority by 1800

Significant dates

Progress

1701 Extensive missionizing of the Mari and the Siberian tribes in Russia by the Orthodox. Many of the conversions were the result of either compulsion or enticement.

1705 Foundation of the Danish-Halle Mission and the sending out of the first Protestant missionaries

1722 Count Ludwig von Zinzendorf founded Hernhut as a small Moravian settlement in Saxony. After revival broke out there, it became the base for the first major church-based missionary movement in Protestantism, sending its first missionaries to St Thomas in the W Indies (1732), Greenland (1733), Suriname (1735), northern Russia (1736), the US state of Georgia, Ghana and S Africa (all in 1737), Ceylon (1738) and Labrador (1750). A total of 2,000 missionaries went out over the next century or so.

1725 The beginning of the "Great Awakening" in New England. One of its great leaders was Jonathan Edwards, a strong advocate of both prayer and missions. "Concerts of prayer" for revival and world missions began in Britain in 1782 and then, in 1790, in the US. The spiritual basis for the worldwide missions expansion of Protestants was prayer.

1732 John and Charles Wesley started the Holy Club in Oxford, England, which ultimately became the Methodist Movement. The British Great Awakening began through the preaching of the Wesleys and George Whitefield (who was to become one of the greatest preachers in history, speaking to over 18 million people on both sides of the Atlantic). It became the foundation of modern evangelicalism—a largely, but not exclusively, Protestant phenomenon.

1783 Charles Simeon began the Evangelical Movement in Cambridge, England.

1792 Foundation of the Baptist Missionary Society in London, the beginning of the modern missions movement which was to change the world radically over the next two centuries. William Carey, its co-founder, arrived in India in 1793.

1799 Foundation of the evangelical Anglican Church Missionary Society (CMS)

Setbacks

1701 Catholic missions were in decline in India. In 1700, there were 2.5 million Christians in that country; by 1800, the number had fallen to 450,000.

1716 Christianity was banned in China. Severe persecution followed, and the number of Catholics dwindled.

1722 Many Catholics in Ceylon were forced to become Protestant. Christians at this point constituted 21% of the population, but thereafter their numbers fell.

1754 Increasing Ottoman persecution of Orthodox in Romania, Crete and elsewhere

1759 Portugal began to suppress the Jesuits on account of their perceived political influence and interference. Spain followed suit in 1767, and the Pope himself in 1773. The Jesuits were eventually reinstated in 1814.

1764 Massacre of Catholics in Thailand

Key Statistics: 1700–1800	1700	1800
World population (millions)	618	903.7
Christians (millions)	129.7	205
Christians as % of world population	21%	22.7%
Christian martyrs during 1701–1800	190,000	

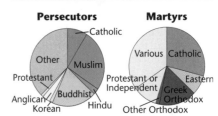

Persecutors — Catholic, Other, Muslim, Protestant, Anglican, Buddhist, Korean, Hindu

Martyrs — Various, Catholic, Protestant or Independent, Eastern, Greek Orthodox, Other Orthodox

Fig 2.32 *Who persecuted whom in the 18th Century*

Prayer, revival and missions

The Reformation was pivotal in returning the Church to biblical truth but it rarely saw revival, as subsequent politics and wars demonstrate. There was little teaching on world evangelization, and I can find no evidence of a biblical prayer meeting in the first two centuries that followed it. It was the praying of the missionary David Brainerd, the passion of Jonathan Edwards for "concerts of prayer" and the revival and hundred-year "chain of prayer" of the Herrnhut Moravians that changed this. Out of them came the revivals and awakenings of the 18th and 19th Centuries, and the modern missions movement. Praise God!

Burning Question for Today

▲ Can any church or movement truly claim to be biblical and led by the Holy Spirit if there is no teaching on and no practice of prayer and missions?

The Empires of AD 1910

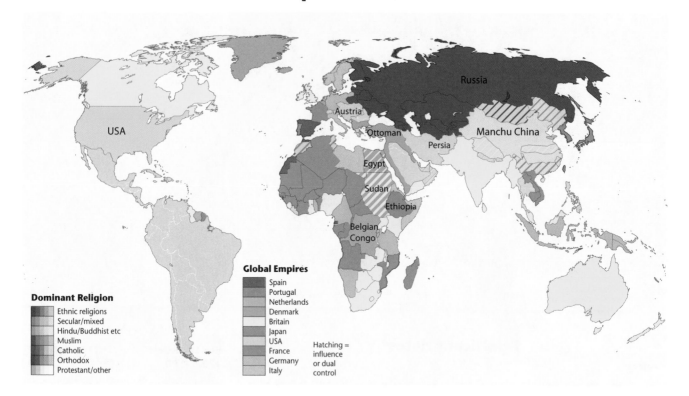

Dominant Religion
- Ethnic religions
- Secular/mixed
- Hindu/Buddhist etc
- Muslim
- Catholic
- Orthodox
- Protestant/other

Global Empires
- Spain
- Portugal
- Netherlands
- Denmark
- Britain
- Japan
- USA
- France
- Germany
- Italy

Hatching = influence or dual control

Significant dates

1801 The formal union of Ireland and Britain (which lasted until 1921) was an imposition on the former's Catholic and Celtic majority. In 1846, the Irish Potato Famine caused 1–1.5 million deaths, while 1–2 million people migrated to Great Britain or N America.

1803 The US purchased from France much of the Mid-West. In 1819 it bought Florida from Spain, and in 1867 Alaska from Russia. In 1898, it won Puerto Rico, the Philippines and Guam in the Spanish-American War.

1809 Russia seized Finland, followed by what are now Kazakhstan (1846) and Uzbekistan (1867) and, by 1885, all of the Caucasus and Muslim C Asia. Defeat by France and Britain in Crimea in 1856 checked Russian advances south to the Mediterranean. Defeat by Japan in 1905 precipitated the eventual fall of Tsarist Russia to Marxism.

1810 Venezuela gained its independence from Spain. By 1821, all of mainland S and C America was free from Spanish rule. In 1822, Brazil gained its independence from Portugal. Latin America in the 19th Century was the only region of the world not dominated by either European powers or the US.

1815 The final defeat of Napoleon led to the reorganization of Europe, a century of relative peace and the vast expansion of Europe's colonial empires, based on industrialization and new wealth.

1828 The decline of the Ottoman Empire in the Balkans continued as Greece gained its independence. Bulgaria followed in 1878.

1830 France seized Algeria, the beginning of its vast colonial empire in W and C Africa.

1834 The decline of Manchu China continued. Defeats by Britain in the Opium Wars (1834–60) forced it to open its ports for trade, cede Hong Kong to the British and admit Christian missions. The colonial powers carved up much of China into "spheres of influence" (see map above). The quasi-Christian Tai Ping Rebellion (1843–64) caused up to 35 million deaths, while the Boxer Rebellion in 1900 led to the collapse of government authority.

1848 The Communist Manifesto published by Karl Marx and Friedrich Engels

1854 Japan opened its ports for trade and ended its centuries of isolation.

1857 Mutiny of the Indian Army against British rule, suppressed the following year. In 1877, Queen Victoria was proclaimed "Empress of India".

1861 The US Civil War broke out, primarily over over the issue of slavery and the right of individual states to secede from the Union. It ended in 1865, after almost a million deaths, in victory for the Unionists.

1870 The Franco-Prussian War resulted in defeat for France and led to the unification of Germany under Prussian leadership.

1881 In Sudan, Mohammed Ahmed announced that he was the Mahdi (for Muslims, the Messiah who will appear in the Last Days) and led a revolution against the British and Egyptians—the first Islamist *jihad* of modern times. In 1898, the British defeated the Mahdi's forces in Sudan and occupied that country until 1960.

1884 Berlin Conference, in which the European colonial powers divided Africa up with no thought of local ethnic and political realities. It sanctioned the Belgian king Leopold II's seizure and plunder of the Congo, causing an estimated 10 million deaths between 1885 and 1908.

1899 Start of the (Second) Boer War between Britain and the two independent Afrikaner republics in S Africa. It ended in 1902, and resulted in the Union of S Africa in 1910.

Food for Thought

God overrules to bring glory to Himself and salvation to the world by unlikely means.

▲ How far will we permit the gains for the Gospel during the colonial era to be eroded by Islam in the 21st Century?

The Church in AD 1815–1910

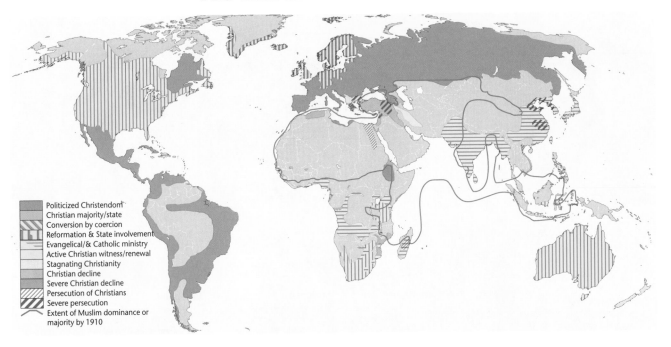

Politicized Christendom
Christian majority/state
Conversion by coercion
Reformation & State involvement
Evangelical/& Catholic ministry
Active Christian witness/renewal
Stagnating Christianity
Christian decline
Severe Christian decline
Persecution of Christians
Severe persecution
Extent of Muslim dominance or majority by 1910

Significant dates

1800 Numerous Protestant mission agencies were founded over the following century. In all, there were fewer than a hundred Protestant missionaries in 1800. By 1900, there were about 45,000 serving missionaries. There were only 270 European Catholic missionaries in 1834.

1804 British and Foreign Bible Society founded in London, to undertake the biggest programme of Bible translation and distribution ever seen

1807 Robert Morrison arrived in Macau, the first Protestant missionary to China. He completed translation of the Bible into Chinese in 1818, but only 10 Chinese were baptized as a result of his ministry. In 1811, proselytization was banned in China, but the country was opened up for missions in 1858. The China Inland Mission (now known as OMF) was founded in 1865 by James Hudson Taylor to evangelize its inland provinces.

1813 In Burma, Adoniram Judson started his remarkable missionary career, though he made a major impact only on the tribal peoples, not the Buddhist Burmese.

1817 Robert Moffatt arrived in Botswana in southern Africa. He completed his translation of the Bible into seTswana after 40 years.

1818 The first Protestant missionaries, from the London Missionary Society, reached Madagascar. They met with great success, including revival; but also, in 1835–61, with persecution.

1822 US missionaries killed by Batak in Sumatra. Subsequently, however, German Lutherans Christianized both the Batak and the Nias islanders.

1827 John Darby founded the Christian Brethren, which became one of the most significant missionary-sending bodies of the 19th Century.

1833 Abolition of slavery throughout the British Empire, the result of four decades of campaigning by William Wilberforce and many others

1844 CMS commenced work in Kenya, followed by British Baptists in Cameroon in 1845, a Malawian missionary in Uganda in 1875, British Baptists in Angola in 1878 and the Paris Evangelical Missionary Society in Zambia in 1885.

1845 Birth of the Evangelical Alliance in Britain, which ultimately led to the formation of the World Evangelical Alliance. Evangelicals became the most dynamic force in the global Church for the next 50 years.

1849 David Livingstone started his missionary explorations in C Africa to end the trade in slaves by Portuguese and Arabs and to open the way for "Christianity, commerce and civilization". He died in Zambia in 1876.

1857 Beginning of the Evangelical Awakening in the US, which spread to many countries in Europe and Asia with a massive increase in evangelism and conversion and great advances in missions

1859 Japan admitted the first missionaries after centuries of isolation.

Key Statistics: 1800–1900	1800	1900
World population (millions)	903.7	1,619.6
Christians (millions)	205	558.1
Christians as % of world population	22.7%	34.5%
Christian martyrs during 1801–1900	1,969,000	

1894 Three hundred thousand Armenian Christians were massacred in Turkey. In all, there were over half a million Christian martyrs under Ottoman rule in the 19th Century.

1899 The Boxer Rebellion broke out in China, in which 48,000 Chinese Christians and a further 188 Protestant missionaries and their children were killed.

Persecutors

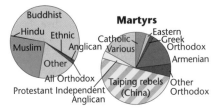

Buddhist
Hindu
Muslim Ethnic
Other
All Orthodox
Protestant Independent
Anglican

Martyrs
Catholic Various
Anglican
Eastern Greek Orthodox
Armenian
Taiping rebels (China)
Other Orthodox

Fig 2.33 *Who persecuted whom in the 19th Century*

Food for Thought

▲ Will Christians of the 21st Century fail in our duty to finish what was started so well, though tardily at first, by our forerunners in the faith?

The Dismantling of Empires by AD 1975

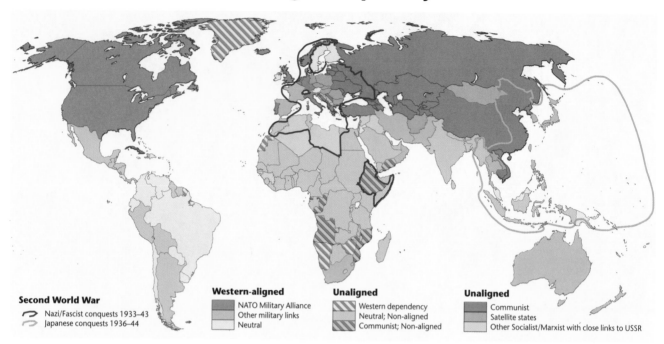

Second World War

↷ Nazi/Fascist conquests 1933–43
↶ Japanese conquests 1936–44

Western-aligned
- NATO Military Alliance
- Other military links
- Neutral

Unaligned
- Western dependency
- Neutral; Non-aligned
- Communist; Non-aligned

Unaligned
- Communist
- Satellite states
- Other Socialist/Marxist with close links to USSR

The end of empires?

In 1914, nearly all of the world's states or territories either were under European or US rule or enjoyed only nominal independence (such as Ethiopia, Thailand and Nepal). Only Japan was truly independent, and it had become an imperial power itself. By 1975, the last major European colonial empire had disintegrated, and 16 years later the Communist empire of the Soviet Union followed suit. We speak of the "end" of empires—but is this true, or even likely? In the past, empires maintained political power by ruling territory and controlling information and finance. Today, television, the internet and mobile phones have lowered the barriers. We live in a "flat" world[17] in which the flow of ideas, information, money—and jobs—has gone global. Even an Islamic jihadist caliphate is unlikely, though still a threat.

Churches, evangelism, literature, leadership, vision, all will need to go global—in a culturally sensitive way—or become irrelevant.

Colonialism and the kingdom of God

Today we abhor the competing nationalisms and the arrogance and greed that drove the colonialism of the supposedly civilized "Christian" nations of Europe. We see the negatives: the subjugation, enslavement and even genocide of peoples, the trading monopolies that transferred the world's wealth to the West, the consumerism, cultural imperialism etc. However, there were distinct positives, too. The Islamic push for global hegemony was arrested for three centuries, and the importance of democracy and human rights, education, health care etc was eventually established worldwide. The greatest benefits were religious freedom and the chance to proclaim the Gospel. Colonialism allowed Western missionaries to sow many seeds; but the indigenization and explosive growth of biblical Christianity came only as the colonial era ended after the Second World War.

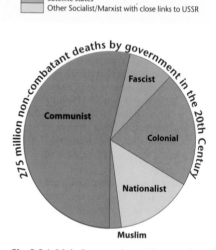

Fig 2.34 *20th Century democides—civilian deaths by types of governments*[18]

Burning Question for Today

▲ Are we ready, as Christians, for this new world—so different from the varying totalitarianisms of Aldous Huxley's *Brave New World* and George Orwell's *1984*?

The AD2000 movement set out to achieve "a church for every people and the Gospel for every person" by AD2000.

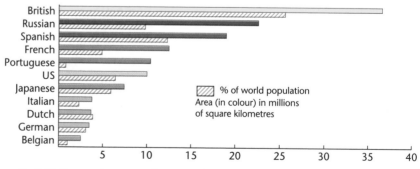

Fig 2.35 *The greatest extent, in area and population, attained by the various colonial empires between 1700 and 1960*

The Church in AD 1910–1975

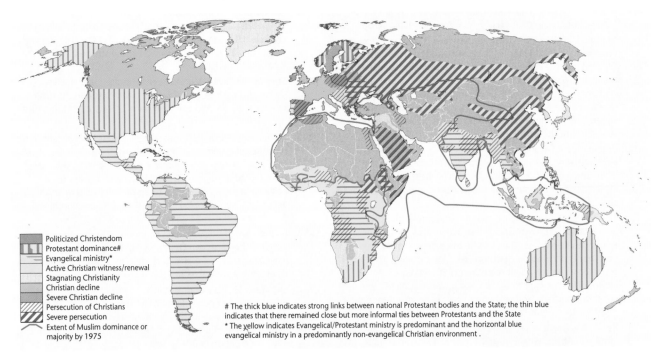

- Politicized Christendom
- Protestant dominance#
- Evangelical ministry*
- Active Christian witness/renewal
- Stagnating Christianity
- Christian decline
- Severe Christian decline
- Persecution of Christians
- Severe persecution
- Extent of Muslim dominance or majority by 1975

\# The thick blue indicates strong links between national Protestant bodies and the State; the thin blue indicates that there remained close but more informal ties between Protestants and the State
* The yellow indicates Evangelical/Protestant ministry is predominant and the horizontal blue evangelical ministry in a predominantly non-evangelical Christian environment .

The Protestant missions movement

The 19th Century saw the belated take-off of Protestant (including Anglican and Independent) mission work. Fig 2.36 shows how a lack of vision for nearly 300 years was followed by strong growth after William Carey and, at the end of the 19th Century, the great boost of the Student Volunteer Movement. This was a century of courageous and costly seed-sowing, though the fruit was more limited. The 20th Century was the one for the ingathering, which also saw the more rapid expansion of the vision for missions.

Chinese believers (photo by P Hattaway)

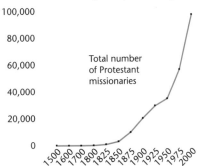

Total number of Protestant missionaries

Fig 2.36 *The dramatic increase in number of Protestant missionaries*

The demise of Christendom and rebirth of Christianity?

The maps on pages 57 and 59 and this page covering the period 1700–1975 show radical changes. The most startling are the expansion of evangelical Christianity (the yellow), the massive increase in persecution (the red diagonal hatching), the decline of Europe (orange) and the ending of the cosy cohabitation of Christendom with national and imperial governments (the huge reduction in the blue shading—both solid and vertical hatching). This last development is closely linked to the other three. By the end of 1975, Christianity was strongly connected to national political processes in only a handful of states (such as Orthodoxy in Greece, Catholicism in Spain and "communist" Poland and Dutch Reformed Protestantism in apartheid S Africa—while in the US, despite the constitutional separation of Church and State, Christianity remains a core value and still operates under the paradigms of Constantinian Christendom). Europe was rapidly adopting secular humanist values, and Christianity was becoming "irrelevant" there. Meanwhile, Latin America, for so long Catholic, was rapidly becoming Pentecostal and evangelical, and the Church was growing in most of the areas where Christians were in a minority.

The 20th Century saw such dramatic change, and not least in terms of Christian growth and decline, that we can only indicate trends here.[19] A fuller timeline can be found on the DVD.

Key Statistics: 1900–1975	1900	1975
World population (millions)	1,619.6	4,074
Christians (millions)	558.1	1,357
Christians as % of world population	34.5%	33.3%
Christian martyrs during 1901–2000		44,933,000

Persecutors

Fig 2.37 *Who persecuted whom in the 20th Century*

Food for Thought

In the 21st Century, the major challenge for the Church is to rediscover its apostolic and prophetic roles, which can change our world and its nations without resorting to political or worldly tools to achieve this.

Significant dates

1900 Reinstatement of Shinto religion in Japan, and beginning of Japan's imperial expansion in E Asia (see the map on p60).

1914 Outbreak of the First World War between the Central Powers (Germany, Austria-Hungary, Bulgaria and the Ottoman Empire) and the Allies, led by France, Britain and Russia. By its end in 1918, 8.5 million combatants and 13 million civilians had perished. It marked the beginning of the end of European dominance in world affairs and the end of the "dream" of a superior Western, Christian civilization that could be exported to the rest of the world.

1917 Britain took Palestine from the Ottomans with Arab help. The eventual outcome was the formation of the state of Israel in 1948 and its conflict with the Arabs. This has had serious ramifications for relations between Muslims and the West ever since.[20]

The Bolshevik Revolution led to the establishment of the Soviet Union under the most destructive, anti-Christian tyranny in history. 1975 was to be the high point of communism's global expansion (see map on p60). The disastrous invasion of Afghanistan (1980–86) and the explosion at the Chernobyl nuclear power station in 1986 contributed to the Soviet Union's spectacular disintegration in 1989–92 (see democide graph in Fig 2.34 on p60).

1922 Benito Mussolini seized power in Italy and sought to build an empire in Africa, where there were already Italian colonies in Libya, Eritrea and Somaliland. His forces invaded Ethiopia in 1935, but held it only until 1941. Half a million Ethiopian Orthodox were massacred by Italian Catholics.

1927 Civil war broke out in China between Nationalists and Communists. It was interrupted by the Japanese invasions in 1930s. but ended in 1949 with Communist victory on the mainland. Over 20 million people perished in this conflict. An estimated 76 million subsequently died in purges and famines induced by the Communist regime between 1928 and 2000.

1929 The Wall Street Crash, caused largely by greedy speculators, resulted in worldwide economic depression and widespread poverty lasting until 1936.

1933 Adolf Hitler elected to power in Germany in the wake of the humiliation of defeat in the First World War and the economic collapse that followed it. Nazism was steeped in pagan and occult beliefs and was virulently anti-Jewish and hostile to any Christian criticism or dissent.

1939 Full outbreak of the Second World War. By its end in 1945, an estimated 72 million people had perished, most of them civilians. Of these, some 42 million died in the struggle with European Fascism and 30 million in the struggle with Japanese imperialism.[21]

1946 Start of the "Cold War" between the West and the Soviet Union and their respective allies, which lasted until 1989 when the Berlin Wall was torn down. The Soviet Union broke up in 1991.

1947 Partition of British India into (initially) two independent states: Hindu-dominated India and Muslim-dominated Pakistan (later split into Pakistan and Bangladesh). Nearly 10 million people were forced to migrate. One million died. The status of Kashmir in India with Hindu rulers but a Muslim majority has led to four wars (1947, 1965, 1971, 1984) and continuous a violent jihadist Islamic guerrilla warfare since 1989.

1958 Foundation of the European Economic Community, later to become the European Union. By 2008, its membership had risen from six to 27 states, including many former allies and three former members of the old Soviet Union.

1962 Outbreak of civil war in Sudan as Muslims in the north attempted to impose Islam on the south by force. Peace was restored in the south only in 2005, after 2 million deaths—many of them of Christians. S Sudan became independent as a separate nation in 2011.

1979 Islamic Revolution in Iran, which replaced the pro-West, modernizing Shah with the Shi'a leader Ayatollah Ruhollah Khomeini. Militaristic Islamism was promoted and exported worldwide.

1980 Iraq invaded Iran. The Iran-Iraq War (sometimes known as the First Gulf War), ended in 1988 and cost a million lives. A second Gulf War, involving a large international coalition led by the US, was fought in 1990/91 after Iraq invaded and annexed Kuwait.

1996 Osama bin Laden, leader of the Islamist network al-Qa'ida, "declared war" on the US and all its "allies" (that is, those perceived as aggressors against Islam). This was followed through in the "9/11" terrorist attack on the USA in September 2001, an event that led to an ongoing war in Afghanistan and the third Gulf War, to oust the Iraqi dictator Saddam Hussein, in 2003, as well as continuing deadly acts of terrorism around the world.

Mobile phones

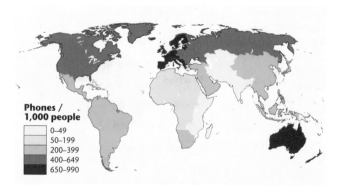

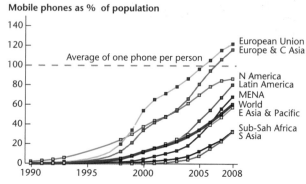

Fig 2.38 *Worldwide mobile phone ownership growth since 1990*

In 1996 there were 136 million mobile phones in use worldwide, but by 2010 this had risen to 5 billion. No other technology has spread so fast or done more to "level" communication.[22] Mobile phone technology has developed an all-in-one solution for phone, camera and computer providing access to the internet and banking. Sadly, it enables new forms of crime; but it also addresses the abuse of power, corruption and economic inequality, as described on page 13. It helps the poor to launch businesses with limited capital and avoid extortionate middlemen and corrupt officials. It is reshaping the world's economy, social life, styles of work and even Christian ministry.

Significant dates for the Church

Revivals that renewed the Church and transformed the world	The 1904 Welsh Revival opened the century and contributed to far bigger revivals in northeast India (1905–), the US (1906–), Korea (1907–1980s), E Africa (1927–1960s), China (1930s, 1940s, 1980–) and Indonesia (1965–1990s), as well as the Charismatic renewal of 1956 (or, among Catholics, 1967) onwards.	See Chapter 5
The rise and decline of liberal Christianity	The strength and optimism of the Evangelicals before the First World War turned to defensiveness as they were marginalized by an ascendant theological liberalism. This daughter of the Enlightenment, with its deification of human reason, dominated much of the Protestant Church for half a century. Its denial of the uniqueness of Christ and the divine inspiration of the Scriptures and its neglect of the core message of the Gospel while focusing on organic church unity and social justice led to a massive decline in the West's major denominations. At the end of the century, "mainline" Christianity had waned to the point where it was globally marginalized.	See page 111
The marginalization and ultimate resurgence of evangelicalism	Evangelicalism's 50 years in the wilderness ended in the 1960s with a multiplication of international conferences[23] and movements,[24] visions and strategies, and a growing global missions force. Christianity will become increasingly evangelical in theology and charismatic in expression and decreasingly Western in culture in the 21st Century.	See Chapter 4
The astonishing harvest gathered into the Church outside the West, and the declines in the West	A comparison of the map on page 61 with those on pages 57 and 59 illustrates this. In the future, we will probably look back at the last decade of the 20th Century as the most fruitful ever for conversions to Christ—in absolute numbers, Evangelicals increased by over 100 million.	See Chapter 6
The increasing focus on evangelizing and discipling the least-reached peoples on earth	As the century progressed, there was more effective outreach to the adherents of the major missionary religions.[25]	This is treated in Chapters 7 and 3
The astonishing levels of persecution endured by the Church around the world	Compare the pie chart and bar chart on persecution in Figs 2.37 (p61) and 2.39 with the summary on democide in Fig 2.34 (p60). Christian martyrs in the 20th Century numbered almost 50 million—65% of all Christian martyrs over the last two millennia.	
The massive growth in missions	This included a huge growth in the number of missionaries and the ultimate globalization of the missions force after the demise of the colonial empires in the 1960s.[25]	See Chapter 8

William Carey, the "father of modern missions"

Evangelical leader John Stott (left), who was included in Time magazine's list of 100 most influential people of the 20th Century, and evangelist Billy Graham (right), who was voted number seven on Gallup's list of admired people for the 20th Century (photo courtesy David Jones)

Food for Thought

Many churches still regard the Great Commission as an optional extra, a fad, an inconvenient relic of the colonial era and not as their core reason for existence.

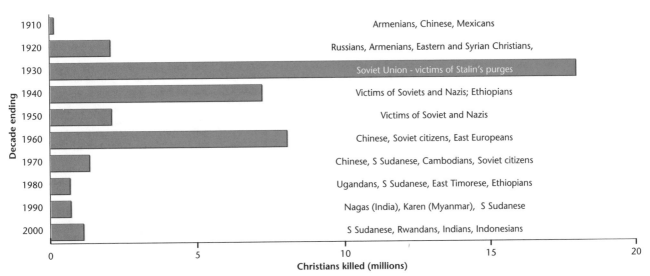

Decade ending		
1910		Armenians, Chinese, Mexicans
1920		Russians, Armenians, Eastern and Syrian Christians,
1930		Soviet Union - victims of Stalin's purges
1940		Victims of Soviets and Nazis; Ethiopians
1950		Victims of Soviet and Nazis
1960		Chinese, Soviet citizens, East Europeans
1970		Chinese, S Sudanese, Cambodians, Soviet citizens
1980		Ugandans, S Sudanese, East Timorese, Ethiopians
1990		Nagas (India), Karen (Myanmar), S Sudanese
2000		S Sudanese, Rwandans, Indians, Indonesians

Christians killed (millions)

Fig 2.39 *Christian martyrs in the 20th Century*

1. See http://www.economist.com/research/articlesBySubject/PrinterFriendly.cfm?story_id=9185774

2. See my book, *The Church is Bigger than You Think*, 1998, Christian Focus, pp33–80 for a listing and explanation.

3. Developments are frequently condensed and presented out of order as a sequence of events over a century under one initial date. They are listed chronologically in the electronic database on the DVD, together with explanatory material.

4. There are persistent oral traditions, and early hints of documentary evidence, that the Joseph mentioned here was the trader Joseph of Arimathea (St Ilid to the Welsh). See http://www.adri-angilbert.co.uk/docus/books/holyking.html. Much of the history of the pre-Saxon Celtic Church has been suppressed by Catholics who wrote history to suit their own claim that Augustine brought Christianity to Britain. How little is written or broadcast about Wales's rich and ancient Christian archeological heritage because it is not politically correct to acknowledge its existence!

5. The Council of Chalcedon condemned both the extreme positions of Monophysitism (in which Christ was one Person in whom the divine and the human were fused completely in one nature) and Diphysitism (purportedly Nestorius' view, in which Christ had two, unmingled natures or essences in one Person). The council took a middle position: that Christ was an indivisible union from two distinct natures. Sadly, the complex shades of meaning over which they argued were more a reflection of the broken relationships between the spokesmen for each position, the different languages they used—Latin, Greek and Syriac—and the different political systems in which they operated. Evangelical Christians of the 21st Century would probably have been closer to the position of the Eastern Church, with its emphasis on the Scriptures and its insistence that Mary was not the Mother of God but only the mother of Jesus.

6. Western Christians and those of Latin origin misuse the term "Orthodox", which covers a wide variety of denominations that differ greatly in history, cultural background and theology. The Holy Apostolic Catholic Assyrian Church of the East is the proper name of the church of Assyrian-Persian origin that became wrongly known as "Nestorian" or "Eastern Orthodox". In this section, I have called it "Eastern", since its constituency was almost exclusively in Asia.

7. There are many books on catastrophism. See "Climate Change, Volcanoes, and Plagues—the New Tolls of History" on the internet at http://www.globalthink.net/global/dsppaper.cfm?ArticleID=96 and other sources given there.

8. At its best, the Celtic Church developed what is possibly one of the finest models for discipling peoples the world has yet seen. Monasteries were more Christian communities to demonstrate Christianity and win pagans to faith through preaching, life witness and education and by ensuring that all enquirers were given a "soulmate" and made part of a care group. See George C Hunter's *The Celtic Way of Evangelism* (Abingdon Press, 2000).

9. The so-called Nestorians are an enigma. Their official name, Holy Apostolic Catholic Assyrian Church of the East, is cumbersome, so I have referred instead to "'Eastern' Christians", though this term sometimes also encompasses the Jacobite Monophysite Christians living in the same areas who for centuries were isolated on the far side of the Muslim world and wrongly condemned as heretics by European Christians. Few records survived their centuries of persecution and (in the end) virtual obliteration, so an accurate picture is hard to

arrive at. Opinions differ widely as to their growth in numbers, the ethnic groups they impacted and their effectiveness as a cross-cultural missionary church. Many commentators are dismissive; others more admiring. This book takes a cautiously positive view. Today, in the chaos of Iraq, these Christians are some of the most sorely persecuted by Islamists, and many have fled that country since the US-led invasion.

10. The Muslim perception of imperial and colonial "Christendom" is also justifiably negative. The 500-year story of Europe's enormous global landgrab is littered with every form of cruelty, intolerance, perfidy, deceit, and so on. The important point to make is that such actions were and are contrary to the principles and doctrines of biblical Christianity and the character and teaching of our Lord Jesus Christ.

11. The best book I have read on this subject is Patrick Sookhdeo's *Global Jihad: The Future in the Face of Militant Islam* (Isaac Publishing, 2007). He cites a wide range of writings and statements by Muslim scholars and leaders to explain their strategies for world domination and the terminology they use.

12. The genealogy of the family of Ghenghis Khan and their interesting relationship with Christianity and other religions can be found in the supplementary documentation on the DVD and also, in brief, in the PowerPoint presentation of the history.

13. Admiral Zheng He, the great explorer of the Ming Chinese Empire, made astonishing voyages to map the world on the orders of the Emperor in the early 15th Century. It is certain he reached Africa, but there is growing evidence that he went further. Gavin Menzies describes the possibilities in his book *1421: The Year China Discovered America* (William Morrow & Co, 2002). (See http://www.1421.tv.) Many people regard Menzies's thesis as too speculative—it threatens academic empires. The major routes he proposed are shown on the map on page 50. It is interesting to note the route round Greenland and Siberia—this was during the Medieval Warm Period, when much of the Arctic ice had melted.

14. A term coined by the political scientist R J Rummel to refer to the murder of any person or people by a government, whether on the grounds of race, ethnicity, religion, language or politics or just indiscriminately.

15. The map here shows how far the reforms of the Reformation were pushed through by its leaders. Where there is more yellow and less blue, there was a larger degree of popular support.

16. Some examples: King Frederick IV of Denmark provided funds for Bartholomaeus Ziegenbalg, a German missionary of the Danish-Halle Mission who translated the Bible into Tamil; the Dutch paid for chaplains in Indonesia to care for both their own people and the Indonesians; and Oliver Cromwell's republican Commonwealth of England was considered responsible for evangelization in N America.

17. Thomas Friedman wrote a book in 2005-07 with the evocative title *The World Is Flat*. It shows how globalization and the internet is "levelling" the world by weakening imperial systems and creating a world market in which country borders have less significance.

18. R J Rummel has meticulously researched the mass murder of civilians by governments throughout history and he is the source of most of the figures I have used. He carefully omits all deaths of combatants in war. His findings are shocking. A large proportion of these deaths were a direct result of the ideologies spawned by the so-called Enlightenment: capitalism, humanism, Fascism,

colonialism, nationalism and, worst of all, Marxism. See http://www.mega.nu/ampp/rummel/dbg.chap1.htm.

19. Many of these will be treated more fully in later chapters and on the DVD. The latter includes Excel spreadsheets of a selective timeline by century, and some accompanying timelines on specific areas and topics found on the internet. The two best books I could find containing exhaustive timelines are David B Barrett and Todd M Johnson's excellent *World Christian Trends AD30–AD2200* (William Carey Library, 2001) and, from a more secular perspective, Bernard Grun's *The Timetables of History* (Simon & Schuster, 1991)

20. The controversial Balfour Declaration stated that the British government "views with favour the establishment in Palestine of a national home for the Jewish people—it being clearly understood that nothing shall be done which may prejudice the civil and religious rights of existing non-Jewish communities in Palestine." The declaration was controversial for many reasons: the identity of its author, the lack of consultation both with the Arabs and within Britain, the objectives of Jewish Zionism and its propaganda, the expected outcome (with some people assuming that it would result in a Jewish state). The Holocaust was to make all the more urgent the need for a homeland for millions of Jewish refugees.

21. The Second World War is generally reckoned to have started with France and Britain's declaration of war on Germany after its invasion of Poland on 1 September 1939, but arguably began with Italy's invasion of Ethiopia in 1935-36, or with Japan's invasion of China in 1931. Casualty figures for the war are much disputed. The most complete and up-to-date data is included in the ChristianChronology2.XLS database on the DVD. Source http://en.wikipedia.org/wiki/World_War_II_casualties. By February 2008 the total had been adjusted to 82 million.

22. Tyrannical rule and extreme corruption of elite leaders have impoverished many nations and held back economic development. The mobile phone is breaking down these barriers. It provides cheap connectivity, makes information freely available and trading conditions transparent; it provides a cheap mechanism for effective banking and transfer of funds.

23. Air travel and the generosity of (particularly US) Evangelicals made possible many hundreds of global gatherings—most of minor significance but some highly influential in bringing Evangelicals together to plan and work for world evangelization. The most important perhaps were those that took place in Berlin in 1966, in Lausanne, Switzerland in 1974, in Manila in 1989 and in Pretoria in 1997. The admirable vision of Billy Graham, the US evangelist, in catalyzing and supporting the first three gave a cohesion and focus to Evangelicals that prepared the ground for the subsequent, massive harvest into the Kingdom.

24. Three major transdenominational global movements must be mentioned: the World Evangelical Alliance (WEA, formerly WEF), the Lausanne Committee for World Evangelization (LCWE, now called the Lausanne Movement) and the AD2000 and Beyond Movement (AD2000). A host of denominational, regional, specialist ministry networks and movements have also developed.

25. Cross-cultural missions multiplied to nearly 3,000 identified agencies in 2000, with over 200,000 missionaries. The members of 10 interdenominational, international mega-missions—AIM, Campus Crusade, Gospel for Asia, Navigators, New Tribes Mission, OM, SIM, WEC, Wycliffe Bible Translators and YWAM—totalled over 50,000.

Religion: The Major Streams

In the 19th and 20th Centuries, the political, industrial, cultural and ideological dominance of Europe and its daughter civilizations in the New World was global. The 21st Century will see the erosion of that dominance. One of the assumptions of secular Western (EuNAPa)-influenced societies[1] has been the irrelevance of religion in a modern world—the USA being an exception—but the increase in population, wealth and influence of non-Western (AfAsLA) societies is eclipsing the Western perspective, and religion has become as key a factor in this century as Western political ideologies were in the previous two. Its influence is fundamental to the world's future. The rise of various expressions of religious nationalism, a global, often violent, Islamist movement and a large, biblically-oriented indigenous Christian church is already impacting our world deeply.

Classifying religions is a challenge. The *World Christian Encyclopedia*[2] lists nearly 10,000 distinct religions and para-religions in the world (many of these being branches, subgroups or denominations). Of these, 270 have followings of over 500,000 individuals. All have been grouped into 19 types in the WCE global table. In *Operation World*, I limited this to nine religions and lumped the smaller, non-traditional religions together in a single "Other" category. These are listed in Fig 3.1. In this volume, only six categories are used. All ethnic religions and the smaller global religions such as Baha'i and Judaism are grouped together. The non-religious are included as a "religious stream" as their belief systems have some of the characteristics of a religion: an unprovable set of beliefs and often a zeal to propagate them.[3] The six streams are distinctively coloured—a colour scheme used throughout this book.

In Fig 3.2, the central pie chart divides the world's population amongst these six categories. Around the periphery, various bar charts further subdivide some of these. These subdivisions are explained more fully in the later sections of this chapter.

Religions	%	Adherents
Christian	32.5	1,973 mil
Muslim	21.1	1,279 mil
Non-religious	15.5	938 mil
Hindu	13.5	820 mil
Buddhist	6.6	400 mil
Chinese	6.3	383 mil
Ethnic	2.9	176 mil
Sikh	0.3	20.5 mil
Jewish	0.2	14.2 mill
Other	1.0	60.8 mil

Fig 3.1 *The six "religious streams" in 2000*

Prayerbeads (photo by E Daymond)

Food for Thought

Globalization is a challenging development that stokes up fears of unsought change. In many parts of the world it is seen as an imposition (thanks to the dominance of its media) of the West's culture, and in particular its materialist values and moral relativism; but for the countries of the more developed world it can mean an influx of immigrants, different world views and religious extremism that could swamp them and their indigenous cultures. Religion is not about to disappear.

▲ How can world leaders be helped to understand the long-term implications of globalization and develop realistic policies that enhance its positives?

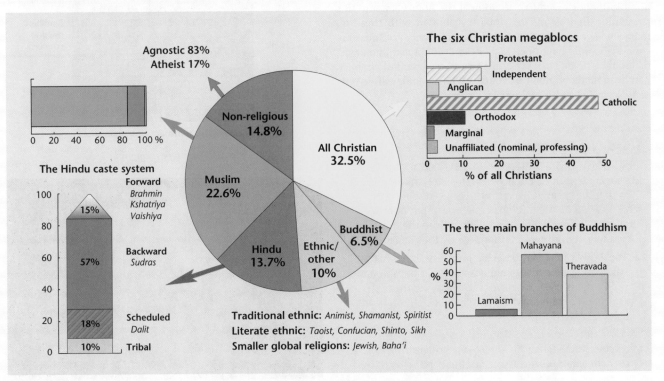

Fig 3.2 *The six major religious streams in 2010*

The Majority Religions by Country in 2000

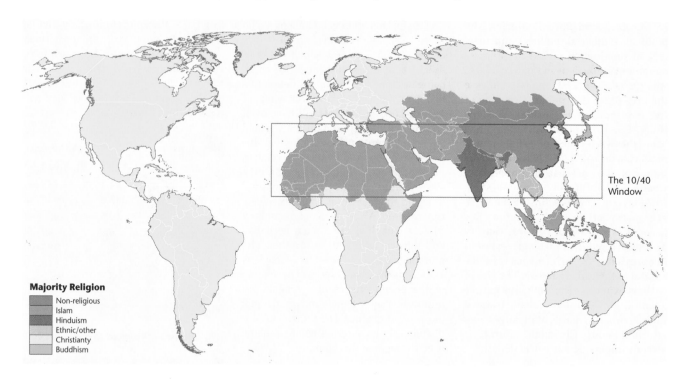

Majority Religion
- Non-religious
- Islam
- Hinduism
- Ethnic/other
- Christianty
- Buddhism

The 10/40 Window

Each country is shaded according to the religious stream with the largest following (which, in some cases, may not comprise a majority of the population). This usually gives an indication of the religious inclination of the country's ruling elite. It is striking to see how Christianity has spread from Europe to encircle the globe. It is also interesting to note that nearly all the "non-Christian" countries of the world—some with very large Christian minorities—lie within or near the so-called 10/40 Window (the blue rectangle on the map).[4]

It's instructive to look back to 1887, the year when Fig 3.3 was published.[5] Its terminology would be frowned on today, but it graphically portrayed the situation at the time. Compare the population figures and religious distribution with those of today on page 65. I suspect that the actual number of "mission converts" would have been higher than the three million estimated then. Even so, it is astonishing to see how little impact had been made on non-Christians a whole century after William Carey began his missionary career.

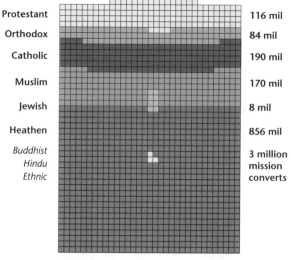

World population was then 1,427 million

Protestant	116 mil
Orthodox	84 mil
Catholic	190 mil
Muslim	170 mil
Jewish	8 mil
Heathen	856 mil
Buddhist / Hindu / Ethnic	3 million mission converts

Each square represents 1 million souls

Fig 3.3 *The major religions in 1887*

Food for Thought

It is the 19th Century that is often described as "the Great Missionary Century", but it was in the latter third of the 20th that the greatest harvest was won—in spite of the scorn heaped on the missions endeavour. That movement has radically changed our world. It has been the most successful enterprise ever undertaken by the Church.

▲ The world today may have big problems, but what would it have been like had not hundreds of thousands of Christians given their lives sacrificially for the education of humankind and to meet its physical and spiritual needs?

We have not finished yet. Billions still grope for peace, forgiveness and eternal life in religious systems that cannot offer them, while we are assured of them in the Lord Jesus Christ.

Church interior, Peru (photo by PJK)

The Majority Religions by Language

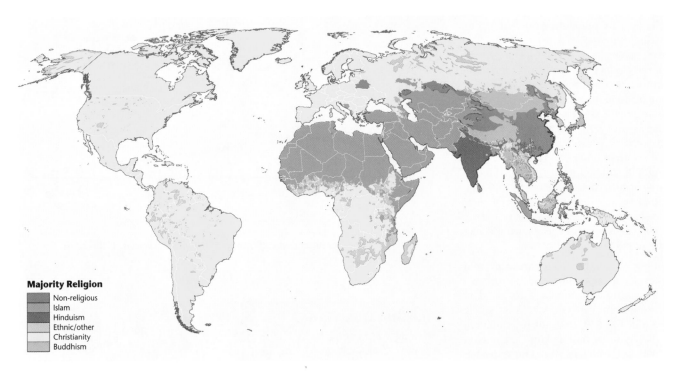

Majority Religion
- Non-religious
- Islam
- Hinduism
- Ethnic/other
- Christianity
- Buddhism

More detail is revealed if we look at the religious affiliation of the world's language groups. Over the past 30 years, there has been a great deal of research into and analysis of the world's languages and peoples (see Chapter 6). The 15th edition of *Ethnologue* listed 6,912 languages, but if we take into account the world's national boundaries we arrive at a figure of 11,233 language communities. Of these, 7,095 both are indigenous and have specific home areas within the countries they inhabit.[6] The languages are coloured according to the largest religious component among their speakers. The line boundaries of these language polygons have been removed. Later on in this chapter, the percentages by religion are given for each of the six religious streams.

Fig 3.4 gives an indication of the changing fortunes of the six major religious streams over the period 1900–2050.

Observations

▲ At the end of this 150-year period, Christians will probably constitute much the same percentage of the world's population as today. What is not obvious from this are the radical changes within the Church over that time—see Chapter 4.

▲ Muslims will grow in number in consequence of their higher birth-rates, and will become more visible as a result of migration or flight to non-Muslim countries. Islamism will add to this visibility by pressuring Muslims to accentuate the cultural aspects of their religion in clothing and lifestyle and creating Muslim "space" by squeezing non-Muslims out of areas where Muslims are concentrated.

▲ Both Buddhism and Hinduism will suffer losses—mainly to Christianity or to no religion.

▲ Primary allegiance to ethnic religions will continue to decline dramatically.

▲ Non-religious will see an even more dramatic change. The rise of anti-Christian ideologies such as Communism and Nazism in the early part of the 20th Century, as well as secular humanism elsewhere in the West, caused many Westerners and E Asians to turn their backs on religion altogether. From 1990 onwards, this trend was reversed—first, because the collapse of Communism in Europe prompted many to return to their forefathers' faith and, second, because those without a religion have fewer children.

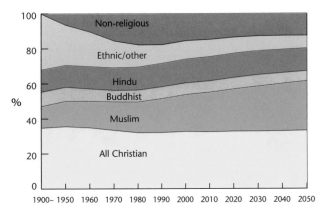

Fig 3.4 *The six major religious streams of the 20th and 21st Centuries*

Burning Question

The 21st Century is developing into what many perceive to be a political, and sometimes even military, confrontation between Islam, secularism and Christianity. Jesus promised: "Blessed are the meek, for they will inherit the earth" (Matthew 5:5).

▲ How can biblical Christians who are politically marginalized inherit the earth without resorting to worldly methods or weapons (2 Corinthians 10:4–5)?

Changes in religious affiliation, 1900–2050

The graphs on this page illustrate changes in population and religious affiliation predicted up to 2050. The first shows the annual rate of growth of the global population, and then, relative to it, the growth rate of the six major religious streams. Global population growth is projected to decrease to near zero by 2050, and all six of these streams will also decline. The growth rate in the number of Muslims will fall but will still be higher than all the others because their higher birth rate. The number of "non-religious" grew massively over the 20th Century, but by 1990 its decade-on-decade growth had dwindled to practically nothing.

In Fig 3.6, the two pie charts represent the global population and the relative changes in the numbers affiliated to the different religions over this whole period. In 2050, the global population is likely to be half as large again as in 2000. The bar chart shows the expected rates of growth or decline of the six main religious streams relative to the growth of global population for the first half of the 21st Century (the horizontal, X axis representing global population growth). Only two will continue to grow, by natural growth or conversion: the Muslims and Christians. The Buddhists, Hindus and adherents of ethnic religions will dwindle in number, mainly as a result of a change of allegiance. The same factor will add to the number of the non-religious but will not be enough to compensate for large reductions in their birth rates.

The dominant change over this period will be that nations with majorities following ethnic religions will become predominantly Christian.

No nation has changed from being mainly Hindu or Buddhist to mainly following another religion, but these two belief systems will continue to lose followers to Christianity, Islam and secularism.

Two countries that once had a Christian majority now have a Muslim one. In Lebanon, the high birth-rates of Sunni and Shi'a Muslims are set against both the low birth-rate and the emigration of Christians. In Eritrea, the Marxist-oriented government has aligned itself with the Muslim world in order to gain support in its fight against Christian-majority Ethiopia. This has advantaged the country's Muslims at the expense of its indigenous Christians—and immigra-

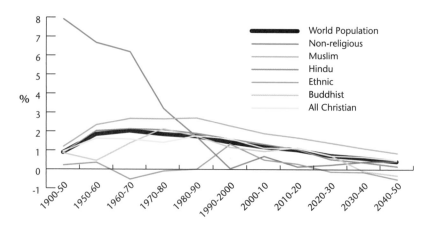

Fig 3.5 *Average annual rate of growth of the major religions, 1900–2050*

Burning Question

The major Abrahamic faiths, Judaism, Christianity and Islam, are likely to increase their representation in the global population from 47.9% in 1900 and 53.9% in 2000 to 61.6% in 2050.

▲ What are the implications for us if we are to relate to non-Christians as both world citizens and Great Commission Christians?

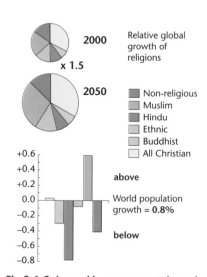

Fig 3.6 *Gains and losses amongst the major religions as a result of natural growth and conversion*

tion and a higher birth-rate have further tipped the scales in their favour.

On the other hand, by 2050 two countries will have shifted from a Muslim majority to a Christian one: Albania[7] and Nigeria[8]

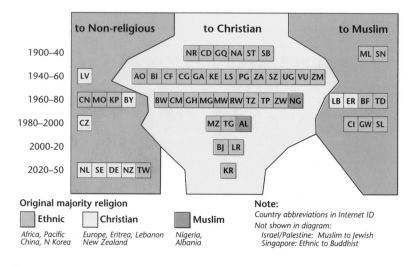

Fig 3.7 *Changes in the religious allegiance of national majorities, 1900–2050[9]*

The Spread of the Non-religious

1900

At the end of the 19th Century, few people openly professed to have no religion. Then, humanism, a child of the European "Enlightenment", went mainstream in the then dominant West. The maps in Fig 3.8 show the impact of this. In the 20th Century, people with no religion were to become a major force in politics and the media. Their ideology is, in effect, a belief system based on evolution (no creator needed), materialism (there is no spiritual world) and humanism (Man is inherently good). Many of the non-religious scoff at religions because "they cause wars", but the 20th Century gave rise to Communism and Nazism, which between them produced the worst democides, ethnocides and wars in history.

1950

The number of people with no religion multiplied amidst the disillusionment of economic catastrophe in the Depression, two devastating world wars and the rise of a militantly atheistic Soviet Union intent on world domination and the destruction of all religious belief. In 1950, the Communists gained control of all of mainland China, the Cold War was at its height and Europe was divided by an "iron curtain" (see map).[10] The European empires were crumbling and the continent was turning away from a Christianity that was in desperate need of reawakening. Marx's prediction that religion would wither away looked ever more plausible.

2000

By 1980, Communism had reached its global peak, but within 10 years it suffered a dramatic collapse as a viable ideology. Its spiritual legacy was mixed, but in many post-Communist countries people turned to religions both old and new. The non-religious element of the global population, though it is still significant, probably peaked in 1980. The principal concentrations of people with no religion (in China and much of the West) were rapidly ageing by 2000, while elsewhere religion (and especially Islam and Christianity) was back in the ascendancy.

2050

In the West, the inexorable rise in the percentage of people claiming no religious affiliation is likely to continue, as the shading on this map shows. Few Westerners today perceive that in the rest of the world the trend is in the opposite direction. The Western secular media, generally hostile to religion and to Christianity in particular, may currently be dominant globally, but for how much longer?

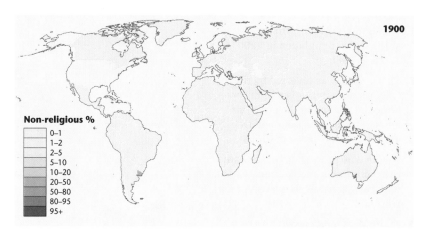

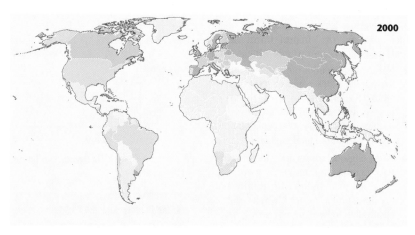

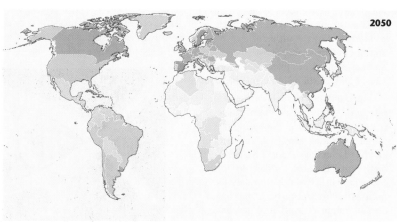

Fig 3.8 *The spread of the non-religious during the 20th and 21st Centuries*

In Fig 3.9, the global spread of the non-religious is broken down by continent and region. Note the following:

1. The dramatic growth from 0.2% of the global population in 1900 to 17.7% in 1980

2. This growth was reversed by the collapse of Communism in Europe, the rapid decline in the birth rate among the non-religious and the growth of the Church in China.

3. People who profess no religion are concentrated in the West and China, with relatively few in the rest of the world.

4. In the West, and elsewhere as affluence spreads, numbers are likely to continue to grow slowly through the 21st Century.

5. A decline in the number of the non-religious as a percentage of global population after 1980 to possibly 12–13%. The non-religious have a lower birth-rate than those who profess a religion.

Europe's demographic and religious changes, 1900–2050

Is Europe committing sociocide? Assuming that there is no major calamity or war in the Middle East that greatly increases the numbers of Muslim immigrants—both possible—recent trends indicate that:

▲ Europe's indigenous population is likely to decline by 28% between 2000 and 2050. The deficit is likely to be made up largely by a threefold increase in immigrants, who by 2050 could comprise nearly 27% of the total population.

▲ Non-religious adults and young people will increase in number as people continue to abandon Christianity, but (as they tend to adopt lifestyles not conducive to bearing or rearing children) not significantly.

▲ The decline in numbers of indigenous Christians is likely to continue, but it will be offset by the influx of immigrant Christians. Those of immigrant stock are likely to comprise 15% of all Christians in Europe in 2050.

▲ Muslims will be the fastest-growing religious community,[11] mainly as a result of immigration (including the import of brides from the homeland in arranged marriages) and a higher birth-rate. There are unlikely to be many converts from the indigenous population (except through marriage and among prisoners). As a percentage of Europe's population, they will triple over this period.

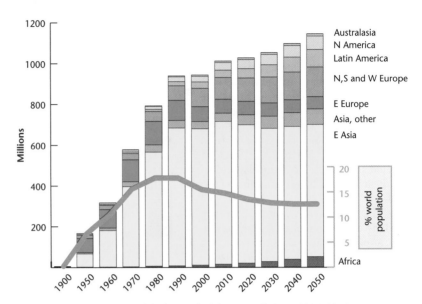

Fig 3.9 *The global spread of the non-religious, 1900–2050*

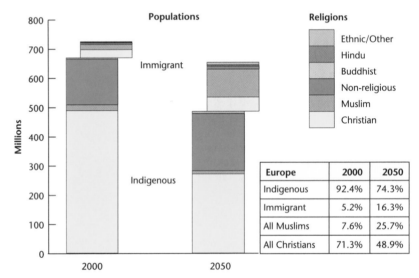

Europe	2000	2050
Indigenous	92.4%	74.3%
Immigrant	5.2%	16.3%
All Muslims	7.6%	25.7%
All Christians	71.3%	48.9%

Fig 3.10 *Demographic and religious changes in Europe, 1900–2050*

Burning Question

People of no religion set much of the world's ideological, political, economic and cultural agenda for most of the 20th Century, but since 1990 it has increasingly been the religious regions of the world that are doing this.

▲ How can the Church worldwide hold to and promote the values of God's Kingdom?

"Darwin" fish (photo by Betty Spackman)

Fig 3.11 highlights the ethnicity, language and religious background of non-religious people globally to illustrate which cultures are most affected (rather than which countries, as shown on page 69). The figures are based on comprehensive ethno-linguistic databases we have developed and represent the 67 largest language groups in the world. Note the following for this sample:

▲ The majority of the non-religious live in Communist countries (especially the Chinese and North Koreans).

▲ In 2008, there were 52 million people who professed no religion in former Communist countries.

▲ Most of the rest of the non-religious are from affluent Western cultures.

▲ There are very few openly non-religious people with a Muslim, Hindu or Buddhist background.

▲ All but 5% of the world's non-religious are either East Asians (78.7%) or Caucasians (16.3%).

Food for Thought

The non-religious communities of the world most responsive to the Gospel are in Asia. They are also the largest.

▲ Is it possible that the most effective missionaries to the aggressively secular West may come from Asia?

Communism

In Fig 3.12, the red line represents the rise and fall of Communism year-by-year by the number of countries that had one-party Marxist regimes. The figure also indicates the major events of the 20th Century associated with this godless ideology. The persecution of Christians was especially severe. Atheists killed nearly 32 million Christians in the 20th Century. After reaching its high point in 1980 after the invasion of Afghanistan, it took only 11 years for the whole edifice of Communism in Europe to collapse.

The blue line shows the number of countries impacted by Communist revolutionary wars.

The remaining rump of Communist countries is Asian (China, North Korea, Vietnam, Laos and, for a time, Cambodia), with the exception of Cuba. China and Vietnam have recently moved rapidly towards a more capitalist economy, while retaining the one-party system of Communism.

The green line charts the emergence of democratically elected Communist governments in multi-party democracies.

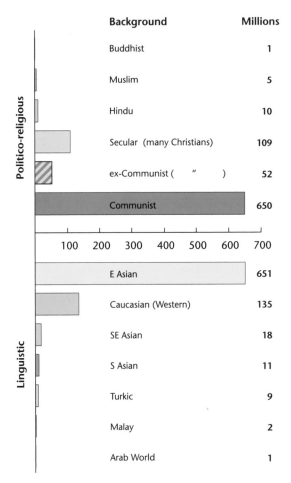

Background	Millions
Buddhist	1
Muslim	5
Hindu	10
Secular (many Christians)	109
ex-Communist (")	52
Communist	650
E Asian	651
Caucasian (Western)	135
SE Asian	18
S Asian	11
Turkic	9
Malay	2
Arab World	1

Representing the 67 national language groups over 2.7 million in 2008 (48% of world population)

Fig 3.11 *The politico-religious and linguistic background of the non-religious in the world's largest ethnic groups*

The hammer and sickle symbolize Communist ideology

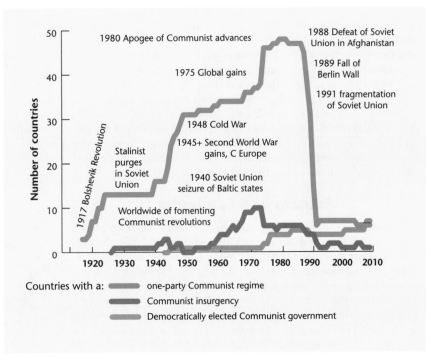

Fig 3.12 *The rise and fall of Communism, 1910–2009*

Communism was an attempt at social engineering on a global scale, but with horrendous social and personal costs. It is helpful to look back over the 20 years since its dramatic collapse around 1990 and see the varying spiritual after-effects. Below I consider 10 countries, grouped in pairs, with some observations about their spiritual demography.

Russia and Ukraine

Imperial Russia was strongly Orthodox, but the church compromised with the Communist rulers who followed. The numbers of the non-religious grew substantially. Since 1991, many Russians have returned to Orthodoxy as an expression of their nationalism. Evangelicals have always been few in number and have often been harshly persecuted. The harassment of minority Christian groups has increased in the 21st Century.

Ukrainian nationalism was crushed for centuries. Independence in 1991 was unexpected, and today conflicting religious, political and ethnic interests dominate the country's life. The non-religious were never strong, because of people's resentment at their mistreatment by the Russians. The plurality of denominations ensured religious freedom after 1991, with a great increase in the number of Evangelicals.

The Czech Republic and Estonia

The peoples of C Europe suffered over the centuries as their lands became buffer zones between neighbouring empires or were swallowed by them. Estonia was invaded and annexed by the Soviet Union in 1940 and 1944, and what was then Czechoslovakia was occupied in 1945 and subsequently taken over by the Communists in a coup in 1948. The non-religious were not so much Marxist as secularist. The disillusionment that resulted from the general suffering encouraged cynicism and disbelief in God, and the eventual fall of Communism did not lead to any return to Christianity. These two states are now the most secular in Europe, and the majority of their peoples are non-religious. Evangelicals have had a long history in both countries, but even so there has been no revival of biblical Christianity since 1990. (The exception among the countries of the old Soviet bloc is Romania, which has seen an increase in the number of evangelical believers.)

China and Ethiopia

The harsh experience of militantly anti-religious Marxism in both countries has had the opposite effect to that seen in C Europe. In both, the hold of religious traditions was weakened and the inefficacy of Communism was demonstrated, causing many to seek solutions elsewhere. Evangelical Christianity has emerged as the most dynamic spiritual movement in both countries. In China, the Communist government is gradually realizing that the increasingly influential Church could actually assist in nation-building. In Ethiopia, Communist rule lasted for 16 years, until 1991, but despite severe persecution the Church there emerged stronger and with greater evangelistic zeal than in any other post-Communist country.

Vietnam and Cambodia

Like those of C Europe, the peoples of Indochina have been pawns in conflicts between empires and superpowers, especially in the 20th Century—France, Japan, the Soviet Union, China and the USA. Yet, despite the traumas of decades of war and the democide in Cambodia's "killing fields"—and despite the tradition of Buddhism—the spread of Christianity here since 1990 has been marked. In Cambodia there is comparative freedom of religion under a post-Communist government, but in Vietnam Communists are still in control and persecution continues, especially for the more Christianized mountain tribes.

Food for Thought

The responses of different populations to systematic, government-instigated persecution have varied so much.

▲ If your country were to undergo such a trial, how would its Christians react? Would they be crushed or emerge as vibrant followers of Christ?

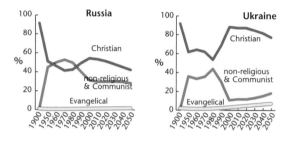

Fig 3.13 *Communism in the Soviet Union*

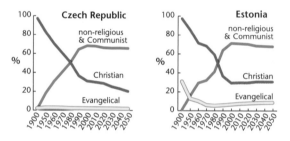

Fig 3.14 *Communism in C Europe*

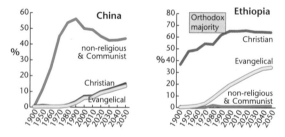

Fig 3.15 *Communism and Christian revival*

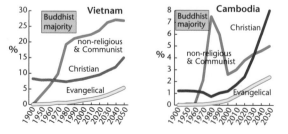

Fig 3.16 *Communism in Buddhist countries*

The Distribution of Muslims by Ethnicity and Language in 2008

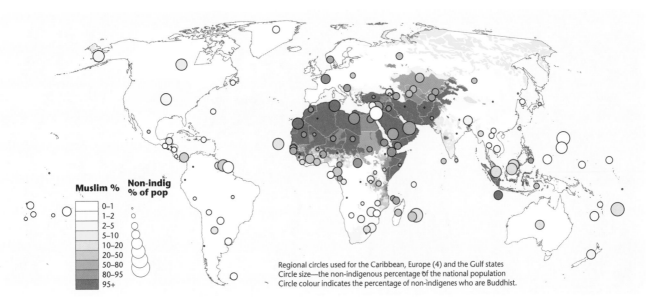

Muslim %

Non-indig % of pop

0–1
1–2
2–5
5–10
10–20
20–50
50–80
80–95
95+

Regional circles used for the Caribbean, Europe (4) and the Gulf states
Circle size—the non-indigenous percentage of the national population
Circle colour indicates the percentage of non-indigenes who are Buddhist.

The Muslim perspective on history and theology as well as Islam's divisions and present distresses are impacting the world today and will continue to do so for many decades. An understanding of Islam is now essential—otherwise, mistakes are inevitable in politics, in communication and in Christian witness.

The map above shows the global distribution of Muslims by ethnicity and language in 2008[12] The intermingling of Muslim and Christian peoples is evident in Africa, C Asia, India and Indonesia—all areas where Muslim-initiated persecution and conflict are more likely. The size of each circle represents the percentage of that country or region's population that is of recent immigrant stock, and their shade of green the percentage of those immigrants that are Muslims. Note the circles with concentrations of Muslim migrants in non-Muslim countries.

The interactions between Christianity and Islam extend back over 1,400 years—and too many have been violent and negative, leaving a legacy of mistrust, fear and even hatred. Fig 3.17 illustrates some of the major events and developments and their duration. This history must not be ignored when we relate to Muslims.

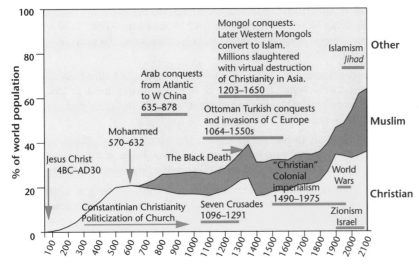

Fig 3.17 *Islam and Christianity: a legacy of hatred, 30–2100AD*

A British mosque (photo by E Daymond)

Food for Thought

The challenge for Christians is to relate to Muslims and share our faith with them with love and confidence in the context both of this negative history and of the present tendency in politics and society towards an inappropriate policy of appeasement and one-sided tolerance. We need to be:

▲ well informed, so that we can influence our governments' policies regarding both Muslim countries and Muslim minorities in our own countries;

▲ suitably equipped for humble ministry to Muslims globally and lead them to the One who alone can give them peace and eternal security in the Gospel.

The Distribution of Muslims by Country in 1900

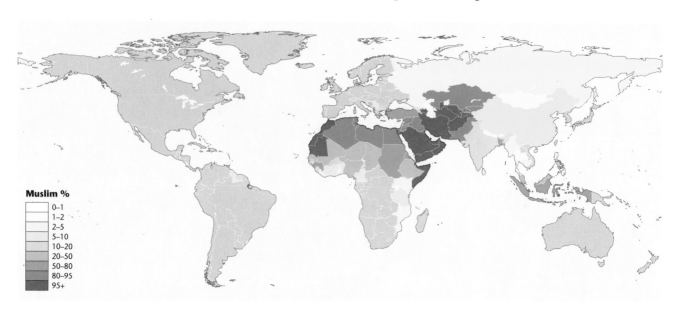

Muslim %
- 0–1
- 1–2
- 2–5
- 5–10
- 10–20
- 20–50
- 50–80
- 80–95
- 95+

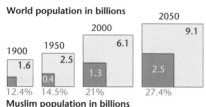

World population in billions

1900 1.6 — 12.4%
1950 2.5 — 0.4 — 14.5%
2000 6.1 — 1.3 — 21%
2050 9.1 — 2.5 — 27.4%

Muslim population in billions

Fig 3.18 *The spread of Islam, 1900–2050*

Food for Thought

The highly visible growth in Muslim numbers can make us fear for the future, yet Jesus promised that His Gospel will be preached to all nations/peoples (NT Greek, *ta ethne*, Matthew 24:14, my translation). Let us have faith in His promise and see these developments as an opportunity for bold witness!

The maps here and on page 75 illustrate respectively the percentage of Muslims in each country's population in 1900 and the extrapolated percentages in 2050. (In both cases I have used the 2000 national borders, for ease of comparison.) The most striking changes are caused by:

1. High Muslim birth-rates globally, so that Muslim minorities become proportionately larger

2. Migration, mainly from the Muslim heartlands to the West and to coastal W Africa. This has increased the number of Muslims where once they were few. Conversely, non-Muslim migrant workers have reduced the percentage of Muslims in the Gulf oil states.

3. Conflict—particularly in the partition of the Indian subcontinent in 1947 and of Palestine in 1949–74 and the seizure of W Papua by Indonesia in 1963. There has been more recent Muslim expansionist violence in Côte d'Ivoire, Indonesia, Nigeria and Sudan.

4. Persuasion, mainly in parts of Indonesia, the Sahel, E and C Africa, plus a few significant conversions in Western countries. Trade, aid and grants for education with strings attached have all played a large part in this process.

5. The persecution of non-Muslim minorities in Muslim-majority countries, which has caused millions to emigrate from Middle Eastern countries—principally Christians from once-large populations, but also Baha'is and Mandeans. This has had the effect of increasing the percentage of Muslims in the Middle East.

Fig 3.18 compares the growth of the global and the Muslim populations. From 1900 to 2050, it is estimated that the former will increase sixfold but the latter 12-fold. Probably 85–90% of Muslim growth will be through reproduction. Muslims comprised just one-eighth of the global population in 1900, but by 2050 they are expected to comprise well over one-quarter.

The growth rate of the global population peaked in the 1960s (the red line) and is expected to continue to decline. There are startlingly differing growth rates for Muslims (the dark green line) and non-Muslims (the brown line). The Muslim populations are subdivided into three categories: countries where Muslims constitute at least 90% of the population (light green), those where they constitute between 50% and 90% (yellow) and those where they are a minority (black). The differences are small, but it is significant that the growth rate is highest in the countries where they are a minority—boosted by immigration.

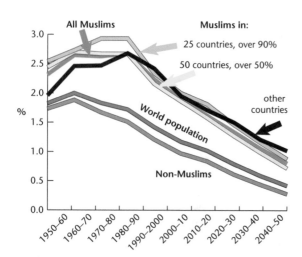

Fig 3.19 *The growth rate of the global and Muslim populations, 1950–2050*

The Distribution of Muslims by Country in 2050

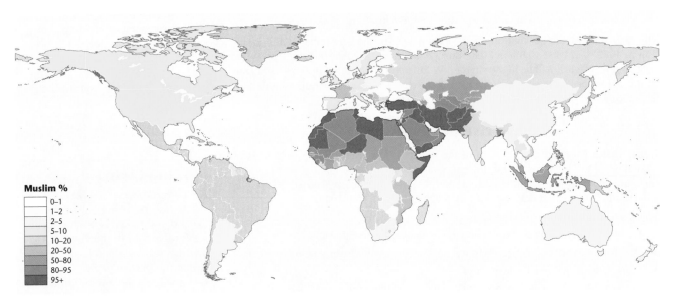

Muslim %

- 0–1
- 1–2
- 2–5
- 5–10
- 10–20
- 20–50
- 50–80
- 80–95
- 95+

It is helpful (if sobering) to look at some of the future implications of the growth in the Muslim population.

The Arab world currently comprises just 25% of all Muslims, yet its language and world view are dominant. Islam developed as a religion suited to an Arabic desert culture but it expects all Muslims to conform to it. Contextualization is not part of its genetic code!

The high concentration of Muslims in S Asia is remarkable. Over 40% of all Muslims live there—a percentage that is projected hardly to change from 1900 to 2050. In recent years, Muslims have not been as successful in winning over Dalits and low-caste Hindus in India as they were when they controlled most of S Asia.

Huge growth in Muslim populations is expected between 1900 and 2050—

rising in Pakistan, for instance, from 21m to 292m, and in Yemen from 2.5m to 59m. This is unsustainable and will cause enormous social, ecological and demographic crises. Many already overpopulated Muslim countries will more than double in population by the middle of the century. The most overpopulated countries are often the ones with the most influential Islamist movements, with potentially serious consequences for the world.

Public prayer, N Africa (photo by ED)

Africa's share of the global Muslim population is projected to expand from 17% in 1900 to 31% in 2050. If we exclude

Burning Question

Since "9/11", the principal preoccupation of the West has been to contain and eliminate the military threat of Islamist *jihad,* but little has been done to deal with the issues that feed the resentment of millions of young Muslims who are being recruited for *jihad.*

▲ How can Christians help to contribute to the equitable resolution of these issues in a culturally sensitive way, and also introduce Muslims to the Prince of Peace?

1900	Country	mil	1950	Country	mil	2000	Country	mil	2050	Country	mil
	India	31.5		Indonesia	58.9		Indonesia	168.0		Pakistan	291.6
	China	23.9		India	37.9		Pakistan	137.1		India	230.9
	Pakistan	20.9		Pakistan	35.7		India	127.6		Indonesia	207.8
	Indonesia	19.4		Bangladesh	32.1		Bangladesh	110.4		Bangladesh	207.2
	Bangladesh	18.8		China	21.9		Turkey	68.0		Egypt	110.8
	Turkey	10.9		Turkey	21.2		Iran	65.7		Turkey	100.4
	Iran	9.5		Egypt	17.5		Egypt	58.2		Nigeria	99.1
	Egypt	8.5		Iran	16.6		Nigeria	48.2		Iran	96.8
	Morocco	5.0		Nigeria	14.3		Algeria	29.5		Afghanistan	94.4
	Afghanistan	5.0		Morocco	8.3		Morocco	29.2		Iraq	61.1
	Nigeria	4.2		Afghanistan	8.0		China	25.0		Yemen	59.4
	Algeria	4.0		Algeria	7.8		Iraq	24.3		Ethiopia	56.7
	Sudan	3.4		Sudan	6.1		Afghanistan	23.2		Niger	48.8
	Russia	3.0		Ethiopia	5.2		Sudan	21.4		Morocco	46.1
	Saudi Arabia	2.7		Iraq	4.9		Ethiopia	21.2		Saudi Arabia	46.0
	Yemen	2.5		Kazakhstan	4.3		Uzbekistan	20.6		Algeria	43.6
	Uzbekistan	2.2		Uzbekistan	4.3		Saudi Arabia	19.9		Mali	37.0
	Kazakhstan	2.1		Yemen	4.3		Yemen	17.9		Sudan	36.7
	Iraq	2.0		Saudi Arabia	3.2		Syria	15.2		Uzbekistan	35.1
	Ethiopia	2.0		Tunisia	3.1		Russia	14.9		China	32.9

Sub-Saharan Africa
E & SE Asia
S Asia
Arab World
C Asia
Non-Arab Middle East

Decline in order
Rise in order
New to top 20
No change

Fig 3.20 *The 20 countries with the largest Muslim populations*

Arab N Africa, the figures become even more significant: up from 6% in 1900 to 20% in 2050. However, the increase of Christians in sub-Saharan Africa should far exceed this—up from 9% to 54%. Religious conflict could become a major destabilizing factor along the fault-line between Muslim and Christian areas.

The EuNAPa Muslim population will rise from 1.6% of these regions' total population in 1980 to at least 10.8% in 2050. Europe is likely to be nearly 17% Muslim by 2050, but this figure will be higher in both W Europe and Russia. These percentages could be higher if there are serious disasters, whether natural or human-induced, in the Muslim heartlands.

> *Islamism:* the view that Islam is a comprehensive political ideology to establish Islamic states under *shari'a* law by any means, including violence. It is characterized by an activist zeal and a desire to adhere to every detail of *shari'a* law and to give one's life as a martyr for the cause.[13]

The rise of Islamism

Hopes that a "new world order" of peace would follow the end of the Cold War were dashed within a decade by the emergence of extreme violence perpetrated in the name of Islam. The events that sparked this were the Iraqi invasion of Kuwait in 1990[14] and the ensuing defeat of Iraq by a US-led coalition in 1991.

The sources of Islamist anger have been:

▲ A sense of impotence and humiliation in an honour/shame culture

▲ The current backwardness, poverty and political failure of Muslim nations

▲ A lost "golden age" of Islamic empire

▲ Western "Christian" colonial, economic and cultural imperialism

▲ A failed Islamic eschatology of an advance to global hegemony

▲ The perceived corruption of the Western world-view, which is also perceived as Christian.

Occasions for hatred include Western support for the foundation and relentless expansion of Israel and for corrupt autocratic regimes in many Muslim countries as well as Western or "Christian" involvement in wars in Afghanistan, Bosnia, Chechnya and Iraq. Dealing with these problems will not remove the anger.

The US and its global power are seen as an embodiment of the source of this humiliation.

In 1996, Osama bin Laden, a Saudi citizen and leader of al-Qa'ida, "declared war" on the US because it had stationed "infidel" troops in the Land of the Two Holy Places (Saudi Arabia). This was followed by a number of terrorist attacks, climaxing in the "9/11" assault on the World Trade Center and the Pentagon. A resolution of this conflict will take decades. It will be a costly diversion of resources from other, more urgent global needs. And it will need more than a military victory—the battle between worldviews or ideologies has to be won in the minds and hearts of people.

Islamism has divided the Muslim world. A radical minority has claimed centre stage in a global propaganda war while the fearful majority remains silent. Fig 3.21 estimates the possible proportion of Islamist sympathizers in different Muslim populations. Samuel Huntingdon[15] has predicted that culture and religion will be the basis of future conflict, with the most significant being between the West and Islam. He sees little hope of a viable future for Christianity before a reinvigorated Islam.

Burning Question

Are our prospects entirely bleak? Are Huntingdon's assumptions correct? He underestimated both the vitality and growth of Christianity in AfAsLA and the instability and division within the Muslim world. There are two possible solutions: reformation of Islam from within or its regeneration through the message of the Gospel of the Lord Jesus Christ. Both are needed.

▲ How can Christians best contribute to these solutions?

The attack on the World Trade Center in New York on the 9th September 2001 (photo in public domain)

Conflicts and divisions within Islam

The demographic prospects for the Muslim world are serious both for Muslim countries and for the rest of the world. Huntingdon controversially wrote of Islam's "bloody borders". It is not only surrounding countries and cultures that are under threat: the scarcity of resources, as well as ideological differences within Islam, will also lead to much conflict. The map at the top of page 77 represents the probable relative sizes of Muslim populations by country in 2050. Also shown are those non-Muslim countries that have significant Muslim populations. The red and orange circles express the nature and scale of current or probable future conflicts.

Islam divided soon after its founding over the issue of the leadership of the Muslim world. From this schism arose the Sunni and Shi'a branches of the faith, which gradually

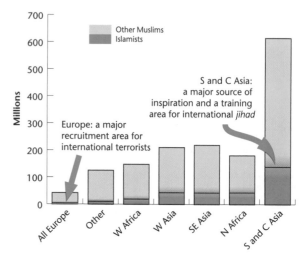

Fig 3.21 Islamist sympathizers as a proportion of Muslims

The Likely Distribution of 2.5 billion Muslims in 2050

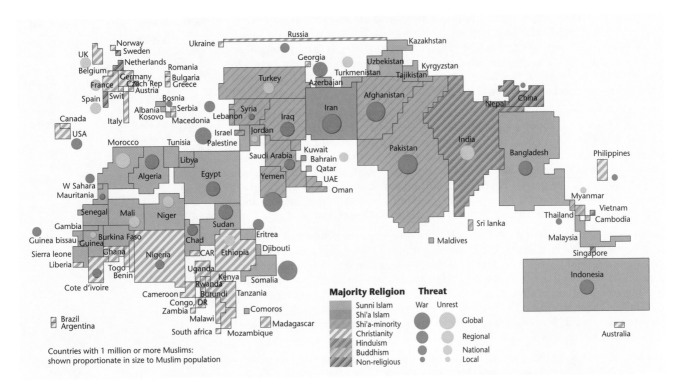

Countries with 1 million or more Muslims:
shown proportionate in size to Muslim population

became polarized between the non-hierarchical and the hierarchical, the secular/military and the theocratic, the largely Arabic and the largely Persian and was cemented also by theological differences. For centuries, the Shi'a were the persecuted minority but the Sunni a threatened majority. The Wahhabi-influenced Sunni Islamists have a passionate hatred for the Shi'a. The rise to regional dominance (possibly backed in the future by nuclear weapons) of Shi'a Iran, which exerts a strong influence throughout western Asia from Egypt to Pakistan, could lead to a Sunni-Shi'a conflict. If this precipitated war in the Middle East, the consequences for the world would be huge.

Burning Question

The imminent collapse of Islam as a result of its own repressiveness, backwardness and internal contradictions is less likely, but wherever Islamists have gained influence, the negative social and economic effects have been severe and increasing disillusionment has followed. The failures of Islamist ideologies are creating a backlash against Islamists and even leading to rejection of Islam itself. Many Muslims long for change and even desire to forsake Islam, despite the danger of persecution and death. Increasing numbers are taking that step and becoming Christians.

▲ Are churches willing to welcome such new believers and give them the support and solidarity they need after giving up everything for their new faith?

Country	Muslim %	Shi'a %	Political Situation	Location; Peoples that are Shi'a
Iran	99.0	93	Shi'a Islamic Republic	All but Arabs, Kurds, Baloch
Azerbaijan	83.0	75	Secular Shi'a rule	Most peoples
Iraq	96.9	65	Conflict	Southern and central Arabs
Bahrain	80.4	61	Sunni rule; tensions	Arabs, Persians
Yemen	99.9	47	Equally balanced	Northern Yemenis; mainly Zaidis
Lebanon	65.0	45	Very tense	Southern Arabs (Hizbollah)
India	12.8	30	Hindu dominance	Large, scattered minority
Tajikistan	91.1	30	Secular Sunni rule	Large, scattered minority
Kuwait	85.9	30	Sunni rule; concerns	Large underclass
Pakistan	96.0	20	Sunni Islamists persecuting Shi'a	Large, scattered minority
Turkey	99.6	20	Largely secular Sunni rule	Mainly Kurds
UAE	63.6	16	Sunni rule	Mixed origins; also Arabs
Afghanistan	97.8	15	Conflict - ethnic and Islamist; less Shi'a	Mainly Hazara- and Dari-speakers
Qatar	76.6	12	Sunni rule	Mixed origins; also Arabs
Saudi Arabia	93.6	12	Wahhabi Sunni rule; Shi'a suppressed	Oil-rich E Province; some Zaidis
Syria	90.4	12	Mainly Shi'a Alawite Arab-minority rule	Mainly Arabs in Latakia Province

Shi'a dominance	Majority	Warfare, suicide bombings, violent sectarian strife within Islam
Sunni dominance	Minority	Possible violence between Sunni and Shi'a or suppression Shi'a
Hindu dominance		Little conflict between Sunni and Shi'a

Fig 3.22 *The conflict between Sunni and Shi'a Islam*

2010	Pop (mil)
Muslims	1,532
Sunni	1,285
Shi'a	226
Other	20

Sunni 84%
Shi'a 15%
Other 1%

Fig 3.23 *The divisions of Islam today*

The impact of the Gospel on Muslims

Maybe as long as 200 years ago, the conversion of Muslims to Christianity was considered virtually impossible. While countless millions of "Christians" were persuaded or coerced to become Muslims, there were only a few passionate advocates[16] to win Muslims to Christ and the results were meagre. It is only since the 1960s that there has been an expanding ministry to Muslims and a steady increase in the number of converts. This has prompted hostility towards any Christian ministry and persecution of those who have turned to Christ.

Fig 3.24 gives conservative estimates for the countries and regions with the most believers from a Muslim background (BMBs). The total number worldwide may exceed 8 million (and could be much higher).[17] The figure indicates countries where persecution is widespread and those where the death penalty is in force for apostasy. It could surprise us on the Day of Resurrection how many people will rise to glory out of Muslim graves! There are significant movements to Christ in Indonesia, Bangladesh, Nigeria and Algeria and among Iranians (both in the diaspora and in Iran), and more are developing in about half a dozen other countries.

Despite the trend towards multi-faith tolerance and a fear of causing offence by witnessing in EuNAPa cultures, this is not the attitude of the AfAsLA Church. Passionate prayer and vigorous witness are achieving significant results. The present turmoil in the Muslim world and the many means now available for outreach (through the internet, satellite television and radio and by mobile phone as well as face-to-face) have increased the response in even the most geographically isolated parts of that world. There is unprecedented openness to the Gospel among Muslims, despite the negatives.

Fig 3.25 shows the 15 main "affinity blocs" of peoples and languages in the world. Each of the pies (which represent also the respective diasporas on other continents[18]) shows the proportion of indigenous Muslims and Christans in its bloc. It is notable that in the seven blocs with substantial numbers of Muslims, only the Iranian-Median and Turkic blocs contain very few indigenous Christians. There are likely to be political and even military confrontations between Muslim and "Christian" components of most of these blocs. True Christians long for the freedom and opportunity to share the Gospel of Christ and to see the Church grow among each people group, Muslim ones too. There are 1,990 people- and language-groups in the world that are 50% or more Muslim. Of these, 281 are entirely Muslim, and in many cases little effort is currently being made to bring the Gospel to them. Of the 1,193 that are 95% or more Muslim, 447 (with a total population in 2008 of 857 million) are less than 0.1% Christian.[19]

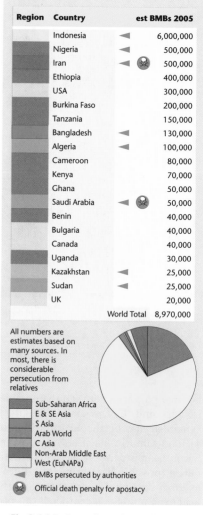

Region	Country			est BMBs 2005
	Indonesia	◄		6,000,000
	Nigeria	◄		500,000
	Iran	◄	☠	500,000
	Ethiopia			400,000
	USA			300,000
	Burkina Faso			200,000
	Tanzania			150,000
	Bangladesh	◄		130,000
	Algeria	◄		100,000
	Cameroon			80,000
	Kenya			70,000
	Ghana			50,000
	Saudi Arabia	◄	☠	50,000
	Benin			40,000
	Bulgaria			40,000
	Canada			40,000
	Uganda			30,000
	Kazakhstan	◄		25,000
	Sudan	◄		25,000
	UK			20,000
			World Total	8,970,000

All numbers are estimates based on many sources. In most, there is considerable persecution from relatives

- Sub-Saharan Africa
- E & SE Asia
- S Asia
- Arab World
- C Asia
- Non-Arab Middle East
- West (EuNAPa)

◄ BMBs persecuted by authorities

☠ Official death penalty for apostasy

Fig 3.24 *Estimated numbers of believers from a Muslim background (BMBs) in 2005*

Burning Questions

▲ Are Muslims too hard for the Gospel?

No! They, too, have a right to hear of the free salvation that Jesus offers. How can we reach these people—some of whom are the least evangelized on earth? And how can we publicize their need in our churches?

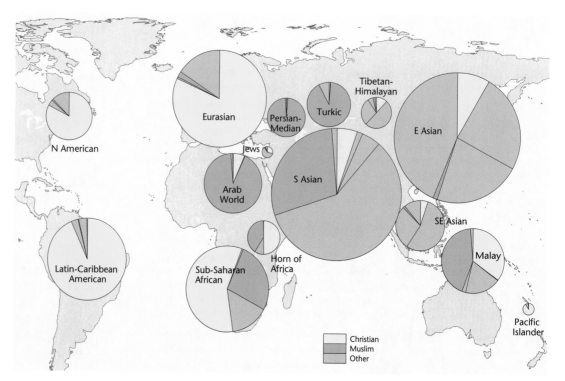

N American

Eurasian

Persian-Median

Turkic

Tibetan-Himalayan

E Asian

Jews

Arab World

S Asian

SE Asian

Malay

Latin-Caribbean American

Sub-Saharan African

Horn of Africa

Pacific Islander

- Christian
- Muslim
- Other

Fig 3.25 *The evangelization of the Muslim world*

The Distribution of Hindus in S Asia

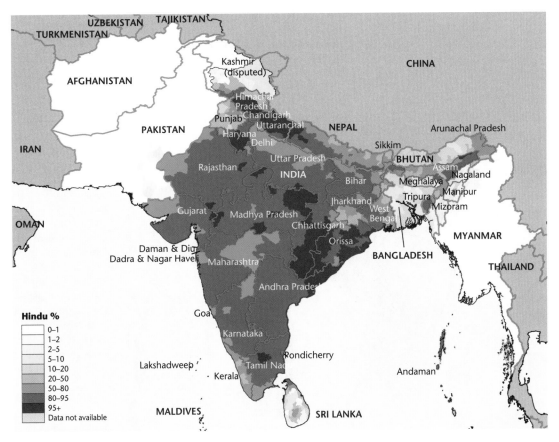

The global spread of Hinduism

In Fig 3.26 below, on this page, the pie chart represents the three countries with the largest Hindu populations and the bars represent the 17 countries with the next-largest. Only three have a Hindu majority: India, Nepal and Mauritius. All the other countries are coloured according to the majority religion. The nationality of the Hindus is shown beside the bars.

When evaluating Hinduism in the 21st Century, it is important to note:

▲ India's growing population, economy and influence as a functioning democracy ensure a crucial role for that country and its majority religion.

▲ The ideas of Hinduism have had and will continue to have wide acceptance and global influence despite their ethnic origins.[20]

▲ There has been an erosion of tolerance among Hindus, with the rise of *Hindutva* (religious nationalism) and increasing oppression of other religious minorities such as Muslims and Christians.

▲ There are likely to be major upheavals and defections to other religions as Dalits and low-caste Hindus increasingly reject social discrimination and poverty.

Shrine, India (photo by PJK)

Food for Thought

India's population is projected to overtake that of China in 2029. Economic development and growing wealth alongside massive poverty and deprivation will impact every aspect of India's life. Changes in religious affiliation will be more likely in India than in any other part of the world.

▲ Which faith is best placed to gain from these upheavals—will it be Buddhism, Islam or Christianity?

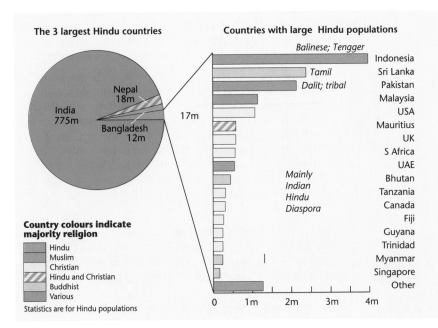

Fig 3.26 *Hindus around the world*

The Languages of the Hindu World

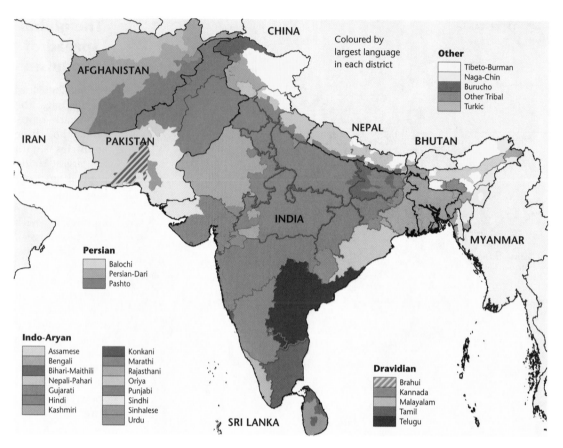

Coloured by largest language in each district

Other
- Tibeto-Burman
- Naga-Chin
- Burucho
- Other Tribal
- Turkic

Persian
- Balochi
- Persian-Dari
- Pashto

Indo-Aryan
- Assamese
- Bengali
- Bihari-Maithili
- Nepali-Pahari
- Gujarati
- Hindi
- Kashmiri
- Konkani
- Marathi
- Rajasthani
- Oriya
- Punjabi
- Sindhi
- Sinhalese
- Urdu

Dravidian
- Brahui
- Kannada
- Malayalam
- Tamil
- Telugu

Total living languages	
India	387
Nepal	120
Pakistan	69
Afghanistan	45
Bangladesh	38
Bhutan	24

This map shows the living languages that are spoken in S Asian countries (some in more than one country). These have been grouped into 28 related people/ language clusters (by colour) and into four larger "affinity blocs" (by legend category). Each different culture has contributed to the present diversity of the region and of Hinduism itself.

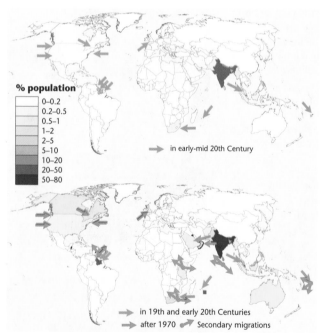

% population
- 0–0.2
- 0.2–0.5
- 0.5–1
- 1–2
- 2–5
- 5–10
- 10–20
- 20–50
- 50–80

→ in early-mid 20th Century

→ in 19th and early 20th Centuries
→ after 1970   ➤ Secondary migrations

Fig 3.27 *The spread of Hindus around the world, 1900–2050*

The S Asian diaspora, 1900–2050

Fig 3.27 shows the historic and future changes in the distribution of Hindus around the world.

Hinduism was once prominent across the whole of S Asia and much of SE Asia. By 1800, however, it was confined to the Indian subcontinent and the Indonesian islands of Bali and E Java. As European imperial control expanded during the 19th Century, many Indians were recruited first as indentured labour and then as settlers around the world. (This is indicated on the first map by the arrows.) Most were Hindus, though some were Muslims. They became the major component of today's influential world-wide S Asian diaspora.

The latter part of the 20th Century saw the beginning of migration of S Asians to the West both from diaspora communities and from S Asia itself. Most of these were Hindus. Generally, people from Hindu communities were more successful in integrating into the host cultures and prospering economically than their Muslim counterparts. Many Hindu S Asians have become well known in the West as academics, engineers, business people or authors or have distinguished themselves in other professions.

Food for Thought

S Asia has the highest concentration of unevangelized individuals on earth. Christians have multiplied in only a few hundred of its thousands of cultures. The 22 million-strong S Asian diaspora has enjoyed success in almost every profession, and 10% are now Christian.[21] Many still retain links with unevangelized cultures in S Asia. The remarkable Lambadi-Rom ("Gypsy") migrations westwards a millennium ago mean that there are 10 million Roma world-wide. Of these, 50% are Christian; but of the 3 million who live in S Asia, only 0.2% are.

▲ How can the diaspora effectively help in evangelizing the whole of S Asia?

The Hindu caste system

There are estimated to be over 6,400 castes in Indian society. Socially, the caste which someone belongs to is more important than the language they speak. In Fig 3.28, the traditional caste names are shown on the right. (The Dalits—formerly "Outcastes" or "Untouchables"—and tribal peoples are outside the caste system.) On the left is a more modern, economic categorization: India's government divides its population into "forward" and "backward" castes. Its middle classes are largely in the so-called "creamy-layer" forward (Sudra) castes, while the Dalits and the tribal peoples are now regarded as "scheduled" castes.

The caste system is controversial. Discrimination on grounds of caste is illegal but socially pervasive. It is a form of religious and social apartheid and it is crippling India's development. This could become an explosive issue as the oppressed increasingly rebel against the strictures it imposes on 60% of the country's population. Urbanization and industrialization as well as democracy, education and law are all helping to break down the barriers of casteism, but what one might call "Hinduist" nationalism seeks to perpetuate this iniquitous system.

Buddhism and Christianity first, and then Islam and Sikhism, all tried to abolish the caste system, but with mixed success. Most of the converts to these religions have come from the lower sections of society (as illustrated for Muslims and Christians in the diagram).

Hindus and Muslims

The history of conflict between Hindus and Muslims is long and sad. The British Raj supplanted a Muslim Mughal dynasty of Persian-Mongol origin that had lasted for centuries (see pp44–54). By that point, a third of the population of S Asia was Muslim. In 1947, at Muslim insistence, India was partitioned with the formation of Pakistan, which was then itself divided with the secession of Bangladesh in 1971. The unresolved issue of Hindu-ruled but Muslim-majority Kashmir has caused over 60 years of conflict and three wars. Internally in India confrontations continue between Hindus and members of the Muslim minority—exacerbated by the rise of both extremist *Hindutva* and Islamism.

Modern political / Traditional

Fig 3.28 *The Hindu caste structure*

Temple, India (photo by PJK)

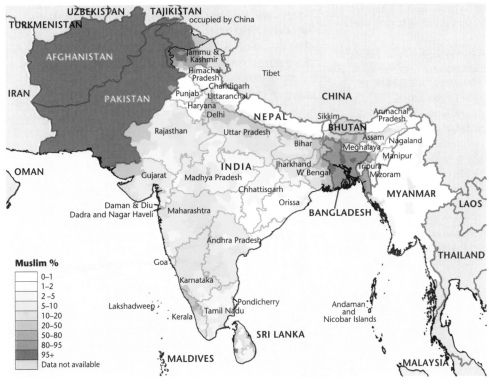

Fig 3.29 *The distribution of Muslims in S Asia*

Burning Questions for Today

What is India's future? At one extreme, it could be a thriving democracy and economic powerhouse; at the other, Hindu nationalism could turn it fascist, and riven with conflicts over caste and religion.

▲ How should Christians handle the issue of caste? It cannot be ignored socially, and must be taken into account in outreach.

▲ Should it be condoned and perpetuated in church planting and leadership?

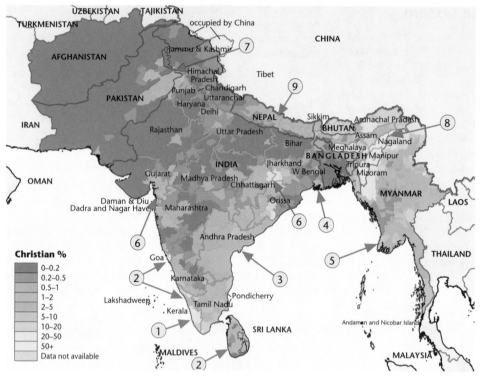

Fig 3.30 *The distribution of Christians in S Asia*

1 S India—Eastern and Syrian, AD 30 to the present

2 SW India, Sri Lanka—Catholics, 16th Century onwards

3 Sri Lanka and SE India—Protestants from the 17th and 18th Centuries respectively

4 William Carey to Bengal in 1793 and then the whole region

5 Adoniram Judson to Burma in 1813; ultimately, mass movements among the hill tribes

6 The tribal peoples of Orissa, Jharkhand, Madhya Pradesh, Meghalaya and Gujarat from the mid 19th Century onwards

7 Punjab: mass movement of low-castes to Christianity, 1870–1914

8 The hill tribes of Assam (now the separate, Christian-majority states of Meghalaya, Nagaland and Mizoram) from the late 19th Century. Nagaland is 90% Christian and 75% Baptist. Mizoram, largely Presbyterian and Baptist, is the most evangelical state in the world.

9 Nepal: see below

Hindus and Christians

Christianity has been indigenous to India for 2,000 years, but had become culturally isolated in the south-west. Outreach in many parts of the subcontinent was renewed by Catholics in the 16th Century, followed by Protestants in the 18th. As Fig 3:30 shows, the response was strongest among low-caste Hindus, Dalits and tribal animists.

The future of Hinduism is illustrated in Fig 3.31. The six countries that comprise the Hindu heartlands are represented. The likely changes in the percentages of Hindus between 1900 and 2050 are given in relation to the year 2000.

▲ India: The erosion of the Hindu component of the population is significant, with losses first to Islam and then to Buddhism and Christianity. The Dalit/low-caste movement is likely to lead to further losses from Hinduism according to the official statistics for Hinduism.[22]

▲ Nepal: Since 1990, Hinduism has lost ground to both Maoist Communism and Christianity. The Church has grown from virtually nothing in 1950 to 700,000-strong in 2005 and to 850,000 in 2010. This growth is likely to continue.

▲ Mauritius, the only Hindu-majority country outside of S Asia: Little change, apart from some probable small losses to Christianity

▲ Sri Lanka: The generation-long war between the Tamil minority and the Sinhala majority has caused perhaps 800,000 Tamils to flee to countries around the world. The Sinhala are mostly Buddhists, the Tamils mostly Hindus, but there are Christians in both communities.

▲ Bhutan: The number of Hindus increased through immigration until the 1990s, when the Buddhist government began to eject Hindus of Indian and Nepali origin in large numbers.

▲ Bangladesh: Many Hindus fled to India between 1947 and 1980. There is now a relatively stable, if marginalized, community in this Muslim-majority country.

Burning Questions

There could be a dramatic mass movement of Dalits and low-caste Hindus to Christianity over the next few decades.

▲ Are the churches ready to welcome and disciple such a movement?

▲ Would this eventuality hinder outreach to the (far less evangelized) middle and upper castes?

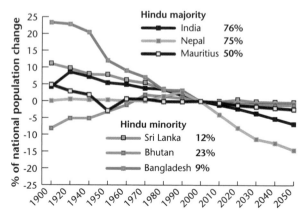

Fig 3.31 *The growth and decline of Hinduism in the Hindu heartlands*

The Distribution of Buddhists by Ethnicity and Language

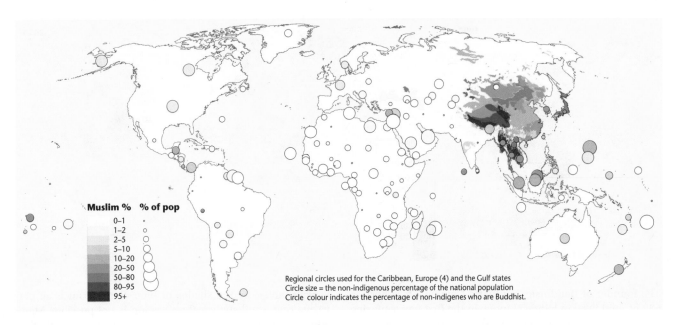

The map shows the global distribution of Buddhists by ethnicity and language.[23] Non-indigenous Buddhists in most countries are represented by circles. Here are some observations:

▲ Buddhists comprise a large majority only among most Tibetan and many SE Asian peoples, the Bhama and Shan of Myanmar and the Sinhala in Sri Lanka.

▲ Large proportions of major Buddhist-influenced peoples, such as the Chinese, Koreans, Mongolians and Japanese, also follow other, indigenous religions or are non-religious.

▲ The great majority of Buddhists in other parts of the world are migrants; most of them are Chinese or, less commonly, Korean, Vietnamese, Laotian or Japanese.

The main branches of Buddhism

Theravada: Practised mainly in SE Asia and Sri Lanka, it is often considered to be the "purest" form of Buddhism. It emphasizes an individual search for enlightenment, and makes no offer of forgiveness for bad karma (the cumulative effects of good and bad actions that determine someone's destiny).

Mahayana: Practised mainly in China, Korea and Japan, it emphasizes universal compassion and the selfless ideal of the bodhisattva, and is more communal in its search for enlightenment. There

is a wide range of different sects and schools of thought.

Lamaism, Vajrayana or *Tantric Buddhism:* This is broadly of the Mahayana branch but involves an array of spiritual techniques designed to enhance Buddhist practice. Much of Lamaism derived from the earlier Bön religion which was absorbed into Buddhism. It is practised today mainly in Tibet, Nepal, Bhutan, Mongolia, Kalmykia (in Russia), areas of India and, to a more limited extent, China and Japan. Bön is characterized by the worship of demons and angry, demanding deities.

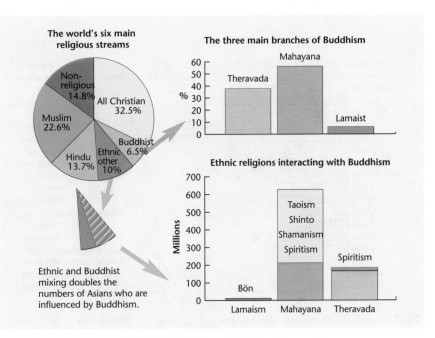

Fig 3.32 *Buddhism and ethnic religions*

The Spread of Buddhists Around the World, 1900–2050

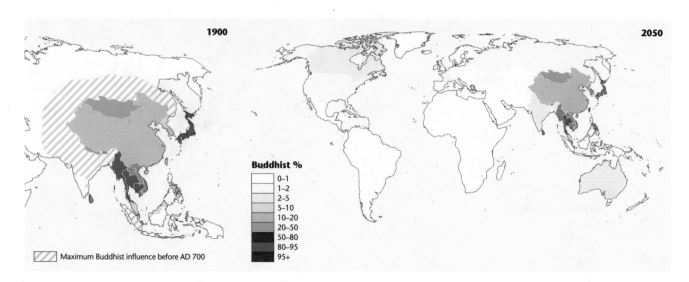

1900   2050

Buddhist %
- 0–1
- 1–2
- 2–5
- 5–10
- 10–20
- 20–50
- 50–80
- 80–95
- 95+

Maximum Buddhist influence before AD 700

The founder of Buddhism, Siddharta Gautama, was born in 632 BC and lived in Hindu N India. In the first few centuries, his teachings spread to much of Asia. The first map shows the area where Buddhism was most influential before AD 700. A slow decline set in with the advent of Islam and the rejuvenation of Hinduism, and has continued with more recent losses also to atheism/secularism and Christianity. By 1900, almost all Buddhists lived in the countries of E and SE Asia.

What does the future hold? There are likely to be gains, with many syncretists in E Asia becoming more firmly Buddhist in profession and millions of Dalit and low-caste Indians embracing Buddhism in protest against Hindu casteism. There will probably be significant Christian growth among some Buddhist peoples—especially the Chinese, Mongolians, Cambodians and Vietnamese—but less markedly among the Thai, Japanese, Sinhala and Bhama.

Buddhist syncretism

The bars in Fig 3.33 represent the 20 most Buddhist countries by percentage of population in 2000. Many Buddhists are at the same time also spiritists, Shintoists, Taoists etc, and this is represented by the shades of blue. Syncretism is so pervasive that a full statistical separation is not possible. Many adherents of ethnic religions could well also be classified as Buddhists.

Buddhist people groups

The three branches of Buddhism are compared in the bar chart in Fig 3.34 on page 85, both by absolute numbers of followers and by the number of people groups regarded as following them.[25] Most of the Mahayana people groups are large and are spread across many countries. It is striking how few people comparatively follow Lamaist Buddhism, but how many small people groups they represent.

The pie charts under the bars in Fig 3.34 represent the whole populations of these Buddhist-influenced people groups but give a breakdown of their religious affiliations. The Mahayana peoples, which include the Chinese, are the ones with the smallest number of Buddhists overall and the largest number of Christians. Most of the least-evangelized Buddhist people groups are Lamaist.

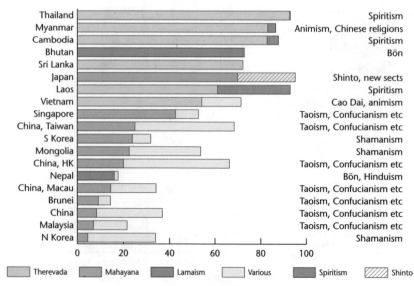

Country	Religion
Thailand	Spiritism
Myanmar	Animism, Chinese religions
Cambodia	Spiritism
Bhutan	Bön
Sri Lanka	
Japan	Shinto, new sects
Laos	Spiritism
Vietnam	Cao Dai, animism
Singapore	Taoism, Confucianism etc
China, Taiwan	Taoism, Confucianism etc
S Korea	Shamanism
Mongolia	Shamanism
China, HK	Taoism, Confucianism etc
Nepal	Bön, Hinduism
China, Macau	Taoism, Confucianism etc
Brunei	Taoism, Confucianism etc
China	Taoism, Confucianism etc
Malaysia	Taoism, Confucianism etc
N Korea	Shamanism

Legend: Therevada | Mahayana | Lamaism | Various | Spiritism | Shinto

Fig 3.33 *The 20 most Buddhist countries in 2000*

Food for Thought

By 2050, there are likely to be more Christians than Buddhists in both China and Korea and they will then comprise a large part of the global missionary force. They will contribute much, but from a very different, Buddhist-influenced perspective and experience of the Gospel.

▲ How can we all best adapt and contribute, in a united way, to the task of world evangelization?

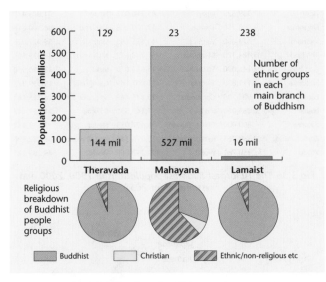

Fig 3.34 *The three Buddhist people groups*

Burning Question

Fig 3.35 below reveals a wide range of peoples. A few of these are now mostly Christian and many have experienced significant spiritual breakthroughs and now have strong churches, but there remain 616 peoples and people groups out of a total of 1,316 in these ABs that are less than 2% Christian. The growing Chinese Church could and should reach the less-evangelized minorities, but (as with any culturally and politically dominant people-group) there are high barriers of past hostilities and present cultural insensitivities the Chinese have to surmount before their message will be accepted among ethnic minorities in their region. Their evangelization has to be a task for the worldwide Church.

▲ Who is willing to take the Good News to these people groups?

Buddhist affinity blocs

Fig 3.35 shows the statistics I have used.[26] Over 96% of all Buddhists are located in three "affinity blocs" (ABs), though many of the peoples within these affinity blocs are not Buddhist. The pies on the map are proportionate to the size of each population and also show their religious composition. The ABs are further subdivided into 35 "people clusters" (PCs), which are represented in the three bar charts alongside. The Buddhist, Christian and "other religions" compo-

nents of each are shown, with the size of the population in millions beside each bar. The figure also gives the number of peoples, Buddhist and non-Buddhist in each affinity bloc, followed by the number of these that are less than 2% Christian. (Below 2%, there are unlikely to be the Christian resources within a people group to evangelize it without outside help.) It is challenging to see how many people clusters and people groups are still largely unevangelized.

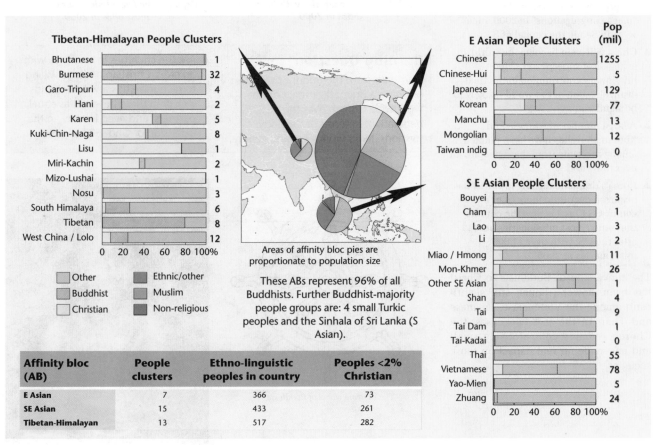

Affinity bloc (AB)	People clusters	Ethno-linguistic peoples in country	Peoples <2% Christian
E Asian	7	366	73
SE Asian	15	433	261
Tibetan-Himalayan	13	517	282

Fig 3.35 *The three Buddhist affinity blocs and their associated people clusters*

The future of Buddhism

Fig 3.36 compares the 10 most Buddhist countries in 1900, 2000 and 2050. A number of comments are relevant:

▲ The "geography" of Buddhism is unlikely to change radically over the next four decades.

▲ The rapidly falling birth rate in E Asia and losses to Christianity and secularism will ensure an overall decline of Buddhists as a percentage of the global population.

▲ Comparatively few Chinese profess to be Buddhists. It is likely that many adherents of traditional religions will become more openly Buddhist. Many Chinese are secular, and increasing numbers are becoming Christians.

▲ The spread of Buddhism in other countries will mainly be the result of immigration from the Buddhist heartlands.

▲ The growing interest in Buddhism in EuNAPa cultures is unlikely to yield many actual converts.

Country	1900	Country	2000	Country	2050
China	59,594,242	China	97,642,594	China	177,983,391
Japan	42,359,625	Japan	85,316,073	Japan	71,806,477
Myanmar	9,060,150	Thailand	57,709,008	Thailand	66,500,816
Vietnam	7,623,000	Vietnam	43,835,665	Vietnam	59,027,026
Thailand	5,484,320	Myanmar	41,748,872	Myanmar	48,379,564
Cambodia	2,145,000	Sri Lanka	13,532,070	India	23,890,560
Sri Lanka	2,111,879	S Korea	11,007,149	Cambodia	19,359,323
Laos	904,500	Cambodia	10,831,449	Sri Lanka	16,525,183
Nepal	885,000	India	7,147,590	S Korea	11,157,147
S Korea	800,000	China, Taiwan	5,427,053	Nepal	7,573,432
Rest of world	2,383,065	Rest of world	18,095,346	Rest of world	43,082,996
World	133,350,781	World	392,292,869	World	545,285,915

Fig 3.36 *The 10 largest Buddhist populations in 1900, 2000 and estimated for 2050*

Believers from a Buddhist background (BBBs)

Estimates of the number of BBBs have been made for each country.[27] Fig 3.37 illustrates the 10 countries with the greatest number. It is clear that the great majority of BBBs are Chinese. The ethnicity of these believers is shown in Fig 3.38. Most of them belong to one of two people clusters, the Chinese and the Koreans. In the latter part of the 20th Century, the Church grew dramatically among these two PCs. This is the evidence:

▲ The number and size of their congregations. Of the world's 10 "mega-congregations" in 2000, nine were in Seoul, the capital of S Korea.

▲ China will soon become the world's evangelical superpower.[28] Its missionary contribution to the final evangelization of the world is likely to be significant.

▲ A large number of Chinese and Korean churches have been planted among migrants from these peoples all over the world.

▲ Korea's dramatic turning to Christ has occurred over little more than a century. S Korea is now the country that sends most missionaries abroad after the US, with over 13,000 missionaries in 2008.

The conversion of Buddhists to Christ has been slower (though still significant) among the Vietnamese, Japanese and Thai. In the last two cases, the Church remains comparatively small and has made no real impact on those societies.

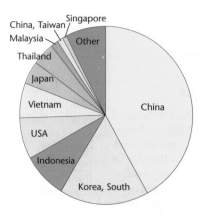

Fig 3.37 *The 10 countries with the most BBBs in 2000*

Estimated total in 2000: 23,800,000

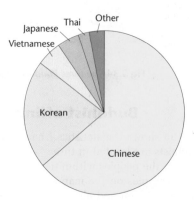

Estimated total in 2000: 23.8 million
Possible total including ethnic religions influenced by Buddhism: 60 million

Fig 3.38 *The five ethnic groups with the most BBBs in 2000*

Burning Question

Christians from the Buddhist world will have a dramatic impact on the worldwide Church over the next generation, in terms of theology, missions, faith, worldview and culture.

▲ Are the churches in countries with an older Christian heritage willing to recognize this and adapt and welcome these believers as equal partners, and even leaders, in the extension of God's Kingdom?

The Dharma wheel of Buddhism

Thai Buddha (photo by PJK)

The Distribution of Adherents of Ethnic and Other Religions by Ethnicity and Language

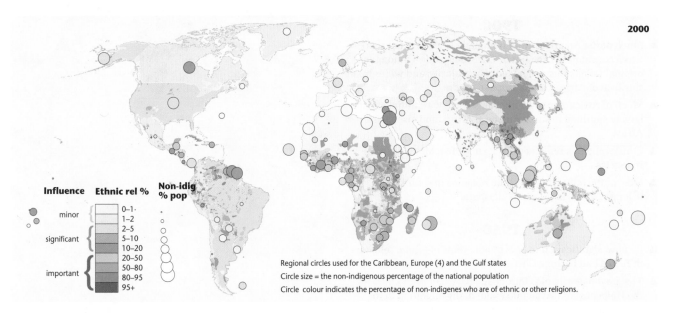

2000

Influence | Ethnic rel % | Non-idig % pop

minor: 0–1·, 1–2
significant: 2–5, 5–10, 10–20
important: 20–50, 50–80, 80–95, 95+

Regional circles used for the Caribbean, Europe (4) and the Gulf states
Circle size = the non-indigenous percentage of the national population
Circle colour indicates the percentage of non-indigenes who are of ethnic or other religions.

All other religions are grouped together in this book in a single category, with four major subgroups:

▲ *Traditional ethnic religions:* usually unwritten beliefs within individual cultures. These include animism, spiritism, ancestor worship, voodoo, shamanism etc.

▲ *Literate ethnic religions,* which include Jainism in India, Sikhism among Panjabis, Taoism and Confucianism in China, Shinto in Japan, Zoroastrianism/Parseeism in Iran and India etc.

▲ *Smaller world religions* such as Baha'i and Judaism

▲ *New religions* such as Sokka Gakkai in Japan, New Age and scientology in the West and Cao Dai in Vietnam

None of these religions has the mechanism for widespread proselytization and they are all unlikely to inaugurate major changes in the world over the coming decades.

The map above shows the distribution by percentage of ethnic religions across the world by ethno-linguistic people group in 2000. Note the following:

▲ The continued resilience of traditional ethnic religions in the Americas and Africa, despite massive losses—especially to Christianity

▲ The influence of Chinese religions even after 60 years of Communist rule. Outside Africa, most non-indigenous communities with a high percentage of adherents of ethnic religions are Chinese (indicated by circles on the map).

▲ The prominent circle representing immigrant Jews in Israel/Palestine

The "ethnic/other" category of religions is further subdivided by type and population. Although adherents of ethnic religions comprise just 10% of the world's population, syncretism is widespread in all religious streams. This includes the Christo-paganism prevalent in Latin America,[29] the notional Christianity of Europe,[30] some African Independent churches that incorporate ancestor worship,[31] spiritism in Thai Buddhism and Bön in Tibetan Buddhism, folk Islam and the religion of the Yezidis of Iraq, the Druze of Lebanon and the Ahmaddiya of Pakistan on the fringes of Islam. That syncretism may include 30–50% of humankind.

Food for Thought

The followers of ethnic religions have been the most fruitful source of new converts to Christianity for two millennia, and yet these religions have also often altered the biblical content of Christianity itself wherever the Church has taken root.

▲ The cultural adaptation and contextualization of the Gospel is biblical, but how far have our own and other cultures diluted or distorted it in church life and witness?

N African mosque (photo by E Daymond)

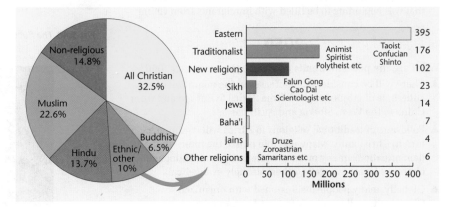

Non-religious 14.8%
All Christian 32.5%
Muslim 22.6%
Hindu 13.7%
Ethnic/other 10%
Buddhist 6.5%

	Millions
Eastern	395
Traditionalist — Animist Spiritist Polytheist etc / Taoist Confucian Shinto	176
New religions	102
Sikh — Falun Gong Cao Dai Scientologist etc	23
Jews	14
Baha'i	7
Jains	4
Other religions — Druze Zoroastrian Samaritans etc	6

0 50 100 150 200 250 300 350 400
Millions

Fig 3.39 *Ethnic and other religions in 2010*

The series of four maps shows the dramatic decline in adherence to ethnic religions worldwide likely over the 150 years from 1900 to 2050. These are some of the more significant factors over the half century leading up to the year of each map.

1900

▲ Much of the Americas were nominally Christian, but there was a considerable amount of Christo-paganism among the original indigenous and mixed-race majority, and widespread spiritism of African and European origin.

▲ Much of Africa remained unevangelized, with initial efforts largely confined to southern and E Africa, and also coastal W Africa.

▲ Ethnic religions remained strong in China, Mongolia and Indonesia.

▲ Most of the adherents of ethnic religions in C Europe belonged to the large Jewish diaspora.

1950

▲ By now, significant numbers of adherents of ethnic religions in Africa had become Christians.

▲ The great majority of C European Jewry had been killed in the Holocaust or driven into exile—many migrating to the Anglophone world or to the new state of Israel.

2000

By now, changes were radical—most of the peoples that once followed traditional ethnic religions had become Christians, in one of the greatest mass movements to Christ ever seen. The most marked declines in adherence to ethnic religions were in:

▲ Africa, with a post-independence surge after 1960

▲ China, where many Taoists either forsook religion altogether or became Christians

▲ Indonesia and the Sahel, where many people embraced Islam

▲ Latin America, where many tribal peoples in Mexico and C America and many of the Highland Quechua and Aymara peoples of the Andean altiplano became evangelical Christians

However, ethnic religions spread:

▲ in Brazil, with the growth in popularity of spiritism

▲ in the Americas generally, with a resurgence of pre-Christian belief systems

▲ with the migration of Asians to N America and (to a lesser extent) Europe

▲ in Russian Siberia, where large-scale migration westwards as well as the general decline in birth rates had left a vacuum that was beginning to be filled with immigrants from China

2050

What are the possible trends as we progress towards 2050?

▲ There will be considerable increases in the migration of adherents of ethnic religions from Africa to Europe and from China to the West, Siberia and Australasia.

▲ Followers of traditional religions in Africa will continue to turn to Christianity. Many will join one of the international denominations; many more will join indigenous Independent churches (some syncretic, others strongly evangelical).

▲ Globally, many people disillusioned with organized Christianity will turn back to pre-Christian religions or to new religious movements.

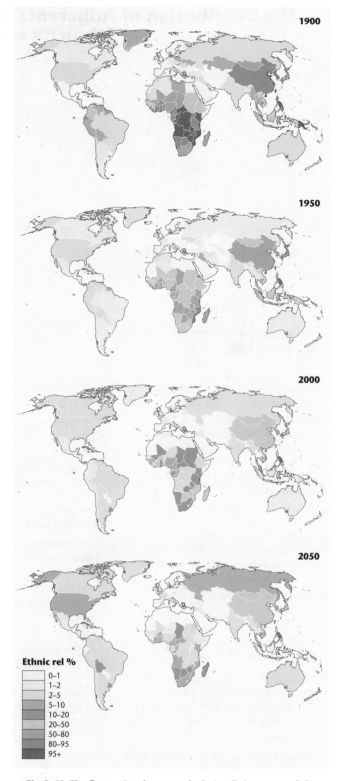

1900

1950

2000

2050

Ethnic rel %

0–1
1–2
2–5
5–10
10–20
20–50
50–80
80–95
95+

Fig 3.40 *The fluctuating fortunes of ethnic religions around the world*

N African shrine (photo by E Daymond)

The future of these other religions

For the last hundred years, these "other" religions have been rapidly losing ground to other belief systems, and in particular to Christianity, secularism and Islam. (The one steep rise shown in Fig 3.41 relates to the measure of religious freedom in China that followed the failure of Mao's Cultural Revolution in 1980, when many Chinese openly embraced the beliefs of their ancestors.) That decline is likely to continue for the foreseeable future.

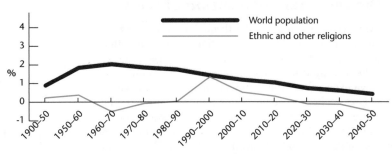

Fig 3.41 *The average annual rate of increase of adherents of ethnic and other religions, 1900–2050*

Sikhism

Sikhs believe:[32]

▲ that there is one God, the Creator, a God of love and not fear who is our Father, Mother, Brother, Husband and Friend

▲ in the brotherhood of humankind, rejecting all distinctions of race, creed, caste and gender. Sikhism is practised almost exclusively by Panjabi Indians, but there are Sikh communities world-wide.

▲ that all religions are good, and all holy books should be read. Sikhism is not the only or the final way, and Sikhs do not proselytize

▲ that morality is a matter of honesty, kindness, almsgiving and commitment to community service

▲ that salvation is through meditation, good works and an eventual merging of each person into God. Jesus is honoured, but is not regarded either as God or as our Saviour from sin.

Sikhs reject idolatry, superstition, fasting, pilgrimage, hierarchy, asceticism, holy war and any concept of a literal heaven or hell.

Baha'i

▲ The world's second most widespread religion, after Christianity

▲ Worldwide, it has 6.8 million adherents in 190 countries.[33] Note its geographical spread in the charts. The small Pacific republic of Nauru is 6.8% Baha'i.

▲ Founded by Baha'ullah in Iran in 1844, much influenced by Shi'a Islam and regarded by some as a Muslim sect

▲ Its core beliefs are in the unity of God, of all religions and of humankind. It is strongly ethical and egalitarian, condemning discrimination, prejudice and war.

▲ Severely persecuted in some Muslim countries—especially Iran!

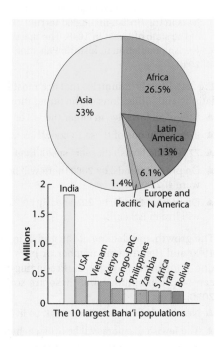

Fig 3.43 *The geographical spread of Baha'i*

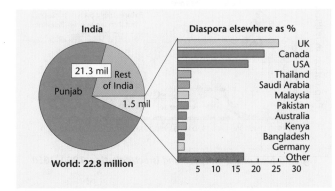

Fig 3.42 *The 12 countries with the largest Sikh populations*

The Khanda symbol of Sikhism

The regional distribution of Jews

The Jews have been controversial throughout their long history. For millennia they have been victims of discrimination, persecution, forced conversion, pogroms and genocide[34]—and in the last hundred years Zionism and the founding of Israel have exacerbated this. They are loved by many Christians as God's "chosen people" and hated by many nationalists, Communists and Muslims and in some quarters of the Christian Church. Their future and that of humankind are intimately linked by political events in the Middle East and by eschatology.[35] Fig 3.44 shows some of the regional fluctuations in Jewish populations in the 20th Century.

▲ Well over half of the Jews of Continental Europe—up to 6 million people—were killed by the Nazis and their allies between 1935 and 1945.

▲ The Anglophone world's Jewish population was massively swollen by refugees from Europe and the Middle East.

▲ The Jewish population of the Soviet Union declined under Communism, but this only accelerated after the collapse of the Soviet Union in 1989 onwards, with many migrating to Israel and the West.

▲ Almost the entire population of Jews in N Africa emigrated during the 1960s to France or Israel.

▲ The controversial emergence after the First World War of a "national home" for the Jews in the British-mandated territory of Palestine led ultimately to the foundation of the state of Israel in 1948. The massive immigration of Jews (*aliyah*) increased the Jewish population in historic Palestine from 55,000 in 1900 to almost 5 million in 2010.

Fig 3.45 lists the countries that are most important for Jews, with their Jewish populations and indications of the population trends.[36] Here are a few salient ponts:

▲ 81% of all Jews live in either the US or Israel.

▲ 97% live in one of these 13 countries.

▲ 77% of the Jewish diaspora speak English.

▲ On present trends, by 2080 there will be very few Jews left in Russia. In 2001, there were 462,000.

▲ On present trends, by 2020 nearly 60% of all Jewish children will live in Israel.

The growth and decline of the global Jewish population after 1900 and the growing number of Jews living in Israel/Palestine are shown in Fig 3.46. Predicting future developments can be presumptuous, but these are some possible trends to 2050:

▲ Nearly two-thirds of all Jews will be living in Israel.

▲ The Jewish diaspora will be overwhelmingly Anglophone.

▲ It is unlikely that the conflict between Palestinian Arabs and Israeli Jews will be resolved politically with an equitable compromise, and the growing hatred between the two populations is likely only to escalate further.

▲ The conflict in Israel/Palestine will continue to poison diplomatic efforts for a wider peace in the region and will polarize Muslims and Christians, the Middle East and the West.

Tourists at the Wailing Wall in Jerusalem (photo by C Pantridge)

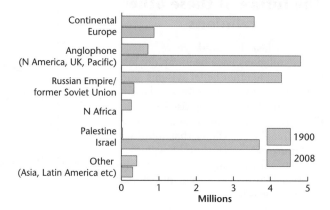

Fig 3.44 *The regional distribution of Jews in 1900 and 2008*

Rank	Country 2006	Populations
1	Israel	5,313,800
2	USA	5,275,000
3	France	491,500
4	Canada	373,500
5	UK	297,000
6	Russia	228,000
7	Argentina	184,500
8	Germany	118,000
9	Australia	103,000
10	Brazil	96,500
11	Ukraine	80,000
12	S Africa	72,000
13	Hungary	49,700

increase   slow increase   rapid increase

Fig 3.45 *The 13 countries with the largest Jewish populations*

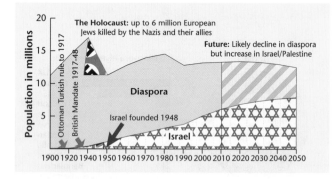

Fig 3.46 *Jews of the diaspora and Israel/Palestine, 1900–2050*

Food for Thought

Paul declared in Romans 1:16 that the Gospel is "the power of God for salvation to everyone who has faith, to the Jew first and also to the Greek".

▲ Was this a statement of fact for his day only, or has it an application to mission work today?

▲ How should Christians relate to Jews today in the political turmoil of the Middle East, in theology, in witness and in eschatological expectation?

▲ Will there be a day when the Jews as a nation will all be converted (Romans 11:26)?

The contribution of Jews to world culture

Despite anti-Jewish prejudice and the traditional caricature of them as mercenary and avaricious, even plotting world domination, Jews have contributed to humankind out of all proportion to their numbers. Their race was the progenitor of the great monotheistic religions, Judaism, Christianity and Islam, whose followers today comprise well over half the world's population. The Son of God Himself became a Jew. Consider Fig 3.47. The Swedish industrialist Alfred Nobel established a fund in 1895 to award prizes in five categories, for physics, chemistry, medicine, literature and peace, and between 1901 and 2007 there were 750 recipients. This composite pie chart breaks down the distribution of the awards over that period in two ways.

By language (outer circle): The prizes originated in Europe and their distribution reflects the dominance of European languages in science and culture in the 20th Century. Over half of the recipients were English-speakers, and most of the remainder spoke another European language as their mother tongue.

By religion (inner circle). Here, Nobel-Prize-winners are divided into Jews, Muslims and others. Secular and religious Jews, who comprised just 0.2% of the world's population in 2007, had by then won nearly 22% (162) of all the prizes, while Muslims, who in 2007 represented 21% of humankind, had won just 1.2% (nine prizes). In the Middle Ages, of course, Muslims made major contributions to science, mathematics, medicine and the arts.

Jewish divisions and losses

There is no consensus about who qualifies as a Jew. Nearly half of all Jews are actually non-religious. Jews who convert to another religion are not considered to be Jews by the state of Israel, but are still regarded as Jews by most rabbis. Is the determining factor ethnicity, religion, culture or even shared suffering? What about Jews who become Christians? The status of Messianic Jews, who claim to be "completed" Jews who have found their Messiah in Jesus, is controversial.

The major cultural division is between the Ashkenazim (C and E European, 80%) and the Sephardim (originally from Spain, N Africa and Asia, 19%).

The major theological divisions are referred to on the left-hand side of the pie chart in Fig 3.48. Other forms of Judaism are losing ground both to a more legalistic Orthodox Judaism and to secularism.

If the global population of Jews in 1910 had continued to grow at the same rate as those of their host countries, today it would have been more than double the actual present figure of 13.4 million. The causes of the discrepancy are:

▲ The Holocaust of 1935–45; up to 6 million killed. By 2010, they and their descendants would have numbered some 7million.

▲ Assimilation—common in the West as Jews marry non-Jews and/or become secularized.

▲ Conversion—mainly to Christianity, more rarely to other religions. Some Jewish Christians maintain cultural links to Judaism as Messianic Jews.

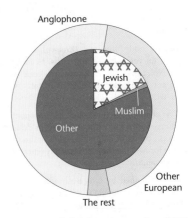

Fig 3.47 *Nobel-Prize-winners since 1901*

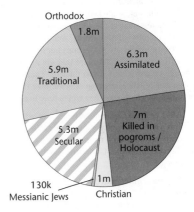

Jewish population in 2010:
Potential = 27.4 mil
Actual = 13.3 mil

Fig 3.48: *Jewish divisions and losses, 1935–2010*

The Temple Mount in Jerusalem, from the Jewish cemetery on the Mount of Olives (photo by C Pantridge)

Burning Questions

This concludes our brief survey of the five non-Christian religious streams. This represents the entire global population still to be brought to Christ. It is to these people that God is sending us as his Church. There are immense challenges, but there is also encouragement in current successes and in the expectation of a completed harvest.

▲ What is the Church in YOUR country contributing to this work of proclaiming the Gospel to all humankind and to all people who do not know Christ as Saviour—whether they are religious or not?

▲ What is YOUR local church doing in teaching, discipling, preparing, sending and supporting a new generation of workers for the task?

1. I include AfAsLA societies that have embraced European ideologies such as Marxism, materialist capitalism etc.

2. Barrett and Johnson's three-volume *World Christian Encyclopedia* of 2001 lists 19 main categories (vol 1, p4), the 270 larger religions (vol 2, pp5–7) and nearly 10,000 religions in total (vol 3, pp 551–612).

3. Try challenging the belief in the spontaneous emergence of life without intelligent design or demanding proof for natural selection as the source of all life forms! The response is usually emotive and not very scientific.

4. A term coined by Luis Bush around 1994 to denote the area of the globe with the greatest spiritual need. It lies between latitudes 10°N to 40°N and between the Atlantic and Pacific Oceans.

5. B Broomhall, *The Evangelization of the World* (London: China Inland Mission, 1887)

6. The research of SIL-WBT in analysing these languages is an arduous, continuing task. Global Mapping International (GMI) then mapped as polygons the home areas of these language communities for each country of the world. Another 779 language communities are indigenous but do not have a specific area polygon (because they are nomads or migrants or are widely disseminated). There are a further 3,365 listed language communities that are not indigenous to the country where they live.

7. After years of Communist tyranny in which all religions were vigorously suppressed, Muslim and Christian communities re-emerged. Albania's ties with Europe mean that Christians may now be in a slight majority.

8. Nigeria's independence in 1960 united the northern, feudal Muslim protectorate with the southern, Christianized colonies. The Muslims had used their freedom under British rule to extend their power over non-Muslim peoples and engineered a Muslim "majority" by manipulating census data. The Muslims have done everything possible to retain power in the face of a growing Christian majority. This has led to corruption, polarization and frequent assaults on Christians, as well as a violent and protracted civil war (see pp178–79).

9. The ISO 3166 Country Codes are widely used as abbreviations for email and the Internet addresses. A full list is available from http://www.theodora.com/country_digraphs.html

10. The term "Iron Curtain" was popularized in a famous speech by Winston Churchill in 1946: "From Stettin in the Baltic to Trieste in the Adriatic, an 'iron curtain' has descended across the Continent." It passed into popular use to refer to the borders of those regions of Europe and Asia controlled by the Soviet Union.

11. Muslim communities vary greatly in terms of where they originate from, where they prefer to settle—S Asians prefer the UK, N Africans France, Turks Germany etc—and how committed they are to their faith.

12. See note 6 above. This and subsequent religion/language maps are layered. The colour fill in the lower layer of this map is based on the percentage of the entire indigenous population of a country represented by Muslims (geographically polygonized and not). The colour fill in the upper layer represents all peoples within a country with a definite home-area polygon, with superimposed circles representing language communities not indigenous in origin. A few surprises and anomalies are explained in the fuller presentation in the PowerPoint notes on the DVD.

13. "Islamic fundamentalism" and "political Islam" are less appropriate synonyms. The anger of Islamists is directed not only against the West and its perceived evils but also against most Muslim governments, whose leaders are often regarded as *kufr* (unbelievers), and any territory that was once dominated by Islam but is no longer (such as India, Spain, the Caucasus, C Asia etc). Their ultimate goal is global conquest.

14. Kuwait helped to fund Iraq's war against revolutionary Iran in 1980–88 and was owed US$40 billion by Saddam Hussein's regime—a problem that would have been solved by its annexation. The use of Saudi soil as the principal base for the subsequent, US-led war on Iraq provoked Osama bin Laden to mobilize al-Qa'ida against the US.

15. Samuel P Huntingdon, *The Clash of Civilizations* (New York: Touchstone, 1997)

16. Samuel Zwemer (1867–1954), a Presbyterian missionary in Arabia for 15 years, became the first great advocate. Two significant consultations in 1978 in Glen Eyrie in the US that focused on evangelizing Muslims, and a further one in 2007 that stressed effective church-planting, have stimulated ministry among Muslims. There are 40 or so mission agencies, with around 10,000 workers, involved directly or indirectly in outreach to Muslims. From these consultations emerged two key books, *The Gospel and Islam* (1978) and *From Seed to Fruit* (2008).

17. Astonishing reports of much higher numbers of BMBs in Saudi Arabia, Iran, Algeria, Nigeria and elsewhere are hard to verify.

18. The one exception is the Eurasians in the Americas, who are included in the two affinity blocs for the Americas.

19. There is much more information on Muslim peoples and the languages they speak on the DVD and the websites listing ethno-linguistic people groups.

20. The nature and beliefs of Hinduism are treated more fully in the PowerPoint notes on the DVD.

21. "S Asians" here refers to the peoples of the S Asian Peoples affinity bloc, and excludes those people from S Asia who belong to the Persian-Median Peoples or Tibetan-Himalayan Peoples affinity bloc. These two affinity blocs have few Hindus, however.

22. In the time of the British Raj the term Hindu was applied to all native Indians, and then to the unconnected medley of religious systems to distinguish the majority from other more organized religious groups. Technically all born and bred in India could be termed "Hindu", but increasingly it has come to mean everyone who is not of a religion defined as such on the decadal census forms. This, by default subsumes the ethnic religions of the Dalits and Tribals as statistical Hindus. The decadal census figures from 1881 onwards thus politicised Hinduism.

23. See note 25 below.

24. Buddhism is essentially an atheistic religion, but most Buddhists effectually deify their founder (there are many images of the Buddha) and seek to appease the gods and spirits of pre-Buddhist religions.

25. All the figures in this diagram are derived from Paul Hattaway's *Peoples of the Buddhist World* (Piquant Editions, PO Box 83, Carlisle CA3 9GR, UK or from www.piquanteditions.com, and in N America available from Authentic Media at www.authenticmedia.com). This is one of the best resources available that describes the peoples of the Buddhist world. The list of peoples and associated information have also been incorporated into the Joshua Project List (http://www.joshuaproject.net).

26. These languages are derived from the JPL statistics. They belong to the three ABs and therefore can't be compared with the figures used in the diagram above. The first relates to Buddhist-majority ethno-linguistic people groups *across* countries, the second to languages spoken *within* countries of all religious affiliations. So, for instance, the 822 million Mandarin-speaking Chinese are counted as one people group in the first case but as 100 in the second because they have identifiable communities in that number of countries.

27. For this book, I made an estimate by country of the number of Christian believers who come from a Buddhist background. The estimates for Chinese and Korean BBBs are less certain because many will have come to Christ from an ethnic religion and not from Buddhism. All the figures are to be found in the Excel database for the Buddhist world on the DVD.

28. Paul Hattaway's 2003 book *Back to Jerusalem* tells the story of the genesis of a vision to send Chinese missionaries westwards along the silk trade routes to the Middle East and Europe. This has yet to be realized, though Christians worldwide are enthused and many groups and networks in China are beginning to turn the vision into reality.

29. The enforced conversion of native Americans by the Spanish in the 16th Century onwards led to a folk Catholicism steeped in the original pre-Christian religions.

30. "Notional Christianity" is a phrase coined by Peter Brierley of the Christian Research Association in the UK in his surveys of Europe since 1983 and used by the more recent Barna surveys in the US. Originally, it covered the many Europeans who would claim to be Christians and who maybe live according to Christian moral values but who probably rarely, if ever, attend a Christian place of worship and have little understanding of the basics of Christian doctrine. The Barna surveys also include all Christians who have no personal relationship with the Lord Jesus Christ and do not trust in His death and resurrection for salvation and eternal life.

31. African Independent Churches (AICs) consist of all denominations originating in Africa, ranging from biblical Evangelicals to highly syncretic groups whose doctrine and practice have minimal Christian content.

32. Source: World Christian Database 2008

33. Source: World Christian Database 2008

34. In 2005, the European Monitoring Centre on Racism and Xenophobia (EUMC), a body of the European Union, arrived at a detailed definition of anti-Semitism: "a certain perception of Jews, which may be expressed as hatred toward Jews. Rhetorical and physical manifestations of anti-Semitism are directed toward Jewish or non-Jewish individuals and/or their property, toward Jewish community institutions and religious facilities. In addition, such manifestations could also target the state of Israel, conceived as a Jewish collectivity. Anti-Semitism frequently charges Jews with conspiring to harm humanity, and it is often used to blame Jews for 'why things go wrong'."

35. Many people see the recent return of the Jews as a fulfilment of biblical prophecy and relate it to the Second Coming of the Lord Jesus Christ. This may be so, but there are serious weaknesses in some of the more exotic interpretations of eschatological promises which embarrass Christians in the Middle East and hinder communication of the Gospel to both Muslims and Jews.

36. Source: http://www.jewishvirtuallibrary.org/jsource/Judaism/jewpop.html

Christianity: Six Megablocs

2010

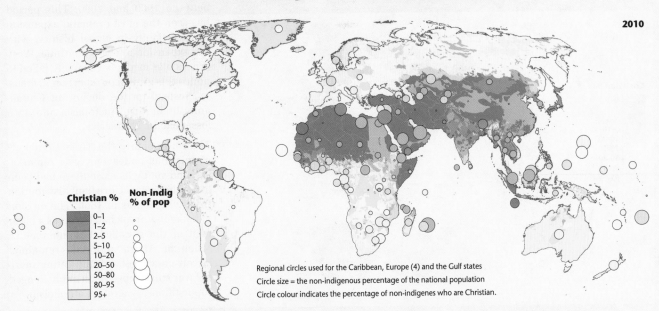

Christian % / Non-indig % of pop

Christian %	
0–1	
1–2	
2–5	
5–10	
10–20	
20–50	
50–80	
80–95	
95+	

Regional circles used for the Caribbean, Europe (4) and the Gulf states
Circle size = the non-indigenous percentage of the national population
Circle colour indicates the percentage of non-indigenes who are Christian.

This chapter reviews Christianity and its expansion since 1900 and then projects further likely developments into the 21st Century. This section covers Christianity in general, while later sections describe first the main streams and then particular denominations and theological groupings.

The map above shows the global spread of Christianity by *language and ethnicity*. It was created in three layers, coloured according to the percentage of a population or people group that is Christian: a lowest layer with single colour for the total *indigenous* population per country; a middle layer patchwork of boundaryless area polygons for *indigenous peoples* with recognized bounded home areas; an uppermost layer with circles for *non-indigenous peoples*. The map visualizes the complexity and unevenness of the spread of Christianity in more detail than any graph of national statistics.

Several local and regional concentrations of Christians stand out: the West African countries where the coastal areas have largely become Christian though the Sahel is Muslim; the Christian "island" of Ethiopia; India, with many Christians in the south and northeast—in the latter, a concentration of tribal Christians spreading into SE Asia and SW China; and Indonesia's religious patchwork. Note the difference between northern and southern Sudan.

Non-Christian areas amidst Christian majorities become plain. Note the non-Christian fringes in China, and the dearth of Christians in northern India, Indonesian Sumatra and Africa's Somali horn. Also significant is the number of less-Christian immigrant communities in Christian-majority areas.

There are about 7,000 spoken languages in the world. Many are spoken in several countries, either because the language area straddles national boundaries or because significant numbers of people using the language have migrated abroad. Allowing for such multiple entries, we obtain the approximate figure of 11,200 languages.

▲ More than 2,000 people groups[1] are over 95% Christian.

▲ Nearly 6,000 people groups have a majority that is Christian.

▲ Over 1,500 peoples have a significant minority of Christians.

▲ 2,500 peoples have a Christian population of less than 2%.

▲ 2,000 peoples have a Christian population of less than 1%.

▲ Over 2.5 billion people belong to people groups that are predominantly Christian.

▲ Around 2.4 billion belong to people groups in which Christians are a significant minority.

▲ Approximately 1.8 billion belong to groups with a Christian minority of less than 2%. They represent the least-reached people groups on earth.

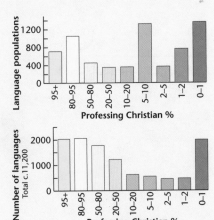

Fig 4.1 *The distribution of Christianity by language*

Christians are people who profess to be Christians.[2]

Christian adherents are people who identify themselves as "Christian" in national or regional surveys or censuses. The children of adherents are also included.

Affiliated Christians are all those who are considered to belong to organized churches or denominations. This includes full members and their children, and attenders regarded as part of the church community.

Adherents + secret believers = Affiliates + nominal believers.

Secret believers are those known to the churches but unknown to or unrecognized by the ruling authorities (whether religious, Communist etc).

Nominal believers are those counted by the authorities but unknown to the churches.

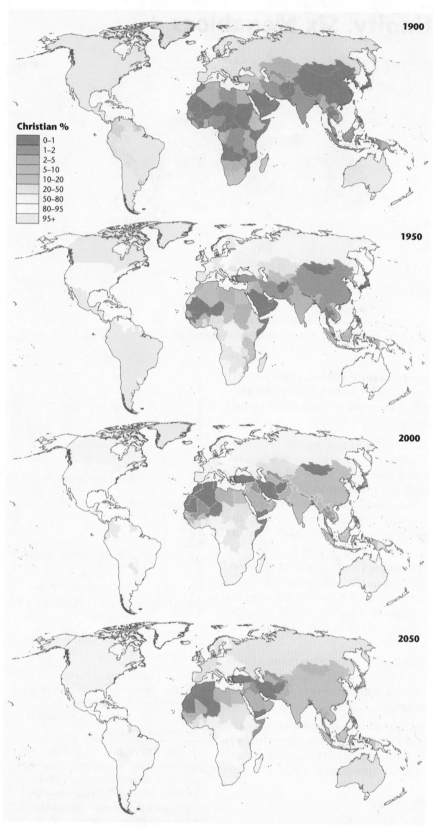

Christian %

- 0–1
- 1–2
- 2–5
- 5–10
- 10–20
- 20–50
- 50–80
- 80–95
- 95+

1900

1950

2000

2050

Fig 4.2 The likely spread of Christianity, 1900–2050

These four maps show the changing percentage of Christians by country between 1900 and 2050. This period has seen the most dramatic expansion of Christianity in global history, with the expansion likely to continue. Western secular media have largely failed to notice this growth or report on it, focusing instead on the decline of Christianity in Europe, Australasia and, to a lesser extent, N America.

The 19th Century, the "Great Century"[3] of missions endeavour, was remarkable, and yet by its close there had been little change in Christian distribution from what it was in 1800. The erosion of belief in Europe had begun as a bitter fruit of the so-called Enlightenment.[4] Much of Africa and Asia remained largely unevangelized, and Latin America[5] was still steeped in an unchallenged superstitious, syncretic Catholicism.

By 1950, the broad trends were apparent:

▲ Secularism was growing in Europe—a legacy of rationalism, Fascism and Communism.

▲ Christianity was spreading slowly but steadily in most of Africa and parts of Asia.

▲ Islam had reached its lowest point in terms of influence, though Christians were making only limited efforts to evangelize Muslims. Evangelicalism was at its lowest ebb after 50 years in which theological liberalism had gained control of the power structures and theological education of much of organized Christianity.

The expansion of Christianity between 1950 and 2000 has no parallel in history. At its heart were the revival of Evangelical and Catholic enthusiasm for missions, and the global growth of Pentecostal denominations and Charismatic networks, all facilitated by global conferences and networking.[6] The result was massive church growth in sub-Saharan Africa and parts of Asia, and the spread of Evangelicalism throughout the Americas. These gains offset the big losses in Europe and the Pacific. The Church truly became worldwide for the first time in history.

Food for Thought

The 21st Century is likely to be defined by a three-way contest for the hearts of humankind between evangelical Christians, Muslims and secularists. Evangelicals will probably have the edge over the other two.[7] Basically, biblical Christians have a cultural flexibility and a core message of present assurance of future salvation that Muslims could never have, while secularists will ultimately decline because of their very low birth rates and their unsustainable dependence on affluence. However, harsher conditions of opprobrium and persecution are likely to become more common for Christians.

▲ How ready are we to suffer shame and pain for the sake of a cause so needful as making Christ known to the nations?

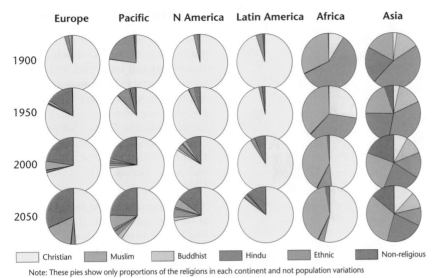

Fig 4.3 *Likely growth and decline of religions per continent, 1900–2050*

The pie charts in Fig 4.3 show the Christian component of the population of each continent in relation to the other five major religious streams, vertically over time and horizontally in comparison with the other continents. The bar charts compare the continental populations.

Note: These pies show only proportions of the religions in each continent and not population variations

Legend: Christian | Muslim | Buddhist | Hindu | Ethnic | Non-religious

Continental Populations — 1.6 billion, 2.5 billion, 6.1 billion, 9.1 billion; Christian / Other

Europe

A "Christian" continent in 1900. Are we witnessing the death of Europe's civilization?

A high degree of nominalism, increasing secularization and growing influence of liberal theology, and disillusion and cynicism following two world wars led to massive decline in church attendance. Increasing pluralism (as a result of immigration and experimentation with new religious ideas), growth of Islam at a time when the Church was discouraged and divided, and rejection of absolutes in society under the banner of "tolerance" resulted in marginalization of Christianity. By 2050, Christians will make up less than 50% of the ageing population, with most being nominal in their adherence.

The Pacific

By 1900, much of the indigenous population was Christian or rapidly becoming so. European settlers in Australia and New Zealand had a Christian majority, but followed Europe into spiritual decline and cynical secularism, albeit more slowly. Asian settlers since 1990 are often more overtly religious—Muslim, Buddhist and also Christian.

N America

The first amendment to the US Constitution ensured the separation of Church and State and created a flourishing free market for religious faith and its propagation worldwide: patterns and methods of US Christianity were then exported globally and adopted even by opponents of Christianity. In 1900, N America was almost entirely Christian,

with a Protestant majority. The 1950s in the USA were characterized by vigorous church life and the immigration of people of other faiths. A growing secularism in the media and public life then contrasted with the strong commitment to faith in US society—these trends are likely to be maintained in the 21st Century, when they will impact the world.

Latin America

By 1900, there was little challenge to the dominance of Catholicism in Latin America: much of the indigenous population was effectually unevangelized, though nominally Catholic, and there was a lot of traditionalism and syncretism. In 1900, Protestants did not regard the continent as a mission field; consequently small numbers. N American missions changed this, with a rapid growth in the number of Protestants after 1970. The advent of Pentecostalism (both indigenous and imported) after 1906 proved astonishingly successful. Secularism has been less evident than in Europe. Losses from Catholicism to Evangelicals stimulated the development of Charismatic theology and worship within Catholicism.

Africa

Only in the 19th Century did most of Africa become open to travel—and the Gospel. Ethiopia, however, had already been Christian for nearly 2,000 years. In 1900, the majority of N Africans were Muslim while sub-Saharan Africa followed traditional religions. Colonial regimes strongly promoted their national brands of Christianity up to the 1960s. The real growth of Christianity came in the chaotic 40 years

that followed the colonial rush to independence. Africa was unique in being the first continent to become Christian-majority in barely a single century.

Asia

Asia is the birthplace of all the major world religions: it is still the most religiously-diverse continent, and the only one on which Christianity does not have the most adherents. Islam and Christianity are the religions in the ascendancy, with the latter outgrowing the former (though from a smaller population base). Asia's huge population and growing economic influence make it a key arena for future Christian ministry: Asian input into every aspect of Christian philosophy, theology and practice is likely to become pivotal by the middle of the 21st Century.

Burning Question for Today

Nearly all of the major world religions have become global in their influence as a result of migration and also of unashamedly winning converts. Many Christians have become embarrassed even to use the word "mission", let alone actually to proclaim the amazing Good News, for fear of causing offence.

▲ How does your own life and that of your local fellowship compare with the challenging words of the Apostle Paul in Romans 1:16? *For I am not ashamed of the Gospel; it is the power of God for salvation to everyone who has faith…*

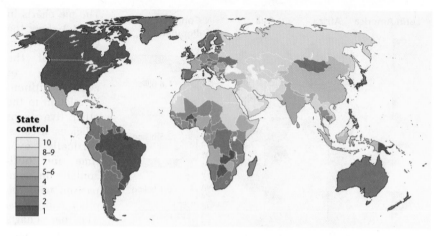

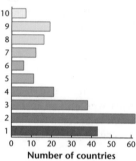

Fig 4.4 *State involvement in religions*

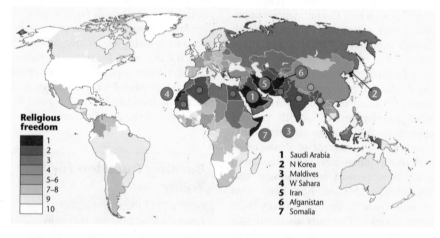

1	Saudi Arabia
2	N Korea
3	Maldives
4	W Sahara
5	Iran
6	Afganistan
7	Somalia

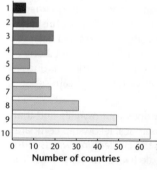

Fig 4.5 *Religious freedom and Christians*

State involvement

The three maps on these two pages show the environment in which Christians lived and witnessed in 2005. The extent of state involvement—and also oppression—is compared country by country across the world. The 20th Century saw the Church advance, albeit amidst much persecution; it is more than likely that the 21st will deliver its share of suffering to those who live for Christ.

The three maps in the series and their scale definitions overlap, but they emphasize different aspects. The scales have been derived and updated from a number of sources.[8]

Fig 4.4 shows state involvement in legislation that promotes or limits religious freedoms. The level of state involvement in religious affairs may be benign: Japan, for instance, enjoys a high degree of religious freedom but is culturally closed to outside religious influences. The USA and about 40 other states—nearly all Christian-majority—have specifically or implicitly made a complete separation between State and religion. A total of over 60 states have not made such a separation and maintain some legal link with their official religions but grant full religious freedom to adherents of other religions. It is sad to note that a number of European countries have moved towards further curbing religious freedoms.

In Fig 4.5, the deeper the colour, the more limited is religious freedom—especially for Christians.

The Universal Declaration of Human Rights charter was adopted by the UN in 1948. Subsequent protocols and a Covenant were signed by 132 nations; many, however, ignore their commitments to safeguarding religious freedom, and curtail it through bureaucratic obstruction, legislation or even persecution. Fig 4.5 identifies the seven countries with the worst record of persecuting Christians. The countries that next most restrict religious freedom are marked on the map with small coloured circles: green if the repressers are Muslim, orange if they are Buddhist, brown if they are Hindu and red if they are Communist.

It is significant that before 1990 the states that most curtailed religious freedom were Communist, but since then the levels of restriction imposed by Muslim states have increased.

The indexes on page 96 are combined in Fig 4.6 to show where the environment for Christian ministry is positive (green) or negative (red). The 20th Century began with most of the world under the control of powers that espoused one or another expression of organized Christianity. The 21st Century is likely to be very different, with a globally growing Church ministering in a more hostile secular or non-Christian religious world. Will this lead to complete separation between Church and State, 17 centuries after Constantine?[9]

Most of the areas where Christian ministry will be obstructed are in the non-Christian world—mainly in Muslim-majority countries. What is more surprising is the number of countries with a professing Christian majority that also limit aspects of Christian ministry. For countries such as Cuba, Mexico and Zimbabwe, this is a historic legacy of Communism or revolution, but in many former Communist countries such as Russia, Belarus and Romania the restriction or oppression comes from Orthodox national churches against non-Orthodox denominations or other religions. Sadly, some W European countries are moving in the same restrictive direction. Future ministry may be more difficult, but the Church will be forced to trust more in God than in state protection and to be willing to suffer in exercising a more prophetic role.

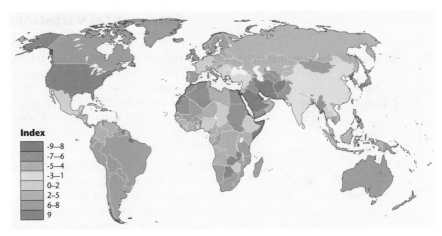

Fig 4.6 *The state of the global environment for Christian ministry*

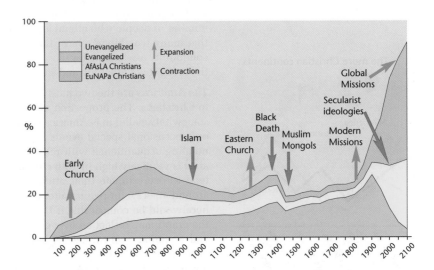

Fig 4.7 *The progress* of world evangelization over 2000 years

World evangelization and the global Church

Fig 4.7 shows the periods of growth and decline of the whole Christian Church in its composition (Christians in AfAsLA vs those in EuNAPa) and outreach (the "evangelized") over the past 2,000 years, with projections into the future. There have been four periods of growth for the Christian Church, and three major periods of decline. It is interesting to note what caused decline: Islam (first with Arabian and later with Mongolian armies), natural catastrophes (the Black Death—possibly after disaster-induced climate change) and, in modern times, Western secularist ideologies. The striking change in the Church's composition in the 21st Century from EuNAPa to AfAsLA is plain to see.

The broad sweep of the fortunes of Christianity over two millennia help us to project that in the future its adherents will continue to increase slowly as a percentage of the world's population but the real growth, initiative, dynamism and leadership will come from AfAsLA nations.

The green band represents that part of the global population that has been evangelized or at least exposed to the basic message of the Gospel over the centuries.[10] This has increased significantly over the last 200 years, but this growth has greatly accelerated in recent decades as a result of mission activity and especially the use of a widening range of media. It is not far-fetched to think that every person on earth could have a meaningful chance to hear the message of the Gospel in a culturally appropriate manner in our times.

Food for Thought

▲ What will be the dominant themes for ministry over the next 40 years?

Asia's economic power, huge population and religious diversity make it the fulcrum for spiritual change. Africa will be the major locus of religious confrontation, between a wealthier, more militant Islam and an indigenous Christianity that is materially poor but vital in its witnessing.

▲ Will this confrontation be violent or peaceful?

Europe's 500-year Renaissance civilization is dying, and along with it European Christendom. It will be seen increasingly by Christians in other continents as a needy mission field.

Continental variations in religious attendance

One way to assess the numbers of adherents claimed both for Christianity and for other religions is by finding out the extent of their involvement in a place of worship (church, temple, mosque etc). Various surveys over the past decade for the larger countries enable us to do this[11] and the results have been taken as representative of entire continents in the graphs below. I have grouped the six continents into three similar pairs. The world average is shown by the black line. The accompanying pie charts show the proportion of worshippers in 2000 who might have been Christian.

The Pacific region and Europe (the majority population of the Pacific being a cultural offshoot of Europe): most of the population claim to be Christian, but generally this does not involve much more than a fuzzy individualistic commitment to some Christian concepts. There is a higher degree of commitment among indigenous Pacific peoples. Over 50% of Europeans claim to be religious but never attend a place of worship. If Christians alone were counted, this figure would be even higher, since the Muslim minorities are more likely to attend a mosque. However, the numbers that go to special events in places of worship show that many who call themselves "Christian" have not severed all links with churches. The low number of people who attend a place of worship more than once a week indicates that many worshippers have little social interaction with others. Fellowship and community are lacking for most, which underlines the personalization of faith and the breakdown of family and social cohesion.

The Americas are the two most Christian continents, so these figures apply mainly to Christians. The proportion of people who do not attend a place of worship is somewhat smaller in N America than in Latin America. The percentage who attend only occasional special events is smaller than for Europe, indicating that a mere nodding acquaintance with religious practice is not so prevalent. Weekly attendance is relatively high in both continents, though various polls[12] show that people tend to overestimate their attendance. Gallup polls in the US consistently gave around 40–42% for regular attenders between 1991 and 2003, and the figures used here would be comparable if the two right-hand values were added together. So, the graph may reflect an over-generous personal assessment, perhaps by 30–40%; and a similar overestimate is likely with all the other continents. Considerably fewer people attend a place of worship more than once a week, which suggests a low level of fellowship and community and a certain dichotomy between one holy day and six secular days a week.

Asia and Africa are the multi-faith continents. *Asia* is the most populous, and so conforms more closely to the world average. Most Asians are involved regularly in religious activity, but of these Christians are a minority. The great majority of those who have no involvement are Chinese. Religious involvement is more important to the average Asian than many Westerners realize.

Africa is very different. There are few people with little or no involvement. The majority go at least weekly to a place of worship (mainly a church or mosque). African cultures generally have an awareness of the spirit world and of the power of prayer.[13] Many of the functions of the state have failed, and religious communities seek to fill the gap. Competition between Islam and Christianity also boosts levels of involvement, with a high proportion of the population professing one of these two religions. Nearly 40% of all Africans participate more than once a week in communal worship, which indicates the importance of social relatedness.

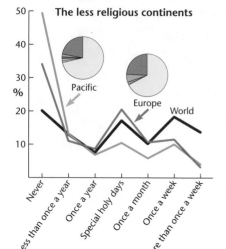

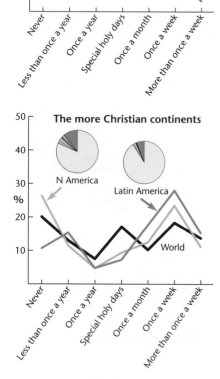

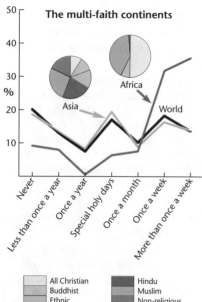

Fig 4.8 *Attendance at places of worship in 2000*

Legend:
- All Christian
- Buddhist
- Ethnic
- Hindu
- Muslim
- Non-religious

Food for Thought

▲ Which will prove more durable— the Western secular, materialistic worldview that has no time for a spiritual dimension or the religious perspective of the rest of the world?

▲ Are we witnessing the demise of Western post-Christian ideologies and the eventual rediscovery of moral and spiritual values—even of despised biblical Christianity?

Continental Christian growth and decline

On this page, the average annual growth rate (AAROG) for Christians is compared to that of the general population in the 20th Century and the projection for the 21st. Where Christians are increasing as a percentage of the population, the red line is above the green. These point to broad ministry goals for the world and for each continent.

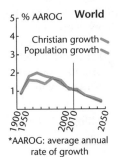

AAROG: average annual rate of growth

The 21st will be the first non-Constantinian century since AD 400. How will the Church function with less state support, fewer privileges and greater opposition? Ties to state structures have long embroiled it in worldly concerns and damaged its witness. Levels of discrimination and persecution are now likely to increase in many parts of the world. Is this the century when the prophetic role of the Church will be restored? Will Christians be willing to suffer persecution in fulfilling it? The decline of state-aligned denominations and the growth of Independent churches globally indicate that this is possible.

The Christian growth rate broadly parallels that of the world population. In the 20th Century it was a little lower, but since 1980 it has increased and will probably remain at this higher level to 2050. In a more hostile environment created by other religions (especially Islam) and a vocal secularism, learning to thrive is vital. Ministry priorities must include discipling believers both new and old, godly mentoring of new leaders and winning successive generations to a living faith.

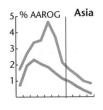

Africa's great Christian growth was in the 20th Century. This will slow rapidly in the 21st. Most of Africa will then be Muslim or Christian. These are the main ministry challenges:

▲ handling an aggressive Islam wisely, and being effective in winning and discipling Muslims

▲ developing biblical leadership-training and handing over to new leadership

▲ discipling children more effectively

▲ influencing those who wield power in a dysfunctional continent.

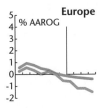

Asia is the one continent where the Church has grown in the 20th Century, and will probably experience significant growth in the 21st. Much of this would be through conversion. The main ministry challenges are:

▲ a focus on persistent, loving evangelistic outreach

▲ effective biblical discipling of those from very different religious backgrounds

▲ dynamic involvement in world missions across Asia and to Europe.

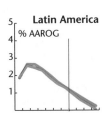

Europe's slower Christian growth rate turned into absolute decline by 1980. This has rapidly accelerated and is likely to far exceed even the general population decline. Ministry challenges for the future are:

▲ restoring expectant faith to Christians

▲ praying for revival

▲ re-evangelizing Europe (many parts of which have *never* been effectively discipled).

Other Christians will see Europe as a "prodigal" continent in need of help from abroad.

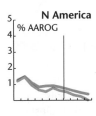

In *Latin America and the Caribbean*, Christians will remain a majority, so the Christian growth rate and that of the general population are almost the same. The ministry challenges are:

▲ can the Church be freed from traditionalism, nominalism and superficiality to become a catalyst for cultural and social change?

▲ there needs to be an emphasis on holy living, dynamic discipling and effective missions outreach.

N America's Christian majority will be eroded by secularization and non-Christian immigration. Note a reduction of the Christian growth rate to almost zero in 2050—lower than that of the general population. The ministry challenges are:

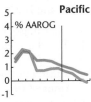

▲ how to develop a dynamic Christian witness that is not dependent on being privileged

▲ how to increase a biblical longing for God's kingdom principles to be put into action in society and the world at large, particularly among the rising generation.

In the *Pacific*, Christians increased in number faster than the general population until the latter part of the 20th Century. This trend then reversed and will probably become a decline by about 2040 unless there is revival. The ministry challenges are:

▲ new life for an increasingly nominal and notional Christianity

▲ evangelizing migrants and winning the youth of local cultures to a living faith.

Fig 4.9 *Average annual growth rates (AAROG)*

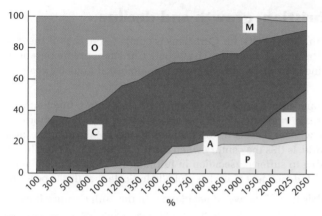

Fig 4.10 *The six Christian confessional megablocs as a proportion of all Christians, over two millennia*

Six Christian streams

Fig 4.10 visualizes the following developments:

C: The Western Church based in Rome was Latin in language and liturgy. For centuries, church councils recognized the "primacy among equals" of the See of Rome, along with the other patriarchal seats of Antioch, Alexandria, Jerusalem and Constantinople. Perhaps more than any other internal factor, the issue of papal authority has caused disputes and wars between Christians and the persecution of those who have rejected it.[15]

O: The Eastern or Orthodox Churches worshipped in Greek, Aramaic/Syriac or their own national language.

A: The Celtic Church in the British Isles had links with the Western Church but developed its own culture, theology and visionary missionary enterprise, which contributed to the emergence of the Anglican megabloc.

P: Protestantism arose through the ministries of John Wycliffe in England, Jan Hus in Moravia, Martin Luther in Germany, Ulrich Zwingli in Switzerland and John Calvin in France and Geneva during the 14th–16th Centuries.

I: The rise of the Independent churches, the growing edge of the Church, is a modern phenomenon that is reshaping global Christianity.

▲ The Council of Ephesus in 431 led to schism and the emergence of a separate Assyrian-Persian Church of the East (Diphysite).

▲ The Council of Chalcedon (451) led to the ejection of the Monophysite Churches (Jacobite, Coptic, Armenian, Georgian etc). These are known as the "Oriental Orthodox".[16]

▲ The Great Schism in 1054 divided the Chalcedonian Greek Orthodox and Latin Churches.

▲ The Reformation (finalized in 1648) was a schism from the Roman Catholic Church of both the Protestants and the Anglicans over doctrine and papal authoritarianism.

Generally good denominational figures for 1950–2000 are used as a basis for projecting to 2050.[17]

Both *Catholics and Orthodox* (and particularly the latter) are declining as a proportion of the Church. The global Catholic population is likely to show a very slight increase over the next three decades before beginning to decline. The global Orthodox population looks set to fall by perhaps 20% between 2000 and 2050.

Anglicans are in a period of decline, but the number of African Anglicans is likely to grow during the 21st Century. The Anglican population may nearly double between 2000 and 2050.

The *Protestant* Church is growing predominantly in AfAsLA countries—that growth more than compensates for losses in EuNAPa countries. In absolute numbers, Protestants are likely to increase by around 80% between 2000 and 2050.

The growth of the *Independent* Churches is startling—numbers may triple between 2000 and 2050. This has major implications for the future of the Church. Christianity has rapidly become indigenous to many cultures through these new denominations. It is these newer expressions of Christianity that are going to have a big impact in the 21st Century; and most of them are Evangelical and most are Charismatic in persuasion.

Definition: Christian Megabloc[14]

A major ecclesiastical stream, bloc, tradition or confession within Christianity that shares commonalities in one or more of the following: origins, doctrine, ecclesiology and leadership structures.

There are six such megablocs used in this book to encompass the 38,000-plus denominations and multi-congregational post-denominational networks: Protestants (P), Independents (I), Anglicans (A), Catholics (C), Orthodox (O) and Marginals (M). X = unaffiliated Christians. Statistics for the P, I and A megablocs are often combined because they overlap so much—hence the order followed here.

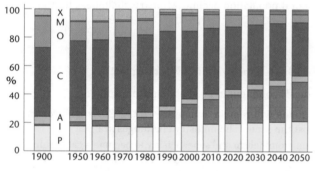

Fig 4.11 *Christian megablocs as a proportion of all Christians, 1900–2050*

Food for Thought

The fragmentation of Christianity over the centuries has generally been attributed to key doctrinal disagreements, but too little attention has been given to the influence of church and secular politics or personal animosities. Even less has been given to the differences in culture and language between the protagonists. The early schisms over the nature(s) of Christ revolved around a very precise use of language that did not necessarily carry over in translation between Latin, Greek, Aramaic and Coptic. The 21st-Century Church, as it develops and becomes less dominated by Western languages, may face similar serious controversies in the future.

▲ How aware are Westerners of this—especially those who speak only English?

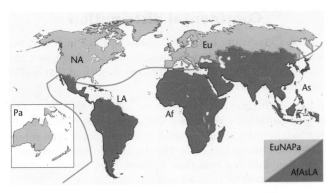

Fig 4.12 *The "North-South" divide, 1900–2010*

The stark divide on the map in Fig 4.12 illustrates the challenge for globalization in the 21st Century. How can the world's wealth (including its material resources, intellectual property, human rights and responsibility for its ecology) be shared fairly and sustainably? Individual and national greed, selfishness and bigotry make any effective agreements on trade, finance, water and food or climate change a distant dream. Christians see hope only in a spiritual solution through the life-changing impact of the Gospel in individuals and nations.

Few realize that the EuNAPa/AfAsLA divide extends to religion—and, more particularly, Christianity. Christian credibility and influence are waning in the former but thriving in the latter. This will be fully shown in the pages that follow.

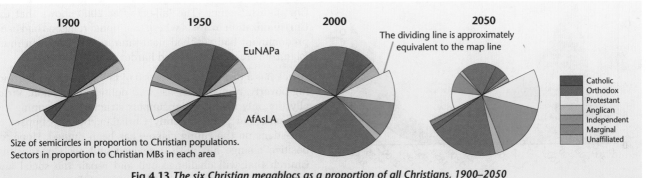

Fig 4.13 *The six Christian megablocs as a proportion of all Christians, 1900–2050*

1900 Most Christians were found in Europe or N America. The Pacific is included with EuNA because the majority of the populations of Australia and New Zealand were European immigrants, while many of the indigenous Pacific Islanders (with the exception of the people of Papua New Guinea) had been Christian for nearly a century.

1950 Most of the Catholics in the AfAsLA semicircle were in Latin America, whose population was then comparatively small in global terms. Christian growth in AfAsLA was due partly to higher birth rates but also to conversion. The two world wars seriously interrupted mission activity and slowed that growth. Evangelical Christians were disorganized and on the defensive during this period, which limited new advances and church planting.

2000 The 50 years that followed have proved to be the most astonishing harvest time the world has ever seen. During this period, the rate of conversion in AfAsLA nations far outstripped even the high population growth rate and shifted the centre of gravity of Christianity to AfAsLA (as the reversal in the relative size of the semicircles shows). A large part of this growth was amongst Evangelicals in the P, I and A megablocs and also Catholics in Asia and Africa. Over this period, Western liberal churches lost interest in mission.

2050 Trends evident in 2000 will probably continue to 2050. They have gained a momentum that even major political changes are unlikely to affect greatly. The Church will then be very different from that of 1900 or even 2000. For good or ill, the baton for witness will have been largely passed from EuNAPa to AfAsLA nations.

The next two pages show, continent by continent, the very different changes in the fortunes of the six megablocs over two millennia.

The Global North-South Divide—how best to refer to it?

Terms widely used are inadequate and arguably patronizing:

First, Second and Third Worlds: The Second World (the Soviet bloc) is no more—and the terms suggest class, as in "third-class".

The distinction between West and non-West is inaccurate and exclusive.

The distinction between developed and developing is divisive and inaccurate.

The Global North and South is not geographically accurate.

I have used two-letter abbreviations for the continents which can be conveniently linked together to form a range of new words such as "AfAsLA" and "EuNAPa". This is comprehensible and neutral.

Food for Thought

The influence of Western Christianity, with all its quirks and distortions, will diminish, and a new series of theological and ethical challenges will arise that are not necessarily derived from Greek philosophy or bankrupt Western ideologies.

▲ How willing are EuNAPa Christians to recognize and honour these massive demographic shifts now taking place in the Christian world?

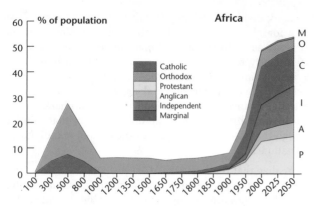

Fig 4.14 *Christians by megabloc in Africa, 100–2050*

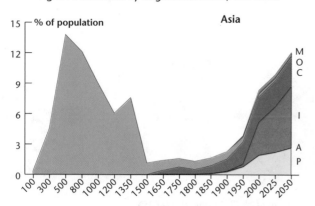

Fig 4.15 *Christians by megabloc in Asia, 100–2050*

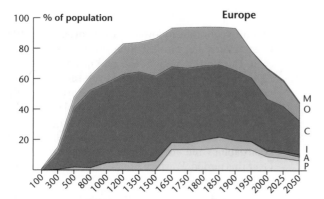

Fig 4.16 *Christians by megabloc in Europe, 100–2050*

Burning Questions for Today

Christianity, with all the faults it had acquired, nonetheless provided the basis for a new era of learning, industry and civil order. The Reformation was followed by a vigorous worldwide export of products and ideas, and eventually biblical missions, too. In the 20th Century, Europe's civilization began its precipitous decline, losing its empires and its bedrock of faith and even developing a societal "death wish". Fig 4.16 shows the astonishing, close parallel between that process and the decline in adherence to Christianity. By 2050, less than half of Europeans are likely to claim any allegiance to Christianity. There are uncomfortable parallels between the situation in Europe today and the collapse of the Greco-Roman civilization.

▲ Could a very different new civilization emerge with a fresh mingling of races and a vigorous Christianity as its catalyst?

▲ How could Christians, in Europe and worldwide, prepare for it?

Continental distribution

Africa. Christianity has long had strong roots in N and NE Africa. The apostle Mark was the pioneer in Egypt, and the Ethiopian eunuch was the first representative of that nation to become a Christian (Acts 8).

Catholic Christianity peaked across N Africa in AD 500 and Coptic Orthodox Christianity spread down the Nile valley to the northern highlands of what is now Ethiopia. The subsequent long trough was caused by the Muslim Arab conquests. Christian Ethiopia was then isolated from the rest of the Christian world for nearly a millennium.

All six megablocs experienced massive growth across sub-Saharan Africa over the last two centuries. The greatest growth came after the ending of colonialism, which left a legacy of political instability, economic distortion and strong Christian influence. The tail-off after 2000 shows that the Christianization of areas where traditional religions had been predominant had reached near-saturation. Growth in more Islamized areas is slower and harder to achieve.

Africa has a dismal recent record of failed states, with grinding poverty, rampant disease and political confusion. Virtually the only viable social support structures remaining are religious, and predominantly Christian; but the impact of Christians on the ruling classes has been limited. Hope for positive change lies with a revived and socially sensitive Church that will challenge evil and repair the social and moral fabric of society—but will this happen?

Asia. The spread of Syrian and Persian Orthodox Christianity across much of W, C and even E Asia is one of the most remarkable episodes in church history,[18] but it is little known today. This 1300-year development is shown in Fig 4.15. So much of the evidence of it was obliterated, first by Islam and then by the Mongols—especially after the western Mongols became Muslim. The figures are estimates, but only now is the Church in Asia beginning to attain the continental percentages of the 8th–10th Centuries.

Arab Muslim invasions after AD 700 caused the first decline. Christians were subjugated and reduced to second-class citizens and suffered waves of persecution. The second decline came in the 14th Century after the Muslim Mongol ruler of Persia, Timur the Lame, set out to destroy all trace of Eastern Christianity. He almost succeeded.

Portuguese and Spanish Catholic missions after 1500 bore fruit in parts of India, China and Japan. Protestants followed after 1793, but most of their success came in the 20th Century. It is the Church in China that has made the biggest difference in recent years. Asia will be the major growth area for the Church in the 21st Century. Its population is huge and it is the one continent left where many peoples have yet to be exposed to the Gospel. It is also likely to be a major source of theological development, recruits for Christian service and funding for expansion.

Europe. Europe's Greco-Roman civilization lasted for 900 years (500 BC–AD 400) until its demise at the hands of pagan and, later, Muslim invaders. About half of Europe was Christianized by then. The Dark Ages that followed were a millennium of limited global influence, but the Celtic Christians were a source of Gospel light to evangelize the invaders in W and C Europe. For all its backwardness, Europe was also the sole remaining area of the world where Christianity was able to develop a new civilization and eventually flourish.

Latin America. The story of how Catholic Christianity was imposed on Latin America while the continent was plundered is a sad and shameful one, though some missionaries tried in vain to challenge iniquitous official policies. It is hard to imagine the trauma suffered by those concerned and then passed on to future generations as a new, mixed race emerged, the fruit of enslavement, rape and exploitation rather than colonization. N America by contrast was invaded by immigrants who intended to settle there—though its colonization also had its awful chapters.

Within a century, most of the indigenous population had become superficially Christian, but it was far from evangelized. The diagram illustrates this Catholic dominance, diluted with syncretism and nominalism. Catholic political power and spiritual tyranny were challenged by the arrival of Protestant missionaries in the 20th Century and the later emergence of a culturally relevant indigenous Christianity. Catholic harassment and persecution of Evangelicals was a reality until the late 1960s or, in some places, even later. A 'vigorous grassroots Protestant/Independent charismatic Christianity is likely to be a dominant influence and is already impacting the Catholic Church itself. If Christian standards are carried into public life by committed Christian leaders and politicians, there is hope that biblical principles could change society and free it from its traumatic past. The non-religious are unlikely to grow in number as significantly as in Europe.

N America. Two centuries of Protestant immigration and numerical growth with periodic revivals—moulded the US as a nation. The founding fathers bequeathed a heritage of religious freedoms. Canada remained ambiguous as a bicultural nation—Catholic Francophone and Protestant Anglophone—with strong links to Europe. European and later global immigration has made N America increasingly multicultural. The separation of Church and State in the US freed churches to be innovative and relevant to gain and retain followings.

The forward-looking, market-oriented US Christianity that emerged has led to huge variety in church life, teachings and worship styles. Many new denominations and networks have appeared that are predominantly Protestant in origin and evangelical in theology. It also resulted in massive input into local, national and international evangelism and missions. New marginal religions and pseudo-religions of US origin such as Mormonism, Jehovah's Witnesses and Scientology have flourished, too. The Catholic Church has adapted and grown—in part due to European and Hispanic immigration—but faces crises in the lack of vocations to the priesthood and the exposure of paedophilia and other immorality among some priests. The influx of non-Christian immigrants and the rise in the number of the non-religious have somewhat reduced the percentage of Christians in the population. Secularists actively seek to apply the principle of the separation of Church and State to mean freedom *from* religion.

The Pacific. The influence of British missionaries and British and Irish settlers on the indigenous peoples of the Pacific in the 19th Century shaped present religious patterns which are similar to those of the UK and Europe. By 1900, most of the indigenous populations across the Pacific had become Protestant with the exception of that of Papua New Guinea. Increasing nominalism among Polynesians opened the way for the spread of Mormonism. In Australia and New Zealand, religious decline, secularism and non-Christian immigration

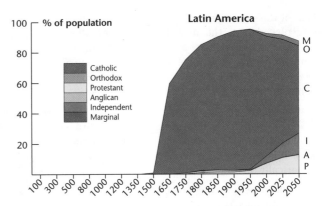

Fig 4.17 *Christians by megabloc in Latin America, 100–2050*

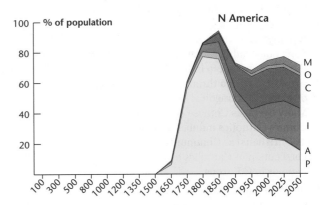

Fig 4.18 *Christians by megabloc in N America, 100–2050*

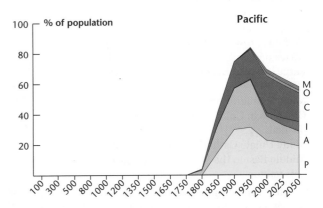

Fig 4.19 *Christians by megabloc in the Pacific, 100–2050*

are eroding the Christian influence in society. Unless spiritual revival comes to the nations of the Pacific, large and small, these trends are likely to continue.

Each of the six megablocs and their global spread is displayed over the next 11 pages. The shading indicates what percentage of each country's population they constitute for each half-century between 1900 and 2050. A few select developments or changes are listed for each 50 years.

First, we look at the Catholic Church over this period, in which its local dominance in Europe and Latin America is challenged at the very time when it is expanding geographically and growing numerically on other continents.

By 1900: Growth through empire

1. Catholic heartlands in S Europe
2. Uniate Churches from 12th Century onwards
3. Catholicization of the Americas after 1500
4. The Counter-Reformation regains many losses.
5. Spanish Catholicization of most Filipinos
6. French Catholics colonize N America after 1541, but then lose their possessions in Canada to Britain in 1759 and sell Louisiana to the US in 1802.
7. Irish Catholic emigration in the 19th Century
8. French conquest and colonization of Algeria
9. French colonization and Catholicization of C Africa, Madagascar, Indochina etc in the 19th Century

1900–50: Coping with advances in times of war

1. Europe's Catholics, traumatized by war and tyranny, are in great need of change.
2. Slow but steady growth of the Indian Church
3. Further outreach to indigenous peoples
4. Growth in Africa through a widespread system of schools and medical services
5. Many overseas Chinese embrace Catholicism.
6. China's Catholics number 3 million (75% of all its Christians) as Communism triumphs.
7. Persecution of Catholics by Communist regimes in C Europe

1950–2000: Modernization and renewal

1. Vatican II (1962–65): a watershed development, bringing the Church into the 20th Century
2. Severe decline in attendance at Mass on both sides of the Iron Curtain
3. French leave Algeria when it becomes independent in 1962.
4. Catholic growth in Indonesia in 1960–90
5. Africa descends into conflict and instability.
6. Large losses to Evangelicals in Latin America after 1960
7. Major immigration of Hispanics into the US
8. Catholics in China number 12 million, but are divided.
9. Many Uniate Catholics emigrate from the Middle East to the West after increased persecution.

2000–50: Possible future developments

1. A leadership crisis caused by a lack of priests
2. A moral disaster unfolds as a result of long-concealed paedophilia in the US and elsewhere.
3. In Africa, growth slows as syncretism and nominalism increase. (Some of Africa's worst leaders have been nominal Catholics.)

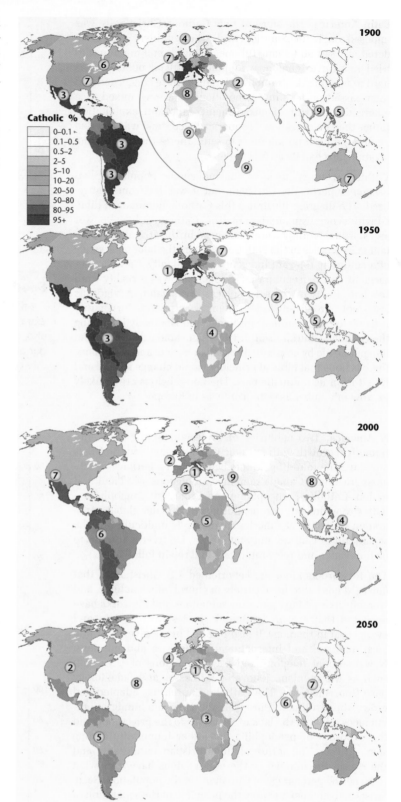

Fig 4.20 *Global spread of Catholics, 1900–2050*

4. Continued decline in Europe and the Pacific is likely.
5. Continuing losses to Evangelicals and sects in Latin America, and diminishing political and social influence
6. Continuing slow growth in Asia is likely.
7. China's divided Catholics may be able to reunite as its freedoms gradually increase.
8. Catholics will decline from 48% of all Christians in 2000 to perhaps 37% in 2050.

1900	Country	mil	1950	Country	mil	2000	Country	mil	2050	Country	mil
1	France	40	1	Brazil	51	1	Brazil	127	1	Brazil	122
2	Italy	33	2	Italy	45	2	Mexico	89	2	Mexico	102
3	Germany	20	3	France	38	3	USA	59	3	USA	83
4	Poland	19	4	Germany	31	4	Italy	46	4	Philippines	64
5	Spain	19	5	USA	31	5	Philippines	46	5	Congo, DR	57
6	Brazil	17	6	Spain	28	6	France	40	6	Colombia	48
7	Mexico	13	7	Mexico	27	7	Colombia	38	7	Uganda	42
8	USA	11	8	Poland	23	8	Argentina	34	8	Nigeria	33
9	Czech Rep	7.3	9	Philippines	17	9	Poland	30	9	Argentina	32
10	Belgium	6.6	10	Argentina	16	10	Spain	27	10	Venezuela	32
Other Countries (191)		86	Other Countries (216)		163	Other Countries (221)		410	Other Countries (221)		617
World Total (201)		272	World Total (226)		469	World Total (231)		948	World Total (231)		1,129

Fig 4.21 *Top 10 countries for Catholics, 1900–2050 (see legend for Fig 4.22)*

Fig 4.21 shows the changing face of the Catholic Church: once largely European, with seven countries in the top 10 in 1900, no European country will remain in the list by 2050.

▲ Hispanic Catholicism will become dominant, from just two entries in the top 10 in 1900 to four in 2000 and five in 2050. Catholic Charismatics are a growing phenomenon.

▲ Brazil became the world's largest Catholic country around 1945. It will remain the largest for the foreseeable future, despite enormous losses to Evangelicals.

▲ Africa will be of rising importance for the Catholic Church, with no entries in 2000 but three by 2050. However, each of these three faces huge demographic and economic challenges.

▲ The Catholic population of the US will probably continue to grow, but this may tail off faster than I suggest if radical changes are not made in its public image and its relevance to popular concerns.

▲ The Philippines is the only Asian entry in the top 10, but here, too, Evangelicals have multiplied fast.

The growth of the Catholic Church over this period is shown in these pie charts. The area of each pie and its continental segments reflect the size of the population.

The Catholic Church will probably grow in number from 948 million in 2000 to 1,129m in 2050, but as a percentage of the global population is likely to fall from 16.8% in 1900 to 14.4% in 2050—and as a percentage of all affiliated Christians, from 48% to 37%.

In *Europe*, Catholics numbered 184 million in 1900 but by 2050 will probably total 144 million. The Catholic Church is likely to be marginalized—though some once saw the European Union as a plot by Catholics to regain control of the continent after the Great Schism of 1054 and the 16th-Century Reformation.

In *N America*, the big influx of Hispanics has helped to bolster the numbers of Catholics, but bad publicity following various sex scandals (and resulting pay-outs) and the reluctance of the hierarchy to acknowledge wrongdoing have so damaged the Church that nothing short of revolutionary change could restore any of its credibility.

The West (EuNA) will have only 21% of all Catholics by 2050. Will this be reflected in the Church's life and leadership?

Latin America's maintenance of its share of all Catholics is due largely to higher, but declining, population growth rates. Continued failure to recruit Hispanic Catholics for service in the Church and widespread nominalism and superstition do not bode well for its future health.

Asia and Africa's rising numbers of Catholics are due both to population growth and to conversion. By 2050, one-third of all Catholics will be either Asian or African, and the Church on those continents will be providing an ever higher proportion of EuNAPa's priests and church workers.

Globally the Catholic Church is suffering a crisis of identity in the modern world as it faces up to ethical, moral and social issues, and has lost much of its relevance and credibility. Historic patterns of leadership, recruitment and decision-making need to change, but the Church is limited by its tradition and Catholic doctrine.

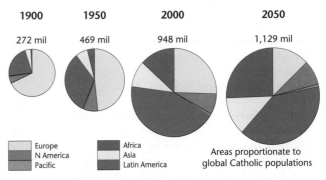

Fig 4.22 Catholic growth per continent, 1900–2050

Food for Thought

A moral tragedy has devastated the Church, first in the US, then around the world, as the media have gleefully exposed paedophile priests long protected by the hierarchy. This has brought into question the appropriateness of a celibate priesthood and has underlined the need for the hierarchy to be accountable to those below them. It has also hastened a massive reduction in church involvement and an already catastrophic decline in the number of parish priests. This issue is not unique to the Catholic Church—few denominations have a clean record on this. The Catholic Church has at least stood against abortion and same-sex immorality.

▲ How can the Church hold the moral high ground in a fallen world if it does not live by biblical standards?

Orthodox Christianity fascinates many Western Christians—it has an air of mystery that is a legacy of centuries of separation in theology, culture and history. Some Protestants are attracted by its multiculturalism and mysticism, its reverence for the Bible and its continuity with the past. The Orthodox have borne the brunt of centuries of persecution and suppression by non-Christians (Muslims, Mongols, Communists). No other part of the Church has contributed so many martyrs. Yet there are other issues: a common ethnocentrism, lack of vision for missions and bigotry where Orthodoxy is dominant. Today, Orthodoxy is in crisis and severe decline. What is its future?

1900: A glorious past but uncertain future

1. Greece heir to the heritage of Byzantium; today still many Greeks in Turkey
2. A millennium of Slavic Orthodoxy in Europe
3. Russia the centre of Orthodoxy; eastward expansion by settlement and conversion of indigenous peoples
4. Coptics in Egypt survive under Islam
5. 2,000 years of Orthodoxy in Ethiopia
6. Oriental Orthodoxy right across Asia, now a shadow of its past greatness
7. Russian Empire; Slavic immigrants in C. Asia
8. Greek and Slavic Orthodox immigrants in NAPa
9. Orthodoxy in 1000-year decline, from 54% of Christians worldwide to 22% in 1900

1900–50: Decades of disaster

1. Orthodox persecuted and manipulated in Soviet Union; millions perish in gulags etc
2. In C Asia forced Orthodox Slavic immigration to dilute Muslim majority
3. Communist control of Orthodox countries in E Europe
4. Massacres and emigration of Orthodox from Middle East
5. Restricted freedom in Egypt
6. Many Orthodox immigrants from the Middle East to NAPa
7. Orthodox missions begin in E Africa.
8. Orthodox decline from 22% of worldwide Christians to 13% in 1950

2000: From subjugation to restoration

1. Orthodox Church regains political influence in Russia.
2. Many Orthodox leave Muslim C Asia after 1990.
3. Orthodox-majority countries in E Europe harass other Christian minorities—especially Belarus, Bulgaria and parts of former Yugoslavia.
4. Exodus of Orthodox to escape persecution and war in Iran, Iraq, Lebanon, Palestine, Syria etc
5. Islamic persecution increases in Egypt.
6. EuNAPa Orthodox immigration, not least into the EU
7. Christians survive in Ethiopia and thrive after the 1975–91 trauma of Marxist persecution.
8. Some US Evangelicals convert to Orthodoxy.

2050: Crisis looms—some possible scenarios

1. Population decline in Russia and disillusion with Orthodox Church lead to large losses.

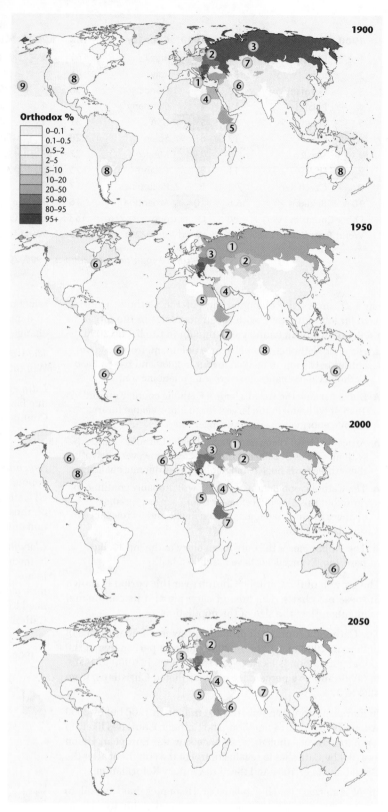

Fig 4.23 *Global spread of the Orthodox, 1900–2050*

2. Orthodox authoritarianism curbs other Christian ministry and outreach in E Europe.
3. Attrition by materialism in EU
4. Continued attrition of Orthodox communities in Middle East
5. Low birthrate and discrimination reduce and marginalize Orthodox Christians in Egypt.
6. Ethiopia and Eritrea favour Orthodox Christians; non-Orthodox Christians persecuted in Eritrea
7. Orthodoxy celebrates 2,000 years of history in India.

1900	Country	mil	1950	Country	mil	2000	Country	mil	2050	Country	mil
1	Russia	62	1	Russia	36	1	Russia	60	1	Ethiopia	56
2	Ukraine	21	2	Ukraine	21	2	Ethiopia	39	2	Russia	32
3	Romania	10	3	Romania	14	3	Ukraine	31	3	Ukraine	13
4	Belarus	5	4	Ethiopia	8.7	4	Romania	17	4	Egypt	11
5	Bulgaria	3	5	Greece	7.4	5	Greece	9.6	5	Romania	9.5
6	Turkey	3	6	Bulgaria	5.8	6	Egypt	7.9	6	USA	7.9
7	Ethiopia	2.7	7	Egypt	3.9	7	USA	5.9	7	Greece	7.4
8	Greece	2.5	8	Yugoslavia	3.7	8	Bulgaria	5.7	8	Yugoslavia	3.6
9	Yugoslavia	2.5	9	Belarus	3.1	9	Yugoslavia	5.4	9	Eritrea	2.9
10	Poland	2.3	10	USA	2.5	10	Belarus	5	10	Bulgaria	2.8
Other Countries (48)		9.3	Other Countries (74)		14	Other Countries (104)		25	Other Countries (101)		26
World Total (58)		124	World Total (84)		120	World Total (114)		213	World Total (111)		172

*Yugoslavia used here for 1900–2050 comprises the Yugoslavia of 2000—now Serbia, Montenegro and Kosovo

Fig 4.24 *Top 10 countries for Orthodox, 1900–2050*

How little the list changes! In 2050, most countries in the top 10 will be European still, and all will be traditionally Orthodox. The common concerns will be ethnocentrism and survival, not missions.

Fig 4.24 reveals extraordinary trends over this period:

▲ Ethiopia was the only non-European country in the list in 1900. By 2050, its Orthodox population will have grown from 2.7 million in 1900 to maybe 56m—then the largest in the world.

▲ The multicultural Ottoman Empire, of which Turkey was the heart, had a large Armenian minority. Millions were killed or driven out between 1894 and 1916, which explains the big fall in numbers by 1950.

▲ Russia has been the Orthodox "superpower" for centuries, but will lose its numerical supremacy by 2050.

▲ In E Europe the Orthodox are likely to suffer significant decline over the next four decades, with losses to the non-religious and possibly also to the Evangelicals.

▲ The USA is of growing importance to the Orthodox, offering more freedom than both Muslim and Orthodox countries. (Few Orthodox countries tolerate breakaway churches or new churches serving ethnic minorities.) Many branches of Orthodoxy now have their headquarters there.

The ongoing decline of the Orthodox population over this period was only reversed during 1980–2000, after the collapse of Communism in Europe. The only part of the Orthodox world showing consistent growth is *Ethiopia*.

N America's Orthodox are boosted mostly by immigration, and also some by conversion. Only in Alaska, when under Russian rule, has Orthodox mission work made an impact on indigenous populations.

Orthodox missions have been limited over the past 500 years to work among indigenous peoples across *Siberia*, using the

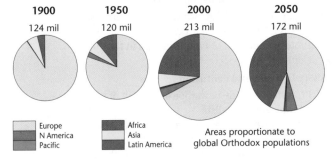

Fig 4.25 *Orthodox growth per continent, 1900–2050*

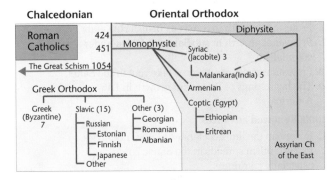

Fig 4.26 *Orthodox origins*

Russian language since the 1700s, and a little Coptic mission work in *Ethiopia and E Africa*.

There were three great schisms (in 424, 451 and 1054),[19] each contributing to the diversity within Orthodoxy. Note the red schism lines.

Burning Questions for Today

▲ Are Orthodox-majority countries evangelized—or a needy mission field?

There is much to respect in Orthodoxy: its tenacity in suffering, its New Testament heritage and its spirituality. Some well-known Evangelicals have become Orthodox. Yet are the Orthodox Churches right to insist that they have sole spiritual authority for the countries and peoples where they have the majority? A whole population may be baptized and yet in most such countries few go to church or have any understanding of the biblical way of salvation. Accusations of proselytism by Christians, and especially Evangelicals, are hollow. Discriminatory legislation, and even persecution, is still a reality in many Orthodox countries.

▲ Can we neglect nominally Orthodox populations that their churches do not evangelize and leave them without a personal knowledge of Christ?

In the 16th Century the Reformation led to a rediscovery of biblical truth, a new dynamism and, for millions in Europe, a personal faith, though it took nearly three centuries and several evangelical "awakenings" before it became an outward-looking missions movement that had an impact on the rest of the world. These maps show the progress made since 1900.

1900: After a century of advances

1. N Europe the heart of the Protestant Reformation
2. The UK: the main missionary-sender of the 19th Century
3. The USA: increasingly the hub of Protestant Christianity
4. The Pacific: the first non-Western Protestant countries
5. Some peoples in the Dutch Indies have already been Protestant for 300 years.
6. India the first target of modern Protestant missions
7. Livingstone's explorations make southern Africa a gateway for the Gospel into C Africa.
8. Costly sowing in W Africa with little fruit; disease makes it "the white man's grave".
9. Protestant neglect of Latin America in the 19th Century

1950: Division and confusion

1. Protestant decline in Europe as a result of both tyranny and liberalism
2. Tragic wars and dramatic revivals in Korea
3. Decline in US mainline denominations
4. Severe persecution of illegal Protestant churches in the Soviet Union
5. Protestant revival and growth in China, but missions are suppressed by the Communists in 1950.
6. Protestant growth in S Asia as British rule ends
7. Protestant growth in sub-Saharan Africa under colonialism
8. Protestant mission advances take root in the Sahel.
9. The beginnings of Protestant growth in Latin America

2000: Renewed advances

1. European decline accelerates in most countries.
2. Protestantism spreads in the Slavic lands, especially Ukraine.
3. Mainline denominational divisions in USA; Evangelicals grow in numbers and influence.
4. S Korea develops as a major sender of missions.
5. Indonesia: revival and growth despite Islam
6. Protestant growth in S Asia, but increased persecution from both Hindu and Muslim extremists
7. Numerical growth and geographical expansion in the Sahel
8. Protestant growth and revival under Muslim and Communist persecution in Sudan and Ethiopia
9. Much Protestant growth and vigour in Latin America; more missionaries sent abroad

2050: Facing a globalized world

1. European Protestants are in a minority in Protestant countries.
2. Small but significant Protestant growth in Middle East
3. Protestant mainline denominations decline in USA.

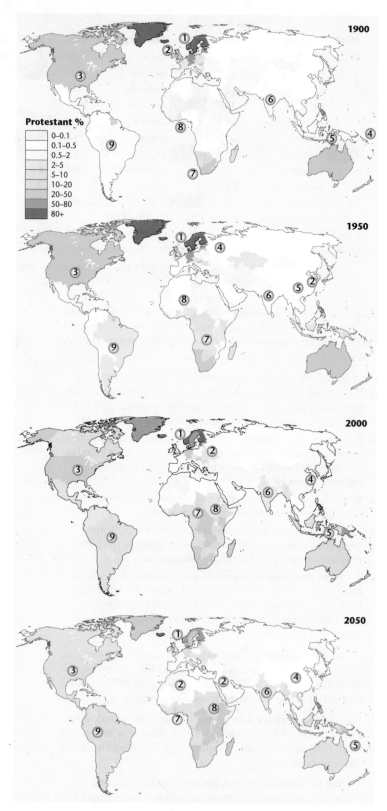

Fig 4.27 *Global spread of Protestants, 1900–2005*

4. Most growth in China amongst Independents, but many still treasure their pre-1949 Protestant roots.
5. Decline in both the Pacific islands and Australia/New Zealand due to nominalism and secularism
6. Significant Protestant growth in India is likely as the oppressed poor turn to Christ.
7. Dynamic Protestant growth in W Africa amidst economic and political failure
8. A maturing, growing Protestant Church in Sudan and Ethiopia
9. Latin American Protestant Evangelicals gain greatly in influence as Catholic influence wanes.

1900	Country	mil		1950	Country	mil		2000	Country	mi.		2050	Country	mil
1	USA	35		1	USA	36		1	USA	69		1	USA	63
2	Germany	22		2	Germany	21		2	Germany	28		2	Ethiopia	49
3	UK	9.1		3	UK	14		3	India	21		3	India	48
4	Sweden	5.1		4	Sweden	8.7		4	Nigeria	19		4	Congo, DR	43
5	Netherlands	3.2		5	Canada	5.0		5	Indonesia	18		5	Nigeria	41
6	Finland	2.7		6	India	4.6		6	Korea, S	17		6	Brazil	33
7	Denmark	2.4		7	Denmark	4.1		7	Ethiopia	13		7	Indonesia	29
8	Canada	2.3		8	Netherlands	4.1		8	Congo, DR	12		8	Kenya	17
9	Norway	2.2		9	Finland	3.8		9	Brazil	12		9	Philippines	17
10	Switzerland	1.9		10	S Africa	3.8		10	S Africa	10		10	Uganda	17
Other Countries (160)		14		Other Countries (207)		35		Other Countries (220)		141		Other Countries (222)		285
World Total (170)		100		World Total (217)		158		World Total (230)		358		World Total (232)		644

Fig 4.28 Top 10 countries for Protestants, 1900–2050

In 1900 the 10 countries with the largest Protestant populations were all Western, but of these only the USA may still be on the list in 2050. The other nine will probably be African, Asian or Latin American. Two of these are non-Christian (Hindu India and Muslim Indonesia) and three are Catholic-majority.

The US tops the list throughout this period. Its influence on global Christianity is often underestimated but (despite the growth of AfAsLA Protestants and Independents) the worship styles and use of technology in US churches are imitated by Christians and non-Christians[20] alike around the world—which has both its positives and its negatives!

In 1900, eight of the top Protestant countries were European. By 2000, Germany was the only one left in the top 10, and that was mainly because membership statistics are linked to the system of church tax levied by the government.[21] By 2050, no European country is likely to remain on the list. Many European Protestants speak of "a post-Christian world". This is inaccurate: only Europe will merit that description—though Canada and the Pacific countries are heading in the same direction.

The sixfold increase in the number of Protestants worldwide between 1900 and 2050 is considerably larger than the not quite fourfold increase in the global population over the same period. However, in AfAsLA Protestants will have increased almost a hundredfold, from 5.4 million to perhaps 524m—which brings home how successful the 200-year Protestant missions movement has been. If we also take into account the majority of the Independent Churches that are essentially Protestant in origin or inspiration, this success appears even more remarkable.

Europe's Protestants peaked at 83 million in 1960 but will probably have declined to 44 million by 2050. (As a percentage of Protestants worldwide, they will have dwindled from a clear majority in 1900 to 45% in 1960 to a likely 7% in 2050.)

N America's Protestants have increased in number but have not seen the sort of growth the newer Independent church networks have. Disputes over sexuality and women in leadership have torn apart many of the larger denominations, boosting the new Independent denominations—most of them evangelical in theology.

The major growth has been in *Latin America, Africa and Asia*. AfAsLA countries had 5% of all Protestants in 1900, but in 2000 this figure had grown to 59% and it may reach 81% by 2050.

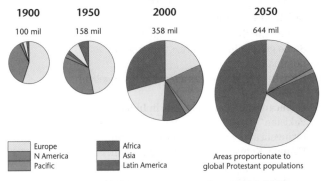

1900	1950	2000	2050
100 mil	158 mil	358 mil	644 mil

Europe
N America
Pacific

Africa
Asia
Latin America

Areas proportionate to global Protestant populations

Fig 4.29 Protestant growth per continent, 1900–2050

By 2050, over 44% of all Protestants will probably be Africans—a figure all the more astonishing given that Independent indigenous groups have grown even more at the same time. This has enormous significance for the future of Protestantism, as African Protestants are likely to have a global influence in leadership and the direction of theological reflection and denominational life.

Cape Town 2010 (photo courtesy Lausanne Movement)

Burning Question for Today

These figures and charts show that the lands of the Reformation will have little spiritual impact on the world in the 21st Century.

▲ What has caused the loss of the cutting edge, the spiritual authority and the visionary enthusiasm that gave rise to one of the most significant efforts in history to obey the Great Commission?

The spiritual need of Europe will now become the focus of attention of the non-European Christian world that Europe once blessed.

Anglicanism is a unique blending of five Christian streams (see p111). Fig 4.30 shows how this very English Church has morphed into a global denomination, the third largest in the world.

To 1900: Church and Empire

1. In the UK strong Anglican influence in the Victorian era
2. Episcopalians in the USA, a church of the elite
3. Anglicans followed British colonial expansions in the Caribbean (to grow sugar using slave labour)
4. Autonomous in Canada, gaining its own synod in 1893
5. Growth under British rule in India
6. White settlers in S Africa; mission outreach
7. Growth among both settlers and indigenes in Australia, New Zealand and the Pacific islands
8. Anglican growth in British colonies in W Africa
9. Anglicanism takes root among overseas Chinese in Malaya, Borneo and Singapore.

1950: Moving beyond empire

1. Majority in the UK still baptized as Anglicans
2. Some growth in N America, but much nominalism
3. Growth in S America as a result of Evangelical missions
4. Anglicans into church unions in India and Pakistan
5. Evangelical revivals in Rwanda, Burundi, Uganda, Kenya etc lead to much growth.
6. Anglican expatriate community in the Gulf states
7. Anglicans become a leading voice against apartheid in S Africa.
8. Strong and expanding Anglican Church in southern and central Nigeria

2000: After empire

1. Rapid decline in UK numbers and influence, but a growing Evangelical wing
2. Divisions threaten the Church in N America.
3. Continued advances and growing effectiveness in S America
4. SE Asia: overseas Chinese; dynamic growth; increasingly Charismatic and Evangelical
5. Massive growth in E Africa, especially in Uganda
6. Australian decline—except in the diocese of Sydney
7. Global Anglican expatriate community in the Gulf states
8. Sudan: huge growth in the south after decades of *jihad* and Muslim persecution
9. 12 million Anglicans in Nigeria

2050: A global but divided communion?

1. Disestablishment and renewal in the UK?
2. Accelerated, suicidal decline in the USA?
3. Evangelical growth to continue in Latin America?
4. Evangelical/Charismatic growth with vigorous national leadership in SE Asia?
5. E Africa: the centre of gravity of Evangelical Anglicanism?
6. Worldwide: schism, followed by decline or revival?
7. Sudan divided between the Muslim north and a largely Christian south?
8. Nigeria: a source of global leadership sharpened by the confrontation with Islam?

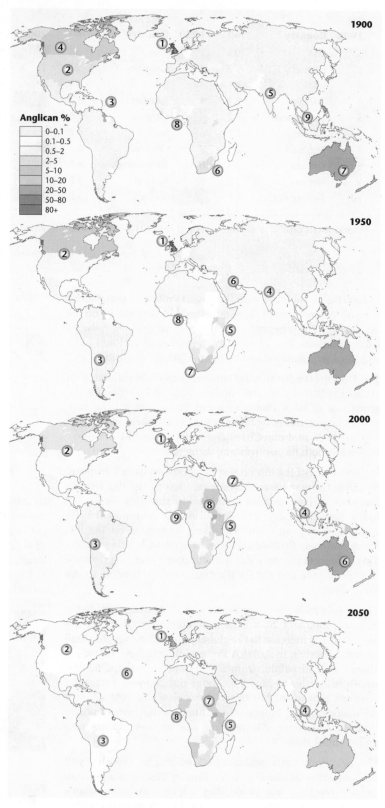

Fig 4.30 *Global spread of Anglicans, 1900–2050*

Food for Thought

The Anglican Church in 2050 is likely to be overwhelmingly African, largely conservative and mostly evangelical in its churchmanship.

▲ Has the English-speaking part of the Anglican Communion fully grasped the implications of such developments?

▲ Should the Archbishop of Canterbury automatically be regarded as the overall leader?

1900	Country	mil	1950	Country	mil	2000	Country	mil	2050	Country	mil
1	UK	25	1	UK	28	1	UK	25	1	Uganda	41
2	USA	1.6	2	Australia	3.2	2	Nigeria	12	2	Nigeria	33
3	Australia	1.5	3	USA	2.8	3	Uganda	9.6	3	UK	14
4	Canada	0.6	4	Canada	1.1	4	Australia	3.9	4	Sudan	8.7
5	New Zealand	0.3	5	New Zealand	0.8	5	Kenya	2.8	5	Tanzania	7.6
6	Jamaica	0.3	6	S Africa	0.8	6	Tanzania	2.7	6	Kenya	7.1
7	Ireland	0.3	7	Uganda	0.6	7	USA	2.4	7	Australia	3.4
8	S Africa	0.2	8	Nigeria	0.3	8	Sudan	2.3	8	Burundi	2.6
9	Barbados	0.1	9	Trinidad	0.1	9	S Africa	1.8	9	Rwanda	2.2
10	Uganda	0.1	10	Kenya	0.1	10	Rwanda	0.8	10	S Africa	1.4
	Other Countries (59)	1.2		Other Countries (92)	1.5		Other Countries (129)	6.4		Other Countries (126)	9.5
	World Total (69)	31		World Total (102)	40		World Total (139)	70		World Total (136)	130

Fig 4.31 Top 10 countries for Anglicans, 1900–2050

Nominalism is a particular problem in the English-speaking world. Active Anglicans may constitute only about 10–15% of the totals cited. The high figures for Anglicans in the UK during the 20th Century include many who rarely, if ever, went to church.

In the 20th Century it was no surprise that the great majority of Anglicans were in the UK. In 1900 over 80% of all Anglicans lived in the British Isles, but by 2000 this had fallen to 36%. The 21st Century will be the century of African Anglicans, and UK Anglicans will constitute only about 10% of the total worldwide.

By 2050, eight of the top 10 Anglican countries will probably be African.

Around 1985, the majority of Anglicans were in AfAsLA, and often they were more involved in the Church than Anglicans elsewhere.

Only a small percentage of non-Anglophone Anglicans are indigenous to AfAsLA countries that were never ruled by the British. The principal countries concerned are Burundi (2.6m in 2050), Rwanda (2.1m), Congo, DR (1m), Madagascar (600,000), Angola (400,000), Brazil (250,000), Mozambique (220,000) and Haiti (180,000).

Anglicans constituted

▲ 5.5% of all Christians in 1900

▲ 4.4% in 1950, and were in decline because of the loss of nominal Anglicans

▲ 3.5% in 2000—but possibly increasing to 4.3% in 2050. Any such increase would be mainly in Africa, as a consequence of both population growth and conversion.

In 1900, the Anglican Communion was 96% Caucasian and almost entirely English-speaking. By 2050, this percentage is likely to have fallen to just 16%. The transformation of an Anglophone denomination into a global, largely non-Western family of churches in the space of 150 years is an unusual story. It was one of the legacies of the British Empire, an empire built on trade and greed but by a people long committed to freedom of religion and speech. The inconsistencies between these two commitments provided the catalyst for this unexpected development—one never conceived by Anglican leaders and missionaries of the past!

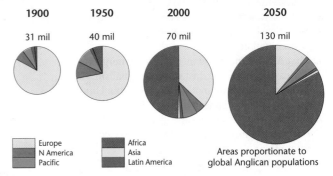

1900	1950	2000	2050
31 mil	40 mil	70 mil	130 mil

Europe · N America · Pacific · Africa · Asia · Latin America

Areas proportionate to global Anglican populations

Fig 4.32 Anglican growth per continent, 1900–2050

AfAsLA Anglicans constituted just 4% of the total in 1900, but by 2000 this percentage had risen to 52%, and it could reach 84% by 2050. The impact of AfAsLA Anglicans, and especially Africans, will determine the Church's theological direction.

Note how few in numbers and small in influence *N American* Anglicans will be in 2050, in contrast to the wider communion. The theological vagaries of the US Episcopalian Church have looked so important in recent years, but current trends show them to be a damaging digression.

Anglicanism: its roots

▲ the Celtic heritage from Patrick, the apostle to Ireland, and Irish missionaries to Britain

▲ unreformed Catholicism within Anglicanism—the Anglo-Catholic or High Church stream

▲ John Wycliffe's teaching and Bible translation and the influence of his followers, the Lollards, over a century before the Reformation

▲ the Reformation, with input from the Lutherans and Calvinists of mainland Europe

▲ the legacy of the political involvement of Henry VIII, king of England from 1509 to 1547. The British monarch still has a limited legal role as "the Supreme Governor" of the Church of England.

The Anglican Communion is an association of 44 autonomous national and regional churches in agreement with the Church of England on "essential" doctrines, with the Archbishop of Canterbury as symbolic, not legal, head.

Independent Christianity represents a paradigm shift in how to "be" church, often driven by ethnic or generational indigenization rather than doctrinal principles. It includes elements of protest against tradition, paternalistic leadership, formality, rigid liturgies and historic divisions within Christianity that are seen as no longer relevant.

In the West, this has become known as "*post-denominationalism*". With flatter structures, less bureaucracy, it is more relational and impatient with historic labels. All new denominations, networks and single congregations that show some of these traits are classified as *Independents*.[22]

To 1900: Small beginnings

1. Close Church-State links limit development of Independents to a few European countries.[23]
2. Religious freedom allows new expressions of church life to develop in the USA.
3. Freed slaves start their own churches in Liberia.
4. W Africa: beginnings of Independent denominations
5. First African Independent churches emerge in S Africa as a protest against white paternalism.
6. Independent denominations emerge from Hindu and Orthodox origins in India.
7. Independent "Old Believers" ejected from the Orthodox Church in Russia in the 17th Century retain their old liturgy.

1950: The expanding edge of the Church

1. Many new denominations and networks emerge in the 20th Century in the USA.
2. Independent churches heavily persecuted in the Soviet bloc
3. Rapid growth of large Independent Churches in Nigeria, Ghana and Côte d'Ivoire
4. Many new Pentecostal Independents in S and C Africa
5. Rapid growth of Independent Churches in the Philippines
6. S Asia: many secret believers among Hindus, unknown to mainline churches
7. The Church in China has to become indigenous as Communist persecution grows.
8. Chile: many new indigenous Pentecostal denominations after 1906
9. Rapid growth of Independents in Brazil

2000: The fastest growing part of the Church

1. Europe: newer churches still marginalized
2. Muslims coming to Christ in the Middle East
3. W Africa: expansion of large Independent Churches[24]
4. S and C Africa: many new Pentecostal Independents
5. Independents a near-majority of active Christians in N America; post-denominationalism
6. Local missions in India plant many churches.
7. Dramatic Independent growth in China
8. Problem of Pentecostal nominalism in Chile
9. Rapid growth of Independents in S America

2050: A post-denominational Christianity

1. Eclipse of most denominational structures as post-denominational Independency grows in the USA
2. Europe: Independent churches primarily among migrants

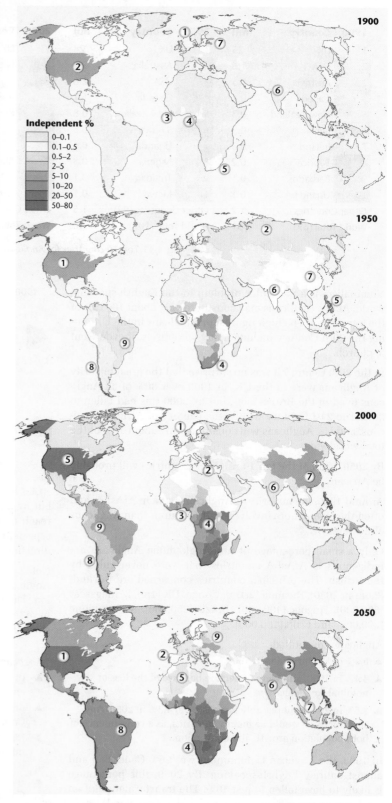

Independent %

	0–0.1
	0.1–0.5
	0.5–2
	2–5
	5–10
	10–20
	20–50
	50–80

Fig 4.33 *Global spread of Independents, 1900–2050*

3. Independent Christians in China have global impact.
4. Independent Christianity is now the main expression of church life in Africa and a channel for missions
5. BMB churches likely to multiply in the Middle East
6. Dalit-Bahujan movement to Christ in India likely to accelerate
7. SE Asia: dynamic new church life and witness among Indonesians, Chinese etc
8. Rapid growth of Independents in Latin America
9. E Europe: persecution likely to increase again, stimulating more church growth

1900	Country	mil	1950	Country	mil	2000	Country	mil	2050	Country	mil
1	USA	5.9	1	USA	15	1	China	87	1	China	194
2	Philippines	1.8	2	Philippines	1.8	2	USA	69	2	USA	116
3	India	0.1	3	S Africa	1.4	3	Nigeria	21	3	Nigeria	62
4	Latvia	0.1	4	Russia	1.2	4	S Africa	17	4	India	48
5			5	Congo, DR	1.1	5	India	14	5	Congo, DR	46
6			6	China	1.1	6	Philippines	12	6	Brazil	46
7			7	Nigeria	1.0	7	Congo, DR	11	7	Philippines	33
8			8	Czech Rep	0.8	8	Brazil	10	8	Kenya	27
9			9	Kenya	0.6	9	Kenya	7.0	9	S Africa	23
10			10	Brazil	0.5	10	Zimbabwe	4.6	10	Mozambique	14
Other Countries (25)		0.1	Other Countries (87)		2.5	Other Countries (198)		50	Other Countries (212)		232
World Total (29)		8.0	World Total (97)		27	World Total (208)		303	World Total (222)		840

Fig 4.34 *Top 10 countries for Independent Christians, 1900–2050*

The prominence of China in the list is significant. One result of the persecution by the Communists after 1949 was the enforced indigenization of Chinese Christianity. A biblical and mission-minded indigenous Church is emerging.[25]

These lists are fascinating in what they reveal about the changes in Christianity in the 20th and 21st Centuries.

In 1900, Independent Christianity was a major factor in the USA, where (unlike almost all other countries at the time) new expressions of church life faced few restrictions. The increase in the number of post-denominational or Independent Christians in the US maintains its position, alone among Western countries, in this list.

By 1950, Independency in Africa was becoming significant. At first it was more of a protest movement, but as the colonies rushed to independence in the 1960s, missions and international denominations began to realize that they, too, had to give their daughter churches autonomy. A third generation of Christians in dynamic indigenous movements formed churches that were more biblical and often charismatic and evangelical in their expression. This later growth has had global impact as Africans engage more in world evangelization.

The growth I have projected for India assumes that much of the Dalit population will turn to Christ. Time will tell whether this expectation is justified!

The growth of Independents since 1950 is extraordinary.

This has gone largely unnoticed in the West because it is largely unconnected with Western churches and missions. It is, nonetheless, a measure of the success of the modern Protestant missions movement, which sowed the seed of the Gospel and nurtured it—especially by translating the Bible into local languages. There has been growth in the Protestant denominations, but the real growth has been in their Independent offshoots.

The rise of Independent Christianity is the major source of church growth globally and more than compensates for the decline in the other, denominational megablocs.

Independents have increased from 1% of all Christians in 1900 to 3% in 1950 and 15% in 2000, and may reach 25% by 2050. The major growth areas are the *USA and AfAsLA*, with the former having huge influence on expressions of church life in the latter.

About 50–60% of these Independent churches are (broadly speaking) evangelical in their theology, but many are not, having marginal, syncretic, liberal or sacramental roots.

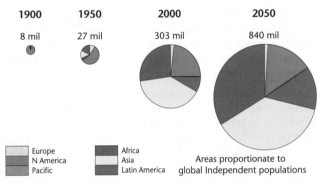

Fig 4.35 *Independent Christian growth per continent, 1900–2050*

There are many *African* Independent Churches that are pentecostal/charismatic in expression but not necessarily evangelical in theology.

The small sliver that represents *Europe* shows how European Christianity, not realizing that the Holy Spirit has moved on and blessed the rest of the world, has failed (and will probably continue to fail) to adapt old patterns for a new generation that has a very different culture and worldview that need new expressions of the unchanging Gospel.

Food for Thought

What impact will these dynamic Independent Christians have on our world? David Aikman subtitled his book *Jesus in Beijing:* "How Christianity is transforming China and changing the global balance of power".[26] This identifies China's Christians as the ones who will change our world, as missionaries, theologians and humble, sincere believers—but it is not only the Chinese but the Brazilians, too, with their heart for evangelism, the Indians with their missionary zeal, the Nigerians with their innovative outreach to non-Christians in hostile countries, the Filipinos with their willingness to live and even die for Jesus in Muslim lands. Most will represent Independent churches that are strong on faith, believe in miracles and expect God to answer prayer.

▲ Will this new wave also bring new life to older streams of Christianity?

▲ And will they welcome it?

1900	Country	mil
1	Philippines	1.8
2	USA	0.8
3	Romania	0.05
4	Belgium	0.02
5	UK	0.01
6	Canada	0.01
7		
8		
9		
10		
Other Countries (17)		0.1
World Total (23)		2.8

1950	Country	mil
1	USA	3.9
2	Philippines	1.2
3	UK	0.2
4	Canada	0.07
5	Switzerland	0.06
6	S Africa	0.05
7	Zambia	0.05
8	Netherlands	0.05
9	Romania	0.05
10	France	0.04
Other Countries (79)		0.36
World Total (89)		6.1

2000	Country	mil
1	USA	10.7
2	Philippines	6.6
3	Mexico	2.3
4	Brazil	2.0
5	China	2.0
6	Korea, S	1.7
7	UK	1.3
8	Nigeria	1.1
9	Peru	0.8
10	Japan	0.8
Other Countries (202)		11.8
World Total (212)		41

2050	Country	mil
1	USA	21.3
2	Philippines	7.6
3	China	6.8
4	Mexico	5.4
5	Brazil	5.3
6	Nigeria	3.6
7	Peru	2.1
8	Congo, DR	1.6
9	Argentina	1.5
10	UK	1.5
Other Countries (211)		28
World Total (221)		85

Fig 4.36 *Top 10 countries for Marginal Christians, 1900–1950*

The term "Marginal" is controversial! Some would prefer to classify these bodies as something other than Christian. However, this violates one of our basic principles, that we count people according to their self-profession—even if we regard their beliefs as unbiblical.

The changing order of countries (and continents) in Fig 4.36 is interesting. *The USA* now heads the list yet again—freedom of religion generates freedom to diverge into error. *The Filipino Independent Church* is a 19th-Century breakaway from the dominant (Spanish) Catholic Church. It is the largest Marginal denomination listed in the Philippines but probably should not have been classified as such. *China's Marginals* may ultimately prove to be far more numerous than I have projected for 2050. *Latin American Marginals* are likely to increase rapidly in both number and variety in the next few decades. Most *British and European Marginals* in 2000 were among immigrant communities.

The challenge of errant Marginal groups has always been with us. The New Testament often refers to the problems they presented to the early Church. In the 21st Century, the globalizing influence of migration, widespread access to the internet and higher literacy levels have combined with the negatives of overpopulation, ecological degradation and poverty to make many hearts and minds open to the "solutions" that such groups offer. Many African Independent Churches could also have been classified as Marginal according to our definition in the coloured box to the right.

Marginal groups flourished in the 20th Century, with the US setting the pace for a global increase in religious freedom. Note their remarkable growth worldwide since 1900. The largest included here—Jehovah's Witnesses and Mormons—are US in origin but have spread their message worldwide. (Scientology claims to be a Church but is not included here as it does not claim to be Christian.)

Some sections of Protestant denominations are even more marginal doctrinally than those counted here. Christians in mainline denominations who deny such basic, biblical doctrines as the personhood of God, the nature of Jesus Christ as equally God and man, His atoning death for sin, His bodily resurrection and His second coming, the existence of the Trinity and salvation by grace through faith are themselves, in effect, Marginal, even if this is not how their denomination is described.

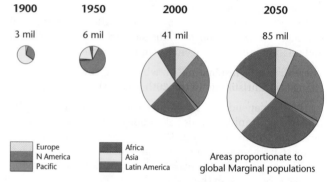

1900	1950	2000	2050
3 mil	6 mil	41 mil	85 mil

Europe
N America
Pacific

Africa
Asia
Latin America

Areas proportionate to global Marginal populations

Fig 4.37 *Marginal Christian growth per continent 1900–1950*

Definition: Marginal Christian Group

Any group that claims to be Christian but displays one or more of the following characteristics would be classed as Marginal:

▲ a non-Trinitarian Christology or anti-Trinitarian position

▲ a rejection of some doctrinal statements in all the historic creeds of the Church

▲ a claim to be the sole possessors of truth and of salvation

▲ a reliance on a further source of revelation equal in authority to the Bible, or greater than it

▲ an authoritarian leadership that claims unique access to God and knowledge of His will.

We use "Marginal" rather than "cult" or "sect", both of which are often pejorative and also rather ambiguous.

Food for Thought

Jesus warned us that false prophets would arise and lead many astray (Matthew 24:11). Church history is full of such people, as is the Christian world today. Much evangelism and good church growth do not mean that new believers become true disciples. Only people who have an intimate walk with the Lord, dig deep into the Scriptures and are daily filled with the Holy Spirit are able to discern error.

▲ How many of those who are linked with our ministries and churches have been so discipled that they can recognize a false prophet's teachings as wrong?

▲ Are we more interested in good attendance figures than in the costly effort of training true disciples?

The Christian megablocs and Christian denominations

Based on statistics for the Christian world's 38,000 denominations in 2000, this diagram shows the denominational origins of the six Christian megablocs and the basic links between them.[27]

Catholicism, Orthodoxy: The Great Schism of 1054 divided the Eastern and Western Church. Then, 54% of all Christians were Orthodox, but big losses to Islam and Catholicism followed and today only 10% of Christians are Orthodox.

Protestantism arose in the 16th Century as a protest against the error and decadence of the medieval Catholic Church. The Reformation has had a huge impact on the world since 1729, the year when Protestant missions began.

Anglicanism originated in England at the time of the Reformation—the three main streams of churchmanship are Reformed (Low), Catholic (High) and liberal (Broad).

Independents: As mission-related churches multiplied, so did indigenous movements—over 90% of Independent Christians have roots in Protestantism. The other 10% come from the Catholic, Orthodox, Anglican or Marginal megablocs.

Marginals: Many deviant forms of Christianity have arisen—most out of Protestantism.

The three most closely linked megablocs (P, I and A) are broken down by major denominational type. Note how many of these straddle two megablocs.

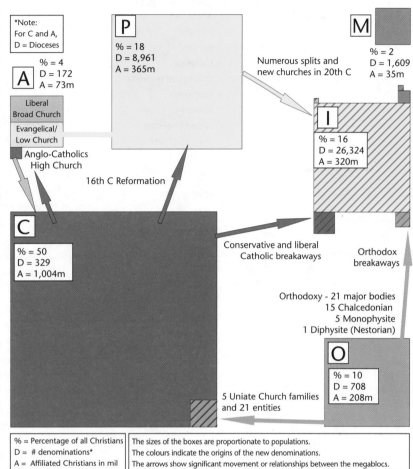

Fig 4.38 *The denominational make-up of the Christian megablocs in 2000*

I have listed 12 major denominational types in Fig 4.39, including those Independent denominations whose ecclesiology and theology are similar to that of Protestants. Bear in mind that every national denomination is counted—a denomination with branches in 30 countries will be recorded as 30 denominations.

It is not easy to predict developments for each denominational type, but the situation in 2050 will be very different from that shown here for 2000, with Pentecostal and Charismatic denominations showing continued growth but some, such as the Methodists, much reduced in numbers. More liberal denominations such as the United Protestant groups and the Lutherans will also see significant decline. The variations between the six continents are shown on pages 116 and 117. I have not included figures for the Catholics and Orthodox here.

Pentecostal denominations and *Charismatic* networks far outnumber all other types in terms of their affiliates, congregations and, above all, "denominations". The abundance of the last can be considered both good (in terms of variety, flexibility, cultural sensitivity, hardiness in times of persecution etc) and bad (in terms of perceived error, misuse of funds etc—and because schism usually arises out of a breakdown of leadership or clash of personalities). If this variety is increased by rivalry or sin, it is tragic; but if the diversity is character-

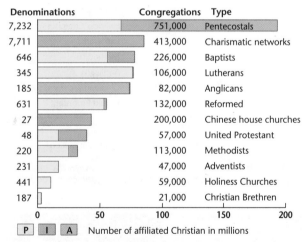

Fig 4.39 *The major denominational types for P, I and A globally in 2000*

ized by a spiritual unity and cooperation in ministry for the growth of God's Kingdom, it can be a blessing.

In 2000, the *Baptists* had the most denominations, congregations and affiliates of all the largely non-Charismatic streams—though many Baptist congregations were also Charismatic in practice.

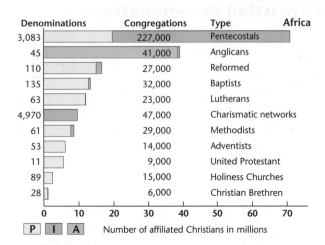

Denominations	Congregations	Type	Africa
3,083	227,000	Pentecostals	
45	41,000	Anglicans	
110	27,000	Reformed	
135	32,000	Baptists	
63	23,000	Lutherans	
4,970	47,000	Charismatic networks	
61	29,000	Methodists	
53	14,000	Adventists	
11	9,000	United Protestant	
89	15,000	Holiness Churches	
28	6,000	Christian Brethren	

P   I   A   Number of affiliated Christians in millions

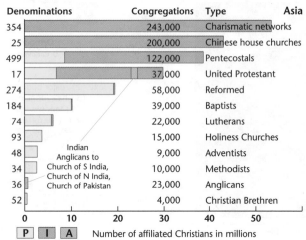

Denominations	Congregations	Type	Asia
354	243,000	Charismatic networks	
25	200,000	Chinese house churches	
499	122,000	Pentecostals	
17	37,000	United Protestant	
274	58,000	Reformed	
184	39,000	Baptists	
74	22,000	Lutherans	
93	15,000	Holiness Churches	
48	9,000	Adventists	
34	10,000	Methodists	
36	23,000	Anglicans	
52	4,000	Christian Brethren	

Indian Anglicans to Church of S India, Church of N India, Church of Pakistan

P   I   A   Number of affiliated Christians in millions

Denominations	Congregations	Type	Latin America
2,472	273,000	Pentecostals	
49	12,000	Adventists	
203	12,000	Charismatic networks	
155	20,000	Baptists	
62	10,000	Reformed	
162	12,000	Holiness Churches	
64	59,000	Lutherans	
56	56,000	Methodists	
46	24,000	Anglicans	
39	48,000	Christian Brethren	
6	4,000	United Protestant	

P   I   A   Number of affiliated Christians in millions

Fig 4.40 *AfAsLA continental differences between the main denominational types for P, I and A megablocs in 2000*

Cape Town 2010 (photo courtesy Lausanne Movement)

Africa

What stands out is the predominance of *Pentecostals*. About half of the Independent Pentecostals are not Evangelical in theology but more syncretic. Newer indigenous Pentecostal groups have been more willing to confront syncretic practices but can have other problems: charismatic leaders who are unaccountable and make no plans for their succession, misuse of funds, infatuation with "prosperity" teaching etc.

Anglicans are the second-biggest group—especially in E Africa, Nigeria and southern Africa.

The *Reformed* group is also large—primarily a legacy of the strong influence of southern Africa's Afrikaners.

The *Lutherans* have large communities in Ethiopia, Tanzania, Madagascar, Nigeria, S Africa and Namibia. Both Ethiopia and Madagascar have seen significant revivals.

Baptists are widespread, the fruit of both Baptist and interdenominational mission agencies. The countries with the most Baptist affiliates are Ethiopia with 4.2 million (largely thanks to SIM missionaries) and Nigeria with 1.8 million.

Asia

The three largest denominational types in Asia are predominantly Independent. Most are Evangelical in theology.

China's networks of unregistered churches are large and growing. Figures released in 2009 show that their memberships total about 47 million.[28]

The *United Protestant Churches* include China's Three-Self Patriotic Movement. The government monitors it closely and places restrictions on its churches' ministry. Many of these were among China's original Protestant denominations; half or so are probably broadly evangelical, but some are liberal in their theology. India and Pakistan also have key United Churches. The Anglican contribution to these unions is shown in blue on the graph.

Reformed Churches are strong in S Korea and Indonesia—the former has over 100 Presbyterian/Reformed denominations, the latter 38 regional Reformed Churches.

One remarkable Reformed Church is that of Mizoram State in India. After a century of revival, today most of the Mizo are enthusiastic Christians. A 750,000-strong Church (in a population of about 1 million) has sent some 2,000 missionaries out to India and beyond.

Latin America

In Latin America (and the Caribbean), almost all other denominational types have had to adapt to the success of the *Pentecostal* culture and style of worship that so suit the people and are such a contrast to the often distant clergy and the formalism, superstition and syncretism of the Catholicism that was originally imposed on them. Latin America now has one of the largest Catholic Charismatic communities in the world.

Adventism has also been very successful, probably on account of the legalistic demands it makes of its adherents. Many nominal Adventists still take care to keep the Sabbath and refrain from eating pork, but attach little importance to avoiding a sinful lifestyle.

Holiness denominations have also done well, especially the Christian and Missionary Alliance, Church of the Nazarene and Church of God (Anderson).

Europe

The Lutherans are the most numerous type, but many listed as members of churches have no meaningful connection with them. All the Scandinavian countries and parts of Germany are mostly Lutheran, but those majorities are melting away. Pietistic awakenings in Norway, Finland and parts of Sweden and Germany have left an Evangelical legacy.

The Reformed Churches are strong in the northern Netherlands, parts of Switzerland, Scotland and N Ireland. Most denominations are in decline and liberal in theology, but all have an Evangelical minority.

The Methodists are in serious decline across Europe wherever they have a presence. Most are in the UK.

The Baptists are generally holding their own where most of their churches are Evangelical in theology, but their numbers and influence in Europe are quite small.

The Pentecostal/Charismatic Churches are small and have generally been on the margins of Christian life in Europe.

Indigenous *Independent* movements were relatively insignificant before the 1970s. Many *Independents* are immigrants from the Caribbean or Africa.

N America

The Baptists are the most numerous type. In the USA, their structure and ecclesiology suit a culture that prizes individualism and democratic decision-making. Most successful are the Southern Baptists, who have remained largely Evangelical in theology and have an extensive global mission outreach.

Modern *Pentecostalism* was born in the USA and has had some success in N America (though more in AfAsLA).

Charismatic Christian networks have become important. Many flourishing newer churches are run like business corporations in terms of their structure and marketing, but this can be at the expense of a biblical leadership style, effective discipling and adequate accountability.

More traditional types such as *Reformed, Methodists, Lutherans and Anglicans* have been split by suicidal divisions over the authority of the Bible, sexuality, abortion and the place of women in leadership. This has weakened their message, damaged their credibility and decimated their membership.

Extensive use has been made of radio, television and the internet to communicate the Gospel and impart teaching. This has become a highly successful industry, though the behaviour of some televangelists has brought the Church into disrepute.

The Pacific

Over 60% of the region's population live in Australia and New Zealand, the majority of them being European (and largely British or Irish) in origin. Denominational types reflect that heritage. The same denominations were also the evangelizers of the indigenous peoples.

Anglicans are the most numerous, followed by the *United Protestant* groups (mainly in Australia and Papua New Guinea).

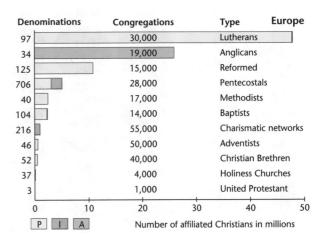

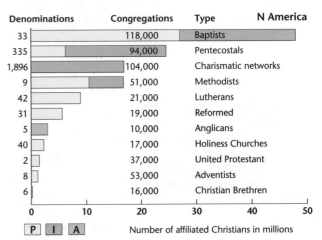

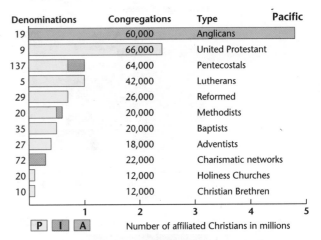

Fig 4.41 *EuNAPa continental differences between the main denominational types for P, I and A megablocs in 2000*

Independents—and especially *Charismatics*—have until recently played a minor role but are now the one growing element of a Church in general decline.

Burning Questions for Today

▲ What is the future for denominations, both old and new, in a changing, globalized world?

▲ How can stability, continuity and tradition be balanced with change, flexibility and innovation and yet have the cultural relevance to win and retain the emerging generation?

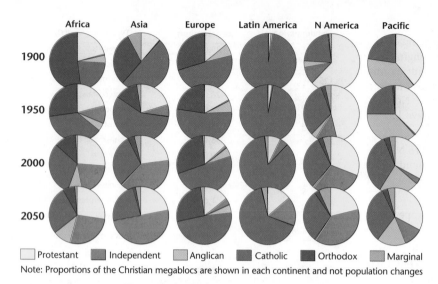

Fig 4.42 *Megabloc Changes per continent, 1900–2050*

Note: Proportions of the Christian megablocs are shown in each continent and not population changes

These last two pages draw together strands from earlier pages. Overall the percentage of the world's population that is Christian looks set to show little change, but since 1900 the shape of Christianity has continued to change dramatically. The pie charts illustrate this by megabloc and continent. The block charts show the changing proportions of the six megablocs and their geographical shift from EuNAPa to AfAsLA.

In Fig 4.42, the analysis of the changing proportions of the six megablocs by continent reveals some interesting facts:

▲ The dominance of some continents by a single megabloc is yielding to diversity. Discrimination against or persecution of Christian minorities by Christian majorities was common a century ago but, except in some Orthodox-majority areas, has now diminished.

▲ In Europe and the Pacific, the relative strengths of the megablocs have changed little (but as shown earlier, this is in a context of a decline in absolute numbers).

▲ All continents have seen a growth of Independents, but this growth has been least marked in Europe.

The last two facts are related.

In Fig 4.43, the vertical scale shows the percentage of all professing Christians affiliated to each megabloc. (The unaffiliated are not shown as such, but are represented by the gap between the Marginal block and the 100% mark.) The relative decline of the Catholics, Anglicans and, especially, Orthodox contrasts with the relative increase in Protestants, Marginals and, especially, Independents.

The horizontal scale shows the percentage of each megabloc found in the two regions EuNAPa and AfAsLA. Note that the central vertical line is 0%. The dramatic shift from the "old" Christian world to the "new" is plain to see.

The success of the different megablocs in maintaining their share of the world's Christian population is closely related to their success in transplanting Christianity in AfAsLA. The Protestant, Independent and Anglican megablocs are all likely to be over 80% AfAsLA by 2050, with the Catholics and Marginals not far behind. It is striking how unsuccessful the Orthodox have been in engaging in missions even when not engaged in a fight for survival—as they were for much of the 20th Century.

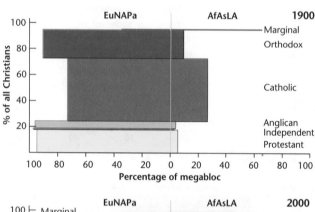

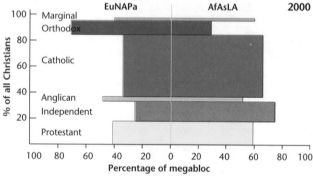

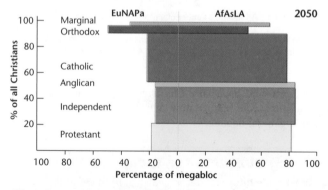

Fig 4.43 *Megabloc shifts between EuNAPa and AfAsLA, 1900–2050*

What about the future?

Present trends are likely to continue, but with less dramatic changes, due to the slowing of population growth:

▲ Christian areas will see their majorities eroded by losses to secularism and diluted by non-Christian immigration.

▲ There will be continued growth in Africa and Asia—especially China, India and SE Asia.

▲ There are likely to be increasing numbers of conversions to Christianity in some countries with large Muslim populations (most probable in Iran, N Africa, Indonesia and possibly India) and to Islam among disadvantaged people in Christian-majority countries (in Western prisons, for example, and poorer African states).

The top 20 Christian countries

Fig 4.44 lists the 20 countries with the largest Christian populations at 50-year intervals between 1900 and 2050. The colour behind the number of each entry indicates its continent, and this device highlights some of the major changes that will affect the life and ministry of the Church in the decades ahead. The significance of the changing order

▲ *The Americas and Europe* (shades of pink and red) dominated the list in 1900, but by 2050 a cluster of Asian and African countries may well have become prominent. The biggest surprise is India—assuming there is a high conversion rate among the Dalit.

▲ *The USA and Brazil* will be the largest nations with Christian majorities. The US contribution to missions will continue, and Brazil's may grow considerably—the youth of its population and its increasing wealth make that likely. In all, four Latin American countries will be in the top 20.

▲ The rise of *AfAs* countries up the list will be the result of both higher population growth and conversion. Conversely, the

eclipse of *European countries* will be the result of low birth rates, a loss of faith among adult Christians and a failure to disciple their increasingly dysfunctional children.

▲ As Christianity becomes increasingly global, there will be greater congruence in the top 20 between the absolute size of a country's Christian population and its total population.

▲ Four of the top 11 will be *Asian countries*. (Surprisingly, S Korea is unlikely to make the list.) By 2050, the Christian populations of those four countries could total 530 million.

▲ There will probably be four *African countries* in the top 20—but, given how many smaller countries there are in the continent, this does not reflect the numbers of African Christians, already great in 2000 and set to be much greater into the future.

Pressing issues in the 21st Century

1. *The disparity between rich and poor countries:* Some Latin American and Asian countries are likely to get stronger economically and join the wealthier Western countries. However, in India, Nigeria, Congo-DR and Ethiopia many will still be mired in poverty. The disparities will create turmoil as population pressures increase and climate change accelerates. Christians will have many opportunities to be involved in caring ministries locally and internationally.

2. *Violence and war:* In the first decade of the 21st Century there were wars, civil wars or inter-communal violence in eight of the top 20: Congo-DR, the Philippines, China, India, Indonesia, Russia, Ethiopia and Colombia. There are ample opportunities for Christians to be peacemakers.

3. *Islam:* In the 2050 list there is one Muslim-majority country, Indonesia, five with large indigenous Muslim minorities (China, India, Nigeria, the Philippines and Ethiopia) and many others with Muslim immigrant communities. Will the interactions between Christians and Muslims be peaceable or violent? Opportunities to demonstrate Christ's love for Muslims will never have been so extensive.

4. *Discrimination and persecution* against Christians have increased worldwide since 2000. In six of the 2050 top 20 there is already active persecution at local or national level which the authorities are encouraging or condoning. How will Christians handle such pressures?

Burning Question for Today

Never before has Christianity been geographically, culturally and linguistically so diverse. The Church has gone global. We can praise God for astonishing successes.

▲ How can we best overcome the inevitable differences of theology and denomination, for the good of our world and God's Kingdom?

The environment for our ministry is likely to become more hostile and less receptive than in recent decades. If we are to thrive in the 21st Century, much grace will be needed if we are to avoid internal strife and reach out to one another to bear witness together to our needy world.

	1900			1950			2000			2050	
Rank	Country	mil	Rank	Country	mil	Rank	Country	mil	Rank	Country	mil
1	USA	73.3	1	USA	146.1	1	USA	240.2	1	USA	292.3
2	Russia	67.3	2	Germany	66.2	2	Brazil	156.6	2	Brazil	210.9
3	Germany	41.4	3	Brazil	52.7	3	Mexico	94.5	3	China	205.4
4	France	40.7	4	Russia	52.1	4	China	86.5	4	India	159.3
5	UK	37.1	5	UK	45.6	5	Russia	79.2	5	Congo, DR	158.1
6	Italy	32.9	6	Italy	44.8	6	Philippines	70.5	6	Nigeria	151.2
7	Ukraine	26.9	7	France	37.8	7	India	64.5	7	Mexico	126.9
8	Poland	22.0	8	Spain	28.0	8	Nigeria	61.9	8	Philippines	110.6
9	Spain	18.8	9	Mexico	27.1	9	Germany	57.2	9	Ethiopia	108.9
10	Brazil	17.3	10	Poland	23.3	10	Congo, DR	47.7	10	Colombia	58.9
11	Mexico	13.5	11	Ukraine	22.9	11	Italy	44.6	11	Indonesia	54.1
12	Romania	10.4	12	Philippines	18.7	12	Ethiopia	44.6	12	Russia	46.9
13	Czech Rep	7.8	13	Argentina	16.6	13	Ukraine	43.3	13	Argentina	41.2
14	Belgium	6.6	14	Romania	15.5	14	UK	42.0	14	S Africa	35.0
15	Philippines	6.6	15	Canada	13.4	15	France	40.2	15	Germany	31.4
16	Belarus	6.4	16	Colombia	12.0	16	Colombia	40.2	16	UK	30.9
17	Hungry	6.4	17	India	10.7	17	Poland	34.9	17	Poland	25.9
18	Austria	5.8	18	Ethiopia	8.8	18	Argentina	34.3	18	Italy	24.1
19	Canada	5.5	19	S Africa	8.6	19	S Africa	33.5	19	France	23.2
20	Portugal	5.4	20	Belgium	8.4	20	Indonesia	33.5	20	Ukraine	20.3

The top 20 countries are listed for each half century, but the names and areas are extrapolated from their values for 2000. The Pacific is not included here since no Pacific nation is in the top 20.

Continents largely Christian before 1900:

☐ Europe ☐ N America ☐ Latin America

Continents more recently evangelized:

☐ Asia ☐ Africa

Fig 4.44 *The top 20 countries for Christians, 1900–2050*

1. The people lists of WCD, JPL and the IMB are ethno-linguistic. Ethnicity and language are not the same, but in the case of those mapped by the *Ethnologue* and GMI the overlap is probably over 95%, so sometimes peope (group) and language are used interchangeably.

2. For many this definition is too vague. It is a self-designation. We may have serious doubts about the theological or statistical validity or meaning of such a profession but it is valid for comparison of Christian statistics with those of other religions.

3. The great US church historian K S Latourette coined the phrase. He wrote after the Second World War but before the post-1960s Christian expansion—an expansion that few could ever have predicted.

4. The Enlightenment of the 18th Century derived its values from the premise that human reason is the final arbiter and authority. At its core was a critical questioning of traditional institutions, customs, morals and also theology. Its origins: the forbidden fruit in the Garden of Eden!

5. Latin America has always been hard to categorize—Christianized, but far from being evangelized. In the 1910 Edinburgh Missionary Conference, the spiritual needs of the continent were ignored in deference to the scruples of the Anglican Anglo-Catholic delegates. The number of Protestant or Evangelical believers was then extremely small.

6. The impact of Billy Graham can hardly be overestimated. He became the great ambassador for evangelism and world missions and helped to restore Evangelicalism to centre stage in world Christianity by 2000.

7. The basis for this evocative statement will be found in Chapter 6.

8. The WCD scale formed the basis, but modified and updated from Operation World information and the Open Doors religious persecution index.

9. See Chapter 2 for a fuller picture of this "Constantinian" captivity in which so much of Christendom was bound to or controlled by the State.

10. The percentages used for this green band are derived and adapted from the WCD statistics and represent those likely to have had some contact with a Christian witness. They should only be seen as an approximation that compares populations over time. See *World Christian Trends* by Barrett and Johnson (William Carey, 2001), p321.

11. The organization World Values Survey (http://www.worldvaluessurvey.org) in 2005 conducted an investigation of attitudes including frequency of social involvement in a place of worship. The 87 countries surveyed represented a great majority of the population of the world (though Africa was least comprehensively covered). I added up figures for each continent, on the assumption that the totals from this sample would be comparable to the actual continental totals.

12. *American Sociological Review*, December 1993, vol 58; and Gallup polls 1992–2004

13. There are few atheists in Africa. If an African claims to be one, any offer to pray that God might strike him in judgement because of this would probably elicit an impassioned plea not to do it!

14. The term "megabloc" for a Christian tradition was first used in the *World Christian Encyclopedia* of 1981, which detailed seven such blocs. In the following 20 years this methodology was adapted to incorporate schismatic Catholics (who constituted a separate bloc in 1981) in the Independent bloc. We decided to use the same terminology in the 2000 Operation World database, though there were some denominations that we thought better assigned to a different bloc (which means that Operation World figures are not always comparable with those in the *World Christian Encyclopedia* and World Christian Database). There has been a large, two-way flow of information between the two databases, but both have independently developed networks of sources and informants.

15. The doctrine of papal supremacy in the Church has several sources: Jesus' naming of Peter as the rock and the holder of the keys of the Kingdom, the claim that Peter was the first Pope in Rome, the primacy accorded to Rome by the five major centres of Christianity before its fall in 410, and the Church's assumption of some secular imperial powers after the fall of the Western Empire.

16. The intense debates of the early Church over the nature(s) of Christ led to a three-way schism. The Diphysites maintained that Christ had two separate, unmingled natures, one divine, one human. The Monophysites, in contrast, held that He had a single nature, part divine, part human. The Chalcedonian position was that He had two natures (divine and human) in one person. The deeper issue was not so much theological as linguistic, reflecting differences between Greek and Syriac. Although I have used these terms, they are no longer considered as divisive as they were then.

17. The DVD and website related to this book contains the Operation World database of denominations. The data took more than 20 years to assemble, from many sources—primarily the denominations themselves but often via secondary sources or deductive derivation. Figures are given for every five-year period from 1960 to 2000; many of them are also interpolative or extrapolative estimates.

18. This story is covered more fully in Chapter 2. See also Philip Jenkins' 2010 book *The Lost History of Christianity: The Thousand-Year Golden Age of the Church in the Middle East, Africa, and Asia*.

19. The three main schisms were: a) the *Diphysite*—the Assyrian Church of the East, b) the *Monophysite*—three main bodies and several offshoots such as the Indian, Ethiopian and Eritrean Orthodox. The Indians once had links with the Church of the East but later developed links with the Syriac Church, c) the *Great Schism* between the Roman Catholic and Chalcedonian Orthodox Churches, which resulted in over 25 separate Orthodox bodies. The largest branch of Orthodoxy is the Slavic, which includes the Russian Orthodox Church.

20. Islamist organizations such as al-Qa'ida hate the USA, but gladly use its technology and communications and finance systems and imitate the style of its religious organizations in terms of publicity, use of media, autonomous structures and commitment to a cause!

21. Germany, along with other German-speaking and Scandinavian countries, funds churches through a special church tax levied on members of recognized churches, who may legally opt out but often do not. This forms the basis of the country's Protestant and Catholic church membership statistics, even though many people have no involvement in church life apart from paying the tax.

22. The real divisions within Christianity are less well identified by denominational labels than by issues that cut right across denominational boundaries such as the opposition between Evangelicals and liberals and that between social conservatives and social liberals, the Pentecostal/Charismatic movement etc. This is examined more fully in the next chapter on "trans-megabloc" groups.

23. The closed nature of European society 100 years ago seems incomprehensible in today's emerging post-Christian Europe. For much of the 19th Century most of the continent was ruled by elites and dictatorships (both Communist and Fascist). Religious conformity was expected or even required by the governing powers or state church, and often any form of dissent that threatened the *status quo* was resisted or even severely persecuted.

24. Early African Independent Churches (AICs) were often strong protest movements that had semi-literate leaders and were syncretic, but after the 1960s most of the newer Churches became more biblical and mainstream Evangelical in theology, and usually Pentecostal in practice.

25. Chinese Christianity has two main streams of Independents, which emerged from 19th- and 20th-Century Protestant mission work. The first, the official, government-supervised Church (the Three-Self Patriotic Movement and the China Christian Council), is the successor to the various Protestant denominations and has both liberal and Evangelical components. The second stream is the "house churches" or unofficial (and often heavily persecuted) groups that refused to submit to the limitations the government wanted to impose. Both streams are included in these figures.

26. *Jesus in Beijing*, David Aikman (Regnery Publishing, 2003)

27. Every significant denomination that could be identified within a country is listed. Denominations with branches in many countries are therefore listed many times, which greatly increases the apparent number of denominations. This was necessary to derive country totals. Also, each national expression of an international denomination has its own theological perspective and character—for instance, what percentage of it is Evangelical in theology. The Operation World database has over 7,000 separate records for denominations in a country, but many single congregations and small networks of congregations are aggregated into single records in the above 7,000 (each with the aggregate number of contributing component Churches or networks also given). The database covers the period 1960–2002, but the new edition extends that to 2010. Those figures were not completed in time for this publication and so have not been used here.

28. Paul Hattaway of Asia Harvest spent several years reviewing the numbers of Christians of all types in China by province and district. This is by far the most accurate assessment to date. See p155.

Christianity: Renewal Growth

In Fig 5.1, the *oval* covers the five main streams of Christianity but excludes the Marginals. It shows the range of transconfessional types and their relationship to the Bible. The *central circle* represents the Bible and how closely Christians hold to its truths and authority. The *vertical axis* shows the range between the "spiritual" (the heart) and the intellectual (the mind), and the *horizontal axis* that between cultural and political Christianity. The *terms at the oval's edge* refer to emphases in churchmanship.

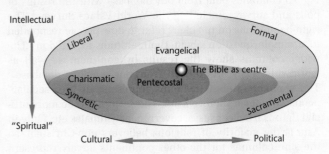

Fig 5.1 *Transconfessional Christianity and the Bible*

Worldviews in Christianity

People's worldviews, and their relationship to churchmanship and the Bible, are often more important than their denominational affiliations. Worldviews spread across denominational boundaries, and four tendencies are shown in the diagram that are transconfessional:

Formal. Many Christians have church links that range from nominalism—a problem across the denominational spectrum—to loyal but rarely life-changing involvement. Biblical truth is often little understood.

Sacramental. Predominantly Catholics, Orthodox and some traditional Protestant denominations may look to the sacraments rather than the Scriptures for their inspiration.

Liberal. Some Christianity is formed more by Western Enlightenment thinking and its virtual deification of human reason. Destructive biblical criticism and rejection of the miraculous or any need for personal salvation crippled the spiritual life of many mainline denominations in the 19th and 20th Centuries. Churches and denominations that espoused such teachings had gone into severe decline by the end of the 20th Century.

Syncretic. Elements of local culture incompatible with the Gospel have been interwoven into Christianity, so that its very message is corrupted or compromised. A global problem, though most prevalent in Latin America, Africa and parts of Asia and the Pacific.

Evangelicals and Charismatics are generally more Bible-centred, though the latter may be less so and may place more emphasis on spiritual experience. Both are found in all five main streams

of Christianity, though the majority of Evangelicals are P, I or A.

There is a close relationship and an overlap between Evangelicals, Pentecostals and Charismatics. *Evangelicals* will be defined and numbered more fully in the next chapter. Evangelicalism is characterized by a theology based on the inerrancy of the Bible, a personal experience of salvation by faith through grace and a desire or obligation to witness to that salvation.

Pentecostals are, by theological definition, all Evangelicals. They are also here defined as Charismatics. The pentecostal oval is located within the lower part of the evangelical oval since Pentecostalism emphasizes an experience of the filling or baptism of the Holy Spirit and the present exercise of spiritual gifts.

Charismatics who are not affiliated to a specifically pentecostal denomination generally belong to other denominations with a range of theological persuasions. Most will be Evangelicals, but not all—some 70–80% will probably be of an evangelical persuasion. That range is shown by the greater width of the charismatic oval across the Christian spectrum—many being also C or O or even syncretic (the last being found especially, though not exclusively, in Africa).

The first four categories in Fig 5.2 are more traditional, and these will include a large number of fringe Christians of various kinds (such as nominal and notional Christians, backsliders and even apostates). The first of the following pages aims to map out the extent of that fringe.

The last three categories refer to the major renewal movements in the Church that have contributed so much to its dramatic growth since the 1960s. It is in these, rather than in the six particular streams of Christianity covered in chapter 4, that the real dynamism of

Seven trans-confessional systems within Christianity

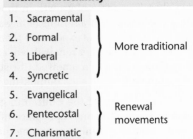

1. Sacramental
2. Formal   } More traditional
3. Liberal
4. Syncretic

5. Evangelical
6. Pentecostal   } Renewal movements
7. Charismatic

Fig 5.2 *Transconfessional Christianity*

the worldwide Church is to be found. From chapter 6 onwards, my focus will be largely on Evangelicals—whether pentecostal or non-pentecostal, charismatic or non-charismatic.

Nominalism

Fig 5.3 combines data from our database with the results of polls and surveys, including the World Values Survey.[4] The right-hand terms on the chart refer to how people responded to a simple question about their attitude to religion. The wider columns show the results by continent as well as worldwide. They are derived from our religions database.[5] The slimmer rainbow columns represent all "non-secular" people, whatever their religion. They represent the more official figures from censuses, government estimates etc. Only in Asia is the majority of religious believers non-Christian, so the slim columns for the other continents largely represent the attitudes of Christians. The difference between the wider dark blue columns and the slim columns is an indication of the extent of nominalism.

The same WVS survey assessed the importance of God to the sampled individuals. The results are even more startling. God is very important to 80% of respondents in AfLA and to nearly 60% in NA, but to only about 25% in EuPa. To two-thirds of Christians in EuPa, He is not so important. Nominalism is a serious issue there.

The results are more ambiguous in Asia because of different perceptions of the meaning of the word "God". Muslims are monotheistic, Hindus polytheistic, wherease Buddhism at its core is a religion without a Creator God.

Europe's spiritual need is shown in Fig 5.4. These composite figures compare and contrast official figures with the findings of various polls that come much closer to the truth.

According to official figures, 23% of Europeans profess to be non-religious, but polls suggest that the true figure is more like 51%, of whom 31% once had some link with a church but no longer do so.

However, of the 40% who claim to be Christians, only about 16% have any current involvement in church life.

The solemn fact is that over half of all Europeans are loosely termed "Christian" but have either rejected Christianity or have no meaningful relationship with it. Truly, Europe is the "prodigal" continent!

These figures also show why Europeans and Americans do not understand each other when talking about faith in the public arena. European politicians dare not speak about their personal Christian faith if they hope to be elected—but a US politician must do so.

Nominalism is a growing problem in the Church as the Christian population ages and the proportion of young people diminishes. The surge of growth in the late 20th Century is likely to be followed by a serious falling-away of young people in the 21st if they do not experience their own, fresh quickening of the Spirit. Further renewals are essential. The extraordinary growth rates of a renewed Christianity are unlikely to be maintained without such outpourings of God's Spirit.

A sad characteristic of the Church in general is a failure to recognize the paramount importance of winning young people and resourcing ministries among them. In many African and Asian congregations, little is done to actively attract and disciple young people and involve them in ministry. Church is seen as an adult activity and children as a distraction. The appeal of a global culture of "netizens" using mobile phones will require radical new approaches to make the Gospel relevant to them.

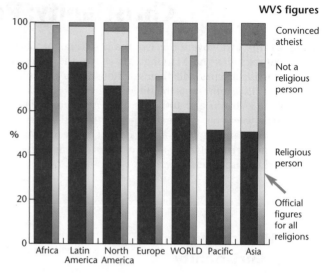

Fig 5.3 *Nominalim and religious adherence, ca 2000*

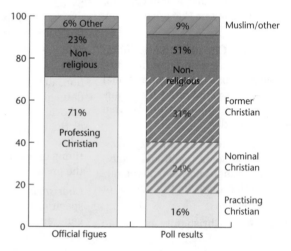

Fig 5.4 *Europe's Christian composition—official and informal*

Food for Thought

Christianity is the only world religion that requires each individual to repent and believe in order to inherit salvation as a free gift and become part of God's eternal Kingdom. God has no grandchildren. Sadly, Muslims, secularists and Hindus notice the licence and sin of the large numbers who are drifting from the Christian faith of their forebears and denying their heritage—and they are scornful. The term "Christian" has often acquired a negative connotation. For many Muslims, "a Christian" conjures up an image of a pork-eating, fornicating drunkard.

▲ A third of the world's population professes to be Christian, but how many are true followers of Christ?

The influence of the Bible

Attitudes to the Bible over the centuries are a key determinant of how receptive non-Christians are and how committed Christians are. The graphs on these pages draw on four different streams of data.[6] The first graph represents all the people in the world who could have had or have had access to the Bible and divides them into those with a positive view of Scripture (those above the 0% X-axis) and those with a negative view (those below it). These are further divided into non-Christians and Christians. Note the rapid expansion both of evangelized non-Christians[7] and of those who resist the Gospel. Note also the increase of Bible-centred Christians and the decline of Christians who are not.

Fig 5.5 shows the following trends and events:

1. The status of the Bible in medieval Christianity—the impact of the Scriptures was limited.

2. The Reformation leads to increasing interest in the Bible and access to it among those it touches. However, few non-Christians were affected by the Reformation.

3. The multiplying of Bible-centred Christians with the start of the six evangelical awakenings from 1727 onwards

4. The rise of the modern missions movement expands the witness of the Church to new, unevangelized areas.

5. The spread of deadening liberal theology in mainline Protestantism causes a decline among Evangelicals and an increase of liberal Christians after 1860.

6. Decline in the influence and numbers of liberal Christians in hitherto mainline Protestant denominations

7. After 1964, the Sixth Global Awakening leads to the translating of the Bible into many new languages and a big increase in the number of evangelized non-Christians.

The growth curve for evangelized non-Christians is extraordinary. After little increase before 1850, the acceleration was then spectacular. This testifies to the success of the modern missions movement, but is also closely connected with the availability of the Scriptures. Before the Reformation, Bibles were handwritten and rare, and available in few languages. Printing transformed this situation in the areas touched by the Reformation, where many people now had direct access to the Bible. Elsewhere, William Carey's pioneering work in India translating Scripture into other languages gave impetus to the Gospel after 1800 and enabled the emergence of truly indigenous churches, a process that greatly accelerated in the 20th Century. Those hostile to the Bible are mostly secularists and atheists in EuNAPa and Muslims in AfAsLA.

The Christian component of Fig 5.5 is expanded in Fig 5.6. All Christians are classified according to their source of ultimate authority. Above the 0% X-axis are those I have counted as Evangelicals in this book—though they fall into various categories. Note that evangelical Catholics and Orthodox—and also post-Evangelicals—hesitate to accept the label "evangelical" because of its political and theological connotations. I have included the first two in "Other biblical" believers.

Christians below the 0% line consider the Bible as subordinate to Church tradition (mainly Catholics and Orthodox), culture (syncretists), subsequent revelation (Marginals) or human reason (liberals and deists).

Charismatics come largely above the 0% line, but many —and especially Catholic Charismatics—also stand within the traditionalist worldview.

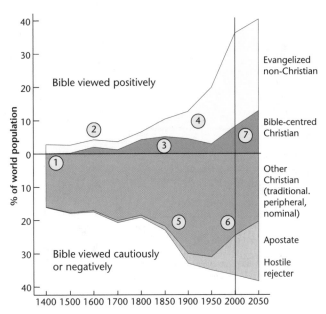

Fig 5.5 *The Bible and the world*

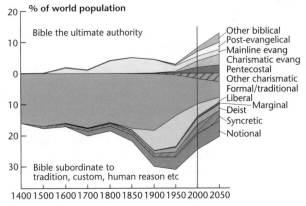

Fig 5.6 *The Bible and Christians*

Food for Thought

The century-long fall in the relative numbers of Bible-centred Christians was dramatically reversed after 1960, with a surge in evangelical outreach and missions coinciding with a massive decline (both numerical and spiritual) in mainline denominations. The old liberalism that so contaminated mainstream Christianity was a spent force. Evangelicalism in its varied forms is becoming mainstream in Christianity. Now, the challenge is that a rising generation could become nominal Christians yet still be called Evangelicals, Pentecostals and Charismatics.

▲ How can a Church that has relied on hierarchical structures and control for so long become truly biblical in the 21st Century, with effective and accountable discipling, mentoring and coaching of new leaders in accordance with 2 Timothy 2:2?

Renewal movements

The Christian renewal movements are the main focus here—by which I mean the evangelical, pentecostal and charismatic movements that transcend the divides between the main Christian confessions.[8] Fig 5.7 compares their combined growth with that of the population of the world and of Christians in general. Fig 5.8 compares the growth of these three movements with each other. Bear in mind that these three movements are not mutually exclusive and many Christians will be represented in more than one of them.

Fig 5.7 visualizes Christian renewal growth—it assigns each population in 1960 the value "1" and indicates the factor by which it has since increased. The figures for 2000 are based on actual numbers, whereas those for 2050 are based on reasonable but cautious extrapolation from present numbers and trends. Note the following observations on trends to 2050:

▲ The population of the world will almost triple, from approximately 3 billion in 1960 to 9 billion.

▲ The total number of Christians will also grow, but at a rate just under that of the global population.

▲ Non-renewal Christians will increase in number marginally but will decline as a percentage of the world's population. Except for Catholicism, what was once mainstream Christianity will become more marginal.

▲ The total number of renewal Christians will increase more than fifteen-fold over the same period. It is these transconfessional movements that will determine the health and growth of the Church in the 21st Century.

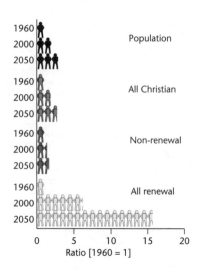

Fig 5.7 Renewal growth ratios over 90 years

Christians are likely to maintain their position as a percentage of the world's population in the foreseeable future, but the long dominance of organized Christendom looks set to end, with a lingering decline into comparative irrelevance in the battle for the hearts and minds of humankind. The whole character of the Church is being transformed through the renewal movements within it, which increasingly will take centre stage in the unfolding drama.

Many people who watch developments in the Muslim world have the impression that Islam is the fastest-growing religion in the world. This is due largely to, first, the higher birth rates and larger families in countries where Muslims constitute the majority and, second, the high visibility of increasing Muslim immigration into non-Muslim areas. Islam is not attracting many converts. The number of Muslims worldwide will increase approximately fivefold over the same period. Renewal Christianity will far outstrip this growth—and much of that will be through conversion.

Counting those involved in renewal is a challenge! The Operation World database contains information on 38,000 denominations from 1960-2010. Each denomination is assigned a charismatic or evangelical percentage for every five-year period. For many this is either 0% or 100% by their own theological definition. For theologically plural denominations this figure often varies over time. This enables us to calculate for each denominational network, country, region and the world the statistics for the renewal movements.[9] Pentecostals are counted separately and include all P and I denominations that describe themselves as pentecostal. Charismatic percentages are less accurate and with more estimates than those for Evangelicals.

The numerical growth of the renewal movements is an astonishing development that has gone largely unremarked in both the secular and the Christian media. Evangelicals and Charismatics are often regarded as the Church's lunatic, fundamentalist fringe. A significant reason for this is the unavailability of accurate, verifiable statistics. The Operation World database is the only global source for such information that is based on grass-roots statistics from national denominations.

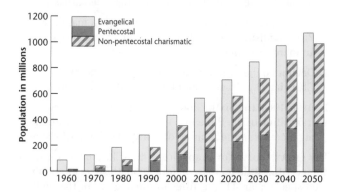

Fig 5.8 Renewal population growth by type, 1960–2050

The World Christian Database now uses a definition of Evangelicals that differs from the general usage by Evangelicals, and so its figures are not comparable. It also does not show time-related changes by denomination.

The bar chart in Fig 5.8 displays the findings from the Operation World database. It presents Pentecostals as a subset of all Charismatics, but they are also no less a subset of Evangelicals (though not shown as such here). It must be stressed that perhaps 20% or more of Charismatics are not theologically evangelical (see p121).

Burning Questions for Today

▲ Can this seemingly optimistic projection of continued growth for renewal movements be realized?

▲ What dangers may threaten this growth?

(The slowing of population growth worldwide has been taken into account.)

Persecution is likely to increase, but this could, conversely, stimulate growth, as it has in China and Iran. Acrimonious divisions, generational change with a loss of passion for Christ, doctrinal error that leads many astray and major human or natural catastrophes are all possibilities to be guarded against or prepared for.

Charismatic renewal by country

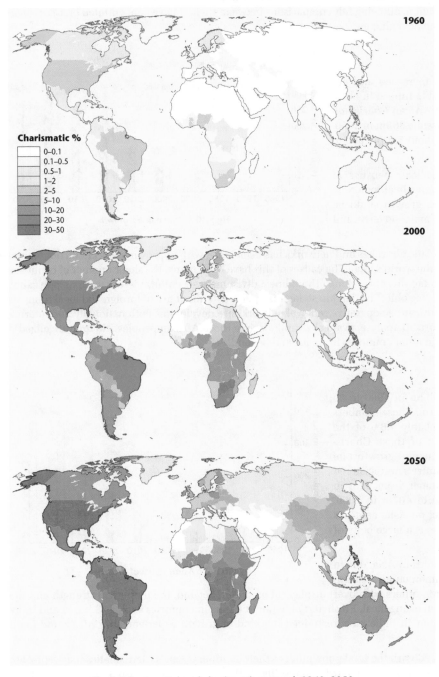

Fig 5.9 *Pentecostal and charismatic renewal, 1960–2050*

These maps show the growth of *charismatic renewal* by country. Pentecostalism is treated here as a component of the wider charismatic renewal movement—in 1960 it was virtually the only denominational type involved; the subsequent Third Wave[10] signified charismatic renewal in non-pentecostal denominations.

1960. Pentecostalism emerged as a denominational movement in the USA in the 1900s. Up until 1960, it spread chiefly in Latin America (especially Brazil and Chile) and sub-Saharan Africa (especially Anglophone W, southern and E Africa and—though here it was often more syncretic—Congo-DR). It had little impact on Europe, with the exception of Scandinavia and the Roma (Gypsy) populations of France, Spain and C Europe.

2000. The combined impact of rapid pentecostal growth after 1960 and the spread in other denominations of the emergent charismatic movement becomes apparent in Latin America and sub-Saharan Africa; also in the Pacific, and China, Indonesia and S Korea (though in Asia in general less so). Charismatic Christianity is now one of the more visible expressions of Church life.

2050. The likely future of charismatic Christianity is one of growth in all the above areas, with India, too, becoming important. Altogether, Charismatics will probably increase from nearly 6% of the world's population in 2000 to an influential 11%. Many significant breakthroughs and conversions in hostile religious environments, such as those that at present are Communist, Hindu or Muslim,[11] are likely to have a more charismatic flavour.

If present projections prove accurate, by 2050 charismatic Christians will comprise one-third of all Christians and one-tenth of the world's population. Significant elements of the leadership in most streams of Christianity will have been influenced by renewal. What impact might this have in the areas where charismatic Christians are the most prominent? Pentecostalism has had a long history of non-involvement in politics but, with the broadening of the movement by so many non-pentecostal Charismatics as well, this will surely change. Politicians will not be able to ignore such a development and charismatic Christianity is likely to shape the worldviews of many nations and influence politics in Latin America and Africa. It will also provide some of the strongest alternative social support structures in increasingly broken societies, as is already happening in Africa. How will China change, given its high proportion of Christians—most of them of a more charismatic persuasion?

Food for Thought

▲ Will charismatic and pentecostal Christians withdraw from wider society and emphasize both this-worldly wealth in a "prosperity gospel"[12] and other-worldly, eschatological escape,[13] or will they become a major influence for social change and uplift as Evangelicals did after the Third Great Awakening in the late 18th Century?

Continental Christian renewal

On these two pages, renewal in each of the six continents is covered in turn for the same period of time, 1960–2050. The vertical scale is roughly the same for each population, allowing fair comparisons between them. I have concentrated on *Charismatics* here as Evangelicals are the subject of the next chapter.

Africa

Both Evangelicals and Charismatics have increased and are likely to continue to do so for the foreseeable future. In absolute numbers, there were in all 2.4 million African *Charismatics* in 1960, rising to 88m in 2000—and a possible 368m in 2050. *Evangelicals* multiplied more slowly, from about 5m in 1960 to 120m in 2000 and perhaps 350m in 2050.

Charismatics are likely to outstrip Evangelicals because of the large numbers associated with non-evangelical syncretic charismatic bodies. Possible constraints on growth could be political instability, violent Islamism, endemic poverty and inadequate health services.

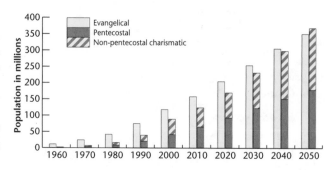

Fig 5.10 *African renewal growth*

The proliferation of pentecostal and charismatic churches and networks has been huge, with approximately 11,000 denominations identified in 2000, or nearly a third of the world's total. The causes of this have been many: the sheer number of countries in Africa, almost a quarter of the world's total; divisions along ethnic lines; divisions over cultural issues such as polygamy, with many groups holding syncretic beliefs; "big chief" leadership styles; disagreements about use of foreign and local finances etc. Amidst all this confusion, however, significant co-operative renewal networks are developing, both nationally and internationally across Africa. Among these are efforts to analyse, evangelize and disciple those African peoples still unevangelized[14] and a burgeoning involvement in missions in other countries in Africa and beyond.

Asia

Asian *Charismatics* increased from 1.6 million in 1960 to 89 million in 2000, and by 2050 may reach 251m. These numbers represent respectively 0.1%, 2.4% and probably 4.8% of the continent's population. A high proportion of these Charismatics are in mainland China, so the continental growth rate is closely linked to the future of that country's unregistered churches. Asian *Evangelicals* grew in number from 12m in 1960 to 118m in 2000, and may increase to 407m in 2050. *Pentecostalism* has not had such an impact on Asia, as it has generally been more successful where there is a large body of traditional and nominal Christians.

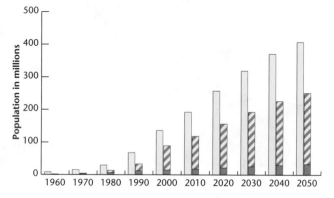

Fig 5.11 *Asian renewal growth*

Evangelicals are likely to outstrip Charismatics in Asia, due to a number of factors. First, there is the common cultural desire not to lose face or to cause embarrassment to others with overt displays of emotion. Second, the numerical strength and the missionary zeal of non-charismatic, but often evangelical, Presbyterian denominations in countries such as S Korea and Indonesia and also non-pentecostal denominations in India have restrained the kind of growth experienced in Africa and Latin America.

Nonetheless, though few in number compared with the total population of their continent, Asia's Charismatics may represent 30% of the global total in 2050 and will make a decisive contribution to the further spread of the Gospel to less-evangelized parts of the only continent without a Christian majority.

Europe

Europe's *Charismatics* numbered just 1 million in 1960, but this climbed to 14 million in 2000 and may reach 27m in 2050. Most of the growth will be among Catholics and new churches started by young people.

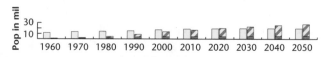

Fig 5.12 *European renewal growth Europe*

Evangelicals and Charismatics are increasing in number at a time when overall numbers of Christians are in decline, but since renewal movements represent such a small proportion of Europe's Christian population, this has not reversed the wider trend. There is a close link between the massive decline of Christianity as a whole on this continent and the very small numbers of both Evangelicals and Charismatics. Europe needs a radical Christian awakening that changes cultures and nations.

Pentecostalism has generally had a cold welcome. Many earlier pentecostal churches in Europe were of Anglo-Saxon origin, while those established more recently are usually pastored by Brazilians, Nigerians or Ghanaians and often have more immigrants among their members. The main indigenous pentecostal denominations are among the marginalized Roma population, with those of France and Spain being the largest.

Latin America

The number of *Charismatics* in Latin America has grown astonishingly. In 1960, there were just 4 million. By 2000, this had grown to 87 million—a 22-fold increase. By 2050, it could exceed 200m. Much of this projected growth is likely to be among Catholic Charismatics, who could number 70m in 2050. It is the Catholic Charismatics, most of them not being theologically evangelical, who raise the numbers of Charismatics well above those of Evangelicals. *Evangelicals* are found largely in Baptist, Presbyterian and Seventh-day Adventist denominations. The first two have seen many denominations break away on account of the charismatic issue. A high percentage of Evangelicals are also charismatic in orientation—in many countries, around 90% of all members of P, I and A denominations.

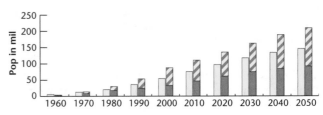

Fig 5.13 *Latin American renewal growth*

As a proportion of the continent's Christians, Charismatics have increased proportionally from 1.8% in 1960 to 16.6% in 2000 and may exceed 25% in 2050. Charismatic Christianity is decisively affecting the cultures and worldviews of these nations and, increasingly, their politics, too. However, evangelical politicians have often proved to be almost as venal as any others.

The wealth and spiritual dynamism of Latin American Charismatics will have an ever-greater impact on both the Christian and non-Christian world. Already the missions contribution of Latin America, and especially Brazil, is considerable.

N America

The USA is effectually the source of modern renewal movements—of Evangelicalism, Pentecostalism and the charismatic movement, too. Many of the values of these exported Christian cultures will continue to mould renewal well into the 21st Century, even as their relative importance in N America declines. All of the continent's renewal movements will continue to grow in numerical terms, but more as a result of birth rates and immigration than conversion. A large proportion of African Americans are *pentecostal* or *charismatic*.

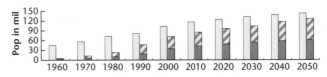

Fig 5.14 *N American renewal growth*

The USA's renewal Christians represented over half the global total in 1960 and exerted an extraordinary influence over the rest of the world. They provided the leadership in initiatives for world evangelization, funded global conferences to stimulate co-operative endeavours for mission outreach and modelled patterns of worship and church structures for the rest of the world. The generosity of US Christians became legendary—and also created problems by exerting an influence that threatened indigeneity and bred dependence among churches and ministries in poorer parts of the world. The proportion of the world's renewal Christians found in N America dropped to a quarter in 2000, and will fall further to perhaps one-seventh in 2050. Leadership and initiative will increasingly pass to Asia, which will have about 40% of all Evangelicals by 2050.

The Pacific

Charismatics in the Pacific totalled around 100,000 in 1960 but by 2000 this had grown to 3.3 million, largely as a result of a strong surge in New Zealand in the 1960s and thereafter in Australia. On the other hand, *Evangelicals* increased from 2.6 million in 1960 to 5m in 2000.

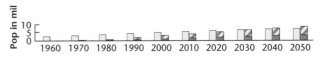

Fig 5.15 *Pacific renewal growth*

Renewal movements in the Pacific have mirrored (and are likely to continue to mirror) developments in the USA, but tempered by the negatives of Europe. As in N America, Evangelicals will increase more as a result of birth rates and immigration. Charismatics are likely to outstrip them, partly because of the growing number of Catholic Charismatics.

Bolivian Christians meet for prayer (photo courtesy Samaritan's Purse)

Food for Thought

The various forms of Christian renewal highlighted here constitute the only fast-growing religious movements in the world today. Among organized religious bodies, Muslims and Protestants are growing fastest—but still at a much lower rate than these movements. The Muslim growth is primarily the consequence of higher birth rates.

If present trends continue, by 2050 Christian renewal movements will have advanced from a marginal 3% of the world's population in 1960 to an influential 12%. The almost unnoticed but very real explosive growth of 1960–2000 will slow in the 21st Century, but the influence of this renewal in all areas of life will almost certainly increase. Renewal will probably embrace well over one-third of all Christians by 2050.

These two pages provide two further perspectives on the growth in numbers charted on pages 126 and 127. They show the percentages and the average annual growth rates of the three renewal types, first by continent and then worldwide.

The *graphs on the left* chart the increase of renewal Christians as a percentage of the whole population (with the increase of Evangelicals shown by a yellow line and that of all Christians—in some cases, on a different scale—by a blue line). The renewal movement is represented by the red areas (Pentecostals) plus the red-and-yellow-hatched areas (non-pentecostal Charismatics). Bear in mind the double counting of those who are both charismatic and evangelical.

The *graphs on the right* compare the average annual growth rates of the three renewal movements with those of the whole population to determine a "conversion rate".[15] The green areas represent growth through natural increase and the yellow areas growth through conversion. The graphs thus actually chart the increase in accession to the renewal movements of both adults and their dependants.[16]

Note that the growth rates in the right-hand graphs can fluctuate, and in several cases I have manually adjusted some points to give a more consistent flow for the decadal statistics I have used.[17]

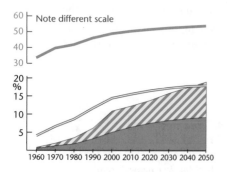

Africa. Leaving Muslim N Africa aside, the percentages of the population that are Christian and renewed are even higher. By 2050, over 50% of Africa's Christians will be renewed.

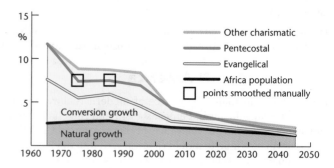

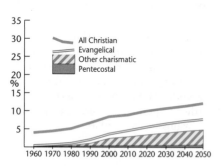

Asia. Renewal continues to spread in Asia, but perhaps with a slower rate of conversion. The future may be more fruitful than projected here.

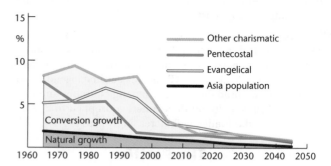

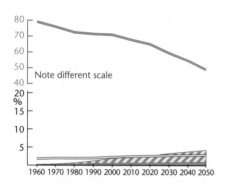

Europe. Renewal movements are likely to continue growing slowly, despite population decline, as a result of both conversion and immigration into Europe.

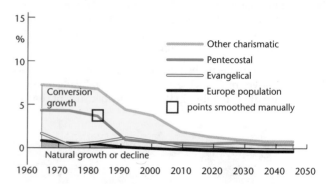

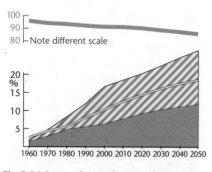

Latin America. Renewal is likely to show further significant growth as it spreads to P and I churches and as the number of Catholic Charismatics also increases.

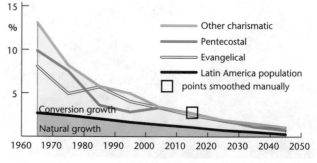

Fig 5.16 *Renewal growth as % of population*

Fig 5.17 *Average annual growth rates for renewal Christians*

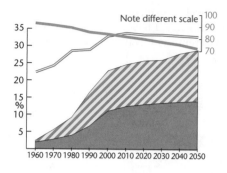

N America. Evangelicals (and Christians) will gradually decline due to non-Christian immigration, but Hispanic converts will probably boost the Charismatics.

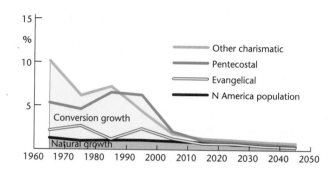

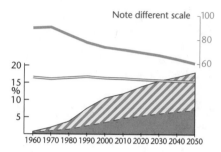

Pacific. Christians will decline due to non-Christian immigration and secularization, but charismatic numbers will be augmented by converts and Catholics.

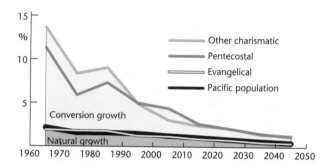

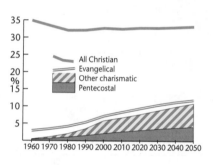

World. Renewal Christians constituted only 8% of all Christians in 1960, 26% in 2000 and is estimated 45% in 2050.[18] There are major implications for the future of the faith.

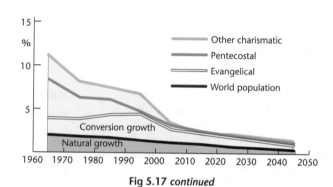

Fig 5.16 *continued*

Fig 5.17 *continued*

Note the considerable differences between the *continents* in terms of percentages of Christians in renewal movements and patterns of growth. Yet there are striking similarities, too. Every continent is likely to show some effects of renewal— even as the growth of both the global and the Christian population slows or even goes into reverse. It is also apparent that the period 1960–2000 saw extraordinary growth in every continent. (This was less obvious in Europe, because of the small numbers involved in renewal, but nonetheless real.) Such growth is unlikely to be maintained without divine intervention, in answer to prayer, in revivals or break- throughs in hitherto resistant areas.

The rate at which the *global population* is growing is steadily declining, and this will affect all religions and their rates of growth, too. It is a simple fact that most people who become Christians do so in their childhood or youth. Smaller families and shrinking populations will mean proportionally fewer young people in the general population, and therefore a reduction in the conversion rate, in all but a few countries. Other negative factors are the possible levels of nominalism, declension and even rejection of the faith among the children of those recently added to the Church. I have tried to reflect all these influences in my cautious growth projections here— which nonetheless still generate high figures for renewal in the 21st Century as a result of the momentum built up in the decades of growth in the late 20th Century. Future figures

(for both all and renewed Christians) could be even higher than projected here.

Charismatic and evangelical Christian renewal movements are the *only* religious movements in the world today that are growing through conversion.

Burning Questions for Today

Change is inevitable, and globalization ensures that it will continue. Few people realize that massive changes have already occurred—not least transforming the nature and composition of the Church. Liberal, traditional, Constantinian Christendom is dying. Present trends indicate that future Christians could be more spiritual, dynamic and prophetic, but also more persecuted. This is far more a New Testament Church!

▲ But will it happen?

▲ Will there be godly, prayerful leaders who help their people to embrace that future and inherit the kingdom that Jesus promised?

The block charts on the next two pages show the past and likely future growth of renewal movements—first evangelical and then charismatic—between 1960 and 2050 within the six main Christian confessional streams. I have used the charts I also used on page 118, but here softened the colours and differentiated the yellow and red to represent Evangelicals, Charismatics and Pentecostals respectively.

Evangelicals

1960. *Evangelicals* were only just beginning to emerge from a half-century of marginalization; but from then on Evangelicalism became the most dynamic belief system in the world and its fast-growing numbers put it at the centre of global Christianity. Evangelicals are now a significant component of three megablocs (P, I and A). Originally, that presence was mostly confined to EuNAPa countries, but subsequent growth has been in AfAsLA countries, where Evangelicals have even become the majority of Christians.

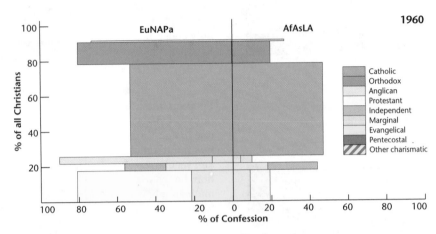

2000. *Evangelicals* have become a majority in the P and I megablocs, and nearly among Anglicans, too. For the most part, that has been as a result of growth in AfAsLA. Evangelicals in EuNAPa have seen a slight rise in numbers, though they now constitute almost half of all P, I and A Christians there. Evangelicals have also become more significant within Catholicism, in both EuNAPa and (especially) AfAsLA. Within Orthodoxy, Evangelicalism is concentrated in certain national churches.[19]

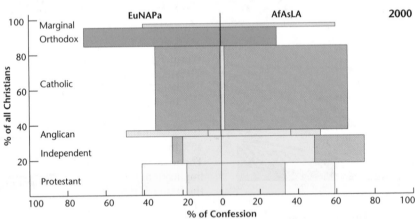

2050. It is likely that the three megablocs P, I and A will be predominantly *evangelical* in theology. Traditional P and A denominations in EuNAPa will still be mostly non-evangelical but will be in severe decline, both in absolute terms and relative to the size of their megablocs worldwide. Theologically, Evangelicalism (even if, increasingly, other terms are used) will have become the mainstream of Christianity in both EuNAPa and (especially) AfAsLA.

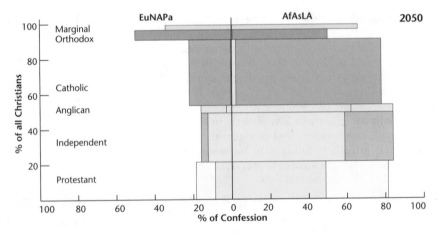

Fig 5.18 *Evangelicals by Confession, 1960–2050*

Evangelicalism has seen an astonishing change in fortunes. After the Great Awakenings of the 18th and 19th Centuries, evangelical Christians were in the forefront of the fight to promote democratic freedoms and social reform, abolish slavery and lay the foundations of a more humane, moral capitalism. Then came the erosion of confidence as philosophical Darwinism dominated science and a liberal theology crippled mainline denominations. There followed a century of decline. What a turnaround since 1960! Once-rampant liberal Christianity has suffered such decline that today its influence is ever more irrelevant, and exposed as little more than a distorting Western form of syncretism. Many scientists today admit that believing in a Creator is not so far-fetched, given the evidence that the universe began with a "big bang", and that even the quasi-religious faith in Darwinism has a shaky basis in science. Evangelicals are becoming the dynamic hub of global Christianity and could remould the worldviews of nations.

Compare and contrast these charts with those on page 130. Pentecostals are a subset of both Charismatics and Evangelicals (shown in these diagrams as red-and-yellow hatched areas). The growth of these charismatic renewal streams is even more dramatic than that of Evangelicals, though less easy to quantify accurately.

Charismatics and Pentecostals

1960. After 1905, Pentecostals grew steadily in number to constitute over half the membership of the Independent denominations, though still a fairly small element in the Protestant ones. In 1960, the Third Wave of Charismatics was barely apparent in the mainline non-pentecostal denominations, but as the decade wore on it became a massive surge sweeping through them. Perhaps 90% in P, I and A denominations would be evangelical in theology, but fewer C and O Charismatics.

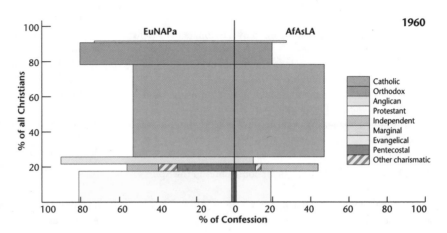

2000. Forty years of remarkable growth followed, in the pentecostal denominations, in charismatic movements within mainline denominations and also in new networks.[20] By 2000, non-pentecostal Charismatics exceeded Pentecostals both in number and in confessional spread. Charismatics are now a majority in Independent denominations and networks. A more charismatic style of worship is now widespread throughout the Church—even among those who did not embrace the movement.

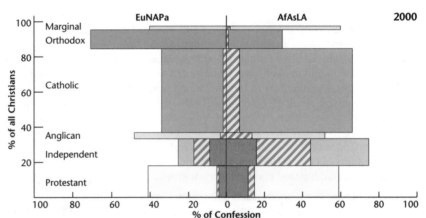

2050. Here are some possible future outcomes:

▲ AfAsLA Charismatics will constitute 50% or more of all P, I and A Christians.

▲ EuNAPa Charismatics will constitute possibly 35% of all PIA Christians, but the latter will make up only 20% of all PIA Christians worldwide.

▲ Pentecostal denominations will continue to multiply and expand in AfLA countries, but less so in Asia and EuNAPa.

The projected growth of Catholic and Orthodox Charismatics is based on two main assumptions:

1. that charismatic renewal will continue at present rates (it may prove to be a passing phenomenon)

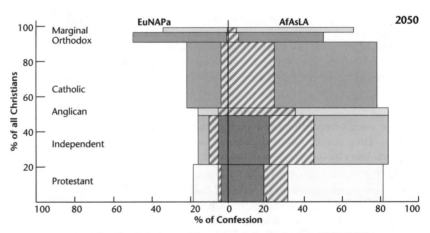

Fig 5.19 *Charismatics and Pentecostals by confession, 1960–2050*

2. that all who are no longer actively involved in charismatic meetings as they get older will still consider themselves as Charismatics.

Food for Thought

By 2050, a high percentage of all Christians will be more charismatic in both worldview and lifestyle. How will non-charismatic denominations and churches adapt to maintain their cutting edge and their numbers? Catholicism, Anglicanism and many Protestant denominations will be fundamentally affected, and even damaged (depending on how their leaderships handle the changes). Current cultural trends all over the world favour an expression of faith that is more emotional than intellectual.

▲ How will we preserve and develop a biblical theology that will still be regarded as relevant by the more charismatic Church that is emerging?

Church history parallels Israel's experience in the Book of Judges, with human falling away followed by divine intervention. Such cycles have occurred often over the past 500 years—the next six pages cover those of the last three centuries. First, however, we must define the terms used about these extraordinary workings of God among His people.

A revival is

▲ a sovereign work of the Holy Spirit among God's people, the Church

▲ usually preceded or accompanied by passionate corporate intercessory prayer

▲ often accompanied by a deep conviction of sin, repentance and restitution

▲ often followed by a manifestation of God's presence and power, a feeling of joy and a spirit of worship

▲ fruitful in a deepening or resurgence of Christian life and witness.

A revival is not

▲ of human origin, though prayer contributes to the Spirit's outpouring

▲ organized by Christians who obey a set of principles

▲ a series of evangelistic meetings.

An awakening

▲ is a wider movement of the Holy Spirit that often begins with the revival of a group of Christians but then touches nominal and backsliding Christians

▲ stimulates a deep concern about a relationship with God among nominal Christians and unbelievers previously careless about sin and ungodliness

▲ usually leads many to seek God and attend a place of worship and increases church membership

▲ produces new visions and new structures, and new networks and movements to spread the Gospel

▲ prompts many to volunteer for Christian work and go out as missionaries to the ends of the earth.

A people movement

▲ is often the result of revival in the home cultures of the missionaries who first bring the message of the Gospel to a people who have no knowledge of it or the Bible

▲ is a turning-to-Christ of many in a people group that previously had little or no contact with the Gospel

▲ is a work of the Holy Spirit within a culture, which not only makes the Gospel relevant to that culture but changes the culture so that it conforms more closely to biblical standards

▲ should be followed by careful discipling, leadership development and translation of Scripture.

Above is an explanation of what revival is and is not. The laws of God's Kingdom are so different to either human laws or the laws of nature. Charles Finney, a great revivalist evangelist in the USA, taught in his revival lectures: *"[A revival] is not a miracle, nor dependent on a miracle, in any sense. It is purely a philosophical result of the right use of the constituted means—as much as any other effect produced by the application of means."*[21] This may have seemed to be the case in his time because God was at work, but this leaves out the sovereign interventions of God in *His* time. Finney gives too much of an impression that humans can have revival at will.

The Church desperately needs such miraculous interventions! We have identified about 200 instances over the last 1,000 years.[22]

An awakening, beginning with revival, may then spread to have a wider impact on non-Christians in the area and further afield. Most of the six awakenings listed below had an international impact. They set up the spiritual dynamics that led to waves of expansion worldwide of today's Church.

A people movement is a special form of God's working in which large numbers of an ethnic group turn to Jesus. There may have been several thousand such events over the last 300 years. They usually follow decades of hard, costly seed-sowing and tears by the pioneers of the work.

Over the last three centuries there have been six waves of new life and growth followed by years of decline and backsliding. Without these awakenings, the Church would have withered away to a small remnant in a few countries. Yet these amazing, Holy Spirit-initiated awakenings mean that we are witnessing advances for the Church worldwide. Such facts are rarely reported by the media.

Summary of the definitions of the interventions of the Holy Spirit:

When God touches	It is
an individual	a renewal
a community of faith	a revival
wider society	an awakening
an ethnic group	a people movement

These six awakenings produced new life, new structures, new advances and the present reality of a Church growing around the world in countries that previously had few if any Christians.

Food for Thought

Each awakening led to a range of local and national revivals of believers and people movements among those evangelized by missionaries sent from the revived countries. Sadly, there is often opposition: internally, from those rejecting the centrality of Scripture, or externally, from the those who do not want to give allegiance to King Jesus.

No.	Main Areas	Dates	Main Impact	Cause of Decline
1st	Germany, Britain, USA	1728 – 1790	Moravian Missions, Methodist revival	Deism, revolutions
2nd	UK, USA, Scandinavia	1791 – 1812	Modern Missions movement	War and social upheaval
3rd	USA	1813 – 1859	Mass evangelism	Social upheavals
4th	N America	1860 – 1899	Surge in church growth and missions	Liberal Ideology
5th	Wales, USA, many lands	1900 – 1914	Global revivals, Pentecostal growth	Colonialism, World Wars
6th	Africa, Asia, Latin America	1964 –	Evangelical resurgence, Charismatic renewal	Globalized secularization?

Fig 5.20 *Summary of the six evangelical awakenings*

18th-Century Revivals: The First Awakening

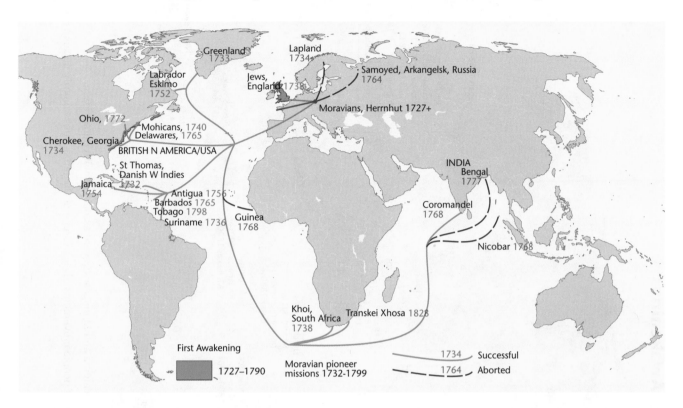

First Awakening
1727–1790

Moravian pioneer missions 1732-1799

| 1734 | Successful |
| 1764 | Aborted |

The *Moravian (Herrnhut) Revival* sparked the First Awakening, which is a story of faith, tenacity and sacrifice with few parallels in the history of the Church. Christian refugees fleeing persecution in Moravia took refuge on the estate of Count Ludwig von Zinzendorf in Herrnhut in Germany. God granted revival to this little community of a few hundred in 1728. They started a chain of prayer that went on for 120 years, and through it the world was changed. They sent missionaries all over the world—on average, two for each 58 members. The Moravians today are a small global denomination of some 500,000 people, but their impact has been immense.

One of their greatest contributions was their influence on the Wesleys and the Methodist revival that followed, which made the Anglophone world the greatest source of missions in history. It was in a Moravian meeting in London that John Wesley had his heart-warming experience of assurance of salvation.

The Moravians' influence on the development of the modern missions movement was pivotal, shaping the thinking of William Carey and the early stream of missionaries who went out after 1792. The areas affected by the Moravian missionaries and this First Awakening are indicated on the map.

The anointed preaching of George Whitfield, John Wesley and many others who followed them resulted in astonishing numbers of converts and witnesses who transformed the Anglophone world and much beyond.

The willingness of revival preachers to travel widely under harsh conditions by foot, horse and ship and to suffer for the cause of the Gospel was exemplary. Their preaching in the open air was a novel but highly successful approach.

The impact of the Methodists on the development of the USA was extensive. From 1,000 members in 1770, they had become the largest US denomination by 1830. This led to the emergence of lay ministries rather than a reliance on professional clergy.

The awakening led to the formation of new structures to spread the Gospel. Chief among them was the denomination the Methodists formed after the Anglican Church rejected them. The Methodist revival transformed the Anglican Church as well by bringing revival to it and stimulating the emergence of a strong evangelical movement within Anglicanism.

Crucial to producing lasting fruit was the effective way in which the Methodists' system of classes discipled new believers, which emphasized personal conversion, prayer and holiness of life. Ministry was through camp meetings, itinerant preachers and good use of lay Christians—a return to the best practices of the Celtic Church. One outcome was a host of societies to spread the Gospel and address the social ills of the time.

Food for Thought

Prayer and revival have been the vital ingredients for the rejuvenation and growth of the Church since its millennium of decline (500–1500). Yet this blessed combination was not a product of the Reformation but came two centuries later. The awakenings point up a link between prayer and the outpouring of the Holy Spirit in reviving power and the resulting surge of missionary endeavour.

Burning Question for Today

"May the Lamb that was slain receive the reward of His suffering!" was the cry of one young Moravian missionary as he set sail for St Thomas in the W Indies in 1731, to become a slave for life voluntarily in order to reach African slaves. It became the motto of the Moravians.

▲ Are we willing to make comparable sacrifices so that the world may be reached?

19th-Century Revivals and Awakenings

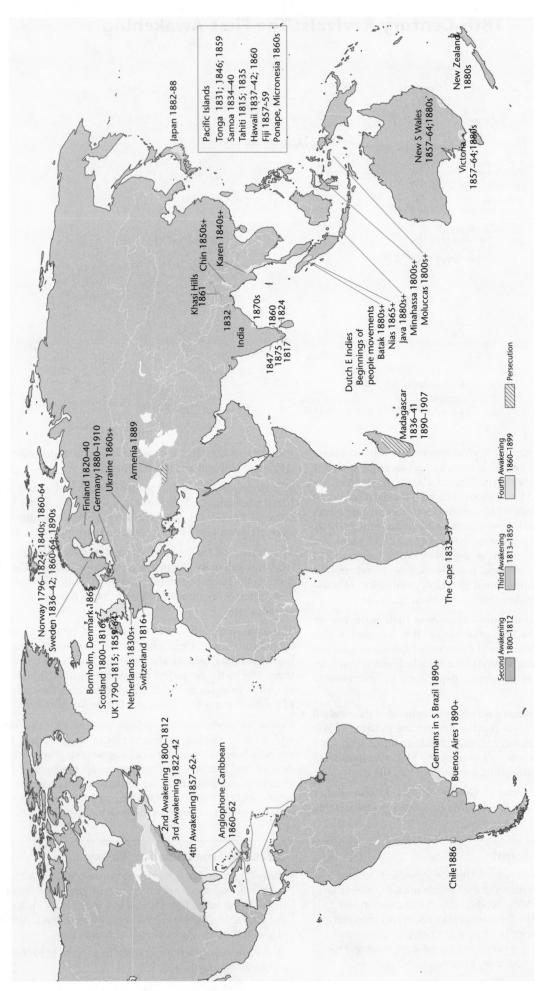

Pacific Islands
Tonga 1831; 1846; 1859
Samoa 1834–40
Tahiti 1815; 1835
Hawaii 1837–42; 1860
Fiji 1857–59
Ponape, Micronesia 1860s

Japan 1882–88

New Zealand 1880s

New S Wales 1857–64; 1880s

Victoria 1857–64; 1880s

Khasi Hills 1861
Chin 1850s+
Karen 1840s+

1832
India
1870s
1860
1824

1847
1875
1817

Dutch E Indies
Beginnings of
people movements
Batak 1880s+
Nias 1865+
Java 1880s+
Minahassa 1800s+
Moluccas 1800s+

Madagascar
1836–41
1890–1907

Armenia 1889

Finland 1820–40
Germany 1880–1910
Ukraine 1860s+

Norway 1796–1824; 1840s; 1860-64
Sweden 1836–42; 1860-64;1890s

Bornholm, Denmark1865
Scotland 1800–1816
UK 1790–1815; 1859–65
Netherlands 1830s+
Switzerland 1816+

The Cape 1832–37

2nd Awakening 1800–1812
3rd Awakening 1822–42
4th Awakening1857–62+

Anglophone Caribbean
1860–62

Germans in S Brazil 1890+

Buenos Aires 1890+

Chile1886

Second Awakening
1800–1812

Third Awakening
1813–1859

Fourth Awakening
1860–1899

Persecution

The 19th-Century revivals we could identify are located on this map. Note that some of them, those in Armenia and Madagascar, were associated with persecution.

Most of the revivals in southern Africa, the E Indies, NE India and the Pacific were more in the nature of people movements, though some of the latter subsequently became revivals.

The Second Awakening

From 1790 onwards, this had a deep impact on major denominations in Britain, the USA and Scandinavia and was instrumental in launching the modern missions movement—on the back of the First—with William Carey as advocate.[23] Within a relatively short time, the islands of the Pacific were largely Christian and missions were begun in many other parts of the world.

The Third Awakening

It primarily affected the USA from 1813 onwards and made mass evangelism a major factor in church growth for the next 170 years. Charles Finney was the first in a long line of illustrious modern evangelists such as Dwight L Moody, Billy Sunday, Gypsy Smith and Billy Graham. In the UK, it stimulated social reform: the ending of the slave trade and child labour and the advent of universal education and Sunday Schools, prison reform, trades unions etc. It also led to the founding of a host of trans- and interdenominational agencies to promote social welfare and missions and the printing and distribution of Bibles.

The Fourth Awakening

The revivals of 1859–64 across the Americas and N Europe were dramatic. In each of the UK, the USA and Scandinavia over a million people were converted. The countries affected saw a rise in moral standards (often with legalistic expectations labelled "Victorian"!). One outcome was a massive growth in the missions effort around the world. It became, as K S Latourette, the great historian of the Church, said, "the Great Century". (The latter part of the 20th Century far surpassed the 19th, but Latourette did not live long enough to see this, or even predict it!) Its demise was brought about by the rise of philosophical Darwinism (no need for God) and the liberal theology that dominated most mainline denominations.

Prayer

The link between *intercession* and *revival* is strong, as many historical accounts bear witness.[24] Fig 5.21 plots the intensity and geographical impact of both, decade by decade, to show the extent of the correlation between them.[25]

Concerted corporate prayer for God's intervention is recorded in the Bible (Acts 2, 4 and 12) but there is little record of the Church continuing with it. I have searched in vain for any evidence of such prayer before the Moravian Revival of 1727 and the Scottish Cambuslang Revival of 1742–44. Jonathan Edwards promoted it in New England in his *Concerts of Prayer*.[26] Since then, prayer movements for missions and revival have been a growing phenomenon, especially towards the end of the 20th Century. As Hans von Staden of the Dorothea Mission said in 1975: *"Much prayer, much blessing; little prayer, little blessing; no prayer, no blessing."*

Each of the six evangelical awakenings was preceded and accompanied by passionate prayer for God to rend the heavens and come down in power. Each wave of awakenings advanced the Kingdom significantly around the world, as maps on the preceding and following pages show. However, each one was also followed by opposition, a cooling of spiritual ardour and even a falling-away within a generation or so.

The map on page 134 shows the location and extent of 19th-Century revivals and awakenings. Most of them made their

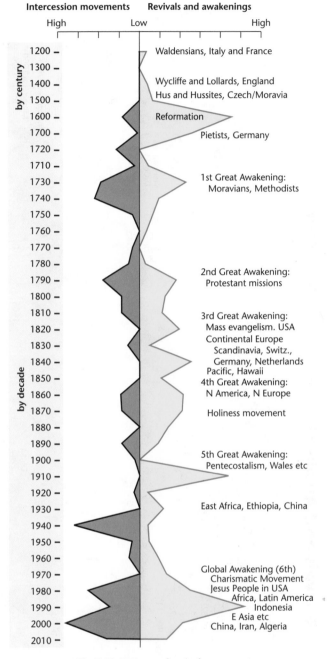

Fig 5.21 *Prayer and revival movements*

impact in EuNAPa—only a few areas in AfAsLA were affected. *Each of the three 19th-Century awakenings* made its own unique contribution to world evangelization. However, there was a growing sense of big advances and the promise of more in the 20th century.

Food for Thought

In the 19th Century, European empires reached their peak. "Christian" nations controlled almost all the world. The British navy dominated the oceans—that made it easier and more affordable for missionaries to traverse the globe. However, there were cruelty and exploitation. Opposition to Christianity increased with the rise of secularism and revolutionary Marxism and signs of a resurgence of other major religions.

Evangelical Revivals and Awakenings in the 20th Century

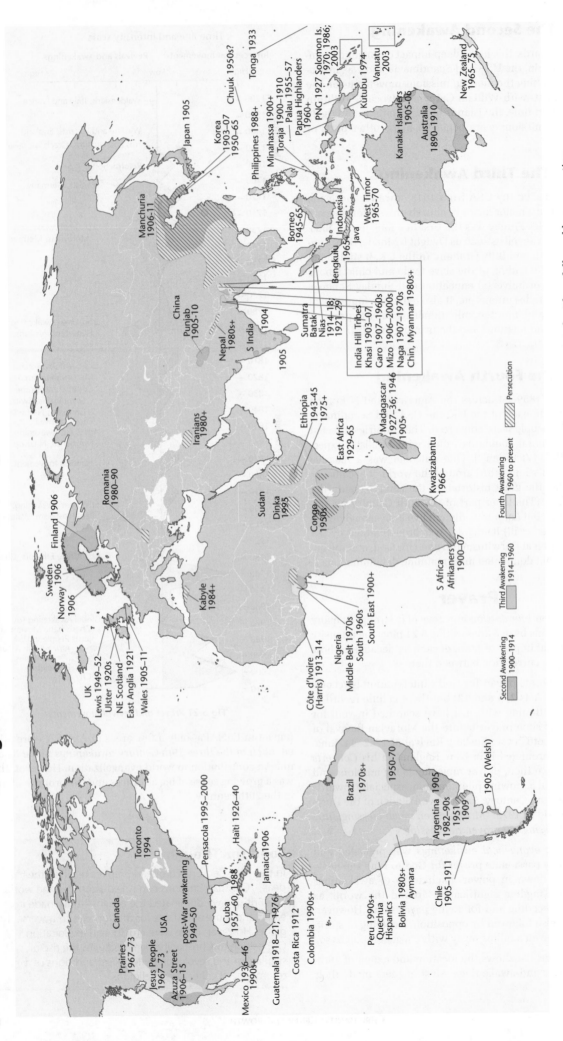

The 20th-Century revivals we could identify are located on this map. The red-hatched shading indicates those that were associated with or followed by persecution.

The Fifth Awakening had a global impact, but the Sixth was largely confined to AfAsLA—principally E Asia and Latin America.

The Fifth Awakening

In 1905, a revival broke out among the coal miners in the valleys of S Wales that was to spread around the world. This Fifth Awakening became the first truly worldwide awakening. It spread to expatriate Welsh communities in Patagonia in Argentina and in Australia and through missionaries of Welsh origin serving in India, Madagascar and the Caribbean. News of the Welsh revival stimulated prayer among concerned Christians in such places as S Africa, Manchuria, Korea, Japan, and the Punjab and (especially) Mizoram in India. Among the Mizo the spirit of revival has returned again and again—long after the spiritual tide ebbed in Wales—and persists today. There were links also to the pentecostal outpouring in San Francisco in 1905, which gave birth to the modern pentecostal movement.

The 30 years of world war and depression from 1914 to 1945 cut short these remarkable events—and yet even in those 30 years some significant revivals occurred. The most notable were:

E Africa: starting in Rwanda in 1929 and spreading to all E Africa and eastern Congo and lasting 35 years

Ethiopia: following the Italian invasion in 1935

China: before Communism in 1946–49

Korea: during and after the Korean War, in 1947–65

Latin America: especially Brazil

The USA: a post-war surge among Evangelicals

The Sixth Awakening

The diversity and worldwide growth of evangelical Christianity are so great that few people recognize this as an awakening. Most Westerners have been largely unaware of the extraordinary outpourings of the Holy Spirit around the world. The bars in Fig 5.22 show the increase in numbers decade-by-decade for each of the three (overlapping) renewal movements.

1964: The Sixth Awakening really began to take off when the Charismatic Movement exploded across the world, propelled especially by the Jesus Movement from New Zealand and the W Coast of the USA. Pentecostal growth around the world also accelerated, touching parts of Latin America and many countries in Africa.

1965–66: Amidst great political upheavals, millions in Indonesia became Christians, especially among the nominally Muslim Javanese and the animistic tribal peoples. A revival also broke out in the very nominal Reformed Church in W Timor, with thousands converted and hundreds of missionaries then going out across Indonesia and around the world.

1980 onwards: The most significant event of all followed the disastrous so-called Cultural Revolution in China and the growth of both legal and illegal churches there. Four million Christians in 1949 had become 105 million by 2010.

People movements have taken on the nature more of revival in countries such as Nepal, the Philippines, Nigeria and Sudan and among the Quechua and Aymara peoples of Peru and Bolivia.

Single-church revivals have also had a big impact due to the global circulation of news of unusual events, which has attracted much Christian "tourism" to the Yo-I-Do Church in Seoul, Kwasizabantu in S Africa, the Airport Church in

Burning Questions for Today

The vital core of Christianity is vigorous and growing. It could become a determining force in the 21st Century. Serious questions need to be asked about Christian ministry in the years ahead:

▲ Can the vitality of this renewal generation be passed on to the next, or will growth be crippled by division, compromise and nominalism—or be followed by decline?

▲ How can these remarkable global trends be best communicated in a world dominated by a hostile media culture that denigrates or ignores anything that looks like successful, vibrant, vigorous Christianity?

▲ Is enough being done by current leaders to prepare their successors, and in due course let them take the lead?

▲ Will passion for God's glory and for the fulfilment of His heart's desire of a Church complete be sustained at a time when on one side globalization is imposing a tyranny of "tolerance" and on the other religious extremism threatens that is based on exclusivism and hate?

Both the "tolerant" and the "extreme" need to hear a relevant account of the unique Gospel of love and grace.

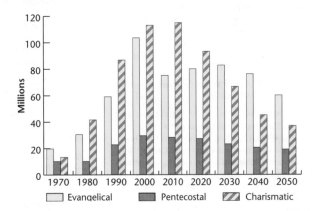

Fig 5.22 *Christian growth through the 6th Awakening*

Toronto and the Assemblies of God Church in Pensacola, Florida. For the first time, significant numbers have turned to Christ from Islam, most notably in Indonesia, Iran, Nigeria and Algeria.

The failure of Communism as an ideology was caused partly by a resurgent Christianity and much prayer. Revivals even occurred under Communism in Romania, China and, most powerfully, Ethiopia. It was in the last of these that the Church emerged least compromised from persecution and tyranny.

A Christian bookshop in China (photo by PJK)

1. The trauma of the Reformation and its aftermath led to bitterness, war and lasting division. The necessary corrections the Reformation made in terms of theology, Christian praxis and practical holiness also led to the loss of much that was good and wholesome, such as the monastic orders, which were agents of mission endeavour, the tradition of confession, which encouraged personal godliness and accountability etc. In recent years, Evangelicals have been more open to Catholic spirituality in such respects as disciplines of spiritual direction and the writings of early saints (e.g. in writings by the Protestant authors Richard Foster and Dallas Willard or the Catholic Henri Nouwen).

2. The Orthodox Church in various places has borne the brunt of some of the worst persecutions suffered by the Church throughout history. Yet it survived, though it has provided by far the greatest number of martyrs for the Christian faith (see ch2). That has profoundly affected the Orthodox understanding of spirituality.

3. The Celtic Church from the time of Patrick (c.389–461) drew on the spirituality of the pre-Constantinian Latin Church and also the Eastern Desert Fathers. Its unique, indigenous expression of the faith, with its poetry, music, love of nature and vigorous missionary vision, leavened the Christianity of the British Isles. The effects are still evident today, despite the deadening impact of centuries of Medieval Catholicism.

4. The comprehensive World Values Survey (http://www.worldvaluessurvey.org) gathered data from 54 countries (containing 75% of the world's population) over the period 2005–08 and analysed a representative sample. The figures for the continents covered were then added up separately to produce the figures used here. Africa was the continent covered least fully.

5. See the Operation World database, File: ReligionsAll6major28Nov08.xls.

6. Statistics for evangelized individuals, and some of the theological category statistics, come from the WCD, Christian figures from the Operation World database and a survey by Carlos Villar, no longer available online, of theological persuasions within Christianity. The website on which the last was posted is no longer accessible, but the data is stored in File: ChristianNominalsWVS-changes.xls. How the figures were derived is explained in this XLS file.

7. "Evangelized non-Christians" is a term coined by the WCD. An extensive methodology was developed to measure the extent of the likely exposure of a population to the Gospel through various Christian ministries. From this was derived a percentage scale representing the number of individuals likely to be evangelized.

8. Terminology for the major Christian megablocs is not widely agreed. The *World Christian Encyclopedia* and *Operation World* have used "megablocs". This is clumsy! The 2010 *World Christian Atlas* uses "Christian traditions". My preference is the term "confession". They are all synonymous.

9. The full sets of statistics for the denominations and the renewed Christians in them are available in the MS Excel database section of the DVD. A fuller description of the methodology is also given there.

10. This refers to the three waves of Pentecostalism since the 19th Century, the Third Wave being that of charismatic renewal after 1960.

11. Persecution, hardship and social pressure erect many barriers to conversion and make the cost of discipleship high. Many new Christians have testimonies of divine intervention in healings, dreams and visions that confirm their faith and steel their ongoing walk in Christ. This reinforces an expectation of the present miraculous working of the Holy Spirit, which places these Christians in the charismatic stream even if they do not apply that term to themselves.

12. The spiritual impact of renewed Christians has often been compromised by the way that some preachers stress material wealth as a sign of God's blessing, overemphasize physical healing (inducing feelings of guilt in those not healed) and blame all negative influences on demons (downplaying personal responsibility for sin).

13. The expectation of the imminent return of Christ to take His people to glory and to judge the world is indeed a blessed hope for Christians, but it can lead to an interpretation of Scripture that Christians will experience a sudden, secret "rapture" 1,007 years before the Judgement and will thus avoid the worst of the tribulation that is coming to the world. Such an emphasis can blunt the desire both to work for world evangelization and to secure present political, social and ecological change and improve the lot of victims of injustice.

14. The most significant is the Movement for African National Initiatives (MANI), which focuses on affirming, motivating, mobilizing and networking African Christian leaders by inspiring them with the vision of reaching the unreached and least evangelized in Africa. www.maniafrica.com

15. To enable valid comparisons with other religions and some denominations, "conversion" does not necessarily mean spiritual new birth here, but refers to everyone (including dependent children) who becomes linked to a church involved in renewal.

16. Any growth rate higher than those shown represents an increase above the rate at which the world population is growing—perhaps as a result of people embracing Christianity as new converts or of existing believers having larger families. Family size is a smaller factor among Christians than among, say, Muslims, but it remains a valid point that religious people tend to have more children than the non-religious.

17. The Operation World database contains data from many sources and covers a wide range of assessment dates. Distortions can occur that become particularly obvious when handling growth rates. These can be due to time lags in reporting (sometimes up to seven years!), differing date points for large bodies of data, under-enumeration or enthusiastic overestimation. This last was the case particularly with data before 1970; much of our data came from the *World Christian Handbooks* of 1962 and 1967, which overlooked many pentecostal denominations in the listings of denominations by country.

18. Percentages involving Charismatics need to be qualified. Most Christians actively involved in charismatic-oriented gatherings tend to be young, and as they get older that involvement may well become less frequent or cease altogether. Nevertheless, they carry that influence with them into later life and so are still included in statistics for Charismatics. This is the case particularly for Catholic Charismatics. Thus, figures for non-pentecostal Charismatics in historic denominations are far more fluid than for those linked with pentecostal or charismatic denominations or churches.

19. Post-Vatican II Catholicism made way for a greater range of theological views, and among these was that of evangelical Catholics. This is a worldwide phenomenon and indicates a greater theological pluralism within Catholicism in contrast to past centuries. However, evangelical Catholics are especially significant in a few countries such as the USA, Ireland and Chile. The losses of Catholics to evangelical denominations have been huge, especially in Latin America and the USA; but some have chosen to remain Catholic as a witness. Many, but not all, evangelical Catholics also have a charismatic background. In Orthodoxy, there are biblical wings within national churches, such as the Lord's Army within the Romanian Orthodox Church, which was one of the founding members of the Evangelical Alliance in that country. The Egyptian and Ethiopian Orthodox Churches have significant minorities of warm-hearted, soul-winning Bible believers whose theology is largely evangelical but who would not use that term because of its association with "proselytizing" Western evangelical missions.

20. These newer networks were often termed the "house church" movements in the 1960s and '70s, or in more recent times the "newer churches". They became prominent in N America, Europe and China, the great majority being charismatic in style and emphasis.

21. Charles Finney's 1835 *Lectures on Revivals of Religion* can be found at http://www.ccel.org. The quotation used here was obtained from Lecture I: "What a Revival of Religion is".

22. The Revivals database has these events listed and categorized on the DVD.

23. The list of these events was derived from many sources, but principally the World Christian Trends section on cosmochronology and the series of books on awakenings and regional revivals written between 1949 and 1981 by J Edwin Orr.

24. The records on prayer movements are incomplete and the evident correlation between them and awakenings is not as high as it possibly should be.

25. Edwards preached a series of sermons to his congregation concerning concerted prayer and then published a book in 1748. The title sums up its content: *An Humble Attempt to Promote Explicit Agreement and Visible Union of God's People, in Extraordinary Prayer, for the Revival of Religion and the Advancement of Christ's Kingdom on Earth.* This compelling entreaty for the practice of unified prayer for revival was widely received and acted upon by Christians of all denominations.

26. Carey is rightly called "the Father of Modern Missions". It was his example and his writings that challenged and inspired many to go overseas.

Christianity: The Evangelical Explosion

From here onwards, the major focus of this book is on Evangelicals. As one of the three major renewal movements, Evangelicals have already been covered in the previous chapter. However, it is chiefly the broader evangelical movement, in all its varied forms across the Christian confessional megablocs, that is providing the main thrust for world evangelization. The overview of Evangelicals will be followed by careful definitions and statistics on growth, which will then lead, in the next chapter, into the challenge of the unfinished task from an evangelical perspective.

Each continent is shown in a distinct colour. Each rectangle represents a UN region, positioned roughly where it usually appears on a world map. The size of each rectangle is proportionate to the number of Evangelicals in that region in 1960, 2000 and (according to careful projections) 2050.

In 1960, Evangelicals were predominantly in EuNAPa, with relatively small numbers in AfAsLA.

By 2000, massive growth of Evangelicals in AfAsLA and also NA, contrasted with a sad lack of growth in EuPa

By 2050, if our projections are correct, and unless there is a significant intervention by the Holy Spirit, evangelical

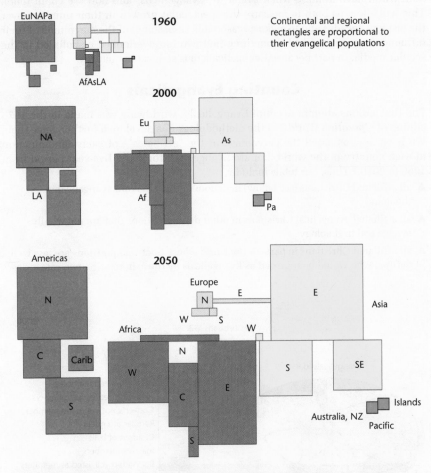

Fig 6.1 *Distribution of Evangelicals by continents and UN regions, 1960–2050*

representation in EuPa will have remained static or will be in slow decline, whereas in AfAsLA and, to an extent, NA Evangelicals will lead in terms of numbers, vision and mission outreach to the rest of the world. The latter developments give real hope for progress towards world evangelization in the coming generation.

Religious growth worldwide

The world. The black bar and the red line indicate the average annual growth rate of the world's population. The various religions can be compared with this.

Five world religions.[1] Muslims, Hindus and Christians have been growing in number faster than the global population. Islam was the fastest-growing religion in 2000, and this is set to continue but at a slower rate because families in most Muslim societies are decreasing in size. Ethnic religions and Buddhism have been growing at a slower rate—largely through losses to other religions.

Five Christian megablocs. The slow growth rates for Orthodox and Catholics are for differing reasons.[2] Independents, Anglicans and Protestants are growing in number faster than the world average—mainly because of their evangelical components.

Christian renewal. Charismatics, Pentecostals and Evangelicals are displayed at the top. Bear in mind that these categories overlap a good deal and that each of them is also a component of all the Christian confessional blocs above them. These renewal movements are largely or entirely evangelical and are the most dynamic, and growing, religious force in the 21st Century.

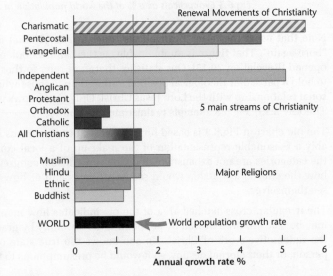

Fig 6.2 *The average annual growth rate of religions, 1990–2000*

The *definition of Evangelicals* and the statistics relating to them are so fundamental to the contents of this book and the related website that it is important to clarify both who I have in mind when I refer to "Evangelicals" and how we count them. This will allow us both to measure the spectacular growth in their numbers over the last few decades and to make a reasonable assessment of the magnitude of their influence in today's world—something that is often overlooked or belittled in the secular media, in part because Evangelicalism is so hard to quantify.

Counting Evangelicals

The first serious attempt to count Evangelicals[3] worldwide was made in the 1978 edition of *Operation World*, but the methodology has developed further since then. We have now assessed the percentage of the "affiliates"[4] of each denomination in each country in the world that are Evangelicals for every five-year period from 1960 to 2010.[5] Thus, our totals include:

▲ all affiliated Christians (see below) in denominations that are evangelical in theology

▲ all affiliated evangelical Christians in other denominations that are not wholly evangelical in theology

▲ all affiliated Christians in parts of the world where doctrinal positions are less well defined who would be regarded as Evangelicals by those in the first two categories.[6]

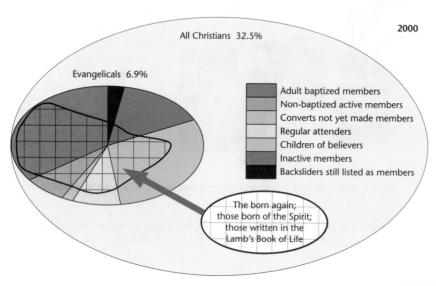

Fig 6.3 *Evangelicals as a % of the world population in 2000*

Note that using the term "Evangelicals" does NOT imply that all such people are "born-again". That figure is unobtainable, as the Lamb's Book of Life has yet to be opened (Revelation 20:15). Our statistics therefore refer to those who might claim to hold a particular theological position, rather than to those who have a living, personal relationship with the Lord Jesus Christ. Only God knows who the Elect are (2 Timothy 2:19). Fig 6.3 attempts to illustrate that reality.

The pie chart in Fig 6.3 is based on hypothesis, but its various segments are probably a reasonable representation of the make-up of a local congregation (though the categories are not exhaustive). It divides up a whole congregation according to how the church leadership would see its affiliates and/or how its affiliates would see themselves.

The irregular, cross-hatched area of the pie indicates how many in each category may be true children of God by adoption into His family by grace through faith in the redemptive work of Christ. No one knows the true state of heart of another person, or their eternal destiny, so it would be presumptuous to try to count them!

Evangelicals: all those who generally emphasize

▲ the Lord Jesus as the sole source of salvation, through faith in Him

▲ personal faith, conversion and regeneration by the Holy Spirit

▲ the authority of the Bible as the inspired word of God and the only basis for faith and Christian living

▲ a commitment to biblical witness, evangelism and mission that brings others to faith in Christ.

A brief elaboration of this definition:

1. The Lord Jesus is unique, the only way to the Father (whereas the modern trend is to regard other religions as equally valid routes to salvation).

2. Personal faith in Christ contrasts with a Christian commitment that is merely notional, nominal or traditional and based on culture, education, family background or place of birth or residence.

3. The Bible is authoritative and without error, and is relevant to the whole of humankind.

4. Everyone urgently needs to hear the Gospel, which must be proclaimed worldwide (a position strongly taken in this book).

Food for Thought

▲ As evangelical Christians, how concerned are we about the current spiritual health and eternal destiny of the people closest to us, in our family, social and work life?

▲ Has the two-edged sword of the Gospel, which has the power both to convict people of sin and to set them free, been blunted by uncertainty about its uniqueness or by the pressures imposed by society?

Cape Town 2010 (photo courtesy Lausanne Movement)

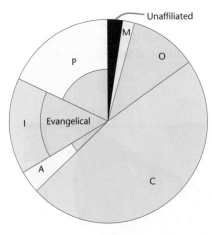

Fig 6.4 Evangelicals by confession in 2000

At the beginning of the 21st Century, Evangelicals constitute the most dynamic and vigorous renewal movement in the worldwide Church. The following pages demonstrate the variety within Evangelicalism. First, we look at the six confessional megablocs.

The pie chart represents the Christian megablocs, according to their global numbers in 2000, and shows the proportion of Evangelicals in each one. There is generally a far greater willingness to embrace the authority of the Bible in cultures that have not been shaped by the Enlightenment, a worldview that exalts human pride.

Evangelicals are predominantly *Protestant, Independent* or *Anglican (PIA)* and, to a great extent, can be grouped together (as they often are in this book) because they have so much in common in terms of vision and beliefs, which for most of them are more important than denominational tags. Indeed, the emerging church networks tend to be non-denominational or post-denominational.

Evangelical Catholics and Orthodox are relatively few as a proportion of their confessional megablocs, and they are also somewhat marginalized, both within their own confessions and among PIA Evangelicals. Many of the latter have reservations about the term "Evangelical" being applied to Catholics or Orthodox, though the growing influence of a more biblical orientation is apparent in sections of both megablocs.

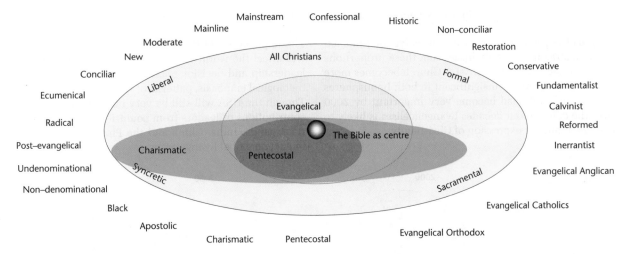

Fig 6.5 Evangelicals by theological emphasis

We turn next to the theological variations within Evangelicalism. A half-century in the wilderness after 1910 ended around 1960. Since then, Evangelicals have bounced back with renewed energy, increasing in number rapidly as a result of vigorous evangelism and a major investment in cross-cultural missions, which made them a dominant force in the worldwide Church. Success has resulted in many calling themselves Evangelicals who have a questionable commitment to the inerrancy of the Bible and evangelical theology. Fig 6.5 illustrates this.

There are maybe 70 different adjectives used to qualify the broad term "Evangelical", and I have used 26 of the commonest here. I have used the diagram from page 121, but placed these adjectives appropriately around the outermost oval. (It would be more appropriate still to place them around the yellow "Evangelical" oval in the middle, but less easy to read.) The diversity is astonishing, and therein lies a threat to the future health of Evangelicalism. There is no guarantee that the next 50 years will continue the successful growth of the last 50. What are the dangers? Here are three:

▲ The success, and even popularity, of the movement has caused many people to join it, or at least to copy its methodology, but without a genuine commitment to the core values listed on page 140. This has created openings for many fringe teachings, such as the "prosperity gospel",[7] a creeping universalism and exotic eschatologies.

▲ The powerhouse for evangelical renewal has been the USA with its freedom of religion, its dynamism and its wealth. Diversity is a passing luxury that cannot be enjoyed in many countries where there is persecution. The "successes" of US Evangelicalism—its management styles, its mega-churches, its business ventures and so on—have all too often become models for church life elsewhere in the world. How much of this is more cultural than biblical?

▲ There has been a loss of a sharp focus on obeying the Great Commission. The great variety of items on the agenda at global evangelical conferences means that many people downplay or even ignore the primacy in ministry of world evangelization.

Burning Question for Today

God has graciously given us an awakening over the past 50 years that has impacted many countries and peoples. The principal human instrument for this has been evangelical Christians. Future projections in this book assume moderate further growth.

▲ Are the very successes of Evangelicalism sowing the seeds of its spiritual demise by grieving the Spirit of God through pride, division, disobedience, carnality, moral laxity, theological error or prayerlessness?

North-south spread

The immense changes in the Christian world as its weight has shifted from the North and West to the South and East can be seen in the two rows of pie charts below, whose two halves compare the Christian populations of EuNAPa and AfAsLA by confessional megablocs.

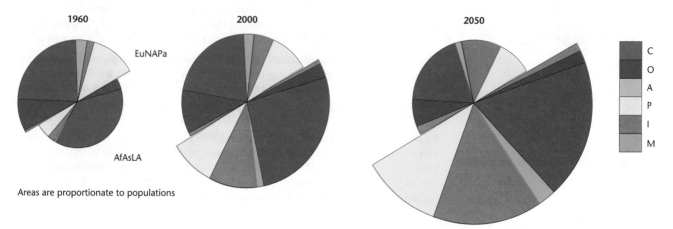

Fig 6.6 *The Christian confessional megablocs distribution, 1960–2050*[8]

Fig 6.7 adds the proportion of Evangelicals (yellow) in each confessional stream. As we shall see later, these proportions are increasing steadily as the AfAsLA Church becomes more prominent. Comparatively insignificant in both hemispheres in 1960, Evangelicals had become very important by 2000 and over the coming four decades Evangelicalism is likely to become the dominant expression of Christianity.

The implications of these developments are many, and they will affect the worldwide Church at every level—in terms of leadership and decision-making, missiology, spirituality and theological emphasis, patterns of worship, new initiatives etc. Though the USA will still be very influential, the increasing contributions of leaders from countries such as Brazil, Nigeria, Uganda, India, China and the Philippines will make an impact on global Evangelicalism.

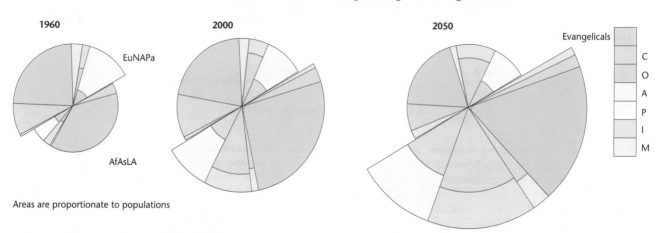

Fig 6.7 *The evangelical components of the confessional megablocs, 1960–2050*

Food for Thought

The unipolar evangelical world dominated by the USA is passing away as a multipolar, global Evangelicalism emerges, with more regional networking.

▲ Will future evangelical leaders be culturally-sensitive enough to work with the complexity of teams and networks of different nationalities?

▲ Will leaders from EuNAPa be willing to give those from AfAsLA room and respect for new initiatives to evangelize the world that is emerging?

Cape Town 2010 (photo courtesy Lausanne Movement)

Evangelicals used to be concentrated in the (largely Anglophone) countries of N America, the Pacific, the UK and S Africa. There were also many in Scandinavia, Germany and Switzerland.

In 1900, the Catholic world was hostile to Evangelicals, and their numbers there were small. Elsewhere, the seed-sowing of the 19th Century's missionaries was only beginning to bear fruit.

Meanwhile, in lands with strong evangelical communities, whole denominations were succumbing to the deadening influence of liberal theology.

By 1960, the devastating impact of liberal theology, hostile ideologies and world wars can be seen in the declining percentages of Evangelicals in EuNAPa populations.

However, over the same 60 years growth was apparent in parts of Africa, Latin America and Asia. It was most evident in the world's most populous Catholic country, Brazil, as well as in C and E Africa, stimulated by revivals that transformed whole denominations.

By 2000, significant and dramatic growth had led to times of harvest. The collapse of Europe's empires, whether colonial or Communist, stimulated an indigenization and vitalization of Christianity—often in times of severe social disruption, war and persecution. The lighter shading on this map bears witness to this.

The growth was mainly in Africa, the Korean Peninsula and Indonesia in the 1960s, in Latin America in the 1970s and in E Asia and China in the 1980s. In the 1990s, it became more global.

The vigour of evangelical growth in the 1990s is to be sustained well into the 21st Century, but at a slower rate. The projections given here are modest. It is likely that, as the century matures, the increase in numbers of Evangelicals in China, India and even some Muslim-dominated countries will accelerate. Africa will probably see further growth as well—as a result of conversion, a higher birth rate among Evangelicals and the impact of Evangelicalism on its social structures.

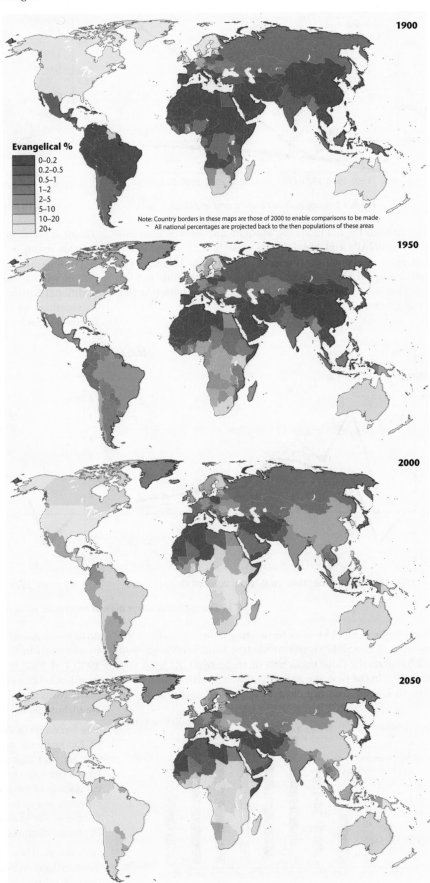

1900

Evangelical %
- 0–0.2
- 0.2–0.5
- 0.5–1
- 1–2
- 2–5
- 5–10
- 10–20
- 20+

Note: Country borders in these maps are those of 2000 to enable comparisons to be made. All national percentages are projected back to the then populations of these areas

1950

2000

2050

Food for Thought

Evangelical growth has been remarkable and gives us cause to praise God.

▲ There are grounds for optimism—but could things all go badly wrong, as so often in the past?

It is essential that we pray for spiritual unity, the rejection of error, a commitment to Christ and a passion for world evangelization if even projected growth-rates are to be sustained.

Fig 6.8 *Evangelical growth by country, 1900–2050*

The graphs on this page present different aspects of evangelical growth worldwide and compare and contrast the growth in EuNAPa and AfAsLA. They convey something of the dramatic reversal of earlier trends for Evangelicals and illustrate why they have become such an important component of the 21st-Century Church.

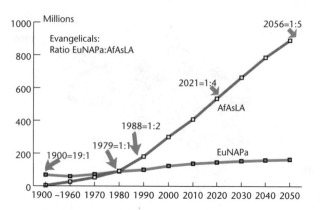

Fig 6.9 *Evangelicals in EuNAPa and in AfAsLA*

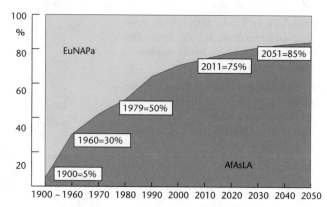

Fig 6.10 *AfAsLA Evangelicals as % of all Evangelicals*

The lines in Fig 6.9 chart the absolute numbers of Evangelicals in EuNAPa and AfAsLA. The growth in EuNAPa, steady but slow, has been far exceeded by that in AfAsLA. The ratios marked along the AfAsLA line further points out the contrast: evangelical Christianity has done far better in that hemisphere.

The area graph in Fig 6.10 shows the percentages of all Evangelicals living in EuNAPa and AfAsLA from 1900 to 2050. According to our projections, the ratio between the two populations will almost be inverted in the space of 150 years. The additional figures in the white boxes give the AfAsLA total as a percentage of all Evangelicals. AfAsLA Evangelicals will in future be much more influential.

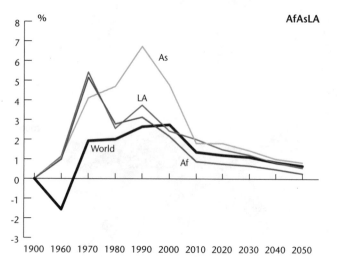

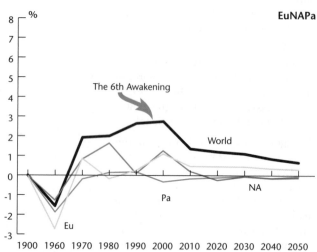

Fig 6.11 *Evangelical average annual conversion rates, 1900–2050*

The graphs in Fig 6.11 show the average annual growth in the number of Evangelicals worldwide (the black line) compared with that on the three continents of, respectively, AfAsLA and EuNAPa. In the first, the peaks in growth in Africa, then Latin America, then Asia are clear to see.[9] (The apparent dip in

2010 is due more to our caution in making projections country by country!) In the second graph, the steep decline between 1900 and 1960 is in startling contrast to subsequent growth worldwide. The global peak is evidence of the harvest of the Sixth Awakening. Future growth in EuNAPa is likely to be small, but this will be at a time of overall population decline.[10]

The bar chart in Fig 6.12 shows the total increase in numbers of Evangelicals decade by decade. The peak in the 1990s reveals that that decade saw more evangelical converts to Christ than any other in history. It may prove to be the greatest decade of harvest there will ever be—in part because most converts are young and the proportion of children and young people in the global population will continue to shrink as the birth rate declines.[11]

In contrast, it is sobering to note that in the six decades from 1900 to 1960, AfAsLA saw an increase of two million only—the breakthroughs had scarcely started—while EuNAPa saw a small decline in numbers during a time of population growth.

Fig 6.12 *Evangelical growth in millions by decade since 1960*

The top 20 countries for Evangelicals

We now focus on the countries with the largest populations of Evangelicals in each successive half-century between 1900 and 2050. These lists give an extraordinary insight into what God has been doing in the world. The colour behind the number of each entry indicates the continent concerned, and countries that have a Muslim majority have also been marked with hatching.

In 1900, over 71% of all the world's Evangelicals lived in two countries: the USA and the UK. There was subsequently a massive decline in numbers in the UK and only a small increase in the USA as a percentage of the national population. The other lands of the Reformation in Europe had remarkably few Evangelicals—most prominent being the three Scandinavian countries with their recent histories of revival. Numbers in Germany were surprisingly low, as nominalism and liberal theology were already taking their toll on the country's spiritual life. Of the 20 countries with the largest evangelical populations in 1900, only four were largely non-Caucasian: India, China, Madagascar and Jamaica. S African Evangelicals were mostly white.

By 2000, there were only three Caucasian-majority countries in the list—and by 2050 there will be just one: the USA. The two most populous countries on earth, China and India, appear on all four lists, and rise steadily to first and third places respectively in 2050.

In 1900 there were no *Latin American countries* on the list, but by 2050 there will be four. Both Brazil and Mexico will by then exercise a global influence.

The increasing number of *African countries* listed is significant—in 1900 just two, in 1960 five, in 2000 ten and in 2050, most likely, 11. Several African countries have experienced revival, including, on this list, Uganda, Kenya, Ethiopia and parts of Congo-DR, Tanzania and S Africa.

In 2000 and 2050, two *Muslim-majority countries* are listed that have large Evangelical minorities. By 2050, there could conceivably be a third, if the present religious tyranny in Iran continues to turn its people against Islam. Sudan has been split during 2010, into a Christian-majority south and a Muslim-majority north.

The evangelical population of *China* will probably have far surpassed that of the US by 2050. What will that mean for the world? By then, China will have a rapidly ageing population but will still be the world's workshop and its largest exporter, as well as a military and political superpower. On top of all this, it will have acquired such a strong Bible-believing Church that this will have a large say in the country's affairs and a leading role globally in theology and missions.

The "wild card" is *India,* where evangelical Christianity has been growing rapidly in the early years of the 21st Century, far exceeding the estimates made by the (rather distorted) census mechanism for quantifying religious adherence. There are two major forces: the Hinduization of India, which is leading increasingly to the persecution of the Church, and the rejection of Hinduism among the downtrodden lower castes and the Dalit underclass. The potential for a harvest has never been greater—if this is handled aright by the Church. The projections here assume a high rate of conversion, but things could turn out very differently.

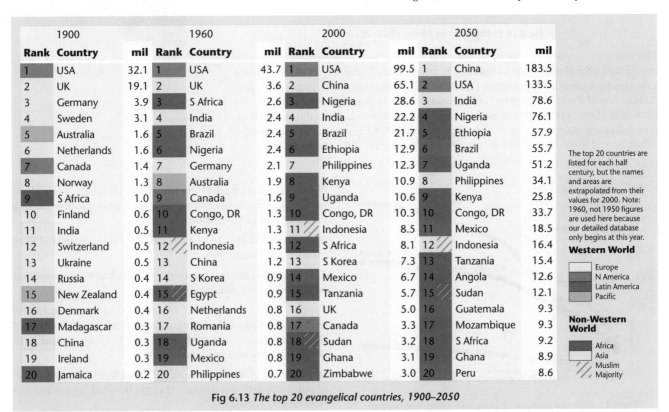

1900			1960			2000			2050		
Rank	Country	mil	Rank	Country	mil	Rank	Country	mil	Rank	Country	mil
1	USA	32.1	1	USA	43.7	1	USA	99.5	1	China	183.5
2	UK	19.1	2	UK	3.6	2	China	65.1	2	USA	133.5
3	Germany	3.9	3	S Africa	2.6	3	Nigeria	28.6	3	India	78.6
4	Sweden	3.1	4	India	2.4	4	India	22.2	4	Nigeria	76.1
5	Australia	1.6	5	Brazil	2.4	5	Brazil	21.7	5	Ethiopia	57.9
6	Netherlands	1.6	6	Nigeria	2.4	6	Ethiopia	12.9	6	Brazil	55.7
7	Canada	1.4	7	Germany	2.1	7	Philippines	12.3	7	Uganda	51.2
8	Norway	1.3	8	Australia	1.9	8	Kenya	10.9	8	Philippines	34.1
9	S Africa	1.0	9	Canada	1.6	9	Uganda	10.6	9	Kenya	25.8
10	Finland	0.6	10	Congo, DR	1.3	10	Congo, DR	10.3	10	Congo, DR	33.7
11	India	0.5	11	Kenya	1.3	11	Indonesia	8.5	11	Mexico	18.5
12	Switzerland	0.5	12	Indonesia	1.3	12	S Africa	8.1	12	Indonesia	16.4
13	Ukraine	0.5	13	China	1.2	13	S Korea	7.3	13	Tanzania	15.4
14	Russia	0.4	14	S Korea	0.9	14	Mexico	6.7	14	Angola	12.6
15	New Zealand	0.4	15	Egypt	0.9	15	Tanzania	5.7	15	Sudan	12.1
16	Denmark	0.4	16	Netherlands	0.8	16	UK	5.0	16	Guatemala	9.3
17	Madagascar	0.3	17	Romania	0.8	17	Canada	3.3	17	Mozambique	9.3
18	China	0.3	18	Uganda	0.8	18	Sudan	3.2	18	S Africa	9.2
19	Ireland	0.3	19	Mexico	0.8	19	Ghana	3.1	19	Ghana	8.9
20	Jamaica	0.2	20	Philippines	0.7	20	Zimbabwe	3.0	20	Peru	8.6

The top 20 countries are listed for each half century, but the names and areas are extrapolated from their values for 2000. Note: 1960, not 1950 figures are used here because our detailed database only begins at this year.

Western World

Europe
N America
Latin America
Pacific

Non-Western World

Africa
Asia
Muslim Majority

Fig 6.13 *The top 20 evangelical countries, 1900–2050*

Burning Questions for Today

These projections suggest a very different evangelical world to the one we have known. There is a double challenge:

▲ How can we facilitate the changes they imply, such as a major breakthrough in India, continued revivals in Africa and the spiritual maturing of Brazil?

▲ Do we just sit back and accept current trends or trust and labour for a backsliding Europe or an unresponsive Muslim world?

▲ What countries should we pray for that are missing from the list because of decline or the absence of a breakthrough?

African Evangelicals increased over the period 1900–2050, but the greatest growth was between 1960 and 2000, the very period in which the European colonial powers relinquished their empires and Evangelical Christianity became indigenous.

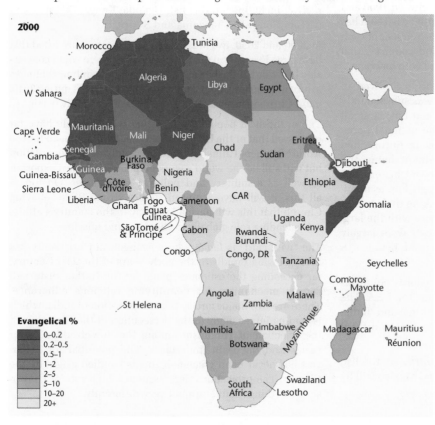

Fig 6.14 *Evangelicals in Africa, 1900–2050*

The colonial carve-up of Africa in the 19th Century imposed borders with little regard for cultural and political realities, to create today's countries. On the positive side, this provided the opportunity for Christianity to advance in Africa—with a predominance of Protestants (many being Evangelicals) in Anglophone countries and Catholics elsewhere. On the negative side, it led to nepotism, corruption and warfare following independence in the years after 1957.[12] Competing ethnic groups, religions and ideologies were too complex to allow for stability and growth.

Fig 6.15 represents the five UN-designated regions of Africa.

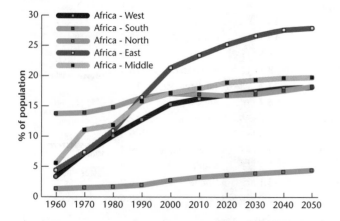

Fig 6.15 *Regional evangelical growth in Africa, 1960–2050*

North: culturally part of the Muslim Arab world; evangelical growth as a result both of indigenous Berber peoples coming to Christ and of northward migrations

South: the first area to be impacted by Evangelicals, but very little growth since 1960

East: massive growth as a result of revival; limited opposition from the Muslim minority

Centre: strong evangelical missions effort leading to the planting of many different churches, which became the most stable component of societies reduced to chaos by war, economic collapse and political failure

West: slower growth as a result of French colonial and, later, Muslim-majority opposition, though boosted by revivals in Nigeria and Ghana

Food for Thought

We may all be of African descent![13]

▲ Westerners have been dismissive of the failings of Africa, but how many realize that their own countries were major contributors to these failures?

The colonial powers created unviable states, while post-colonial Cold War politics supported dictators, condoned corruption, promoted unfair trade policies and provided inappropriate aid. Amidst all the chaos, evangelical Christians are growing and could soon become a major source of Christian workers and missionaries to the world.

Africa's zone of religious conflict

Africa's 2,110 languages are mapped according to the religion practised by the majority of their speakers.[14] Christians (yellow)—of whom Evangelicals are a large component—dominate in the South and Centre and on the western coast, Muslims (green) dominate in the North and on the eastern coast. The zone between, where these two groups overlap and interact, is where most African peoples live who still predominantly practise ethnic religions (blue). It is these peoples that Islam and Christianity compete to win, and it is in this zone that the two religions clash—at times violently, sadly.[15]

Muslims have increased in number in Africa, but the means by which they have achieved this have not always been good—including trading in slaves (like many Western nations), dominating trade systems, migrating to non-Muslim areas, imposing harsh

restrictions and *shari'a* law where they have political power, making financial aid (including student grants) conditional on the recipients embracing Islam and, at times, resorting to armed force. Their greatest successes have been in far W Africa, Tanzania and Mozambique.

Christians have grown in number more rapidly than Muslims, Evangelicals most of all. In the past, it was advantageous to become a Christian to gain access to health care and education. More recently, the principal means of winning people has been evangelism and, often, the godly example of Christians themselves. Translating the Bible helped to preserve cultures, and this made Christianity indigenous to Africa. Islam tends to suppress cultural variety.

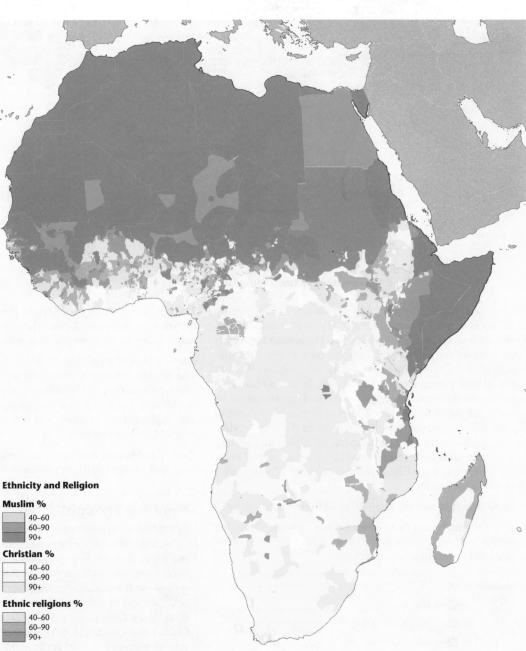

Ethnicity and Religion

Muslim %
- 40–60
- 60–90
- 90+

Christian %
- 40–60
- 60–90
- 90+

Ethnic religions %
- 40–60
- 60–90
- 90+

Fig 6.16 *Religious affiliation by language group in Africa in 2000*

Food for Thought

The rise of Islamism has impacted both the Muslim and the non-Muslim world. It is on this continent that the interactions between Islam and Christianity are the most extensive. In most African countries the two faiths co-exist peaceably, and there are even some families that include Christians and Muslims and adherents of ethnic religion![16] In some countries this has led to conflict, as in the long and bloody civil war in Sudan, the continuing violence in Nigeria, the murder of Christians in Somalia, Egypt etc and the severe persecution of Christians in Algeria. Yet Christians have been successful in boldly winning many Muslims for Christ. African Christians are not afraid to witness to Muslims.

▲ Are we?

Asia was for 500 years the continent where the Church was growing most vigor-ously—and also most persecuted. This was followed by over 800 years of decline. In 1900, fewer than 2% of all Evangelicals were Asian. However, by 2000 this figure had increased to over 29%, and by 2050 it could exceed 33%. Most of these Evangelicals live in a wedge of E and SE Asia bounded by Indonesia, the Philippines, the Korean Peninsula and central China. Asian Evangelicals are still the most persecuted.

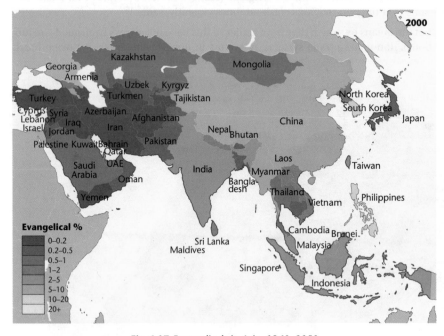

Fig 6.17 *Evangelicals in Asia, 1960–2050*

We rejoice at the dramatic growth of evangelical Christianity in China (see p167 for more details of this phenomenon), S Korea, Indonesia and the Philippines. These countries with large evangelical populations have become major contribu-tors to global Christianity: *China* with its godly spirituality under severe persecution, *S Korea* with its mega-churches, now the world's second-biggest sender of missionaries to other countries, *N Korea*, once a land of revival but subject to the most severe persecution of Christians in the world today, *the Philippines* with its huge diaspora, adaptable and willing to serve the Lord under harsh working conditions, and *Indonesia*, which has more Christians from a Muslim background than any other country.

Fig 6.18 demonstrates the spiritual need that remains in Asia.

East: great growth, but there remains the challenge of the two Buddhist countries, Japan and Thailand, that are so open to witness but unresponsive to the Gospel

The further west one goes in Asia, the harsher the conditions for witness and church life. These parts of Asia must be a major focus for us if our world is to be fully evangelized:

South and Southeast: The Buddhist lands of Laos, Myanmar and Bhutan are largely sealed off from the Gospel; in Hindu India, persecution of Christians is steadily increasing; and in the Muslim lands of Indonesia, Bangladesh, Pakistan, C Asia and Afghanistan, Muslims are making strenuous efforts to restrict Christian witness.

West: The Muslim lands of Iran, Turkey and the Arab world once had a large Christian presence.

Food for Thought

In the first millennium of the Church, Asian Christians suffered periods of severe persecution, with many martyred, and yet they increased and spread. The last 100 years have seen a similar pattern. Revival and church growth on the Korean Peninsula were accompanied with and followed by persecution, first by the Japanese and then by the Communists. The unprecedented growth of China's evangelical Church happened in the midst of terrible persecution, which climaxed in Mao's Cultural Revolution of 1966–76. Indonesia's rapid church growth followed the abortive Communist coup in 1965 and subsequent slaughter by vengeful Muslims. Shi'a Muslim Iran's opening up to Christianity began with the Islamic Revolution of 1979. India's recent growth parallels increased persecution by Hinduists.

▲ Is this to be the pattern of the 21st Century, too?

▲ Are we prepared, as Bible believers, to live by the biblical truth that "all who want to live a godly life in Christ Jesus will be persecuted" (2 Timothy 3:12)?

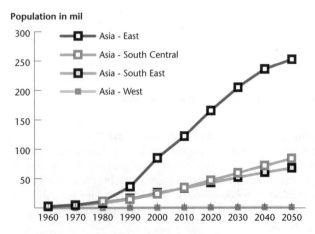

Fig 6.18 *Regional evangelical growth in Asia, 1960–2050*

Asia's zone of religious conflict

SE Asia highlights the future challenge for Evangelicals, though there are a number of similar situations in other parts of the continent. Two trends characterize Indonesia, Malaysia and S Philippines (shown on this map). One is the embrace of Christianity by many peoples, often followers of ethnic religions, over the past century; the other is an aggressive Muslim expansion that also protests at the successes of Christianity.

Islam spread largely through eastward trade from the sultanates of northern Sumatra between the 14th and 19th Centuries. By 1900, most of the coasts of Malaya, the islands of Sumatra, Java and parts of Sulawesi were largely Muslim, replacing the earlier Hinduism, Buddhism and animistic ethnic religions. Islam was often tolerant and syncretic, especially in Java. It is only since the 1990s that Muslims have become increasingly Islamized, leading to discrimination against and persecution of Christians as well as aggressive efforts to convert the entire population of both Malaysia and Indonesia.

Certain ethnic groups are strongly Muslim, notably the Malay throughout the whole region and, in Indonesia, the Aceh, Minang, Rejang, Lampung in Sumatra, the Sundanese and Madurese in Java, the Banjar and Malay in Kalimantan and the Bugis, Kaili and Gorontalo in Sulawesi (see Fig 6.19).[17]

The Javanese are the most numerous ethnic group at nearly 100 million. They are nominally Muslim, but have proved the most responsive to Christianity.

Christianity arrived with colonial rule four centuries ago—the Portuguese brought Catholicism (a majority in Flores and E Timor) and the Dutch brought their Protestant Reformed faith (strong in Maluku, W Timor, Minahassa, Java etc).

More recently, some peoples have become Christian—the Batak and Nias peoples of Sumatra being Lutheran, the Toraja of Sulawesi Reformed, and the Dayak of Borneo and tribal peoples of Malaysia Protestant of various denominations.

The failed Communist coup of 1965 was one factor that prompted the Javanese and Chinese in the region to turn to Christ.[18] Millions have since done so, adding to Muslim hostility—especially to the largely Christian "wealthy" Chinese community.

The major challenges for Indonesian Christians are to reach every people group in their country (about 60% of its population belong to 103 still unreached non-Papuan peoples—most of them Muslim) and to find ways to reach the Malays of Malaysia and Brunei and the Muslim peoples of the restive island of Mindanao in the Philippines.

W Papua, the Indonesian half of the island of New Guinea was once known as Irian Jaya. The Indonesian dictator Sukarno succeeded in gaining control of it from the Dutch in 1963, when it was unilaterally incorporated into Indonesia despite a promise to the UN to hold a full referendum of its population. The many indigenous peoples became marginalized as Muslim immigrants from other islands poured in, and mission work—rapid evangelization and Bible translation—was severely limited.[19] Out of 270 languages, only 30 have a New Testament and around 100 have no Bible portions; yet, significant numbers have turned to Christ.

Fig 6.19 *Religious affiliation by language group in SE Asia in 2000*

Burning Question for Today

Indonesian Christians are now doing most of the missions outreach, but they are unevenly distributed across the country and hampered by Islamist persecution and the blind eye the authorities turn to the burning of churches and the closing of Christian institutions. In Malaysia and Brunei, the Christians are largely non-Malay Chinese and S Asians and are forbidden by law from proselytizing Muslims. Foreigners have great difficulty in gaining entry visas.

▲ How are we to bring the Good News to so many people groups that live behind such formidable barriers?

Most of the Reformation lands in Europe experienced awakenings in the 18th and 19th Centuries, with recent revivals in the UK, Norway, Sweden and Finland. Evangelicals helped to mould more equitable, democratic societies and a capitalism based on biblical principles—a "Victorian" morality much derided today. Yet the 20th Century saw a massive collapse of Evangelicalism in these countries, followed by a slow recovery—with its advance elsewhere in Europe. Here we see the sobering figures.

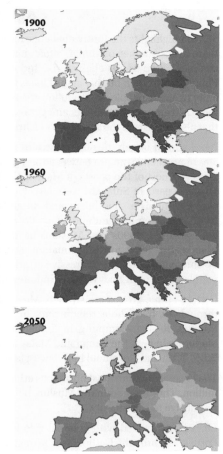

Evangelical %
- 0–0.2
- 0.2–0.5
- 0.5–1
- 1–2
- 2–5
- 5–10
- 10–20
- 20+

Fig 6.20 *Evangelicals in Europe, 1900–2050*

20th-Century decline

Europe's Evangelicals constituted 45% of the world's Evangelicals in 1900 but only 4% in 2000—and by 2050 could be less than 2% unless God intervenes. Note the change in colours on the map. Not all was failure, however, and there were brighter aspects:

▲ The actual decline ended in the 1960s and was followed by slow growth at a time when a wider Christian commitment and church attendances were in free fall. The erosion of autocratic control in both the political sphere and the Church in Catholic and Orthodox countries provided new openings for the spread of Evangelicalism, with churches being planted in S and E Europe.

▲ By 2050, Europe's spiritual need as "the Prodigal Continent" will be plain to see.

North: early huge decline followed by some stabilization but few conversions and little effective evangelism. Most of the growth in future will be as a result of immigration and of the tendency of Christian families (both immigrant and indigenous) to be more stable and to produce more children, who are more likely to embrace their parents' beliefs.

West: early declines in Germany, the Netherlands and Switzerland followed by the same trends as in the north

South: slow growth from a very small base; waning opposition from the Catholic Church. Future growth will be principally the result of immigration from AfAsLA.

East: Most evangelical growth has occurred (and will probably continue to occur) in Romania, Moldova and Ukraine. Orthodox Churches in Greece, Serbia, Russia and elsewhere have often opposed evangelical ministry, whether foreign or indigenous, through restrictions and discriminatory legislation.

Food for Thought

Religion is a taboo subject for most Europeans. In the 17th and 18th Centuries, two hundred years of wars motivated largely by state involvement in religion fuelled a massive change in worldview. Secularism, humanism and tolerance were deified in the Enlightenment. Today, any form of criticism of religion, especially evangelical Christianity, is freely allowed and even applauded, but rarely do Evangelicals enjoy the same freedom to explain their faith either in the media or person-to-person. The discrediting of biblical Christianity by the media so marginalizes believers that the demons of society that are destroying Western civilization go unchallenged. The bare survival of biblical Christianity in Europe is obvious here.

▲ Are we too humbly submitting to this discrimination?

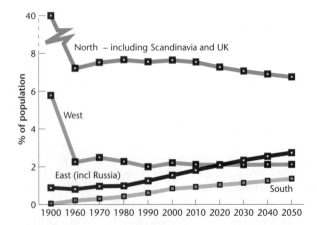

Fig 6.21 *Evangelical growth and decline in Europe, 1900–2050*

Religious conflict in the Caucasus

The Caucasus Mountains separate Europe from Asia, but straddling them are some of the most intractable political, economic, linguistic and religious problems in the world today. For evangelical Christians, this is also one of the most spiritually needy regions. The six countries through which the range runs—Russia, Turkey, Iran, Azerbaijan, Georgia and Armenia—are so different, yet all are in need of God's grace and power.

For centuries, the regional superpowers *Iran, Turkey* and *Russia* have fought one another for control of this strategic but impoverished part of the world.

After the collapse of the Soviet Union in 1991, its three republics south of the Caucasus became independent states.

The oil riches of the Caspian basin and its vital communication routes ensure its continued politico-economic importance far into the future. Over the years since 1991, there have been significant conflicts (marked with stars on the map).

The war between Orthodox Armenia and Muslim Azerbaijan over the Nagorno-Karabakh enclave and Russia's military interventions in Georgia over its ethnic-minority territories of Abkhazia and South Ossetia have left festering wounds that are likely to flare up again some day.

Eight Caucasus republics remain an unwilling part of the Russian Federation. Wars between the Russians and Chechens in Chechnya, with spillovers into Ingushetia and Dagestan have fur-

ther fuelled the Islamists' dream of an Islamic state in the N Caucasus.

The Kurds continue to revolt against the Turks and Iranians who control their homelands.

The Caucasus is a major frontier between the Christian Orthodox and Muslim worlds, whose confrontation there has lasted a full millennium.

The *Armenians* and *Georgians* were the first of what has since emerged as nation states to become Christian—in the 4th Century. All the other peoples in the region but the Ossetians and Udi became Muslim a few centuries later. The Kalmyks are descendants of the Mongolian armies of Genghis Khan, and are Europe's only indigenous Buddhist people.

Fig 6.22 *Religious affiliation and conflict in the Caucasus in 2000*

There are about 50 ethnic groups, speaking 37 local languages. Most are these are ancient Caucasian languages, but there are several that are Turkic (Azeri, Karachay) or Persian-related (Osetin, Kurdish and Domari Gypsy [not shown on map]).

The Armenians and Georgians have long had the whole Bible, but the New Testament has been translated into just five other languages. There are some portions of the Bible available in a further seven languages, but in at least 21 others there is nothing.

Ancient Orthodox traditions dominate in the churches of the region. Nominalism is widespread, and few even among the Christians have any understanding of the true nature of the Gospel. There is a great lack of a clear evangelical witness in this complex area, and most of the many Muslim peoples must be counted among the least evangelized on earth.

Discrimination against and persecution of Evangelicals, whether foreign or indigenous, are commonplace.

Burning Questions

▲ How will this corner of Europe ever be evangelized?

There are several dozen ethnic groups with no known Christian believers and others with only a handful. Visas for foreign workers are almost unobtainable.

▲ Who will go to these peoples for their eternal blessing despite the dangers?

The maps show the growth of evangelical (especially Pentecostal) Christianity in Latin America. Breakthroughs began in Argentina and Brazil. By 2000, 10% of the continent's population was evangelical—by 2050 this will have risen to over 19%.

Fig 6.23 *Evangelicals in Latin America, 1900–2050*

Latin America's spiritual need was ignored at the 1910 Edinburgh Missionary Conference. However, N American Christians took up the challenge and by 2000, through their input, the continent's share of the global population of Evangelicals had risen from less than 1% to 14%.

Fig 6.24 also includes N America. There are a number of important observations:

North: There was a decline in the number of Evangelicals between 1900 and 1960, though not as steep as in Europe. Then came the reawakening through the Jesus Movement, Billy Graham and a general evangelical resurgence.

The Caribbean: slow, steady growth, largely among Pentecostal Evangelicals, though the legacy of African-Caribbean slavery still affects family life

South and Central: Spanish- and Portuguese-speaking in the main. This is where significant growth has occurred, mainly since 1960—to which revival in Argentina and significant breakthroughs in Bolivia, Peru and C America have added.

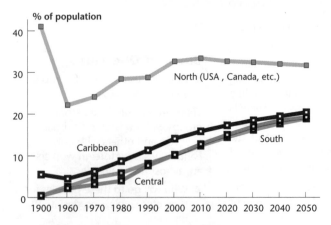

Fig 6.24 *Evangelical growth in the Americas, 1900–2050*

Food for Thought

There are several aspects of Latin Evangelicalism that are praiseworthy:

▲ *willingness* to suffer discrimination and persecution for the name of Jesus—formerly from a dominant Catholic Church, latterly in wars in Colombia and El Salvador; *enthusiasm* in worship, prayer and evangelism; *cultural relevance* with effective, caring social networks to which people gladly belong.

However, there are other areas of challenge:

▲ *commitment* in service and in support of those who go as missionaries; *biblical literacy*—many pastors have not even read through the whole Bible, and few have had adequate theological training or effective mentoring; *being agents of social and political change*—without being compromised in the process. Few Evangelicals who go into politics retain their spiritual integrity.

▲ How will the Latin American Church address these issues?

Brazil: an emerging evangelical superpower

With its abundance of land, water and strategic minerals and its recent industrial growth, *Brazil* is an economic powerhouse. It is the most populous Catholic country in the world, and may also have its third-biggest evangelical population (see below). The large Charismatic/Pentecostal movement also has a massive following in the Catholic Church. All this makes Brazil important for the future of Christianity. It may be a trendsetter for AfAsLA countries.

Fig 6.25 shows the distribution of Evangelicals in each of the country's states. The lowest growth has been in the poorer, drier northeast. The areas of the most growth have been in the wealthier southeast—especially in the triangle formed by the cities of Rio de Janeiro, São Paulo and Belo Horizonte in Minas Gerais.

It is also interesting to note that the sparsely populated western Amazon states have high percentages of Evangelicals. However, what are not shown here are the many long-neglected, small Amazonian tribes that remain unevangelized, especially in the western border areas where much is still to be done if strong indigenous church networks are to emerge. It has been estimated that there are around 150 unevangelized tribal peoples in the Amazon River basin.

The great challenge for Brazil's Evangelicals is to do more than provide a secure social network for their own people and actually become a catalyst for change in a society long blighted by inequality, immorality and corruption.

Fig 6.26 demonstrates the uncertainty of statistics in a large country such as Brazil! Both Brazilian researchers and the 1991 census seemed to indicate that many (especially Pentecostal) denominations were exaggerating their membership figures, so we reflected this in the *Operation World* of 2001 (the blue line). Later, the 2001 census showed that those figures were not so exaggerated after all (note the column). The statistics used in *Operation World* 2010 are represented by the purple line, which gives a count for Evangelicals almost double the earlier estimate. This means that the number of Evangelicals in Brazil could be nearly 20 million higher than the figure being used in this book![20]

The growth of the Brazilian missions movement in the 1980s was spectacular. Though recently the growth has slowed, the movement has become more stable and mature. Many godly missionaries with evangelistic and church-planting gifts have gone out all over the world—in 2000, this reached 4,754 missionaries in 132 agencies in 100 countries. Yet this growth has slowed even as the national economy has expanded. For every church that sends a missionary, there are probably 99 that do not—and even from those churches that do send missionaries, the support is often spasmodic. The challenge is for the Brazilian Church to be mobilized effectively for world evangelization.

Fig 6.25 *Regional distribution of evangelicals in Brazil in 2001*

Evangelical %
- 0–0.2
- 0.2–0.5
- 0.5–1
- 1–2
- 2–5
- 5–10
- 10–20
- 20–50
- 50+

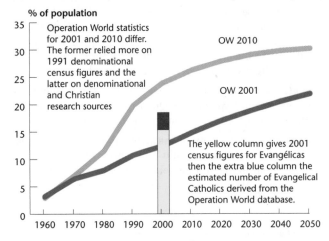

% of population

Operation World statistics for 2001 and 2010 differ. The former relied more on 1991 denominational census figures and the latter on denominational and Christian research sources

OW 2010

OW 2001

The yellow column gives 2001 census figures for Evangélicas then the extra blue column the estimated number of Evangelical Catholics derived from the Operation World database.

Fig 6.26 *Evangelical growth in Brazil, 1960–2050*

Burning Questions for Today

We can praise God for the spectacular growth in recent decades of the evangelical witness in Brazil.

▲ Is that growth going to founder on the lack of godliness and commitment among Christian leaders and the materialism often evident in evangelical congregations?

▲ Will the enthusiasm, vision and prayerfulness of the past be maintained, to make Brazil a blessing to the world?

There are only five countries/territories in N America—all of them Christian in name. What contrasts in size and in spiritual experience (see map below)! Evangelicalism originated in the Anglophone world, but it has gone global from the USA. The influence of US Evangelicalism is enormous, affecting almost every aspect of Christian life worldwide—worship styles, evangelistic methods, theological emphases, models of church life and spirituality.

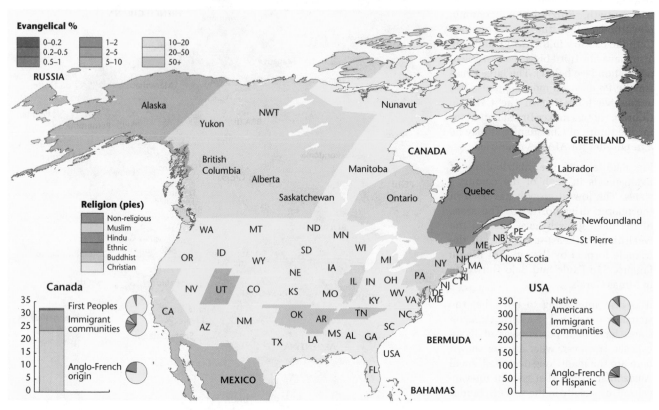

Fig 6.26 *Distribution of Evangelicals in N America in 2010*

The USA: There are significant variations in the percentages of Evangelicals between the Bible belt in the southern states, for example—see the green—and more liberal New England, the Mormon home state of Utah and Alaska with its mix of indigenous and immigrant peoples. The graph below shows the dip for Evangelicals in the early 20th Century, but also the effects of the Awakening of the 1960s onwards.

Canada: Note the stark contrast between the Anglophone provinces[21] and Francophone Quebec, which remains largely Catholic with only a small evangelical population.

Greenland: The majority of the population of this overseas territory of Denmark are Inuit and mostly nominal Lutherans. Spiritual life is at a low ebb, similar to Denmark, with few Evangelicals.

St Pierre and Miquelon: There is almost no evangelical witness in this French overseas territory.

Bermuda: The culture, and spirituality, is more Caribbean than British in this wealthy overseas territory of the UK.

Fig 6.27 looks at Evangelicals as a percentage of the general population and shows the fluctuations in each of the five countries of N America between 1900 and 2050.

What is startling is the wide differences, both between the five countries and over time in the US and Canada.

Figs 6.26 and 6.27 do not show the smaller percentages of Evangelicals among Native Americans (First Peoples)—a reflection of their merely nominal acceptance of the Christian religion of their oppressors.

The small pie charts in Fig 6.26 illustrate the (still) very high numbers of immigrants[22] to N America and hint at the strategic implications of bringing the Gospel to them, and then, in turn, to their lands of origin. It is interesting to note the high proportion of Christians among them.[23]

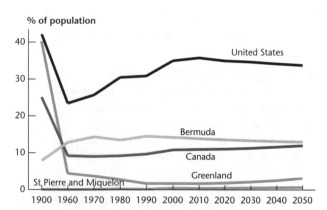

Fig 6.27 *Evangelical growth and decline in N America, 1900–2050*

Burning Question for Today

For over a century, the USA has been the source of much of the culture, theology, funding and ideas of the evangelical movement across the world. This is changing as a result of the growth of Evangelicals in AfAsLA.

▲ Are evangelical leaders in the USA prepared to accept and adapt to a multipolar global leadership with other theological emphases, strategies and practices?

Comparing Evangelicals in the USA and China

It is helpful to compare the two likely superpowers of the mid 21st Century. Not only will their economies, their military power and their influence be well matched by then, but so too will their spiritual impact be. China's evangelical population will far exceed that of the US, though the percentages may be lower.[24] Fig 6.28 shows the situation in 2008. China's Bible belt in the central eastern provinces is clearly seen. There are larger-than-average evangelical populations in the northeast[25] and in Yunnan in the southwest.[26] Henan is the hub of many of the major unregistered church works (see Fig 6.29). The percentage of each county's population that is evangelical is shown. A third of the population in the south are Evangelicals.

Burning Question for Today

China is becoming an evangelical giant.

▲ Will Chinese missionaries play a key role as part of the global mission force of the Church in completing the task of Jesus' Great Commission?

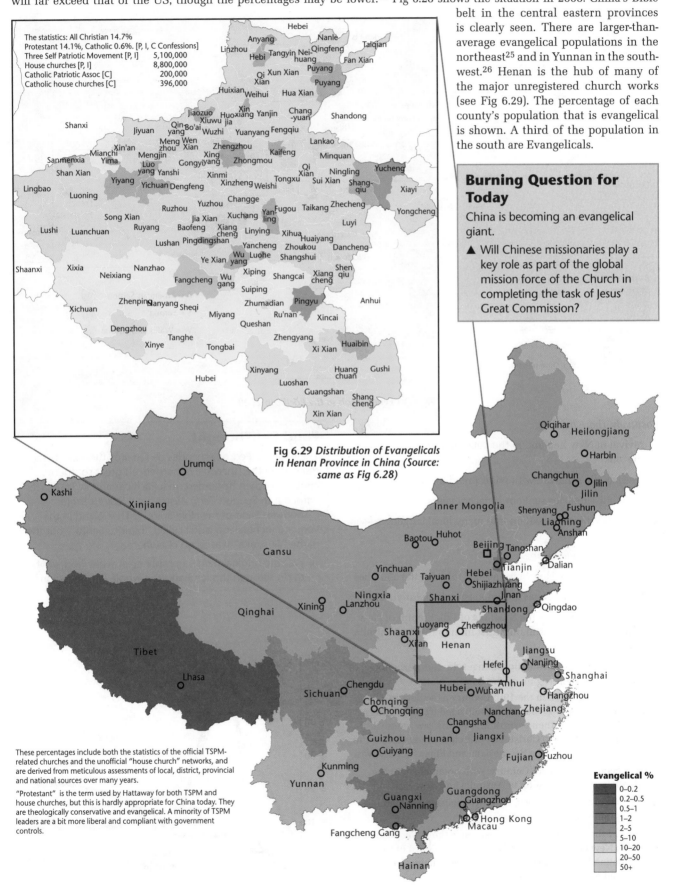

The statistics: All Christian 14.7%
Protestant 14.1%, Catholic 0.6%. [P, I, C Confessions]
Three Self Patriotic Movement [P, I]   5,100,000
House churches [P, I]   8,800,000
Catholic Patriotic Assoc [C]   200,000
Catholic house churches [C]   396,000

Fig 6.29 *Distribution of Evangelicals in Henan Province in China (Source: same as Fig 6.28)*

These percentages include both the statistics of the official TSPM-related churches and the unofficial "house church" networks, and are derived from meticulous assessments of local, district, provincial and national sources over many years.

"Protestant" is the term used by Hattaway for both TSPM and house churches, but this is hardly appropriate for China today. They are theologically conservative and evangelical. A minority of TSPM leaders are a bit more liberal and compliant with government controls.

Evangelical %
- 0–0.2
- 0.2–0.5
- 0.5–1
- 1–2
- 2–5
- 5–10
- 10–20
- 20–50
- 50+

Fig 6.28 *Evangelicals in China in 2008 (Source: Paul Hattaway, Used with permission[27])*

The first great breakthrough of the modern missionary era was in the Pacific. After 1800, missionaries came to an ocean world where Christians were few in number. By its end almost the entire region had become Christian. It was a dramatic story of people turning from greed to godliness, with convicts and cannibals becoming committed Christians and enthusiastic missionaries. The 20th Century was one of decline, nominalism and secularization.

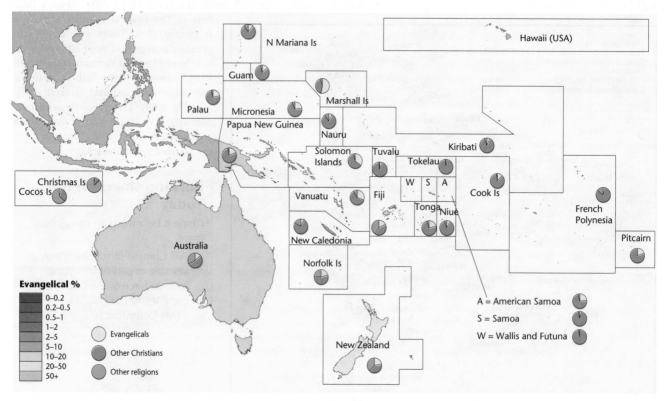

Fig 6.30 *Evangelicals in the Pacific in 2000*

Positively, there has been:

1. revival in New Zealand in the 1960s and the Solomons in the '80s

2. charismatic renewal, with widespread impact

3. many missionaries sent out in recent years

4. extensive Bible translation into many local languages—see page 157.

Challenges that remain, are:

1. a new work of the Holy Spirit needed to revive the churches

2. Mormonism, which has grown massively in Polynesia

3. the less evangelized—the S Asians of Fiji, French of New Caledonia, Muslim and Buddhist immigrants to Australia and New Zealand.

Fig 6.31 shows the dramatic changes in the percentage of Evangelicals in each region of the Pacific. Note:

▲ the amazing growth in the 19th Century as settlers in Australia and New Zealand were impacted by awakenings and Polynesia and then parts of Micronesia saw massive people movements to Christ. The principal evangelists of the Pacific were, in fact, the Polynesians and Fijians themselves.

▲ the declines in the 20th Century, with nominalism in the Islands and secularization in Australia and New Zealand

▲ the stabilization after 1960, with Evangelicals maintaining their numbers but not growing much

▲ the way the post-war effort to evangelize the many peoples of Papua New Guinea began to bear fruit, with most of the population becoming Christians—at least in name. They included many Evangelicals.

Food for Thought

The explorer Pedro Fernandes de Queirós thought he had discovered the (then still hypothetical) great southern continent when he landed on a Pacific island in 1606. He named it in Spanish *Terra Australis del Espiritu Santo* ("Southern Land of the Holy Spirit"). That island in the Vanuatu archipelago is still called "Espiritu Santo", but the name "Australia" was to go elsewhere.

▲ Was the original name a prophecy of what God wants to do through this land and the whole Pacific region?

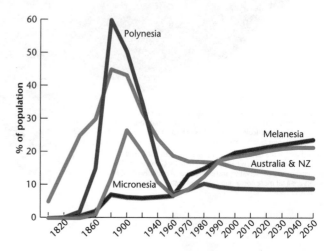

Fig 6.31 *Evangelical growth and decline in the Pacific, 1800–2050*

Bible Translation in Papua New Guinea

Here is a good opportunity to highlight the ministry of Bible translation. In 2010, the Pacific region had a population of 35 million people, but speaking 1,362 languages. Papua New Guinea (PNG) has a population of 5.9 million, but 815 languages. The availability of the Bible in these languages is mapped in Fig 6.32. How can a people become mature disciples of Jesus without the Bible in their own language? It is a major task to translate the Bible into an unwritten language.

PNG is the meeting point for eight tectonic plates, which created its high, steep mountains. It is subject to frequent earthquakes and has 60 volcanoes, 19 of which have erupted in the last century. High rainfall produces thick tropical forests and great rivers, and nurtures diseases. Life is a battle for survival, with limited food resources. Travel between valleys and along rivers is usually difficult, if not impossible. It is often practicable today only in small aircraft, landing on tiny airstrips. Flying is dangerous; engine failure is usually fatal, as there are few open areas. Ethnic diversity has been the result as each new immigration of settlers over the millennia has pushed their predecessors further up the river valleys and into the mountainous highlands. The Stone-Age tribes inland remained undiscovered and unknown until the Japanese invasion in 1942 and the years of war that followed exposed them to the modern world. Cannibalism was practised in some areas until the 1950s.

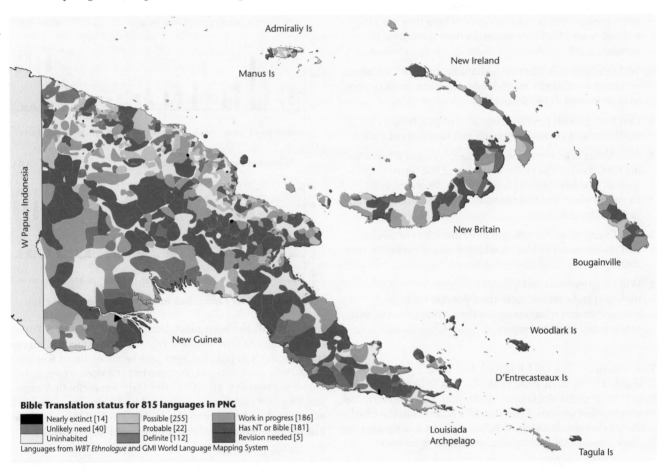

Bible Translation status for 815 languages in PNG

- Nearly extinct [14]
- Unlikely need [40]
- Uninhabited
- Possible [255]
- Probable [22]
- Definite [112]
- Work in progress [186]
- Has NT or Bible [181]
- Revision needed [5]

Languages from *WBT Ethnologue* and GMI World Language Mapping System

Fig 6.32 *The state of Bible translation in PNG in 2010*

Challenges of Bible translation in PNG:

1. The exploration and survey of the many people groups and their languages—done mainly by missionaries—have been a major achievement.

2. Nearly all peoples have been Christianized—Bible translation then becomes vital. Several missions have undertaken this work. The largest, Wycliffe Bible Translators, has active projects in most of the 186 current translation programmes.[28]

3. Providing a people with a New Testament can take 12 years or more. It involves learning the language and analysing it, designing an alphabet, training local people for translation work (and the hard slog of finding appropriate ways to express concepts and objects unknown locally), running literacy programmes etc.

4. The time, effort and materials needed are costly. Careful research reveals the viability or otherwise of a translation project. Out of this comes the information used in Fig 6.32.

5. The ministry of missionary pilots and their support teams is no luxury, for without them the work could never be undertaken.[29]

Food for Thought

The cost of producing a NT for a preliterate people is huge.

▲ Is it worth the effort?

Some people reckon that, of the world's 6,500 languages, 3,000 could be lost in the 21st Century. The best way to preserve a culture is when people become Christians and can take pride in possessing and using a Bible in their own language. So, Bible translation enables not only the preaching of the Gospel but also the preservation of languages and cultures.

Various aspects of evangelical growth worldwide are drawn together here. The bar charts on these two pages show the likely conversion rates[30] for each continent and UN region, with a regional and then a global assessment of the possible trends underneath. The implications for ministry are explored alongside the graphs. But why should we accept these projections as a given? God can step in, as in the past, to change the situation in revival in answer to prayer!

Africa. Recent spectacular growth among Evangelicals in *E, C* and *W Africa* will slow as the proportion of those who are neither Muslims nor Christians diminishes. *The North* is likely to see the largest increase in numbers of Evangelicals, but from a small base in an overwhelmingly Muslim area. Most of these will be Imazighen (Berber). *The South* is likely to see decline rather than growth.

Challenges for ministry:

1. Evangelicals form an important caring network in often corrupt and broken societies, where they act as a social "glue". Will they maintain their integrity and commitment?

2. Will evangelical leadership be humble and godly or carnal and power-seeking? Church leaders in some countries are as little trusted as politicians are.

3. Can Evangelicals provide a ministry of prophetic challenge and address the social and moral ills of society?

4. Syncretism is an ever-present danger, whether it involves old traditions or the modern version of the "prosperity gospel" that has taken Africa by storm. How can Evangelicals affirm their African identity without bowing to syncretic practices?

5. Can Evangelicals become effective disciplers of adults and children—something in which they are currently very deficient?

6. Will congregations and individual Christians in Africa maintain and even increase their passion for local evangelism and missions across the continent—especially to the many Muslim peoples of Africa?

The Americas. *The USA* has long had a high percentage of Evangelicals, so their growth in the '60s is likely to be followed by gradual decline as disillusion with modern US Evangelicalism spreads. *Latin America* (C and S in the chart), is likely to see continued growth, but will it be at a slower rate because subsequent generations lose the early fervour?

Challenges for ministry:

1. Disillusion with evangelical and denominational cultures in NA is debasing even the term "evangelical", with its cultural and theological baggage. What changes could come as a result, and how biblical will they be? Will NA Evangelicals lose their cutting edge?

2. How will LA Evangelicals wield their new-found strength and influence? Will they have the theological and spiritual depth to be prophetic in speaking out on social inequality, corruption and drug trafficking or will they succumb to the temptations of wealth and power?

3. Since 1980, the vision for missions in LA has grown, with many missionaries being sent out. Will these good beginnings peter out, or will churches and individuals maintain their passion for world evangelization?

4. Historic injustices against the original peoples of the Americas must be faced—by Catholics, but by Evangelicals too. Will these be addressed?

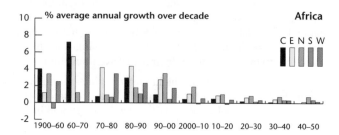

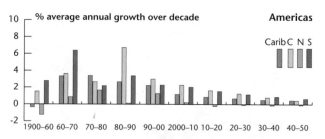

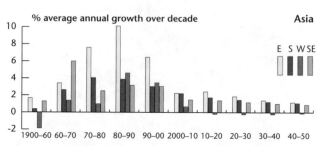

Fig 6.33 *AGR for Evangelicals in Africa, the Americas and Asia*

Asia. Growth has been most dramatic in *E Asia*. In *S Korea*, that growth has now stopped. Will it do the same in China as that country's population ages and becomes more wealthy? In *SE Asia*, growth could continue but at a slower rate. *S Asia* could see massive growth if the Dalit emancipation movement against casteism is welcomed by Christians. The small evangelical community in the *Middle East* (W Asia) is growing, but persecution and emigration could lead to decline.

Challenges for ministry:

1. The global impact of China's evangelical population is only beginning to be perceived. How can this develop for the best for God's Kingdom, and how willing are other Evangelicals to embrace Chinese input?

2. Persecution is a major factor for many Asian Christians. Will it blunt or sharpen the vision for evangelism?

3. Many Asian cultures value harmony in society. How will this affect Asian evangelical theology as it addresses the lostness of the lost or challenges syncretic thinking and practices?

4. How Evangelicals handle the Dalit-Bahujan protests in India may determine the future of Christianity in that land—an immense harvest or a debacle.

5. Asian missions have become influential worldwide. Can they learn from the mistakes of past mission movements?

Europe. Growth through conversion in *S Europe* is from a very small base and has only followed the decline of the once dominant Catholic Church. In *E Europe*, growth through conversion has followed the collapse of Communism. In the *West and North*, Evangelicals are stagnant in the lands once most impacted by the Reformation. Non-Evangelicals have experienced massive decline.

Challenges for ministry:

1. Ministry has been crippled by negativism after years of little fruit and a developing "minority complex". Where are the leaders of vision and faith?

2. Aggressive secularists are marginalizing and even persecuting Evangelicals in particular. There is need for a holy relevance and boldness in witness to them.

3. Declining indigenous populations are pulling in immigrants who need to be evangelized—especially Muslims. Children need to be reached—few nowadays are exposed to anything Christian.

4. Evangelical ranks are being swollen by immigrants. All Evangelicals need to be able to work together for the re-evangelization of Europe.

5. Vision for missions has declined among Evangelicals in the face of a prevailing pessimism and creeping universalism. How can it be revived?

The Pacific. The dramatic declines in *Australia, New Zealand* and *Polynesia* halted temporarily in local revivals in the 1960s and '70s, but are likely to resume. The people movements in *PNG* led to growth through conversion that peaked in the late 20th Century. The future is likely to see relatively static evangelical communities with few conversions.

Challenges for ministry:

1. How can stagnation be ended and ground lost in the 20th Century be regained by Evangelicals in the 21st?

2. An evangelical nominalism is evident across the Pacific. How can these churches be brought back to their first love and the passion for world evangelization that their forebears had?

World. The peak of conversions during the Sixth Awakening from the 1960s to 2000 can be seen here, most strongly in *AfAsLA* countries. Future growth through conversion will inevitably decline with the reduced birth rate worldwide— the majority of conversions to Christ occur among the under-18-year-olds. May we trust for a further, global great awakening that would significantly change this picture?

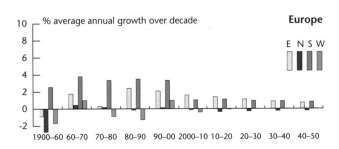

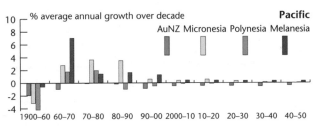

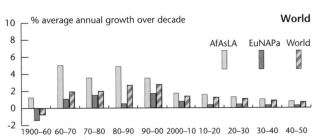

Fig 6.34 *AGR for Evangelicals in Europe, the Pacific and globally*

Challenges for ministry:

1. Global conferences, usually inspired and funded from the USA, have unified and motivated the worldwide evangelical movement for co-operative efforts in world evangelization. This form of dependence is passing. New ways of working together are needed.

2. How can the evangelical world maintain and develop spiritual fellowship and unity amidst its diversity?

3. The drive to make disciples of all nations is seen by many as a fad of the 1990s rather than essential obedience to the Great Commission. How will Evangelicals maintain that primary focus?

4. The globalization of the world's peoples through large-scale population movements and the widespread use of electronic media (satellite technology, mobile phones etc) give us numerous ways to share our faith with the least reached. There has to be global evangelical partnership if the nations are to be discipled as soon as possible.

Burning Questions for Today

This concludes our survey of Christianity and its current renewal, and the major responsibility that Evangelicals bear to take the biblical Gospel to every part of the world and make disciples of all nations. It has been a tale of exciting advances, considerable encouragement and hope for the future.

▲ *In their present state, are Evangelicals worldwide fit for the task?* Or are we seeing a dying of the old order and should we await something new that God must do to realize His passion to evangelize the world and prepare a people of His own as a Bride for His Son?

We cannot rest on past glories, but need to ask God afresh that His Holy Spirit would enflame us once more. Should we fail, God will need to turn to a new generation of Christians that is more obedient and has a new range of skills and gifts. There are too many once dynamic movements that have turned into machines—or monuments full of dead bones. Evangelicals!

▲ What of your future?

Let us turn now to the unevangelized world!

1. The sixth religious stream, the non-religious, is not shown. The non-religious are in significant decline. The large numbers of people who became secular or non-religious in the 20th and 21st Centuries are being reduced by much lower birth rates (as a result of marital instability and a lack of desire to have children) and earlier death rates (as a result of, for example, alcoholism and drug/tobacco abuse in Russia). The religious tend to live longer and have more children.

2. The Orthodox are declining primarily as a result of population decline in the Slavic world, and especially Russia, the largest Orthodox nation. For Catholics, the causes are primarily losses to secularism in Europe and to Evangelicalism in Latin America, as well as a slowing of population growth (despite the papacy's opposition to birth control). The actual losses are higher than official figures suggest since these are based on infant baptism statistics.

3. The 1981 *World Christian Encyclopedia* adopted the 1978 *Operation World* methodology, but in the 2001 edition the definitions were changed, with "Evangelicals" being defined by direct descent from the Reformation and "evangelicals" being classified according to their relationship to the Great Commission and not to theology. The first gives a figure lower than those derived for *Operation World* 2001, and the second gives a much higher figure.

4. We count *affiliates* as the only fair way to make comparisons between numbers of Evangelicals and the figures for other religions and Christian denominations which make no distinction between children and adults or active and inactive adherents.

5. Our databases have been made available for others to study and assess our sources, statistics and estimates, including our evangelical percentages. Occasionally this has led to corrections by people who are knowledgeable about local situations. So, we believe there is a good degree of integrity in these statistics.

6. The term "evangelical" originated in Germany at the time of the Reformation. The German *evangelisch* is equivalent to the more negative English "Protestant". Large-scale departure of Reformed and Lutheran Churches from biblical theology to liberalism emptied the word of its meaning, and modern Germans use *evangelicale*. The term "Evangelical" came into vogue as a label for revived Christians at the time of the First Evangelical Awakening in the 18th Century. It therefore had less relevance to countries where biblical Christianity blossomed in the 20th Century, often in indigenous movements in other parts of the world, and where the term would not be used or even understood.

7. The prosperity gospel, with its strong emphasis on obedience ensuring personal wealth, healing and escape from suffering, gained prominence in the teachings of some US Pentecostal preachers and has spread worldwide. It has had a big impact in countries such as Brazil and Nigeria. Following these teachings leads to a self-centred faith and even an animistic syncretism in which every negative in life has to have some external cause.

8. The Operation World database contains data for denominations back to 1960 only, so the data used in this chapter refer to 1960 rather than to 1950.

9. The seemingly erratic lines, with peaks and troughs, are the result of totalling many, many denominational statistics which all vary in accuracy and recency. The important thing is the underlying trends they reveal.

10. The EuNAPa lines indicate almost zero growth, but in a declining population these figures are better than they appear. However, this relative growth will not necessarily be through conversion. Much of it will be because evangelical Christians tend to have more children and more stable families.

11. Many believers expect a final great global awakening before the return of the Lord Jesus Christ. Were such an awakening to occur, all my predictions would become invalid, as they are based on current trends. I would be delighted to be proved wrong in this way!

12. The legacy of the colonial carve-up of Africa lies behind many of the worst post-independence conflicts on that continent—Nigeria (both the Biafra War and the still severe tensions between the Muslim north and the Christian south), Sudan (the long war between the Arab north and African South), Congo-DR (an ungovernable medley of peoples), Côte d'Ivoire (civil war) etc. The same could be said of wars in Iraq, Afghanistan and Indochina.

13. Recent studies of the human genome postulate that all humankind could be traced back to a single man and a single woman living in Africa. But they were not necessarily the biblical Adam and Eve—see http://en.wikipedia.org/wiki/The_Seven_Daughters_of_Eve

14. In some cases there is no majority religion, in which event the language area is coloured according to the strength of the largest religion.

15. The secular media generally ignore or misreport Muslim violence against Christians, which is often, in reality, a mix of "religicide" and ethnocide. On the rare occasions when Christians resort to violence against Muslims, it is often the result of Muslim provocation, This is especially true in Sudan, central and northern Nigeria, N Africa and Somalia in recent years. When violence is reported, it is often spoken of as intercommunal or sectarian as if both sides were equally to blame. This is rarely the case.

16. Syncretism is a problem for both Muslims and Christians. Generations of Muslims have observed both the requirements of Islam and pre-Islamic ethnic religious practices—this is often called "folk Islam". The reforming zeal of the Islamists, backed by Saudi money, has helped to enforce a more uniformly Islamic, Arab enculturation and a rejection of some syncretic practices. Among Christians, it was the increasing availability of the whole Bible in their principal languages that addressed the errors of syncretism. And, whereas first-generation believers did not address cultural issues, and second-generation ones reacted against Western Christianity, third-generation (often charismatic/evangelical) ones began to confront syncretism while also embracing their own culture.

17. *Indonesia: Unreached People Groups of Indonesia* is a superb survey of the spiritually needy peoples of that country published in 2003 by the Indonesian National Research Network, the PJRN. The results were incorporated into the Joshua Project List.

18. Harmony and meekness are highly esteemed in Javanese culture, which is a complete contrast to Arabic Islam with its militancy and, often, vengefulness. This makes the Javanese particularly sensitive to the claims of the Lord Jesus Christ. The Chinese are Indonesia's traders and businesspeople and in times of economic hardship often bear the brunt of the anger of Muslims. This has been exacerbated by the fact that the majority of Chinese have also become Christian—many strongly evangelical, too.

19. The tragic story of this seizure is little known in the outside world, but the suppression of local cultures and of political expression and the environmental damage caused by the plundering of W Papua's natural resources, as well as the strong efforts to Islamize the area both by offering enticements to the indigenous peoples and by bringing in Muslim immigrants, is a sad story. The extensive missionary endeavour to uplift people through education, Bible translation and improvements in health and literacy has been largely closed down.

20. The graphs in the previous chapter and on page 144 show a dip in the growth curve for renewal and Evangelicals. These statistics would help to rectify this. The ranking of Brazil in 2000 and 2050 could be higher than shown in the table on page 145. We have maintained the consistency of the data used here by retaining the statistics for 2001 in our database. We realize that the startling growth rates shown for AfAsLA are based on a cautious use of data!

21. Nunavut is Canada's newest and largest province, formed in 1999. Most of its 33,000 inhabitants are Inuit (Eskimo)—many being evangelical Anglicans, which explains the high percentage of Evangelicals.

22. Many of these immigrant communities, though here numbered separately, have largely integrated with the Anglophone population. Others have retained their social structures and languages longer.

23. Yunnan has many ethnic minorities that have long been responsive to the Gospel. Some of these groups, such as the Lisu, are today largely Christian.

24. An example is that of the Arabic-speaking communities in the USA. Over 62% are Christian, most being Catholics or Orthodox from Egypt, Lebanon, Palestine etc; Muslims make up 32%.

25. The combined populations of the official, TSPM-related and the unregistered house churches are probably 85–90% evangelical in theology. Liberalism is noticeable only in some official seminaries and in the most senior leadership. So, the Protestant-TSPM figures used in these maps approximate closely to the evangelical population.

26. What was Manchuria is now divided into three northeastern provinces. There has been a history of evangelical revivals in the area, and many committed Christian believers.

27. Paul Hattaway [www.asiaharvest.org] has spent many years gathering information on every province and district of China. His findings are probably the most meticulously researched and consistent yet published. These maps incorporate his most recent results. See also Paul Hattaway, *Henan: the Galilee of China* (Piquant Editions, 2009, www.piquanteditions.com).

28. Wycliffe Bible Translators was founded in Mexico by William Townsend in 1942 and now has Bible translation projects in 50 countries, with over 7,000 translators and support workers. One of its biggest branches is in PNG. Other agencies, too, are involved in Bible translation in PNG—notably, New Tribes Mission and Lutheran Bible Translators.

29. Mission Aviation Fellowship is the primary agency, with 54 workers and 20 aircraft in 2000; but JAARS (linked to WBT) and NTM also have their own staff and planes.

30. "Conversion rate" is the term given to the difference between the growth rate for Evangelicals and the growth rate for the general population. Conversion is one aspect of it—but it also includes birth rate, immigraton rate and even life expectancy.

The Unevangelized

Jesus commanded us to "preach the gospel to every creature" (Mark 16:15, NKJV). Over a quarter of the world's population may still be beyond the present preaching of the Gospel. It is important for us to know who the unevangelized are and where they live, so that then we can seek to ensure that everyone has an opportunity to have a personal relationship with God through Christ. This is the main thrust of this chapter. We begin by looking at countries, then at people groups by language.

Evangelized: the state of having had the Gospel presented and explained in such a way that the hearer becomes aware of the claims of Christ and the need to obey and follow Him.

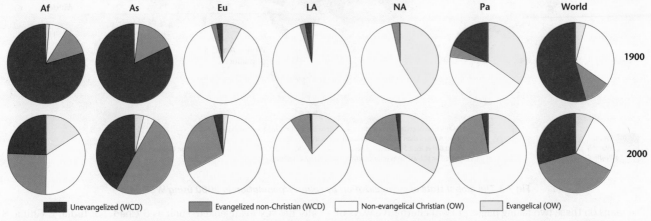

Fig 7.1 *Continents and evangelization in 1900 and 2000, based on WCD and OW data*

Legend: Unevangelized (WCD) · Evangelized non-Christian (WCD) · Non-evangelical Christian (OW) · Evangelical (OW)

Measuring evangelization

We need to define what it means to be evangelized. First, it is important to acknowledge that a person can be evangelized and yet not be a believer. Of course, the process of evangelizing should continue until that person becomes a disciple. The evangelist must so present the claims of Christ that their hearers understand enough of the Gospel to make a meaningful response—whether acceptance or rejection. However, it is not possible to survey whole populations to determine how many individuals have been evangelized, even if we could agree on the criteria.

David Barrett developed a methodology to arrive at approximate figures for the *World Christian Encyclopedia* in 1981,[1] but I have drawn on his results only sparingly in this book. They are useful for comparing the relative exposure of different segments of the population to the Gospel, but less helpful for deriving actual numbers of evangelized.

The pie charts in Fig 7.1 represent the state of evangelization of each continent in 1900 and 2000, using both WCD and Operation World data.[2] The latter introduces the figures for Evangelicals. They give an indication of what was achieved by evangelization in the 20th Century, showing starkly the decline

in belief in Europe and N America as well as the increase of the evangelized in the other four continents. They also show that the number of the totally unevangelized in Africa and Asia fell dramatically over the course of the century—and that the resulting growth of the Church in AfAsLA has been a largely evangelical phenomenon.

The pies on the very right reveal the progress in evangelization globally in spite of the declining percentage of Christians. The disturbing truth is that there may still be nearly 2 billion individuals (out of the 6 billion in 2000) who have never had a chance to hear the Gospel. The command of Jesus in Mark 16 still needs to be obeyed.

The final pie for 2000 in Fig 7.1 is expanded in Fig 7.2 to show the challenge of measuring the unevangelized. In Barrett's methodology, anyone who is a Christian of any kind is by definition evangelized.[3] His statistics on evangelization are fundamental to the widely used classifications for Worlds A, B and C which are examined on page 162.

From an evangelical perspective, more stringent credal criteria would reduce (but not discount) the representation from other theological traditions. Many nominal Christians, and even Evangelicals, may not be evangelized in the sense I have defined above, as the hatching on this pie acknowledges. In

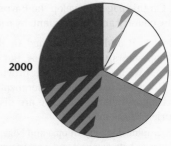

2000

Legend: Nominal Evangelical · Nominal/unevangelized "Christian" · Marginally evangelized Christian

Note: The hatched areas are indicative of impression in statistics and definitions!

Fig 7.2 *The challenge of measuring the unevangelized*

the following pages, I develop a more transparent method to estimate the numbers of the evangelized and unevangelized.

Christian baptism in N India (photo by T Kwant)

Worlds A, B and C

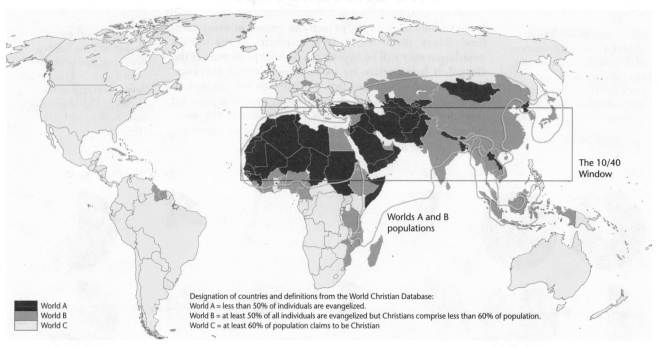

Fig 7.3 *The global state of evangelization by country/population in 2000 using WCE data*

The maps on these two facing pages present alternative ways of looking at the unevangelized world. The final results displayed in the maps are similar, though derived from different sets of data. On this page, I develop the Barrett figures for evangelization by country and, to an extent, by each country's population.

Worlds A, B and C are defined in the legend on the map. The map shows whole countries, but a clearer picture would emerge if we used data for each province or state, or even district. However, nationwide generalizations still yield useful, if surprising, results where there are distinct differences within countries. These may be:

▲ geographical—as in Ethiopia and Nigeria, where there are big contrasts between east and west in one case and south and north in the other[4]

▲ ethnic—as in Suriname and Guyana, which have large populations of Asian immigrants, and Indonesia, with its medley of peoples, Christian, Muslim and Hindu.

The map shows two representations of unevangelized "blocs".

The 10/40 Window (red rectangle) covers an area of the world's eastern hemisphere stretching across Africa and Asia between the latitudes 10°N and 40°N. The term was coined by Luis Bush when he was leader of the AD2000 and Beyond Movement[5] and highlights countries which are characterized by poverty, few Christians and limited access to Christian resources and are therefore least evangelized. It was widely used in publicity after 1990 to redress the relative neglect by churches and agencies to focus prayer and ministry on these parts of the world. Its simplicity was good for publicity purposes but less good for planning strategy. Many areas within the "Window" were actu-

ally heavily evangelized, such as S Chad, NE India, E China, S Korea and the Philippines, while others that lie outside it (such as Mongolia, C Asia, Somalia, the coast of E Africa, the Comoro Islands and Indonesia) were, and still are, among the least evangelized parts of the world.

For these reasons the term has been less used since 2000, but it is still a useful way to give ordinary Christians a simple overview of parts of the world most in need of evangelization.

The Worlds A and B populations line (orange line) links together in a more or less contiguous bloc those populations that could be regarded as belonging to Worlds A and B. This gives a more accurate, if more complex, approximation of the least evangelized parts of the world, which avoids some of the deficiencies of the 10/40 Window. Several features are worth noting:

▲ The line cuts across those countries in Africa that straddle forested areas that are largely Christianized and areas of the Sahel and Sahara that are largely Muslim.

▲ It extends south along Africa's eastern seaboard, where many people are Muslims.

▲ It takes in C Asia.

▲ There are extraordinary concentrations of the evangelized in the eastern Himalayas of India, Myanmar and SE China.

▲ There is a complex mix of evangelized and unevangelized in the islands of Indonesia.

▲ In E Asia, there is a great contrast between the heavily evangelized populations of S Korea (where there are many Christians) and E China (where today people respond to the Gospel with enthusiasm) and Japan, where there has been a great deal of Christian input but little response.

Burning Question for Today

We may have questions about counting the number of the unevangelized, but this is a secondary issue. The broad picture that emerges is of a great and continuing need for massive investment in cross-cultural mission in the 21st Century. All of us who believe in Christ are under obligation (Romans 1:14) to bring the Gospel to the unevangelized.

▲ How can we remain unmoved by the tragedy, both now and for eternity, of those who have no chance to hear about the Saviour?

The 2 billion unevangelized await our response.

Christians, Evangelicals and World Evangelization

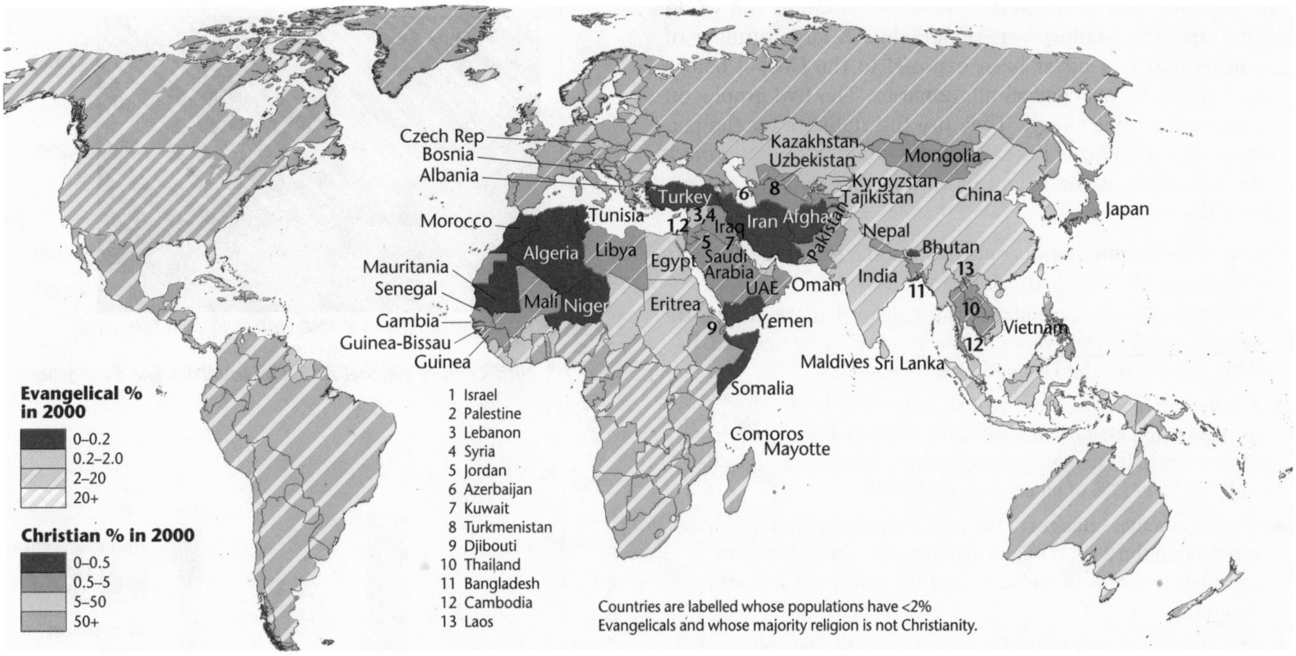

Evangelical % in 2000
- 0–0.2
- 0.2–2.0
- 2–20
- 20+

Christian % in 2000
- 0–0.5
- 0.5–5
- 5–50
- 50+

1 Israel
2 Palestine
3 Lebanon
4 Syria
5 Jordan
6 Azerbaijan
7 Kuwait
8 Turkmenistan
9 Djibouti
10 Thailand
11 Bangladesh
12 Cambodia
13 Laos

Countries are labelled whose populations have <2% Evangelicals and whose majority religion is not Christianity.

Fig 7.4 *World evangelization using statistics for known Christians and Evangelicals*

Another way to assess the numbers of the evangelized and unevangelized is by using our statistics for known Christians and Evangelicals, which are readily available and verifiable. The sizes of both traditional Christian and evangelical Christian populations indicate past or present responses to the Gospel and have been used to indicate the extent of evangelization of a country in the map above.

In the 1980s and '90s, there was much discussion about what constituted "unreached". It was generally decided to adopt a compromise: that any population segment that has both less than 5% Christians and less than 2% Evangelicals would be considered unreached or (the term I prefer) "unevangelized". This was then commonly used as a criterion when listing "unreached peoples"—which dismayed many who were involved with less-evangelized peoples who didn't quite qualify. I have therefore differentiated further by then dividing the two categories of "Christian" and "Evangelical" at both one-10th and 10 times the percentage used as the cut-off value. The two-layered map in Fig 7.4 shows four "densities" of Christians in solid colours and four of Evangelicals in varying thicknesses of yellow hatching.

These categories group countries in a more helpful way and clearly show which are least evangelized. They also differentiate between more traditional Christian populations (in which, often, there are fewer people actively witnessing) and evangelical populations (where

there are more people actively witnessing).

▲ Christians <0.5%, Evangelicals <0.2%: with the Christian presence almost insignificant, the population therefore counts as unevangelized.

▲ Christians 0.5–5%, Evangelicals 0.2–2%: there is significant Christian witness, but most of the population is unevangelized.

▲ Christians 5–50%, Evangelicals 2–20%:[6] a large proportion of the population is likely to be aware of the Gospel.

▲ Christians >50%, Evangelicals >20%: non-Christians are likely to be regularly confronted with the Gospel.

Below are some comments about these different groupings.

The least evangelized countries (with Christians and Evangelicals <0.5% and <0.2% of the population respectively) are coloured dark blue.

The less evangelized countries are a lighter shade. Though there are Christians in the population, they constitute a small

percentage and are often marginalized. Local resources to evangelize the whole population are likely to be inadequate. Note that in the Middle East a high proportion of the Christians are expatriate migrant workers, while in C Asia the Christians are found in minority Slavic communities. The countries in these two categories have been named on the map.

Many countries with a large Christian minority (light blue) also have a higher proportion of Evangelicals, often because the Church there is younger and is generally growing through conversion. Countries such as India, China, Sudan, Chad and Indonesia come into this category.

Countries with a large, traditional Christian population but few Evangelicals are coloured orange with thin yellow hatching. Russia, parts of both Catholic and Protestant Europe and Greenland all come into this category. Their populations may need re-evangelizing. However, these countries are not labelled on this map because its purpose is to highlight the un- and under-evangelized.

Burning Question for Today

Much of the discussion about identifying the unevangelized has revolved round external matters: church affiliation, regular attendance, growth, number of workers, the effort and expense of evangelism. These are comparatively easy to measure, but superficial. The Lord Jesus commanded us to make disciples—and disciples are not made by attendance at church meetings or great celebrations but by intercession and deliberate "alongsiding" new believers so that Christ may be formed in them and their lives transformed. This process is not completed in weeks, but rather takes years of committed mentoring.

▲ Does your church disciple new believers?

20th-Century progress

The improvement in the state of evangelization of the world during the 20th Century was remarkable. A large number of countries that had never been exposed to the Gospel before were entered by evangelical missionaries. The two graphs on this page show this clearly. They use the statistics for the percentage of Evangelicals in each population, to give an approximate indication of the extent of the disciple-making process among the nations.

Fig 7.5 plots the number of countries in each of my four categories relating to Evangelicals. Note the following:

▲ Two-thirds of today's countries were still less than 2% evangelical in 1900 and, from an evangelical perspective, unevangelized. By 2000, this fraction had been reduced to one-third.

▲ Nearly half of all countries (107) came in the "least evangelized" category in 1900, with less than 0.2% Evangelicals. If current trends continue, this number may be reduced to 17 (7% of all countries) by 2050.

▲ The spectacular changes of the 20th Century are unlikely to be repeated in the 21st, though current trends towards a more complete coverage of the nations of the world will probably continue.

▲ The number of countries with more than 20% Evangelicals fell during the first half of the 20th Century, but has since increased.

The changes in the 20th Century become clearer when we add up the populations of these countries in 1900 and 2000 and extrapolate to 2050. In 1900, fewer than 15% of the world's population lived in countries where they were likely to have contact with an evangelical believer (that is, where Evangelicals constituted more than 2% of the population). In other words, more than 85% were *unlikely* to have such contact (many, of course, being in Catholic S Europe or Latin America). By 2000 that second figure had fallen to around 25%, while just under 7% (down from 50% in 1900) lived in countries where Evangelicals constituted less than 0.2% of the population. However, unless there is a supernatural intervention from the Holy Spirit, these figures are unlikely to have changed very much by 2050.

Fig 7.6 presents this data in a different format and compares the years 1900 (the narrow purple column) and 2000 (the broader blue column) to show the dramatic advances made by Evangelicals (yellow hatching).

Only a few more countries were over 20% evangelical in 2000 than in 1900, but their location had changed. In 1900 they were in N America, N Europe, the Caribbean and the Pacific, but by 2000 the USA and the Faroe Islands were the only Western countries in the list, which was now dominated by Africa and C America.

By 2050, most of the bigger countries with large evangelical populations will be in Africa or Latin America, such as Uganda, Burundi, Ethiopia, Zimbabwe, Guatemala and Brazil. What a change over just a century and a half!

The most remarkable movement is in the number of countries that had a minimal evangelical presence and virtually no one evangelized and the number that qualified as evangelized with 2–20% Evangelicals—almost a complete reversal between 1900 and 2000. The success of the missions enterprise in the 20th Century is plain.

It is interesting to compare the population figures and percentages quoted above with those used on page 161. The least evangelized constituted 54% of the world population in 1900 according to the WCD data, compared with 89% here, and

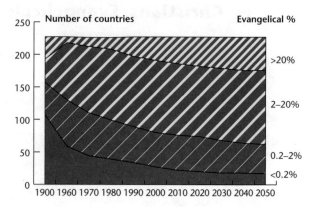

Fig 7.5 *20th-Century evangelization by countries and Evangelicals*

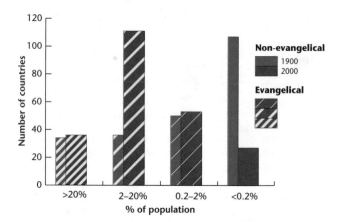

Fig 7.6 *Comparing evangelization in 1900 and 2000 by Evangelicals and non-Evangelicals*

Food for Thought

Despite having a deep spiritual heritage and an effective ministry in winning people to a personal faith in Christ, it is possible, after a generation or two, if parents do not live for Christ and disciple their children and if there is no new reviving work of the Holy Spirit, that nominalism, traditionalism and false teaching take root. Nominalism is not the preserve of more traditional churches—it is increasingly a problem for third- and fourth-generation Evangelicals. In many countries with growing evangelical churches, little is done to disciple children. Unless they, too, come to a living faith, the Church has no future.

▲ Are children a distraction for adults in your church or are they seen as the next generation of Christians?

29% (WCD) or 25% (Operation World/FGC) in 2000. The high figure here for the unevangelized in 1900 is due largely to the limited impact of Evangelicals outside their heartlands in N Europe and N America in traditionally Catholic or Orthodox countries—which is no longer the case. Today, many traditionally Catholic countries have more evangelical congregations, pastors and church attenders than Catholic. Thus, although the methodologies differ, the results are reasonably comparable. The advantage of the OW database is that the figures are derived from statistics that are relatively easy to verify, rather than based on assumptions about the presence of possible outreach mechanisms and ministries.

It is helpful to look at the least evangelized countries from the two perspectives. The tables below show respectively:

▲ the 37 countries where *both* criteria apply (Christians constitute less than 5% of the population and Evangelicals less than 2%)

▲ the 38 countries (omitting several mini-states such as Monaco) where fewer than 2% are evangelical but more than 5% are Christian.

Of the countries listed on the left, 30 are Muslim-majority, six Buddhist-majority and one Jewish-majority. It is the Muslim-majority countries here that present by far the greatest challenge—and yet 18 of them were once largely Christian. Christians included in the percentages for some Arab World countries are primarily non-permanent migrant workers. In C Asia (that is, parts of the former Soviet Union) in 2000, most of the Christians were non-indigenous Russians, Koreans etc, but this is changing as more indigenous people become Christians and as the largely nominal Orthodox Slavs emigrate. By 2010, the number of Christians in Iran and Mongolia had increased through conversion but in Iraq and Palestine there had been a fall in numbers as indigenous Christians flee persecution.

The list on the right is very different. Most of these countries have large Christian populations. There are 18 that are at least nominally Catholic, six Orthodox and one Protestant, but their populations are less than 2% evangelical and in need of new church-planting movements.

Of the seven Muslim-majority countries in this list, three have large numbers of expatriate Christians, though their presence has little impact on the wider population. Bosnia, Lebanon and Guinea all have significant indigenous Christian minorities.

Many Evangelicals regard these countries as unevangelized and feel deep concern for them. The regions that present the biggest challenge are S and C Europe, C Asia and Russia.

There are only three African countries in this list.

<2% evangelical and <5% Christian

Country	Evang %	Christian %	Main religion
Tunisia	0.00	0.21	Muslim
Somalia	0.01	0.05	Muslim
Yemen	0.01	0.08	Muslim
Morocco	0.02	0.11	Muslim
Turkmenistan	0.02	2.41	Muslim
Mauritania	0.03	0.14	Muslim
Maldives	0.03	0.12	Muslim
Afghanistan	0.03	0.04	Muslim
Iran	0.03	0.36	Muslim
Turkey	0.04	0.36	Muslim
Syria	0.06	4.62	Muslim
Tajikistan	0.07	1.23	Muslim
Iraq	0.08	1.47	Muslim
Mayotte	0.11	3.00	Muslim
Senegal	0.11	4.68	Muslim
Comoros	0.15	0.86	Muslim
Algeria	0.16	0.36	Muslim
Israel	0.19	2.23	Jewish
Djibouti	0.19	4.19	Muslim
Palestine	0.20	1.68	Muslim
Azerbaijan	0.21	4.37	Muslim
Niger	0.21	0.48	Muslim
Libya	0.30	2.56	Muslim
Uzbekistan	0.33	1.23	Muslim
Oman	0.35	2.52	Muslim
Jordan	0.39	2.55	Muslim
Gambia	0.40	4.35	Muslim
Japan	0.46	1.63	Buddhist
Bhutan	0.48	0.67	Buddhist
Pakistan	0.51	2.43	Muslim
Bangladesh	0.53	0.72	Muslim
Cambodia	0.79	1.73	Buddhist
Saudi Arabia	0.82	4.83	Muslim
Mali	0.91	2.02	Muslim
Thailand	0.92	1.69	Buddhist
Mongolia	1.14	1.33	Buddhist
Laos	1.55	2.41	Buddhist

<2% evangelical but >5% Christian

Country	Evang %	Christian %	Main religion
San Marino	0.01	90.30	Catholic
Bosnia	0.12	32.62	Muslim
Slovenia	0.16	81.60	Catholic
Poland	0.20	89.19	Catholic
Andorra	0.22	91.19	Catholic
Macedonia	0.23	65.45	Orthodox
Luxembourg	0.34	91.38	Catholic
St Pierre & Miquelon	0.36	96.00	Catholic
Cyprus	0.38	73.49	Orthodox
Austria	0.39	85.52	Catholic
Albania	0.41	40.50	Mixed
Spain	0.45	59.40	Catholic
Kuwait	0.45	9.22	Muslim
Lebanon	0.47	26.57	Muslim
Liechtenstein	0.49	84.85	Catholic
Greece	0.50	92.46	Orthodox
Croatia	0.65	93.95	Catholic
UAE	0.72	9.52	Muslim
Kyrgyzstan	0.81	7.93	Muslim
Russia	0.82	53.00	Orthodox
France	0.90	62.39	Catholic
Wallis & Futuna Is	0.94	97.30	Catholic
Kazakhstan	0.95	24.80	Muslim
Italy	0.97	73.34	Catholic
Czech Republic	1.05	29.11	Non-religious
Guinea	1.14	5.50	Muslim
Monaco	1.15	85.19	Catholic
Belgium	1.16	63.41	Catholic
Guinea-Bissau	1.20	14.67	Ethnic
Gibraltar	1.35	87.40	Catholic
Georgia	1.57	66.31	Orthodox
Slovakia	1.60	80.83	Catholic
Greenland	1.64	95.85	Protestant
Serbia	1.65	66.98	Orthodox
Sri Lanka	1.70	8.12	Buddhist
Malta	1.72	93.91	Catholic
Vietnam	1.75	8.83	Buddhist
Eritrea	1.95	47.30	Mixed

Fig 7.7 The least evangelized countries of the world in 2010

Burning Question for Today

"Prayer for the nations" is the focus of *Operation World*. The dramatic fall in the number of countries still unevangelized *is* an answer to prayer, and yet the task is only partly complete. These lists should inspire us to intercede for these countries until all are evangelized and have significant indigenous communities of committed believers to preach the Gospel to their compatriots. Few of these countries have the resources to achieve this without outside help—but too many congregations in the evangelized world have localized their vision and forgotten countries such as these.

▲ Do you have a vision for the unevangelized?

Romania and Moldova and their Evangelization

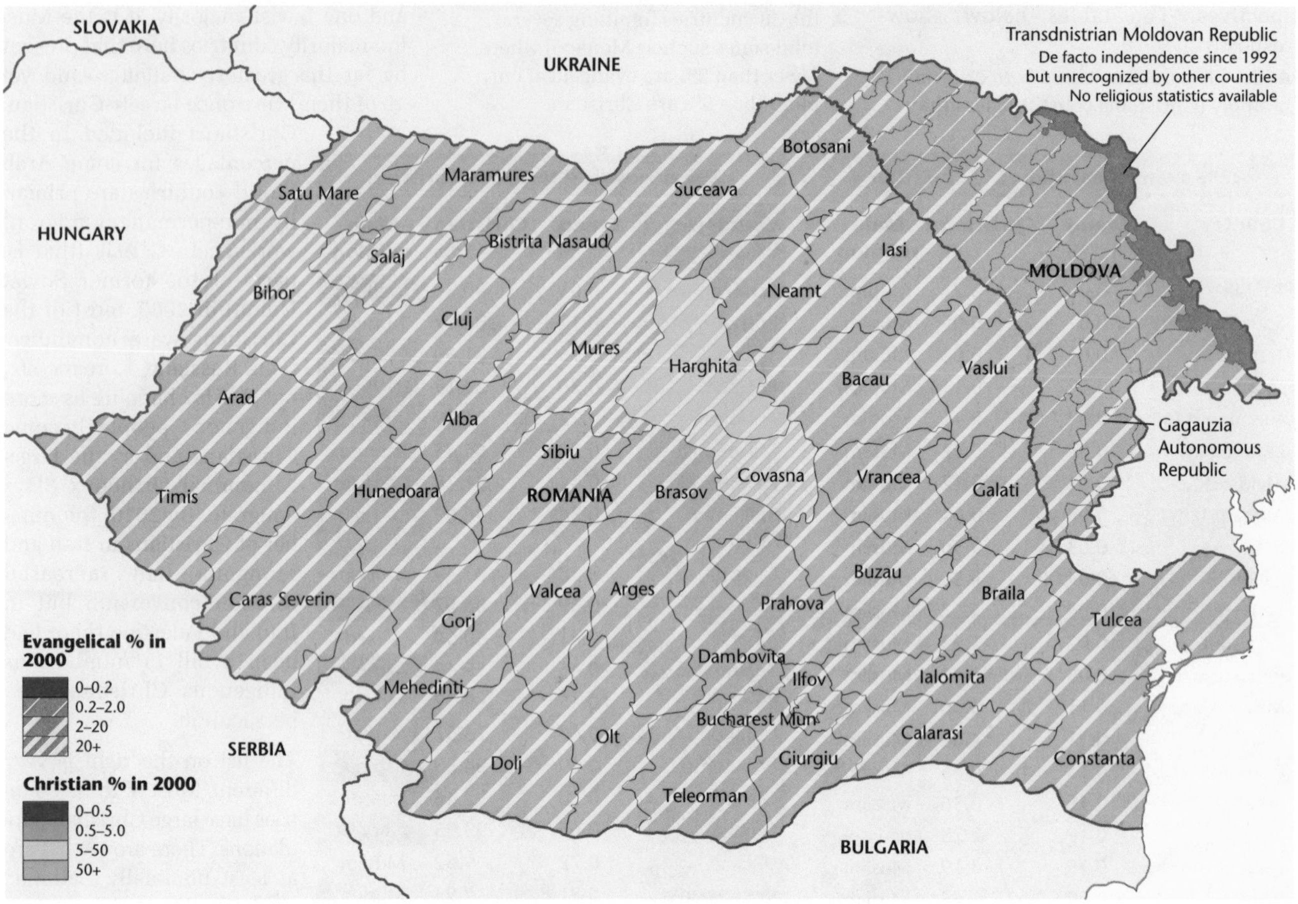

Fig 7.8 *The evangelization of Romania and Moldova*

Two pairs of countries make good case studies in evangelization,[7] based on census results: Romania and Moldova in 2004 and Ethiopia and Eritrea in 2007.[8] The statistics on religion gathered then have been further refined with the aid of the OW database. These four countries well illustrate the impact of politics and the challenges of a partial evangelization of the world's nations. On this page, I look at the results for Romania and Moldova.

Romanians and Moldovans are descended from Roman settlers 1,900 years ago and are largely traditional Orthodox believers.[9] Their recent history has been blighted by the moral and economic impact of Communism, in Moldova's case as part of the Soviet Union. The Orthodox Church gained great political influence after the collapse of Communism in 1990 and has, sadly, proved hostile to any other church. Both countries have been responsive to the Gospel and now have many evangelical churches.[10]

The map shows how Christians constitute a majority in nearly every province of both countries. Nominal adherence to Orthodoxy is common—and yet even among the Orthodox there is a strong evangelical wing, the Lord's Army.

Evangelicals are growing in number, but are more prominent in the centre and northwest. Of the 9,500 villages without any evangelical witness, 7,000 are in southern or eastern provinces.

Among *Romania's* less evangelized are:
▲ the 200,000-strong Turkish Muslim community
▲ the marginalized but numerous Roma population, which numbers between 800,000 and 2 million.

Since 1990, some 10–20% of the Romanian population have sought employment and better economic prospects in other lands—mainly Italy, Spain, Germany and N America.

Moldova is Europe's poorest country and alcoholism, abortion and hopelessness are widespread. About 25% of the population have emigrated and sought employment elsewhere. A large number of women and children have been trafficked as "sex slaves" and forced into prostitution all over Europe and the Middle East.

Transdnistria, the unrecognized breakaway statelet east of the river Dniester, is predominantly Slavic (mainly Russian and Ukrainian) and Evangelicals are few in number.

The Gagauz Turks are predominantly Orthodox Christians but there are some evangelical believers. They have an autonomous republic within Moldova.

Other less-evangelized communities include the 600,000 Roma.

Food for Thought

These countries endured years of Communist tyranny until 1990. All have a strong Orthodox Christian heritage going back a millennium or more. Evangelicals then struggle against official obstructionism, lack of recognition and even severe persecution.

▲ Why has Orthodoxy shown such an ugly face, after itself suffering so much under Communism?

The Horn of Africa and the Unevangelized

The four countries that make up the Horn of Africa are strikingly different, both politically and spiritually. *Somalia* is a failed Muslim state, afflicted by years of inter-clan war and *jihad* and famine in the south. Puntland and Somaliland in the north are quasi-states with separate administrations; the latter's declaration of independence is not internationally recognized. *Djibouti* is a Muslim statelet, a former French colony. *Eritrea* is half Christian and half Muslim and is run by a dictatorship. *Ethiopia* is an authoritarian democracy based on ethnic federalism since 1996. Its eastern lowlands are Muslim, the southwest is largely evangelical Christian and the northwest is Orthodox. Most of the 45 people groups in the SNNP Region are strongly Christian and have missionary-sending churches. It is largely from this area that the main thrust of Ethiopia's missions movement has come.

The evangelized. The highlands of both Eritrea and Ethiopia have been an island of Christianity in a sea of Islam (note the orange area) and have been cut off from much of the Christian world for nearly a millennium. The Amhara and Tigrinya are Oriental Orthodox with close relations with the Coptic Church of Egypt.

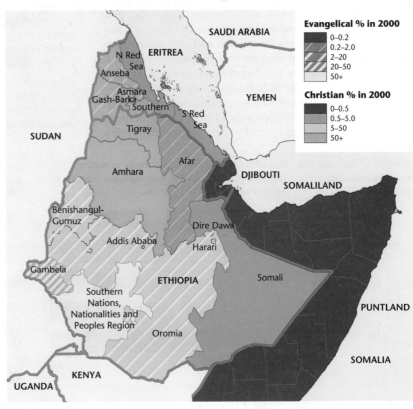

Fig 7.9 The evangelization of the Horn of Africa

Since 1940, the southwestern quadrant has seen dramatic growth of Evangelicals and times of revival[11] among the Omotic and some Oromo and Nilotic peoples. In some districts, more than 70% of the people are evangelical. There is considerable freedom for ministry.

Evangelicals have deeply influenced parts of the Orthodox Church in terms of theology and practice, though evangelical congregations are relatively few among the Amhara and Tigrinya.

In Eritrea, Evangelicals are being severely persecuted, with many imprisoned for their faith.

The unevangelized Muslim east. The swathe of blue on the map above shows how little has been achieved.

Coastal Eritrea and Djibouti are almost entirely Muslim. The Afar, Bilen, Saho in the south, the Tigre in the centre and the Beja and Nara in the north are some of the hardest peoples on earth to reach with the Gospel.

Somalia itself in 2010 was gradually coming under the control of Islamists after years of clan warfare, economic collapse and many abortive foreign interventions, latterly by Ethiopia. The few courageous indigenous Somali Christians have either been tracked down and murdered or had to flee for their lives. The Somalis are handled in more detail on pages 194–5.

The Ogaden desert in E Ethiopia is sparsely populated by Somalis, who wage a low-level war against the central government. Christians are few.

The unevangelized areas of Ethiopia. Recent research has found that there are 30 people groups, totalling 25 million people, yet to be evangelized. They represent 29% of the population of Ethiopia.

The southern deserts and savannah are home to a medley of Oromo people groups, many of which are Muslim. In the western half of Oromia, many of the Oromo people groups have turned to Christ.

Along the borders of Sudan there are a number of isolated nomadic and semi-nomadic peoples who are only now beginning to respond to the Gospel.

The cities of Addis Ababa, Harari and Dire Dawa are of strategic importance and present a major challenge to those trying to reach the unreached. The last two are largely Muslim.

Ethiopia's missions movement. The vision for missions was forged in the fires of Communist persecution in the 1970s and '80s. The Evangelical Churches Fellowship of Ethiopia coordinates the wider effort to mobilize national churches for missions to unevangelized areas and peoples both at home and abroad. The Ethiopian Church is likely to make this one of the great sending countries of Africa in coming decades. By 2010, Ethiopia had more than 600 serving missionaries.

Food for Thought

How important Ethiopia is in Scripture! It is the first existing country to be mentioned in the Bible (as the land of Cush, in Genesis 2:13). The first Gentile convert mentioned in Acts was an Ethiopian (Acts 8:26–39). God made a remarkable promise about this land 3,000 years ago: *"Ethiopia shall soon stretch out her hands unto God"* (Psalm 68:31, KJV). This was one of the first countries to become Christian, and it has steadfastly remained so. Of all the countries that were subjected to Communism, it was Ethiopia's Church that came out of persecution best, revived and eager to send out missionaries.

When Jesus commanded us to "make disciples of all nations" (Matthew 28:18–20), the Greek word He used is *ethne*. It is an ethnic challenge. It is not enough to have a Christian presence in every place: there must be followers of Jesus in every people. For 2000 years, the Church has had only a dim understanding of how big and complex such a task would prove to be. The first full list of the people groups of the world was published only in 2001 in the WCE, though many people had been working on its compilation over several decades. On this page, I define some key terms and provide a brief timeline of recent developments in listing the world's least evangelized peoples.

People group: a significantly large sociological grouping of individuals who perceive themselves to share an affinity with each other. For the purposes of evangelization, a people group is the largest group within which the Gospel can spread as a church-planting movement without encountering barriers of understanding or acceptance.

Ethno-linguistic: (of an ethnic or racial group) defined primarily by language. Such groupings of individuals are based on the language they speak but sub-divisions are possible based on differences of dialect or culture.

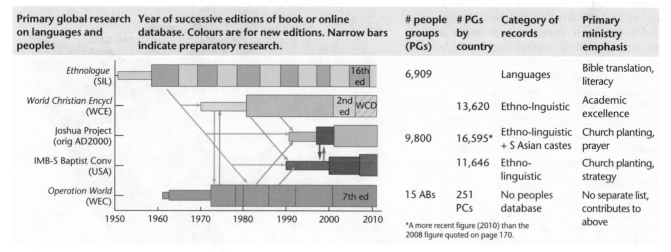

Primary global research on languages and peoples	Year of successive editions of book or online database. Colours are for new editions. Narrow bars indicate preparatory research.	# people groups (PGs)	# PGs by country	Category of records	Primary ministry emphasis
Ethnologue (SIL)	16th ed	6,909		Languages	Bible translation, literacy
World Christian Encycl (WCE)	2nd ed / WCD		13,620	Ethno-Inguistic	Academic excellence
Joshua Project (orig AD2000)		9,800	16,595*	Ethno-linguistic + S Asian castes	Church planting, prayer
IMB-S Baptist Conv (USA)			11,646	Ethno-linguistic	Church planting, strategy
Operation World (WEC)	7th ed	15 ABs	251 PCs	No peoples database	No separate list, contributes to above

*A more recent figure (2010) than the 2008 figure quoted on page 170.

Fig 7.10 *Summary of research to list the languages and peoples of the world*

The Lausanne Congress in 1974 first brought the challenge of hidden, unreached or unevangelized peoples to the attention of the Church and mission agencies. There followed years of research and discussion to refine these definitions. The result was a burst of activity aimed at discipling the world's remaining unevangelized peoples. There have been many successes.

Lists were drawn up to facilitate this effort. The primary focus was on defining people groups to establish where it would take a specific cross-cultural mission outreach to make disciples and begin a church-planting movement.

The concept of "unreached" or "unevangelized" is difficult to quantify, and in models designed to measure the input of the Gospel or the extent or the depth of the response to it, many have criticized the researchers for failing to assess the quality of discipleship and commitment. But that is extremely hard to do, and any findings should be treated with caution![12]

I prefer to use the term "unevangelized" because it does have an idea of response built into it. The fact that someone identifies themselves as being a Christian, or (more specifically) an evangelical Christian, says something about their commitment—however superficial it is, or however deep.

In the pages that follow, I have used a refinement of the "5% Christian" criterion, setting out four categories: less than 0.5% (<0.5%,), 0.5–5%, 5–50% and more than 50% (>50%). We simply do not have the information yet to compile data on Evangelicals among all peoples so that that measure can be applied globally. However, we can do this with the "Christians" criterion.

These lists owe so much to the original research of SIL and its Ethnologue database and David Barrett and the *World Christian Encyclopedia*. However, each list is unique, with its

Reached/unreached: a term widely used today to denote people groups or areas that have/have not responded to the preaching of the Gospel. Strictly, the level of reachedness should refer to the effort expended to expose a people group or area to the Gospel. I prefer using the next set of terms.

Evangelized/unevangelized: having had/not had the Gospel so presented that you are made aware of the claims of Christ and the need to obey and follow Him. In this book, I have used a simple (if crude) set of criteria to define "unevangelized": a people group that has less than 5% Christians and less than 2% Evangelicals.[13] See also my definitions on page 163.

Burning Question for Today

We are privileged today to have a clearer picture of what has been done and what remains to be done. This places a great responsibility on the Church of the 21st Century to use this information for prayer and mobilization to disciple all the people groups of the world. Many younger, postmillennial churches see this vision as a fad for the 1990s.

▲ Is it?

own particular information providers and users and intended applications. This explains some of the divergent numbers derived from this research. (See the information on p241 for ways to access these.)

The contribution of the main global researchers are indicated by the arrows in Fig 7.10. The level of cooperation and exchange of data, and the correlation between lists, have increased in recent years, but it is a complex business that takes time. There are further lists, derived from these, used by networks such as Etnopedia, Finishing the Task etc.

The need for a classification of the world's peoples is evident. There are nearly 7,000 languages spoken and some 13,000 ethno-linguistic people groups, but such numbers are hard to grasp, or even to communicate effectively in order to involve other Christians. I have studied (and edited) these lists for years and have found that a combination of the language trees used by the Ethnologue and WCD databases and the latter's "culture codes", along with a good deal of information gathered for *Operation World*, helped me to begin creating such a hierarchy. I coined the terms "affinity bloc" and "people cluster" in the 1990s to facilitate this, and they are gradually gaining acceptance by researchers and mission agencies.

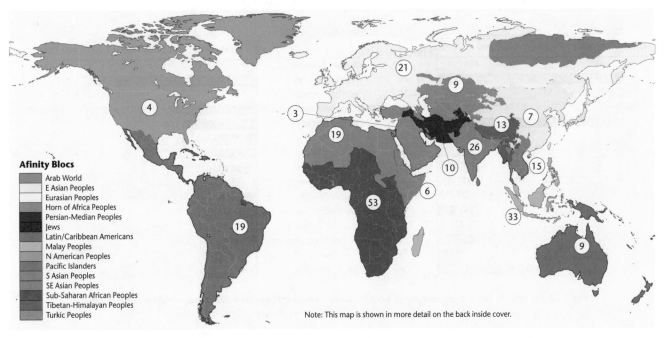

Afinity Blocs
- Arab World
- E Asian Peoples
- Eurasian Peoples
- Horn of Africa Peoples
- Persian-Median Peoples
- Jews
- Latin/Caribbean Americans
- Malay Peoples
- N American Peoples
- Pacific Islanders
- S Asian Peoples
- SE Asian Peoples
- Sub-Saharan African Peoples
- Tibetan-Himalayan Peoples
- Turkic Peoples

Note: This map is shown in more detail on the back inside cover.

Fig 7.11 *The affinity blocs, indicating the number of people clusters per bloc*

In this book, I divide the world's population into 15 affinity blocs. My allocations are pragmatic and are open to change to accommodate new knowledge or to facilitate strategy in the field. The aim is to make these categorizations as useful as possible.

There are 247 associated people clusters, accounting for all 13,000 or so of the world's ethno-linguistic people groups and its 6,909 languages. The number of clusters in each affinity bloc is given on the map above.

Each affinity bloc that includes many unevangelized people groups is covered in more detail in the pages that follow. Of the four blocs not covered, the N American, Latin/Caribbean American and Pacific Islander peoples are all largely professing Christian, while the Jews have been covered more fully on pages 90–1 in Chapter 3.

The following points will help to elucidate the affinity bloc system:

▲ *The Arab World* encompasses all areas in which Arabic is the dominant language, even though many peoples that speak languages that pre-date the Arab invasions are included in this bloc.

▲ *Mongolians* are included in E Asian Peoples for reasons of cultural affinity, though their language is related to the Turkic languages.

▲ *Caucasians living in N America or Australasia* whose primary language is English are grouped with local indigenous peoples in a single bloc, rather than in Eurasian Peoples. Other Caucasian minorities that have retained their original cultures are not.

People clusters are numbered on the map as subsets of their respective affinity blocs. Note the following points:

▲ This system of classification allows rapid identification. For many people groups, different individuals use different names. Grouping peoples in this way helps us to spot duplicates.

▲ Migration of peoples becomes more obvious when they are grouped by people cluster. Emigrant communities can then be included in a global strategy—especially if some of them live in lands that are difficult to access.

▲ Often, a list of obscure names becomes comprehensible when the cluster name is used—for example, if we identify the Kurmanji and the Sorani as Kurdish peoples.

▲ It is much easier to use a generic cluster name in communicating with churches. Congregations can grasp the idea of 247 clusters more readily than 13,000 people groups.

Affinity bloc: a wide range of people groups, which have in common that they are all shaped in a defining way by some or all of the following: geography, language, culture, history and religion.

People cluster: a sub-set of an affinity bloc, made up of more closely related people groups that have many things in common, such as identity, culture, language branch and history. People clusters often have a common name. An affinity bloc contains many people clusters.

Burning Question for Today

If we use our knowledge that many people clusters have "gone global" in their migration patterns, it can revolutionize our cooperation in sharing strategies, resources and personnel in the ministry of churches and missions on all continents.

▲ Are church and mission leaders courageous enough to think globally, to risk such sharing and thereby hasten the spread of the Gospel to the least evangelized?

No one can accomplish what has to be done without such a commitment.

People groups and populations

The next three pages give a statistical summary of the 15 affinity blocs, 247 people clusters and their constituent people groups, before we look in more depth at the less evangelized affinity blocs. This page uses ethno-linguistic statistics from the 2008 Joshua Project listing, which also includes the caste groups of S Asia—a total of 15,861. Page 173 uses statistics relating more to language that ignore both caste groups and multiple ethnic groups that speak the same language to arrive at a figure of 11,233 peoples/languages. It also makes use of the global language polygons prepared by GMI[14] using data from the Ethnologue. Below are statistics relating to the Joshua Project list.

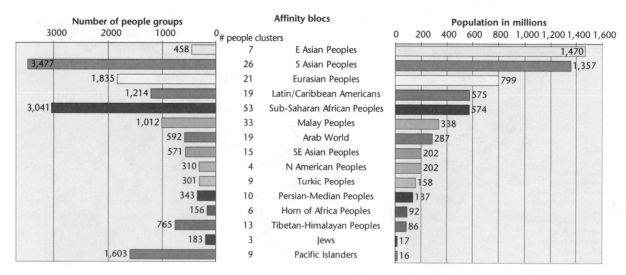

Fig 7.12 *The affinity blocs: their number of people clusters, people groups and size of populations using JP data*

Concerning the *number of people groups*, note the following:
▲ the high number of *Hindu peoples*, owing to the inclusion of over 2,300 Hindu caste groups
▲ the high number of people groups in the *Pacific and in Africa*, where many tribal groups are small
▲ *the many Eurasian peoples*—the result of three centuries of European emigration (for example, the British and the French who have numerous expatriate communities that are listed separately).

Concerning the *populations* of the affinity blocs, note:
▲ The affinity blocs are listed in order of population size.
▲ The E Asian Peoples affinity bloc is the largest, but has relatively few people groups and fewer languages—the number of people groups is swollen by Chinese and Korean emigrant communities.
▲ The Pacific Islanders have many languages, though their numbers are small. Many of these languages are spoken in Papua New Guinea, Vanuatu and the Solomons.
▲ The global population of Jews is small. Their 183 people groups represent their diaspora across most of the world.

Note the following:
▲ Nearly 6,000 of the approximately 16,000 people groups have a majority that professes to be Christian.
▲ Just over half as many have Muslim majorities. Their populations are more intensely concentrated in people groups that have been Islamized.
▲ Nearly 3,000 people groups mostly follow ethnic religions. Bear in mind that this category of religion includes both traditional religions and the likes of Sikhism and Judaism, which are based on ethnicity.
▲ Mostly non-religious people groups are few, but as Europe becomes more secular, their number is likely to increase over the next 40 years.
▲ There are more than 700 people groups that have no religious majority.

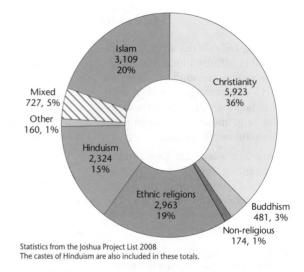

Statistics from the Joshua Project List 2008
The castes of Hinduism are also included in these totals.

Fig 7.13 *The majority religions of the world's 15,861 people groups*

Food for Thought

Religion is likely to prove a potent force for both good and ill. Fig 7.13 illustrates that reality. We need to live among and minister to people groups that are already religious. Blind tolerance is esteemed in Western society, but whereas as Evangelicals we respect other people's beliefs (whether they follow other religions or other streams of Christianity) and ought to love them whatever their opinions are, we cannot embrace a tolerance for which all views have equal validity. Nothing should hold us back from boldly proclaiming the truths of the Gospel to other people.

The pie charts on this page present a more detailed breakdown of the religious affiliations of each affinity bloc. Each pie is proportionate in size to the total population of the bloc it represents, and appears on the map in approximately the right geographical position. Fig 7.14 shows the affiliation of each bloc to the six main religious streams, and Fig 7.15 divides the Christian population of each bloc between the six Christian "confessions". We can now make useful comparisons.

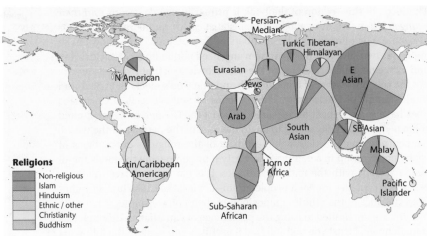

Fig 7.14 *Affinity blocs and the main religions*

The challenge of Asia. The sizes of the pies for S Asian and E Asian peoples and their non-Christian segments highlight the spiritual need there. The non-religious segment in the E Asian peoples bloc is larger than that in the Eurasian peoples bloc, but is under pressure as interest in religion—and, in China, Christianity in particular—is increasing. In S Asia, Hinduism, too, is aggressively defensive in the face of Christian growth. And yet in both regions many peoples are still unevangelized.

The three Muslim-majority affinity blocs present a challenge because of an increasing Islamization that is ever less tolerant of any Christian activity and even the presence of indigenous Christians. That the Malay peoples affinity bloc is not one of this group is largely because of the many Christians in the Philippines and Indonesia. In the sub-Saharan African peoples bloc, Muslims are in a minority overall but constitute a majority in many people groups.

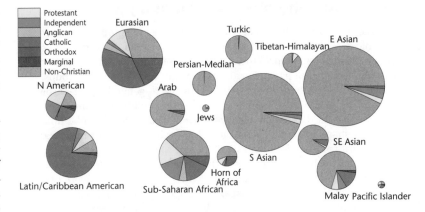

Fig 7.15 *Affinity blocs and the Christian confessions*

The six Christian-majority affinity blocs have a crucial role to play both in sending missionaries and receiving immigrants. Many people from the least evangelized people groups have been migrating, and will continue to migrate, from their homelands in the less-evangelized blocs to those blocs where Christians are in the majority. The rate of migration is likely to increase over the next few decades as populations grow larger and resources become scarcer.

The Christian population of each affinity bloc is analysed here. With all other religions coloured grey, the six main Christian streams are identified in colour. The Christianization of many peoples in Africa continues, but the continent remains a huge challenge with the long fault-line between the Muslim- and Christian-majority areas across the Sahel and down the east coast. There is likely to be tension and strife for decades to come.

There are four affinity blocs with few Christians. Note how almost invisibly small the Christian segment is in the Turkic and Persian-Median peoples pies—so small that no differentiation has been made between the various confessions. God is at work in all four of them, and in some of their people groups there is a growing Church, predominantly evangelical Protestant or Independent—though the numbers are still small.

The small *Jewish affinity bloc* continues to decline. Nearly one-third of all people of Jewish birth or descent have become Christian, and most of those have joined evangelical, Catholic or other churches and are no longer counted by Jews as Jewish. There is not space here to consider this bloc fully.

No statistics on Evangelicals are given here, because we do not yet have adequate data for Evangelicals in all people groups worldwide. Most Evangelicals belong to the Protestant or Independent streams of Christianity. They have a strong presence in the American, African and Asian affinity blocs—it has been Evangelicals rather than other kinds of Christians whose numbers have been growing among these people groups over the past century. In the traditionally Christian blocs of Europe and the Pacific, the Evangelical component of the Church is smaller but still growing.

As the presence of Evangelicals continues to increase in almost every bloc, their witness and the quality of their lives become a vital determinant of the future spread of biblical Christianity.

Burning Question for Today

It is very important to consider the world's peoples by affinity bloc and people cluster. It is strategic to reach out to people groups in many countries by evangelizing local immigrants—who in turn can evangelize those from other less accessible groups in their cluster. Most churches think of missions in terms of local outreach *or* perhaps overseas ministry.

▲ The big question is how many churches, even when they see the need for outreach to immigrants, are prepared to extend a warm welcome to their immigrant neighbours?

The focus of this section of the book is primarily *people groups and their evangelization*. We have good national statistics, for numbers of adherents of each major religion and for numbers of Evangelicals. This allows us to apply our two simple criteria for unevangelized populations: <5% Christian and <2% evangelical. The first of these acknowledges that Evangelicals are not the sole possessors of biblical truth and that God's elect are to be found in all streams of Christianity. The presence of non-evangelical Christians does have some impact in revealing truths of the Gospel, however limited some people may believe this to be. In the case of the peoples of the world, we can now make a reasonable estimate of the religious percentages of each people group in a country and verify it by comparing the totals for all people groups with the national statistics. It is harder to derive the evangelical percentages for each people group—not least because few churches keep statistics of the ethnic composition of their congregations. So, for the present, we are limited to using the percentage of Christians. Although this is inadequate, I trust you will still find it useful as you explore the following pages.

Affinity blocs and languages

From page 168, we have looked at ethno-linguistic people groups and their affinity blocs, which included the caste groups of S Asia. Now, our focus moves on to languages used. In these terms, the total number of groups per country is smaller (see p173). For 85–90% of the world's people groups, language and ethnicity are almost the same thing—generally, a tribe or people speak a single "mother tongue". With more widespread languages, especially those used as national languages or in trade, a number of ethnic groups may share a common language but differ in culture. For instance, only a minority of Irish, Scots and Welsh people speak their original Celtic languages; most people in Ireland and the UK now use English—and so in this section English-speakers belonging to those ethnic groups would be included under the English language. This approach does not help us to identify all unevangelized people groups but it does enable us to create language maps and record the extent to which the peoples that speak these languages have been evangelized. The term "peoples/languages" appears frequently in the following pages, therefore.

Given that the statistics for Evangelicals for all people groups are not yet available, I have used the simpler criterion of the percentage of the population that professes Christianity. In the 1990s, 5% became accepted as the dividing point between "unevangelized" and "evangelized". This is not really adequate, but it's a reasonable approximation. There is no sudden transformation when an unevangelized people group passes the "5% Christian" point to become "evangelized"—the change is gradual. Thus, from here onwards I shall use four categories, defined as follows:

▲ The *less evangelized* people groups or peoples/languages are <5% Christian.

▲ Of these, the *least evangelized* are <0.5% Christian.

▲ The *more evangelized* are >5% Christian.

▲ Of these, the *largely evangelized* are >50% Christian.

Fig 7.16 shows the number of people groups, counted by country, in each category:

▲ Almost 6,000 peoples/languages (more than 52% of the global total) have a Christian majority of some kind. In most of these there is also a significant proportion that are active Evangelicals.

▲ A further 2,400 people groups have probably experienced a missiological breakthrough at some period of their history, so that the Gospel has impacted their cultures significantly. Examples would be the Han Chinese and the S Koreans.

▲ Some 1,135 people groups will have many churches and an active Christian witness, but will be unlikely to have seen the sort of missiological breakthrough that would indigenize Christianity. For these less evangelized peoples, further cross-cultural effort from outside their culture is probably needed.

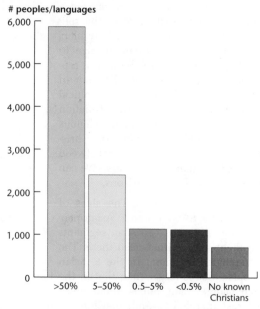

Fig 7.16 *The number of people groups and their state of evangelization in 2008*

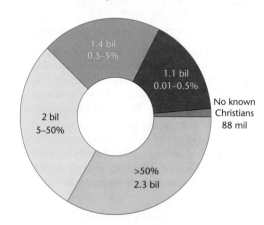

Fig 7.17 *The state of evangelization of the global population in 2008*

▲ The 1,120 people groups in the <0.5% category will almost certainly have some Christians, but they may be very few in number, marginalized and even secret believers.

▲ One final category is added here, but is not used hereafter: people groups that, so far as we know, may have no indigenous Christians at all. Many of these are small or isolated behind substantial geographical, social or political barriers.

Fig 7.17 shows the total populations in each category. It is interesting to see that the number in the red segment ("no known Christians") is comparatively low at 88 million. Nonetheless, each of these people groups—and the people in them—is important to God and should be a concern for believers.

Note: People lists are constantly being updated as research continues. Some statistics quoted in this chapter may appear to be inconsistent—mostly because I have introduced recent figures without giving a detailed explanation.

The bar chart and table below provide a summary of the constituent peoples/languages of the 15 affinity blocs and their religious affiliation and state of evangelization. The same format will be used for each of the 11 affinity blocs examined in the rest of this chapter.

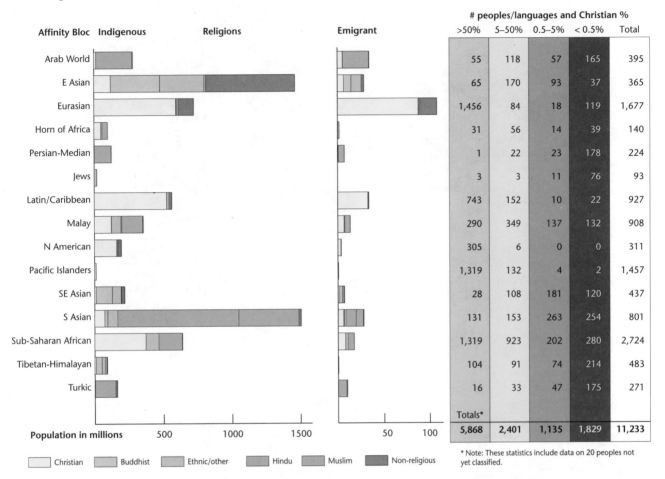

Affinity Bloc	# peoples/languages and Christian %				
	>50%	5–50%	0.5–5%	< 0.5%	Total
Arab World	55	118	57	165	395
E Asian	65	170	93	37	365
Eurasian	1,456	84	18	119	1,677
Horn of Africa	31	56	14	39	140
Persian-Median	1	22	23	178	224
Jews	3	3	11	76	93
Latin/Caribbean	743	152	10	22	927
Malay	290	349	137	132	908
N American	305	6	0	0	311
Pacific Islanders	1,319	132	4	2	1,457
SE Asian	28	108	181	120	437
S Asian	131	153	263	254	801
Sub-Saharan African	1,319	923	202	280	2,724
Tibetan-Himalayan	104	91	74	214	483
Turkic	16	33	47	175	271
Totals*	5,868	2,401	1,135	1,829	11,233

Population in millions 500 1000 1500 50 100

Legend: ☐ Christian ☐ Buddhist ☐ Ethnic/other ☐ Hindu ☐ Muslim ☐ Non-religious

* Note: These statistics include data on 20 peoples not yet classified.

Fig 7.18 *The evangelization of the world's peoples/languages*

In Fig 7.18, the population of each affinity bloc is divided into "indigenous" and "emigrant" communities. All the people groups with communities outside their home language areas or countries are classified as emigrants here and in the pages that follow. (Earlier in the book when considering countries, populations were considered either indigenous or non-indigenous, but such terminology is not appropriate when considering affinity blocs.) Each pair of bars represents the religious affiliations of the affinity bloc concerned, "at home and abroad". In some cases, there are marked differences between these "indigenous" and "emigrant" peoples.

Note that both here and in similar charts hereafter a different scale is used for the two sets of bars.

The statistics for the small Jewish bloc are incomplete, since many Jews are well integrated into host populations in the West and do not show up in language-based databases.

The table is based on individual records for every known language community in every country in the world, and so for widely disseminated peoples such as the Han Chinese, the Filipinos, the English etc there are many entries. The table lists a language only once per country, even if multiple ethnic groups use it, and India's caste groups are not included (as the lists on page 168 did).

What is shown are the totals of the number of peoples/languages in each of my four "percentage Christians" categories, which gives some indication of their level of evangelization.

There are nearly 3,000 people groups counted here that are less-evangelized, whose Christians are unlikely to have the spiritual or material resources to complete the evangelization of their own peoples without some outside help.

Food for Thought

Affinity blocs with less-evangelized people clusters are the main focus for this chapter. This is only an overview, but it gives us a new perspective on the unfinished task that has never before been considered in this way. In each bloc covered here, more detailed coverage is given to a specific people cluster or group of clusters. May these stimulate further research and the development of new resources and initiatives for their evangelization!

So much information can overwhelm us, yet these figures tell a remarkable story of great achievements and also many remaining challenges. If we are passionate about world evangelization, we have no excuse for holding back from doing anything out of ignorance.

▲ How willing are churches and individual Christians actually to obey Christ's Last Command?

People Clusters of the Sub-Saharan African Peoples Affinity Bloc

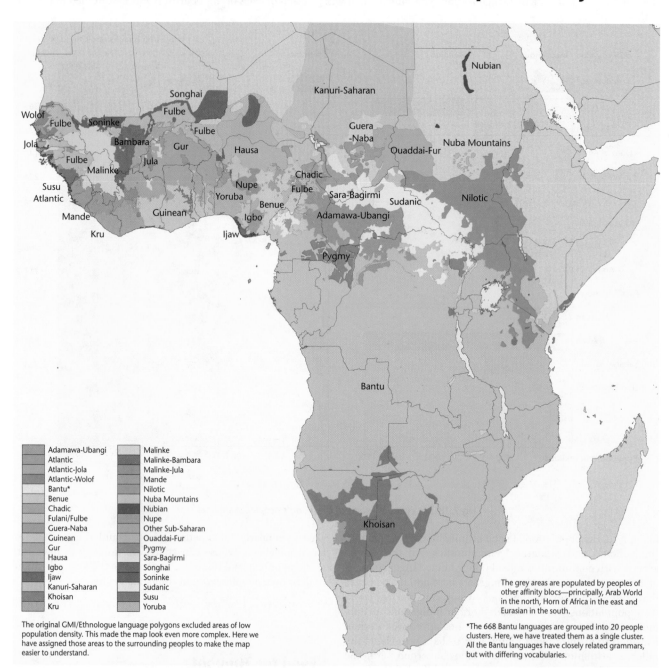

The original GMI/Ethnologue language polygons excluded areas of low population density. This made the map look even more complex. Here we have assigned those areas to the surrounding peoples to make the map easier to understand.

The grey areas are populated by peoples of other affinity blocs—principally, Arab World in the north, Horn of Africa in the east and Eurasian in the south.

*The 668 Bantu languages are grouped into 20 people clusters. Here, we have treated them as a single cluster. All the Bantu languages have closely related grammars, but with differing vocabularies.

The ethnic and linguistic variety in Africa is overwhelming. More than 4,000 people groups are represented on the map above. This is based on language areas, but in Africa languages equate to ethnic groups as well. It is helpful to group these peoples/languages together in people clusters and mark them with different colours, but without demarcating their areas.

The Sahara desert has long separated Asian and Mediterranean cultures from the rest of Africa, where a rich variety of cultures emerged. There is a further barrier across the continent: the Sahel, the belt of semi-arid savannah that stretches from the Atlantic to the Nile, dividing the Sahara itself from the forested regions to the south. Very different cultures emerged here and in the wetter rainforests.

Peoples such as the Malinke migrated to W Africa, possibly from the Nile valley, 2,000 years ago. Islam crossed the Sahara with the Arabs and, once the Malinke, the Fulbe, the Tuareg and the Songhai had embraced it, spread across the whole Sahel. Most Sahel cultures are largely Muslim today.

Note how Western colonialism drew the frontiers of today's countries in Africa but in doing so paid scant attention to the prevailing cultures or religions of the indigenous populations.

Food for Thought

It was the blood-sucking tsetse fly and the diseases it carries that killed the horses of the Muslim armies and prevented their conquest of the forest areas. The peoples there resisted Islam, and over the last century have largely become Christian. This helps to explain the north-south tensions that exist in nearly every country that straddles this Sahel-forest divide.

▲ Africans must be responsible for finding solutions to their own problems, but how many of these were created largely by the greed and insensitivity of colonialists and Muslims invaders?

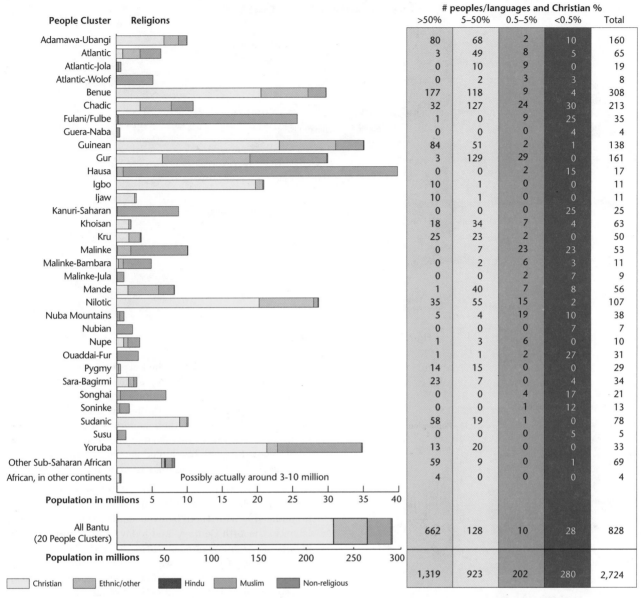

People Cluster	# peoples/languages and Christian %				
	>50%	5–50%	0.5–5%	<0.5%	Total
Adamawa-Ubangi	80	68	2	10	160
Atlantic	3	49	8	5	65
Atlantic-Jola	0	10	9	0	19
Atlantic-Wolof	0	2	3	3	8
Benue	177	118	9	4	308
Chadic	32	127	24	30	213
Fulani/Fulbe	1	0	9	25	35
Guera-Naba	0	0	0	4	4
Guinean	84	51	2	1	138
Gur	3	129	29	0	161
Hausa	0	0	2	15	17
Igbo	10	1	0	0	11
Ijaw	10	1	0	0	11
Kanuri-Saharan	0	0	0	25	25
Khoisan	18	34	7	4	63
Kru	25	23	2	0	50
Malinke	0	7	23	23	53
Malinke-Bambara	0	2	6	3	11
Malinke-Jula	0	0	2	7	9
Mande	1	40	7	8	56
Nilotic	35	55	15	2	107
Nuba Mountains	5	4	19	10	38
Nubian	0	0	0	7	7
Nupe	1	3	6	0	10
Ouaddai-Fur	1	1	2	27	31
Pygmy	14	15	0	0	29
Sara-Bagirmi	23	7	0	4	34
Songhai	0	0	4	17	21
Soninke	0	0	1	12	13
Sudanic	58	19	1	0	78
Susu	0	0	0	5	5
Yoruba	13	20	0	0	33
Other Sub-Saharan African	59	9	0	1	69
African, in other continents	4	0	0	0	4
All Bantu (20 People Clusters)	662	128	10	28	828
	1,319	923	202	280	2,724

Population in millions 5 10 15 20 25 30 35 40

Population in millions 50 100 150 200 250 300

African, in other continents — Possibly actually around 3-10 million

Legend: Christian · Ethnic/other · Hindu · Muslim · Non-religious

Fig 7.19 *Sub-Saharan African people clusters—their religious affiliation and state of evangelization in 2008*

The map on page 174 shows the 33 non-Bantu people clusters, plus the Bantu (whose 20 clusters are conflated into a single cluster here). The Bantu peoples have a great variety of closely related but mutually unintelligible languages, but they are nearly all Christianized and few need pioneer evangelism today. The bar chart above indicates the religious affiliations of the people of each cluster, and the table tells, as an approximate guide to their spiritual need, how many people groups come in each of my four "percentage Christian" categories.

The Christians among the *more evangelized* people groups (those in the two columns to the left) constitute one of the fastest-growing parts of the global Church. Moreover, they are taking on the responsibility for evangelizing their own peoples and nations. However, many of the *unevangelized* (the two columns to the right) are Muslims, with whom more Christianized peoples may have to overcome a legacy of centuries of animosity and conflict as well as immense cultural differences. The complete evangelization of Africa must continue to be a common, global responsibility.

The less evangelized people groups (those in the two columns to the right) are still numerous, with 482 being less than 5% Christian. Few of these have indigenous churches with the resources to evangelize their own or neighbouring peoples, and 202 people groups are still very much work in progress. The greatest challenge of all is presented by the 280 people groups in which there are almost no indigenous believers. The people clusters in question are the Hausa in Nigeria, the W African Fulani/Fulbe, Wolof and Malinke and, in northern Chad, the Naba, Kanuri, Bagirmi and Ouaddai. Most of these are Muslim.

Burning Question for Today

For over a century, Africa has been a major focus in missions. Astonishing indeed has been the measure of success. Seed sown in hardship, sickness and tears has borne fruit. The emergence of a strong, increasingly missional Church in Africa is cause for praise. However, there is a widespread feeling around the world that the job there is finished—and that is not true. The continent's present traumas highlight an unmet spiritual need we cannot ignore.

▲ Can the Church overcome prejudice against Africa, fear of its dangers and misconceptions about it to take up this challenge?

The Fulbe people cluster

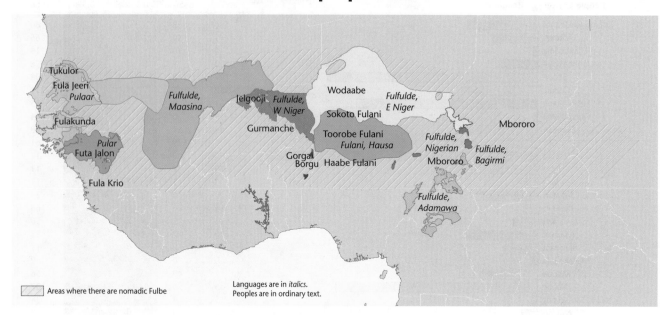

Fig 7.20 *The Fulbe people groups and languages*

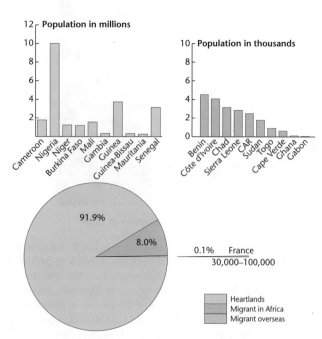

Fig 7.21 *The distribution of the Fulbe by country*

The Fulbe are also known as the Fulani Nigeria, the Fula or, in Francophone W Africa, the Peul. They are a cluster of people groups who have a unique culture and value system. Their principal languages and ethnicities are shown above. Their origins are obscure, but their generally lighter skin colour indicates a mixture of races. They emerged in the region of what is now Senegal, but spread east across the Sahel. Their language is W African and links them to the Bantu peoples.

At 31 million strong, the Fulbe are the largest nomadic pastoralist people in the world: nearly half of them still live the nomadic life with their beloved cattle. Many converted to Islam in the 14th Century, and today they are proud of their history as spreaders of Islam through *jihad* all over W Africa; and yet aspects of their original religion are still evident. Many of the more nomadic Fulbe are only nominally Muslim, and some still follow their old ethnic religion.

The pie chart separates the Fulbe by country into three:

▲ those living in their peoples' heartlands (green)—the countries where they wield real political influence and make up a significant proportion of the indigenous population. Powerful Fulbe-dominated emirates arose in many of the countries listed in the green bar chart. Many Fulbe settled down as farmers, traders and city dwellers. They continue to hold great power in the north of Nigeria and in its federal government. They have largely lost the use of their own language and become Hausa-speaking. Only in Guinea are they the largest ethnic community.

▲ those living in countries where they are generally more recent immigrants or live as nomadic pastoralists (orange). The advance of the Sahara is forcing the nomads further south and into the coastal states of W Africa. Growing populations in cultivated areas together with this migration is causing more frequent and ugly clashes between nomads and farmers.

▲ those who have emigrated to other continents (blue). These are comparatively few, though their numbers are probably far higher than official statistics indicate. Few governments in other continents gather statistics on the ethnicity of their African residents. Also, illegal immigration into Europe is high—and likely to increase.

Burning Question for Today

Modern Christian missions have been singularly unsuccessful in evangelizing and discipling nomads. Planting churches that function in nomadic communities is rare, and yet the Old Testament is full of references to godly people who lived in tents, such as Abraham! It is only among the Wodaabe Fulbe in Niger and the Fulbe in Chad that some have become believers.

▲ How can we enable indigenous nomad churches to emerge and multiply?

The Fulbe languages form a continuum of dialects across the Sahel, but they differ enough to make it necessary to produce a separate translation of the Bible for each group listed in Fig.7.22. Furthermore, each of these languages includes speakers from several distinct ethnic groups of Fulbe, such as the Tukulor, the Fula Jeeri and the Fulakunda of Senegal and the Wodaabe of Niger. These, too, are shown on the map opposite and counted in the table below.

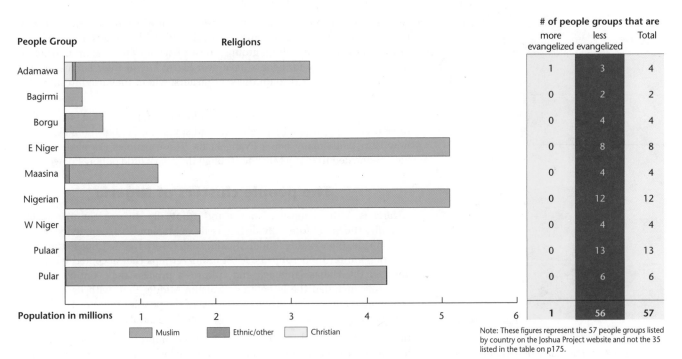

People Group	Religions	# of people groups that are		
		more evangelized	less evangelized	Total
Adamawa		1	3	4
Bagirmi		0	2	2
Borgu		0	4	4
E Niger		0	8	8
Maasina		0	4	4
Nigerian		0	12	12
W Niger		0	4	4
Pulaar		0	13	13
Pular		0	6	6
Population in millions		**1**	**56**	**57**

Muslim · Ethnic/other · Christian

Note: These figures represent the 57 people groups listed by country on the Joshua Project website and not the 35 listed in the table on p175.

Fig 7.22 *The Fulbe people cluster—religious affiliation and state of evangelization of its people groups in 2008*

The religious affiliations of the Fulbe are indicated here. The numbers that adhere to either Christianity or an ethnic religion are very small, and almost everyone would claim some allegiance to Islam (though there is a great deal of syncretism).

Some of these languages already have a Bible (Nigerian, Adamawa) or New Testament (Pulaar, Fulakunda) or portions of Scripture (Pular etc); but much remains to be done. The challenge is the scarcity of indigenous Christian translators.

The table reveals a sad situation. Only one Fulbe people group can be regarded as "more evangelized"—a very small community in Cape Verde who are mostly Christians. All the other 56 groups still come in the "least evangelized" category. In most countries where Fulbe live, there is Christian outreach going on—notably in Senegal, Guinea, Guinea-Bissau, Mali, Burkina Faso, Niger, Nigeria and northern Cameroon. In nearly all of these it is the settled Fulbe rather than the nomads who are reached. The work among the Fulakunda in Senegal started 70 years ago, but there are still only two tiny congregations.

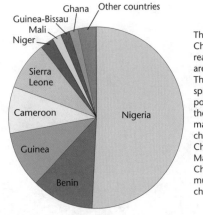

The number of Fulbe Christians is not really known. These are estimates. Their widely spread-out populations and their mobility do not make it easy to plant churches or count Christians. Many Fulbe Christians meet in multi-ethnic churches.

Estimated total Christian population among Fulbe: 40,000 (based on Operation World data) or 155,000 based on the World Christian Database

Fig 7.23 *The distribution of Fulbe Christians by country*

Fulbe cattle herders (David Phillips, Peoples on the Move*)*

Burning Questions for Today

▲ This strategic people cluster presents the Church with a series of huge challenges, yet what could ensue if the long-prayed-for harvest were granted by the Lord?

There are now a thousand believers among the Wodaabe in Niger.

▲ Is this the first fruits of a wider ingathering?

This widespread and influential people could make a great impact for God's Kingdom were they to become believers in the Lord Jesus Christ.

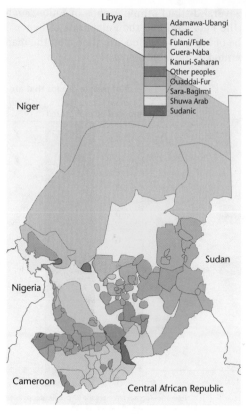

Adamawa-Ubangi
Chadic
Fulani/Fulbe
Guera-Naba
Kanuri-Saharan
Other peoples
Ouaddai-Fur
Sara-Bagirmi
Shuwa Arab
Sudanic

Fig 7.24 *The people clusters of Chad*

The people clusters of Chad

Chad extends deep into the sparsely inhabited Sahara desert in the north. It is actually the tribes that live there that control the country's government and the new-found oil deposits in the far south.

Across the centre of the country there is a belt of sandy scrubland that is used for rainy-season agriculture and by Shuwa Arab nomads. It is the home of a medley of small ethnic groups, most of whom are Muslim and totally unevangelized. Few foreigners have ever learnt any of their languages. The Muslim peoples here disdain the southerners, whom they used to subject to slave raids.

In the deep southwest live numerous peoples of a totally different background. Most used to practise ethnic religions and some still do, but the majority are now Christians—many being Evangelicals. These peoples are also generally better educated than the Muslims, though they have little political power.

The people clusters of Nigeria

Nigeria is Africa's most populous and ethnically diverse country. It, too, straddles the Sahel-forest divide that is also a Muslim-Christian divide. Under British rule, the existing feudal Muslim rulers were free to impose their rule and religion on their subjects. Most ethnic groups that accepted Islam also adopted the Hausa language and culture—a process that continues today. That rule included the largely non-Muslim Middle Belt, with its extremely fragmented and diverse ethnic mix. Most of the peoples there resisted Islam, and many have since embraced evangelical Christianity.

In the south, British colonial rule ensured improvements in education, health and the economy and allowed the Gospel freedom to flourish. Most of the peoples that live there are now Christian.

Shortly before Nigeria gained independence in 1960, Britain encouraged the formation of a federal government system to include the Muslim north, the Yoruba-dominated southwest and the Ibo-dominated southeast. This led to many years of Muslim control, a long civil war and the misappropriation of the oil wealth of the southeast. The state has barely functioned since the end of the Biafra War in 1970. Many are the woes of this complex country created in the death throes of the British Empire.

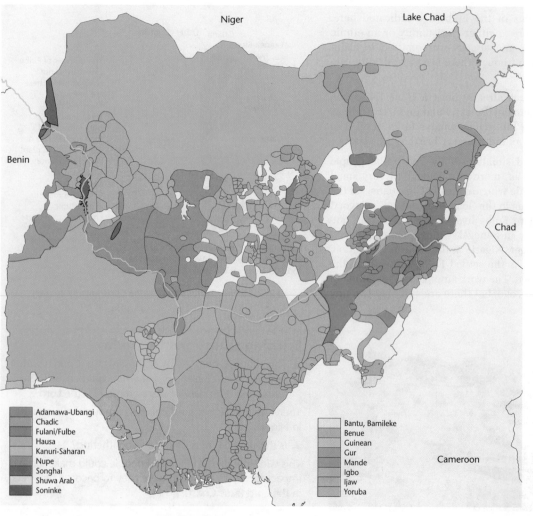

Adamawa-Ubangi
Chadic
Fulani/Fulbe
Hausa
Kanuri-Saharan
Nupe
Songhai
Shuwa Arab
Soninke

Bantu, Bamileke
Benue
Guinean
Gur
Mande
Igbo
Ijaw
Yoruba

Fig 7.25 *The people clusters of Nigeria*

The two maps on this page refer to the same peoples as those opposite, but indicate their respective states of evangelization. These two adjoining countries are separated by Lake Chad and a narrow strip of Cameroon. It is striking to see the Sahel-forest divide in both countries reflected in the response to the Gospel. The least evangelized peoples are almost entirely Muslim.

The unevangelized in Chad

Chad was a creation of France's African colonial empire, bringing together three totally different geographical and ethnic components into a single, poverty-stricken, land-locked state. The Catholics and evangelical Protestant missions assiduously evangelized the forest peoples of the southwest, and had a huge response. There are now 2 million Christians and 6,000 or more congregations, with "islands" of Chadians deep in the Muslim areas in the centre and north (though these serve only southerners and are culturally far removed from the local indigenous peoples). Chad remains one of the most open countries for mission work and yet it has many totally unevangelized peoples. The middle and north of the country are home to dozens of peoples with no local resident witness. In several areas of the Guéra, in the centre of Chad, there has been a response. Along the border with Sudan there are thousands of totally unevangelized Sudanese ethnic groups who have fled the fighting in Darfur.

The unevangelized in Nigeria

Nigeria has seen amazing growth in its Church and has become the foremost missions-sending country in Africa. Revival and strong evangelical mission work have resulted in the Gospel taking root among peoples far into the north of the country—it is surprising to note this on this map. The major challenge is to evangelize the large Hausa and Kanuri populations effectively, in the northwest and northeast respectively, as well as many smaller northern peoples that for the most part have not been open to the Gospel.

Christians are actually the majority in Nigeria, but by manipulating census data Muslims have managed to create the impression that they are—and that they thus have the right to rule the whole country. This has provoked a backlash against Christians and southerners in the north and has led to the unconstitutional imposition of *shari'a* law in most of the north.

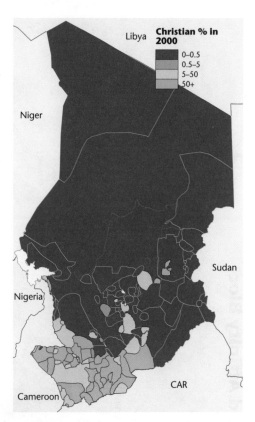

Fig 7.26 *Chad's unevangelized peoples*

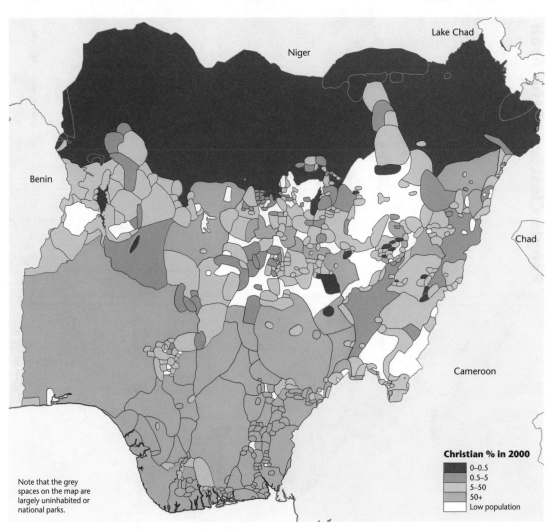

Note that the grey spaces on the map are largely uninhabited or national parks.

Christian % in 2000
- 0–0.5
- 0.5–5
- 5–50
- 50+
- Low population

Fig 7.27 *Nigeria's unevangelized peoples*

People Clusters of the Arab World Affinity Bloc

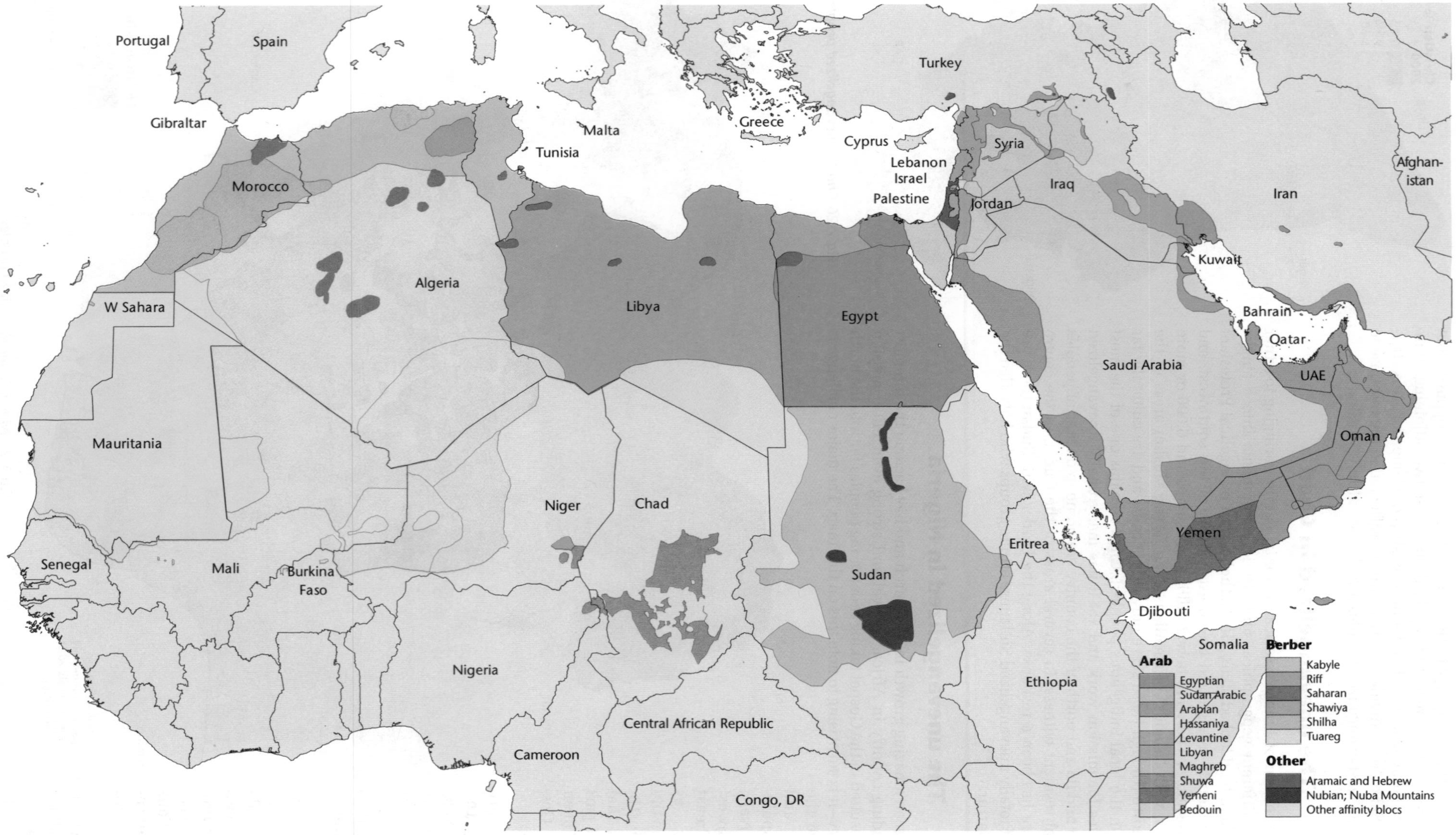

Berber

- Kabyle
- Riff
- Saharan
- Shawiya
- Shilha
- Tuareg

Other

- Aramaic and Hebrew
- Nubian; Nuba Mountains
- Other affinity blocs

Arab

- Egyptian
- Sudan-Arabic
- Arabian
- Hassaniya
- Levantine
- Libyan
- Maghreb
- Shuwa
- Yemeni
- Bedouin

Arabic culture and language dominate in the 20 countries highlighted on this map, which also shows nearby countries with indigenous Arabic and related languages (Hebrew and Aramaic-Syriac) belonging to these Arab World people clusters.

Not shown here are people clusters of the Persian-Median and sub-Saharan African peoples affinity blocs—note the pale brown areas. The one exception is the Nilo-Saharan peoples of northern Sudan, whose links with the Mediterranean world go back 4,000 years.

Countries and regions labeled on the map: Portugal, Spain, Gibraltar, Morocco, W Sahara, Mauritania, Senegal, Mali, Burkina Faso, Niger, Nigeria, Cameroon, Chad, Central African Republic, Congo, DR, Libya, Algeria, Tunisia, Malta, Greece, Cyprus, Turkey, Lebanon, Israel, Palestine, Syria, Jordan, Egypt, Sudan, Ethiopia, Eritrea, Djibouti, Somalia, Iraq, Iran, Afghanistan, Kuwait, Bahrain, Qatar, UAE, Saudi Arabia, Oman, Yemen

The population and religious affiliations of each of the Arab World's people clusters are indicated in the bar chart below. The Arabic-speakers are represented in the first 12 bars, and then the Berber groups. The peoples are divided into those living in their homelands and those that have emigrated, either to other parts of the Arab world or further afield. (The cluster I have named "Arab, generic" encompasses all those undifferentiated Arabs who live outside their home areas as minorities of mixed origins.) The table on the right gives the total number of peoples/languages in each cluster. Of the total of 395, there are 165 peoples/languages in the "least evangelized" category (less than 0.5% Christian).

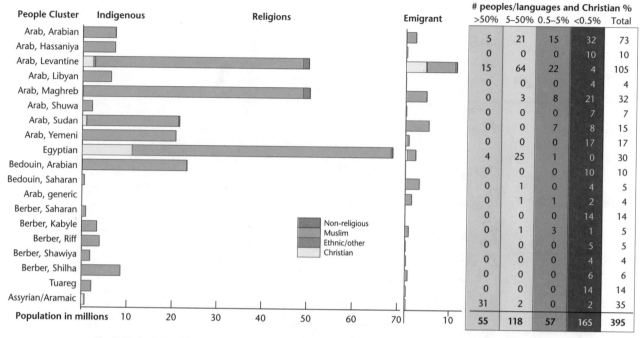

| People Cluster | # peoples/languages and Christian % | | | | |
	>50%	5–50%	0.5–5%	<0.5%	Total
Arab, Arabian	5	21	15	32	73
Arab, Hassaniya	0	0	0	10	10
Arab, Levantine	15	64	22	4	105
Arab, Libyan	0	0	0	4	4
Arab, Maghreb	0	3	8	21	32
Arab, Shuwa	0	0	0	7	7
Arab, Sudan	0	0	7	8	15
Arab, Yemeni	0	0	0	17	17
Egyptian	4	25	1	0	30
Bedouin, Arabian	0	0	0	10	10
Bedouin, Saharan	0	1	0	4	5
Arab, generic	0	1	1	2	4
Berber, Saharan	0	0	0	14	14
Berber, Kabyle	0	1	3	1	5
Berber, Riff	0	0	0	5	5
Berber, Shawiya	0	0	0	4	4
Berber, Shilha	0	0	0	6	6
Tuareg	0	0	0	14	14
Assyrian/Aramaic	31	2	0	2	35
	55	118	57	165	395

Legend (Religions): Non-religious, Muslim, Ethnic/other, Christian

Fig 7.28 Arab World people clusters—their religious affiliation and state of evangelization in 2008

The more evangelized are the Egyptians and Levantine Arabs. There are many Christians among these peoples—Orthodox, Catholics and Evangelicals, though Evangelicals are fewer in number and, as we do not have accurate statistics for them, are not represented here. The Assyrians are historically Christian and have retained much of their original Aramaic culture that predates the Arab Muslim conquest.

The least evangelized: The other 15 people clusters—encompassing more than 222 people groups and languages—remain little impacted by the Gospel. Many of their ancestors were Christians before Islam came, but this generation needs to receive the Good News! Pride, prejudice, the distortion of history and the current political turmoil in the region make this a difficult part of the Muslim world to evangelize.

Arab World emigrants are numerous—note the pies in Fig 7.29, which are proportionate to population.

The opportunity. Many have migrated to nominally Christian countries, where there is great potential for witnessing, planting churches and preparing ministry tools such as satellite broadcasting and literature to evangelize the heartlands of the Arab world —many of which are closed to most forms of Christian outreach.

The tragedy. Many of these emigrants are Christians (as the bar chart above suggests). There is a steady haemorrhage of both ancient Christian communities and of members (and leaders) of younger evangelical churches as a result of heightened persecution, as Islamists seek to rid Muslim lands of all Christian communities.

Breakthroughs for the Gospel have been few but significant. The most dramatic has been the growth of the Church in Algeria, first among the Kabyle and then among Arabic-speakers. Concerns about the cruelty of Islamists in the civil war have created a greater responsiveness. There has been a steady stream of new believers in Christ, due partly to satellite TV,[15] partly to the internet, partly to witnessing by tourists. In recent years, expectations of a larger harvest have been rising.

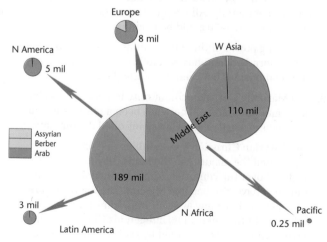

Fig 7.29 Emigration from the Arab World

Food for Thought

Albert Hourani's acclaimed book *A History of the Arab Peoples* begins with the Prophet Mohammed—as if all previous history was irrelevant. This bolsters their pride as the peoples among whom Islam began, but sidesteps much of what the Bible says of the Arabs as descendants of Abraham. This ignorance distorts Muslims' perceptions of both their own origins and the nature of the Gospel. How different history might have been if the Bible had been translated into Arabic before the time of Mohammed!

The Levantine Arab people cluster

The 61 million Arabs and over 100 people groups that inhabit or originate from the Fertile Crescent between the Persian Gulf and the Mediterranean constitute one of the world's strategic people clusters. In AD 600, nearly all the ancestors of these peoples were, at least nominally, Christian.[16] Most have now become Muslim, though there are still significant Christian minorities among them. The area, extending across Iraq, Syria, Jordan, Lebanon and Israel/Palestine, has been a focal point for some of the most sensitive and intractable geopolitical crises of the 20th and 21st Centuries. These have complicated the evangelization of the Levantine Arabs and will deeply impact the future.

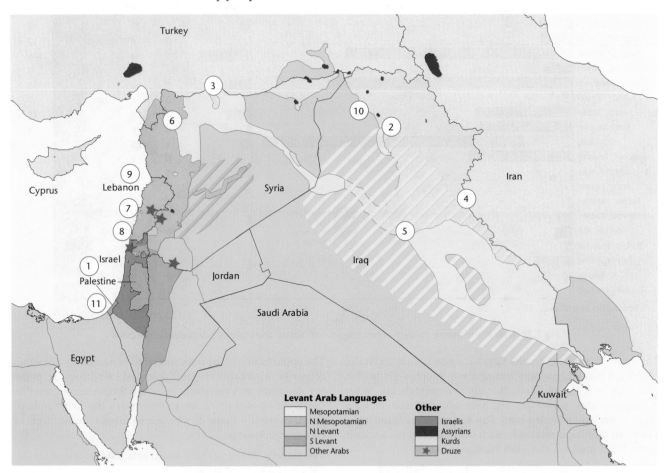

Fig 7.30: *World-impacting conflicts across the Fertile Crescent*

1. The Israeli-Palestinian conflict has frustrated all attempts at resolution and has been the cause of retaliatory wars, uprisings and terrorist attacks. Many of the 10 million Palestinian Arabs live as refugees in surrounding countries and around the world. The rise of the Islamist resistance movement Hamas (**11**) has divided the Palestinians and exacerbated the conflict.

2. The Kurds of northeast Iraq have long been oppressed by the Arabs. The dispute over the oilfields of Kirkuk is a cause of deep division between Kurds and Sunni Arabs and a likely source of future conflict.

3. The Arab-Turkish confrontation over the damming and use of the waters of the rivers Euphrates and Tigris, which both rise in Turkey, could become ugly.

4. The conflict between Iran and the Arab world is centuries-old. The removal of Saddam Hussein as dictator of Iraq in 2003 allowed the ascendancy of revolutionary Shi'a Iran, which seeks to dominate the region. A major war is possible.

5. In Iraq, the long subjugation of the Shi'a by the Sunni minority was ended by the US/UK invasion of 2003. The country is now likely to be virtually ungovernable for the foreseeable future.

6. Syria's politics have been dominated since 1971 by its Shi'a minority, whose Alawite version of Islam is regarded by many Muslims as deviant. They retain power with an elaborate system of controls, but for how long?

7. Lebanon's 18 recognized religious communities include Sunni and Shi'a Muslims, the Druze and various kinds of Christians as well as the large and restive Palestinian refugee community. All vie for power, and the devastating civil war of 1975–90 could be resumed.

8. The rising power of the radical, militant Shi'a Hezbollah in southern Lebanon has destabilized both that country and relationships between Arabs and Israelis.

9. The Maronite Christian community in Lebanon has lost its former dominance. There has been a massive exodus of Lebanese, particularly Christians of all denominations.

10. The Assyrian Christian communities that once constituted the majority in the lands they inhabit have declined over the centuries. Many have adopted Arabic, and most have also become Muslim. The Assyrians are now confined to a few areas in Iraq, Iran, Turkey and Lebanon. In Iraq, like all its indigenous Christians, they have been heavily persecuted by radical Muslims since 2003.

Religious communities functioning almost as ethnic groups is a legacy of the Ottoman Empire, whose "millet" system organized populations under its control according to their religious affiliation.[17] This has contributed to much of the current political division and civil strife. Generally, it has ensured Muslim dominance and discrimination against Christians. Islamism has put further pressure on Christians and has made any form of witness to Muslims more difficult, let alone their conversion.

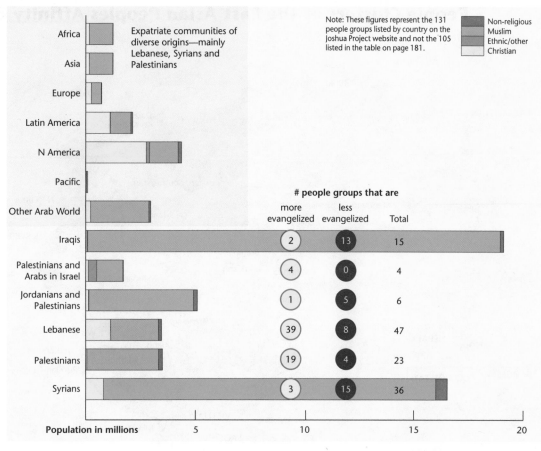

Note: These figures represent the 131 people groups listed by country on the Joshua Project website and not the 105 listed in the table on page 181.

Expatriate communities of diverse origins—mainly Lebanese, Syrians and Palestinians

Legend: Non-religious, Muslim, Ethnic/other, Christian

Fig 7.31 *The Levantine Arab people cluster—religious affiliation and state of evangelization of its people groups in 2008*

The Palestinians: The loss of much of their land occasioned by the creation of the state of Israel in 1948 and its subsequent expansion remains a focus of contention locally, regionally and globally. Half their population lives outside their homeland. In 1900, more than 10% of Palestinians were Orthodox or Catholic Christians. By 2000, this was reduced to 1.9% (with only a few thousand evangelical Christians)—and this decline continues. This tragic, dysfunctional people is largely unevangelized today.

The Levantine Arab diaspora accounts for 23% of their total population. There are three main reasons for such a large emigration:

▲ *Economics:* Lebanese and Syrians have followed their Phoenician forebears as global traders. More recently, others (including many Muslims as well as Christians) have sought employment in the oil-producing Gulf states.

▲ *Social unrest:* The many regional and civil wars since 1945 have forced millions to flee in search of safety and a better environment for their families, principally in the West. This exodus could increase further, given the instability of the region.

▲ *Persecution:* A disproportionately large percentage of the emigrants have been Christians, who had suffered years of discrimination as second-class citizens, Muslim hostility (because of the "Christian" West's support for Israel) and, latterly, violence from Islamists determined to rid the region of Christians.

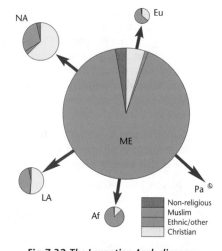

Fig 7.32 *The Levantine Arab diaspora*

People Clusters of the East Asian Peoples Affinity Bloc

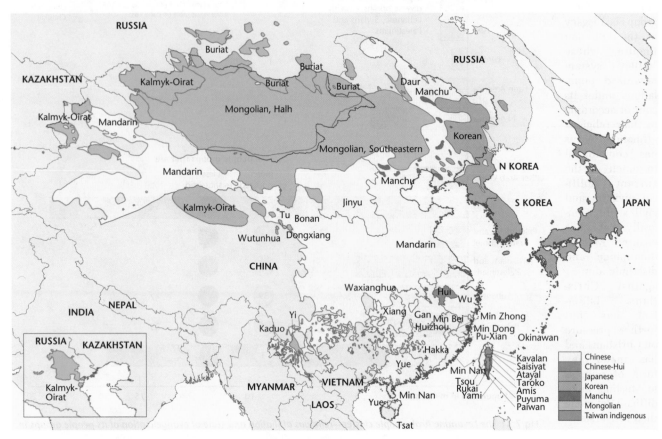

One defining characteristic of the E Asian peoples affinity bloc is the cultural influence of the Chinese on the other peoples in the region and vice versa. The Great Wall was built to keep out the peoples of the deserts and steppes to the north and west, and yet the Mongols and later the Manchu conquered and ruled China for many centuries. In return, however, China's wealth, power, technology, religion and learning deeply affected these invaders, and those who settled were soon assimilated into its culture.

The map above is essentially a language map, and so some ethnic people groups are not shown. There are seven people clusters in this affinity bloc:

The Chinese inhabit the fertile and densely populated eastern half of present-day China. For most of recorded history, the peoples of this land have been great thinkers, inventors and innovators. Over three millennia, a wide range of other peoples have gradually been absorbed into the main Han Chinese population—a process that continues today. Many different Han languages are spoken in the south of the country, but all of them use the same script.

The Hui are descendants of the soldiers and traders, first Arab and then Persian, who settled in China after the eastward advance of the Muslim armies petered out in the northwest of the country. They intermarried with the Chinese but retained their Muslim faith. They are now scattered all over China.

The Japanese are a unique blending of several racial streams since 500 BC. Their civilization owes much to the influence of the Chinese, from whom they learnt to write in the 5th Century.

The Koreans have a long history, much of it relating to being a smaller nation fiercely trying to maintain its independence between two superpowers, China and Japan. The latter occupied Korea from 1910 to 1945. At Stalin's insistence, Korea

was divided after the Second World War, which led to the destructive Korean War and continuing tensions between N and S Korea ever since.

The Manchu are an Altaic people who used to dominate Manchuria, in NE China. In 1611, they conquered the whole of China, and Manchu emperors ruled it until 1912 as the Qing Dynasty. In the process, the Manchu were largely absorbed into the Han Chinese, though they have retained some of their cultural distinctions.

The Mongolians are another Altaic people. Most live in Mongolia or in N China along a 3,000 km arc of territory south of Mongolia. Nine other, smaller groups of Mongol peoples live scattered across China—remnants of the Mongol armies that conquered the land in the 13th Century. Mongol emperors ruled China from 1294 to 1420. Some Mongols live in Russia around Lake Baikal and in the Caspian area of Russian Europe (see map inset).

The 25 indigenous tribes of Taiwan are that island's original inhabitants. They live in the mountains. Many have now become Christian.

Food for Thought

▲ How has China's geography determined its worldview and its attitude both to other countries and to its own ethnic minorities?

Despite its wealth and inventiveness and its huge population, China has always been vulnerable to predatory attacks from its periphery.

▲ How will this determine its policies in the 21st Century as it regains its status as a superpower?

The map below illustrates a remarkable record of successes and failures in the evangelization of these peoples, and also the remaining challenges. Such a map 100 years ago would have been coloured almost entirely dark blue. The lighter blue areas on this map testify to a growing Church among most of the larger peoples of the region.

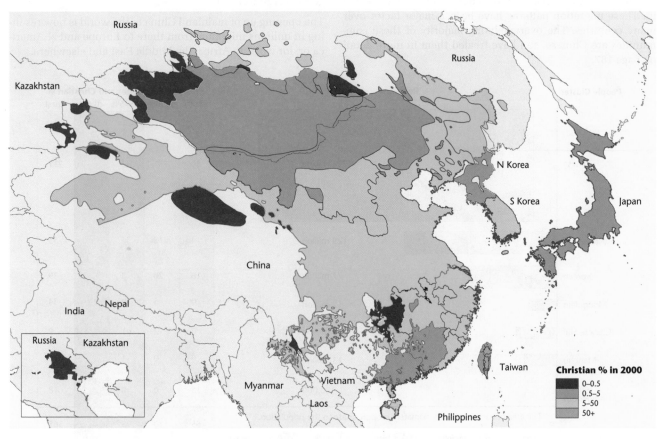

Christian % in 2000
- 0–0.5
- 0.5–5
- 5–50
- 50+

Fig 7.33 *The E Asian people groups and their evangelization*

The successes. *The Chinese* have had many bad experiences with "Christian" countries over the past 500 years. Even after more than a century of intense mission work between 1830 and 1949, China's Christians still numbered around 5 million. It took suffering under Communism for the Church in China to become the dynamic, indigenous movement it is today (as illustrated in the maps on p155). However, the spread of churches across the country is still uneven, with many less evangelized areas.[18]

The Koreans have gone from rejecting the Gospel to embracing it wholeheartedly—one of the more amazing stories in the history of the Church. Just over a century ago Korea had no Christians, but today S Korea has 20,000 churches and 242 denominations and now has the second-largest foreign-missions force in the world—though in N Korea believers languish under severe persecution.

Taiwan's tribal peoples began to turn to Christ in people movements during the Japanese occupation. Today, more than 80% profess Christianity.

The Mongolians under Communism were among the least evangelized peoples on earth, with only a handful of known believers in 1990. Today, there are some 46,000 Christians in the country.

The challenges. *The Taiwanese and Hakka Chinese* on Taiwan have proved far more resistant to change, and the Church has grown very slowly over the past 50 years. About 0.35% of the Hakka are evangelical Christians.

The Japanese were exposed first to Catholic Christianity, an experience that helped to shut off the land and its people from receiving the Gospel despite the current freedom to proclaim it. The real breakthrough has yet to come, and Christianity is still a marginal religious movement in Japan.

The Muslim Hui are China's third-largest ethnic minority. They have received little attention until quite recently, but efforts to reach them with the Gospel have yielded only sparse results. There may now be about 1,000 Christians among them.

The Mongols of N China are a minority in their own region of China (where they constitute 17% of the local population), but their 7 million far outnumber the 2 million in Mongolia itself. Most churches in the region are Han Chinese, and relatively few Mongolians there have become Christians.

Other Mongolian peoples—notably, the Kalmyk-Oirat of W China and European Russia—remain largely unevangelized. The Mongol-related Daur, Tu, Dongxiang, Bonan, Kaduo, Yugur and Wutunhua in China are without any adequate witness to Christ.

> ### Burning Question for Today
> The great missionary Hudson Taylor's mobilization of workers and impassioned pleas for intercession for China's unevangelized in the 19th Century have borne ample fruit in their response to the Gospel in recent years.
>
> ▲ How passionate are we in praying for the remaining unevangelized peoples of E Asia?

There are early 30 million emigrants in diaspora communities around the world (see Fig 7.35)—which could be 50 million if we counted those Chinese and others who have become largely assimilated in the countries they have settled in. These migration patterns have been a major factor over many centuries. The overwhelming majority of these communities are Chinese, so I have treated them in more detail on page 187.

Most of these emigrants live in E and SE Asia, but over the past 100 years many Japanese have moved to Latin America and in the last 50 years millions of Koreans and Chinese have gone to N America.

The opening up of mainland China to the world is now resulting in millions migrating from there to Europe and N America or, for work, to Africa, the Middle East and elsewhere.

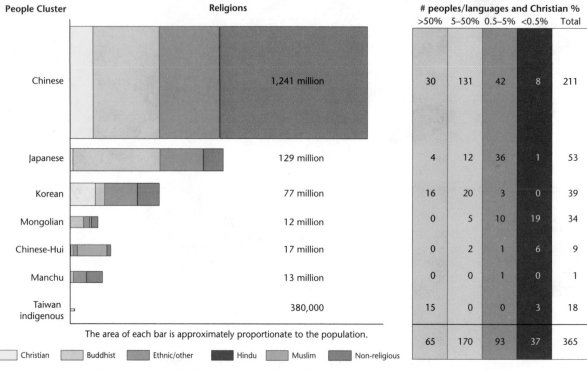

People Cluster	Religions	# peoples/languages and Christian %				
		>50%	5–50%	0.5–5%	<0.5%	Total
Chinese	1,241 million	30	131	42	8	211
Japanese	129 million	4	12	36	1	53
Korean	77 million	16	20	3	0	39
Mongolian	12 million	0	5	10	19	34
Chinese-Hui	17 million	0	2	1	6	9
Manchu	13 million	0	0	1	0	1
Taiwan indigenous	380,000	15	0	0	3	18
		65	170	93	37	365

The area of each bar is approximately proportionate to the population.

Christian   Buddhist   Ethnic/other   Hindu   Muslim   Non-religious

Fig 7.34 E Asian people clusters—their religious affiliation and state of evangelization in 2008

These people clusters vary so much in population that this chart is different from the others in this series. I have made the area of each bar approximately proportionate to the population it represents (the figure is also given). Indigenous and emigrant communities are here taken together and not represented separately.

The comparative responsiveness of the Koreans, Taiwan's tribal peoples and the Chinese both overseas and, latterly, in mainland China is reflected in the Christian percentages. It is notable that so many Chinese are non-religious as a result of Communism, but notable, too, is the strength of both indigenous ethnic religions and Buddhism among the Chinese, Koreans and Japanese.

The lack of response among the Japanese, the Chinese Hui, the Mongolians and the remnants of the Manchu is apparent, though with the Mongolians the situation is now changing for the better.

The large number of Chinese people groups reflects their emigration to many countries on every continent.

The table records that 37 people groups in the E Asian peoples affinity bloc remain in the "least evangelized" category.

Nearly a quarter of all E Asian emigrants are now Catholic, Protestant or Independent Christians. Generally they have done well economically and could make a dynamic contribution to world evangelization.

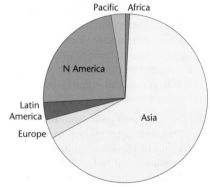

Note: Not counted here are the many E Asians who are integrated into the country they live in—some of whose ancestors arrived there centuries ago.

Fig 7.35 E Asian peoples and their emigration

Food for Thought

There are now millions of young people of E Asian origin living in affluent countries, and they themselves, with their more stable family structures and their drive for educational and economic success, have prospered. They straddle two cultures, with the cultural versatility this gives them.

▲ As Western Christians and churches increasingly renege on their commitment to world evangelization or concentrate on shorter-term goals, is it this new generation of Christians of E Asian origin that will provide a large part of the needed mission force of longer-term workers?

The Chinese diaspora

This has been one of the world's most influential diasporas and has been a major economic factor in Asia for the last 60 years. Most of the emigrants originate from the more outward-looking trading cultures of S China. It is difficult to predict the impact of the growing numbers of mainland Chinese, many of them from N and C China, who are migrating to other countries, whether legally or illegally, or travelling abroad as labourers or businesspeople. It will certainly help to shape the 21st Century.

Earlier migration began in earnest some 600 years ago as China's trading interests expanded. In Fig 7.36, the list of the 10 countries outside China with the largest Chinese populations includes eight around its periphery. Through hard work, business acumen and effective international networking, the overseas Chinese have generally become extremely wealthy and, in many cases, a key component in the economies of these other Asian countries. Singapore, the only Chinese-majority state apart from China itself, has since independence become one of the world's biggest success stories. Many of the Chinese who have migrated to N America or Europe went originally as labourers or to work in the catering trade, but many of those have become important in a variety of professional careers.

The degree of assimilation of the Chinese has varied, depending on the local culture and the extent to which they have been discriminated against or resented for their prosperity. In Thailand they are well integrated, but in Malaysia they live in almost complete separation.

Their response to Christianity has been equally varied. The majority in Latin America are now Christian (in this case, mainly Catholic), as are large minorities in Indonesia, the Philippines, Singapore and N America (where many are Evangelicals)—but few in Vietnam and Myanmar.

The new migrations have been largely from Hong Kong to N America, though now many people are going from mainland China all over the world. As many as 2 million students to date have studied in the West; many don't return to China—and many also become Christians, which is having a big impact on China's educated. Other Chinese have gone as labourers to many countries (including large numbers who are illegal immigrants to Europe or N America). Chinese engineers and businesspeople are working in the Middle East and in massive infrastructure developments in Africa, and many other professionals have gone to the West, with large-scale migrations to New Zealand, Europe, N America etc.

Fig 7.37 looks at the three major components of the world's Chinese population: the mainland Chinese, those of three autonomous parts of China (Taiwan, Hong Kong and Macau) and the overseas Chinese (including those of Singapore).

The left-hand pie represents the religious affiliation of the global Chinese population and the three pies on the right that of its three main components. The differences are striking. Nearly a quarter of all overseas Chinese are now professing Christians—in some areas (Latin America, Europe) predominantly Catholic and in others (Singapore, Indonesia) including many Evangelicals. The numbers in the autonomous parts of China are pulled down by the spiritual need of the people of Taiwan and Macau. The growth of the Church in mainland China was described earlier.

The diaspora and mainland China. China's post-Communist industrial revolution, which has made it the world's leading manufacturer, was in large part enabled by the investment, expertise, trade links and professionalism of the overseas Chinese and those of Hong Kong—now supplemented by the impact of the large number of Chinese trained in Western universities, who are changing old structures and attitudes.

Given that a large minority of these people are active Christians, the implications for China and the growth of the Church there are enormous. Before 1989, the Chinese Church was largely rural, but by 2010 this had changed and churches are now mushrooming in the cities and among the educated.

China's future impact worldwide. The massive industrialization of China has created a growing middle class, as well as some of the world's richest individuals. It has also made China a massive purchaser of the world's mineral stock and agricultural produce. Everyone feels the economic impact of the rise in commodity prices this has led to. Armies of engineers and labourers are upgrading Africa's roads and railways to bring out its mineral wealth, while China is buying up Western mining companies and vast areas of agricultural land all over the world. As Russia's population contracts sharply over the decades to come, Siberia will become depopulated. Will the Chinese move in to take its huge, underexploited resources?

Country	Population	Christian %
Indonesia	9,179,588	43.00
Malaysia	6,732,323	8.31
Singapore	2,216,905	18.00
Vietnam	1,780,750	1.17
USA	1,760,150	21.02
Thailand	1,491,048	8.47
Canada	1,027,255	25.00
Philippines	975,169	89.83
Myanmar	954,740	2.39
Other	3,943,000	24.30

Fig 7.36 *The Chinese diaspora—top 10 countries in 2008*

All Chinese
7.9%

Overseas Chinese 30–40 mil

Hong Kong Macau Taiwan 30 mil

Mainland Chinese 1,200 mil

23.4%

5.1%

7.6%

Non-religious
Muslim
Ethnic / other
Buddhist
Christian

The Christian % is given for each pie chart.

Statistics are for 2008

Fig 7.37 *The Chinese and their religious affiliation*

Food for Thought

The world of 2050 will be very different from today and it will be shaped, increasingly over the coming decades, by China and India.

▲ What influence will Christians exercise in formulating China's policies with regard to foreign relations, the environment, human rights and genetic engineering?

▲ How much will Chinese Christians contribute, both to a better future for humankind and to the world's full evangelization?

People Clusters of the Eurasian Peoples Affinity Bloc

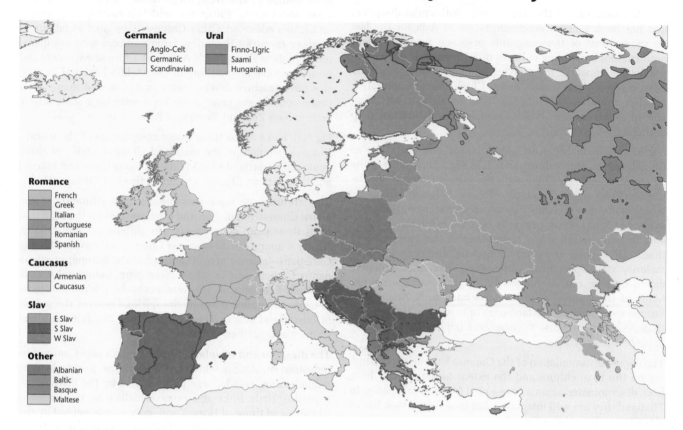

Germanic
- Anglo-Celt
- Germanic
- Scandinavian

Ural
- Finno-Ugric
- Saami
- Hungarian

Romance
- French
- Greek
- Italian
- Portuguese
- Romanian
- Spanish

Caucasus
- Armenian
- Caucasus

Slav
- E Slav
- S Slav
- W Slav

Other
- Albanian
- Baltic
- Basque
- Maltese

The map shows the Eurasian people clusters. These peoples probably spread out originally from the Caucasus area, and hence they are often called "Caucasians".[19] Most of them settled in Europe over the past 4,000 years, but some have their homelands in what is now defined as Asia—Georgia and Armenia, which are south of the Caucasus mountains. This and the eastward spread of Russians to the Pacific Ocean are the reasons the term used here is "Eurasian" rather than "European".

The clusters are grouped into five larger agglomerations of related languages, which are identified on the map by the shading. Most of the languages used in tertiary education worldwide—and hence of vital importance for the future—are represented here.

The Romance languages are, generally, those that developed from Latin and were modified by invading Germanic tribes after the collapse of the Roman Empire in AD 410. However, Greek, which was one of the most important languages of the Western Roman Empire, is often also included in this family of languages. Some 720 million people speak one or other of these languages. Spanish and Portuguese are the most important internationally.

The Germanic languages were probably first spoken in Scandinavia and spread southwards around 750 BC. One of these, English, became in due course the common language of N America and Australasia, and the mother tongue of some 460 million people as well as the official or main language of a third of all the world's states and territiories. It is now the world's preferred second language and dominates the internet internationally.

The Slavic languages probably emerged around 1000 BC in C Europe, and spread south and east. In all, 290 million people today speak one of them as their first language. In the following pages, they are considered in three separate groups. The most important internationally is Russian.

The Ural languages are spoken mainly in northern Scandinavia and across the north of European Russia. The most important languages are Hungarian and Finnish.

The Caucasus languages are spoken in S Russia, Georgia, Armenia and northern Azerbaijan. What is remarkable is the number of languages and dialects spoken—around 50—and the small number of people that speak each one. The most important are Armenian, Georgian and Chechen. See page 191 for maps and a fuller description of this, Europe's least evangelized area.

Other languages include the Indo-European language Albanian and the Baltic languages Latvian and Lithuanian. Basque is unique in having no known relation—it was probably spoken long before the Indo-Europeans arrived. Its speakers are also among the European peoples with the fewest evangelical Christians. Maltese is basically a Semitic language related to Arabic, but with many borrowings from other Mediterranean languages.

The map shows the areas where the main languages are spoken but not all the dialects. The boundaries of the principal regional languages of France, Italy and Spain are marked, but not those of the Netherlands, Germany and Britain.

Food for Thought

Only an estimated 39 languages are used as a teaching medium in the world's universities, and 27 of these are European. Just four are used in more than one continent: English, Spanish, French and Portuguese. These languages will continue to exercise enormous influence for at least another generation and probably more. What a weight of responsibility rests on everyone able to teach overseas in their own mother tongue to use their languages for good and for God!

Europe and Christianity

The language areas in the map are coloured according to the percentage of people in each who profess to be Christian. There is not yet an adequate breakdown of language groups by theology or level of Christian commitment, so I cannot show here the extent either of active evangelical witness or of nominalism. Refer to the national statistics and maps in Chapter 5 for the situation country by country. What this map portrays is largely a Christianized Europe—for the moment.

Fig 7.38 *The Eurasian people groups and their evangelization*

Over the first millennium AD, Europe was Christianized but not necessarily evangelized, and yet Christianity (however distorted) moulded its various cultures. By 1450, the continent had become the last refuge of what could have been a dying faith, with just a few beleaguered outposts in India, Ethiopia and the Muslim Middle East (as I have amply shown earlier in this book).

There is no room for smug complacency about "Europe's Christian heritage"—and "Christian" majority. The map shows the start of the process that could rapidly turn the continent post-Christian. Most people in the Czech Republic and Belarus now no longer claim to be Christian, and by 2050 the blue areas of this map (where non-Christians are in the majority) will have expanded to include many, if not most, of Europe's major peoples. If we take as the criterion for being evangelized that a population should be more than 2% evangelical, there is no country bordering the Mediterranean that comes even close to that figure, even including evangelical Catholics. In fact, only 16 of Europe's 47 countries do.

Burning Question for Today

▲ How does one begin to re-evangelize the ageing peoples of Europe, who are jaded and cynical and think they understand the Christianity they are rejecting?

They are still searching for meaning, but exploring everything except the way to peace, purpose and real life that can be found in Jesus alone.

▲ *The Bosniak Muslims* are probably Europe's largest least-evangelized people. Among a population of 3 million spread over 19 countries, there may be only about 500 evangelical believers with over 200 of these outside Bosnia.

▲ *The Albanians* suffered until 1990 under one of the most repressive Communist regimes in Europe. All religions were banned. By the time the Communists fell, the number of known Evangelicals was reduced to about 10 individuals. Since then, there has been a great deal of mission activity in Albania and there are now some 14,000 Evangelicals, and nearly 200 congregations. About 32% of the population is nominally Christian, but 62% is Muslim. Kosovo, with its 80% Albanian majority, declared itself independent of Serbia in 2008. In 2010, there were about 2,000 evangelical believers in 35 congregations.

▲ *The Caucasus* people groups are the least evangelized in Eurasia. The two great mountain ranges of the Caucasus lie between the Black Sea and the Baltic and have long been considered the boundary between Europe and Asia.[20] Their high peaks and deep valleys have provided a refuge for peoples from many different ethnic backgrounds, and have also permitted the development of numerous local languages and dialects (see p191).

▲ *Non-Eurasians*: The grey areas on the map represent indigenous peoples who belong to other affinity blocs—Turkic peoples in SE Europe, Altaic peoples in N Russia, Mongolian Kalmyk in S Russia and Iranian Ossetians in the Caucasus.

Note: The "Eurasian" affinity bloc is so named because Russian Siberia, Georgia and Armenia are culturally European but technically part of Asia. I have used "European" as an interchangeable term to include all these people groups.

The last five centuries have been astonishing for the flowing tide that spread European peoples and their influence all around the world. Its impact has been huge, bringing wide-ranging industrial, political, economic, cultural and religious changes that have moulded the modern world. It is good to examine these even as we observe the ebbing of that tide. That half-millennium of expansion has now given way to a contraction as populations decline and age.

The two pie charts in Fig 7.39 reveal something of the flood of emigrants to every continent that really began with the Industrial Revolution in the mid 18th Century. The pies divide the present global population of all that are of European descent into three categories:

▲ The pink two-thirds of the lower pie represents the 656 million Europeans living in Europe. The 21 European people clusters are shown in the tables below.

▲ The multicoloured third of that pie represents European settlers in other continents who are now assimilated into the indigenous population.

▲ The smaller pie represents two kinds of European immigrants: those who have only recently settled in another country, and those who have retained much of their cultural identity over generations such as the Armenians in many countries and the Poles in the USA and EU. There are 108 million people in this category.

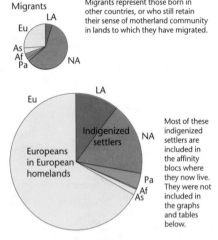

Migrants represent those born in other countries, or who still retain their sense of motherland community in lands to which they have migrated.

Most of these indigenized settlers are included in the affinity blocs where they now live. They were not included in the graphs and tables below.

Fig 7.39 The European diaspora

An amazing 40% of all the 1,090 million people of European descent now live outside Europe, reflecting a scale of migration unprecedented in human history. In this book N Americans, Australasians and Latin Americans of European origin are included in their regional affinity blocs and are therefore not represented in the bar graphs and tables below. The blending of these Europeans with both indigenous and other immigrant peoples has progressed furthest in Latin and N America.

Fig 7.40 indicates the population and religious affiliations of each of the Eurasian people clusters, divided into those people groups living in their homelands and those that have emigrated. The table on the right gives the numbers of people groups in countries of the constituent peoples and indicates their state of evangelization. It is striking that most of the "least evangelized" people groups belong to the Caucasus people cluster—which is examined next.

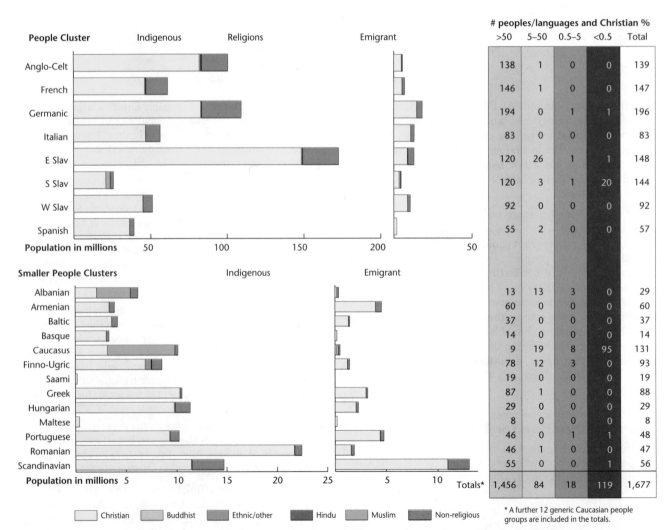

People Cluster	# peoples/languages and Christian %				
	>50	5–50	0.5–5	<0.5	Total
Anglo-Celt	138	1	0	0	139
French	146	1	0	0	147
Germanic	194	0	1	1	196
Italian	83	0	0	0	83
E Slav	120	26	1	1	148
S Slav	120	3	1	20	144
W Slav	92	0	0	0	92
Spanish	55	2	0	0	57
Albanian	13	13	3	0	29
Armenian	60	0	0	0	60
Baltic	37	0	0	0	37
Basque	14	0	0	0	14
Caucasus	9	19	8	95	131
Finno-Ugric	78	12	3	0	93
Saami	19	0	0	0	19
Greek	87	1	0	0	88
Hungarian	29	0	0	0	29
Maltese	8	0	0	0	8
Portuguese	46	0	1	1	48
Romanian	46	1	0	0	47
Scandinavian	55	0	0	1	56
Totals*	1,456	84	18	119	1,677

Legend: Christian, Buddhist, Ethnic/other, Hindu, Muslim, Non-religious

* A further 12 generic Caucasian people groups are included in the totals.

Fig 7.40 Eurasian people clusters—their religious affiliation and state of evangelization in 2008

The Caucasus people cluster

Origins. These peoples have lived in the region since prehistoric times and their ancestors may be the progenitors of most of the indigenous peoples of Europe.

Over the last 2,500 years, Persian, Muslim Turkic and Mongol conquerors also left their mark, and some of their descendant peoples (such as the Persian-related Ossetians and Tat, the Turkic Karachay, Kumyk and Azeris and the Mongol Kalmyk) are now indigenous to the area. The Georgians and Armenians have a history in the area going back nearly 3,000 years.

Conflict. Throughout recorded history, the region has been an arena for conflict between superpowers. The story of its peoples is one of fighting for survival and freedom. This continues today with, most recently, war in Chechnya and between Armenia and Azerbaijan, and Russian interventions in Georgia.

Religion. Persian and Turkic conquest and political domination ensured the conversion of most of the region's peoples to Islam—which has since been a factor in uniting them to resist Russian rule. Today, Islamists dream of an Islamic state encompassing the seven Russian republics of the N Caucasus. To the north, Kalmykia is Buddhist-majority.

Christianity first arrived in apostolic times. The Armenians and Georgians are the two extant nations that first became Christian, early in the 4th Century. Their possession of the Bible and a culture moulded by it ensured their survival as distinctive peoples despite persecutions and massacres by Zoroastrians, Muslims and Mongols. The only other peoples in the Caucasus with a Christian majority are the Migrelians, Svan, Ossetians and Abkhaz. The last two look to Russia for support for independence from Georgia.[21]

The *least evangelized* peoples and areas:

▲ *The Chechens* have resisted "Christian" Russian rule since it began in the area in 1783 and have suffered greatly as a result, not least in the recent wars. This struggle affects the whole region, as well as (with terrorist attacks) other parts of Russia. Only about 100 Chechens have believed in Christ—most of them living in other parts of Russia.

▲ *The Ingush* identify strongly with the Chechens. There is only a handful of believers among them.

▲ *Dagestan* on the Caspian Sea is home to 34 people groups and is 90% Muslim. Violence is rife—overspill from Chechnya, inter-ethnic conflict—and

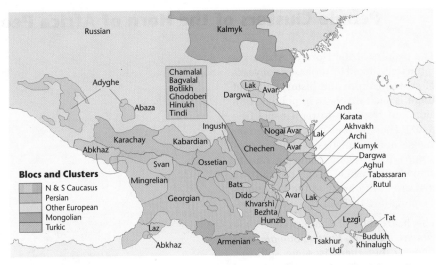

Fig 7.41 *The languages of the Caucasus people cluster and other peoples of the region*

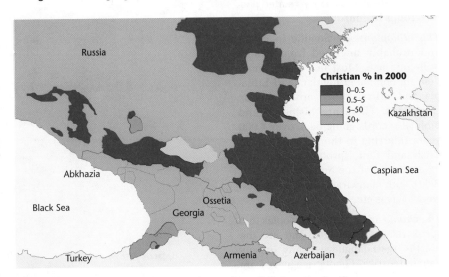

Fig 7.42 *The Caucasus peoples and their evangelization*

kidnapping is commonplace. There are several multi-ethnic churches, but few believers among indigenous peoples.

▲ *The Adyghe and the Cherkess* (Circassians) are related, but were separated into two republics by the Russians in 1920. They were Christians for a thousand years, but converted to Islam in the 15th Century. The once numerous Adyghe were decimated by the Russian wars and invasion after 1770, and most were driven into exile in the Ottoman Empire (which they

were to provide with some of its finest soldiers). To this day, they remain an influential minority throughout the Middle East, where they currently number about 600,000. There is only one Adyghe-speaking church, but there are other Adyghe Christians in Russian-language churches.

▲ The 50 people groups of the region, and their 40 or so expatriate communities all over the former Soviet Union, constitute the least evangelized group of peoples in Europe.

Burning Question for Today

It is hard to conceive of a more difficult region to evangelize than the Caucasus. Local wars, ethnic rivalries, interreligious hatred, harsh Russian control and very high levels of corruption, suspicion and abduction of foreigners make this a dangerous part of the world for any outsider to enter. Then there is the diversity and complexity of local languages spoken only by a few, the dearth of active churches and Christians and even the lack of any Scriptures in most of these languages.

▲ Who is willing to risk everything so that, in this generation, these peoples loved by God have the chance to become followers of the Lord Jesus?

People Clusters of the Horn of Africa Peoples Affinity Bloc

The peoples of the Horn of Africa are intimately linked by thousands of years of shared culture and history—and yet there is such diversity in politics, religion and response to the Gospel (see p167). Here, I concentrate on the languages and ethnicities of these people groups. This region could be said to embody the whole range of conflicts that are at the heart of the key issues shaping the 21st Century.

The heartlands of these people clusters are *Ethiopia, Eritrea, Somalia and Djibouti*, but there is some spillover into neighbouring *Kenya, Sudan and Egypt*. There are also three related people groups in *Tanzania*.

The Ethiopians are Semitic in origin and probably migrated from Arabia millennia ago. Most live in the more densely populated highlands of Ethiopia and Eritrea. Most are Orthodox Christians. There are historical and biblical records going back over 4,000 years referring to the Ethiopians and Cush and Punt (probably inhabited by ancestors of the Somalis, Afar and Beja), with many trade links for spices, wood, slaves etc.

The Oromo are a cluster of peoples that speak related languages, and are the fourth-largest language family in sub-Saharan Africa. Omotic languages are distantly related to Oromo, but vary widely (note the complex lines on the map!).

The Beja, the Afar, the Somalis and *the eastern and southern Oromo* live in the dry savannah or desert lowlands. Many of these peoples have embraced Islam.

For much of recorded history, Ethiopians and their ancestors have dominated the politics of the region. The Communist revolution of 1976 destroyed the old structures and the imperial leadership and installed a cruel dictatorship. Rebellions by the Tigrinya and other ethnic groups ended Communist rule in 1991. In 1996, the Ethiopian government recognized the country's ethnic diversity by creating a federal system based on language. The issue of language is also key for Eritrea and Djibouti.

In the last 80 years, the whole region has become a byword for famine and war, which have periodically devastated it. The effects have been dreadful, with millions dying. The most recent wars (which are still unresolved) have

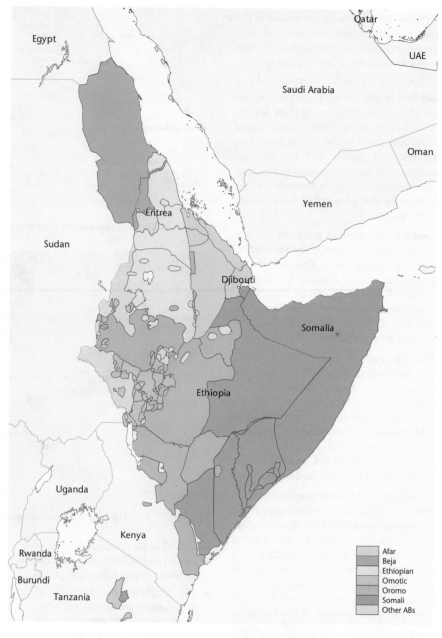

been between Ethiopia and first Eritrea and then Somalia. Eritrea is a failing dictatorship and Somalia a failed state. These factors complicate any effort to evangelize the people of the region.

Food for Thought

The years of conflict and disaster have held back every people group from developing their infrastructure and making economic progress. Any form of Christian ministry, whether material or spiritual, is fraught with difficulty and danger.

▲ How can foreign input be most effective and lead to long-term—and, indeed, eternal—benefit?

Good news from Eritrea: the OT editor of the Africa Bible Commentary *and his wife in their Eritrean national dress (photo by PJK)*

The bar chart indicates the population and religious affiliations of each people cluster of the Horn, divided into those people groups living in their homelands and those that have emigrated. The numbers superimposed refer to constituent people groups that are more evangelized (more than 5% Christian) or less so. Of the region's 161 people groups, as listed in the JPL, 99 are reckoned to have viable churches and a Christian witness, while the remainder are still largely unevangelized.

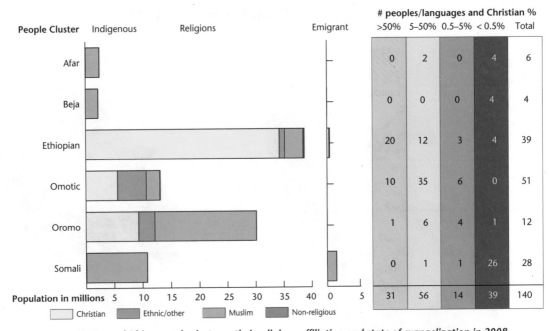

People Cluster	# peoples/languages and Christian %				
	>50%	5–50%	0.5–5%	< 0.5%	Total
Afar	0	2	0	4	6
Beja	0	0	0	4	4
Ethiopian	20	12	3	4	39
Omotic	10	35	6	0	51
Oromo	1	6	4	1	12
Somali	0	1	1	26	28
	31	56	14	39	140

Legend: Christian, Ethnic/other, Muslim, Non-religious

Fig 7.43 *Horn of Africa people clusters—their religious affiliation and state of evangelization in 2008*

More details on each people cluster and people group can be found on the Joshua Project website (see p240).

The *more evangelized*:

Ethiopians were among the first peoples on earth to hear and respond to the Gospel. There are comparatively few Evangelicals, but these have had a big impact on some parts of the Orthodox Church.

The western Oromo and Omotic peoples are part Muslim and part Christian. Many Oromo are either Orthodox or Evangelical. The Omotic peoples are now largely evangelical after years of faithful witness by missionaries and nationals, and after awakenings and revivals over the past 20 years. The main churches are Lutheran, Word of Life (SIM) and Pentecostal. Growth continues.

The *less evangelized*:

The Afar live in northeast Ethiopia, northern Djibouti and southern Eritrea. Very few have heard the Gospel, and even fewer have responded to it.

The Beja live in the deserts along the coast of the Red Sea and have proved to be one of the more difficult peoples on earth to evangelize. There is little current witness to them, and no known church.

The Somali are strongly Muslim but after years of war, famine and social and political upheaval have a broken and dysfunctional society. They are one of the world's least evangelized people clusters. See page 194 for more.

Burning Question for Today

The key to evangelizing the region is the revived Church, south and west of the Ethiopian capital, Addis Ababa. However, these Christians are physically isolated and economically impoverished, and the peoples they need to reach are Muslim—and there has been 1,500 years of hostility locally between Christians and Muslims.

▲ How can these obstacles be overcome?

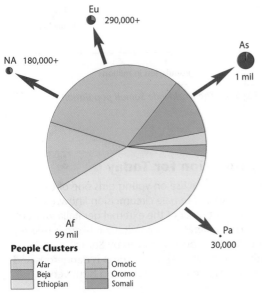

Eu 290,000+
As 1 mil
NA 180,000+
Af 99 mil
Pa 30,000

People Clusters
- Afar
- Beja
- Ethiopian
- Omotic
- Oromo
- Somali

Fig 7.44: *The Horn of Africa people clusters and their level of emigration*

Nomadic Arabs in Eritrea (David Phillips, Peoples On the Move)

The Somali people cluster

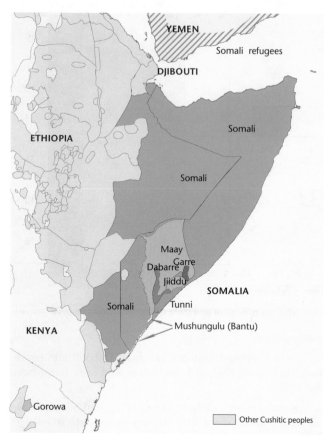

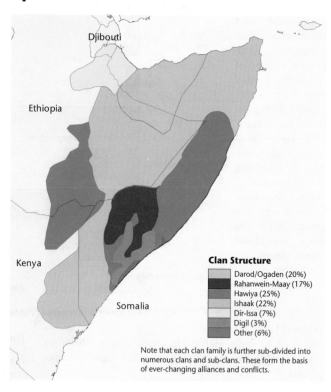

Fig 7.45 *The Somali people cluster
—languages (left) and clans (right)*

For several decades, *the Somalis* have rarely been out of the news. Their state collapsed into anarchy in 1991, which led to clan wars, foreign interventions and terrible disasters, both man-made and natural. By 2010, they had gained an unenviable reputation for violence, including piracy, and as a fertile recruiting ground for Islamist extremists.

Clan loyalty is more important than language in differentiating Somalis. Their six clan families have numerous sub-clans, and the volatility of the allegiances between them are a fundamental cause of the continuing conflict and chaos.

The greatest conflict since 1991 has been located in the area around the capital, Mogadishu, where many different dialects of the Somali language are spoken. Virtually all non-Somalis, both foreign and indigenous (including the Mushungulu), have been driven out of the country. Many of the Somalis now living in the US are, in fact, not ethnically Somali but Bantu Mushungulu. The latter are agriculturalists, whereas the Somalis are largely pastoral and partly nomadic.

All figures for Somalis are estimates, and it is likely that the commonly used statistics for their home areas are too high while those for those living abroad are too low.[22] All we could glean is presented in Fig 7.46, which for most countries gives an upper and a lower figure.

What is shocking is the number of refugees. There are estimated to be 1.4–1.6 million in their homelands, and some 1.6 million Somalis have fled abroad—especially to Yemen. Note the hatching that shows the concentrations of Somalis in that country.

Somali refugee communities have grown rapidly in the Middle East, Europe and N America. Sadly, some of these people have turned to drug-dealing and other crime, and, increasingly, Islamist terrorism.

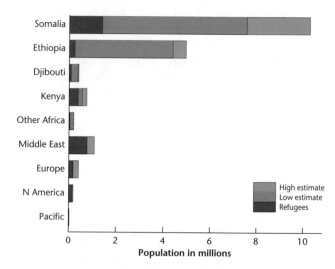

Fig 7.46 *The worldwide Somali population*

Burning Question for Today

Somalis commonly practise on young girls one of the most barbaric forms of female circumcision known, which involves cutting out most of the external genitalia without anaesthetic. They claim that this cultural custom is Islamic, but it is not—and it is observed even by Somali communities in the West. The mutilation is dangerous and makes both sexual intercourse and giving birth very painful.

▲ What can be done to address this issue?

The Gorowa of Tanzania live far from other Somali peoples and were never Islamized. Most of them follow their own ethnic religion, but about 40% have become Catholic or Protestant Christians.

All other Somali people groups are Muslims. Many efforts have been made to evangelize them, but only a few hundred or so Somalis have accepted Christ, and most of those have had to flee for their lives. Islamists actively seek out and kill as "traitors" any Somali Christians they can find in Somalia

and elsewhere, and the few believers in Somalia today have to live in hiding. There are several Somali Christian groups in Kenya and the US, but none now in Somalia.

Somalia—a failed state. For 20 years (as at August 2010), the country has had no single government and has been in chaos with rival warlords, clans and gangs fighting each other and any foreign military intervention. The US, then the UN and finally the Ethiopian army have sought to establish some sort of peace and organized government, but had to give up and leave.

Most of the fighting and the social collapse has been in the south. There are now four distinct political entities:

Somaliland occupies much of the area once ruled by the British. It declared its independence after the collapse of Siad Barre's dictatorship in 1991, but the Maakhir area in the east split off in 2007 and was then incorporated into Puntland in 2009.

Puntland considers itself an autonomous part of Somalia and has its own government. It is the principal base for Somali pirates operating in the Indian Ocean (the shaded area on the map in Fig 7.48).

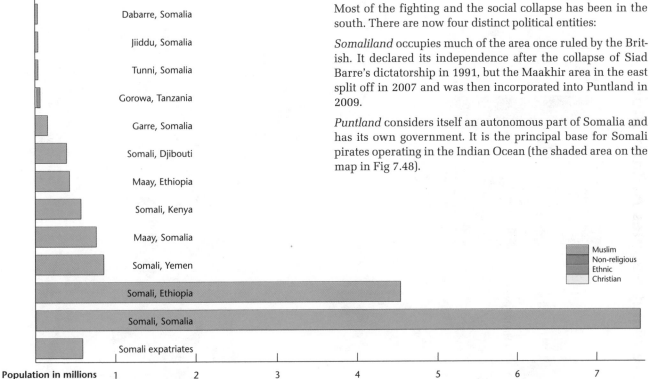

Fig 7.47 *The Somali people cluster—religious affiliation and state of evangelization of its people groups in 2008*

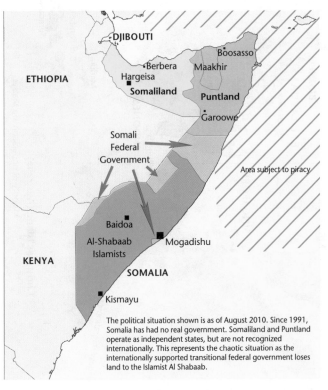

Fig 7.48 *Somalia, a failed state*

The *Somali Federal Government* controls part of the capital, Mogadishu, and some border areas, but survives only through international support. Many refugees live in these areas, where they depend on foreign aid.

Al-Shabaab Islamists now control most of the south of the country, and impose strict *shari'a* law. They are closely linked with al-Qa'ida, and this part of Somalia is becoming a haven for international terrorism.

Burning Questions for Today

We could write off the Somalis as a lost cause, but…

▲ Can we look beyond the hatred and violence, the piracy, kidnapping and Islamism, to see a broken, traumatized people who desperately need to hear of the love, forgiveness and peace that the Lord Jesus alone can give?

▲ Can we develop a global perspective, to reach the scattered Somali people wherever they have taken refuge?

▲ Can we trust that their sufferings may yet lead them to salvation in Christ?

The ethnic and linguistic diversity of the Malay peoples is remarkable, though hardly surprising. Over the centuries, numerous migrations by sea have resulted in many thousands of island communities. Today, there are more than 900 peoples/languages living on some 7,000 islands (principally the Philippines and Indonesia). I have followed the assignation of people clusters developed by Indonesian Christian researchers.[23]

The main divisions in Malaysia, the Philippines and Brunei are between the original, proto-Malay peoples (often tribal) and the later Malay peoples.

Papua was ruled by the Dutch but seized by Indonesia in 1963. Its indigenous peoples are very different, and are not included in this survey of the Malay Peoples affinity bloc.

People Clusters of the Malay Peoples Affinity Bloc

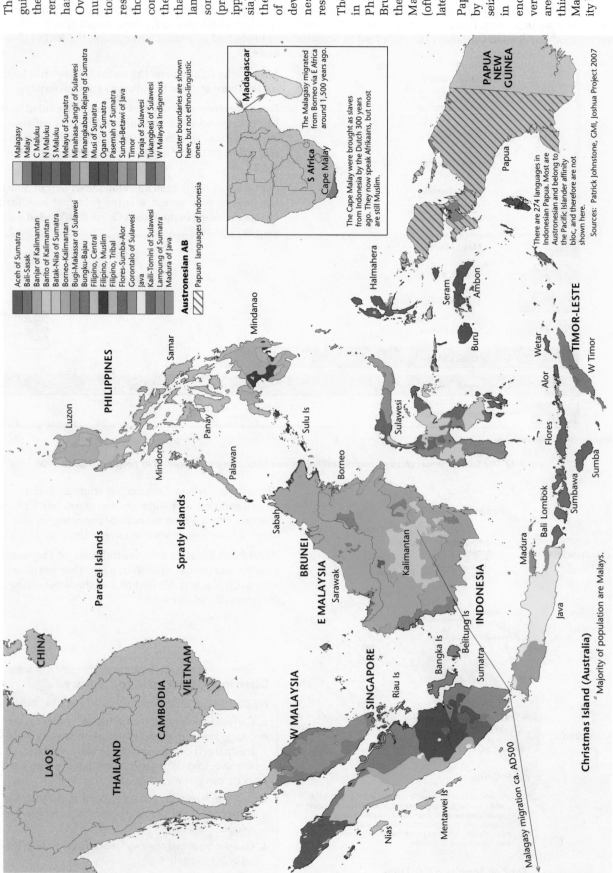

Austronesian AB
Aceh of Sumatra
Bali-Sasak
Banjar of Kalimantan
Barito of Kalimantan
Batak-Nias of Sumatra
Borneo-Kalimantan
Bugi-Makassar of Sulawesi
Bungku-Bajau
Filipino, Central
Filipino, Muslim
Filipino, Tribal
Flores-Sumba-Alor
Gorontalo of Sulawesi
Java
Kalli-Tomini of Sulawesi
Lampung of Sumatra
Madura of Java

Malagasy
Malay
C Maluku
N Maluku
S Maluku
Melayu of Sumatra
Minahasa-Sangir of Sulawesi
Minangkabau-Rejang of Sumatra
Musi of Sumatra
Ogan of Sumatra
Pasemah of Sumatra
Sunda-Betawi of Java
Timor
Toraja of Sulawesi
Tukangbesi of Sulawesi
W Malaysia Indigenous

Cluster boundaries are shown here, but not ethno-linguistic ones.

Papuan languages of Indonesia

The Malagasy migrated from Borneo via E Africa around 1,500 years ago.

The Cape Malay were brought as slaves from Indonesia by the Dutch 300 years ago. They now speak Afrikaans, but most are still Muslim.

Madagascar

S Africa
Cape Malay

There are 274 languages in Indonesian Papua. Most are Austronesian and belong to the Pacific Islander affinity bloc, and therefore are not shown here.

Sources: Patrick Johnstone, GMI, Joshua Project 2007

CHINA
LAOS
THAILAND
CAMBODIA
VIETNAM
W MALAYSIA
SINGAPORE
Paracel Islands
Spratly Islands
PHILIPPINES
Luzon
Samar
Mindoro
Panay
Palawan
Sulu Is
Mindanao
Sabah
BRUNEI
E MALAYSIA
Sarawak
Borneo
Kalimantan
Halmahera
Seram
Ambon
Buru
Sulawesi
INDONESIA
Bangka Is
Belitung Is
Riau Is
Sumatra
Nias
Mentawei Is
Java
Madura
Bali Lombok
Sumbawa
Sumba
Flores
Alor
Wetar
W Timor
TIMOR-LESTE
Papua
PAPUA NEW GUINEA

Malagasy migration ca. AD500

Christmas Island (Australia)
" Majority of population are Malays.

Seafarers

The Malay peoples live mainly on islands or peninsulas. They are one of the greatest seafaring races on earth, whose ancestors came from the island of Taiwan and migrated south to what we now know as the Philippines, Malaysia and Indonesia. The related Malagasy peoples sailed west to the African island of Madagascar, while the Polynesians moved east across the Pacific Ocean as far as the now Chilean-ruled Easter Island. The sea (and migration across it) remains a vital part of their cultures.

Fig 7.49 shows the spread of Malay peoples at the start of the 21st Century. The African component mainly comprises the Malagasy peoples who made the amazing journey by canoe across the Indian Ocean to mainland Africa and then Madagascar about 1,500 years ago. The Malagasy are mixed Malay and African, but their language is closest to Barito, spoken today in central Kalimantan. Those in Latin America (Suriname) and S Africa are primarily descended from slaves and indentured labourers taken from the E Indies in the 17th–19th Centuries by the Dutch, who ruled those islands until they became independent as Indonesia in 1945. Malay peoples in EuNAPa are primarily economic migrants.

The four pies in Fig 7.50 represent four key Malay populations. Expatriate populations of these countries come from their often over-populated island homelands. In Indonesia and the Philippines, underdevelopment and endemic corruption have hindered economic growth. Filipinos have scattered across the world, with communities in more than 55 countries on every continent, while Indonesians have generally sought work in neighbouring Singapore and Malaysia. In Malaysia, Malays have benefited from economic progress (in contrast to the large, mobile Chinese community) and emigration has been on a smaller scale.

Indonesian transmigration was a massive social experiment begun by the Dutch and was resumed by the Indonesian government in 1979. In the latter period, more than 2.5 million people were moved from crowded Java, Bali, Lombok and Madura to the less densely populated Sumatra, Kalimantan and, latterly, Irian Jaya/Papua. Java-Madura constitutes 7% of Indonesia's territory but has 60% of its population. The policy was not a great success. Many of the areas settled do not have the same fertile volcanic soil as Java, and

serious social problems arose between the indigenous peoples and the new arrivals. In Papua, it was an obvious attempt also to forestall any demand for independence and it has led to serious oppression and to overexploitation of the island's resources. New "transmigrants" now number about 60,000 a year.

The nautical character of the Malay peoples is reflected in the statistics for seafarers in Fig 7.51. These figures, based on UN statistics,[24] include only people involved in international shipping. Over a quarter of all seafarers, both officers and crew, are Filipinos, and the Malay peoples account for more than one-third (though they constitute only about 5% of the world's population). Here we have both a large mission field in itself and a possible recruiting ground for missions and church planting among them.[25] With their high standards of education and their fluency in English, Filipinos could excel as evangelists.

This also highlights the need to use ships in evangelizing and discipling people on the thousands of isolated islands in these vast archipelagos. There are many islands in E Indonesia where the population has been nominally Christian for centuries but the church buildings today stand empty.

Languages and evangelization

The increasing use of the national languages Indonesian, Malay and Tagalog (the principal indigenous language of the Philippines), inhibits evangelism and Bible translation in the many local languages and dialects. Evangelizing and discipling adequately all the peoples of these people clusters is a major challenge.

We can praise God for the strong, indigenous Church in each country of the Malay world, but often this is limited to particular people clusters such as the Chinese, the Batak, the Javanese, the Toraja or the Timorese. Visas are now much harder for foreigners to obtain and therefore much of the pioneer work has to be done by nationals—but they, too, have big cultural and religious obstacles to overcome.

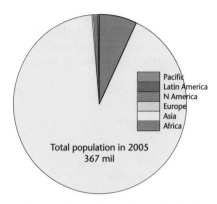

Fig 7.49 *The continental spread of Malay peoples*

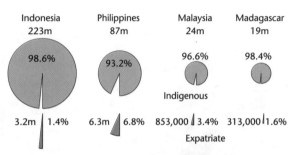

Fig 7.50 *Malay affinity bloc indigenous and expatriate populations in 2005*

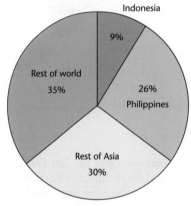

The number of registered seafarers in 2005 was 1,347,000. Of all the seararers in international shipping, 65% were from Asia.

Fig 7.51 *The world's seafarers*

Burning Question for Today

In each Malay-majority country there is a large, lively Christian Church, and yet Islamism has reared its ugly head in Malaysia, Brunei, Indonesia and, in the Philippines, in S Mindanao. In Indonesia, many churches have been destroyed.

▲ How can local Christians be effective and winsome in their witness in these negative situations?

The map below illustrates the remarkable contrasts within the Malay world, both on individual islands and within particular people clusters. Much of the Philippines, Timor-Leste and Flores in E Indonesia have had a Catholic majority for centuries, and much of northern Sulawesi and E Indonesia have had a Protestant one just as long. Nonetheless, vast areas have been scarcely exposed to the Gospel if at all. Meanwhile, Islam has extended its influence further east and has deepened its roots.

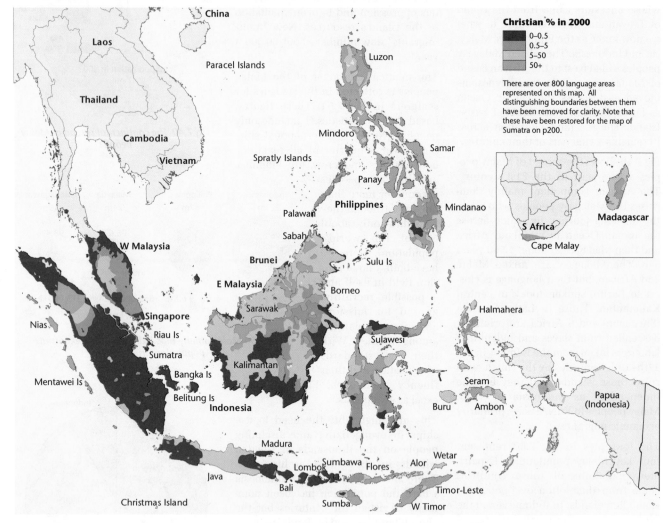

Fig 7.52 The Malay people groups and their evangelization

The response. Over the last century, it has been the tribal peoples of the Philippines, Borneo/Kalimantan, Sulawesi and W Malaysia who have responded most strongly. There have been significant revivals and people movements among the Javanese, W Timorese and tribal peoples in E Malaysia and the Philippines since 1965, and there has also been much evangelical church growth among Filipinos and Indonesian Chinese. Among Muslims the response has been mixed, with the Gospel having the greatest impact among the Javanese, who practise a folk Islam. However, persistent, fervent evangelism by Indonesian Christian missionaries is bearing more fruit among some other peoples and the number of believers from a Muslim background has increased across Indonesia. Persecution has, sadly, become an ever-growing problem, involving both discrimination and violence. Many Muslims are also dismayed by this development.

The challenges. The darker areas on the map identify the greatest need. These are:

▲ *the coastal areas of Malaysia and the larger islands of Indonesia*, where many people speak Malay and are fervent Muslims

▲ *W Java*, where the Banten and Sunda peoples have shown little response

▲ *E Java*, where the Madura people have shown considerable hostility to anything Christian

▲ *parts of Sulawesi*—especially the Buginese in the southwest of the island and the Gorontalo in the north

▲ *Bali*, whose people have remained ardently committed to Hinduism (once the religion of most Sumatrans and Javanese) and few have responded to the claims of Christ

▲ *Brunei*, the tiny, oil-rich, strongly Muslim state on the northern coast of Borneo, where all forms of witness are illegal

▲ *parts of E Maluku*, where there has been some Muslim violence against the Christian majority.

Timor-Leste (E Timor) became an independent country only in 1999, after 25 years of brutal Indonesian occupation. It is nominally Catholic, but most of its 19 indigenous peoples are ignorant of the Gospel.

Mindanao and the Sulu Islands are the least evangelized parts of the Philippines. Many of their tribal peoples are responding; the Muslim areas are the neediest but are restive and suffer from Islamist guerrilla warfare.

There are 33 people clusters in the Malay Peoples affinity bloc. Most are specific to countries or larger groups of islands in the region, so I have put them into nine geographical groups in the bar chart and the table. Below is a brief description of some of the challenges for the 21st Century.[26] The seven people clusters of Sumatra are examined on pages 200–01.

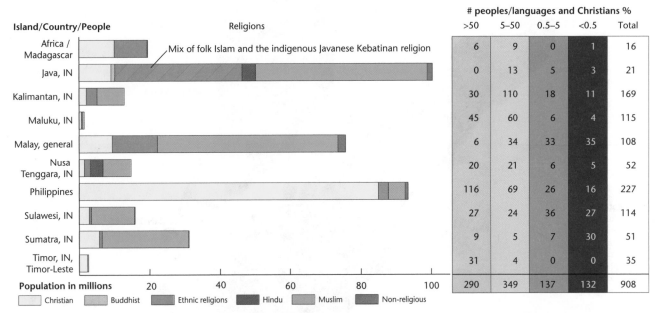

Island/Country/People	Religions	# peoples/languages and Christians %				
		>50	5–50	0.5–5	<0.5	Total
Africa / Madagascar	Mix of folk Islam and the indigenous Javanese Kebatinan religion	6	9	0	1	16
Java, IN		0	13	5	3	21
Kalimantan, IN		30	110	18	11	169
Maluku, IN		45	60	6	4	115
Malay, general		6	34	33	35	108
Nusa Tenggara, IN		20	21	6	5	52
Philippines		116	69	26	16	227
Sulawesi, IN		27	24	36	27	114
Sumatra, IN		9	5	7	30	51
Timor, IN, Timor-Leste		31	4	0	0	35
Population in millions 20 40 60 80 100		290	349	137	132	908

☐ Christian ☐ Buddhist ☐ Ethnic religions ☐ Hindu ☐ Muslim ☐ Non-religious

Fig 7.53 *Malay people clusters—their religious affiliation and state of evangelization in 2008*

Africa: The highland Malagasy have been Christian for over a century, and have experienced periods of revival. Some of the coastal peoples are less evangelized, and the northeast of Madagascar is more strongly Muslim.

Java: The Javanese have generally been quite responsive—many follow the traditional ethnic religion, Kebatinan, but they are officially classified as Muslims. Among the Sundanese and Banten in the west and the Madurese in the northeast there are only a few thousand evangelical believers. The Tengger peoples of E Java are largely Hindu.

Malays have settled around the coasts of *E and S Sumatra, Kalimantan* and other parts of Indonesia. Little has been done to evangelize them and their response has been minimal. The Malay of Brunei are among the least reached peoples on earth.

Borneo-Kalimantan: The inland Dayak and Barito tribal peoples have responded to the Gospel, but many in both the Malaysian and the Indonesian parts of the island still hold to their ethnic religions.

Nusa Tenggara is the province of Indonesia east of Java that includes Bali (largely Hindu), Lombok and Sumbawa (Muslim), Flores (Catholic) and Sumba and Wetar (Protestant). There are few Evangelicals in these islands, and many of the Christians are nominal. About 1% of the Balinese are Christians, but there are few, if any, groups of believers among the Bali Malay, Bima, Sasak and Sumbawa peoples, and few people are seeking to reach them.

The Philippines: Filipinos were Catholicized assiduously during the centuries of Spanish rule. Over the last century, Protestant mission work has made great headway among tribal peoples and has also won many Catholics to a personal faith. Now, 92% of the population are Christians, including 12% who are Evangelicals. There are still less-evangelized tribal peoples in Luzon and Mindanao, but the greatest challenge remains the Muslim areas of Mindanao, the Sulu Islands and Palawan. The Muslims there number about 4.1 million in 12 people groups, the largest being the Maguindanao, the Maranao, the Tausug, the Sama and the Yakan. For years,

Muslims have been fighting for independence to escape Christian rule. More than 10% of Filipino Muslims are now refugees in E Malaysia.

Sulawesi has a mix of Christians and Muslims, with a large minority still unofficially following traditional religions. The principal people clusters are the Bugi (26 people groups, two of them mostly Christian and 24 Muslim-majority), the Gorontalo (5, 1 and 4), the Kaili (24, 7 and 16), the Minahasa (14, 12 and 2), the Tukangbesi (17, all Muslim) and the Toraja (15—nine Christian, five Muslim and one that practises an ethnic religion). There has recently been much persecution of Toraja Christians in central Sulawesi.

Timor: W Timor, which is part of Indonesia's Nusa Tenggara province, has been largely Protestant for four centuries. E Timor (now Timor-Leste) was ruled by the Portuguese until 1974 and is nominally Catholic, though very little evangelized.

An outdoor church service in W Indonesia (photo courtesy Langham Partnership International)

Food for Thought

Like Nigeria, Indonesia has seen great revivals and huge church growth and developed an increasing vision for missions—and yet in both countries Christians live alongside Muslim peoples who have been greatly influenced by radical Islamism, and discrimination and persecution are rife.

▲ What helpful theological perspectives and methods of witnessing to Muslims can believers elsewhere learn from the Christians in these two countries?

Sumatra—the largest unevangelized island on earth

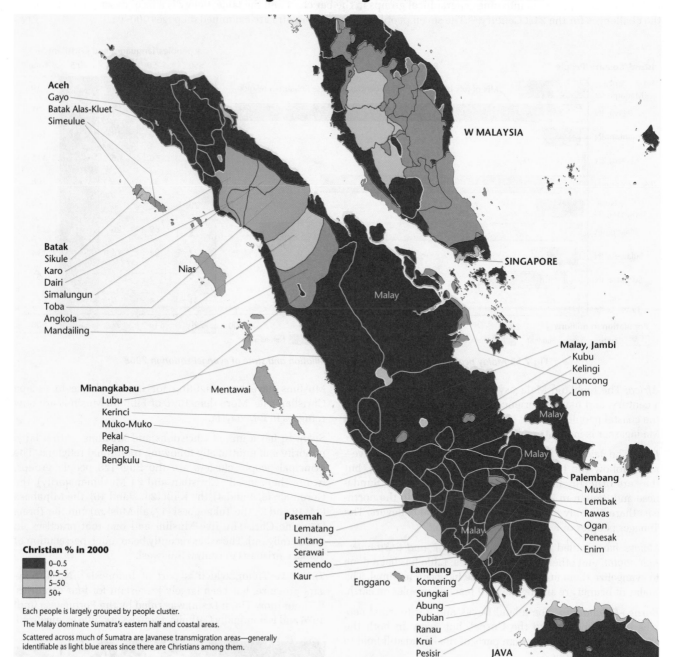

Fig 7.54 *The peoples/languages of Sumatra and their evangelization*

At 473,000 km^2 Sumatra is the world's sixth-largest island, but in terms of population it is third, with nearly 50 million people.[27] It has some 52 indigenous people groups in eight people clusters, nearly all of which are represented on the map above, which is coloured according to the percentage of each people group that is Christian. The contrasts are striking.

The Christianized areas stand out clearly. Here, Christians constitute some 10–12% of the population, and they are in a majority among most of the Batak peoples and the peoples on the chain of islands off Sumatra's west coast. Among the Angkola and Mandailing Batak there has been a more limited response to the Good News, and there was a limited people movement among the Muslim Serawai in 1965 that did not develop. Several small tribal forest peoples, such as the Kubu and Lulu, still practise their ethnic religions, but have heard little of the Gospel.

Unevangelized peoples constitute the majority in Sumatra. Islam took root first in Aceh about 800 years ago and has

since spread gradually across Sumatra and then to much of the rest of Indonesia. It has become more deeply embedded in Sumatra than in any other part of the country. Christian missionaries have been largely confined to the non-Muslim areas of the island, and there has never been a strong witness to its Muslim peoples. There are very few believers.

Burning Question for Today

The history of Aceh is one of centuries of conflict with Dutch and British colonial powers and, since 1949, the Indonesian army (in which many Christian Batak serve)—all seeking control of its strategic position and abundant natural resources. This made the Aceh people hostile to Christianity.

▲ How can people with such a background be evangelized and discipled?

The population and religious affiliations of each of Sumatra's eight people clusters are indicated in the bar chart below. The table gives the number of people groups in each that comes into each of my four "percentage Christians" categories, which gives some indication of their level of evangelization.

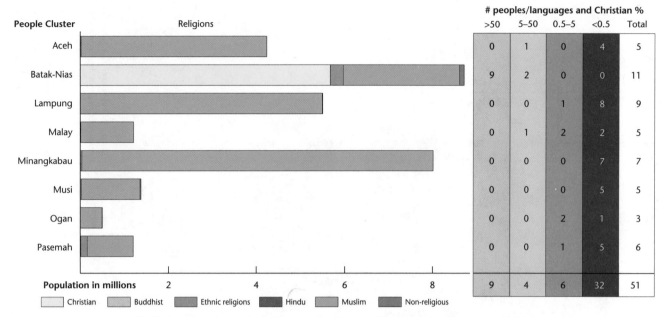

People Cluster	Religions	# peoples/languages and Christian %				
		>50	5–50	0.5–5	<0.5	Total
Aceh		0	1	0	4	5
Batak-Nias		9	2	0	0	11
Lampung		0	0	1	8	9
Malay		0	1	2	2	5
Minangkabau		0	0	0	7	7
Musi		0	0	0	5	5
Ogan		0	0	2	1	3
Pasemah		0	0	1	5	6
Population in millions	2 4 6 8	9	4	6	32	51

Christian Buddhist Ethnic religions Hindu Muslim Non-religious

Fig 7.55 *Sumatra's people clusters—their religious affiliation and state of evangelization*

Aceh: The 2004 Asian tsunami was a catastrophe which killed over 200,000 people. Most of the victims lived in Aceh. It effectively ended the decades-long uprising of the Aceh against Indonesian rule, which was then sealed by a peace agreement in 2005. Aceh gained a high degree of autonomy and today is the only part of Indonesia that has instituted *shari'a* law. There are five people groups in this cluster, but there were fewer than 400 Christians before the tsunami and most of those lived outside the province. Many Indonesian and foreign Christians came to the aid of the victims, which gained considerable credit for the Gospel. A number of conversions to Christ have been reported as a result.

The Batak live mainly in the mountainous interior of northern Sumatra. They were once known for cannibalism, and indeed the first missionaries (from the US) were killed and eaten in 1837. German Lutheran missionaries arrived in 1862 and the Toba, the Simalungun, the Dairi and later the Karo Batak became Christians. The Lutheran Rhenish Mission also evangelized the neighbouring islands of Nias and Mentawai. Today, Batak congregations can be found all over Indonesia. Only a minority of the Mandailing and Angkola are Christians, however; most are Muslims.

The Lampung: These nine peoples are almost entirely Muslim. Little mission work has ever been undertaken among any of these peoples; there are no known churches, and fewer than 200 Christians. Many Javanese transmigrants live in this area, some of whom are believers.

The Malay dominate along Sumatra's east coast and on the nearby islands Riau, Bangka and Belitung. There are fewer than 100 Christians and little witness to the Malay. The Jambi Malay people cluster is included in these statistics.

The Minangkabau-Rejang: The seven peoples in this cluster are strongly Muslim, and there are fewer than 1,600 Christians in a population of 8 million. The Minang are well known for their matriarchal society and for their commercial skills—Minang traders are found across Indonesia. The 1 million Rejang are a major unevangelized people with no known churches and only a handful of believers.

The Musi inhabit an area that includes the regional capital, Palembang, which is named after the largest people of this area. There is only a handful of Christians among these five Muslim peoples, and no indigenous churches—the many churches in Palembang serve other people groups.

The Ogan: These seven peoples live south of Palembang in southern Sumatra. They, too, are almost entirely Muslim, with just a few dozen scattered Christians.

The Pasemah are the largest of nine groups in the people cluster, with a total population of 1.2 million. There are no known Christians or churches except among the Serawai. In their case, there was a small people movement in the 1960s that was the first significant turning to Christ among Muslims ever seen in Sumatra, though, sadly, it ended not long after it began. Today, there are three churches and about 2,000 Christians among the Serawai.

Note: The numbers and assignation of people groups and languages in Indonesia, particularly in Sumatra, change as more information becomes available. For example, the language areas on page 200 were drawn a decade ago; the text on this page includes more recent information.

Food for Thought

Indonesia presents a complex mix of Gospel breakthroughs and seemingly impossible challenges. Some of the largest least-evangelized people groups in the world are here—and many of these live in Sumatra.

▲ How can missions, both national and international, engage meaningfully with these peoples who are hedged about with so many barriers to their evangelization?

People Clusters of the Persian-Median Peoples Affinity Bloc

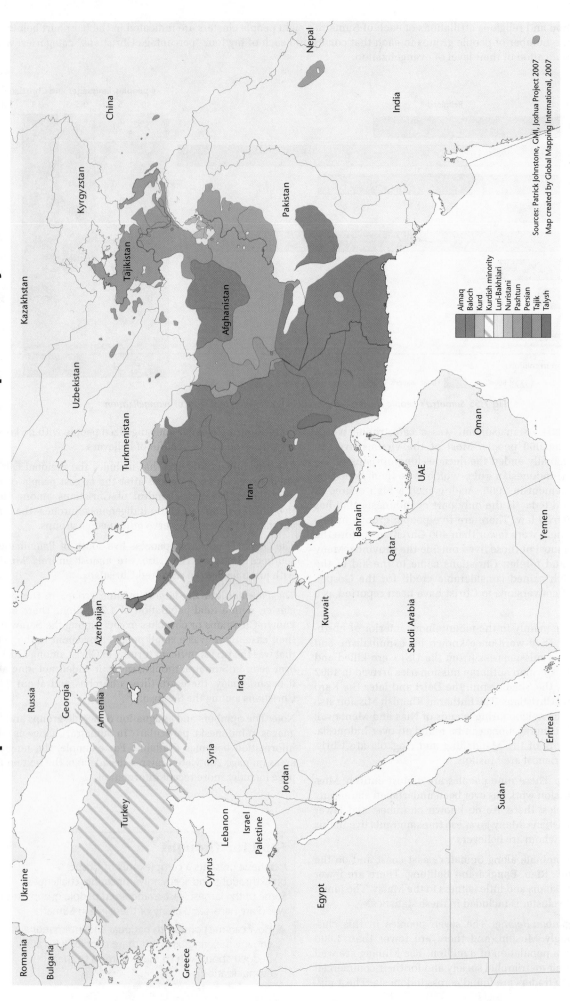

These peoples all speak related languages that have their origins some 3,500 years ago. Ten people clusters are represented on this map. Many of these peoples, such as the Persians, the Pashtun in Afghanistan and Pakistan and the Kurds in Iraq, Iran and Turkey, are much in the news today.

Historically, they have been very important. The Persians were a superpower for a millennium or more, and now Iran, under revolutionary Shi'a rule, is seeking to regain some of that ancient influence. A large proportion of these peoples were Christian before the coming of Islam, but today there are very few Christians among them.

Legend:
- Aimaq
- Baloch
- Kurd
- Kurdish minority
- Luri-Bakhtiari
- Nuristani
- Pashtun
- Persian
- Tajik
- Talysh

Sources: Patrick Johnstone, GMI, Joshua Project 2007
Map created by Global Mapping International, 2007

The bar chart in Fig 7.56 indicates the population and religious affiliations of each of these people clusters, which are divided into those people groups living in their homelands and those that have emigrated to other parts of the world.

The table shows that, apart from 23 Persian people groups which are more than 5% Christian, all of these peoples fall into the category "least evangelized". Nearly all are nominally Muslim, though this has to be qualified (see p205).

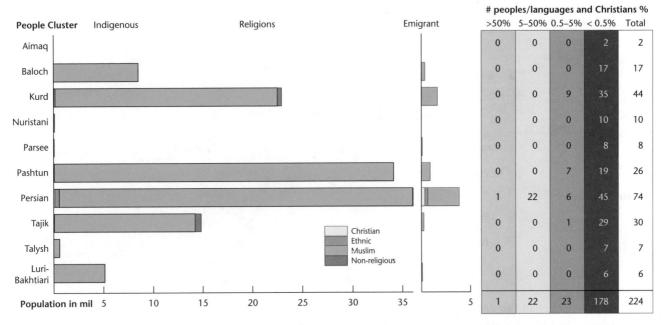

People Cluster	# peoples/languages and Christians %				
	>50%	5–50%	0.5–5%	< 0.5%	Total
Aimaq	0	0	0	2	2
Baloch	0	0	0	17	17
Kurd	0	0	9	35	44
Nuristani	0	0	0	10	10
Parsee	0	0	0	8	8
Pashtun	0	0	7	19	26
Persian	1	22	6	45	74
Tajik	0	0	1	29	30
Talysh	0	0	0	7	7
Luri-Bakhtiari	0	0	0	6	6
	1	22	23	178	224

Legend (bar chart): Christian, Ethnic, Muslim, Non-religious

Population in mil: 5 10 15 20 25 30 35 5

Fig 7.56 *Persian-Median people clusters—their religious affiliation and state of evangelization in 2008*

Fig 7.57 represents the response of these people clusters to the Gospel, both in their homelands and abroad. Their homelands are a difficult environment for any form of Christian witness, foreign or indigenous. However, the decades of war and social upheaval in the Middle East and Afghanistan have led to an exodus of millions fleeing persecution, tyranny and economic hardship, and in the lands where they have taken refuge a growing number of these people have sought and found in Christ the answers to their deepest needs. These figures are only estimates, as a census of Christians would be impossible, and possibly dangerous. However among the Aimaq, Baloch, Nuristani, Talysh and Luri-Bakhtiari there are no churches and maybe just a handful of believers.

Fig 7.58 represents the percentage of Christians in each of these people clusters. Most notable is the reaction of Iranians to the Shi'a Islamist revolution of 1979 and the wars and oppression that followed it—many became open to the Christian Gospel. Some observ-

ers claim that large numbers in Iran have come to Christ and little house churches are multiplying there, despite persecution and even the death penalty for those discovered to have converted. The bigger response, however, has been among those who have emigrated. There are now networks of Persian-speaking churches across the free world. Electronic evangelism via the internet, mobile phones and satellite TV has played a significant role.

Iranian women in a shop
(photo courtesy OM International)

Indigenous Christians est 170,000

Emigrant Christians est 360,000

Legend: Baloch, Kurd, Pashtun, Persian, Tajik

Fig 7.57 *The estimated number of Christians among indigenous and emigrant communities*

Fig 7.58 *The Christian % of indigenous and emigrant communities*

(chart) % of population — Christians: Emigrant, Indigenous — Aimaq, Baloch, Kurd, Nuristani, Parsee, Pashtun, Persian, Tajik, Talysh, Luri

The Kurds

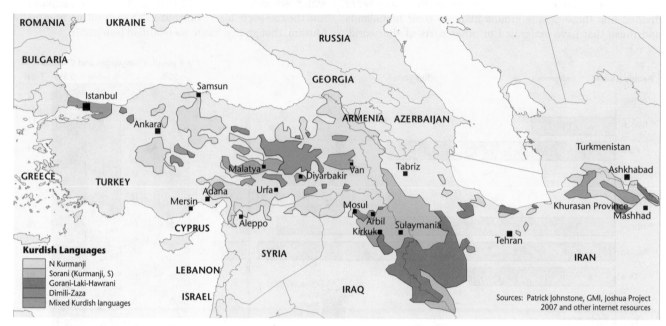

Fig 7.59 *Languages of the Kurdish people cluster*

From the Persian-Median Peoples affinity bloc, I have chosen to examine the Kurds because of their widely publicized struggles for political freedom and also their spiritual need.[28]

The Kurds are a mountain people with a history extending back many millennia. They are the descendants of many different peoples, but notably the Hurrians,[29] Medes and Scythians. The geographical distribution of their languages and widely differing dialects reflects their complexity, as the map bears witness. There are four main languages, but more than 45 recognized ethnic subgroups. The Joshua Project lists 12 people groups scattered across 35 countries. Their population numbers are a sensitive political issue: here we suggest 31 million, but there may be a further 5–15 million ethnic Kurds now speaking Turkish, Persian or Arabic.[30]

After the First World War, the victorious British and French failed to keep their promise to create a Kurdish state following the collapse of the Ottoman Empire, and in the 1923 Treaty of Lausanne the Kurdish homelands were carved up between Turkey, Iran, Iraq and Syria. Each of these countries now has its own Kurdish separatist movement, which has resulted in uprisings and wars to this day. The current, long-standing conflict between Turkey and its Kurdish separatists and the debacle in Iraq where Arabs and Kurds are both claiming control of the cities of Kirkuk and Mosul and their oilfields are examples.

The pie chart indicates the likely numbers of Kurds in the four main countries whose borders take in what might have been the state of Kurdistan. Each of their governments has its own reasons to downplay the size and influence of their large Kurdish minorities. Generally, their policy has been to try to enforce the assimilation of the Kurds into their majority communities. Many Kurds have moved to other countries to escape political and religious oppression, or else to better their economic prospects. Those who remain tend to be poorer than their compatriots, as a result of both the difficult terrain of their lands and its underdevelopment. The "exploded" part of the pie represents the regions of the world where emigrant Kurds live today. There are probably 2–3 million people in this diaspora, though many are classified as Arab, Turkish or Iranian on account of

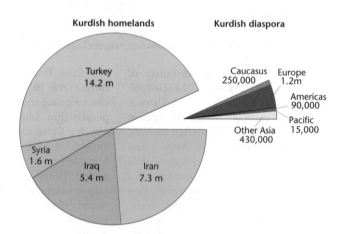

Fig 7.60 *The Kurdish homelands populations*

their country of origin. Some Kurds living in the West have become involved in either nationalist or Islamist terrorism.

A modern Kurdish ethnicity is now emerging as a result of present-day communications and population movements. The older diversity of language and dialect is giving way to the widespread use of Kurmanji, which ties in with the decline of the old Kurdish religion and a stronger Muslim identity. Great Kurdish leaders of the past include the Muslim leader Saladin (Salah-ad-Din), the victor over the Crusaders in the 12th Century who became the ruler of much of the heartlands of the Islamic world.

The Kurds and Christianity. The apostle Andrew was probably the first evangelist to the Kurds. Many of them in time became Orthodox Christians, and in some areas Christians were actually in a majority. After the arrival of Islam, the Kurds gradually became Muslims, but a few remnants of the old Christian population survived into the 19th Century. Today, a number of Kurds in both Turkey and post-Saddam Iraq have become evangelical Christians. There are now Kurdish congregations in Iraq, while elsewhere Kurdish Christians meet in Turkish or Persian churches.

Fig 7.61 gives a breakdown of the Kurdish population by language and people group regardless of national boundaries. The column at the side shows the number of people groups, which here includes each country where they have a presence.

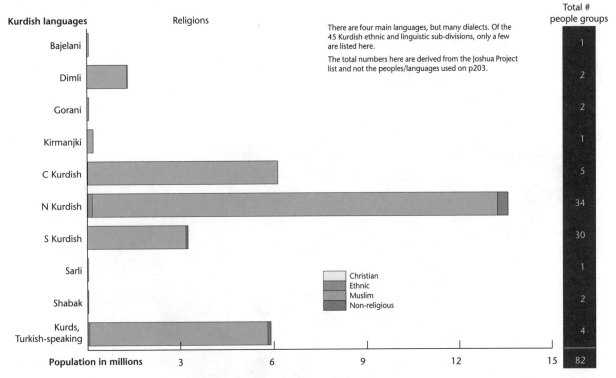

Fig 7.61 *Kurdish peoples—their religious affiliations and state of evangelization*

The overwhelming majority of Kurds would call themselves Muslim, but over a quarter of them still adhere to either their original ancient religious beliefs or a more modern version of them. Christians are very few in number, and all Kurdish people groups fall into the category "least evangelized".

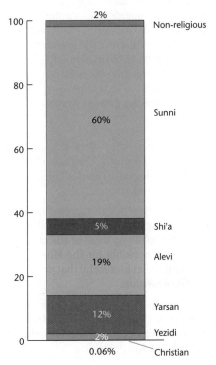

Fig 7.62 *Religions of the Kurdish peoples*

The main religious groupings are:

▲ *The non-religious*, who constitute a small, passionate and vocal minority whose perception is that the Kurds are victims of religion, which has brought them nothing but hatred and war. Given that they live on the fault-line between, in the past, the Orthodox and Muslims and, today, the Sunni and the Shi'a, this is not hard to understand.

▲ *The Sunni* make up the majority of all Kurds.

While nominal adherence to Islam is common, that is not the whole picture, for Sunni Islam is growing, often at the expense of other groups:

▲ *The Shi'a* are not numerous, but are concentrated mainly in Shi'a-dominated Iran (with some also in Iraq). However, many of the fringe Muslim groups listed below would align themselves loosely with Shi'ism.

▲ Most "fringe" groups are influenced by pre-Islamic, pre-Christian religious beliefs known as *Yardanism*. Many of these groups have links to Muslim Sufi orders but are highly syncretic. All are in gradual decline.

▲ *The Alevi* live mostly in Turkey (where up to 25% of the populace, including many Kurds, adhere to this deviant form of Islam) or Syria.

▲ *The Yarsan* live mainly in Iraq and western Iran. They believe in the transmigration of the soul and practise many non-Muslim rituals.

▲ *The Yezidis* are concentrated in northern Iraq, though many have fled north to the Caucasus republics, where they now make up a large part of the Kurdish population. Many others have migrated to the West. They are syncretic, and not really Muslim at all. They have been classified as an ethnic religion in this book.

▲ *Christians* now make up an insignificant part of Kurdish society.

Burning Question for Today

▲ How can the Kurds be evangelized despite the challenges presented by geography, history and their minority status in countries already hostile to any form of Christian witness?

There was a time when many Kurds were Christians, but it took nearly 2,000 years for the first translation of the Bible into their language to be published.

▲ Who will take the Kurds to heart?

People Clusters of the S Asian Peoples Affinity Bloc

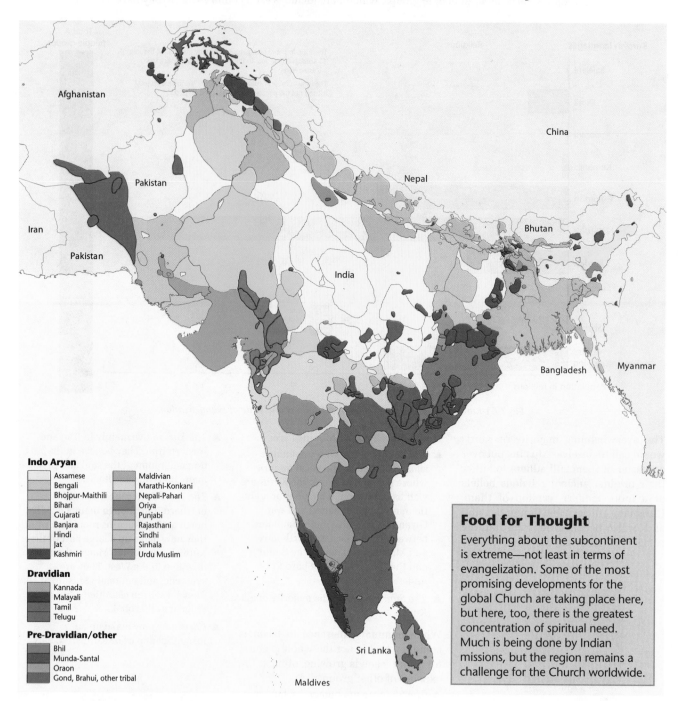

Indo Aryan

Assamese	Maldivian
Bengali	Marathi-Konkani
Bhojpur-Maithili	Nepali-Pahari
Bihari	Oriya
Gujarati	Punjabi
Banjara	Rajasthani
Hindi	Sindhi
Jat	Sinhala
Kashmiri	Urdu Muslim

Dravidian

Kannada
Malayali
Tamil
Telugu

Pre-Dravidian/other

Bhil
Munda-Santal
Oraon
Gond, Brahui, other tribal

Food for Thought

Everything about the subcontinent is extreme—not least in terms of evangelization. Some of the most promising developments for the global Church are taking place here, but here, too, there is the greatest concentration of spiritual need. Much is being done by Indian missions, but the region remains a challenge for the Church worldwide.

The greatest challenge for world evangelization is presented probably by the peoples of the S Asian affinity bloc. It has more unevangelized individuals and people groups than any other region of the world, and yet in some segments of its societies the Church is growing vigorously. Its ethnic, linguistic, religious and social complexity defies representation on a map such as this. Overshadowing all is the pervasive caste system that blights India and Nepal especially. The aspect I shall focus on here is language.

People clusters are based mainly on ethnic origin, language and (to an extent) religion. It is helpful to see the sub-continent in this way, but we need a three-dimensional model that also incorporates caste— a classification that still needs further refinement.[31]

There are three main groupings of S Asian clusters:

The pre-Dravidian/tribal clusters principally comprise tribal peoples, together with a few others not yet categorized. This map represents most accurately tribal peoples such as the Bhil, Gond etc, as they are not part of the Hindu caste system.

The Dravidian peoples were probably the second major wave of settlers in India, and today they constitute a majority in the south. The main clusters are the Malayam-, Tamil-, Telugu- and Kannada-speakers.

The Indo-Aryan peoples arrived in India from the northwest about 3,000 years ago. They make up most of the clusters, and are responsible for the Hindu religion and social hierarchy that dominate the whole region.

The grey areas on the map show where peoples of other affinity blocs (mainly Persian-Median, Tibetan-Himalayan and SE Asian peoples) live.

The map in Fig 7.63 illustrates the extent to which S Asian peoples have responded to Christianity. The figures behind it are based on the 2001 government census, though these are manifestly an undercount[32] as most new Christians now come from lower castes. The Dalit-Bahujan protest against Hindu oppression has been a factor in many becoming Christians, but Christian Dalits lose many of their constitutional privileges and so it is not in the interests of those who convert to declare it to the government.

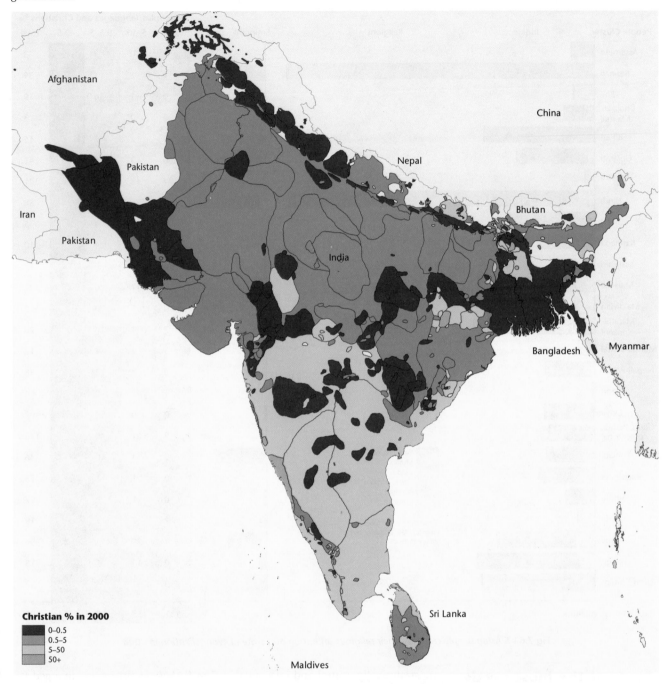

Christian % in 2000
- 0–0.5
- 0.5–5
- 5–50
- 50+

Fig 7.63 *The S Asian peoples and their evangelization*

The successes (note the orange and light blue areas) are:

▲ With an almost-2,000-year history in India, *Orthodox Christians* now make up 19% of the population of Kerala. Most speak Malayam. They have been at the core of the expansion of Christianity in India in recent centuries.

▲ *The Catholic advances of the 16th Century* were largely in the southwest.. The orange areas on the coast are a reflection of this. Catholics officially constitute 1.55% of India's population. About 10% of India's Catholics are Charismatics.

▲ *The Protestant Church* arrived in the 18th Century and flourished mostly in the south of India; but later spread to the north, where it has seen a lot of growth in tribal areas and in Punjab.

▲ *Independent and pentecostal churches* have multiplied over the past 30 years, almost all of them among tribal peoples and Dalits. Most of this growth is the fruit of work by indigenous evangelists and missionaries.

The challenges (note the darker areas) are:

▲ *The less evangelized plains and cities in the north*

▲ *The Muslim clusters* in Pakistan, the plains of N India and the Deccan Plateau in the south

▲ *The "forward" castes (see p81)*, with 50 million people but probably only around 18,000 Christians

▲ *The rising middle classes*—few have been evangelized, and most see Christians as poor and largely Dalit.

The bar chart and table provide more detail on S Asian people clusters. There are some 800 people groups in this bloc, but this total is based largely on language and if ethnicity and caste as well were taken into consideration, there would be nearly 3,000. Note that well over half of the peoples listed here qualify as "less evangelized". As before, each people cluster is divided into those people groups living in their homelands and those that have emigrated to other parts of the world. Note that the population scale for the latter is 10 times that for the former.

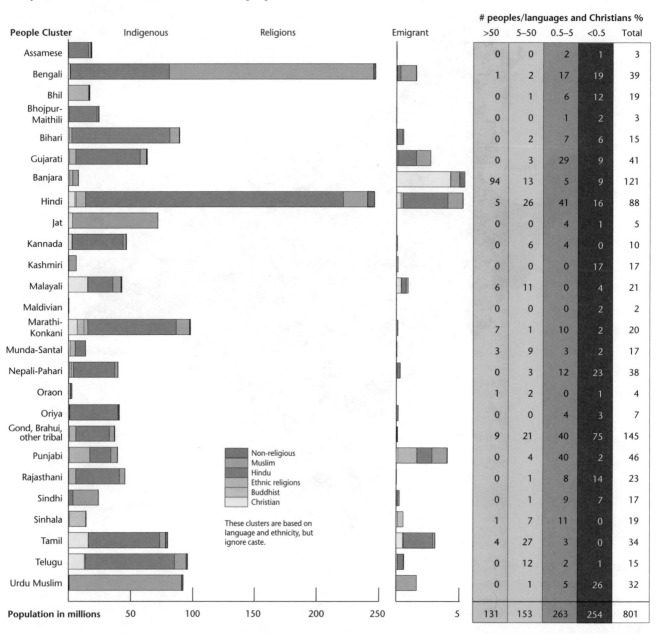

Fig 7.64 S Asian people clusters—their religious affiliation and state of evangelization in 2008

Some of the most needy people clusters

Muslims: There are Urdu-speaking Muslims all over India; most Bengalis (in India and Bangladesh) are Muslim, as are the great majority of Kashmiris, Sindhis and Jats. Nearly 30% of S Asia's population (that is, 447 million individuals) are Muslims but, even though it is comparatively easy to reach them in India, there are very few believers from a Muslim background.

Hindi-speakers represent the core of the challenge of the unevangelized. They are strategically central and influential but speak a wide range of languages and dialects. Their heartlands are in Uttar Pradesh and surrounding states. Most Indian missionaries are from non-Hindi-speaking areas of the country, which makes it harder for them to witness to Hindi speakers.

The many other Hindu-majority people clusters need to be evangelized— the Nepali, Bihari, Bhojpuri, Oriya, Rajasthani, Hindu Bengali and Gujarati of N India.

The Sinhala of Sri Lanka emerged triumphant (and militant) in 2010 after a long civil war against Tamil separatists. There are comparatively few committed believers among them.

The Maldivians of the Maldive Islands and the Indian territory of Lakshadweep are solidly Muslim, and only a handful have ever become Christians.

The Nepali-Pahari: Despite amazing church growth among Hindus of all castes in Nepal, many of these peoples are still unevangelized, both in Nepal and along the foothills of the Himalayas.

For a thousand years, the subcontinent has been a source of migrants to other parts of the world. The extent of this emigration is illustrated in Figs 7.65 and 7.66. The S Asian diaspora may even total 40 million today, if recent population movements and illegal immigration are taken into account. These communities form a strategic global network that allows a two-way flow of trade, information, technology—and the Gospel. This has big implications for the evangelization of S Asia.

Africa's Indian population is largely descended from the indentured labourers brought in by the British in the 19th Century to build railways in E Africa and harvest sugar in S Africa and Mauritius. Gujarati traders then followed.

In the Pacific and Latin America, Indians were imported for similar reasons. Their descendants now make up nearly half the population of Fiji, and more than half in Guyana and Trinidad. Many of them are now emigrating to the West, especially Australia and New Zealand.

Europe and N America: First came the Roma, and then, since 1947, economic migrants and refugees. A high percentage of the IT experts working in the US—including some brilliant scientists—are from India.

Asia: There are large communities of Indians in Malaysia and Singapore, and more recently many have sought work in the oil-producing states of the Middle East.

The table lists the 24 countries worldwide that have received most immigrants from S Asia. These have arrived in a number of waves:

Lambadi/Roma ("Gypsies") from India began migrating west a thousand years ago to the Middle East and Europe. They retain aspects of their nomadic cultures, which differ from other European cultures. Most of them became nominally Christian in Europe, or Muslim in the Ottoman Empire. In recent years, there have been people movements to Christ, especially in Spain and France—they now represent a large proportion of the Evangelicals of those two countries.

Indentured labour: The British exported labour from the subcontinent, as its then rulers, to many parts of the Empire, including Fiji, Malaya, Mauritius, E Africa, S Africa, Guyana and Trinidad. Many of these migrants went on to establish S Asian communities that contributed to the economies of these colonies (and, later, independent states). Many of these communities have now been evangelized, and churches have multiplied—especially in the Caribbean and S Africa.

Traders and businessmen also chose to migrate to many other parts of the British Empire and even further afield. This was especially true of Gujaratis and Sindhis, who became the chief traders in many countries in Africa and elsewhere. Most of their communities are Muslim or Hindu, and few have ever been reached.

Economic migrants to the West increased in number after Indian and Pakistani independence in 1947. The large numbers of S Asians in the UK (including Punjabis and Bengalis), Canada and now the US are testimony to that. Vancouver today has more Sikhs than any other city in the world.

Refugees: Worldwide, some 700,000 Tamils have fled the violence of civil war in Sri Lanka.

Illegal immigrants have multiplied in recent years, whether Bangladeshis and Pakistanis moving to the West or Nepali children being trafficked to India for the sex industry.

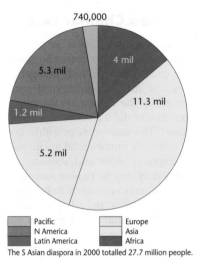

740,000
4 mil
5.3 mil
11.3 mil
1.2 mil
5.2 mil

Pacific
N America
Latin America
Europe
Asia
Africa

The S Asian diaspora in 2000 totalled 27.7 million people.

Fig 7.65 *The S Asian diaspora*

Country	Total
USA	4,136,000
Malaysia	2,230,000
UK	2,082,000
Pakistan	1,870,000
S Africa	1,440,000
Saudi Arabia	1,404,000
Canada	1,194,000
Myanmar	1,185,000
UAE	966,000
Bangladesh	791,000
Spain	684,000
Mauritius	592,000
Hungary	550,000
Brazil	514,000
Oman	463,000
Tanzania	428,000
Fiji	379,000
Uganda	325,000
Egypt	311,000
Kenya	286,000
Singapore	286,000
Germany	235,000
Australia	233,000
Yemen	231,000

Fig 7.66 *The top 24 receiving countries for S Asians*

Food For Thought

Strong anti-foreign sentiment highlights the urgent need for indigenous missionaries.

All the expatriate communities mentioned on this page present opportunities to reach the people clusters they belong to—they can plant churches among them after becoming evangelized in their receiving countries and then being sent as missionaries to their lands of origin. Moreover, many S Asians in the UK and N America are now among the wealthiest people in their adopted countries.

▲ How well does the Church in the top receiving countries understand the importance of their immigrant communities for the evangelization of the world?

Burning Question for Today

Hindutva nationalists want to eliminate all "foreign" religions in India. Islam and Christianity are their main targets—and yet the latter has been part of Indian culture for nearly two millennia.

▲ How can Christians and their churches become more Indian in their worship and witness so that they can be recognized as truly belonging to their land?

India's Chamar caste

The caste system. This is so pervasive in India that it simply cannot be ignored if the country is to be fully evangelized. Its origins are fiercely disputed—was it imposed by the Aryans on the original population or did it evolve out of a tribal culture? The answer is probably both. The system is fundamental to Hinduism and imposed order and stability on a rural society, but its rigidity and unfairness are a brake on modern India's social, political, economic and religious development.[33] The country's constitution guarantees equality for all. Affirmative action and job reservation for the underprivileged have sought to redress what is, in effect, a form of religiously sanctioned *apartheid*. Modernization, urbanization and education have weakened its hold, but it is still a powerful fact of social life. Other religions such as Sikhism, Islam and Christianity have all sought to abolish the caste system but often have ended up conforming to it. Here, I take as an example one of the most influential "scheduled" castes, the Chamar.

The Chamar. These people were traditionally leather-workers, though today many are farmers. Upper-caste Hindus consider them unclean. They are the second-largest caste in India, with a population of more than 45 million. There are many subdivisions.

Some 64% speak one of the many variants of Hindi, but 60 other languages also serve as their mother tongue—7% speak Bhojpuri, 2.5% Chhattisgarhi, 2.2% Punjabi etc. Castes straddle language boundaries, and people's attachment to their caste is more important than their language.

As Fig 7.67 shows, their heartlands are in N India, and especially the states of Uttar Pradesh (where they make up 14% of population), Madhya Pradesh (10%), Chhattisgarh (9%), Haryana (9%) and Punjab (11%).

The Chamar have gained considerable influence through important Chamar leaders and, as a result of democracy, some political power.[34] The state of Uttar Pradesh was won in 2007 by the largely Dalit *Bahujan Samaj Party*, which was led by a Chamar woman, Mayawati. Chamars also are in the forefront of the movement to liberate the 300 million poor Dalits and Bahujan—the backward castes—from Hindu casteism. One of the defining issues in the 21st Century will be how India changes under pressure from this protest movement and how it develops both politically and in its religious affiliations.

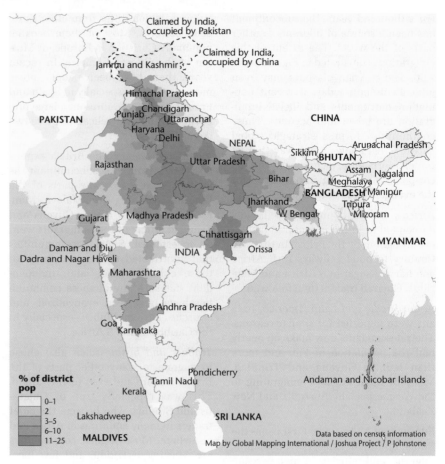

Fig 7.67 *Distribution of the Chamars*

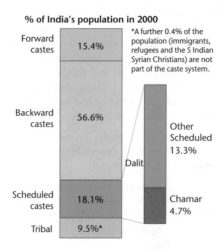

Fig 7.68 *The position of the Chamars in the caste system in India*

The Chamar have set the pace in challenging the caste system and will probably continue to do so as the 21st Century unfolds.

The caste system and the Chamars. The larger bar in Fig 7.68 represents the broad divisions in Indian society. There are about 4,700 castes (or *varna*, which means "colour"), and 25,000 sub-castes or *jati* ("birth lineage").

The "forward" castes include the traditional three main divisions of Brahmins (priests), Kshatriyas (warriors) and Vaishyas (merchants). Below these are

Food For Thought

The British Raj saw in the caste system a reflection of the UK's own class structure and reinforced its rigidity as a means both of understanding India and of controlling its population. Caste was an item in some of the 10-yearly censuses, which conferred some respectability on the system.

▲ Do Christians unwittingly support and perpetuate such a system, which the Gospel should dismantle, in the way we research, strategize and plant churches along caste lines?

a fourth, the servant Sudras or "backward" castes—though the upper levels of Sudras are increasingly treated differently as a "creamy layer".

Beneath them all are those that were never part of the caste system and were considered "untouchable"—now called "Dalits"—who have now been incorporated into the Hindu system by law as "scheduled castes".

The tribal peoples are not regarded as part of the caste system, though Hinduists seek to woo them to their cause.

The Chamars and Christianity. Fig 7.69 shows the distribution of Christians in absolute numbers by district across the countries of the region. Hitherto outreach to Chamars has been sporadic and localized. As the 2001 census figures suggest, there are areas where there had been a significant response by 2000—notably in Uttar Pradesh, W Bengal, Chhattisgarh, Punjab etc. The prevailing Hinduist discrimination (and even persecution) against Christians means that official statistics are likely to be lower than the true total. In recent years, the number of Indian evangelists and missionaries serving among Chamars has increased and so has the response. The potential for rapid church growth is great and if there were such a response, its impact on both this and other castes would probably be significant. Less has been done to reach Chamars in Pakistan, southern Nepal and Bangladesh.

Other religions. Most Chamars are Hindus, but they worship their own particular gods and in general are excluded from higher-caste temples, but still join in many of the celebrations and rites of Hinduism. The burgeoning Dalit-Bahujan movement for their emancipation is causing many Chamars to question their affiliation to Hinduism—is their traditional religion even Hindu at all? Census assessments have assumed (in order to boost Hindu statistics) that anyone who doesn't practise a minority religion is automatically a Hindu.

As part of the protest against the centuries of Hindu oppression, increasing numbers are turning to other religions—Christianity and Buddhism especially, but also Islam. All three offer the chance to be part of a casteless community.

The early great leader of the protest movement was Dr B R Ambedkar, who himself converted to Buddhism. Since 2000, there have been some public mass conversions to Buddhism. There have been many who have become Christians too. These are not reflected in the statistics cited here. Unlike those who officially become Christians, those who embrace Buddhism do not lose their legal privileges as Dalits (in terms of reserved jobs and aid). This movement to Buddhism is likely to gain momentum in future decades.

The Chamars present one of the major hopeful prospects for church planting in the 21st Century.

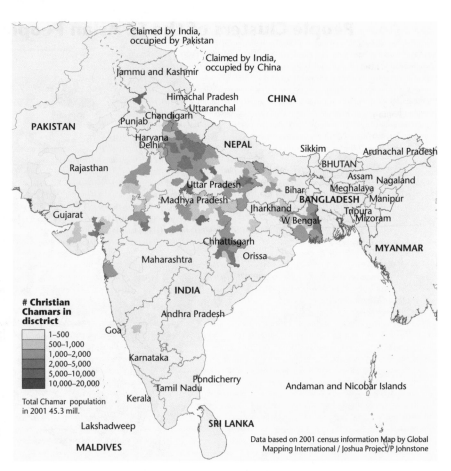

Fig 7.69 *The distribution of the Chamars*

Casteism and the future

The countries of S Asia are in a state of massive flux. Not the least of the issues is the future of casteism in India, which suffocates its society. Will it adapt and survive in the country's race to become a modern industrial and IT giant—and if so, how? With all the oppression, corruption and social rigidity it imposes, casteism is one of the strongest brakes on such progress. Some observers think it is possible that 300 million of the lower and scheduled castes may renounce Hinduism in this generation. How would that be handled by the government, by Hinduists and by Buddhist and Christian religious leaders? Are churches ready to cope with such an influx?

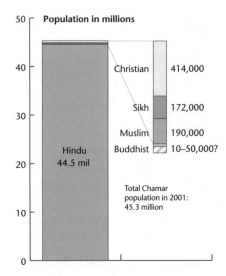

Fig 7.70 *The religious affiliations of the Chamars*

Burning Question for Today

Most of the response to Christ in India has been among the disadvantaged. The more privileged castes, the political elites and the rising middle classes all associate Christianity with the poor and have very little exposure to the Gospel.

The background and culture of most Indian missionaries give them readier access to the tribal peoples and the less privileged.

▲ How will the more privileged castes be evangelized?

People Clusters of the SE Asian Peoples Affinity Bloc

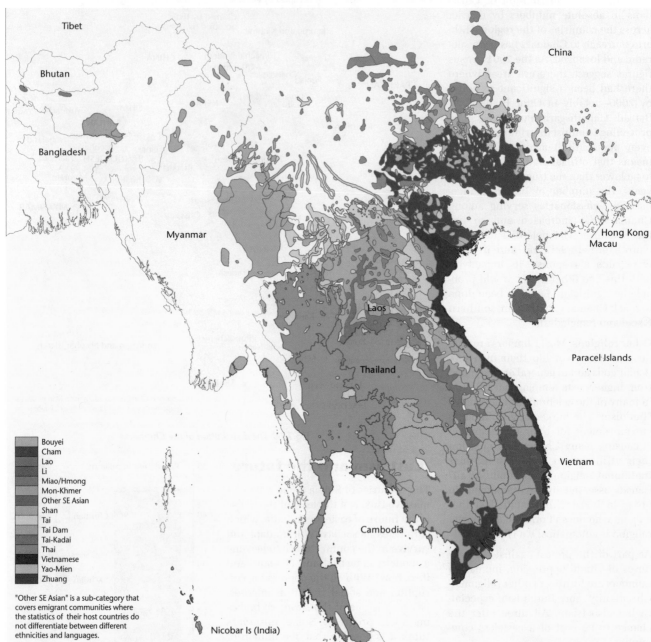

Bouyei
Cham
Lao
Li
Miao/Hmong
Mon-Khmer
Other SE Asian
Shan
Tai
Tai Dam
Tai-Kadai
Thai
Vietnamese
Yao-Mien
Zhuang

"Other SE Asian" is a sub-category that
covers emigrant communities where
the statistics of their host countries do
not differentiate between different
ethnicities and languages.

The origins of the principal ethnic groups of SE Asia and the interactions between them are complex—as the medley of peoples and clusters shown on this map suggests. Included here are the major language families of the Tai (the Thai of Thailand being the largest), the Mon-Khmer (the Khmer Cambodians being the largest), the Hmong (of northern Laos and S China) and the Vietnamese. The Thai, Khmer, Lao and Vietnamese all live in the fertile lowlands, while many smaller peoples have migrated and settled in the many less fertile mountains. Many apparent gaps have been settled by Tibeto-Burman peoples (see p216).

The populations of SE Asia probably originated in Taiwan, China and Indonesia. In earlier centuries, there were strong influences from India (which has given the region its principal religions, Hinduism and, later, Buddhism, and their original written scripts). China's population pressure and its political and economic power have driven many ethnic groups to migrate south into this region. For much of its history, Vietnam has periodically been invaded by China and either ruled directly or made a vassal state.

Thailand resisted Western colonial rule. Indo-China (now Vietnam, Laos and Cambodia) was colonized by France in the mid 19th Century, laying the foundations of many modern aspects of its culture; but continued resistance culminated in the expulsion of the French in 1954. The Communist North was ultimately successful in defeating the

Food for Thought

Across the region, small ethnic groups have been subjected by politically dominant cultures to assimilation, suppression and, frequently, violence. Many of these minorities are going through trials even now in Laos, Myanmar and Vietnam. Peoples that have become partly or largely Christian have suffered even more.

non-Communist South in the bloody and destructive Vietnam War, which became part of the wider Cold War. The effect on the peoples of the region has been traumatic (see p215).

The centuries of foreign intervention have all contributed to the religious variety displayed below. The SE Asian affinity bloc's 15 people clusters have been divided into two groups: those with smaller populations and those with larger ones. The tables indicate the size of the Christian presence in each of the 437 people groups (each people group is specific to a country and counted as many times as the number of countries in which it appears). Each cluster is also divided into indigenous and emigrant groups.

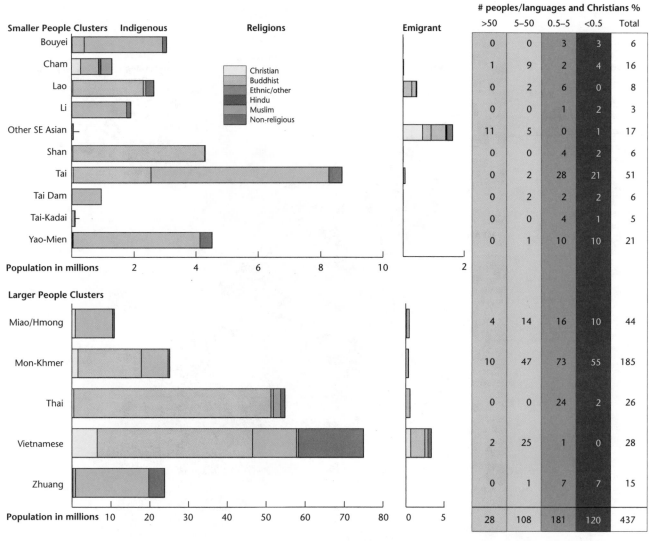

Smaller People Clusters (Population in millions)	# peoples/languages and Christians %				
	>50	5–50	0.5–5	<0.5	Total
Bouyei	0	0	3	3	6
Cham	1	9	2	4	16
Lao	0	2	6	0	8
Li	0	0	1	2	3
Other SE Asian	11	5	0	1	17
Shan	0	0	4	2	6
Tai	0	2	28	21	51
Tai Dam	0	2	2	2	6
Tai-Kadai	0	0	4	1	5
Yao-Mien	0	1	10	10	21
Larger People Clusters					
Miao/Hmong	4	14	16	10	44
Mon-Khmer	10	47	73	55	185
Thai	0	0	24	2	26
Vietnamese	2	25	1	0	28
Zhuang	0	1	7	7	15
	28	108	181	120	437

Religions: Christian, Buddhist, Ethnic/other, Hindu, Muslim, Non-religious

Fig 7.71 *Religious affiliation of the SE Asian people clusters and their state of evangelization*

Discipling successes and challenges

The 20th Century was a time of harvest, despite the violence and the trauma of war, and official opposition from successive ruling powers. Only in Thailand has there been a high degree of freedom.

▲ *The Vietnamese:* Many became Catholic under French rule, or Protestant more recently—especially among some of the mountain tribes of central and southern Vietnam. Lately, unregistered churches have multiplied and grown significantly all over the country.

▲ *Cambodians* were scarcely touched by the Gospel until just before their nation succumbed to the infamous Pol Pot regime and its policy of genocide. Since the demise of that regime in 1978 as a result of Vietnam's invasion, some freedom has come to this traumatized country and many people have become Christians.

▲ *Thailand* has welcomed missionaries, but the response of the Buddhist Thai has been unenthusiastic, and interest in the Gospel is mostly limited to the urban Chinese and some of the mountain tribes around Thailand's borders.

▲ *Laos* has never really had much exposure to the Gospel and remains subject to a repressive Marxist government hostile to

Christians. The principal response has been among the Hmong, who have resisted the Communists and suffered greatly as a result. About half the Hmong population fled the country— many now live in the US.

▲ *The emigrants* have proved to be the most responsive, and significant Cambodian, Vietnamese and Hmong church networks have sprung up in the West.

However, 120 of the bloc's peoples are less than 0.5% Christian and a further 181 are less than 5%. In discipling, church planting and Bible translation, the unfinished task remains large—and yet any overt witness is prohibited in S China, Laos and Vietnam. God is providing ways around this problem, but the challenges in reaching these peoples are many.

Tourists experience Buddhist spirituality in Thailand (photo by PJK)

This map shows the state of evangelization of the SE Asian Peoples affinity bloc in geographical terms. A lot has been achieved by pioneer mission work throughout the 20th Century, and especially after the exodus of missionaries from China in 1947 after it fell to Communism. A number of these missionaries relocated to Thailand and Laos—often to unevangelized populations of the same people groups for whom the pioneering work had been done in China.

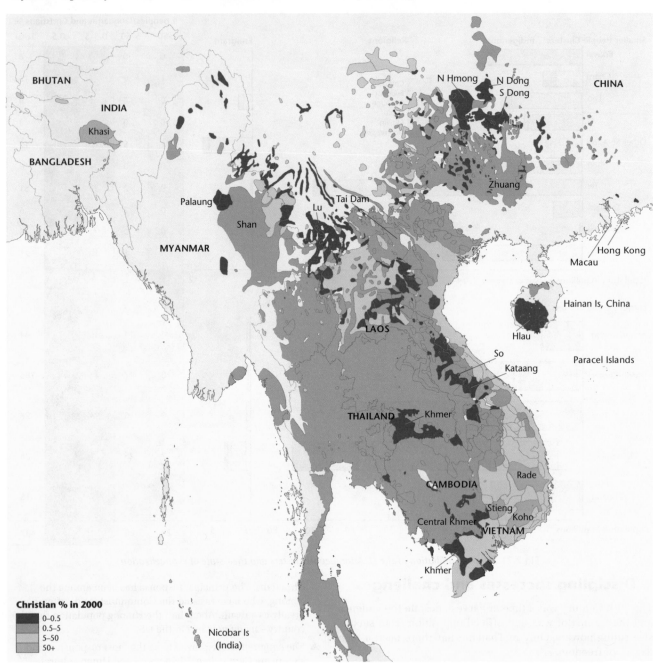

Fig 7.72 *The SE Asian people groups and their evangelization*

Politics and evangelization. Apart from Thailand, every country that is home to these peoples has suffered severely from war and oppression. In Myanmar, it has been the hated military dictatorship, which has favoured Buddhism. Elsewhere, it has been Communism. As in China, the Church in Laos, Cambodia and Vietnam was largely driven underground but has ultimately grown vigorously. This is especially true of Vietnam, where the Stieng, Koho and Rade are more than 50% Christian today, and a further 19 tribes are more than 20%. Tribes of this affinity bloc in India and Bangladesh also have large Christian populations.

Opposition has made many peoples in S China and on Hainan Island, in N Vietnam and many parts of Laos inaccessible to Christian witness (see the dark blue areas). Among the peoples of the SE Asian bloc, there are probably 38 or more with no known church and few believers. The following peoples (all numbering at the very least 100,000 individuals) are less than 0.5% Christian:

▲ *China:* Five of the six people groups of the 4.7 million Zhuang, China's largest ethnic minority, are unevangelized, as are two people groups among the 3.7

Food for Thought

In many of these countries, Christians who are in a minority in their people group are often severely persecuted—and yet in many cases their churches are growing, with little outside help.

▲ Apart from the essential prayer, what can we do to help them?

million Dong and a further 12 other peoples. Officially, China has 55 recognized ethnic minorities, but the true number is far higher. Among the peoples of the SE Asian bloc, there are probably 38 or more with no known church and few believers.

▲ *Laos:* the Kataang (121,000), So (150,000), Lu (152,000) and Tai Dam (114,000) Laotians, who are part of the Thai cluster, are largely Buddhist, but many are atheistic Communists. Only about 1% are Christians of any kind.

▲ *Myanmar:* the Palaung (four people groups, totalling 600,000). The 4.2m-strong Shan, who are related to the Thai, are less than 1% Christian.

▲ *Thailand and Vietnam:* the Khmer (1.1m and 1.2m respectively). Thai people are warm and welcoming to everything but the Gospel.

Furthermore:

▲ The Cham (after whom Cambodia is named) are the only Muslim-majority people in the bloc. Only a handful of them are Christians.

▲ Many of the mountain tribes remain without any resident Christian witness, and there are few if any Christians—there are 24 such tribes in Laos and three in Vietnam.

The Impact of the Vietnam War

Vietnam, Laos and Cambodia have had a long history of invasion, conquest and loss of independence. The history of the last 150 years has been traumatic. The French invasions of 1858–67 precipitated Indochina into a century of conflict—resistance to French rule, Japanese occupation during the Second World War and subsequently 30 years of war in which Communist insurgents gained control of all three countries.

In the Vietnam war—first against France (1945–54) and then the US (1954–75)—there were an estimated four million Indochinese killed. Millions were forced to flee, even after the Vietnam War had ended. Many readers will recall the "boat people" and the crowded refugee camps in Thailand and elsewhere.

▲ *The Vietnamese government* severely repressed the mountain peoples—many of whom have embraced Christianity. Recent years have seen a softening of this harsh approach along with economic liberalization.

▲ *The Cambodians* suffered the massacre of maybe 2 million people by the Khmer Rouge in the so-called Killing Fields of 1975–79.[35] The small Church was obliterated. After the Vietnamese invasion in 1979 and the institution of a new government, freedoms have gradually increased and the Church has grown. Christians today represent more than 3% of the population.

▲ *The Lao:* The Pathet Lao Communists retaliated against the *Hmong* peoples of the north, who had opposed them during the Vietnam War, and also persecuted Christians (a few Lao, but most tribal) vigorously. About half the Hmong fled the country, but many—in Laos as well as among the refugees—have become Christians.

During the Vietnam War and the decade that followed, millions of people fled to the surrounding countries. A minority of them were gradually assimilated, but most moved on to N America, Europe or Australia—or even, in the case of the Hmong, French Guiana—where they came to form significant communities. Fig 7.74 indicates how many went to each continent.

The children of these refugees have often done well, both educationally and economically. Many of them have become Catholic or evangelical Protestant Christians.

In many cases, ethnic-minority refugees have not retained their separate cultures and networks and have become quite integrated into the wider society they live in.

Few SE Asian people from Myanmar, China or India have become refugees, so they do not figure in these statistics.

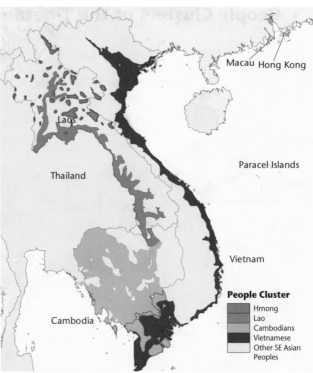

Fig 7.73 *The peoples of Indochina*

People Cluster
- Hmong
- Lao
- Cambodians
- Vietnamese
- Other SE Asian Peoples

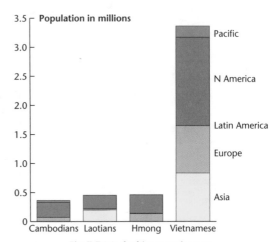

Fig 7.74 *Indochinese emigrants*

Food for Thought

The 1972 photograph of a girl burnt by napalm in S Vietnam became one of the most famous images of the 20th Century and contributed to the growth of the anti-war movement. The girl in question became a Christian 10 years later and forgave those who had caused her suffering. She now lives in Canada.[36] Her story is symbolic of what God can do in spite of the cruelties of war and the agonies—and long-lasting trauma—of its victims.

▲ How best can the millions of descendants of these refugees around the world contribute to the evangelization of their lands of origin and others beyond?

People Clusters of the Tibetan-Himalayan Peoples Affinity Bloc

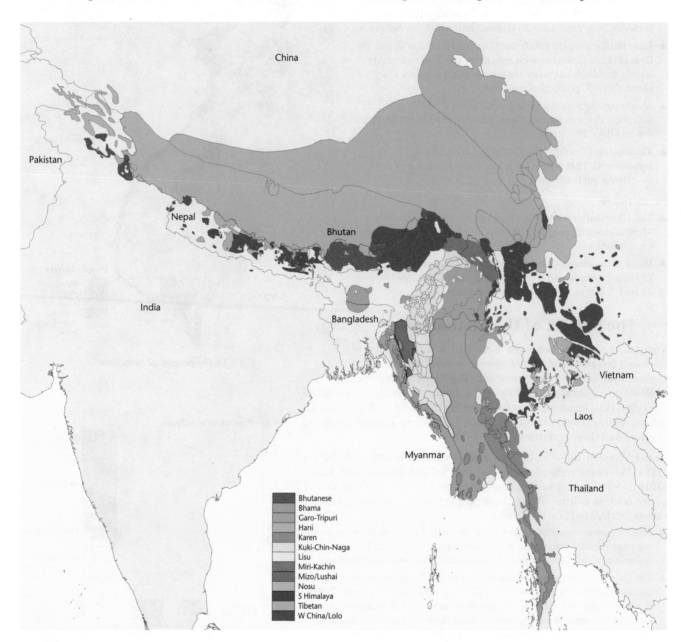

Legend:
- Bhutanese
- Bhama
- Garo-Tripuri
- Hani
- Karen
- Kuki-Chin-Naga
- Lisu
- Miri-Kachin
- Mizo/Lushai
- Nosu
- S Himalaya
- Tibetan
- W China/Lolo

These two facing maps reveal striking contrasts between these people clusters. Their homelands are split by the soaring heights of the Himalayas, and over time their political and spiritual histories have diverged considerably. These peoples are indigenous to nine countries, but only in Myanmar and Bhutan do they constitute a majority. Tibet itself lost its independence when invaded by the Chinese in 1950—a continuing source of unrest and international opprobrium.

The vast mountain ranges that cover the whole area are the cause of such ethnic and linguistic diversity. The many small people groups that live in Nepal, SW China and the mountains around Myanmar's borders are represented in the map above. Many of them live intermingled with SE Asian peoples in eastern Myanmar, Thailand, Laos, northern Vietnam and SW China or with S Asian peoples in Nepal and India. These other peoples are not shown in this map.

The government of Bhutan strictly protects the cultural and religious heritage of that country, which is one of the least evangelized and most strongly Buddhist in the world. The Bhutanese practise the Mahayana form of Buddhism.

The government of Myanmar is a military dictatorship that stamps on any political or religious dissent and persecutes Christian and Muslim minorities. The Bhama (Burmese) people, who make up 63% of the population, favour Theravada (Hinayan) Buddhism.

Burning Question for Today

There are many obstacles that prevent the flow of the Gospel to all these peoples. The terrain itself is a huge factor, and nearly all these peoples live in sensitive border regions or under the rule of oppressive governments. Only in one of these nine countries, Thailand, is there considerable freedom. Communism is dominant in China, Laos and Vietnam, Bhutan and Myanmar have no real religious freedom and Nepal's 2008 revolution has led to an uneasy stand-off between the Communists and Hindu-oriented parties.

▲ How will these lands be opened up so that all might hear the Good News?

Although these people groups have common origins, the contrasts in their receptiveness to the Gospel are startling. Some are among the least evangelized peoples on earth, while others have been swept into God's Kingdom in mighty movements of His Spirit. However, almost every people that has responded positively has experienced persecution or else serious social unrest.

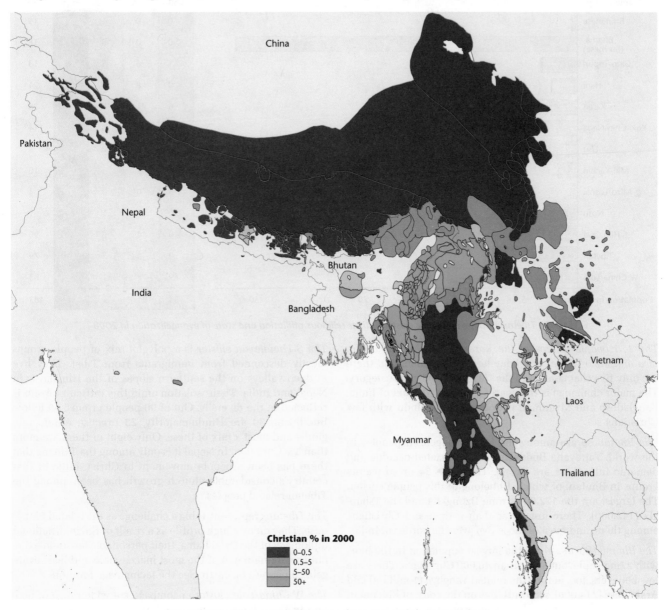

Fig 7.75 *The Tibetan-Himalayan people groups and their evangelization*

The evangelized: Adoniram Judson, the great missionary pioneer to Burma (present-day Myanmar), began his ministry in 1813. His burden for the Bhama majority to come to Christ was never realized, but over the next two centuries there were conversions to Christ among the hill tribes first of Burma, then of NE India and Bangladesh and next, in the 20th Century, the peoples of SW China. After China fell to Communism in 1949, the mission work there was aborted (though the churches that had been planted survived and grew). Expelled missionaries worked among similar peoples in Vietnam, Laos and Thailand. Again, it was the tribal peoples in these countries who responded more than the predominantly Buddhist ethnic majorities. In more recent years, new movements to Christ have occurred in remote Arunachal Pradesh in NE India, Sikkim and Nepal. Most conversions to Christ in Nepal since 1960 have been among Hindu peoples, and fewer among the Buddhist Tibetan-related peoples. Mizoram and many parts of Nagaland have for many years enjoyed outpourings of the Spirit of God and revivals. Missionaries from there have been taking the Gospel to new areas in India and beyond.

The unevangelized:

▲ *The Bhama* have been exposed to the Scriptures for nearly 200 years—Judson's translation of the whole Bible into their language was so good that it is still the principal version used—and yet only some 40,000 (or 0.1%) are Christians today.

▲ *There are 14 other unevangelized minorities* in *Myanmar*, the largest being *the Arakanese and the Yangbye.*

▲ *Bhutan* is a seemingly impregnable fortress for Buddhism. All forms of evangelism are illegal.

▲ *China* has more than a hundred Tibetan-related people groups that are unevangelized—notably, the 3.1 million Nosu, the Bai (2.3m), the Nisu (1.2m) and the Guizhou Yi (1.7m). All of those practise ethnic religion, not Buddhism; there are few active Christians. Other groups are very small; some are Buddhist.

▲ *China's Xizang Autonomous Region (Tibet)* remains a major challenge. Among the 6 million Tibetans, with three major languages and 30 people groups, there are at most 16,000 Christians. Some analysts put the figure much lower, at 1,000 Evangelicals and 2,000 Catholics only. See page 219 for more.

Below, I assess each people cluster in the Tibetan-Himalayan Peoples affinity bloc. The diversity is interesting.

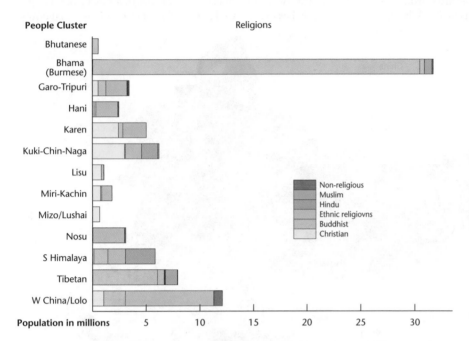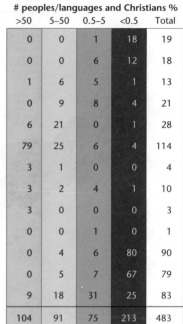

Fig 7.76 Tibetan-Himalayan people clusters—their religious affiliation and state of evangelization in 2008

The 175 people groups of the Karen, Chin, Naga, Kachin, Lisu and Mizo/Lushai are today largely Christian, and there are only five that come into the "least evangelized" category. The major challenge is the nearly 2 million Meithei of India, Bangladesh and Myanmar, who are largely Hindu with few Christians.

The Bhutanese are among the least evangelized peoples in the world. Vajrayana Buddhism and associated occultic and demonic influences are strong. There are 24 or so people groups in Bhutan, of which 19 belong to this people cluster. The largest are the 172,000-strong Dzongkha and the Tshangla (142,000). There are fewer than a thousand Christians among them, and most of those live over the border in India.

The Bhama (Burmese) are the largest population in the bloc, with 27m people, but fewer than 40,000 Christians. There are few believers, too, among the related Yangbye (1 million) and Arakanese (214,000), who both live on the coast of Myanmar. In some areas the Bhama have been well exposed to the Gospel for two centuries, but the breakthrough has yet to come.

The Garo-Tripuri number about a million and live almost entirely in India (where 37% are Christians) and Bangladesh (more than 60%). The 820,000 Chakma also straddle the border and have Christians and churches, though most are Buddhist. There are two largely Hindu peoples, but in most of the other people groups the majority practise ethnic religions. All but the Deori and Tiwa—both in India—are more than 1% Christian.

The 800,000 Hani are unevangelized. Many related peoples live in the border regions of China, Myanmar and Thailand. There has been some response among the Akha in Myanmar and Thailand and the Biyo, Honi and Kadu in SW China, but most have not been evangelized and are still animists.

The Nosu number more than 3 million, in at least seven people groups. The Gospel has been presented to these polytheistic peoples on many occasions, but the response has been small. Only about 1% are Christians.

The S Himalayan cluster is a polyglot mix of people groups mostly descended from immigrants from Tibet. They live in deep valleys on the southern slopes of the Himalayas in Nepal and India. Their isolation amid this difficult terrain is reflected in the diversity. Out of 90 people groups, 45 follow Buddhism, 30 are Hindu-majority, 23 practise ethnic religions—and most a mix of these. Only eight of them are more than 1% Christian. In Nepal it is only among the Tamang that there has been a people movement to Christ. Little of that country's considerable church growth has been among the Tibetan-related peoples.

The Tibetans represent as big a challenge as the related Bhutanese. They enjoy a high profile as a result of the international diplomacy of the Dalai Lama, their personable leader-in-exile; but they remain one of the most inaccessible and least evangelized peoples on earth. See the facing page for more.

The W China/Lolo cluster encompasses a wide range of peoples in W and SW China as well as northern Myanmar and Thailand who are Tibetan-related but speak a variety of mutually unintelligible languages. Of these, eight are mostly Christian (including the Lahu, Jingpho, Lipo and Maru), but 56 are less than 5% Christian and 25 less than 0.5%. Of the latter, "least evangelized" people groups, the largest are the 2.7m-strong southern Bai, the Nisu (1.5m) and the Yi (1.7m).

Food for Thought

The complexities of language and ethnicity, together with the challenges presented by geography, culture and politics, make it hard to give all these peoples an opportunity to hear the Good News. The task must fall mainly to local Christians, whether from these ethnic minorities or the Han Chinese themselves.

▲ How can this be done?

▲ What is the most appropriate way for local people and expatriates to work together to achieve this?

The Tibetan people cluster

It is an astonishing fact that of the 90 million individuals who belong to the Tibetan family of peoples, most live as minorities in countries where they have no political power. Only two countries are the exception to this: tiny, xenophobic Bhutan (with its large, marginalized Nepali population) and Myanmar (with its history of conflict with ethnic minorities). Nonetheless, Tibetans and their Buddhist religion have a high profile worldwide. In most of the other countries shown in Fig 7.77, Tibetan-related peoples form only a small part of the population. Some have migrated to other lands—most of them refugees from Chinese repression in Tibet itself or from Myanmar's harsh military rule. This makes it even harder to reach any of these peoples with the Gospel.

Most of us associate these peoples with Buddhism—and indeed the Bhama of Myanmar are major exponents of Theravada Buddhism, as Tibetans are of Lamaistic Mahayana Buddhism. However, both of these are steeped in the occult and pre-Buddhist religions, and in general Buddhists are actually in the minority. Of all the Tibeto-Burman people groups, a quarter openly practise various ethnic religions. Many in India and Nepal are actually Hindu, and in northern Pakistan the Balti and the Purik are Muslim. Surprisingly, more than 10% of the total population are Christians. Some in Nepal and (especially) China have become non-religious as a result of Communist ideology. The Maoist movement in Nepal has great influence and its atheistic propaganda has affected even some Tibetans.

Fig 7.79 shows the Tibetan people cluster. Besides its three principal people groups, there are many smaller people groups, here represented by the green areas (and mostly identified). There are few Christians, mainly among the Chepang and Mundari in Nepal and the Balti and Purik in Pakistan, though there are a handful of illegal congregations of Tibetans in Tibet and scattered believers elsewhere. The Amdo, Khampa and Lhasa (Central) Tibetans remain a great challenge for the Church.

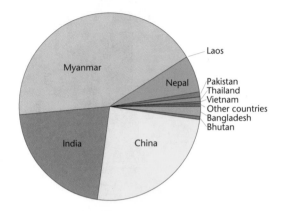

Fig 7.77 *Geograhical distribution of the Tibetan peoples*

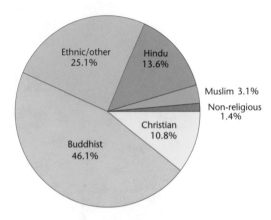

Fig 7.78 *Religious affiliation of the Tibetan peoples*

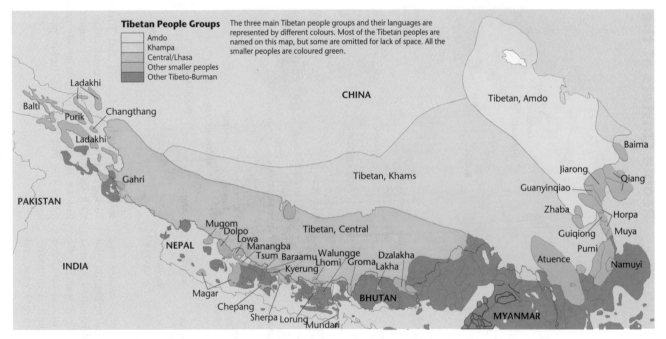

Fig 7.79 *The Tibetan peoples/languages*

Burning Question for Today

Tibetans were first exposed to the Good News over a millennium ago, but the spiritual breakthrough has not yet come. However, for the first time a few communities of indigenous believers have now emerged who worship, sing and pray in Tibetan.

▲ Can we trust God to break the spiritual bondage that binds these peoples?

People Clusters of the Turkic Peoples Affinity Bloc

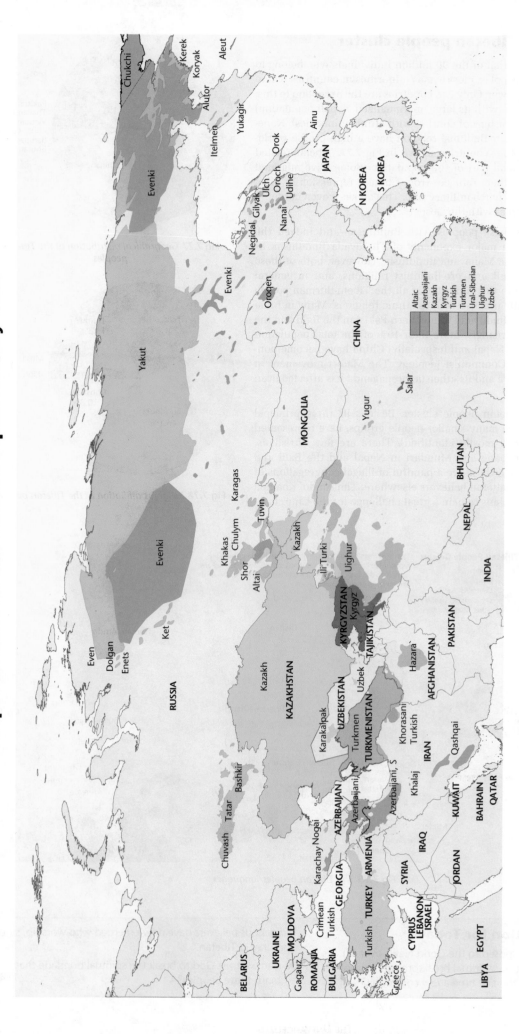

The nine Turkic people clusters are represented here. For several millennia, the Turkic-Mongol peoples dominated what is now Russian Siberia, and it was largely because of their periodic attacks on China that the Great Wall was built. A thousand years ago, Turkic tribes moved west and

subjugated much of C Asia and Turkey. Turkic and Mongol forces combined in the 13th Century to form the all-conquering Golden Horde. This history largely determines the distribution of Turkic peoples today.

Mongol peoples have been linked with the E Asian Peoples affinity bloc on account of more recent cultural, economic and religious ties to China. The gap between the northern and southern Turkic clusters was caused by the eastward Russian advances over the last four centuries. Many parts of

N Siberia and C Asia are desert or Arctic tundra and very sparsely inhabited. The map cannot show the ethnic diversity in each area, such as the Kurds among the Turks in Turkey and the mix of peoples throughout the former Soviet Union.

Four empires have determined the present distribution of Turkic peoples and their migration patterns:

The Muslim Seljuk Turk and Ottoman empires (1055–1307 and 1299–1923 respectively) were centred in Anatolia or Asia Minor, in what today is Turkey. The Ottoman Empire was a global superpower for centuries, and for much of that time encompassed most of the western Muslim world as well as SE Europe. Turkey has always straddled East and West—Istanbul stands astride the Bosporus, in both Asia and Europe—and much of its economic and cultural life has been shaped by both the Arab world and Europe. As a result, most of the 4 million Turks who have emigrated have moved to the West—especially, Germany and W Europe.

The Russian/Soviet Empire (1721–1917 and 1921–80 respectively). The Russians gradually subjugated the homelands of seven of these people clusters, and ultimately drew the boundaries of what are now independent states. In consequence, these peoples have typically migrated all over the former Soviet Union but relatively rarely to the West.

The rest of the Turkic peoples now live in countries where they form a minority of the population: Iran (26%), Afghanistan (22%) and China (1%—but 56% of the restive Xinjiang Uighur Autonomous Region).

From about 1517, the Ottoman Turkish Sultan was generally recognized as the Caliph, the secular leader of the Sunni Muslim world.[37] This ended with the establishing of the modern state of Turkey in 1924—but Sunni Islamists hanker after a restoration of the Caliphate, to have a single, secular leader of the Islamic world, and this is one of their principal political goals.

Religion. Over 90% of the Turkic peoples are now Muslims. For several centuries before the advent of Islam, many of their ancestors in C Asia were Eastern Christians; but that history has, sadly, been forgotten, as for hundreds of years Turks became the principal guardians of Islam. The legacy of the militant atheism of Communism in the 20th Century can be seen in the percentage of C Asian Turkic people who are non-religious. The small number who follow ethnic religions are mainly among the peoples of N Siberia.

Christianity. Less than 1% of all Turkic people are Christians of any kind. Most of those who call themselves Christian are nominally Orthodox—their ancestors were pressured by the Russian authorities to become Christian. In the former Soviet Union's C Asian republics, the indigenous peoples were some of the least evangelized on earth in 1990. In some of these lands, 20 years of comparative freedom for the Gospel followed and there has been significant growth in the number of churches and Evangelicals.

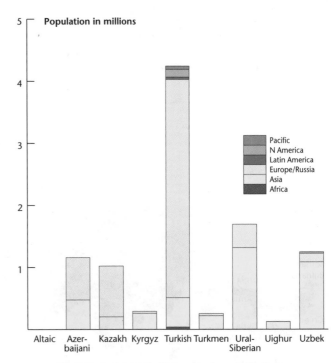

Fig 7.80 *Emigrant Turkic peoples by people cluster*

Kazakh women (photo by Elizabeth Hempel)

Food for Thought

As part of the Byzantine Empire, what is now Turkey was once a bastion for Christianity. After 1453, however, it became the centre of power in the Muslim world, and today the Turks are among the world's least evangelized peoples. There are only about 4,000 evangelical believers in their country, though this is a great improvement on 1960 when there were only a handful. Even so, nearly all of Turkey's hundred or so indigenous congregations are dependent on foreign support.

▲ How can this be changed?

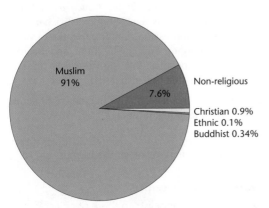

Fig 7.81 *The religious affiliations of the Turkic peoples*

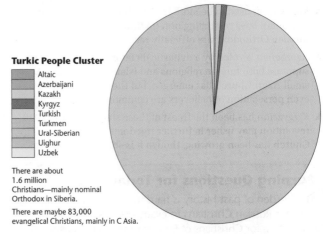

Turkic People Cluster
- Altaic
- Azerbaijani
- Kazakh
- Kyrgyz
- Turkish
- Turkmen
- Ural-Siberian
- Uighur
- Uzbek

There are about 1.6 million Christians—mainly nominal Orthodox in Siberia.

There are maybe 83,000 evangelical Christians, mainly in C Asia.

Fig 7.82 *The Christian distribution of the Turkic people clusters*

The Turkic peoples represent one of the great challenges for the Church today. For most of the last 800 years, they have been among the least accessible to the Gospel—chiefly as a result of the intertwining political and religious opposition to anything perceived as Western, including Christianity. The collapse of the Muslim Ottoman Empire in 1920 and the Marxist Soviet Union in 1991 created new opportunities to reach some of these peoples.

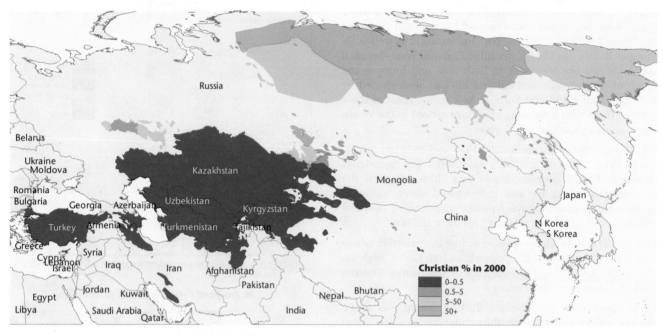

Fig 7.83 *The Turkic people groups and their evangelization*

The Turkic-majority countries are six in number—the de facto state of N Cyprus is not recognized internationally.

▲ *Turkey* is the only one of these countries that has never been Communist. It was formed in 1922 out of the ethnic-Turkish-majority remnant of the polyglot Turkish Ottoman Empire. History has left a difficult legacy that makes it hard for Turks to become Christians—over the past 120 years, the large ethnic Christian Armenian, Greek and Assyrian minorities in this land have been persecuted, expelled or even massacred. Despite official and popular hostility, the last 30 years have seen the emergence of a network of Turkish-speaking congregations, but most of Turkey's 81 provinces have no established witness or congregations. It remains the least evangelized country in Europe.[38]

▲ *Turkmenistan* moved in 1991 from Communism to a nationalist dictatorship that has sought to suppress every form of religion except Russian Orthodoxy and a tame Sunni Islam.

▲ *Uzbekistan* has pursued a similar course, with non-Orthodox Christians falling victim to efforts by the government to control the growth of violent Islamism.

▲ *Kazakhstan* used to be more free but has recently passed draconian laws restricting non-traditional religion. Islam and Russian Orthodoxy are officially recognized.

▲ *Azerbaijan* is ruled by a dynastic dictatorship that seeks to suppress both foreign religions and Islamic extremism. A small Azeri Church has emerged, but the intimidation and even persecution of believers are common.

▲ *Kyrgyzstan* has been the freest of these states—and the 2010 revolution may usher in further freedoms. The Kyrgyz Church has been growing, though it is still small.

The Turkic peoples of the Russian Federation

There is a long history of Russian conflict with the Turkic and Mongol peoples. The subjugation of the Russians by the Mongols and Tatars from 1237 to 1505 was reversed as the Russian Empire expanded east and gradually conquered all the territory that now comprises the Russian Federation. The rulers of Russia have long worked closely with the Russian Orthodox hierarchy, except for the 70 years of state persecution under Communism. Today, constitutional freedom of religion exists more in theory than in practice and any expression of Christianity other than Russian Orthodoxy is regarded as a hostile intrusion. As a result, the spread of evangelicalism among the Russian majority has been much slower than in Ukraine. Russian Orthodox missions in the past tried assiduously to both Christianize and Russify all the ethnic minorities which then became superficially Orthodox Christians. They still seek to prevent evangelization by any others. Advancing the Gospel among these peoples remains a massive challenge.

The Ural and Siberian minorities have large Orthodox minorities—or even majorities—but for the most part really practise shamanism or other ethnic religions or are non-religious.

The 60 indigenous Muslim peoples in the Caucasus and also the *Tatar and Bashkir* of the Urals see Orthodox Christianity as a component of Russian oppression. Small networks of evangelical churches are emerging among the Tatar and Bashkir and some of these other peoples, but the Caucasus remains Europe's least evangelized area (see also p191).

Muslim communities of C Asian origin live in cities right across Russia. Little is being done to reach them.

Burning Questions for Today

The burden of past history is hard to escape, which makes it hard for Russian Christians to evangelize their ethnic minorities, for Christians of European origin to witness to

Turks and for Chinese Christians to reach the Uighurs of NW China.

▲ How can we get over these barriers?

▲ Who could be the best evangelists to these peoples?[39]

The bar chart and table below provide more details on the nine Turkic people clusters. No breakdown of their Christian populations is given, since few government or denominational statistics are available.[40] This affinity bloc and its constituent people groups represent one of the biggest challenges for evangelization in the 21st Century. After some liberalization, legal restrictions for Christians have steadily increased since 2001.

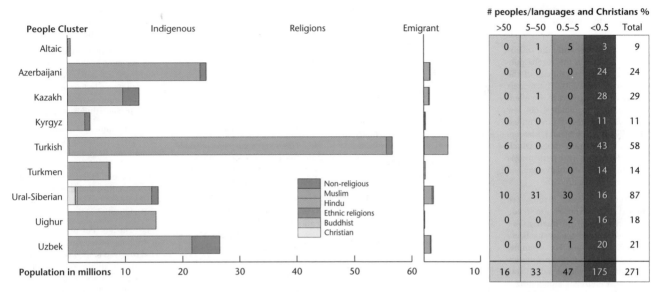

Fig 7.84 *Turkic people clusters—their religious affiliation and state of evangelization in 2008*

People Cluster	# peoples/languages and Christians %				
	>50	5–50	0.5–5	<0.5	Total
Altaic	0	1	5	3	9
Azerbaijani	0	0	0	24	24
Kazakh	0	1	0	28	29
Kyrgyz	0	0	0	11	11
Turkish	6	0	9	43	58
Turkmen	0	0	0	14	14
Ural-Siberian	10	31	30	16	87
Uighur	0	0	2	16	18
Uzbek	0	0	1	20	21
	16	33	47	175	271

Legend: Non-religious, Muslim, Hindu, Ethnic religions, Buddhist, Christian

Population in millions: 10 20 30 40 50 60 10

There are 96 Altaic and Ural-Siberian people groups in total, many of them small and scattered across Siberia and N China. Most have been only marginally evangelized. The majority are superficially Christian but really shamanists (435,000 Yakut). The 270,000 Tuvinians, 80,000 Khaka and 80,000 Altai are Buddhist. Others, such as the 7m Tatars, 6m Crimean Turks, 1.8m Bashkir and 80,000 Nogai, are largely Muslim. There are some evangelical congregations among the Tatar and Bashkir, but most of these peoples have had very little exposure to the Gospel.

The Azerbaijanis live in both Azerbaijan and northwest Iran. They speak two main dialects. Almost all are Muslim, though many are fairly secular. There are only around 6,000 active Christians in Azerbaijan, and slightly fewer in Iran. They suffer discrimination and persecution in both countries.

There are 13 million Kazakhs worldwide. Evangelical believers have grown in number from almost none in 1990 to about 15,000 today, but they are increasingly disadvantaged by restrictive laws. The 700,000 related *Karakalpak* live in Uzbekistan to the south of what remains of the Aral Sea. Several thousand have lately become Christian and now meet in underground churches, but they are severely persecuted by the authorities. Most of the Muslim majority remain unevangelized.

The 4.7 million Kyrgyz have enjoyed more religious freedom. There were no known churches in 1990, but today they exist and have maybe 15–20,000 believers. Islam is not so strong among the Kyrgyz, and many still practise their old shamanistic religion.

The Turks are by far the largest and most influential of these people clusters, and are admired by the whole Turkic world for their entrepreneurial culture and comparative freedom. Secularism has been strongly enshrined in law for 80 years, but this is weakening as Muslim zeal grows. Despite difficulties, indigenous Turkish-speaking Christians have increased in number from 10 or so in 1960 to about 4,000 today, though most Christians in Turkey belong to an ethnic minority. However, this remains one of the least evangelized countries on earth. There are Turkish believers in Bulgaria and among the other communities of the diaspora, and the Gagauz Turks of Moldova are largely Christian (though those in Turkey are mainly Muslim).

The Turkmen have never had religious freedom and very few have ever had the chance to hear the Gospel. Evangelical believers number only a few hundred or so—their homeland needs to be evangelized!

The 11 million Uighur constitute a minority in China who resent the influx of Han Chinese into their province of Xinjiang. They are mostly Muslims, though centuries ago there were Christians among them. Few Uighur now have heard the Good News and it is difficult to witness to them, and yet there are some 2,000 evangelical believers, mostly in the large cities. The *Hazara* of Afghanistan are a related Muslim Turkic people that speak Dari Persian.

The Uzbeks number 28 million with 21 million in Uzbekistan. The government of Uzbekistan is a secular Muslim dictatorship that persecutes both Islamists and indigenous Christians. Most Uzbeks are unevangelized. There are over 10,000 Evangelicals in their country.

Food for Thought

Before 1991, C Asia's Muslims were sealed off from any form of Christian witness. Apart from a few persistent intercessors, no one expected this situation to change—and yet the disintegration of the Soviet Union and the ideology that underpinned it created a 20-year window of opportunity. In 1991, there were probably fewer than a hundred Christians among the C Asian Turkic people groups, but today that number has increased to maybe 65,000. Let us pray that God will open up these and other countries and peoples!

1. Barrett expands on the measuring of evangelization in *World Christian Trends AD 30–AD 2200*, pp739–69, in which he gives a detailed history of various attempts to devise and refine models and scales. I was involved with him in this, especially between 1975 and 1980.

2. I appreciate all the effort expended to obtain the results published in successive editions of the *WCE* and in the *WCD*. The models developed by Barrett are excellent for comparing populations, but few people who use these figures understand the definitions and assumptions that lie behind them, which largely determine the percentages and absolute numbers of evangelized these models come up with.

3. Very different results are obtained if allowances are made for the theology, spirituality and churchmanship of the evangelizers and their ministries. For example, in 1900, almost all of Latin America was defined as "evangelized". It was then almost entirely Catholic, there were hardly any Protestants or Evangelicals—and the great majority of the population were Christo-pagans. This same broad ecumenical perspective also led the 1910 Edinburgh Missionary Conference to ignore the continent's spiritual need.

4. The eastern half of Ethiopia and northern third of Nigeria are almost entirely Muslim; the other areas are largely Christian.

5. This term became a missions focus in the 1990s to plant churches in the most spiritually needy parts of the world. It also led to some discrimination by churches against agencies and missionaries engaged in valid mission work outside that Window.

6. Many sociologists take 20% as the point at which a population segment begins to impact the worldview of the wider society.

7. These countries have much in common historically but were divided by the imperial politics of the 19th and 20th Centuries. Italy seized control of Ethiopia's Red Sea coast in 1890, while the Soviet Union took over Bessarabian Romania to form the Communist Republic of Romania at the end of the Second World War. All have considerable populations of Orthodox Christians, as well as many unevangelized areas and peoples.

8. Eritrea has become a one-party nationalist dictatorship which severely represses political dissent and persecutes Evangelicals. There has been no census since independence in 1993.

9. The claim of direct descent from Roman soldier-settlers is hotly debated, but the fact remains that, despite the influence of many incoming peoples over the centuries, the

Romanian-Moldovan language closely resembles Italian.

10. Romania has Europe's fourth-largest population of Evangelicals. Moldova and Ukraine were the centre of the spread of Evangelicalism in the former Soviet Union.

11. The story of the evangelization of Ethiopia is thrilling. The work of SIM and Lutheran, Baptist and Pentecostal pioneer missionaries has had dramatic results despite wars, famines and 14 years of Communist persecution.

12. A fuller list of resources can be found in the short bibliography in this book and also on the website.

13. David Barrett developed such a model to assess the numbers of individuals evangelized. It is better when used in making comparisons than in deriving actual numbers, since it is not based on head counts.

14. Some years ago, Global Mapping International patiently compiled an amazing set of language polygons based on SIL's Ethnologue database. This included every language with a definable geographical home area and covered almost the entire world. This resource has been used for these maps.

15. The impact of Christian satellite television in the Arab world has been remarkable—it has helped to change the worldview of millions of Muslims and to create a steady stream of conversions to Christ. One of the most notable channels is SAT-7 (http://www.sat7.org).

16. The present Levantine Arab population is largely descended from the Chaldeans, Assyrians, Phoenicians and other ancient indigenous peoples of the area.

17. This system was an effective instrument for control of diverse populations, with each religious community being granted a measure of autonomy. The present divisions of Lebanon are the most prominent result of this legacy. Interestingly, the Muslim millet did not allow for separate millets for the Sunni, Shi'a or (more deviant) Alawite communities that have subsequently become important. The Druze, however, did constitute a separate millet.

18. The greatest successes in China have been among some of the tribal peoples of the southwest, such as the Lisu; but these are not shown here as they are part of the SE Asian peoples affinity bloc.

19. The label "Caucasian" should perhaps also be applied to the Berber peoples of N Africa and the Indo-Aryan peoples of C and S Asia.

20. Georgia, Armenia and Azerbaijan lie largely between the two Caucasus ranges but nowadays are classified as part of Asia. Culturally, Georgia and Armenia belong to Europe but Turkic Azerbaijan to Asia.

21. Russian hostility to Georgia's attempts, as a former republic of the Soviet Union, to align itself with the West and NATO brought retribution in the form of military support for the secessions of the mini-states of S Ossetia and Abkhazia from Georgia.

22. The wars and famines in Somalia have caused the deaths of huge, but uncounted numbers and thousands of unrecorded Somali refugees have made their way to Europe, N America and elsewhere.

23. See the PJRN survey "*Indonesian People Profiles: Unreached People Groups*" (Indonesia: 2003).

24. These statistics were obtained from the UN Economic and Social Commission for Asia and the Pacific in 2005 (www.escap.org).

25. Martin Otto has written two excellent books, on evangelism to seafarers (*Seafarers! A Strategic Missionary Vision* [Carlisle: Piquant Editions, 2002]) and church planting among seafarers (*Church on the Oceans* [Carlisle: Piquant Editions, 2007]).

26. Far more information can be obtained by looking up the relevant countries for these peoples in *Operation World* and visiting the Joshua Project website.

27. Java has 136 million people but is 30% the size of Sumatra. The Japanese island of Honshu is second in terms of population, with 103 million people, and 48% the size of Sumatra.

28. One of the best sources for Kurdish history and culture is Professor Mehrdad Izady, much of whose writing can be found on the internet. Also useful is Gérard Chaliand's book *A People Without a Country: the Kurds and Kurdistan* (Northampton, Ma: Interlink Publishing Group, 1993).

29. The name of the Hawrani Kurds is derived from the Hurrians, whose empire lasted from 1500 to 850 BC. Some three-quarters of Kurdish clan names are of Hurrian origin. Even the term "Kurd" goes back to pre-Median times (before 1000 BC) as "Kurti".

30. In every country in which Kurds now live, there are many who speak the majority language in the home. This adds to the difficulty in counting the Kurdish population. Some analysts reckon that the true number is nearer 52 million.

31. Language is vital for communication, and so for all ministries involving language this perspective is needed. However, to give a realistic picture for church planting, a caste perspective is more helpful—even if the whole system needs to be expunged from Christian and national life (see pp210–11). The current subdivision of languages and peoples into these categories is a continuing process—especially for this region.

32. This is explained more fully on page 92, note 22. Census figures indicate that 2.3% of the population are Christians, but the most recent estimates by Indian researchers vary from about 4% right up to 9%. Such high figures are not reflected here, but certainly far more is happening than this map shows.

33. One of the most lucid and objective accounts of the origins, development and present state of casteism written by an Indian can be found at http://www.hindu-website.com/Hinduism/h_caste.asp.

34. Dr Bhimrao Ambedkar (1891–1956) was a Chamar Dalit who overcame great prejudice to become the first Dalit to obtain a college education in India. He eventually chaired the committee that drafted the Indian Constitution. He, too, converted to Buddhism.

35. The Pol Pot regime instituted a forcible restructuring of society that involved emptying the cities and destroying all links to Cambodia's past—including everyone who had been part of the old governing and educational system. Estimates for the death toll from execution, starvation and disease vary from 1 to 3 million. The whole nation was traumatized for decades.

36. The story of Kim Phuc, the girl in the photograph, is told on many websites, such as http://www.nytimes.com/2000/06/29/news/29iht-kim.2.t.html.

37. The Caliphate is based on the political system instituted by Mohammed, which aimed to choose his successors as leader by election or general consensus. The Caliph was also known as *Amir al-Mu'minin* ("Commander of the Faithful"), which has military connotations. The eventual outcome was a series of Sunni caliphates that were, in effect, imperial dynasties. This has been the cause of much division. A high percentage of reigning caliphs were assassinated.

38. Only 3% of Turkey's surface area is in Europe, but for many centuries it ruled a large part of SE Europe and it is often considered a European state—and a legitimate applicant for membership of the EU, though its Muslim culture and large population make its application unlikely to succeed.

39. The Ukrainians in Russia have been most successful among its minorities—they are Slavs like the Russians—but they, too, have a history of being oppressed by them. African and Asian Christians are more likely to get a hearing untainted by history from the Turkic and other Muslim peoples of the Middle East and C Asia.

40. The statistics for Evangelicals used here were derived from the research done for the 2010 edition of *Operation World*.

Christian Missions and the Future

The Church and missional structures

The Ministry of Jesus / The Early Church

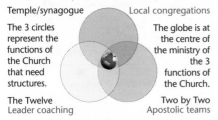

Temple/synagogue — Local congregations

The 3 circles represent the functions of the Church that need structures.

The globe is at the centre of the ministry of the 3 functions of the Church.

The Twelve — Leader coaching

Two by Two — Apostolic teams

The Medieval Catholic Church

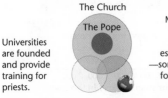

The Church

The Pope

Monastic orders were established —some were focused on missions.

Universities are founded and provide training for priests.

The Church after the Reformation

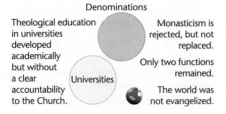

Denominations

Theological education in universities developed academically but without a clear accountability to the Church.

Universities

Monasticism is rejected, but not replaced.

Only two functions remained.

The world was not evangelized.

The Protestant Church in 20th C

The local churches were often regarded as a source of funding and workers, but stayed passive in the process.

The 3 functions of the Church developed their own separate identities with little mutual accountability.

Denominations

Theological training institutions

Mission agencies

"parachurch" organizations

The Missional Church Model

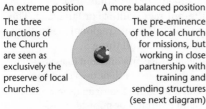

Congregations rightly should have missions at their heart

An extreme position

The three functions of the Church are seen as exclusively the preserve of local churches

A more balanced position

The pre-eminence of the local church for missions, but working in close partnership with training and sending structures (see next diagram)

A 21st C Missional Church/Congregation

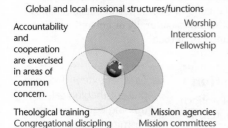

Global and local missional structures/functions

Accountability and cooperation are exercised in areas of common concern.

Worship Intercession Fellowship

Theological training Congregational discipling

Mission agencies Mission committees

Fig 8.1 *The development of missionaries and missions in response to the Great Commission*

We now turn to the workers needed for world evangelization. Throughout its history, the Church has been only intermittently obedient to the Last Command of Jesus; yet much has been achieved, despite limited vision and resources. First, we will look briefly at the biblicality of having a missions structure in the Church.[1]

Jesus left few instructions about the structure of the Church He was instituting, but patterns in His own ministry were continued in the early Church. The circles alongside represent the functions and structures in both His earthly ministry and the emerging churches in Acts.[2] The functions of gathering, training and sending were equally important but distinct. How rarely has the Church kept that balance and focus! The statement of John Piper is valid: *"Missions is not the ultimate goal of the church. Worship is. Missions exists because worship doesn't."*[3] Our passion should be to increase the number and diversity of worshippers giving glory to God.

Over time, the original apostolic fervour waned and the Church became institutionalized and politicized—especially in the Western Latin Church portrayed in this diagram. The Catholic Church was ruled by an authoritarian pope in Rome. The three structures of the early Church survived but were distorted. Universities were established in the Middle Ages to provide a more educated priesthood. From the 4th Century onwards, monastic institutions and orders became the principal means in all Christian traditions by which any mission work was undertaken. Note how the globe is no longer central but the preserve of monks. Reformation was desperately needed.

In the 16th-Century Reformation, the essentials of biblical theology were recovered but the Reformers did not develop a biblical missiology. Sadly, they also did not address the need for a structural reformation and they retained many of the distorted forms of the past. Monasticism was rejected and for 300 years no missions structures were set up to replace it for the churches of the Reformation. The Reformation was, in fact, a structural "deformation". It was not until the Moravians in the early 18th Century that the world was again placed at the heart of church life. This was followed by the evangelical awakenings that inspired some Protestant churches to engage in missions.

For the next 200 years, Protestant missions spread around the world, becoming the growing edge of a dynamic global Church. Sadly, the three functions developed autonomous structures with little accountability between them. This was true for both denominational and, even more, interdenominational training and sending agencies. Churches regarded the training and sending functions as "parachurch" and often saw agencies as taking away their funds and their most useful members. The idea that the three functions were all essential to the ministry of the Church was not understood. Globalization, the ease of travel, regular involvement in short-term mission trips and the accessibility of information through the internet led to many local churches demanding fuller involvement with and greater accountability from mission agencies deploying their church members.

During the 1990s, the concept of a "missional church" spread widely. Some churches went further and claimed that all functions must be controlled by the local church and that any structure apart from the local church is unscriptural. This diagram represents that more radical view. The more balanced position is shown in the diagram below. The extreme position does not take into account what developed in the very first missional church, in Antioch, where there was a balance between the responsibilities of the local church and the Holy Spirit's guidance of the apostolic team, who were nonetheless clearly accountable to the local church.[4]

Here is a suggested model for the restoration of the original balance for the Church both globally and locally. We are still far from this, but some leaders and agencies are moving in this direction. If biblical patterns are to be restored for the sake of world evangelization, we need to repent in humility, call an end to years of mistrust and begin to work closely together in the common cause of obedience to Jesus' Last Command. The body of Christ must have the three functions working harmoniously and prayerfully together. There needs to be great respect for the primacy of local churches but also respect for the special gifts the Holy Spirit provides for each function.

Half a century ago, "missionary" was a title of honour for those who sacrificed much to go to the ends of the earth for the sake of the Gospel. Today, it is associated more with embarrassment and even opprobrium, with an aura of old-fashioned imperialism and intolerance in wanting to change the religious beliefs of others. Even the word "mission" has to be replaced by more innocuous synonyms, and it does not appear in most translations of the Bible into English. The term "missions" accordingly has a wide variety of meanings and interpretations among Christians today.

Fig 8.2 indicates some of the uses of the term "missionary". The upper pair of bars represents all Christians and their potential involvement in missions, and the lower pair all Christian workers. These two groups have been further divided into Christians living or serving in their own or a "near" culture and those in a "distant" one.

The top bar represents all church attenders of all streams of Christianity. Many people say that all Christians are missionaries, or should be. There is some truth in this, in that we are all called to be witnesses; but not all witnesses are really missionaries, nor do all church attenders necessarily witness or even have a living faith. Most church attenders "in distant cultures" are refugees or migrants.

The second bar represents Christians in all religious streams reckoned by the *World Christian Encyclopedia* to know about the Great Commission and to seek to further missions either by sup-

porting it or by going as missionaries themselves. However, "Great Commission Christians" is too vague a term.[5]

The third bar represents all Christian workers recognized by local churches or denominations. Most serve within their own cultures, but a few serve in other cultures as missionaries.

The explosion of interest in short-term mission and mission trips over the past few decades has prompted some people to promote them as the future of missions. This is questionable. Such trips can have value in the field in a support capacity, but are more valuable in inspiring and educating those who take part in them and and preparing them for possible future service.[6] Participants in mission trips are not included in the statistics in the following pages.

Mission has moved a long way from its early simplicity, as the complexity of our globalized world makes it vital to have a wide range of ministries. Fig 8.3 shows the six main facets of ministry and lists in each triangle a range of ministries that relates approximately to that facet. Missions can only function effectively if there is a partnership at every level between:

1. local churches and agencies at home and in the field

2. trainers and deployers (local churches and agencies)

3. agencies in the field, for team building and use of resources

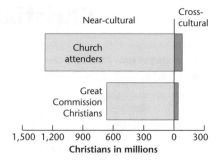

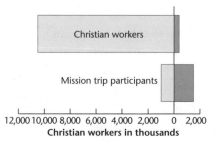

Fig 8.2 *Christians and Missions in 2000*

4. different nationalities, within agencies and between agencies.

We operate in an environment where our wired world makes key the issues of security and cultural sensitivity. The internet, and especially Facebook, can imperil life and ministry.

The unity of the body of Christ amid all this diversity is essential if we are to make progress in the task of world evangelization.

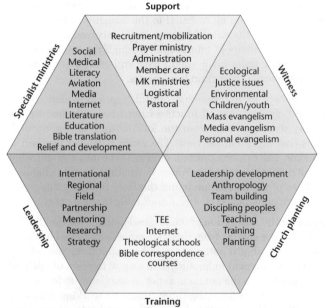

Note: Many of these categories are not exclusive to one triangle, and many missionaries have multiple roles. This is just to help give some understanding of the scope and complexity of missions today.

Fig 8.3 *The ministries of missions*

Missionary: one who is sent with a message. This word of Latin derivation has the same basic meaning as the Greek word "apostle" in the New Testament. It is incongruous that we use the term "missionary" and ignore the biblical term "apostle". The Christian missionary is someone commissioned by a local church or denomination to evangelize and disciple people outside his or her home area, and often among people of a different race, culture or language. The term has three somewhat different, regional definitions and our missions database covers all three:[7]

1. The stricter N American usage: anyone sent to evangelize, plant churches or minister outside their own country

2. The broader European and Latin American usage: anyone sent to evangelize, plant churches or minister cross-culturally, whether in their own country or outside it

3. The even broader African and Asian usage: anyone sent to evangelize, plant churches or minister outside their home area, whether cross-culturally or not and whether in their own country or abroad.

Burning Question

The early church at Antioch was a missional church. It was multicultural—as modern urban churches should be.

▲ To what extent does our present theological training equip workers for ministry both with and to people of other cultures?

The role of the local church in missions

A local church that wants to be biblical and obedient to the Holy Spirit should be passionate in its commitment to Jesus' Last Command. Sadly, this is rarely the case and only a small minority of churches are directly and meaningfully involved in spreading the Gospel worldwide. On this page, we analyse the level of involvement of churches in sending missionaries and also the real cost of initiating and maintaining a long-term mission effort that bears lasting fruit.

Here is a list of many of the more significant missionary-sending countries and how many thousands of P, I and A missionaries each has sent (the red bars on the left).[8] Most of these churches are evangelical in theology. The USA tops the list, followed by India, S Korea, Canada and the UK.

The countries are listed according to the average number of churches needed to send ONE missionary. This changes the order significantly. Only one country sends out more missionaries than it has churches—Singapore. Some smaller countries and territories, such as Finland, New Zealand and Norway, are also high on the list, as is Hong Kong. More than seven churches are needed to send a single missionary from the US. These figures are only averages, of course. In practice, it is often a handful of churches with a large missions programme and budget that sends most of the missionaries, while many have little or no meaningful involvement in missions. It is also interesting to see how the rapid growth of churches in Africa has not yet led to a massive increase in missions involvement.[9]

The cost in preparing and sending missionaries into a distant cross-cultural situation is rarely well understood. For both wealthy and less wealthy countries, it is expensive—yet essential. 'Field visits' and short-term involvement have value but are more supportive or motivational. Learning languages and cultures is a long-term requisite for fruitful ministry.

Fig 8.5 shows an average career path of a missionary, whether short-term, single or married. On the right are the statistics for cross-cultural missionaries. The bands of colour indicate the percentage of all missionaries in that period of ministry.[10]

At any one time, over half of all serving cross-cultural missionaries are in the process of preparation for mission, with maybe only a third fully engaged in a discipling ministry in a distant culture. It often takes between 11 and 13 years from leaving a secular career to reach that point—including seven years after one's appointment to a field of ministry. Yet in the 1990s the average couple stayed in place for only seven or eight years, while single (usually female) missionaries averaged 14–16. Thus, anything that local churches and mission agencies can do to keep missionaries in the field and lengthen their useful ministry is a good investment, though it may mean providing support for their children, pastoral care, further training etc.

In many fields, experience and maturity are more likely to be found among the longer-serving single female missionaries. How can missions and ministries better recognize this reality and capitalize on it?

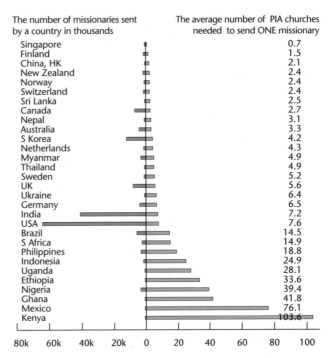

Fig 8.4 *Churches and the sending of missionaries*

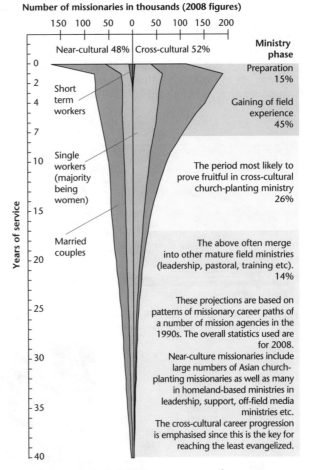

Fig 8.5 *Missionary career paths*

Food for Thought

▲ Is it more cost-effective to support nationals?

They know the culture and need less funding—yet there are few, if any, Christians from the least-evangelized peoples to do the job. Cross-cultural missionaries from distant cultures are still essential.[11]

The expansion of the mission force in the 20th Century

The mobilization of Christians in missions since 1900 has been astonishing. From 17,400 in 1900, the number rose slowly to 43,000 in 1962, but then came the explosive growth that followed the Awakening around that time, with some 200,000 in 2000 and maybe even 300,000 in 2010. This has happened even as non-evangelical denominational missions collapsed, with the new wave of fervent evangelical missionaries more than replacing them.

This growth has not been so apparent in the media, secular or Christian, partly because so much of it has come in new forms of "crazy" youth missions such as Campus Crusade, YWAM and Operation Mobilisation, or from countries that had not traditionally sent out missionaries.[12]

The graph in Fig 8.6 shows that growth. Note that from 1980 onwards the massive increase in missions was in AfAsLA, and especially Asia. Note the dark blue line, which indicates the percentage of the world's missionaries coming from AfAsLA countries (with the actual figures given at intervals). Before 1980, the figures for AfAsLA were probably undercounted.[13]

The globalization of the mission force, along with this increase, is an unprecedented phenomenon. If the statistics were available, the number of Catholic missionaries would show similar growth—until the last 20 years, when vocations to both domestic and foreign missions declined dramatically. We have therefore restricted our statistics to the three Christian streams P, I and A, since nearly all of the missionaries from these are evangelical in theology and are linked with denominational or interdenominational missions in which

there is no distinction between the three streams but they relate closely together in ministry.

As I was writing this chapter, the latest statistics gathered for the 2010 *Operation World* became available. These were incomplete,[14] but they testify to a further dramatic increase during the first decade of the 21st Century. The graph in Fig 8.7 shows this development by continent. In Europe and the Pacific there has actually been a small decline, while growth has been modest in Latin America, where an initial fervour for missions subsided as the tough demands of missionary life became more apparent—but could build up again. The countries that have shown the greatest growth over the ten years are listed between the columns.

The US has seen growth, but a large proportion of this has been in short-term workers and those who train and facilitate their ministry overseas.

China is included for the first time as the vision for missions there increases. No figures were available for 2000 in our database.[15]

Growth in *S Korea* continues but is likely to slow rapidly as a result of low birth rates and little church growth.

The continued growth of missions in *India* is the most striking—about half of it to near cultures and half to distant cultures within India.

The 20th-Century growth began with much fervour for missions while the influence of the Student Volunteer Movement was at its height.[16] The missions movement was largely Anglophone and was dominated by the British and N Americans and, to an extent, other European Protestant nations. Even then, there were differences in strategy and working that made cooperation a challenge. The century ended with missionaries going all over the world from almost every country that had a Christian presence.

The whole paradigm of missions has now changed. The old, Western ways of forming relationships and strategies and working in the field will no longer do now that missionaries are being sent out from all over the world. Increasingly, everyone will need to deal with multiple initiatives aimed at the same populations; agencies and networks will have to cooperate across cultures, and multicultural teams will become the norm. This is no longer an option, but essential. Care will be needed to ensure that all peoples are discipled. Multicultural teams work well only with a lot of tears, hard work, humility and frequent repentance—but it is worth the effort!

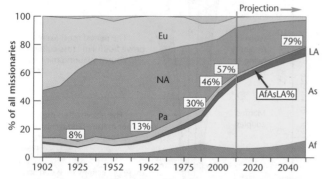

Fig 8.6 *The sending of missionaries by continent, showing the growth of the AfAsLA component, 1900–2050*

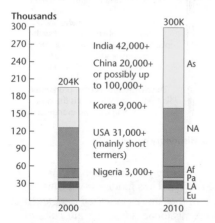

Fig 8.7 *Missionary growth between 2000 and 2010*

Chinese home Bible-study group
(photo P Hattaway)

Burning Question

Western countries found it hard to work together in missions in the 20th Century.

▲ How much more challenging is it likely to be with Africans, Asians and Latin Americans all involved with Westerners in missions?

Western agencies and churches may have to change their organizational structures, leadership styles and ways of making decisions, handling moral failure, resolving relational breakdowns etc for the sake of unity in ministry.

From Where Were Missionaries Sent in 2000?

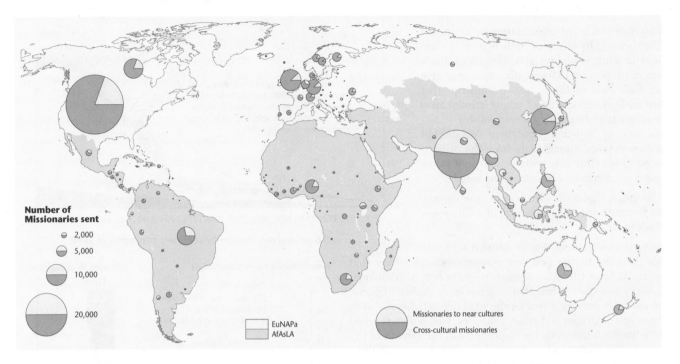

Number of Missionaries sent

- 2,000
- 5,000
- 10,000
- 20,000

EuNAPa
AfAsLA

Missionaries to near cultures
Cross-cultural missionaries

The map above gives more detail about the sending of missionaries, which it shows by country, divided into the two major continental groupings of AfAsLA and EuNAPa. Each country's contribution is represented by a pie, whose size is proportionate to the number of missionaries it has sent—the legend gives an approximate measure. Each pie is divided into two segments: those missionaries working or living in a near culture and those in a distant culture (whether in their own country or abroad).

Near-culture missionaries. Information gathered from agencies about where their missionaries are working and in what ministries has enabled us to make reasonable estimates of the numbers serving cross-culturally and in distant cultures. Approximately 30% of PIA missionaries are serving either in their own countries and cultures or among closely related peoples in other countries. They fall into several categories of ministry:

▲ church planters in largely unevangelized areas who speak the local language or one very like it. This is a global phenomenon, but especially it involves many Indian and Chinese missionaries.

▲ specialists in Bible translation, literature, the media, the internet, aviation, aid, relief, development, medical ministries etc, working from bases in their own countries. This is more common in N America and Europe.

▲ missionaries assigned to preparing new missionaries for the field as short- and long-term workers

▲ full-time leaders, strategists, researchers etc

▲ support workers—who represent the work of missions, raise and channel support, provide pastoral care for missionaries etc. The range of ministries needed to undergird the work of the global mission force is impressive.

Cross-cultural missionaries. Over 70% of the global mission force is serving in distant cultures. Without such cross-cultural workers, the world will never be fully evangelized. They fall into four categories:

1. missionaries serving in other countries among peoples not their own—as church planters, in aid, health or development programmes, or in specialist ministries whose ultimate aim is to establish indigenous churches or church-planting movements

2. professionals whose secular skills can be a witness in themselves but also create opportunities for witnessing or church planting. This can be a way to obtain a visa to a "closed" country, and an increasing proportion of missionaries are serving in this way. In some cases, this work also supports them financially.

3. missionaries serving in their own countries among less evangelized indigenous people groups—for example, Brazilians working among indigenous Amazon peoples and Nigerians working among unreached people groups in Nigeria[17]

4. missionaries serving in their own countries among immigrant groups. This is a major area of ministry in Europe, Australasia and the Americas.[18]

S Korea is a surprising country. Out of the fires of 20th-Century revival, 35 years of Japanese occupation, the division of their land in 1945 and the subsequent devastation of the Korean War (1950–53) emerged a strong, dynamic Church, a highly successful economic boom and an explosion in the number of missionaries sent out. There were few Korean missionaries in 1980, but by 2000 there were over 12,000, mostly in cross-cultural work—and by 2010 that number had climbed to over 21,000. S Korea is second only to the US in sending out missionaries to other lands. Now, its missionaries are reaching out to nearly every nation on earth.

Food for Thought

The Korean missions movement has had a deep impact on the world. S Korea is largely monocultural and until recently was isolated from the rest of the world. Its missionaries face huge challenges in adapting to other cultures, and not least the cultures of other missionaries.

▲ How can this two-way culture shock best be handled and the dynamic Korean missions movement fully integrated into the global Church and the world missions movement?

The distribution of missionaries

The distribution of missionaries by continent is revealing, in terms of both how many are sent to each continent and how many there are in proportion to its population. It may give an indication of the range of ministries that are really needed, and of where missionaries may be inappropriately deployed—for example, among Christian populations. We did not gather detailed enough data from the original surveys to refine this analysis, and so it raises many questions that remain unanswered.

The graph shows the distribution of missionaries by continent from 1900 to 2010, with projections to 2050.

Note the under-reporting of AfAsLA missionaries (because in the past few researchers understood that many AfAsLA Christian workers were, in fact, also missionaries[19]) and the red line that suggests more realistic figures. In our later surveys it was harder to obtain reliable statistics from some African and Asian countries, which also resulted in a likely undercount. The importance of the growth of the missions movement in Asia is marked—though this is likely to decline as E Asian populations rapidly age.

The analysis of missionary deployment by continent is inadequate. It is too simplistic in an age of massive intercontinental migration, the rapid development of air travel, mass media and the internet and the rise of an Islamism that actively seeks to eliminate any Christian presence from Muslim heartlands. Many fruitful ministries, such as those that use satellite television and mobile phone outreach, may be based a continent away from the people they serve. Looking at the world by people groups and people clusters rather than geographically is more helpful.

The impact of "9/11" changed the perception and management of ministry in sensitive countries, and especially among Muslim peoples. Security became a major factor, and this in turn led to missionaries keeping a low profile or even trying to remain invisible in order to be able to minister to Muslims. Overt mission in Muslim contexts has often been replaced with off-field ministries or "tentmaker" church planting, and use of the term "missionary" has been avoided. This inhibits both open recruitment and publicity to generate prayer—and yet ministry continues among Muslims, and often is increasingly fruitful.

Charting the number of missionaries per every million people on each continent reveals another surprising fact: their unequal distribution. In Fig 8.9, the black bars show that the density of missionaries in the Pacific is far higher than in Asia

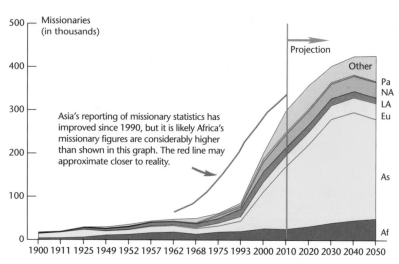

Fig 8.8 *Serving missionaries by continent of ministry in 2000*

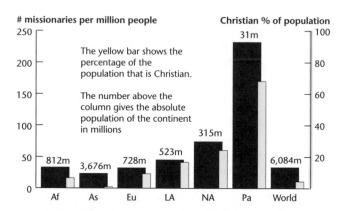

Fig 8.9 *Density of missionaries by continent in 2000*

(a fact not apparent in Fig 8.8 because it is not related to the immense size of Asia's population). One significant reason for this imbalance is that the Pacific has a large number of small people groups and there is a heavy emphasis on providing emerging churches with Scriptures in their own languages.

The yellow bars indicate the percentage of each population that is Christian. It is sobering to see that generally the higher the percentage of Christians in a population, the more missionaries there are, when it should be the other way round.

The range of Christian ministries (including, for example, teaching, Bible translation, literature and development) increases with the extent and variety of church life in a country or among a people. Where the Gospel is a novelty and, often, Christian input is not welcome, too many pioneers can provoke a negative response—especially if they come from many different countries and do not work together. Some mission fields can soon become saturated in this sense.

Evangelical Bolivian believers (photo courtesy of Samaritan's Purse)

Food for Thought

The publicity about unreached peoples after 1990 prompted many missional churches to reassess their deployment policies, and to favour missions engaged in pioneer work with underevangelized nations and peoples. This certainly helped to redress an imbalance, but it often went too far and discriminated against valid ministries elsewhere. All missionary ministries, however, must have "hand-over" and "move-on" strategies if they are to be truly apostolic.

Missionaries and their primary religious environment

There is inadequate data to determine how many missionaries are deployed to specific people groups or religious communities. Many agencies do not categorize in this way. However, we have enough information to indicate how many missionaries work in each country or region and to determine the approximate number actually in contact with peoples of other religions.

Fig 8.10 groups countries according to their principal religion and shows the percentage and the number of missionaries working in each group. This may not be a fair way of counting, because in some countries that have several religions, or a large Christian minority, most missionaries would be working among minorities or exclusively serving the Christian community—though this community may have its roots in the dominant religion. For example, in India the large majority of Indian missionaries work among tribal people groups or the disadvantaged Dalits or low-caste Hindus, and very few among higher-caste groups. This is also true in Brazil, where many Brazilian church-planting missionaries are working in Amazon tribal areas with very small populations.

In many countries that have a sizeable Muslim minority, very little ministry at present is directed to reaching them. This would be true of northern Nigeria, India's Muslim communities, eastern Ethiopia with its Muslim majority etc.

The tally of missionaries working among the non-religious is distorted by the fact that, while most of the people we've counted among the non-religious are in China, our survey in 2000 did not include the missionaries from China working among the non-religious in their own country.

However, these figures do give some idea of the efforts currently being made to evangelize adherents of other religions.

The number of missionaries serving in Christian countries is surprising and needs explanation. An obvious conclusion would be that missions focus far too often on Christians, but this may not be the case. If we compare the figures for all Christian workers in Fig 8.8 on page 230, we have to admit that most effort by far is spent satisfying the needs of churchgoing Christians, with too little expended on outreach and, especially, missions. However, a number of the missionaries serving in "Christian" lands are planting churches among nominal or even notional Christian populations that have few evangelical churches. Others are involved in key ministry to non-Christian immigrants—a growing need today and even more so in the future. Most of these missionaries, however, are involved in ministries of leadership, representation or support, or other specialist ministries—which are all an essential component in taking the Gospel to the world.

The same statistics (still grouping countries according to their principal religion) are treated in a different way in Fig 8.11. This shows how many people on average there are for each religion per each missionary working in a country with that majority religion. It is abundantly clear that people in Muslim-majority countries have far fewer missionaries serving among them, as do those in the mostly non-religious West and China.

Once again, China's figures distort the results: the non-religious are in the majority there, but the figures also include large numbers of Buddhists, Muslims and followers of ethnic religions.

The best-served are those living in countries dominated by ethnic religions, Buddhism or Christianity.

What stands out is the need of the Muslim world, which accounts for a quarter of the world's population. Reaching it is a major challenge. The negative interactions between Muslims and Christians over nearly 1,500 years, the entrenched denials of the essentials of Christianity in Islamic doctrine and the recent traumatic episodes of Muslim violence and terrorism all make the very idea of "proselytizing" Muslims controversial.[20] Nonetheless, in the midst of this, one of the largest missionary efforts ever to Muslims is under way, and there is much evidence of more Muslims becoming followers of Jesus than ever before. So, how many missionaries are there working among Muslims? Fig 8.10 comes to a reasonable figure of over 16,000. A few years ago, I made a brief survey of 20 agencies with extensive involvement with Muslims, and these alone had more than 9,000 missionaries working among Muslims, whether living in Muslim-majority countries or, as migrants in Muslim communities, elsewhere. It is hard to estimate the number of "tentmaker" missionaries serving in the Muslim world, whether sent by churches or having gone there for the sake of Christ without that formal recognition, notably including Nigerians, Filipinos, Iranians and Chinese.

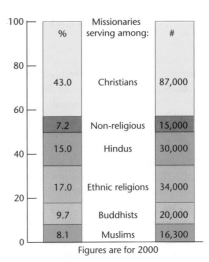

%	Missionaries serving among:	#
43.0	Christians	87,000
7.2	Non-religious	15,000
15.0	Hindus	30,000
17.0	Ethnic religions	34,000
9.7	Buddhists	20,000
8.1	Muslims	16,300

Figures are for 2000

Fig 8.10 *Missionaries per main religion of the country they ministered in*

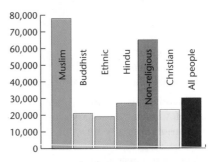

Fig 8.11 *Adherents of each religion per missionary in the countries where that religion was the dominant one in 2000*

A Muslim man (photo by ED)

Burning Question

Islam has clear teaching on *da'wa*, which is the obligation of Muslims to invite people to embrace Islam—yet Muslims vigorously oppose any form of Christian mission. Sadly, many Western governments and even churches discourage it, too, on the grounds that it could "provoke" Muslims. In recent years, the number of missionary martyrs in Muslim lands has risen steeply.

▲ Are we prepared to promote prayer for and missions among Muslims despite the cost?

TO EVERYWHERE

Receiving countries

Listing countries according to the number of missionaries they have received, it is eye-opening to see how the order has changed over the 20th Century. In Fig 8.12, the abbreviation at the head of each column refers to the source of the data.[21] The colour behind the number of each entry indicates its continent, and hatching shows where the majority religion is either Islam or Buddhism. The low numbers of missionaries in 1900 are in strong contrast to 2000. In Fig 8.13 on page 233 there is a similar chart of missionary-sending countries for comparison. Missions did not die with colonial empires but instead has become a major global enterprise.

1900. The goal of the Student Volunteer Movement towards the end of the 19th Century was manifestly unattainable. Just four countries dominated the attention of missions in 1900, of which only one, S Africa, became largely Christian over the century that followed. China and Japan endured traumatic war, revolution and repression, and in Japan and India the major breakthroughs are still to come.

It is interesting to see how few missionaries there were in Africa. At this stage, there were still no answers to the killer diseases malaria[22] and sleeping sickness. Some Muslim countries are listed, but much of the mission effort was to the traditional Christian minorities there.

1960. India still tops the list, but after independence the number of foreign missionaries dropped dramatically owing to visa restrictions. By now, missions to Africa dominated and interest in Latin America had grown considerably. Both of these continents were on the verge of massive church growth.

Muslim countries were thinly covered, and there was still a strong feeling that Muslims were too resistant to the Gospel. Most of the effort was still addressed to Christian and fringe minorities in these lands.

By this time, China had dropped out of the list as the Communists were seeking to dominate and then to eradicate Christianity in the so-called Cultural Revolution.

1975. The huge growth of the mission "industry" after the 1960s Awakening established the USA at the top of the list. The heavy Christianization (albeit apartheid-dominated) of S African society kept that country high in the list.

By this time, the importance of non-Communist Asia had grown—often because these countries were pioneered by missionaries ejected from China in 1949. Despite many visa difficulties, the number of foreign missionaries in Asia was rising.

Africa and Latin America continued to be important, but with large, maturing indigenous church movements emerging.

2000. The situation by 2000 was characterized by huge growth in the number of missionaries in Asia, most of them Asian or indigenous national missionaries. By this time, Nigeria had become Africa's missions powerhouse.

Notable, too, is the appearance of post-Communist Russia and France and parts of C Europe as mission fields receiving missionaries.

A high proportion of the US, UK, German and S Korean missionaries serving in their own countries were servicing those that had been sent abroad. Missions to Muslim countries had by now become a major focus, but for security reasons that is not reflected in this list.

	1900 (WMC)			1960 (WCH)			1975 (WCE)			2000 (OW)	
Rank	Country	#	Rank	Country	#	Rank	Country	#	Rank	Country	#
1	India	3,600	1	India	5,161	1	USA	5,676	1	India	42,023
2	China	3,500	2	S Africa	3,791	2	S Africa	2,900	2	USA	20,219
3	S Africa	1,200	3	Japan	3,144	3	Japan	2,633	3	Brazil	6,966
4	Japan	700	4	Nigeria	2,495	4	India	2,214	4	Philippines	5,051
5	USA	400	5	Congo, DR	2,258	5	PNG	21.7	5	UK	4,179
6	Indonesia	350	6	Zimbabwe	1,972	6	Congo, DR	1,830	6	Japan	3,683
7	Cameroon	300	7	Tanzania	1,559	7	Nigeria	1,716	7	Nigeria	3,584
8	Congo, DR	300	8	Brazil	1,418	8	Ethiopia	1,454	8	Indonesia	3,416
9	Kenya	300	9	Philippines	927	9	Mexico	1,442	9	Myanmar	3,263
10	Nigeria	300	10	Ethiopia	748	10	Philippines	1,334	10	Canada	3,114
11	S Korea	290	11	Indonesia	685	11	Kenya	1,289	11	Australia	2,965
12	Canada	250	12	Kenya	656	12	Indonesia	1,257	12	Kenya	2,870
13	Madagascar	250	13	Pakistan	625	13	Zimbabwe	1,137	13	Mexico	2,695
14	Turkey	250	14	Malaysia	611	14	Tanzania	1,036	14	Russia	2,584
15	Jamaica	220	15	Thailand	592	15	Colombia	888	15	PNG	2,556
16	Hong Kong	200	16	PNG	548	16	Taiwan	877	16	Thailand	2,377
17	Palestine	200	17	Peru	540	17	Thailand	844	17	S Africa	2,344
18	Mexico	200	18	Argentina	500	18	Zambia	830	18	Germany	2,283
19	Myanmar	200	19	Jamaica	482	19	Peru	823	19	S Korea	2,043
20	Syria	200	20	Colombia	466	20	Ecuador	788	20	France	1,746

Fig 8.12 *The top 20 missionary-receiving countries, 1900–2000*

The top 20 countries are listed for 1900 to 2000 but the names and areas are extrapolated from their status for 2000.

Note: By 2000 there was a large increase in the number of Christian workers in Muslim nations, but for security reasons many of these nations are not listed.

Western World

- Europe
- N America
- Latin America
- Pacific

Non-Western World

- Africa
- Asia
- Islam
- Buddhism

Food for Thought

The 20th Century was extraordinary for the change and growth in missions. It began with missionaries focused on some specific parts of the world—mainly S and E Asia and also S and E Africa. By its end, there was scarcely a country in the world without a PIA missionary presence, overt or covert, and only a handful that showed no evidence of the beginnings, at least, of a church-planting movement. In the course of the century the Church became a global force for the blessing of the world.

How much was achieved by so few!

THE FUTURE OF THE GLOBAL CHURCH

Sending countries

The following chart of the top 20 missionary-sending countries is not quite comparable with the one opposite, as the 1975 list is not shown but a list for 2010 is. The changes over the period are again remarkable.

EuNAPa Countries. Anglophone countries dominated, with nine in the top 20 and 80% of all missionaries. *Britain* was the largest sender of missionaries in 1900 but was soon eclipsed by the *USA*. The UK's numbers changed relatively little over the next 110 years. The US has headed the list ever since. *Germany's* contribution was seriously affected by the closure of all mission work during the two world wars in 1914–18 and 1939–45, and never fully recovered. The *Scandinavian countries*, though small, have played a significant role in missions around the world. The contributions of Sweden, Norway and Finland proportionate to their populations have exceeded those of the US and the UK. The *Pacific island nations* do not appear in these lists because of their small size, but much of the evangelization of the Pacific was actually done by Tongan, Samoan and Tahitian missionaries. *S Africa*, though in Africa, has largely sent Caucasian missionaries. Sadly, this is still true today, with the African, S Asian and mixed-race communities contributing little to missions—in part a legacy of the years of apartheid.[23] *Ukraine* appears on the 2010 list as the prime missionary-sending country within the former Soviet Union—especially to other ethnic minorities in Russia, out of a sense of fellow feeling.

AfAsLA Countries. Three of the top four missionary-sending countries in 2010 were Asian—an astonishing change from 1900. A high proportion of India's and China's missionaries today are focused on unreached areas of their own countries, but the Chinese Church is increasingly assuming its global responsibilities.[24] Of the *Caribbean countries*, Jamaica and Trinidad appear on the 1900 list. The contribution of Caribbean missionaries to early mission work in W Africa has been little recognized. The Caribbean churches need a renewed vision for missions. *India* was one of the first AfAsLA countries to become a major sender of missions. Mainly these have gone out from the strong churches established in the south in the 18th and 19th Centuries and the amazing people movements among the tribal peoples of India's northeast. In the last 20 years, the commitment of Indians to missions has deepened, but it is little known because much of this effort is cross-cultural within India itself. *Brazil* was the first Latin American country to take up the challenge of missions, and it remains at the forefront of that continent's mission movement. Brazilians often major on evangelism and church planting.[25] *Nigeria and Ghana* have been the pioneers for missions in Africa, both among their own unreached people groups and in other African countries. Africans are now focusing on ministry to the Middle East and Europe. Nigerian church planters have been some of the most successful in unresponsive Europe. For *S Korea's* impressive missions movement, see page 229. In *the Philippines,* people are often poor, with few resources, but well educated, and many thousands have gone out as tentmaker missionaries to Asia, the Middle East and beyond. Their ministry has been exemplary in their willingness to suffer for the sake of Christ in difficult countries that others could not enter. This is a yet untold story of the spread of Christianity.

	1900			1960			2000			2010	
Rank	**Country**	**#**	**Rank**	**Country**	**#**	**Rank**	**Country**	**#**	**Rank**	**Country**	**#**
1	UK	6,530	1	USA	20,500	1	USA	64,084	1	USA	95,000
2	USA	5,591	2	UK	5,700	2	India	41,064	2	India	82,950
3	Germany	1,833	3	Canada	3,600	3	S Korea	12,279	3	S Korea	21,500
4	India	837	4	India	1,500	4	UK	8,164	4	China	20,000
5	S Africa	531	5	Sweden	1,400	5	Canada	7,001	5	Nigeria	6,644
6	Australia	403	6	Norway	1,200	6	Brazil	5,801	6	UK	6,405
7	Canada	280	7	Australia	1,100	7	Australia	4,167	7	Canada	5,200
8	Sweden	235	8	Germany	1,000	8	Germany	3,953	8	Philippines	4,500
9	Jamaica	156	9	Netherlands	1,000	9	Nigeria	3,351	9	Australia	3,756
10	Japan	146	10	S Africa	850	10	Philippines	3,188	10	Germany	3,712
11	France	132	11	New Zealand	720	11	Myanmar	3,151	11	Brazil	3,438
12	Norway	132	12	Philippines	600	12	S Africa	2,548	12	Indonesia	3,000
13	Ireland	131	13	Switzerland	500	13	New Zealand	1,694	13	S Africa	2,300
14	Netherlands	108	14	Brazil	500	14	Indonesia	1,573	14	Switzerland	2,183
15	China	68	15	Indonesia	400	15	Finland	1,449	15	Netherlands	2,000
16	Trinidad	62	16	Myanmar	400	16	Switzerland	1,404	16	Ghana	2,000
17	Switzerland	51	17	Finland	380	17	Netherlands	1,341	17	Ukraine	1,599
18	New Zealand	48	18	Denmark	200	18	Sweden	1,126	18	New Zealand	1,200
19	Sri Lanka	47	19	Singapore	150	19	Norway	1,045	19	Sweden	1,143
20	Denmark	35	20	France	140	20	Nepal	957	20	Mexico	1,139

The top 20 countries are listed for 1900 to 2010 but the names and areas are extrapolated from their status for 2000.

Note: There has been no projection by country to the future because of the unpredictable fluidity of the missionary sending patterns around the world.

Western World

- Europe
- N America
- Latin America
- Pacific

Non-Western World

- Africa
- Asia
- Islam

Fig 8.13 *The top 20 missionary-sending countries, 1900–2010*

Food for Thought

▲ How can a passion for missions be revived in countries that once made major contributions to world evangelization but now have lost that vision or localized it?

It is tempting to think that it is the turn of other, AfAsLA, countries and to concentrate instead on the urgent local needs of an increasingly nominal Christian and secular society. Yet the Last Command of Jesus remains valid until His return.

The present missions force is working at the growing edge of the Church. Most missionaries are still linked to agencies or national or international networks, but an uncounted number are now also sent out as individuals directly by local churches and others work independently—though their impact is quite limited.[26] Mission agencies are biblical in concept but not necessarily so in practice.[27] Historically, they follow in the line of the monastic orders in the Eastern and Western Church between the 4th and 18th Centuries. Modern mission bodies, developed during the Moravian-Methodist Awakening in the 18th Century, acquired a sharp focus through the writings of William Carey, who proposed the formation of "mission societies". It was this that enabled the long-dormant and ineffectual post-Reformation churches to become the dynamic global Church of today. It is important to recognize that mission agencies are an essential part of the Church, both nationally and internationally, and accountable to it (see p225).

Over the past 20 years we have developed a database of agencies, both for the compilation of *Operation World* and as a way to keep in touch with (and informed by) missionaries on active service. It is global in coverage (as the upper pie chart shows), so we are able to give a reasonable assessment of the world's mission agencies.[28] The two pie charts in Fig 8.14 summarize our findings. The 3,180 "national missionary-sending entities" range from large, multi-department mission headquarters to the supporters of a single missionary serving with an international agency. The continental spread of these entities demonstrates that there are missionaries going out from almost everywhere to almost everywhere. Both our database and our coverage of each country provide these figures for sending and receiving. However, heightened security since 2001 means that such an analysis is unlikely to be repeated.

The second pie chart gives the statistics for agencies selected for a more detailed listing in *Operation World* 2001. In general, the criteria for selection were the number of full-time workers and the nature of the agency's ministries (though some agencies were includ-

ed that had an especially unique role). These 109 agencies account for more than 70% of known serving missionaries and most of their larger national sending bases, and over half of the total number of bases.

For such a variegated, multinational mission force, the cultural demands are enormous and the time and emotional energy consumed in working together seem, at times, too much. Many agencies, therefore, prefer to function as single-nationality bodies or single-nationality teams in the field. However, this is not the biblical pattern. Christ has broken down the cultural divide between Jew and Greek—indeed, people of all nations (Ephesians 3:10–22). We must live this out and be the answer to Jesus' prayer for unity in John 17. Unity in diversity presents possibly the biggest challenge for missions in the 21st Century.

The two pie charts in Fig 8.15 group the agencies listed in the two editions of *Operation World* according to their core or original ministry. Most, of course, have expanded beyond their initial vision and now have a wide range of ministries. It is interesting to see the increasing and healthy emphasis on church planting.

Very few of the agencies listed are involved in specialized or aid-providing ministries—partly because the former tend to be smaller and, of the latter, few actually send out field workers.

Partnership

The sharing of resources, strategies, support structures and personnel is not optional but an essential component in world evangelization today. Partnerships at every level among agencies have grown over recent decades, whether in the form of larger international conferences, national alliances and international bodies such as WEA and LCWE or (increasingly) of cooperation in the field at the level of regions, countries and people clusters. Many agencies have become increasingly multicultural, or now contribute workers to multi-agency ministry or church-planting teams.

Possibly the most defective partnership is that between mission agencies and local churches. This dysfunctionality is rooted in church history and in the patterns of theological education of pastoral workers where missions played little or no part. It is also the result of two centuries of mission agencies acting as if local churches were just a source of finance and people, and local churches acting irresponsibly in their roles of sending and supporting. The centrality of the local church in missions needs to be emphasized, and agencies must be more accountable to their supporting churches for their ministries and use of workers. However, both are vital components of the Church—and must work together.

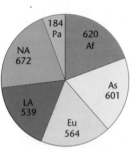

Distribution by continent

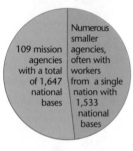

Fig 8.14 *Distribution and division of the national missionary-sending bases listed in* Operation World, *2001*

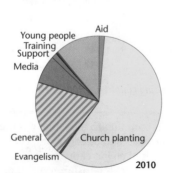

Fig 8.15 *Comparison of core or original ministries of the agencies listed in OW2001 and OW2010*

Burning Questions for Today

Breakdowns in relationships between agencies, theological trainers and local churches have harmed the cause of world evangelization. There are many instances of broken promises, misunderstanding and pain.

▲ How can missions become more sensitive to local churches?

▲ How can local churches become more missional in their vision?

▲ And how can trainers become more aware that academic excellence is no substitute for godliness in those sent out to serve in churches and missions?

Mission name (in 2010)	OW abbrev	Main ministry	Workers	Type of mission	Original/other nationalities	Nationalities in 2000	Fields 2010
Campus Crusade for Christ International	CCCI	yp	9,913	Int	USA/International	118	128
Gospel for Asia	GFA	cp	9,550	non	India	11	9
Operation Mobilisation	OM	gen	6,332	Int	UK/USA/Internat	79	87
International Mission Board (formerly SBC)	IMB	cp	5,512	Den	USA	6	100
Wycliffe Bible Translators	WBT	media	5,021	Int	USA/International	35	50
Youth With A Mission	YWAM	gen	5,000	Int	USA/International	132	154
New Tribes Mission	NTM	cp	2,467	non	USA/International	32	26
Assemblies of God	AoG	cp	2,355	Den	USA	58	153
Gospel Echoing Missionary Society	GEMS	cp	2,205	non	India	1	4
Vishwa Vani	W	cp	2,123	non	India	1	11
Indian Evangelical Team	IET	cp	2,093	Int	India	2	3
Global Mission Society-Presby Ch (Hapdong)	GMS	cp	1,991	Den	S Korea	3	100
Synod Mission Board	SMB	gen	1,826	Den	India	1	1
WEC International	WEC	cp	1,819	Int	USA	53	80
SIM International	SIM	cp	1,600	Int	USA	26	51
OMF International	OMF	cp	1,557	Int	UK/International	23	22
Pioneers	P	cp	1,166	Int	International	27	70
Presbyterian Church (Tonghap)	PC (T-hap)	cp	1,144	Den	S Korea	1	83
Association of Baptists for World Evangelism	ABWE	cp	1,053	Den	USA	3	61
Great Commission Movement Trust	GCMT	cp	1,045	Int	India	1	1
Native Missionary Movement India	NMMI	cp	1,012	Int	India	1	1
Interserve	I	gen	1,006	Int	UK/International	14	22

Fig 8.16 *The world's largest mission agencies in 2010, each with over 1,000 serving missionaries*

Fig 8.16 lists only the world's mega-missions—those with more than 1,000 serving missionaries in 2010—but it is revealing about the new world of missions. It indicates the type of mission in each case (denominational, interdenominational or non-denominational) and also the principal ministries (cp = church planting; gen = general; yp = young people) and the country (if one in particular) from which its original workers came. It also gives the number of nationalities each agency deployed in 2000, and the number of fields it was active in in 2010.

Mission nationalities. It is surprising to see that, of the 22 listed, seven agencies are Indian in origin and two are S Korean.

Most of the others are of US or UK origin, but those that are not denominational have become very international. Note the numbers for nationalities and fields with these missions.

Mission morphing. OM started out as a short-term youth mission, but many of its workers are now reaching retirement age.

GFA started as an aid mission for Indian pastors but has become a pioneer church-planting mission.

YWAM was launched to disciple young people but has become one of the most diverse of missions.

Mission agency challenges for the 21st Century

Here are a few of many I could cite:

▲ The internationalization of missions, though very worthwhile, has not been easy. How can missions structured according to a Western Greek/Renaissance worldview adapt to accommodate workers from relational or oral cultures and cultures based on animist or Confucian worldviews, or cultures where honour and shame are more significant than right and wrong? The process of adaptation is often redemptive and forges strong church-planting teams that demonstrate the power of the Gospel.

▲ Burgeoning S Korean missions come from an isolated monoculture, which also has a strong Presbyterian heritage—there are over 100 Presbyterian denominations in S Korea! How can they avoid the cultural imperialism of earlier Western missions and serve the nations according to the Nevius principles that made their Church so strong?

▲ Dynamic Nigerian missions just failed to "qualify" for the listing in Fig 8.16. How are agencies and churches on other continents going to handle the innovation and dynamism of the coming wave of African missionaries?

▲ Will the emphasis on church planting among the least evangelized be swamped by other current emphases—on disaster relief, ecology and tentmaking missions, the fascination with new technologies etc? How can all these ministries be bonded into a new synergy for discipling the peoples of the world effectively?

▲ The modern desire for short-term involvement and quick results can cripple efforts to give time to learn languages and cultures, build relationships and incarnate the Gospel in other cultures. There are few short cuts in pioneer evangelism and church planting. Breakthroughs often need 20–40 years of hard work to achieve. This is especially true in work among Muslims.

Food for Thought

No doctoral programmes, techniques, strategies, management styles or fund-raising expertise can replace a humble godliness and dependence on the Holy Spirit. Technology is a good servant but a poor master.

▲ Are the internet and mobile phones the most wonderful tools for evangelism or do they maybe hinder the forming of good discipling relationships?

▲ How will we engage in missions in the 21st Century and complete the task set us by our Lord and Saviour in Acts 1:8?

1. This is more fully covered in my book *The Church Is Bigger Than You Think*, pp155–177.

2. The design of these illustrations is based on Venn circles. These are now available on the DVD and online.

3. Quoted from John Piper's book *Let the Nations Be Glad* (Grand Rapids, MI: Baker Books, 1993)

4. The church in Antioch is a superb model for today. It was the Holy Spirit who was in charge. He had already called Paul and Barnabas, and He spoke to the leaders about setting apart Paul and Barnabas as an apostolic team. The local church obeyed, prayed, laid hands on them and released them. Paul and Barnabas built their own team, and sought the Lord about the direction it should take and forms of ministry it should exercise. They later recruited others to travel with them, to be trained as a new generation of workers, but remained accountable to the church that sent them out. The three functions were well structured. See Acts 14–15.

5. The term "Great Commission Christian" was coined by David Barrett in the *World Christian Encyclopedia* in 2001, and used extensively in those volumes. It is based on a constructed model, not on firm field or survey data. It also includes both nominal and committed Christians, from every branch of Christianity, and has limited value for a work such as this.

6. Short-term missions and mission trips are more characteristic of evangelical churches in wealthier countries (particularly EuNAPa and Overseas Chinese)—they are far less common in most AfAsLA countries. Setting aside long-term workers to facilitate short-term recruits is costly in resources and effort. Most of those serving as long-term missionaries today have had a short-term experience, but the value of much of this effort may ultimately be limited if there is not adequate preparation and follow-up of short-termers.

7. In both *Operation World* and this book, we synthesize the three principal definitions of a missionary by dividing all the missionaries from each country and region between the three categories of national/foreign, near-cultural/cross-cultural and sent-out/support ministries. Most foreign missionaries are cross-cultural but not all, as many are actually working within expatriate communities of their own culture.

8. We have included only P, I and A missionaries. Probably about 95% of modern missionaries are evangelical in theology. We have not included the relatively small number of Orthodox missionary priests, or the much larger number of Catholic missionary priests, monks and nuns, because statistics are no longer published on either that would enable us to distinguish between foreign-origin and indigenous workers.

9. The number of true African missionaries is very hard to assess. Much that is done is not analysed, and many Africans go to serve in other lands in secular work but with the full intent of planting churches. It is therefore likely that our figures given here are much too low.

10. *Too Valuable to Lose* and *Worth Keeping* are compendiums of talks given at WEA conferences which were called to address the need to reduce the attrition rate of missionaries in the field. They were edited by William Taylor and published by the William Carey Library in 1997 and 2006 respectively.

11. Many churches in wealthier countries have majored on raising funds to support nationals rather than sending missionaries themselves. The general half-truth is that nationals can do the job far sooner and for a much lower cost than a foreign missionary. This is true but it presupposes that there are nationals within an unevangelized people group who are employable, which is rarely the case. Sending a national cross-culturally can be as expensive as sending someone from Europe or the US, or even more so. However, this philosophy of ministry also has serious dangers: overseas control, dependence, the bypassing of national Christian leadership, misjudgements arising out of cultural differences, the misuse of funds and even the misunderstanding of what the pioneer needs actually are. This does not preclude giving of this kind, but it must be done in such a way as to enhance the long-term spiritual health of local leaders, churches and the workers themselves and strengthen local accountability to the Body of Christ.

12. The data behind these figures come from a number of sources. The *World Mission Atlases* contain global survey figures from 1902 to 1925. For 1949–1967, we drew on surveys in the successive *World Christian Handbooks* edited by Kenneth Grubb. For 1975, it was the *World Christian Encyclopedia* of 1981, and from then onwards it was the global surveys we made for successive editions of *Operation World*. This explains the irregularity of the year scale.

13. The undercount of missionaries from AfAsLA countries was a serious error that arose from a rather paternalistic view that only Westerners counted. The figures for Africa also include S Africa, which for much of the 20th Century provided the bulk of African missionaries, but these were nearly all Caucasian Afrikaners and English-speakers.

14. The *Operation World* data for 2010 covered most, but not all, major missionary-sending countries. Where there were significant gaps, I added an estimate extrapolated from 2001 data.

15. Paul Hattaway of Asian Harvest has strong evidence that in 2010 the actual number of longer-term missionaries sent out by Chinese churches may have exceeded 100,000.

16. The Student Volunteer Movement was founded in 1886 to mobilize Christian students for mission. It greatly raised the profile of missions and led to thousands of new recruits going overseas, even if its aims were simplistic and very optimistic. Nonetheless, it contributed to making the 20th Century the greatest century of missions ever.

17. The Brazilian government has excluded foreign workers from many areas in the Amazon River Basin where indigenous peoples live.

18. Many returning missionaries seek out opportunities for ministry among immigrant communities from their original field. They are often not counted, and yet this important area of ministry will gain in significance as the 21st Century unfolds.

19. It took many decades to break down the assumption that a missionary had to be a Westerner or function in a Western-style mission agency. Major missions congresses convened by the LCWE and AD2000 and Beyond Movement in the 1970s to 1990s, as well as the wide distribution of *Operation World* in many languages helped as much as anything to change this.

20. Muslim propaganda and political leverage have been effective in the West. The constant reminders of the threat of civil unrest or violence certainly make politicians careful to avoid provocation, and in the process reduce their ability to take firm action in future where necessary. Christian churches and ministries have also severely compromised their own position by changing their vocabulary (to cut out militant biblical language), diluting the theology of the Gospel and making no overt attempts to witness. There are many aspects of our faith that cannot be negotiated or watered down. We will need to be both loving and firm in our proclamation that in Jesus alone is there salvation and Muslims can and should come to Him.

21. The World Missions Conference in New York in 1900 was the spur to produce data on missionaries, and we have used its figures. The 1962 *World Christian Handbook* provided the data for the second column, the *World Christian Encyclopedia* of 1981 the third and the 2001 edition of *Operation World* the final column.

22. There is a little ditty that highlights the short lifespan of traders and missionaries on Africa's tropical coasts: "Beware, beware the Bight of Benin, for few come out though many go in." The casualty rate among missionaries was so high that in the 19th Century they were expected to live just two years.

23. The revival conditions in S Africa among the Caucasian Afrikaners and (to a lesser extent) English-speakers at the turn of the century stimulated missionary vision that resulted in many new advances. There was an unspoken paternalism in mission work among the non-Caucasian communities in S Africa that inhibited a vision for missions in those communities, and even led to a rejection of the concept of missions, which was seen as signifying cultural oppression..

24. The "Back to Jerusalem" vision of some Chinese leaders in the 1920s—to take the Gospel from China westwards towards Jerusalem—has gained new impetus in recent years but still largely remains a vision.

25. COMIBAM (Cooperación Misionera Iberoamericana) was launched in 1987 in São Paulo as the first Hispanic missions network. It was the moment when Latin America moved from being primarily a receiver of missionaries to being a sender.

26. See Chapter 16 in my book *The Church is Bigger than You Think* for a fuller treatment of this.

27. Proving the biblicality of the concept should not therefore condone wrong practices by mission agencies.

28. The Operation World team garnered further data for the 2010 edition, which builds on the work of previous editions.

An Evangelized World?

Countries by Christian %	Major Religion	Indig Pop in 2008 (000s)	Christian %	Evangelical %
Turkmenistan	Muslim	4,669	0.0	0.0
Comoros	Muslim	838	0.0	0.0
Maldives	Muslim	302	0.0	0.0
Mayotte	Muslim	116	0.0	0.0
Afghanistan	Muslim	27,962	0.0	0.0
Yemen	Muslim	20,884	0.0	0.0
W Sahara	Muslim	374	0.0	0.0
Tajikistan	Muslim	6,323	0.0	0.0
Mauritania	Muslim	3,043	0.0	0.0
Somalia	Muslim	8,742	0.1	0.0
Morocco	Muslim	30,522	0.1	0.1
Uzbekistan	Muslim	25,172	0.1	0.1
Tunisia	Muslim	7,959	0.1	0.1
Djibouti	Muslim	697	0.1	0.1
Libya	Muslim	4,969	0.1	0.1
Niger	Muslim	13,830	0.2	0.1
Turkey	Muslim	74,544	0.2	0.1
Bhutan	Muslim	542	0.3	0.2
Algeria	Muslim	34,157	0.3	0.3
Saudi Arabia	Muslim	19,932	0.5	0.5
Iran	Muslim	71,327	0.5	0.5
Bangladesh	Muslim	160,293	0.5	0.4
Oman	Muslim	1,903	0.7	0.2
Cambodia	Buddhist	13,364	0.8	0.7
Mongolia	Buddhist	2,589	1.1	1.0
UAE	Muslim	562	1.1	0.3
Thailand	Buddhist	62,150	1.2	0.5
Bahrain	Muslim	498	1.5	0.3
Palestine	Muslim	3,484	1.6	0.2
Kuwait	Muslim	1,531	1.7	0.3
Total		**603,278**		

	Persecution	Moderate	Severe

Fig 9.1 *The 30 countries with the smallest percentage of Christians*

Countries by Evangelical %	Major Religion	Indig Pop in 2008 (000s)	Christian %	Evangelical %
Bosnia	Catholic	3,861	40.8	0.1
Montenegro	Orthodox	468	91.8	0.1
St Pierre & Miquelon	Catholic	6	95.1	0.1
San Marino	Catholic	28	91.4	0.1
Slovenia	Catholic	1,805	92.7	0.1
Syria	Muslim	20,230	5.6	0.1
Azerbaijan	Muslim	7,992	1.8	0.2
Iraq	Muslim	28,576	1.9	0.2
Macedonia	Orthodox	1,888	68.0	0.2
Senegal	Muslim	12,472	4.9	0.2
Jordan	Muslim	5,694	2.1	0.3
Kuwait	Muslim	1,531	1.7	0.3
Poland	Catholic	36,651	96.6	0.3
Andorra	Catholic	61	90.8	0.4
Croatia	Catholic	3,981	95.2	0.4
Greece	Orthodox	10,669	93.3	0.4
Israel	Jewish	3,264	4.1	0.4
Albania	Muslim	3,078	48.1	0.5
Austria	Catholic	7,510	89.4	0.5
Japan	Buddhist/ Shinto	126,423	1.9	0.5
Kosovo	Muslim	1,909	7.4	0.5
Lebanon	Muslim	3,201	34.9	0.5
Liechtenstein	Catholic	27	97.0	0.5
Luxembourg	Catholic	369	91.8	0.5
Qatar	Muslim	200	2.5	0.5
Pakistan	Muslim	163,654	2.5	0.6
Serbia	Orthodox	7,616	79.1	0.6
Czech Rep	Catholic	9,733	56.3	0.7
Guinea	Muslim	9,261	4.5	0.7
Kazakhstan	Muslim	13,296	11.0	0.7
Total		**485,454**		

Fig 9.2 *The countries with the smallest percentage of evangelical Christians*

How can we know when Jesus will return with the task of world evangelization complete? We can't, though we may discern when the time draws near. Jesus spoke these words just before His death: *"This gospel of the kingdom will be preached throughout the whole world, as a testimony to all nations; and then the end will come"* (Matthew 24:14, RSV). The timing of His return seems to be intimately connected with the evangelizaton of the world—and therefore with our own obedience.

Matthew 24 is a chapter full of predictions by the Lord Jesus about the state of the world between His two comings. He spoke of many trials and a great deal of suffering from heresy, war, natural disaster, persecution, as well as apostasy and other failures among believers. Nonetheless, He told us not to be alarmed, but to press on with fulfilling His Last Command, given in the verse quoted above. Preachers and witnesses are needed for this to be achieved.

There are two specific criteria for completion that He gave—the first geographical ("the whole world"), the second ethnic ("all nations"). The tables here and on the following page identify those least evangelized in our generation based on those criteria. The tables on this page look at them in geographical terms.

Fig 9.1 lists in ascending order the 30 countries with the smallest percentages of *professing* Christians. The percentages of Evangelicals are also given. The statistics cited are specifically for the *indigenous population*, since in many cases the large number of Christian migrant workers obscures the spiritual poverty of local people. The exceptions here are the oil-producing Arab countries, where many migrant Arabic-speaking Christians work who are subsumed in statistics for the indigenous. The orange and red indicate the level of persecution that converts face, suggesting the difficulties that missionaries must overcome. Nearly all these countries are Muslim-majority.

Food for Thought

The magnitude of the unfinished task is daunting. Most of the countries in the tables on this page are Muslim-majority, and nearly all are unevangelized as a result of governmental and social oppression, discrimination and persecution. The barriers can be broken down only by prayer followed by innovative and courageous action.

Affinity Bloc	People Cluster	Main Religion	# People Groups	Total pop (mil)	Emigrant %	Christian %
Persian-Median	Luri-Bakhtiari	Muslim	6	5.2	1.7	0.001
Persian-Median	Baloch	Muslim	17	8.9	4.2	0.002
Horn of Africa	Beja	Muslim	4	2.2	0.4	0.003
Persian-Median	Aimaq	Muslim	2	1.6	0.0	0.004
Arab World	Berber, Saharan	Muslim	14	0.9	0.0	0.006
Persian-Median	Talysh	Muslim	7	0.6	0.4	0.006
Turkic	Turkmen	Muslim	14	7.7	3.3	0.007
Sub-Sah African	Kanuri-Saharan	Muslim	25	8.8	4.1	0.007
Turkic	Azerbaijani	Muslim	24	25.4	4.6	0.008
Malay	Musi of Sumatra	Muslim	5	1.4	1.0	0.008
Arab World	Arab, Hassaniya	Muslim	10	7.3	3.0	0.010
Malay	Lampung	Muslim	9	5.5	0.0	0.010
S Asian	Maldivian	Muslim	2	0.3	0.0	0.011
Turkic	Uighur	Muslim	18	15.5	0.8	0.011
Arab World	Berber, Shawiya	Muslim	4	2.1	10.7	0.011
Arab World	Tuareg	Muslim	14	2.8	22.6	0.011
Turkic	Kyrgyz	Muslim	11	4.2	6.9	0.018
Malay	Minangkabau	Muslim	7	8.0	0.0	0.018
Sub-Sah African	Soninke	Muslim	13	1.8	10.1	0.018
Persian-Median	Nuristani	Muslim	10	0.1	0.0	0.019
Sub-Sah African	Nubian	Muslim	7	2.2	0.0	0.019
Arab World	Arab, Yemeni	Muslim	17	21.5	3.6	0.022
Malay	Madura (Java)	Muslim	3	12.8	0.2	0.022
S Asian	Kashmiri	Muslim	17	6.2	2.0	0.026
Malay	Melayu (Sumatra)	Muslim	5	1.2	0.0	0.028
Persian-Median	Tajik	Muslim	30	15.1	1.8	0.039
Arab World	Berber, Riff	Muslim	5	4.0	3.1	0.039
Sub-Sah African	Guera-Naba	Muslim	4	0.5	0.0	0.040
Arab World	Berber, Shilha	Muslim	6	8.8	2.9	0.041
Arab World	Arab, Shuwa	Muslim	7	2.3	6.0	0.049
Persian-Median	Parsee	Ethnic	8	0.2	61.9	0.054
Malay	Aceh of Sumatra	Muslim	5	4.2	0.0	0.063
Persian-Median	Kurd	Muslim	44	24.6	6.7	0.067
Turkic	Uzbek	Muslim	21	27.7	4.5	0.083
Turkic	Kazakh	Muslim	29	13.5	7.6	0.085
Sub-Sah African	Malinke-Jula	Muslim	9	1.0	2.6	0.111
Arab World	Arab, Libyan	Muslim	4	6.3	0.3	0.114
Persian-Median	Pashtun	Muslim	26	35.0	2.6	0.128
Sub-Sah African	Hausa	Muslim	17	39.8	4.1	0.132
Tibetan-Himalayan	Burmese	Buddhist	18	31.8	0.7	0.139
Sub-Sah African	Songhai	Muslim	21	7.0	5.2	0.146
S Asian	Urdu Muslim	Muslim	32	93.8	1.7	0.151
Sub-Sah African	Susu	Muslim	5	1.3	0.7	0.172
Tibetan-Himalayan	Bhutanese	Buddhist	19	0.6	0.0	0.180
Arab World	Arab, Maghreb	Muslim	32	55.2	8.5	0.194
Horn of Africa	Somali	Muslim	28	12.2	11.5	0.225
Malay	Ogan of Sumatra	Muslim	3	0.5	0.0	0.231
S Asian	Sindhi	Muslim	17	24.2	1.1	0.234
Sub-Sah African	Atlantic-Wolof	Muslim	8	5.2	2.3	0.262
Tibetan-Himalayan	Tibetan	Buddhist	79	8.0	1.1	0.319
Total			**742**	**577**	**3.8**	
Total <5% Christian			**108 clusters**	**2,203**	**2,152**	**3.3**

Persecution	Moderate	Severe

Fig 9.3 *The 50 least evangelized people clusters*

Fig 9.2 presents a different list of countries: those that have the smallest percentages of known *evangelical* Christians excluding those listed in the first table. Again, Muslim countries predominate, but most of these also have a significant Orthodox or Catholic *indigenous population*. What is striking about this second list is the number of Catholic and Orthodox countries in Europe. There is debate about whether such Christian-majority countries can be considered unevangelized. Many Evangelicals have good grounds for saying that they are, for in some of them Evangelicals face particular discrimination and harassment—note where the colours for persecution differ between the last two columns.

Finishing the task

In Matthew 24:14 and, also, 28:18, Jesus spoke of testifying to and making disciples of all the peoples of the world. The word used in most English translations is "nations". Today, we understand by "nation" a country or territory with a recognized government. NT Greek uses the word *ethne*, from where we derive our English word "ethnic". So, I conclude this book with a list of the least evangelized ethnic clusters of peoples. There are some 12,000 people groups in the world (or 16,000 if we include S Asia's castes), which I have categorized into affinity blocs and people clusters. Fig 9.3 lists the 50 least evangelized clusters. If I also included all 108 clusters that are less than 5% Christian, the number of people groups concerned would be more than 2,200, with a total population of nearly 2.2 billion. (It is not yet possible to give totals for Evangelicals, as a worldwide assessment has yet to be completed; but it should be said that, among these tiny numbers of Christians, a large proportion are evangelical believers.)

Concerning the columns: the first gives the *affinity bloc* to which each cluster belongs. Twenty-nine of the clusters are in Asia, 11 are in Africa and 10 in the Arab World straddle both of those continents.

The second lists the *people clusters*. Almost all of them have significant migrant communities elsewhere.

The third gives the *principal religion* of each cluster. In all but four cases

Burning Question for Today

We are responsible for our generation and its evangelization. We have such opportunity to reach the world for the Lord Jesus Christ—with the means to travel, a multiplicity of tools, a motivated global workforce and the information we need to identify the most needy. Above all, God has given us clear directions as to what we must do, and His Holy Spirit empowers us to accomplish it.

▲ Will we grasp this opportunity or miss it through our indifference or disobedience?

this is Islam, which indicates the seriousness of the challenge we face if we are to evangelize every people group in the world.

The fourth cites the number of *people groups* that, according to the Joshua Project, make up each cluster (see the Project's website for more information). In the Joshua Project listing, there is a separate record for each country in which a particular people group has a presence.

The fifth gives the *total population* in millions of all these constituent people groups.

The sixth gives the percentage of each population that lives in countries other than its homeland(s). This highlights the possibility of ministry to *expatriates*, who could then impact the communities they originally came from.

The last column gives the percentage of each population that is Christian. In most cases, as we noted with the least evangelized countries, many of these *Christians* will be theologically evangelical.

The colour behind this last column indicates the level of *persecution* that Christians face (and restriction that preachers encounter) in each cluster's homeland(s)—orange once again meaning "moderate" and red "severe".

Food for Thought

▲ Will the Church rise to the challenge and improve the predicted outcomes, or will we slide into another decline and these projections prove to have been optimistic?

There are encouraging signs of a rise in some parts of the world in the number of global prayer and missional movements, but there are also less promising trends. Not least is a significant slowing in the growth of evangelical Christianity worldwide. One of the greatest concerns is the decline of Christianity in Europe. It is in this area of the world where my own present ministry is primarily focused as a leader in WEC International. I am passionate to prove my own predictions for Europe wrong. The Lord Jesus has given us the keys of the Kingdom to unlock the doors to the hardest hearts, the most resistant cultures and the most closed countries. Let us go out in faith as William Carey did, two centuries ago, to *"expect great things from God; attempt great things for God."*[1]

Notes

1. Carey preached a fiery message based on Isaiah 54:2 to the ministers of the Northampton Baptist Association, concluding with this famous phrase. It led to the founding of the first modern mission agency and the launch of the missions movement as we know it today.

2. The full text of the Commitment is to be found at http://www.lausanne.org/ctcommitment. It is a comprehensive and inspirational statement.

Finally...

Various trends that are likely to affect the Church in its missional task in the future have been considered in this book and projections made about possible outcomes. I have drawn attention to the astonishing growth and spread of Christianity over the past century, and especially of Evangelicalism over the past fifty years. I have also highlighted the challenge of the unfinished task that must be faced in the coming decades. This task was also the focus of the Third Lausanne Congress on World Evangelization that took place in South Africa in October 2010. There is no better summary than to quote here from the Commitment that concluded that Congress.[2]

In a world which works to re-invent itself at an ever-accelerated pace, some things remain the same. These great truths provide the biblical rationale for our missional engagement.

Human beings are lost. *The underlying human predicament remains as the Bible describes it: we stand under the just judgment of God in our sin and rebellion, and without Christ we are without hope.*

The gospel is good news. *The gospel is not a concept that needs fresh ideas, but a story that needs fresh telling. It is the unchanged story of what God has done to save the world, supremely in the historical events of the life, death, resurrection, and reign of Jesus Christ. In Christ there is hope.*

The Church's mission goes on. *The mission of God continues to the ends of the earth and to the end of the world. The day will come when the kingdoms of the world will become the kingdom of our God and of his Christ and God will dwell with his redeemed humanity in the new creation. Until that day, the Church's participation in God's mission continues, in joyful urgency, and with fresh and exciting opportunities in every generation including our own.*

From the preamble to the Cape Town Commitment (above), and from the section entitled "Discerning the will of Christ for world evangelization" (below).

Let us rise up as the Church worldwide to meet this challenge, and:

Repent of our blindness *to the continuing presence of so many unreached peoples in our world and our lack of urgency in sharing the gospel among them.*

Renew our commitment *to go to those who have not yet heard the gospel, to engage deeply with their language and culture, to live the gospel among them with incarnational love and sacrificial service, to communicate the light and truth of the Lord Jesus Christ in word and deed, awakening them through the Holy Spirit's power to the surprising grace of God.*

Aim to eradicate Bible poverty in the world, for the Bible remains indispensable for evangelism.[3]

Aim to eradicate Bible ignorance in the Church, for the Bible remains indispensable for discipling believers into the likeness of Christ.

Let us keep evangelism at the centre of the fully-integrated scope of all our mission, inasmuch as the gospel itself is the source, content and authority of all biblically-valid mission. All we do should be both an embodiment and a declaration of the love and grace of God and his saving work through Jesus Christ.

3. The Bible poverty is reference to possibly 2,000 languages in which there is no extant translation of any part of the Bible and for which Bible translation may be required. It is almost impossible to conceive of a healthy church without access to God's Word.

SELECT BIBLIOGRAPHY

Barraclough, Geoffrey (ed) Overy, Richard J (author) *Complete History of the World (The Times)*. HarperCollins 2000

Barrett, D B and Johnson, Todd M (eds). *World Christian Encyclopedia*. New York, Oxford University Press, 1982 & 2001

Barrett, D B and Johnson, Todd M (eds). *World Christian Trends*. Pasadena CA, William Carey Library 2001

Beach, Harlan P and Fahs, Charles H. *World Mission Atlas*. London, England: Edinburgh House Press, 1924

Carey, William. *An Enquiry into the Obligations of Christians to use Means for the Conversion of the Heathens*. Leicester, 1792

Chadwick, Henry and Evans, G R. *Atlas of the Christian Church*. London, MacMillan, 1987

Garrett, Laurie. *The Coming Plague: Newly Emerging Diseases in a World Out of Balance*. New York: Farrar, 1994

Grun, Bernard. *The Timetables of History*. New York, Simon & Schuster, 1991

Grubb, Kenneth. *The World Christian Handbook*. London, England: World Dominion Press, 1948, 1952, 1957, 1962, 1968

Friedman, Thomas L. *The World is Flat*. London, UK, Penguin Group, 2005

Hall, Douglas John. *The End of Christendom and the Future of Christianity*. Valley Forge, PA, USA: Trinity Press, 1997

Hattaway, Paul. *Operation China*. Carlisle, England, Piquant, 2000

Hattaway, Paul. *Peoples of the Buddhist World*. Carlisle, England, Piquant, 2004

Hunter, George. *The Celtic Way of Evangelism*. Nashville, TN, Abingdon Press, 2000

Jenkins, Philip. *The Next Christendom: The coming of Global Christianity*. Oxford, England, Oxford University Press, 2002

Jenkins, Philip. *The Lost History of Christianity*. New York, HarperCollins, 2008

Johnson, Todd M and Ross, Kenneth R (eds). *Atlas of Global Christianity 1910-2010*. Edinburgh University Press, 2009

Johnstone, Patrick J and Mandryk, Jason. *Operation World*. Carlisle, Paternoster, 2005

Johnstone, Patrick J. *The Church is Bigger than You Think*. Fearn, Rosshire, Scotland, Christian Focus, 1998

Lambert, Tony. *China's Christian Millions*. London, Monarch, 1999

Latourette, Kenneth Scott. *A History of Christianity*. New York: Harper & Row, 1975

Mandryk, Jason. *Operation World (7th ed)*. Colorado Springs, Biblica, 2010

Menzies, Gavin. *1421: The Year China Discovered America*. UK, Transworld, 2002

Mickelthwait, John and Woolridge, Adrian. *God Is Back: How the Global Revival of Faith is Changing the World*. New York, Penguin, 2009

Moffett, Samuel. *A History of Christianity in Asia* (2 vols). New York, Orbis, 2005

Ostler, Nicholas. *Empires of the Word, A Language History of the World*. London, Harper Perennial, 2006

Pantoja, Luis, Tira, Sadiri J and Wan, Enoch. *Scattered, the Filipino Global Presence*. Manila, Lifechange Pub. 2004

Phillips, David. *Peoples on the Move: Introducing the Nomads of the World*. Carlisle, Piquant, 2001

Rubenstein, James M. *An Introduction to Human Geography*. Upper Saddle River NJ, Pearson Prentice Hall, 2005

Ruthven, Malise. *Historical Atlas of the Islamic World*. Oxford, UK, Oxford University Press, 2004

Schnabel, Eckhard J. *Early Christian Mission (2 vols)*. Downers Grove, IL, Intervarsity Press, 2004

Sookhdeo, Patrick. *Global Jihad, The Future in the Face of Militant Islam*. McLewan VA, USA, Isaac Publishing, 2007

Sanneh, Lamin. *Whose Religion is Christianity? The Gospel beyond the West*. Grand Rapids, MI, Eerdmans, 2003

Yousef, Mosab Hassan. *Son of Hamas*. Milton Keynes, Authentic, 2010

Databases and Reference Sources

Ethnologue: Languages of the World, 2004–10. Published by SIL International, USA. http://www.ethnologue.com

Human Development Report (HDR), 2009. Published by the United Nations Development Programme (USA). http://hdr.undp.org

IIASA migration database. http://www.iiasa.ac.at/Research/POP/docs/Population_Projections_Results.html

Indonesian People Profiles, 2003. Published by PJRN (Indonesian National Research Network)

Joshua Project database, 2004–10. A ministry of the US Center for World Mission, USA. http://www.joshuaproject.net

Omid database. A comprehensive database of castes and tribes of South Asian countries, compiled in South Asia and incorporated into the Joshua Project database. http://www.joshuaproject.net

Operation World database, 2001 and to a limited extent, 2010 update. WEC International, UK. http://www.operationworld.org

The World Factbook, 2004–10. Published by the US Central Intelligence Agency. https://www.cia.gov/

Timechart History of the World (ISBN-10: 3-8290-1705-7). Published by Third Millennium Press, 1999.

United Nations Statistics Division, 2004–2010 (USA). http://unstats.un.org/unsd/default.htm

World Christian Database (WCD), 2005–10. Todd Johnson (ed), USA. Published by Brill Academic, NL. http://www.worldchristiandatabase.org

ELECTRONIC EDITIONS AND RESOURCES

Want more from *The Future of the Global Church*?

Do you want to use it in your presentations and teaching? Or do you want to dig deeper, explore the sources or analyse the facts and statistics behind the book? Perhaps you just want to access the book online or carry it with you on your notebook, eBook reader or smartphone?

Our team is implementing a digital publishing plan to make available a wealth of electronic resources, including:

▲ The full text of the book
▲ PowerPoint presentations
▲ High-resolution images
▲ Database spreadsheets
▲ Supplemental documents.

DVD-ROM

The Future of the Global Church enhanced DVD helps you present the book's content to others and enables you to do your own in-depth analysis. It runs on Windows and Mac computers and provides:

▲ the full text of the book in PDF format – hyperlinked and fully searchable
▲ PowerPoint files with extensive speaker's notes covering the content of the book
▲ high resolution maps and graphs from the book
▲ the book's underlying database files in Excel spreadsheets
▲ a generous license to facilitate use of the materials in your ministry

Website

The Future of the Global Church website www.TheFutureOfTheGlobalChurch.org is designed to be an active, dynamic source of new and revised information that will be updated and improved on an ongoing basis. Here you can access:

▲ background information about the author and the book
▲ free sample PowerPoint presentations and paid-for in-depth presentations
▲ all published electronic products
▲ PowerPoint files with the author's live commentary, to be added in the months following publication of the book
▲ Adobe Illustrator (.ai) and ArcMap (.mxd) files of the book's images
▲ a wealth of supplemental materials—appendices, documents and an expanded glossary—not included in the book or other electronic products

eBooks & Apps

The Future of the Global Church eBooks, downloadable from the website, provide the full content of the book in PDF, ePUB, and Mobi formats for your eBook reader such as Kindle and Nook, as well as for your notebook computer, iPad and other digital devices.

The Future of the Global Church apps deliver the book's content on smart phones, tablets, and other portable devices.

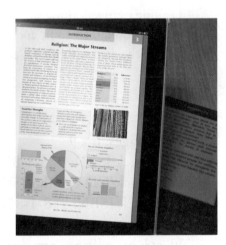

Downloadable components

If you don't need the whole book or DVD, you can easily download the specific content you need as individual components from *The Future of the Global Church book* or *DVD*, such as:

▲ book chapters
▲ images
▲ PowerPoint slides and presentations
▲ Excel spreadsheets
▲ supplemental content found only on the website

All these electronic products are brought to you by Global Mapping International

Strategic Mission Research and Mapping

www.TheFutureOfTheGlobalChurch.org

ALSO AVAILABLE

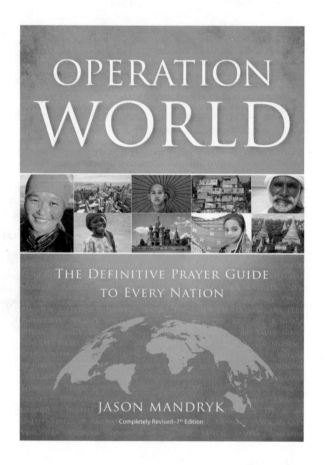

Join millions of praying people around the world using this book to inform, inspire, and ignite their prayers. Engage your heart and mind in global prayer with this thoroughly researched, fully-updated seventh edition. It is loaded with clear, concise, accurate information on peoples, languages, religions, denominations, spiritual trends, and prayer needs—for every country in the world, from the largest to the smallest.

Operation World's easy-to-follow summaries of every nation include:
- Timely challenges for prayer and specific answers to prayer
- Updates on church growth, with a focus on evangelicals
- Population, people group and language statistics
- Charts and maps showing global religious and demographic trends
- Explanations of major currents in economics, politics and society

Leading evangelical mission leaders, scholars, writers, pastors and lay people all over the world rely on this book, refer to it, and quote from it regularly. Every fact, number and statement is checked and re-checked with global and local experts in each field.

www.operationworld.com

1012 pages, 6 x 9
Paperback ISBN: 978-1-85078-862-1
Paperback/CD Combo ISBN: 978-1-85078-875-1
Hardback ISBN: 978-1-85078-861-4

Electronic editions are also available at www.operationworld.com.